Brain, Mind, and Behavior

SECOND EDITION

Floyd E. Bloom
Arlyne Lazerson

An Annenberg/CPB Project

W. H. Freeman and Company
New York

Major funding for the *Brain, Mind, and Behavior* telecourse and for the television series, *The Brain,* was provided by the Annenberg/CPB Project. Additional series funding is provided by the National Science Foundation, the National Institute of Neurological and Communicative Disorders and Stroke, the National Institute of Mental Health, and the National Institute on Aging.

Library of Congress Cataloging-in-Publication Data

Bloom, Floyd E.
    Brain, mind, and behavior.

    Accompanied by a complete set of instructional supplements, prepared by Timothy J. Teyler, North-eastern Ohio College of Medicine, for the text and the television series: The Brain.
    "An Annenberg/CPB project."
    1. Neuropsychology. 2. Brain. 3. Intellect.
I. Lazerson, Arlyne. II. Brain (Television program)
III. Title. [DNLM: 1. Behavior—physiology. 2. Brain.
3. Mental Processes. 4. Nervous System—physiology.
WL 103 B655b]
QP360.B585   1988   612'.82   87-30598

ISBN 0-7167-1863-4

3 4 5 6 7 8 9 DO 9 9 8 7 6 5 4 3 2 1

Contents

Preface

The pace of fascinating scientific discoveries about the brain increases with every year. Much remains to be learned, but in recent decades scientists all over the world have begun to make great inroads in understanding what is perhaps the most complicated living tissue and in relating the brain's functioning to human thought, feeling, and behavior. The goal of BRAIN, MIND, AND BEHAVIOR is to make this ever-growing and exciting body of knowledge about the brain accessible to the interested student who may have had little or no background in either biology or psychology.

For the second edition, we have thoroughly revised the text in light of new discoveries and have added a number of new discussions to make the book more useful to students and teachers. Topics that now receive more extended treatment include: prenatal neuronal development; the senses of hearing and taste; eating disorders—obesity, anorexia nervosa, and bulemia; aggression; sexual behavior; mental retardation; and techniques used in brain research and the treatment of disorders. We have also added summaries in outline form and a list of selected further readings for each chapter. The second edition also includes a complete glossary.

The orientation of the second edition of BRAIN, MIND, AND BEHAVIOR is strongly biological, as it was in the first.

While we describe behavior and psychological phenomena, out aim is always to show how those behaviors and phenomena are related to the brain's cellular structure, chemical signals, and operations. This new edition's basic tenet remains the same: everything that "the mind" does will *ultimately* be explainable in terms of the interactions among the brain's components.

To introduce students to the workings of the brain and its relation to behavior, we begin in Chapter 1 with the basics of overall brain organization, using everyday language and a purposefully simplified scheme. The second chapter presents a more detailed discussion of the brain's components, explaining how the processes of neural transmission work and describing the basic neurotransmitters. A new third chapter has been added, describing the key events in neural development from earliest embryonic unfoldings to changes in old age; as part of the developmental story, we look at sex differences in brain form and function.

The next two chapters (4 and 5) examine how the brain enables the body to sense the world and move through it and how at the same time the brain is able to maintain appropriate internal conditions for optimal physical and mental performance. We then turn our attention to the processes underlying the brain's behavioral responsibilities. In Chapter 6 we see that the ability of the brain to meet the demands of the environment depends on its ability to coordinate the activity of its several functional systems. The brain's varying levels of activity are not merely fluctuations but are, in fact, rhythmic variations in activity that depend on systems that coordinate the body with the world around it.

The places in the brain where these coordinating events take place are also part of larger systems wherein emotional weight is attached to the sensing of specific environmental signals (Chapter 7). These emotional highs and lows help determine which of many possible responses should be given to those signals. Throughout these discussions, the student is urged to recognize an underlying biological basis for complex behavioral phenomena, in essence, to demystify some of the mysteries of the brain. It is in this spirit that the most complex issues of brain function—learning, memory, thinking, and consciousness—are considered in Chapters 8 and 9. The student is offered new insights into the very human aspects of brain research that have emerged from studies of animal nervous systems and from powerful new methods of investigating the brain of human subjects. The examination of mental disorders in the final chapter provides still another avenue for exploring the contributions of biological understanding to our knowledge of brain and behavior. Comparing neurological and behavioral disorders establishes a basis for the understanding of psychiatric diseases in terms of biologically verifiable changes.

The first edition of BRAIN, MIND, AND BEHAVIOR was part of a multimedia teaching package built around the Public Broadcast System's eight-part television series, *The Brain,* produced by WNET in New York. This series is available on cassette and is regularly broadcast on selected stations by the Adult Learning Service of PBS. We are happy to report that a second such series, *The Mind,* is scheduled to begin airing in the fall of 1988.

A complete set of instructional supplements, prepared by Timothy J. Teyler of the Northeastern Ohio College of Medicine, accompanies the second edition of the text and the television offerings. The Instructor's Manual includes suggestions for presenting text material in the classroom, term-paper topics, and an expanded number of test questions for each chapter. For those who use the PBS series in conjunction with the text, the Telecourse Instructor's Manual offers, in addition, suggestions for using the telecourse most effectively. The Study Guide provides students with a synopsis of each chapter and each video program, a list of key terms, self-test questions, and other useful study aids.

Finally, the authors of the textbook were aided enormously in their efforts to simplify the presentation of this often complex subject matter by the informative medical illustrations created especially for this book by the noted *Scientific American* illustrator Carol Donner and by the sketches, charts, and graphs rendered by artist Sally Black.

There are many to whom the authors owe their gratitude—for direct assistance or for directing our efforts toward improving the text. Kevin Morrin gave cheerful and timely library-research assistance and wrote much of the glossary. The following teachers who used the first edition gave us the benefit of their experience in reviews that helped shape our revisions: Alan Auerbach, Wilfrid Laurier University; Donald P. Cain, University of Western Ontario; Edith E. Cracchiolo, Cerritos College; Linda K. Davis, Mt. Hood Community College; David R. Hertzler, State University of New York, Oswego; Alan Kim Johnson, University of

Iowa; Augustus R. Lumia, Skidmore College; William M. Miley, Richard Stockton State College; Maribel Montgomery, Linn-Benton Community College; W. Ronald Salafia, Fairfield University; Michael Sloane, University of Alabama at Birmingham; Lilburn E. Wesche, Seattle Pacific University.

We owe much to our editors—Jonathan Cobb, Cheryl Kupper, and Stephen Wagley— who kept reminding us, and reminding us, of what we owe the beginning student in clarity and background explanation and who found words to provide clarification when we ran out.

La Jolla, California   Floyd E. Bloom
September 1987   Arlyne Lazerson

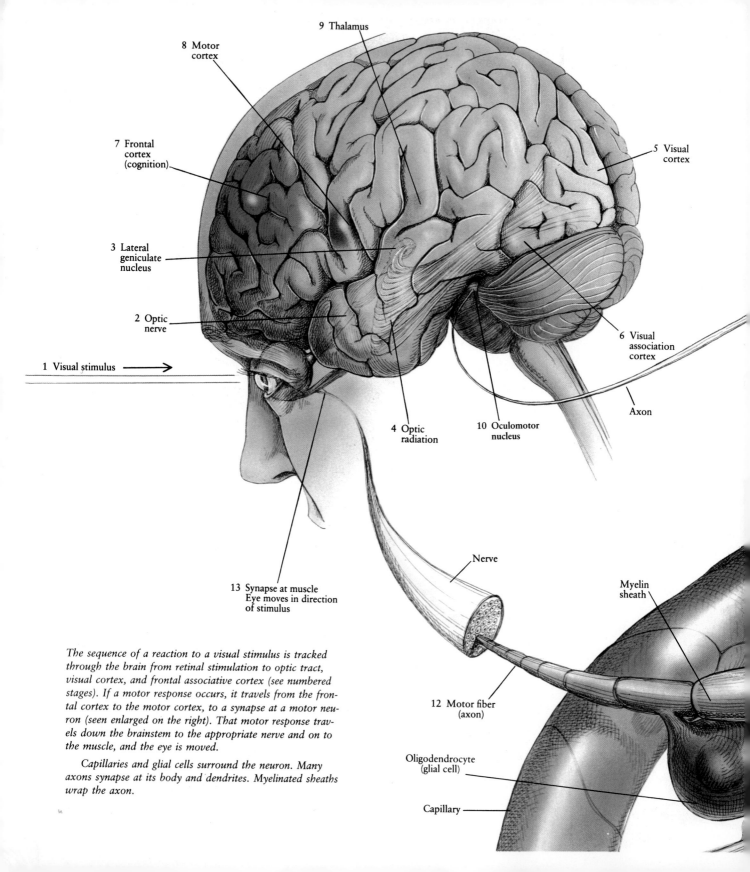

9 Thalamus

8 Motor cortex

7 Frontal cortex (cognition)

3 Lateral geniculate nucleus

2 Optic nerve

1 Visual stimulus →

5 Visual cortex

6 Visual association cortex

Axon

4 Optic radiation

10 Oculomotor nucleus

13 Synapse at muscle Eye moves in direction of stimulus

Nerve

Myelin sheath

12 Motor fiber (axon)

Oligodendrocyte (glial cell)

Capillary

The sequence of a reaction to a visual stimulus is tracked through the brain from retinal stimulation to optic tract, visual cortex, and frontal associative cortex (see numbered stages). If a motor response occurs, it travels from the frontal cortex to the motor cortex, to a synapse at a motor neuron (seen enlarged on the right). That motor response travels down the brainstem to the appropriate nerve and on to the muscle, and the eye is moved.

Capillaries and glial cells surround the neuron. Many axons synapse at its body and dendrites. Myelinated sheaths wrap the axon.

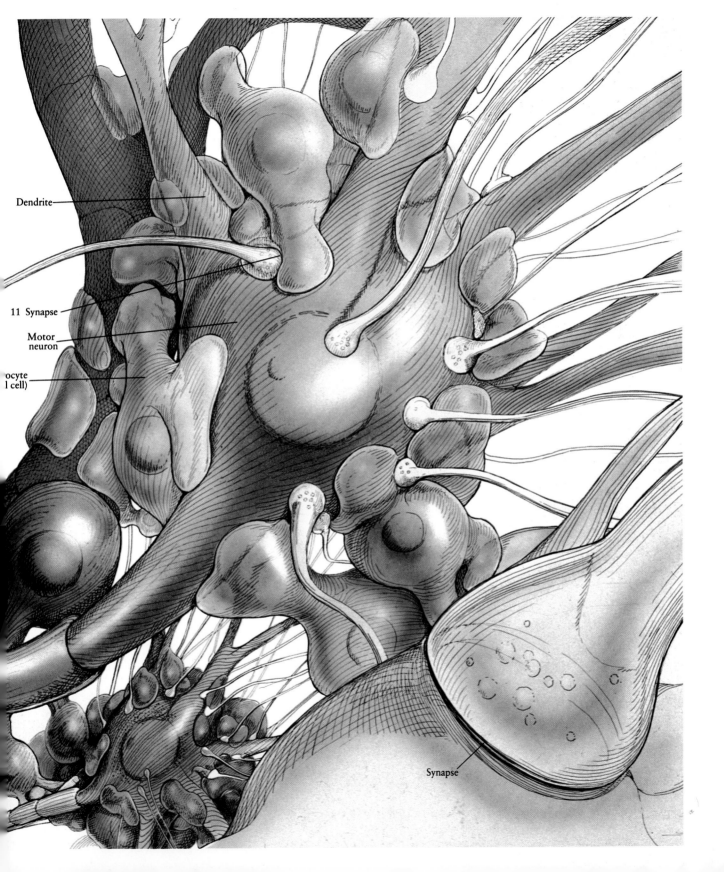

Dendrite

11 Synapse

Motor
neuron

ocyte
l cell)

Synapse

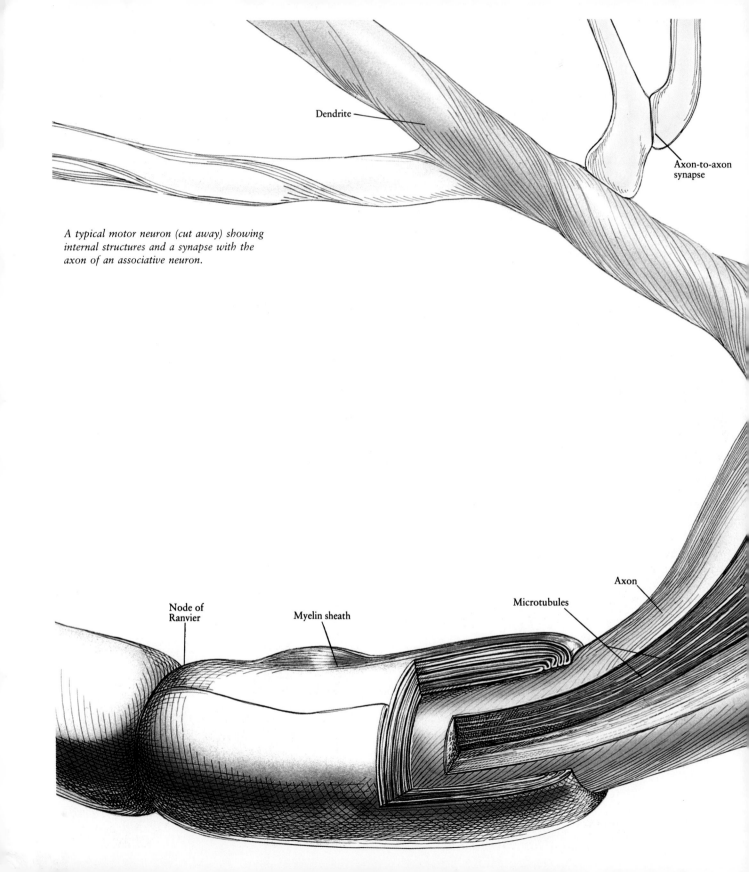

Dendrite

Axon-to-axon
synapse

*A typical motor neuron (cut away) showing
internal structures and a synapse with the
axon of an associative neuron.*

Node of
Ranvier

Myelin sheath

Microtubules

Axon

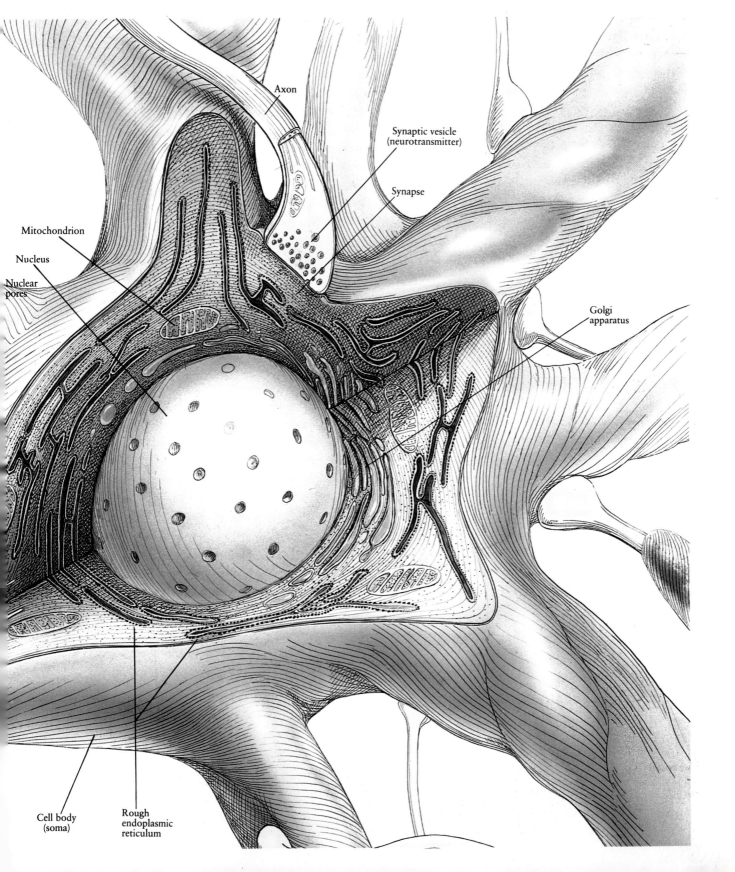

Axon

Synaptic vesicle
(neurotransmitter)

Synapse

Mitochondrion

Nucleus

Nuclear
pores

Golgi
apparatus

Cell body
(soma)

Rough
endoplasmic
reticulum

Brain, Mind, and Behavior

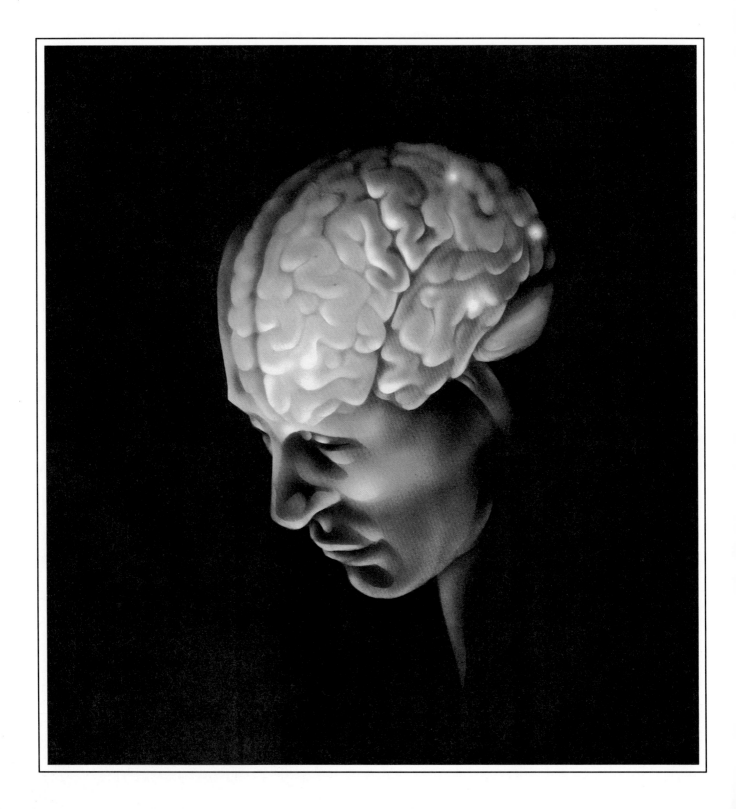

1

Introduction to the Nervous System

1

Why Study the Brain?

The human nervous system consists of the brain and spinal cord (central nervous system) and all the neural tracts that run from the spinal cord out to muscles, organs, glands, and other tissues (peripheral nervous system). Our primary focus in this text is the brain: how the brain functions when we see or learn or speak, and how it malfunctions to produce mental disorders.

Most scientists would answer the question "Why study the brain?" by saying, simply, that it offers the best chance of discovering why and how human beings do what they do. Perhaps this is also your reason for studying the brain. The human brain, however, may be the most complex living structure in the universe. Consider that your brain is packed with billions of nerve cells and that each cell communicates, on average, with 10,000 others. These nerve-cell linkages within the brain and spinal cord make up miles and miles of living wires. The nerve cells communicate with each other by means of chemical signals, and thus far, over 40 chemicals have been identified, although their number is thought to be far greater.

The brain's complexity poses an enormous challenge to the scientists who study it. Nevertheless, for the past two decades, research on the organization and operation of the brain has progressed at an accelerating pace. Scientists from many disciplines have been participating (see box on pages 10 and 11), and because they share a common set of concepts, they benefit from each other's discoveries. All brain researchers, no matter what their discipline or point of view, are now called "neuroscientists."

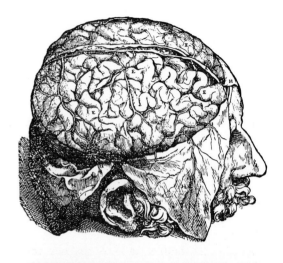

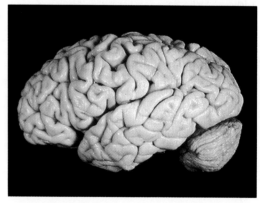

Two images of the brain. Above, Andreas Vesalius revolutionized anatomy with the 1543 publication of De Humani Corporis Fabrica, *which was illustrated by artists of Titian's studio working from the dissected heads of decapitated criminals. Below, photograph of a human brain (side view) removed during an autopsy.*

New experimental techniques and advances in the understanding of brain structure and function have enabled neuroscientists to study some of the more elusive types of behavior, such as memory, in ways not previously possible. Instead of just testing people or laboratory animals to see what they remember after various learning tasks, investigators can now examine specific changes in the operations of brain cells as the events of "remembering" occur. Scientists studying the mysterious state of sleep now know which brain structures and transmitters work together in inducing sleep. New studies are also revealing how the experience of pain is chemically transmitted, or inhibited.

Brain, Mind, and Behavior

The new techniques and approaches that allow direct study of brain mechanisms also shed new light on the study of the mind and behavior. During the first half of this century, before it was possible to know much about the brain besides its gross anatomy, many scientists studied behavior as the only precisely measurable aspect of the psychology of humans and other animals. In fact, the theory based on this approach is called "behaviorism." Behaviorism began to be influential around 1910, and it was the predominant theoretical approach in psychology in the 1950s and 1960s. It was assumed that no one could know what happened inside an organism while it learned or slept or felt pain, so experimenters administered precisely measured stimuli and recorded the organism's observable behavior in response. What happened inside the organism was considered as if it were a "black box"—an unknown.

Now that the brain's workings are open to examination, the term "behavior" takes on new meanings. For example, electrical recordings of a monkey's brain, taken through electrodes precisely implanted to monitor single nerve cells, show that certain cells are active *before* the monkey moves to pick up a certain object during a learning experiment. Thus, besides observing the monkey's behavior in choosing the correct object, we can see that a specific part of its brain is active during the process of *deciding* which behavior to perform.

Historically, investigations of the mind were separated from studies of the physical brain and behavior. This earlier approach, the introspective method, ignored behavior and tried to find scientific techniques for analyzing the contents of consciousness, or mind. "Mind" was an abstract concept that, depending on your beliefs, included the personality, self-identity, or "soul." Even some contemporary observers believe that the lack of a clearly understood physical basis for mental acts means that conscious experience can exist apart from the brain. To them, the mental world exists independently, unconnected to the physical entity of the brain. Others, including the authors of this text, believe that any complete account of mental function must be based on the scientific examination of the brain.

Brain and Mind: A Basic Premise

The lessons of this book are founded on a single basic premise: All the normal functions of the healthy brain and the disorders of the diseased brain, no matter how complex, are ultimately explainable in terms of the basic structural components of the brain and their function.

Everything that the brain does, when it works properly and when it does not, rests on the events taking place in specific, definable parts of the brain. However, many of these events are extremely complicated, and often scientists do not know exactly which parts of the brain are most critical or what these parts do. Yet compared with the almost total ignorance of these subjects that persisted well into this century, we now have a considerable amount of information. The basic pieces of information about how the brain is organized and how it functions form the principles of neuroscience. Eventually, because of the exciting brain research now going on, these principles will be extended so that the more complex acts of the brain can be understood.

Before we look at these principles, however, we need to discuss a controversial concept buried within our basic premise. What does the phrase "everything the brain does" mean? It certainly means moving, sensing, eating, drinking, breathing, talking, and sleeping. But does it include mental acts—thoughts and dreams, musings and insights, hopes and aspirations?

This book takes the view that "the mind" results when many key cells of the brain work together, just as "digestion" results when the cells of the intestinal tract work together. You may disagree with this view, but that should not stop you from being curious. When a scientist confronts a "fact" that does not "feel right," a typical response is "Well, I'll wait and see what the next experiments (or interpretations) show." If you disagree with the statement "The mind is the product of the brain's activity," consider the facts that follow in subsequent chapters and then see what you think.

What Does the Brain Do?

Stop for a moment and make a list of all the actions your brain is engaged in controlling right now. Certainly the action most prominent in your mind is reading. This act can be broken down into several complex subordinate acts: seeing the symbols on the page, assembling the symbols into words, connecting the words with meanings, and then integrating the meanings to form thoughts. While you focus on this book, you are more or less blocking out background sounds—the whispers of those around you, footsteps, the sounds of cars going by, the ticking of the clock. Without thinking about it you simply suppressed those noises while you concentrated on something else. You have also been suppressing a lot of information coming into the brain through other sensory channels—where your arms and legs are and whatever position you have just shifted to without thinking; the location of things in the room; the time of day; the relative position of where you are now to where you live. Your brain constantly monitors all this information, updating it as the sun comes out or goes behind the clouds, waiting for you to turn your attention to something new.

Has your list been exhausted? In fact, we have only begun. Your brain is performing countless actions even farther out of reach of your active awareness. It is controlling your breathing to maintain just the right amount of oxygen in your bloodstream, as well as your blood pressure to keep that fresh, oxygenated blood going to your head. It is monitoring and regulating almost all the other vegetative responsibilities of your body, such as the nutrient content in your bloodstream, which provides one of the signals to eat again; your body temperature; the amount of water your body needs to stay in chemical balance; and the hormonal control of your whiskers or your lack of them. The brain works actively at these and many other duties and still maintains energy for emergency tasks. If a fire were to break out, for example, your brain would enable you to jump up, grab the baby or the dog, run to the door (whose location has just reentered your active awareness), and escape, all while it adjusts your blood pressure and blood oxygen to appropriate levels.

Table 1.1 *Some activities controlled by the brain.*

Interactions with the environment	Actions controlling the body	Mental activities		
Seeing	Breathing	Learning	Creating	Concentrating
Listening	Regulating blood pressure	Remembering	Analyzing	Ignoring
Feeling	and heat	Writing	Deciding	Feeling
Smelling	Regulating body positions	Drawing	Calculating	Sleeping
Tasting	Regulating locomotion, e.g.,	Reading	Imagining	Dreaming
Speaking	moving			
	Regulating reflexes, e.g.,			
	blinking			
	Eating and drinking			
	Regulating hormones			

All these brain activities, which are summarized in Table 1.1, fall into five general categories: sensation, motion, internal regulation, reproduction, and adaptation to the world around us.

Sensation

The major means by which we sense the world are: *vision* (sight), *audition* (hearing), *gustation* (taste), *olfaction* (smell), and *somatic sensation* (touch). Each of these senses has specific organs and segments of the nervous system through which its information is channeled.

One other kind of sensing almost never appears in such lists, partly because its organ is hidden from view, but largely because it seldom malfunctions. Deep within the bony structure at the side of the skull and beneath the ears lies a complex called the *vestibular apparatus* (see Figure 1.1). This structure provides us with the *sense of balance* that we use to monitor the movements of our head and body and to orient ourselves in space.

Motion

The body engages in two different types of movement: *voluntary* motions—those you can control when you want to—and *involuntary* motions—those you cannot control

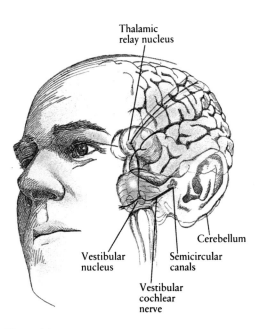

Figure 1.1
The brain parts important for the sense of balance. The fluid-filled semicircular canals sense the head's rotation and relay that information to the vestibular nuclei in the medulla, to the cerebellum, to the thalamus, and to the somatosensory cortex.

(see Figure 1.2). Voluntary movements are those that result when you move your limbs, make a face, or wiggle your tongue. Involuntary movements are generally restricted to

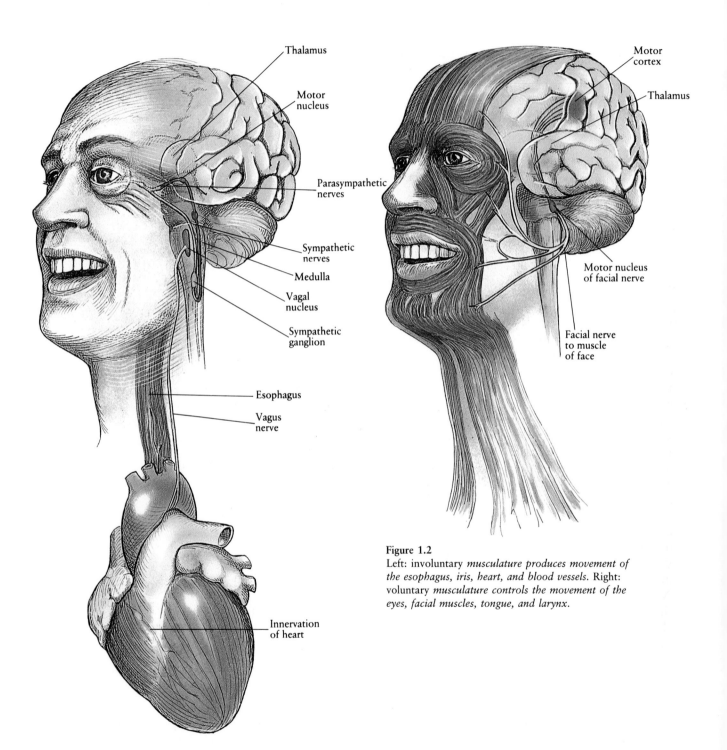

Thalamus

Motor
nucleus

Parasympathetic
nerves

Sympathetic
nerves

Medulla

Vagal
nucleus

Sympathetic
ganglion

Esophagus

Vagus
nerve

Innervation
of heart

Motor
cortex

Thalamus

Motor nucleus
of facial nerve

Facial nerve
to muscle
of face

Figure 1.2
Left: involuntary *musculature produces movement of the esophagus, iris, heart, and blood vessels.* Right: voluntary *musculature controls the movement of the eyes, facial muscles, tongue, and larynx.*

muscles deep within the body, such as the heart and those in the intestinal tract. You can glimpse the involuntary operation of such muscles if you go into a dimly lit room, look at your pupils in the mirror, and suddenly turn on the light. Your pupil contracts almost instantly because your nervous system protects the light-sensing cells of your retina by reducing the amount of incoming light. The goose bumps you get when you are chilled or thrilled are also involuntary movements. The nerves activate small muscles attached to the hairs on your skin and make them literally "stand on end."

Internal Regulation

The precise regulation of your internal organs depends on the active surveillance of the nervous system. Only occasionally do these organs intrude upon your thinking, such as when your stomach gurgles loudly while the class is silently at work—but you cannot do much about it. You almost never need to be concerned about regulating your body temperature; it remains stable despite your level of activity. When you are aware of being too warm or too cold, you invoke a behavioral response—you change your clothes or your locale, or you exercise. As long as you stay in the same general place, your brain can also plan ahead each day, coordinating the internal machinery of your body to the timing of your daily routine of going to work, eating, and sleeping.

Much of the communication between the brain and the internal organs is carried out by hormones, chemicals that are manufactured by organs or glands and secreted into the bloodstream. The brain has special receptor cells for interpreting the messages carried by these chemicals. The brain also manufactures certain hormones, which are released into the bloodstream and activate or regulate certain processes.

Reproduction

The brain coordinates the proper hormonal regulation of the testicles in preparing sperm, the ovaries in preparing ova, and the uterus lining in preparing for implantation of the fertilized egg. The brain monitors the testicles or ovaries by means of a complex set of internal sensing systems. It also issues commands to the reproductive system by means of the hormones secreted from the pituitary gland, part of which is a brain structure. In fact, small differences exist between male and female brains in those parts concerned with reproduction long before the brain urges your body to grow muscular or to become shapely.

Adaptation

The world around us is constantly changing, and if we are to survive, we must accommodate many of these new conditions. Our brains act as our agents in such adaptive responses. We adapt to new problems by remembering how we solved similar ones before, by defending against them or by retreating from them. Sometimes we adapt more simply, without thinking about the process, such as eating when hungry, drinking when thirsty, and sleeping when tired. When an adaptive response leads to a long-lasting change in behavior, we speak of that change as "learning." Usually, adaptive responses benefit those who make them. As the number of our successful adaptations increases, we enlarge our repertoire of behaviors. With practice, many of the responses that we need when we encounter a particular situation become almost unconscious (like coming in out of the rain, or fastening your seat belt before you drive).

Unfortunately, human beings have a tendency to devise ways of adapting that are not good for them, such as habitual overeating or using recreational drugs.

Box: How Scientists Study the Brain

The name for the general field of research that provides the data on which most of this book is based is *neuroscience,* the science of the nervous system. The general purpose of this field of research is to link the biological and chemical properties of the brain and its component cells to behavior.

Many specialists work within the general field of neuroscience, using a wide range of methods to examine different aspects of brain structure and function. We should at the outset distinguish two categories: (a) *experimental* neuroscience, in which the scientist perturbs the nervous system of an organism to yield measurable, predictable, and eventually explicable changes; (b) *clinical* neuroscience, in which a medical physician or other professional observes a change produced by life events (e.g., developmental, infectious, or traumatic events) and tries to understand the effect of the change on brain function.

Throughout history, clinical scientists have identified situations that have revealed previously unsuspected aspects of the normal structure, function, and chemistry of the brain. Many fields of medicine are concerned with aspects of bodily function that are ultimately regulated and monitored by the brain. However, the branches of medicine most closely tied to the study of the brain are neurology (the study of the diseases of the brain), neurosurgery, and psychiatry (the study of behavioral, emotional, and mental diseases).

Clinical neuroscientists study the brain first by talking to their patients and then testing the operations of their special systems of sensing, moving, and remembering. They can also assess mental function by evaluating the performance of more abstract talents like mathematics or drawing. A critical part of these evaluations is the ability to link disorders to specific structures of the brain revealed by conventional x-rays or by the newer imaging methods. *Com-puterized axial tomography* (or CAT) allows the x-ray data of the whole skull and brain to be stored in a computer's memory and then resectioned computationally so that individual planes of "view" can be examined. Unless the problem area is a large one, or is composed of tissue that is considerably different than the brain's composition (like a blood clot or a large abscess), it is often difficult to visualize the nature of a brain lesion with x-ray. *Magnetic resonance* images of the brain provide a much better view, using a totally different principle: a large, brief magnetic pulse in the form of very high-frequency radiowaves is applied to the tissue, and then the electrical signals generated by the tissue in response are measured. The detailed structural picture of the brain provided by magnetic resonance rivals direct visual inspection. Much can also be learned by recording the brain's electrical activity (on an electroencephalogram, or EEG) or by performing chemical tests on the fluids from the internal cavities of the brain (for example, to test for infectious agents or abnormal chemical components). More detailed investigation of the chemistry and structure of the brain in unsuccessfully treated cases is obtained in postmortem examinations.

The experimental neurosciences have traditionally been divided into separate major disciplines:

Anatomists seek to describe the organization of the elements of the brain. These scientists study the brain's shape and form by gross inspection, or by slicing it into very thin sections and examining the sections under a microscope. Using special dyes, they can discriminate one kind of nerve cell from another. Other types of dyes injected into the brain help to define the connections between cells in different places. Still other stains detect the particular chemical that individual neurons use to transmit their intercellular messages.

Physiologists attempt to understand the function of the elements of the brain. These scientists have focused their interest on the electrical activity of the cells in the brain. In some instances, signal detectors (electrodes) are placed on the surface of the scalp to record the activity of millions of cells at a time, as in the EEG. In other cases, very thin electrodes are placed directly within the substances of the brain to record the activity of just one cell at a time. By determining how the single cells or groups of cells alter their activity when the brain is performing a specific task, like processing light signals that enter through the eyes, the physiologist seeks to determine how neurons work together to achieve the complex behaviors of our brains.

Biochemists investigate the chemical properties of the elements of the brain. When very little was known of how the brain worked, biochemists determined how much of the brain was made of fat, protein, and various sugars. Later they focused on identifying specific proteins and other molecules that act as signals between cells or that amplify the effects of these signals. As more and more distinct chemicals were discovered, the biochemists sought to link changes in them to brain development, aging, or to specific diseases. For example, patients dying from the neurological disease called Parkinson's disease (a disease in which it becomes increasingly difficult to initiate or terminate voluntary movements and in which the hands exhibit a prominent trembling motion at rest) lacked normal amounts of a brain chemical called dopamine. Since it was known how the dopamine-containing neurons of the brain actually made this molecule, drugs were developed that allowed other neurons to manufacture the missing chemical and help reverse, at least temporarily, the symptoms of the disease.

Psychologists seek to understand the behavioral operations of the brain. Some psychologists analyze the behavior of normal humans and define the rules by which they sense, discriminate, store, and recall specific information. Others analyze the behavior of experimental animals under the controlled environment of the laboratory. Under laboratory conditions, it is possible to determine which brain structures and chemicals are critical for the performance of a particular kind of task, and to analyze how the brain changes when an animal is taught to give a specific response to a signal (like pushing a lever when a red light is on in order to receive a food pellet).

Although we have described the four major disciplines within the neurosciences as though they were separate, many studies in the field are actually *interdisciplinary*. In this form of research, a given brain system, like the visual system, or a complex structure, like the cerebellum, is studied in terms of its function, chemistry, cellular organization, and behavioral operations.

Frequently, scientists who study the brain take their cues for future studies from clinical observation—for example, why one person who has had a stroke may become depressed yet another does not, or why someone who has had a series of epileptic attacks may suddenly start to lose the ability to remember anything new. Other times, knowledge gained from research on experimental animals—like the discovery of a new chemical signal, or an unexpected connection between parts of the brain—is applied to chemical or brain-function tests on people. Although much has been learned about the brain, there is still much, much more to understand, and much of what we need to know is not yet clear. It is to be expected that the development of new methods for studying the brains of healthy and diseased people will require continuous efforts to improve our abilities to analyze the structure, function, and chemistry of the brain, and behavior.

Some mental disorders are characterized by maladaptive behaviors. For example, people with *phobias,* or irrational fears of particular things or events, choose certain behaviors to alleviate their anxiety. People who develop a morbid fear of germs or infection are the classic example. These people may wash their hands a hundred times a day, spending a large part of their waking hours in unnecessary cleansing.

What Is a Brain?

As discussed, the brain takes care of sensation, motion, internal regulation, reproduction, and adaptation. If you have ever taken biology, you will recognize these properties as characteristic of all animals. Even single-cell organisms, such as bacteria, can sense, move, regulate their internal nutritional and respiratory systems, reproduce, and adapt to changes in their environment. Every cell in our bodies can, in fact, respond to some kind of stimuli in its immediate environment and regulate to some degree its internal environment. Many of our cells can also move independently (white blood cells, for example, chase and capture invading bacteria) and reproduce (such as the cells of our skin). If we left out motion, this list would apply to all plants as well as animals.

If all creatures big and small, with and without a brain, do the same basic things, what is the brain for? Obviously, creatures with brains are capable of behaviors far beyond the reach of simple organisms and cells without brains. Without their brains and the other operating units of the nervous system, humans would quickly become sources of food for smaller-brained animals. But this quick answer may seem deceptively easy.

To examine the question another way, let us say that *the brain is an organ specialized to help individual organisms carry out major acts of living.* How well an organism can succeed in its environment depends on the complexity and capacity of its brain as well as the demands of the environment. Bacteria move toward light and sense the presence of nutrients, but multicelled organisms can do much more. Multicelled organisms contain different groups of cells that allow them to detect changes in the environment and adapt to them in more complex ways. These additional capacities give them many advantages in gaining access to nutrients or fleeing from predators. A shark cannot do arithmetic, but it can sense small changes in the electric charge in the ocean that would escape the notice of sophisticated electronic gear. Animals with complex brains not only remember more experiences but can also solve more complex problems and devise tools with which to make their environment more to their liking.

By comparing the structure and function of the human brain with those of other animals, we can begin to ask what is unique about our brain. We cannot fly like an eagle or see as well, nor can we climb mountains that would be a morning romp for a mountain lion, but we are more skilled than other animals in observing, analyzing, and solving complex problems. We can invent and construct airplanes that fly us higher and farther than an eagle, and we can record the construction plans so that later generations can build the planes and even improve their design.

The human brain's capacity for language eventually led to written languages. Once human beings were able to record their thoughts, many did so at length, for the enlightenment of their contemporaries and to communicate with future generations. Since some of the early writing has been preserved, we are able to gain a historical perspective on what our ancestors thought about the brain.

Historical Views of Brain, Mind, and Behavior

The ancient Greeks kept some of the earliest written records of humans thinking about the ability to think. Heraclitus, a Greek philosopher of the sixth century B.C., referred to the mind as an enormous space whose boundaries could never be reached, even by traveling along every path.

Speculation about the nature of mental activity has probably gone on since thinking began, but agreement on the source of mental activity is a relatively recent accomplishment. In the fourth century B.C., Aristotle wrote that the brain was bloodless and that the heart was not only the source of nervous control, but was also the seat of the soul. (Aristotle is revered today more for his invention of a systematic style of thinking than for his neuroanatomical insights.) The early dissectors of animal brains in the second century A.D. took great care to assure the authorities that they sought only for the center of the system of nerves that caused the body to sense and move. For the next thousand or more years those who examined the brain took the same precautions. The church, after all, retained authority over human consciousness, the "soul," and the soul, wherever it lay, was not subject to direct investigation.

Analysis by Analogy

Historians of science have observed that thinkers in the past tried to explain how the brain and mind worked by using analogies to the physical world in which they lived. This striking observation can be stated more poetically as "the metaphors of mind are the world it perceives" (Jaynes, 1976). The Greek physician Galen, living in the second century A.D., was one of the first to dissect the brains of humans and other animals. The major technological achievements in his day

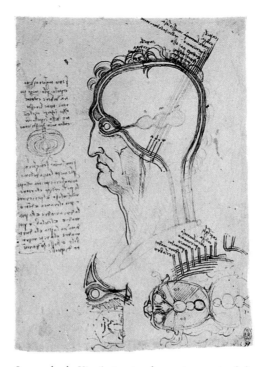

Leonardo da Vinci's passion for anatomy extended to dissection. In sketches like this one he follows the medieval convention of spherical ventricles, the foremost of which he called the "common sense cell," where the soul was thought to reside.

were aqueducts and sewer systems that relied on the principles of fluid mechanics. It is hardly accidental, then, that Galen believed the important parts of the brain to lie not in the brain's substance but in its fluid-filled cavities. Today these cavities are known as the cerebroventricular system, and the fluid that is made there is called cerebrospinal fluid. Galen, however, believed that all physical functions and states of health and ill-health depended on the distribution of four body fluids, or "humors": choler (or blood), phlegm (or mucus), black bile, and yellow bile. Each "humor" had a special function: blood carried the animal's vital living spirit; phlegm caused sluggishness; black bile was

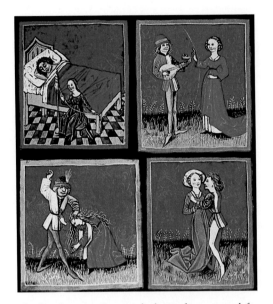

The four humors. Counterclockwise from upper left: too much black bile keeps a melancholic man in bed; yellow bile drives the choleric husband to wife-beating; phlegm makes a reluctant mistress; the high-blooded lover plays the lute for his lady.

responsible for melancholy; and yellow bile aroused the temper. So deeply were Galen's views ingrained in Western thought that the role of humors in brain and other organ functions remained largely unquestioned for nearly 1500 years.

By the eighteenth century, more rigorous-minded observers had begun to attack the natural phenomena of the world "scientifically." The undocumented and hypothetical constructs of the past were replaced by the conviction that everything could be explained in terms of mechanics. It was now a world of machines. The brain machinery of the sensing organs for vision and hearing was the first to be revealed. In the early seventeenth century, the German astronomer Johannes Kepler argued that the eye operated essentially like an ordinary optical instrument, by projecting the image of what

was being seen onto the special sensory nerves of the retina, the light-detecting tissue at the back of the eye. Some 75 years later, the description of the mechanisms of the inner ear by the English anatomist Thomas Willis led to the recognition that hearing was based on the transformation of sound through the air by activation of special receptors of the cochlea, a coiled tube of tissue within the inner ear.

These mechanistic discoveries gave rise to a split in thinking about body and mind, which some scholars believe has caused problems ever since. Philosopher and mathematician René Descartes is often cited as the father of this body-mind dualism. Questions of biological science—that is, of what could be "known" about human beings and other animals—could apply only to those structures they shared in common. The processes of perceiving and examining the images received by these structures belonged to a different and separate "mental" world reserved only for humans. Although this permitted a mathematically accurate portrayal of the transformation of optical and auditory images, it did not answer the deeper questions of how the sensations received were synthesized into meaningful images of the world.

During the sixteenth and seventeenth centuries, scientific advances gave rise to accurate descriptions (but not actual explanations) of electricity. And as seventeenth-century explorers spread out around the world, a more complete notion of the surface of the earth was gained. The principles of both electricity and geography were eventually applied to concepts of how the brain worked. However, change was slow. When the important properties of the nervous system ceased to be regarded as the flow of humors, this explanation was temporarily replaced by the theories of the "ballonists," who considered the nerves to be hollow tubes through which the flow of gases ex-

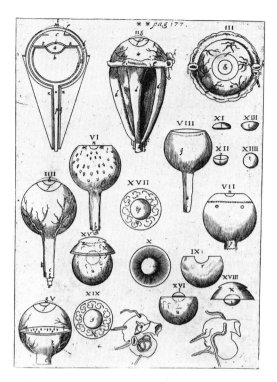

Johannes Kepler portrayed the eye as an optical instrument rather than a divine mystery. This view of body parts as being like other machines was the breakthrough that allowed scientific research to begin.

cited the muscles. How did one disprove such a view? Scientists dissected animals under water. When no gases were observed to bubble up during muscle contractions, the theory went flat.

What new insight was gained from this gruesome experiment? (Remember that although electricity was known, its powers had yet to be applied to practical uses. The industry of this era, mid-seventeenth century, received its power from windmills, flowing rivers, and waterfalls.) Something had to flow from the nerves to cause muscles to contract, so a "vital fluid" theory replaced the gas theory. It was reasoned that an "essence" of the hollow nerves flowed into the

muscle, mixed with its fluids, and caused explosive contractions. This "fluid" hypothesis was one of the first to be issued from the newly formed Royal Society of England, around 1661.

The vital-fluid concept eventually gave way to the view, proposed by the physicist Isaac Newton around the beginning of the eighteenth century, that activity was transmitted by a vibrating "aetherial Medium," one which had all the properties later found to hold for biological electricity. Even with the primitive instruments of the eighteenth and nineteenth centuries, it was rather easy to show that both nerves and muscles were electrically excitable. However, the view that the nerves and muscles themselves actually worked by generating animal electricity was not immediately grasped. The Italian scientist Luigi Galvani solved this problem near the end of the eighteenth century, and the German biologist Emil du Bois-Reymond reexamined it early in the next century. Du Bois-Reymond was the first scientist to attempt an explanation of all functions of the brain on the basis of chemical and physical grounds. He and his coworkers were the first to measure in a convincing way the electrical properties of living, active nerves and muscles.

Analysis by Observation and Experimentation

During the nineteenth century, medical investigators provided the next wave of understanding about the brain. Taking advantage of the unfortunate victims of the expanding technology of war, medical observers could determine the exact locations of destructive injuries, or lesions, in the brains of soldiers with nonfatal head injuries. Clinical observations, which connected specific neurologic or mental problems to specific areas of damage to the brain, continue to serve as a major source of vital information. The "le-

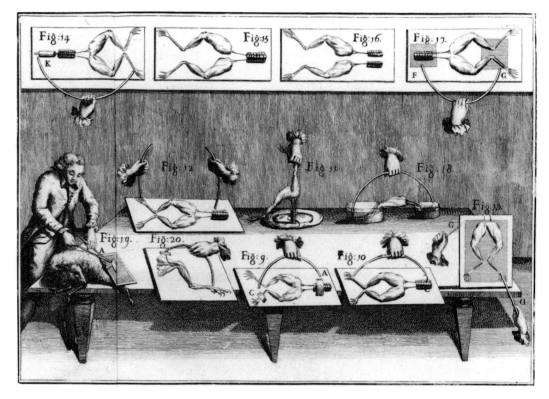

Luigi Galvani's electricity-producing machine one day accidentally sparked a twitch in the leg of a freshly dissected frog. The general observation that electrical stimuli can cause muscles to contract set off the search for "animal electricity."

sion approach" was also applied experimentally to the brains of other animals in order to find the locations of gross functions, such as response to touch or movement of the limbs.

The Austrian anatomist Franz Joseph Gall carried the concept of localized sensory and motor regions in the brain one step further. Perhaps borrowing an idea from geography, Gall proposed that all human mental faculties—from such well-accepted abilities as speech and movement to detailed and inferential skills like dexterity, wit, and veneration of the deity—could be located by charting the bulges in the skull that overlay the pertinent physical structures of the brain. This transient science, known as phrenology, soon fell out of favor. A corresponding strategy of animal brain research, however, was more useful. Its proponents believed that the action for which a brain region was responsible could be determined by seeing what happened when the region was electrically stimulated. By the end of the nineteenth century, these two techniques of research—lesions and stimulation—had enabled scientists to identify large functional segments of the brain.

As physical scientists began to explore beneath the surface of the earth and examine in detail the structural and chemical properties of the soil, brain scientists in the late nineteenth and early twentieth centuries began similar "geological" examinations of what lay below the surface structures of the brain. Lesions and stimulation experiments had shown that the outer layers of the brain were essential for the highest forms of consciousness and sensory responsiveness. By geological analogy, the layers beneath were assumed to represent structures that were laid down earlier in evolution, the most primitive being the deep structures of the midbrain and hindbrain. When these regions were destroyed, animals could not survive.

Further insight came from detailed analyses of brain structure. These efforts were led by the success of the early microscopists, such as the English anatomist Augustus von Waller, who discovered a chemical method that would detect strands of dying nerves (so-called "Wallerian degeneration"). This chemical "stain" helped establish that the long fibers of the nerves outside of the brain and spinal cord were actually extensions of the cells inside the brain and spinal cord. Some of these large cells could even be seen with the aid of the primitive microscopes. Although microscopes were available earlier, the complex and compact cellular structure of the brain was not easily examined. More stains were needed to highlight single cells selectively.

Soon thereafter, by the 1880s, the Italian Camillo Golgi and the Spaniard Santiago Ramón y Cajal began to apply improved staining methods intensively. Now the detailed structures of the brain could be resolved into two main classes of cells: the nerve cells, or *neurons,* and the cells that appeared like glue between the nerve cells, called *neuroglia,* or sometimes just *glia.* Microscopic analysis of the brain and its parts then became a third critical "instrument" in the researcher's tool box.

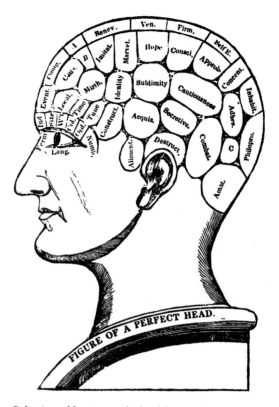

Palpation of bumps on the head became the rage after the introduction of phrenology in 1790. Everyone wanted his or her head read—except, perhaps, those with bumps around the ears, which stood for combativeness, destructiveness, secretiveness, acquisitiveness, and a devotion to food.

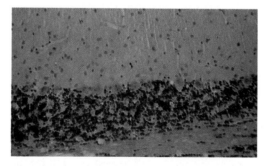

Layering of the cerebellum. At this very low power of magnification, the nerve-cell nuclei appear as deep purple-blue spots. Three basic cellular layers are visible because of the density at which the neurons are packed.

A Golgi-stained neuron from the cerebellar cortex of an adult rat. Following chemical exposure, this large Purkinje neuron has become totally impregnated with silver, giving it a near-black image that makes it stand out from the unstained cells around it. The elaborate dendritic system arising from the cell body is clearly seen.

The recognition that the tissue of the brain was composed of individual cells connected by their extensions led to the question of how those cells worked together to perform the work of the brain. For decades, arguments raged as to whether the process of transmission between neurons was electrical or chemical. By the mid-1920s, however, most scientists were willing to accept the current view, that the activation of muscles and the regulation of the heartbeat and other peripheral organs occurs by the passage of chemical signals arising in the nerves.

This chemical-transmission hypothesis was clearly demonstrated in the experiments of the English pharmacologist Sir Henry Dale and the Austrian biologist Otto Loewi. Their discoveries led directly to the use of a fourth investigative strategy, the application of plant extracts and synthetic chemicals directly to the nerves and muscles in order to compare their effects with those actually produced by the nerve. Although chemical transmission was considered a necessary and sufficient explanation of the responses to nerve signals in the limbs and viscera, its central role in the links between the neurons of the brain and elsewhere took much longer to demonstrate.

A Contemporary Analogy

The complexity of the brain—even the brains of small animals—that has slowly emerged from these hard-won discoveries staggers the imagination. The history of brain science in the twentieth century has yet to be completely written. When it is, the working analogy for the living brain might be the computer.

Analogies often help scientists to model brain experiments according to some other grand design already recognized in nature—either as we find it, as we see and observe it, or as we imagine it to be. But no model, no matter how closely it simulates the operations of the brain, will be completely acceptable until it can predict features of the brain's operation that are not now readily apparent. The objective of brain scientists is not to develop a model or a machine that can merely simulate or explain some of what we already know the brain can do. Rather, the successful model will explain what the brain does and how.

The Scientific Method

A true experimental science of the brain (or any other object of interest) requires a method that allows for the establishment of certain facts, and then uses those facts to ask better questions in order to gain more fundamental insights. The scientific method depends on several separate components: (1) *observation,* the accurate recording of the methods of study, the experimental conditions under which the observations were made, and the results of the experiment; (2) *interpretation,* reasoning about the results in order to generate hypotheses that can be used to frame future experiments, and (3) *verification,* the repetition of the study by others, using the same conditions, in order to confirm or question the results.

The process of working from observations, to formulation of an integrative hypothesis, to evaluation of the hypothesis experimentally is known as *inductive reasoning.* Scientists who believe they work this way argue that they have no fixed ideas at the start but simply allow nature to reveal itself through painstaking observations. A contrasting strategy, attributed to Aristotle, is *deductive reasoning,* in which one starts with a global hypothesis and then formulates experiments to test its truth.

Most scientists probably use both strategies. It is virtually impossible not to have some preexisting impressions, or intuitions, before an experiment, and it is equally impossible to make observations without having these ideas somewhere in the background. Indeed, unless you have some idea of what you are looking for, you probably cannot recognize it when you see it. It is possible, however, when the data are presented according to the rules of science, for one scientist to question another's interpretation. An outsider without the discoverer's biases can, and often does, come up with another explanation of the discoverer's results. The art of science, then, derives from an ability to look at someone else's observations and devise new experiments that will confirm their accuracy or suggest another explanation.

The chapters that follow this introduction describe and discuss the results of scientific studies of the brain and other elements of the nervous system. (The box on pages 10 and 11 describes the many types of methods scientists use in conducting studies of the nervous system.) However, before we can make sense of their discoveries, we need to know, in broad outline, the elements of the nervous system and the basic organization of the brain.

The Organization of the Nervous System

In order to describe "brain" properly, we must understand its relation to the central and peripheral nervous systems. The *central nervous system* (or CNS) includes all the parts of the nervous system that lie within

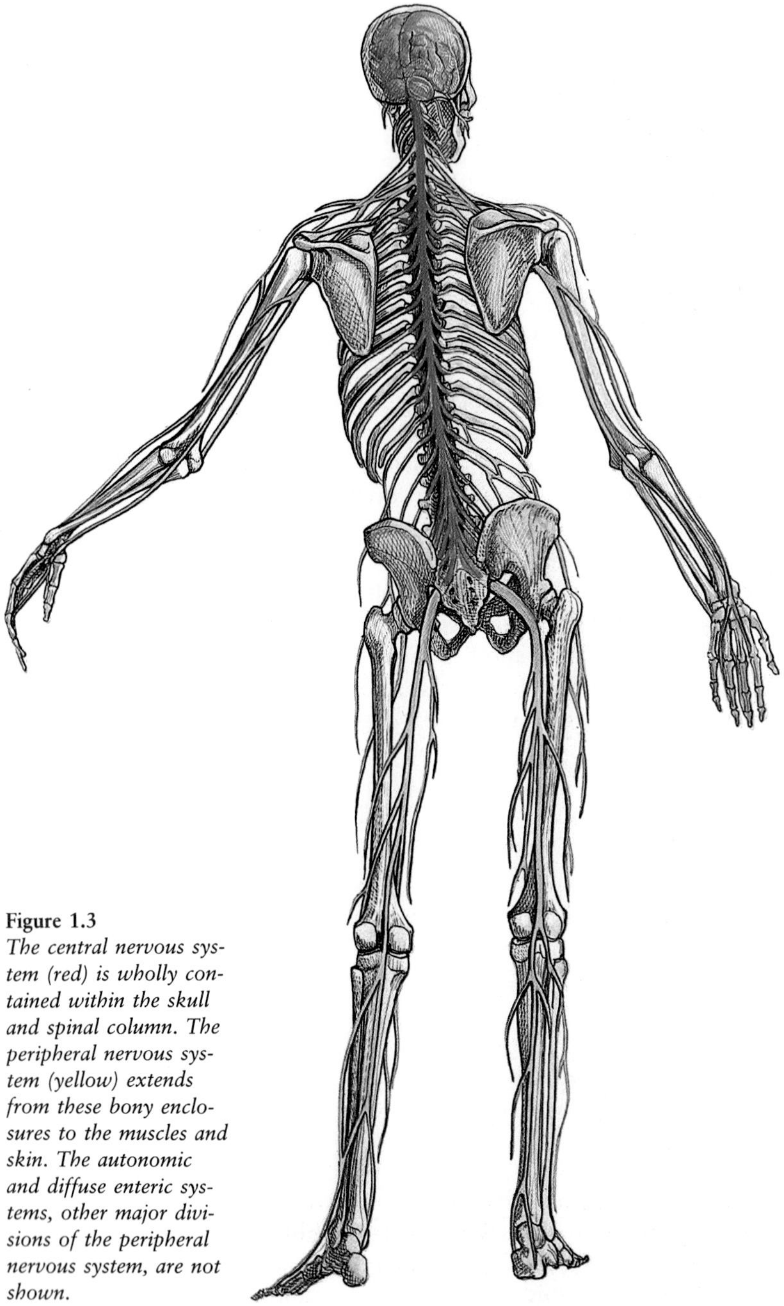

Figure 1.3
The central nervous system (red) is wholly contained within the skull and spinal column. The peripheral nervous system (yellow) extends from these bony enclosures to the muscles and skin. The autonomic and diffuse enteric systems, other major divisions of the peripheral nervous system, are not shown.

the bones of the skull and spine (see Figure 1.3). The brain, therefore, is that part of the CNS enclosed within the bones of the skull. The other major component of the CNS is the spinal cord.

Nerves come into and out of the CNS, and once these nerves are beyond the bony protective shelter of the skull and spine, they are considered to be parts of the *peripheral nervous system* (PNS) (see Figure 1.3). One division of the PNS, the *somatic* (meaning "to the body"), consists of the nerves that carry information from the skin, muscles, bones, and joints to the spinal cord and from the spinal cord to the muscles. Some parts of the PNS, however, have only remote connections with the central nervous system and work with its limited supervision. These nerves are a division of the PNS called the *autonomic nervous system* (or ANS), a set of structures described in later chapters. For now it is sufficient to know that the ANS is largely responsible for regulating the internal environment: the heart, lungs, blood vessels, and other internal organs. In addition, the digestive tract has its own internal autonomous nervous system, the *diffuse enteric nervous system,* which some neuroscientists now consider to be a third division of the PNS.

The Organization of the Brain: An Introduction

We offer in this chapter only the most basic introduction to the brain's organization. The details are given in the context of the brain's operation in later chapters. Table 1.2 identifies the major anatomical regions of the brain and their subdivisions (see also Figure 1.4). These regions can be distinguished during the early stages of embryonic development (described in Chapter 3).

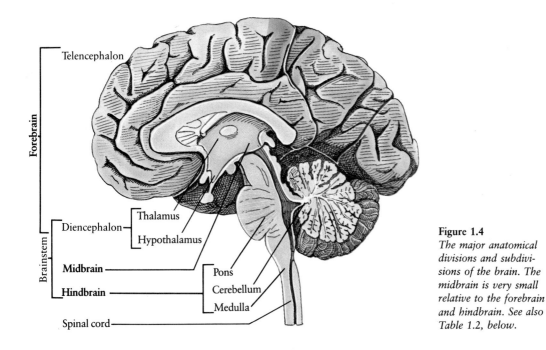

Telencephalon

Forebrain

Diencephalon

Brainstem

Thalamus
Hypothalamus

Midbrain

Hindbrain

Pons
Cerebellum
Medulla

Spinal cord

Figure 1.4
The major anatomical divisions and subdivisions of the brain. The midbrain is very small relative to the forebrain and hindbrain. See also Table 1.2, below.

As seen from the outline form in Table 1.2, the organization of the brain is largely hierarchical. For example, the forebrain is composed of the diencephalon and the telencephalon; and the diencephalon, in turn, is composed of the thalamus and the hypothalamus. These large divisions and subdivisions are just the beginning of the hierarchy. The hypothalamus, for example, is composed of a number of nuclei; a nucleus is a densely packed group of neurons, or nerve cells, that usually function as a collective entity. The nucleus is visually distinct from the surrounding matter. Other distinct groups of neurons—which are not as densely packed as those in a nucleus—are called *fields* or *areas*.

Although the anatomical organization of the brain is hierarchical, its operational organization often is not. Widely separated brain parts may form an "alliance" to carry out particular functions. For example, specific places throughout the brain must work to-

Table 1.2   *Major anatomical divisions and subdivisions of the brain*

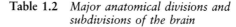

Forebrain	
Telencephalon	
Cerebral hemispheres	
Amygdala	
Hippocampus	
Basal ganglia	
Septum	
Diencephalon	
Thalamus	
Hypothalamus	
Midbrain	Brainstem
Hindbrain	
Medulla	
Cerebellum	
Pons	

gether to construct an accurate interpretation of what our sense organs detect. Table 1.3 lists a number of such functional systems.

Table 1.3 *Some functional brain systems*

System	Function
Sensory	Specific sensing operations
Receptors in skin, muscle	Vision
Relay nuclei in spinal cord, thalamus	Hearing
Cortical areas	Olfaction
	Taste
	Somatic sensation
Motor	Specific motion components
Muscle and spinal motor neurons	Reflexes
Cerebellum, basal ganglis	Movement-pattern initiation and control
Motor cortex, thalamus, and cortex	Complex movement of joints
Internal regulatory	
Hypothalamic nuclei and pituitary	Reproduction
	Appetite
	Salt and water balance
Behavioral state	
Medulla, pons, midbrain, and cortex	Sleeping, waking, attention

Finally, much of the brain's outer layer, the cortex, develops distinctive operational units both in a horizontal and vertical direction. These horizontal layers and vertical columns form a sort of warp and woof texture and perform specific functions, which will be discussed in appropriate chapters.

We started this chapter by claiming that the brain is the most complex living structure in the universe. You may, by now, begin to agree. It is, however, as fascinating as it is complex. For this introduction, we need only examine the main structures listed in Table 1.2.

The Forebrain and Its Parts

The forebrain structures—the telencephalon and the diencephalon—are generally credited with performance of the "highest" intellectual functions: thinking, planning, and problem solving.

The telencephalon When you first look at a brain, the most prominent structures are the two large, paired, left and right hemispheres of the *cerebral cortex,* the brain's outermost layer (see Figure 1.5). The cortex of each hemisphere is subdivided into four sections, or *lobes,* by deep grooves that are called sulci. The lobes are named either for their locations or for the major functions attributed to them (see Figure 1.6): the *occipital lobe* for vision; the *temporal lobe* for hearing and, in humans, speech; the *parietal lobe* for sensory responses; and the *frontal lobe* for motor control and coordination of the functions of the other cortical areas.

Under the cortex lie the smaller regions of the telencephalon: the *amygdala,* or amygdaloid complex (named for its nutlike shape), the *hippocampus* (shaped like a sea horse), the *basal ganglia,* and the *septum* (named for the wall it forms between two of

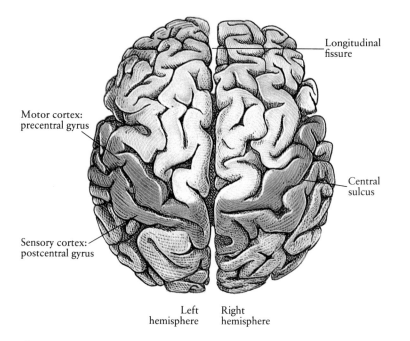

Longitudinal fissure

Motor cortex: precentral gyrus

Central sulcus

Sensory cortex: postcentral gyrus

Left hemisphere   Right hemisphere

Figure 1.5
The hemispheres of the human cerebral cortex as viewed from above.

the brain's fluid-filled cavities, or *ventricles*) (see Figure 1.7).

The amygdala, hippocampus, basal ganglia, and septum function together to help regulate emotion, memory, and certain aspects of movement. Together, they are called the *limbic system*.

The diencephalon   The subdivisions of the diencephalon are the *thalamus* and *hypothalamus* (see Figure 1.4). Both of these structures contain well-defined areas. Specific *thalamic fields* and *nuclei* serve as relay stations for almost all the information coming into and out of the forebrain. Specific *hypothalamic fields* and *nuclei* serve as relay stations for the internal regulatory systems, monitoring information coming in from the autonomic nervous system and commanding the body through those nerves and the pituitary.

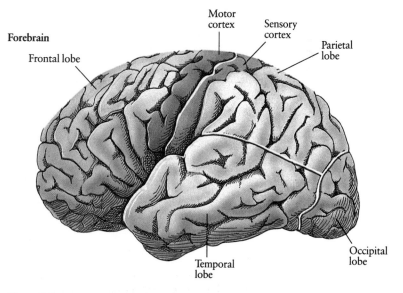

Forebrain

Motor cortex

Sensory cortex

Parietal lobe

Frontal lobe

Occipital lobe

Temporal lobe

Figure 1.6
One hemisphere of the cerebral cortex, showing the location of the four lobes into which it is divided. The divide between the motor cortex and the sensory cortex, the central sulcus, marks the boundary between the frontal and parietal lobes.

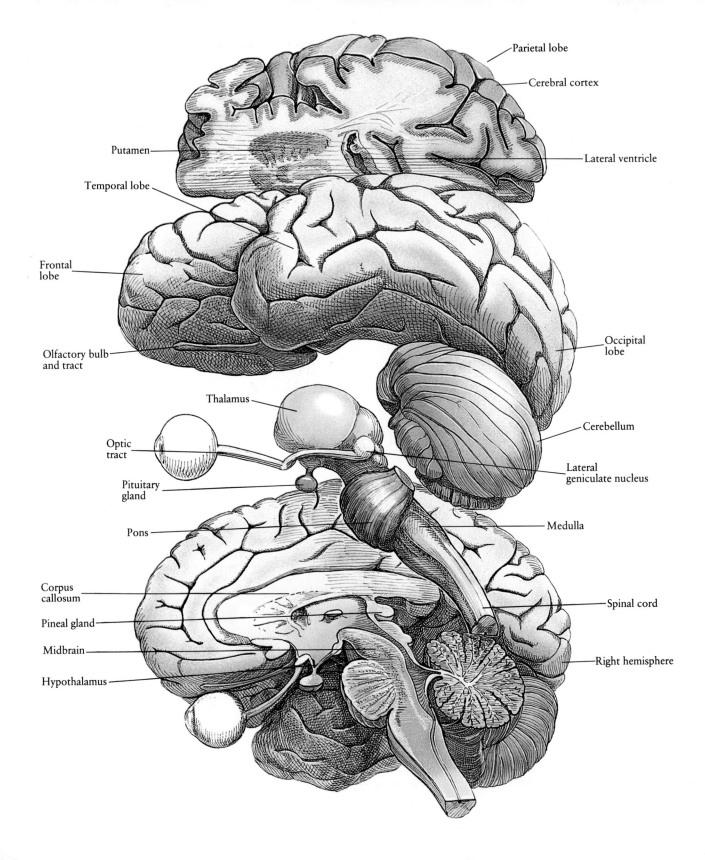

Parietal lobe

Cerebral cortex

Putamen

Lateral ventricle

Temporal lobe

Frontal lobe

Occipital lobe

Olfactory bulb and tract

Thalamus

Cerebellum

Optic tract

Lateral geniculate nucleus

Pituitary gland

Pons

Medulla

Corpus callosum

Spinal cord

Pineal gland

Midbrain

Right hemisphere

Hypothalamus

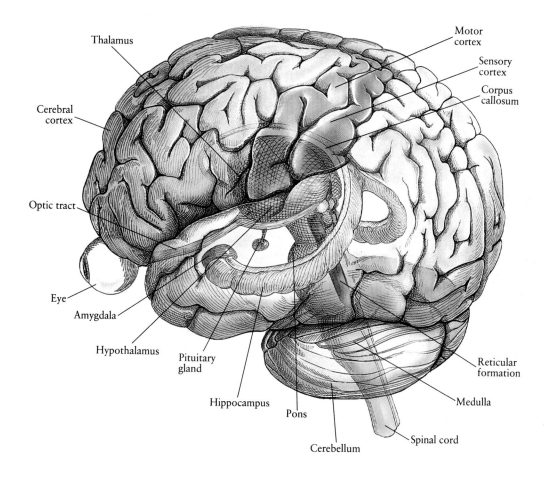

Thalamus

Motor cortex

Sensory cortex

Corpus callosum

Cerebral cortex

Optic tract

Eye

Amygdala

Hypothalamus

Pituitary gland

Hippocampus

Pons

Cerebellum

Spinal cord

Medulla

Reticular formation

Figure 1.7

At left, the major areas, regions, and some specific places can be seen in this view of a sliced and separated human brain. The left and right cerebral hemispheres and the entire set of structures lying along the midline have been bisected. The internal parts of the left hemibrain are shown as they would appear if dissected free. The eye and optic nerve are shown connected to the hypothalamic mass, from the lower surface of which the pituitary emerges. The pons, medulla, and spinal cord extend from its hind surface. The left side of the cerebellum appears below the left hemisphere, exposing the olfactory bulb. The upper half of the left cerebral hemisphere is also bisected, revealing parts of the basal ganglia (putamen) and a portion of the left lateral ventricle. Above, the brain assembled, showing major structures active in sensing and internal regulation, as well as those in the limbic system and brain stem.

The Midbrain and Its Parts

The midbrain is the smallest of the major brain divisions and is the most difficult to recognize when examining the brain. Some scientists believe that the organization of divisions set out in Table 1.2 should be revised to reflect the midbrain's small size and relative lack of distinctive features, but other scientists—purists, perhaps—refuse to consider its annexation. Thus, it remains on its own, as the region between the pons and the diencephalon (see Figure 1.4). On its upper surface are two pairs of small hills (colliculi)—collections of cells that relay specific sensory information from sense organs to the brain. The two closest to the pons—the inferior colliculi—relay auditory information; and the two closest to the thalamus—the superior colliculi—relay visual information.

The Hindbrain and Its Parts

The major parts of the hindbrain are the *pons* (bridge), the *medulla oblongata* (often simply called the *medulla*), and the *cerebellum* (see Figure 1.4, purple area). The structures within the pons, medulla, and cerebellum generally interact with telencephalon structures by relays through the midbrain and the diencephalon, with some exceptions. A parallel term, the *brainstem,* includes all of the hindbrain plus the midbrain and the diencephalon. This "stem" contains almost all of the connections between the cerebral cortex and the spinal cord. The *fields* and *nuclei* of the pons and medulla, which control respiration and heart rhythms, are critical to survival. The attachment of the cerebellum to the roof of the hindbrain has been interpreted to mean that it receives and modifies information related to body and limb position before that information makes its way to the thalamus and cortex. The cerebellum stores the basic repertoire of learned motor responses which the motor cortex may request.

This brief outline of the brain's anatomical organization will be filled in with more detail as you learn, in later chapters, how the brain allows us to sense and move, sleep and awaken, love and fear, think and remember. But before you can truly understand how the brain functions in these activities and experiences, you must gain some familiarity with how individual nerve cells function. We explore these cellular properties in Chapter 2.

Two Basic Concepts of Neuroscience

1. *The nervous system operates throughout the body.* The nervous system is the organ of the body responsible for: (a) sensing and reacting to the world around us; (b) coordinating the functions of other organs so that the body can survive—eating, drinking, breathing, moving, and reproducing; and (c) storing, organizing, and retrieving past experiences.

The two operating divisions of the nervous system are: (a) the central nervous system, consisting of the brain and spinal cord, which is contained within the bony compartments formed by the skull and spinal column; and (b) the peripheral nervous system, which consists of the peripheral nerves in the skin, muscles, bones, and joints, along with two other subsystems—the autonomic nervous system, which regulates the activity of the internal organs, and the diffuse enteric nervous system, which regulates the digestive tract.

2. The separate functions of the nervous system are carried out by subsystems organized according to area of responsibility. Each function of the brain—sensing, moving, and all of the regulating actions—is a responsibility of a separate system. The parts of each system are most easily understood in terms of a hierarchy. In addition, specific—and critical—connections exist between specific parts of the nervous system. As information is processed through the hierarchy, it goes from "lower" levels, such as those in the peripheral nervous system and spinal cord, to "higher" levels, such as those in the cerebral cortex.

Although the operations performed on each level can be detected by observing that the activity of one level causes activity in the next level and by determining some of the actual connections within a rank-ordered system, current knowledge is inadequate to explain these operations in any detail.

Further Reading

Hubel, David H. 1979. The Brain. In *The Brain*. New York: W. H. Freeman. A Nobel-prize-winning scientist looks at the broad problems of studying the brain, touching on the history of neurobiology and the evolution of the brain. He also offers some speculations on the future of brain science.

Hebb, Donald O. 1980. *Essay on Mind*. Hillsdale, N.J.: Lawrence Erlbaum Associates. A famous psychologist offers his thoughts on the relationship of brain and mind.

Worden, F. G., Swazey, J. P., and Adelman, G., eds. 1975. *The Neurosciences: Paths of Discovery*. Cambridge, Mass., MIT Press. A number of noted neuroscientists tell about the paths they took, including blind alleys and detours, in their quest for knowledge about the workings of the nervous system.

Adelman, G., ed. 1987. *Encyclopedia of Neuroscience*, Vols. I and II, Birkäuser Publishers, Boston, An up-to-date compendium of short essays by leaders in the field on a wide selection of topics in the neurosciences.

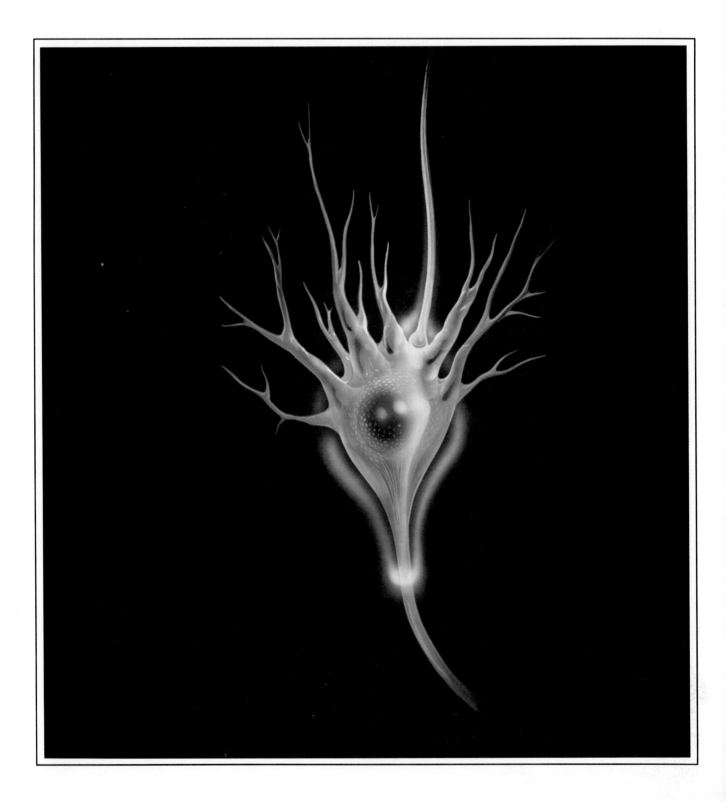

2

The Cellular and Chemical Machinery of the Brain

2

In the preceding chapter, we looked at the sequence of models that people have used over the centuries in attempting to understand and describe the workings of the human brain. It was proposed that the contemporary analogy for the brain's workings may be the computer. Just like us, the computer takes in information, processes it in some way, and offers up its reworking of the original information. At first glance, computers and brains seem to have much in common—both have many very small parts, both perform complicated feats that appear to involve reasoning, and neither seems to have any moving parts.

Some computers appear to be more powerful than the human brain—a computer that handles very complicated mathematical problems and performs all the detailed calculations in the correct order can work all night on them without getting tired and in the end tell us, for example, exactly what time a space shuttle will reenter the earth's atmosphere and, almost to the second, what time it will land back on earth. This computer, however, cannot protect itself against a power blackout, or laugh at a joke, or compose a poem about something it feels.

Like the earlier models for the brain's workings, the computer analogy has shortcomings. For example, a computer's means of operating is extremely rigid, partly because it does not form the same kinds of memory associations that human beings do. If you need a screwdriver and none is at hand, you will think of using a knife, a nail file, a comb, a letter opener, a spoon handle, a coin edge, and so on. These are essentially creative association processes; it is almost impossible to design a computer program

A human nerve cell. The dendrites that branch out of the cell carry electrical impulses to axons, which release chemical messengers to other cells (see Figure 2.4 for details of neurotransmitter release).

that can lead to such nonsequential, nonlogical—but nevertheless useful—associations.

Perhaps the most telling argument against the computer/brain analogy is the fact that our brain sits atop and constantly interacts with a body—flesh and bone, guts and glands, eyes, ears, and nose. This body changes throughout the life span and differs from moment to moment. Our brain and body create a history together. An odor experienced in childhood and suddenly reexperienced in middle age can cause our brain to call up a flood of memories: details of the place where the experience occurred, such as the quality of sunlight, the colors of a patterned carpet, the arrangement of furniture. We might recall how our skin felt against the fabric covering a chair we were sitting on at the time. We usually remember the other people there and the quality of the emotional interaction taking place, and most important, how we felt at that moment, whether our emotion was contentment or fear or anger.

Computers can have no such history. If we are to accept the computer model of the brain's workings, it must be in a very limited way—perhaps at the level of logical reasoning, which is only a small part of what the human brain does.

To know how the brain works, we must first gain an understanding of the different cells that compose this intricate, dense web of tissue. It is only because certain of these cells make signals, chemical and electrical, that we are able to think and feel and are able to recall how we thought and felt. These cells are the neurons.

Neurons

Individual nerve cells, or *neurons,* do not perform local functions in isolated units the way cells of the liver, kidney, or other organs of the body do. The billions of neurons in the human nervous system "work" by receiving messages from and sending messages to other nerve cells. Sending cells and receiving cells are linked to each other in *circuits* (see Figure 2.1 for an overview of the neuronal organization discussed here), roughly like the electrical circuits that link the appliances in your home to a central circuit box where the power company brings in the electricity. In general, a given neuron is connected to only a few specific recipients and has a rather limited number of neurons from which it receives information. However, in some cases, an individual neuron may transmit messages to as many as 10,000 other neurons. There are basically just a few patterns of neuronal circuits, with many minor variations (see

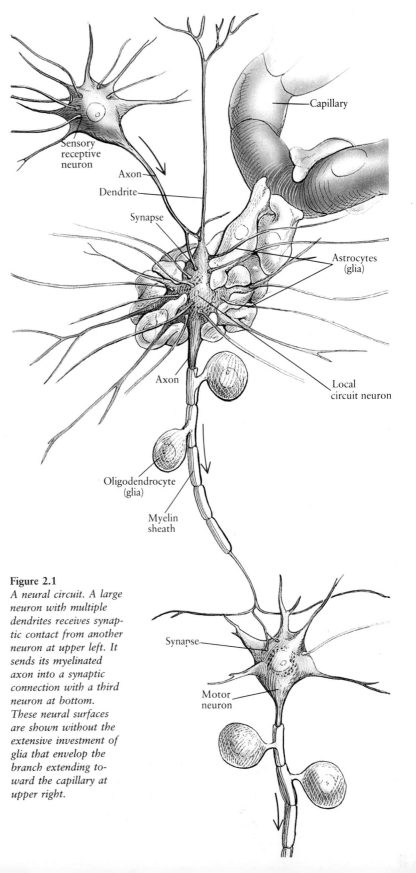

Figure 2.1
A neural circuit. A large neuron with multiple dendrites receives synaptic contact from another neuron at upper left. It sends its myelinated axon into a synaptic connection with a third neuron at bottom. These neural surfaces are shown without the extensive investment of glia that envelop the branch extending toward the capillary at upper right.

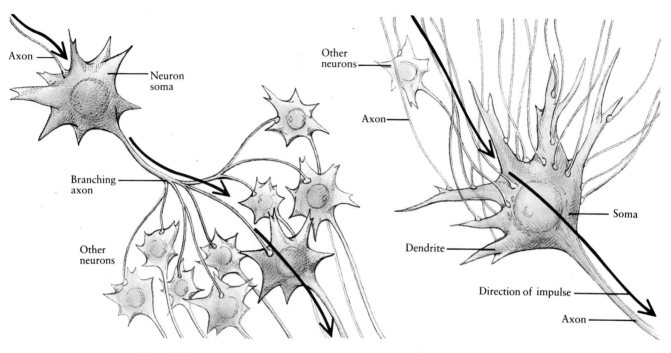

Figure 2.2
Schematic drawings of two of the most common types of neural circuitry. Left, a divergent circuit, where one neuron, through branchings of its axon, sends its signal to many other neurons. Right, a convergent circuit, where one target neuron receives signals from many different neurons.

Figure 2.2). We will explore these basic patterns later in the chapter.

The actual linking sites, the specific communication points on the surfaces of nerve cells, are called *synapses* (see Figures 2.1 and 2.4), and the process of information transfer at such sites is called *synaptic transmission.* When neurons communicate through synaptic transmission, the sending cell secretes a chemical, called a *neurotransmitter,* which carries the message from the sending cell to the receiving cell. The chemical signal bridges the small space (about 20 nanometers—20 billionths of a meter) that separates even the most closely connected cells in the brain. This small space is often called the *synaptic gap.*

After looking at some cellular features of neurons, we will have more to say about the transmission of neural messages.

What Neurons Have in Common with Other Cells

Neurons share some features with virtually every other cell in the human body. The common features are the plasma membrane; the cytoplasm and organelles within it that conduct the business of the cell; and the cell's nucleus.

Plasma Membrane Like all other cells, neurons have an external wall, or *plasma membrane.* This membrane surrounds the cell and forms a boundary between its interior and the external environment. When a neuron interacts with other neurons or

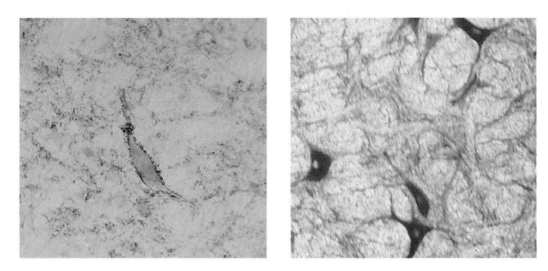

Figure 2.2
Large neurons in a portion of the brainstem called the reticular formation, seen through a light microscope. In left photo, a large cell is outlined by almost continuous synaptic terminals at its surface. In right photo, several large neurons and their major dendrites appear, but the small axons, glia, dendrites, and synapses in the spaces between the cells cannot be seen.

senses changes in the local environment, it does so by means of the array of molecular machinery embedded in the plasma membrane.

Cytoplasm and Organelles All the material enclosed by the plasma membrane is referred to as the *cytoplasm*. Within the cytoplasm are the *cytoplasmic organelles*, little organs that cells need to maintain themselves and do their work (see Figure 2.3). The organelles include the mitochondria, microtubules, ribosomes, and endoplasmic reticulum. The *mitochondria* provide energy for the cell by converting sugar and oxygen into special energy molecules. *Microtubules* are fine "struts" that help maintain the cell's structure.

The network of internal membrane channels by which the cell distributes the products it needs in order to function is called the *endoplasmic reticulum*. Many cells, including neurons, must both distribute products

within the cell and export products for use outside the cell. The products to be secreted to the outside are manufactured by organelles called *ribosomes* that are attached to one kind of endoplasmic reticulum. Because it is studded with these ribosomes, this type of membrane channel is called *rough endoplasmic reticulum*. The vast amounts of rough endoplasmic reticulum contained in the cytoplasm of neurons mark them as cells that are very active in making products for outside secretion (namely, neurotransmitters).

Organelles composed of *smooth endoplasmic reticulum* package the products for outside secretion; these membrane-covered packets are subsequently shipped to the surface of the cell at the point where the secretion takes place. A specialized component of the smooth endoplasmic reticulum is called the *Golgi apparatus*, after the Italian Camillo Golgi, who first developed a method for staining this internal structure so that it could be studied under a microscope. It is

Camillo Golgi (1844–1926). This photo was taken in the early 1880s when Golgi was a professor at the University of Padua. In 1906, Golgi and Ramón y Cajal shared the Nobel prize in physiology and medicine.

Figure 2.3
The internal structure of a typical neuron. The microtubules provide structural rigidity as well as mechanisms for transport of materials synthesized in the cell body and destined for use in the synaptic zone at bottom. Within the synaptic terminal, synaptic vesicles storing the transmitter, along with vesicles that fulfill other functions in transmitter release and conservation, also appear. On the surface of the postsynaptic dendrite, the presumed location of the receptors for the transmitter are seen. (Figure 2.4 shows more detail.)

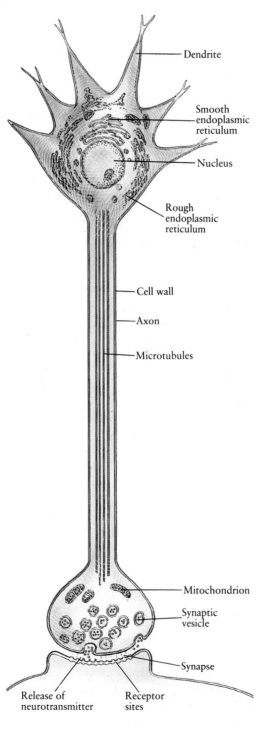

prominent in all cells specialized for secretory activity.

Products for the cell's own use are synthesized in the numerous ribosomes that exist free within the cytoplasm, unattached to endoplasmic reticulum.

Nucleus At the center of the cytoplasm is the cell's *nucleus*. Here, neurons, like all other nucleated cells, contain their genetic information, coded within the chemical structures of genes. Each gene instructs the fully developed cell to make certain products that establish the specific shape, chemistry, and function of that cell. Because mature neurons (unlike almost all the other cells of the body) are unable to divide to form new cells, the genetically specified products of any neuron must be sufficient to maintain and modify that cell's function for its lifetime.

Unique Features of Neurons

Most cells of the body look, more or less, like smooth spheres, cubes, or flat plates. In contrast, neurons have highly irregular shapes, with one or a few or many protrusions extending from their surfaces. These protruding structures—the axon and dendrites—are the living "wires" by which neurons are linked into neuronal circuits (see Figure 2.1).

The structure of individual neurons was first revealed when another staining method developed by Golgi was insightfully applied by his rival, the Spanish microscopist Santiago Ramón y Cajal. This Golgi stain uses metallic silver, which binds to the microtubules; it gives stained cells a black color when light is shone through a thin section of the brain under a microscope (see figure on p. 18). Before Ramón y Cajal's work, some observers, including Golgi himself, thought the brain was composed of giant multinucleated nets, in which the pool of cytoplasm was common and continuous. Using Golgi's staining method, even with the rather primitive microscopes available then, Ramón y Cajal was able to establish the basic features of the cellular organization of the brain and to make the point that the complex structure of the brain depends on individual cells and their connections.

Axons and Dendrites   Each nerve cell has one main protruding element called the *axon*, by means of which it sends information to its partner cells in a circuit. When a neuron must communicate with more than one target cell, its axon branches many times in order to send connecting axons off the main line to each of the intended recipient cells. The branches are called *collateral axons*. Although a neuron may have many collateral axons, only one axon extends from the cell body.

The other protruding elements of a neuron are called *dendrites* (from the Greek root *dendron*, or "tree") because their shape resembles the branching of a leafless tree. The dendrites protrude from the cell body, or *soma*, and both the dendrites and soma constitute the receiving zone for messages from other cells. The actual mechanisms for message reception lie on the outer surface of the plasma membrane covering the dendrites and soma. Here, incoming axons from other neurons make their synapses, establishing the links of a complete neural circuit (see Figure 2.1).

Neuronal Organelles   The arrangement of organelles within the neuron differs from that of other cells, and specific parts of the neuron have different sets of organelles and different molecular products. Rough endoplasmic reticulum and free ribosomes are found only in the cytoplasm of the soma and of the dendrites, not in axons. Since axons lack ribosomes and rough endoplasmic reticulum, they must rely on the soma for the manufacture of proteins needed for their function.

Axons, on the other hand, contain tiny storage bladders, or *synaptic vesicles*, not found in dendrites or the soma. The synaptic vesicles store the neurotransmitter molecules that the neuron secretes. Each vesicle is thought to contain thousands of the transmitter molecules (see Figure 2.3).

Both axons and dendrites contain large numbers of microtubules. The microtubules not only function as "struts," helping the neuron maintain its shape, but also transport substances from the soma to the axon or dendrites and back to the soma from these cell protrusions. For example, the molecules that are produced by the rough endoplasmic reticulum and packaged on the Golgi apparatus are transported by the microtubules to the ends of the axon. Such transport mechanisms are extremely important in cells whose axons may be hundreds of times as long as the cell body.

Labeling of Neurons

Since neurons come in such a variety of shapes and sizes, the early microscopists used these characteristics, along with a cell's location, to identify and name many types of neurons. But succeeding generations of scientists have used other criteria in typing neurons. In fact, sometimes the same neuron can be labeled in different ways, depending on the context of the discussion. This can sometimes be confusing, but it is not very different from the way we identify ourselves, or the people we know. At various times we may refer to the same young woman as a student, a daughter, a sister, a redhead, a swimmer, a sweetheart, or a member of the Smith family. Neurons, too, are burdened by as many labels as they have roles. One scientist or another has probably used almost every observable property of a neuron as the basis for a scheme of classification.

Santiago Ramón y Cajal (1852–1934). A poet and artist as well as a histologist of enormous creativity, Ramón y Cajal taught chiefly at the University of Madrid. He made this self-portrait in the 1920s.

Every unique structural feature of a specific nerve cell reflects the degree to which that cell is specialized to perform certain tasks. One way that scientists label a neuron is by its task, or function. For example, nerve cells linked into circuits that help us sense the external world or monitor events within our body are described as "sensory" neurons. Neurons linked in circuits that produce movement of the body by causing muscles to contract are called "motor" neurons.

The position of the neuron in the linkage is another important criterion for labeling. Those neurons that are lower in a hierarchy (closest to the event being sensed or the muscle being activated) are the primary, or level-1, sensory or motor neurons; next in the chain come the secondary, or level-2, relay neurons; then the tertiary, or level-3, relay neurons; and so on.

An individual neuron, then, may be referred to by its shape (such as a *pyramidal cell*), its specialized function (a sensory cell), or by its position and function in a circuit (a level-2 relay neuron). This practice should give you no great trouble in the discussions that follow, especially now that you know the practice exists. The most important point to remember, however, is that whatever a neuron's name, virtually all neurons do their work in the same way.

Regulation of Neuronal Activity

Neurons do their main work—receive and transmit impulses—by means of electrochemical energy. This energy is generated by the flow of charged chemical particles, *ions,* through the neuron's membrane.

Readers who do not have a strong background in physics or chemistry might, at this point, want to read the accompanying box, Some Basic Chemistry. Those who feel ready to plunge ahead will have the opportunity to test their chemical recall as we examine the process by which neurons can become active.

The Neuron at Rest

In the fluid that surrounds all the cells of the body, positive and negative ions are distributed freely in equal amounts, neutralizing each other's charge. The ions of sodium, potassium, calcium, and magnesium all have a positive charge; the ions of chloride, phosphate (a combination of phosphorous and oxygen), and certain more complex acids made by cells from carbon and oxygen all have a negative charge. Other trace elements, like iron, copper, zinc, and sulfur have much lower concentrations of their ions present.

Inside the neurons (and most other cells) are most of the body's proteins; when in solution, these proteins are usually in the form of ions having a negative charge. Therefore, the inside of the neuron is negatively charged, or *negatively polarized,* with respect to the outside. The relative deficiency of positively charged particles inside the cell means that there is a strong electrical force trying to pull positively charged ions into the cell. However, the plasma membrane does not grant all of the outside substances equal rights of transit to the inside, so when the neuron is at rest, the negative polarity is maintained.

The plasma membrane's selectivity is possible because it has, along its length, openings, or *channels,* that are specialized to allow the passage of specific substances; there are channels for potassium, channels for sodium, and so forth. Most of these channels are normally closed, so that nothing passes through; such channels are said to be *gated.* Some ions, such as potassium, can normally pass through their channels much more easily than others, such as sodium, which can only enter the cell during periods of neuronal excitation (see Figure 2.4).

Some Basic Chemistry: What Is an Ion?

Atoms are composed of protons (positively charged particles), neutrons (no charge), and electrons (negatively charged particles). The atom's nucleus, made up of protons and neutrons, is surrounded by electrons orbiting it in given energy paths, or *shells*. In an element, which is composed of identical atoms, the number of protons in the nucleus is identical to the number of electrons, so the atom is electrically neutral.

Electrons are always arranged in their shells so that the shell closest to the nucleus contains 2 electrons and the succeeding outer shell has at most 8 (the next shells contain up to 18, then 32 electrons). The outermost shell contains the number of electrons left over after the shells of 2, 8 and so on are complete. For sodium, which has 11 protons and 11 electrons, the outermost shell contains only one electron. Such atoms are highly reactive. Atoms in which only one electron is missing from the outer shell are also highly reactive. Chlorine, for example, contains 17 protons and 17 electrons and therefore is missing just one electron from its outermost shell. The reactivity occurs because the atoms with just one electron in their outer shell are eager to give it up, and those missing just one electron in their outer shell are eager to acquire one from other atoms.

When sodium and chlorine combine, for example, to become sodium chloride (table salt), the single electron in sodium's outer shell is given up to chlorine's outer shell. Both atoms then become ions: the sodium ion is positively charged, since there is now one more proton than electrons making it up; the chlorine ion is negatively charged because it has one more electron than the number of protons. Since these opposite charges attract, the two ions can bind together to form sodium chloride. What comes out of your shaker will always be salt. In water, however, the ions can dissociate, and they remain as charged particles while in solution. Many of the body's chemicals also exist in the body's fluids as ions. These positively and negatively charged particles play a major role in the conduction of neural impulses.

Another biological process contributing to maintenance of the negative polarity is the existence of efficient ion pumps in the plasma membrane, powered by energy made by the mitochondria. These pumps exchange extracellular potassium ions for intracellular sodium ions. Although this exchange is electrically neutral, exchanging a positive ion for a positive ion, the pump mainly helps to remove the excess sodium ions that enter during periods of excitation. Since the inside of the cell is relatively rich in potassium, compared to the extracellular fluid, and since potassium can move across the membrane much more readily than sodium, the net result is that more potassium tends to flow out spontaneously than can enter. This diffusion of potassium also helps to leave the inside of the cell in a net negative state.

With the neuron "at rest," then, there is a voltage difference across the membrane, the inside being negative relative to the outside. This voltage difference amounts to nearly a tenth of a volt, or about 5 percent as much electrical energy as there is in a regular flashlight battery—a considerable amount of energy for such a tiny entity. This electrical state of the unstimulated neuron is often called its *resting potential*.

The Nerve Impulse

A neuron is stimulated to fire—to conduct an impulse—by receiving certain chemical signals at excitatory synapses (see Figures 2.4 and 2.5). The immediate effect of such signals is to alter the electrical state on the inside of the cell, making it a bit more positive than it is in its normal resting state. This small shift toward the positive then triggers the gates on sodium channels to open. The sodium ions outside an open channel rush in, pulled by the negative electrical force that still exists inside the neuron, even though it is more positive than it was. (It remains negative relative to the outside.)

The sodium channels at the part of the

38

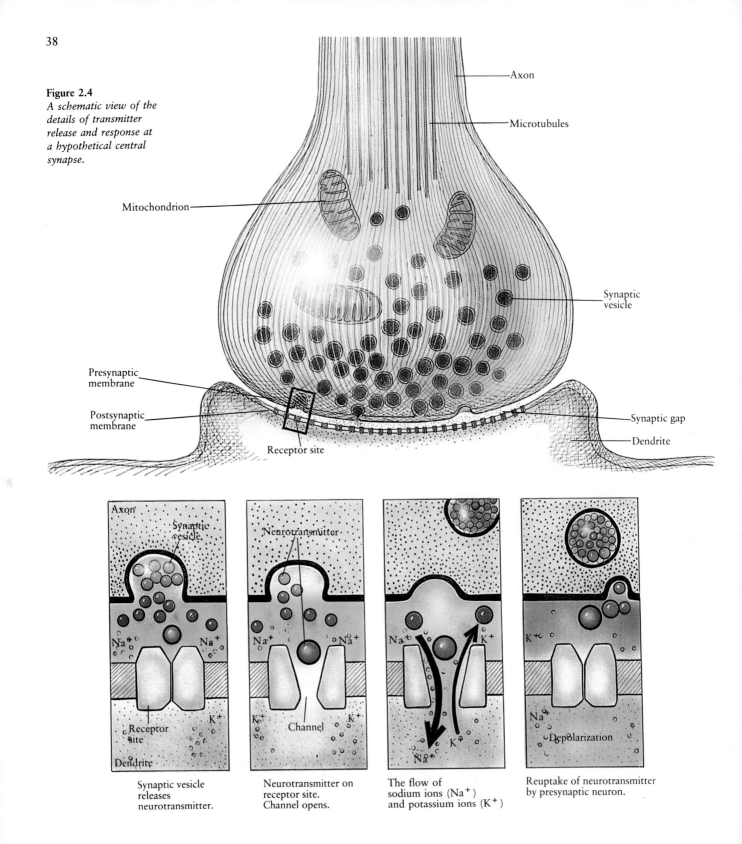

Figure 2.4
A schematic view of the details of transmitter release and response at a hypothetical central synapse.

Axon

Microtubules

Mitochondrion

Synaptic vesicle

Presynaptic membrane

Postsynaptic membrane

Synaptic gap

Receptor site

Dendrite

Axon

Synaptic vesicle

Neurotransmitter

Na^+

Na^+

Na^+

Na^+

K^+

Na^+

K^+

Receptor Site

Channel

K^+

K^+

Na^+

K^+

K^+

Na^+

Dendrite

Depolarization

Synaptic vesicle releases neurotransmitter.

Neurotransmitter on receptor site. Channel opens.

The flow of sodium ions (Na^+) and potassium ions (K^+)

Reuptake of neurotransmitter by presynaptic neuron.

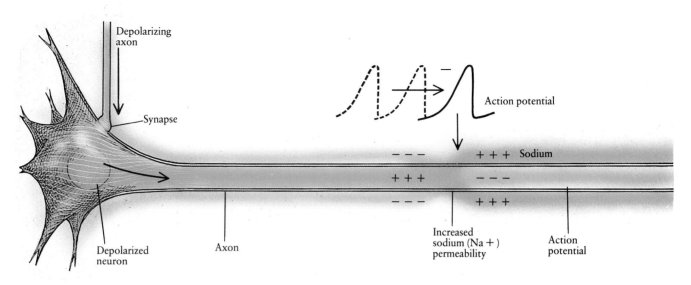

Figure 2.5
When a neuron is activated by an incoming excitatory synaptic connection, the wave of depolarization temporarily reverses the internal negativity of the resting potential. As the wave of depolarization moves down the axon, progressive segments of the axon also undergo this transient reversal. The action potential can be recorded as the positively charged sodium ions (Na+) flow from the extracellular fluid into the excited, depolarized surfaces of the neuronal membrane.

axon nearest the cell body open first, and the sodium ions rush in. In fact, after some sodium has entered, the rush to move sodium and other positive ions (calcium and potassium) into the cell during this brief period of excitation is so successful that the inside of the neuron near the channel becomes positively charged for a very brief period. This positive state then causes the adjacent sodium channels to open. And so on, down to the end of the axon. Each such reversal of the interior membrane's state from negative to positive is called an *action potential,* or *depolarization.*

An action potential lasts less than 1/1000 of a second. It is so brief because the excitation response is self-correcting. During the increased inward flow of sodium and calcium ions, there is also an outward flow of potassium ions and a rapid automatic clos-

ing of the sodium and calcium channels in that vicinity. All three events help to restore the resting potential. Throughout the cycle of activity, the ion pumps also work continuously to maintain the low internal concentration of sodium.

This succession of action potentials down the axon ensures that there is no loss of signal along the way, no matter how long an axon is. When an action potential reaches the synaptic terminals of the axon, it triggers the release of a chemical transmitter across a synapse to the receptors of a target neuron, where, if the signal is excitatory, the process begins again.

Inhibition of Nerve Impulses

While some chemical transmitters signal neurons to fire, others signal them to hold their fire, that is, to inhibit their firing (see

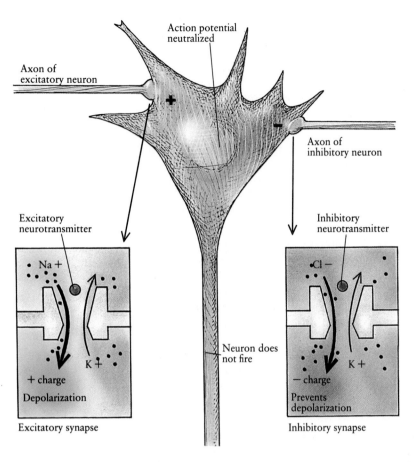

Figure 2.6
The contrasting effects of excitatory (left) and inhibitory (right) transmitters can be illustrated in terms of the different combinations of ion channels that each type of transmitter influences (Na$^+$, sodium ions; K$^+$, potassium ions).

How Neurons Communicate

When people speak to one another, they use words to capture the basic content of their communication, adding subtle emphasis and additional meaning by tone of voice, facial expression, and hand and body movements. When nerve cells communicate, their specific chemical messengers, the *synaptic transmitters,* act as the basic units of content. (A given neuron uses the same neurotransmitters for all of its synapses.)

While verbal communication—conversation—is usually a two-way proposition, information at synapses is transmitted in one direction only—from the axon terminals of the sending neuron across the synapse to the receptive surfaces of the receiving neuron. To understand this process, which is perhaps the most important of all the steps we have discussed so far, we need to take a closer look at the many steps involved in synaptic transmission and at the kinds of signals this process can generate.

What Happens at Synapses

The neuron sending the message is called the *presynaptic* neuron, and the message's recipient is the *postsynaptic* neuron. When the action potential has flowed down the neuron to the end of the axon, the presynaptic neuron releases its neurotransmitter into the synaptic gap. The neurotransmitter has been stored in the synaptic vesicles, and these vesicles find their way to the outer membrane of the axon terminal, fuse with it momentarily, and open, releasing their transmitter molecules into the synapse (see Figure 2.4).

The transmitter molecules diffuse across the gap and find receptor sites on the postsynaptic membrane that they can bind to. Evidently, the transmitter molecules have shapes that lock onto the shapes of the special receptor protein molecules embedded in

Figure 2.6). The chemical signal passed at inhibitory synapses acts by making the voltage inside the neuron even more negative than it is during its resting state. A common way this is accomplished is by triggering the membrane to open, briefly, some channels that allow the inflow of chloride ions. Since these ions have negative charges, they make the inside membrane even more negative relative to the outside, so the neuron cannot fire.

the postsynaptic membrane, much as pieces of a jigsaw puzzle fit together.

More transmitter molecules may be released than the number of binding sites available. This excess transmitter is removed immediately. Sometimes it is destroyed by a special enzyme released from the membrane of the postsynaptic neuron. Sometimes the presynaptic neuron will, thriftily, draw back the excess into its vesicles. The latter process is called *reuptake* (see Figure 2.4).

The amount of transmitter released, however, is monitored by the presynaptic neuron; it has *autoreceptors* to give it feedback about the amount of transmitter in the synapse, and it regulates its production and release of the chemical on the basis of this feedback.

In general terms, there are only two functional kinds of synaptic messages: *excitation* (or loss of polarization), in which one cell commands another to activity, and *inhibition,* in which the recipient cell is prevented from firing. Chronic inhibitory commands keep some nerve cells generally silent until an excitatory transmission stimulates them to become active. For example, the nerve cells in your spinal cord that command your muscles into activity when you walk or dance are generally silent until excited by impulses from the cells of the motor cortex. Spontaneous excitatory commands arouse other nerve cells to activity without waiting for conscious signals. For example, the nerve cells that move your chest and diaphragm in the act of breathing respond to nerve cells located at a "higher" hierarchical level of organization that are activated only by the level of oxygen and carbon dioxide in your blood.

To Fire or Not to Fire

A postsynaptic neuron receiving an excitatory chemical message from another neuron may or may not fire in response to the mes-

sage. (The facts that follow apply as well to inhibitory messages, but for ease of discussion here, we will use only excitatory commands as our example.) One factor in determining the threshold for firing is the amount of neurotransmitter released onto the receiving neuron. A single release from a presynaptic neuron may not be enough to change the receiving cell's resting potential to an action potential.

Often, a *summation* of many impulses is required to produce the potential change necessary. This summation can come in two ways. First, a sending neuron can fire a number of times in rapid succession, so that transmitter accumulates in the gap faster than the mechanisms for removing it can work. Second, since a neuron usually has many axons from other cells forming synapses with it at various points, it will pass the threshold for firing when a number of these other cells fire simultaneously; the combined action then produces enough of a signal to depolarize the postsynaptic neuron.

Conditional Messages

Based on what scientists now know, it appears that the major interactions within the circuits of the brain are largely explainable in terms of these "excite" or 'inhibit" types of synaptic transmitter messages. However, more complex modifying messages also come into play, and they are important because they enhance or diminish the intensity with which a recipient cell responds to other messages from different sending cells.

We will not discuss these mechanisms in detail here, but one way to envision such modifying transmitter messages is to view them as being *conditional*. By conditional, we mean that recipient cells respond to them only under certain conditions, that is, when these transmitters are used in combination with other major excite or inhibit signals

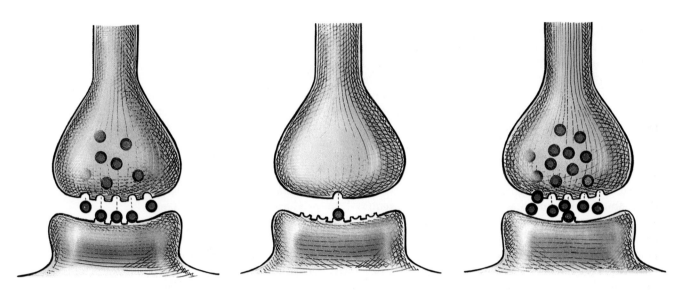

Figure 2.7
Schematic illustration of the adaptive regulatory processes that are used to maintain normal synaptic transmission despite changes, induced by drugs or possibly by disease, in the amounts of transmitter available for release or response. The normal condition is at left. At center, transmitter synthesis or storage is deficient, and the postsynaptic cell increases the number of receptors. At right, transmitter content and release is enhanced, and the postsynaptic cell decreases the number and effectiveness of its receptors.

coming in from other circuits. Musicians, for example, consider the actions of the foot pedals on a piano conditional in that to have any effect, their action must coexist with another action. The mere pressing of a foot pedal without striking a note has no value. It modifies the sound of a note only when that note is struck. Many of the neuronal circuits that are subject to conditional messengers are those whose neurotransmitters are most relevant to treatments for depression, schizophrenia, and certain other brain diseases (a topic that is discussed at more length in Chapter 10).

Modifiability of Neuronal Function

So far we have seen that a neuron must successfully meet certain basic responsibilities in order to function properly as a member of a specific circuit. It must make the transmitter substance(s) it uses to pass along neuronal messages. It must make the surface receptors by which it becomes available to receive incoming transmitter signals. It must also maintain adequate supplies of energy to transport excess ions back across the membrane. Neurons with long branching axons to service must also transport enzymes, transmitters, and other molecules from the synthesis sites in the central cytoplasm to the distant dendritic and axonal spots where they are needed. Generally, the rate at which a neuron performs these functions depends on the mass of its dendritic and axonal systems and its overall rate of activity.

The overall rate of energy production, the cell's metabolic activity, is *modifiable* as the demands of interneuronal traffic vary, however (see Figure 2.7). The nerve cell can increase its capacity to synthesize and transport specific molecules during periods of high neural activity. Likewise, a neuron can turn down its level of function when it is underutilized. This ability to modify fundamental intracellular processes gives the neuron the flexibility to manage its responsibilities at widely different activity levels.

Synaptic Transmitters

All known synaptic neurotransmitters in the human nervous system produce one or another of the conditions described in the preceding section: their signal excites receiving cells, causing them to fire, or inhibits them from firing, or modifies the excitability of the receiving cell. The general characteristics of the major individual transmitters are important to know not only because they perform vital functions in the normal working brain, but also because absence or excess production of some play a major role in brain disease and behavioral disorders. The brain's reaction to drugs also depends on the synaptic transfer system. The surface receptors that enable neurons to respond to incoming synaptic transmitters also render these cells susceptible to chemically similar drugs, which may be taken either to treat a diseased nervous system or to wreak havoc on an otherwise normal nervous system.

The major transmitters introduced here are grouped on the basis of the chemical structure of the transmitter molecule. These transmitters, their function in the brain, and their influence on behavior will be described at greater length in subsequent chapters.

Amino Acid Transmitters

At the simplest chemical level are the amino acids that act as transmitters (see Figure 2.8). The main amino acids that have been established as being neurotransmitters are glutamate and aspartate, which act as excitatory

Gamma-aminobutyric acid (GABA)

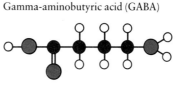

Glutamic acid

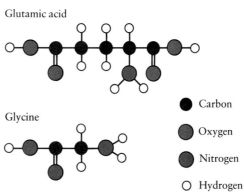

Glycine

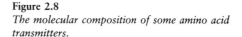

Figure 2.8
The molecular composition of some amino acid transmitters.

signals, and glycine and gamma-aminobutyric acid (commonly called GABA), which act as inhibitory transmitters. These simple amino acid transmitters probably account for the vast majority of transmission signals in the brain. Drugs that are able to produce convulsions, such as strychnine, act by inhibiting neurons' responses to glycine or GABA. That is, the drug prevents glycine or GABA from delivering their inhibitory messages, because it prevents target cells from recognizing the inhibitory messages.

Monoamine Transmitters

The monoamine transmitters are slightly more complicated chemically than the amino acid transmitters (see Figure 2.9). Neurons themselves synthesize these monoamines from amino acids, using enzymes present only in these neurons to make the modifications.

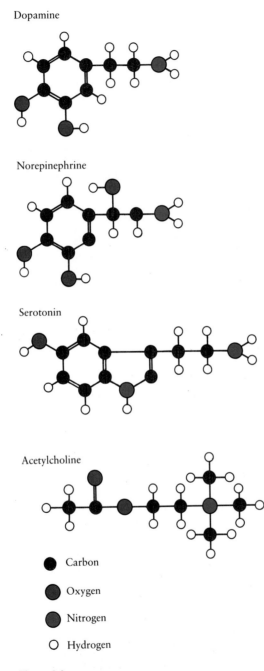

Dopamine

Norepinephrine

Serotonin

Acetylcholine

- Carbon
- Oxygen
- Nitrogen
- Hydrogen

Figure 2.9
The molecular composition of some monoamine transmitters. Neurons themselves manufacture these transmitters from amino acids.

Monoamine signals are much less common in the brain than amino acid signals, with perhaps 1 monoamine message for every 1000 amino acid messages. Still, these signals are vital to human neurological well-being. The five major monoamine transmitters are acetylcholine; dopamine, norepinephrine, and epinephrine; and serotonin.

Acetylcholine *Acetylcholine* is the transmitter that signals your muscles to become active, both the skeletal muscles that allow you to move and the smooth muscles that control some of your hollow organs, such as your stomach. Acetylcholine is historically important because it was the first chemical transmitter identified, on the basis of its ability to perfectly imitate the action of the nerves that can cause the heartbeat to slow down. Curare, a poison used by South American hunters and also sometimes used during surgical procedures, produces paralysis by preventing acetylcholine from exciting the muscles. Acetylcholine is one of the brain transmitters lost in Alzheimer's disease, a disease characterized by progressive loss of higher cognitive functions (see Chapter 10).

Dopamine, Norepinephrine, and Epinephrine These three chemically related transmitters are all synthesized from the amino acid tyrosine. Because of the similarity of their chemical structure, they are often referred to as catecholamines.

Each of these transmitters is found in groups of neurons that are highly localized in distinct clusters and pathways. Neurons containing dopamine, for example, are found in clusters concentrated in certain regions of the midbrain (the substantia nigra and ventral tegmentum). Many of the norepinephrine-containing cells in the brain are concentrated in a small cluster in the pons (called the locus coeruleus). In contrast, neurons containing epinephrine are more scattered

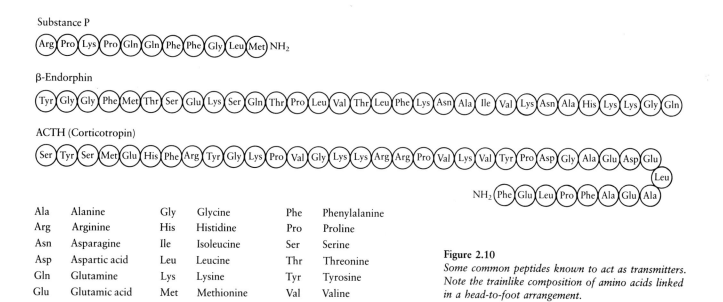

Substance P

Arg Pro Lys Pro Gln Gln Phe Phe Gly Leu Met NH₂

β-Endorphin

Tyr Gly Gly Phe Met Thr Ser Glu Lys Ser Gln Thr Pro Leu Val Thr Leu Phe Lys Asn Ala Ile Val Lys Asn Ala His Lys Lys Gly Gln

ACTH (Corticotropin)

Ser Tyr Ser Met Glu His Phe Arg Tyr Gly Lys Pro Val Gly Lys Lys Arg Arg Pro Val Lys Val Tyr Pro Asp Gly Ala Glu Asp Glu Leu

NH₂ Phe Glu Leu Pro Phe Ala Glu Ala

Ala	Alanine	Gly	Glycine	Phe	Phenylalanine
Arg	Arginine	His	Histidine	Pro	Proline
Asn	Asparagine	Ile	Isoleucine	Ser	Serine
Asp	Aspartic acid	Leu	Leucine	Thr	Threonine
Gln	Glutamine	Lys	Lysine	Tyr	Tyrosine
Glu	Glutamic acid	Met	Methionine	Val	Valine

Figure 2.10
Some common peptides known to act as transmitters. Note the trainlike composition of amino acids linked in a head-to-foot arrangement.

through the medulla. Norepinephrine and epinephrine are also found in cells of the adrenal glands and in the nerves of the sympathetic division of the autonomic nervous system.

Dopamine is thought to play a role in regulating emotional responses. It is known to play a crucial role in the control of complex movements: the brains of people with Parkinson's disease, a disease whose victims suffer from muscle tremors and rigidity and who have great difficulty in moving, contain almost no dopamine. The norepinephrine system seems to be involved in arousal, in attributing a rewarding value to a stimulus, and in regulation of sleep and mood. Not much is known about the relative role of epinephrine in the brain, but its location suggests it may play a role in the way the brain helps to regulate blood pressure.

Cocaine and amphetamine produce their excitant actions on the brain by releasing norepinephrine and dopamine from their synaptic vesicle storage points. Some antidepressant drugs and many blood pressure–regulating drugs act at receptors for norepinephrine and dopamine.

Serotonin Neurons using serotonin as a transmitter are found only in the brain, most of them in a concentrated cluster of cells in the pons (called the raphe nuclei). This transmitter is thought to be involved in temperature regulation, sensory perception, and the onset of sleep.

The serotonin receptors are the sites at which the hallucinogenic drug LSD acts, and at which some antidepressant drugs can also act. Some of the drugs most commonly used to treat severe depression act at serotonin or norepinephrine synapses to prevent the normal reuptake of these transmitters into the terminals that secreted them.

Peptides

Peptides are chains of amino acids linked in a special head-to-foot arrangement like the cars of a train (see Figure 2.10). Peptides are not exclusive to nerve cells; in fact, their role as neurotransmitters has been intensively studied for only the past ten years. Results of such studies suggest that the peptides represent a very primitive form of interneuronal signaling. In cells that can make and secrete a particular peptide signal, the peptide is probably a second signal that modulates the amino acid or monoamine signal also produced by that neuron. Peptides occur in very low concentrations in the nervous system but appear to be quite potent.

Peptide chemical signals are also used by the cells of the pituitary and other tissues that secrete hormones into the bloodstream. Some of the peptides found in the nervous system are also found in the intestines, the kidney, or the cardiovascular system. Since many of the nervous-system peptides were first identified in one of the organs or tissues outside the brain, their names reflect those sources, even though their function in the brain might be very different. For example, *vasopressin* and *oxytocin* are released by the posterior pituitary to regulate blood pressure, uterine contractions, and water excretion by the kidney. These peptides are also present in the brain, but their function there is not yet totally clear.

Cholecystokinin, substance P, and *vasoactive intestinal polypeptide* were first recognized in extracts of the walls of the intestines for their ability to control, respectively, gall bladder contraction, blood flow, and peristalsis, the muscle contractions that move food through the gastrointestinal system. Their general role in the brain remains to be discovered; substance P, however, seems to play a role in the experience of pain, as discussed in Chapter 7. All three of these peptides occur in so many places that they may have more than one general function.

The *endorphins* (a shortened version of their original name, "endogenous morphines") are three related peptides that can all produce certain of the effects of morphine: they can relieve pain; they can slow

the release of transmitters that activate contraction of intestinal muscle; and their actions can be selectively antagonized by drugs used to reverse morphine overdosage. In fact, it is really more accurate to say that the drugs morphine and heroin work their effects by attaching themselves to receptor sites for the endorphins.

The transmitters that neurons make or can respond to are genetically specified, as described in Chapter 3. In fact, most characteristics of individual neurons—their size, shape, and amalgamation with other neurons to form specific brain parts—are largely set by the genes. Certain patterns of neuronal circuitry are also specified by genes, and the final section of this general overview of the brain's cellular machinery looks at three of the most common of these patterns.

Patterns of Neuronal Circuitry

Three main patterns of neuronal circuitry appear frequently in the brain's architecture: hierarchical chain circuits, local-circuit neurons, and single-source/divergent circuits. The billions of neuronal circuits in the human brain are represented by just nine cells in Figure 2.11 to represent schematically the three types of circuits. Although the number of elements varies, these three patterns are found reliably enough to make a useful classification scheme.

Hierarchical Circuits

The most common type of interneuronal circuitry is that found in the major sensory and motor pathways. In sensory systems, the hierarchy is organized in terms of the ascending order of cells in the chain through which information flows *into* the nervous system: primary receptors to secondary relays, to tertiary relays, and so on. The incoming sensory information enters and is then passed on "up" to where the information can be sorted, compared, and attended to. Motor systems are organized in terms of a descending hierarchy for commands coming down out of the nervous system to the muscles: cells figuratively "on high" in the motor system speak to specific motor cells in the spinal cord that, in turn, speak to specific sets of muscles.

Hierarchical systems make for very precise information flow because *convergence*—when several sets of neurons at one level speak to a smaller number of relays at the next level—and *divergence*—when the cells at one level speak to a larger number of cells at the next level—filter and amplify information. But like all chains, hierarchical systems are only as strong as their weakest links. Any inactivation at any level by injury, disease, stroke, or tumor can render the whole system inoperative. Convergence and divergence, however, give the circuit some opportunity for survival in the face of severe damage. If some of the cells at one level are decimated, the surviving cells can maintain the circuit's function.

Hierarchical systems are by no means restricted to the sensory and motor pathways. The same pattern is found in all the circuitry systems dedicated to a specific function, such as the visual system and the central endocrine system, which are considered in more detail in later chapters.

Local-Circuit Neurons

The neurons comprising a local circuit differ in character from other neurons: they have very short axons and thus can fire without the mechanism of an action potential. When they are triggered into action by synapses on their surface, the result is an almost immediate release of their transmitter. Because their axons are so short, these local-circuit neurons are very restricted in their task and their range of influence.

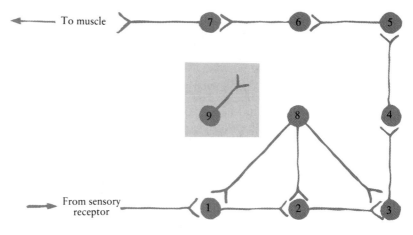

Figure 2.11
A "nine-cell" nervous system. Around the edge, neurons link in the one-to-one hierarchical connections typical of circuits in the sensory and motor systems. At center (8), the single/source-divergent pattern, typical of the monoamine systems, in which one neuron connects with a great many targets appears. At left center (9), is a local-circuit neuron whose major connections are made within its immediate environment.

They essentially operate as filters within one or more levels of a hierarchy to modulate the flow of information. Their effect can be either excitatory or inhibitory. As information flows through a hierarchical circuit, the local-circuit neurons within a level of the hierarchy act to modulate the flow. They further broaden the flow (say, for divergent circuits), further narrow it (say, for convergent circuits), or refocus it.

Single-Source/Divergent Circuits

Some neural circuits involve neuron clusters in which one sending cell has many, many recipients. (Such circuits push the term "divergent" to the ultimate limits of its meaning.) Inquiry into this type of circuit began only recently, and the only sites of these neurons that we know about so far are restricted to specific parts of the midbrain and brainstem. The advantage of such a pattern lies in its ability to influence a very large audience of neuronal targets, communicating with all levels of a hierarchy, for example, and thus often transcending the boundaries of specific sensory, motor, or other functional systems.

Because they do not restrict their output to systems dedicated to specific functions, the divergent paths of these circuits are sometimes referred to as *nonspecific*. However, because these circuits can influence so many different levels and functions, they have great significance in integrating the many activities of the nervous system (see Chapter 5). That is, such systems may act like concert masters, or athletic coaches, to get the best performance out of a big group that must work together. Furthermore, the transmitters associated with these single-source/divergent systems produce "conditional" transmitter actions—that is, the results of the action depend on the conditions under which the action takes place.

Single-source/divergent circuits represent only a small fraction of all neural circuits, but their influence is widespread. They apparently play an integrative role in governing some global behavioral states, such as sleep, arousal, and attentiveness (see Chapter 6).

Other Cells and Structures of the Nervous System

Up to this point, we have dealt solely with the characteristics of neurons and their circuitry. But neurons are not the only cells making up the brain, even though they are the most important. To do its work, the cellular machinery of the brain depends on the active participation of the glia and other structures described in this section.

Glia

The cellular space between the nerve cells and their circuits is filled by specialized support cells called *glia*. By most counts, there

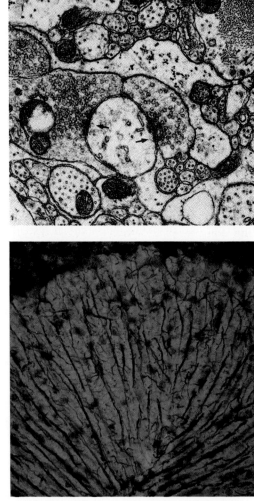

One of the major types of glial cells, astrocytes contribute glucose on demand to the neuronal elements they surround. Above, an astrocyte (outlined in cross-section) containing glycogen granules. Arrows indicate two synapses on the same dendrite. Below, fibrous astrocytes, colored dark brown, surround the dendrites of cerebellar neurons.

are perhaps five or ten times as many glia as there are neurons. The actual function of most glia is unknown, but scientists generally attribute to them some vague "house-keeping" chores. Unlike the neurons, glia do have the capacity to divide to form new cells.

The most common of the two major types of glial cell is called the *astrocyte* for its star-like shape. Astrocytes are thought to "clean up" excess transmitters and ions from the extracellular spaces, thereby helping to keep the interactions that take place on the neurons' surfaces free of background chemical "noise." Astrocytes may also contribute glucose to very active nerve cells; and they may redirect the flow of blood, and therefore the transport of oxygen, to especially active regions. Although nothing about this is certain, these glia may be important in providing some of the signals essential for the regulation of synaptic function. Individual astrocytes do seem to mark off specific regions of synaptic connections on a target cell. It is known that after partial lesions of the brain, astrocytes scavenge the dying pieces of neurons, an action that perhaps limits the spread of toxic substances.

Glia of the other major class are better defined by their function than by their shape. Some axons are insulated in a way that specializes them for rapid conduction of electrical impulses. This cellular insulation, called *myelin*, is a compact wrapping material formed by layers of membrane from a specialized glial cell, the *oligodendrocyte* (see Figure 2.12). In some diseases, including multiple sclerosis, the myelin insulation around the axon becomes unhealthy, exposing ion channels in parts of the axon surface that are normally covered. The result has been likened to short-circuiting between normally unconnected neurons, and this may delay the signals from one brain region to another. As a result of this myelin loss and short-circuiting, victims of multiple sclerosis suffer sensory disorders and loss of muscular control. In the peripheral nervous system,

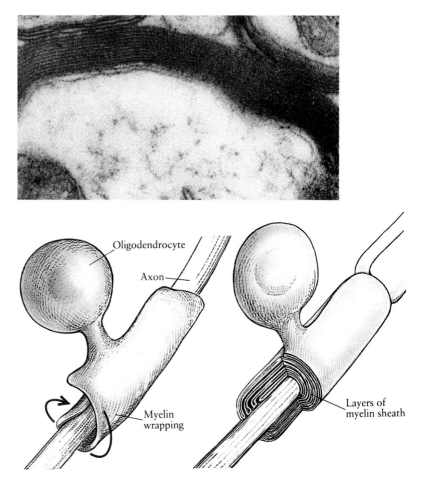

Oligodendroglia, the other major type of glia, form myelin around axons, providing insulation to speed conduction of impulses. Top, the multiple layers of myelin (dark rings) surround a small axon. Below, an oligodendrocyte wrapping its membrane around an axon to form a myelin sheath. Ions flow into the nerve membrane only at gaps in the myelin.

the glial cell that forms myelin, known as the *Schwann cell*, has slightly different synthesizing abilities and chemical properties.

Vascular Elements

Among the other nonneuronal cells of the nervous system are those of the blood vessels—the arteries, veins, and capillaries—

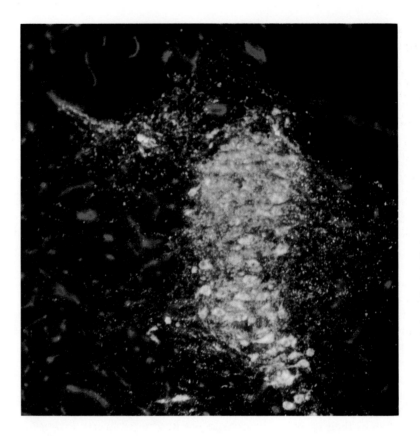

Injection of a dye that produces a red fluorescent image permits the rapid assessment of the degree of vascularization around neurons. Each red spot is a small arteriole, capillary, or venule. The degree of vascularity differs from one region to another, reflecting the underlying metabolic demands of the neurons there.

which make an essential contribution to its vitality. The brain receives a privileged share of oxygenated blood; in fact, all the muscles of your body together, when fully active, draw only about 25 percent more oxygen than the brain does.

The blood vessels of the central nervous system are unlike those of the rest of the body in that they lack the ability to transport large molecules across their walls. These vessels are also more-or-less sealed off on the brain side by the solid attachments of astrocytes to their outer surfaces. These modifications limit what can enter the brain from the bloodstream mainly to the blood gases (oxygen and carbon dioxide) and the small nutritional molecules, including glucose and es-

sential amino acids, that the brain needs to operate properly. This limited access of the blood to the tissues of the central nervous system is so different from its access to other tissues that it has a special name—the *blood/brain barrier.* The existence of this diffusional barrier certainly suggests that it is to the brain's advantage not to be sensitive to all of the chemical signals that might be circulating in the bloodstream. However, a few toxins, like alcohol, nicotine, and nerve gases, can still enter the brain.

The metabolic demands of the brain increase even further during certain mental activities, and the active regions can be partially visualized by modern techniques that spot changes in blood flow or in oxygen or

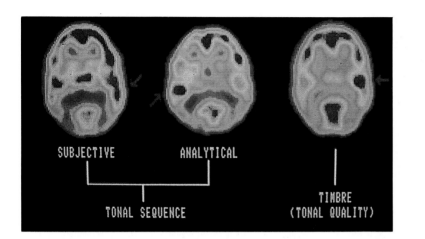

Following injection of a nonradioactive modified glucose molecule, the PETT (Positron Emission Transaxial Tomography) scan detects the relative amounts of glucose being consumed in the cortex while the subject listens to music. This subject, a trained musician, shows increased metabolic demand over both the right temporal and the left parietal areas, suggesting a focused attention to the details of the music.

glucose consumption. These techniques help physicians spot small zones of epileptic activity or other pathological changes such as cancers or vascular tumors. The same methods also have begun to provide information about which parts of the brain become especially active or quiet when a depressed patient or one with schizophrenia is most disturbed by the illness (see Chapter 10).

Connective Tissue Elements

The last nonneural cells we will look at are those that line the outer and inner surfaces of the brain. Within the bony confines of the skull and spinal cord, the central nervous system is sealed into a form-fitting, fluid-filled stocking of membranes called the *meninges,* made up of conventional connective tissues found elsewhere in the body. The fluid is the *cerebrospinal fluid*. The meninges and the cerebrospinal fluid act as a shock absorber system to soak up the twists, turns, bumps, and other insults to the body that would severely hamper the integrity of the nervous system were they to be transmitted full force.

The cerebrospinal fluid fills space continuing from the outer surfaces of the brain and spinal cord to its inner spaces, the *cerebral ventricles,* which, as you saw in Chapter 1, received the lion's share of attention from the ancient students of the brain (see Figure 2.13). The cells lining these inner ventricular spaces are also specialized, and, except for certain key spots, their edges are sealed together tightly, apparently to limit passage of anything across this lining layer. The cerebrospinal fluid itself is produced by specialized blood vessels, the *choroid plexus,* which filter out the blood cells. The choroid plexus is attached to certain parts of the ventricular system, and the fluid that its cells yield circulates from the inner ventricles up over the surface of the cortex and cerebellum and down into the space around the spinal cord.

The function of this internal circulation of spinal fluid is not known, but physicians make use of it when trying to diagnose infections of the nervous system—bacterial meningitis, for example. When infection is present, the spinal fluid exhibits white blood cells and a protein content that is much higher than normal. Because the spinal fluid also contains some of the byproducts of synaptic transmission, diagnosticians and researchers frequently examine its content as they try to

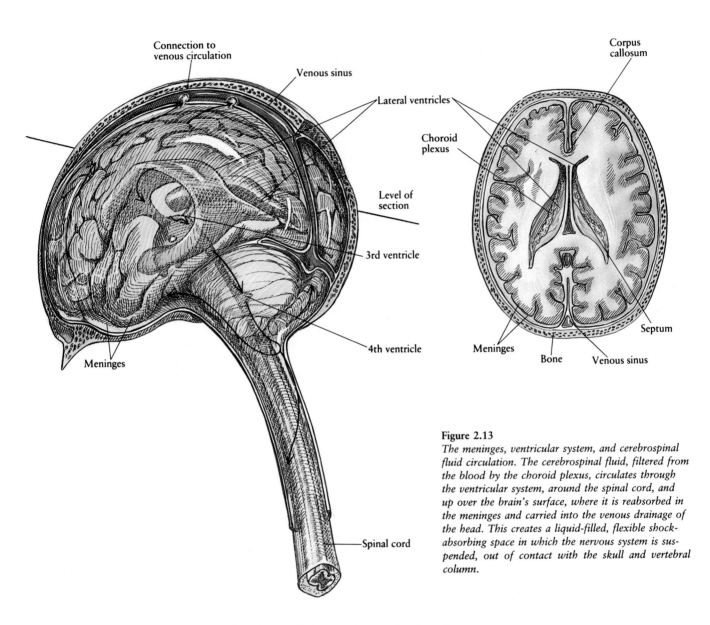

Connection to
venous circulation

Venous sinus

Lateral ventricles

Level of
section

3rd ventricle

4th ventricle

Meninges

Spinal cord

Corpus
callosum

Choroid
plexus

Septum

Meninges

Bone

Venous sinus

Figure 2.13
*The meninges, ventricular system, and cerebrospinal
fluid circulation. The cerebrospinal fluid, filtered from
the blood by the choroid plexus, circulates through
the ventricular system, around the spinal cord, and
up over the brain's surface, where it is reabsorbed in
the meninges and carried into the venous drainage of
the head. This creates a liquid-filled, flexible shock-
absorbing space in which the nervous system is suspended, out of contact with the skull and vertebral
column.*

piece together chemical clues to the unsolved
mysteries of brain disorders. The possibility
that the cerebrospinal fluid might transport
chemical signs of brain abnormality almost
brings us back full circle to the view of the
Greeks and Romans who considered the ventricles and their plumbing functions to be of
premier importance.

Summary

All these facts about cells and circuits have
been organized around a skeleton outline of
the cellular organization and function of the
brain's machinery. Let us review these general statements now that they have been explained to some degree.

1. The basic operating elements of the nervous system are the individual nerve cells, or neurons.

2. Neurons share certain universal cellular features with other cells in the body. All have a plasma membrane, cytoplasm containing organelles, and a nucleus.

3. Neurons also differ considerably from other body cells in several ways. They have characteristic configurations, with protruding parts—an axon and dendrites—that connect with other neurons to form circuits. Also, the arrangement of organelles within neurons differs from that of other cells.

4. The activity of neurons is regulated by the properties of the nerve cell membrane. When chemically stimulated, the membrane's state changes from a resting potential to an action potential, and a nerve impulse is generated.

5. The chemical stimulation of a neuron is in the form of a synaptic transmitter, which one neuron manufactures and releases from the end of its axon across the synaptic gap to a receiving neuron.

6. Synaptic transmitters may have the function of producing a nerve impulse, inhibiting an impulse, or modifying the function of another transmitter.

7. Generally, a receiving neuron requires a summation of many impulses in order for it to receive enough transmitter to effect an action potential.

8. The three major classes of synaptic transmitters are amino acid transmitters, monoamine transmitters, and peptides.

9. Three basic patterns of neuronal circuitry emerge from genetic specifications: hierarchical chains, local-circuit neurons, and single-source/divergent circuits.

10. Besides neurons, the nervous system contains two types of glial cells, one of which forms the myelin sheath covering many types of neural circuits; all the functions of the other type of glial cells are not yet known for certain, but these cells appear to at least play a role in destroying possible toxic substances. Other brain cells are those making up the blood vessels and those composing the membranes surrounding the brain and spinal cord.

Further Reading

Iversen, Leslie I. 1986. The chemistry of the brain. In R. Thompson (ed.), *Progress in Neuroscience: Readings from Scientific American*. New York: W.H. Freeman. A concise presentation of current knowledge about the major neurotransmitters present in the brain and their functions.

Keynes, Richard D. Ion channels in the nerve cell membrane. *Scientific American*, March 1979. Details the flow of sodium and potassium ions through membrane channels as nerve impulses are generated.

Nauta, W. J. H., and Feirtag, M. 1986. *Fundamental Neuroanatomy*. New York; W. H. Freeman. A masterful illustrated explanation of the brain's cellular features and wiring diagrams and how they were worked out.

Kandel, E., and Schwartz, J., eds. 1985. Principles of Neural Science, 2nd edition, Part III: Elementary interaction between neurons: Synaptic transmission (pp. 87-208) New York; Elsevier Scientific Publishing. (An advanced textbook coverage).

3

Life-Span Development of the Brain

3

Virtually all of what we are and do depends on how our brains function, and normal functioning depends in great part on normal processes of development. In this chapter, we will discuss what is known about the brain's development before birth, during childhood and adulthood, and in old age. We have the most information about processes occurring during embryological development, even though much of our data come from studies carried out with animals such as frogs or chicks. Although we cannot state with certainty that these processes are identical to those in human beings, the strong likelihood is that they are much the same across species.

The genes direct these developmental processes, which begin as soon as the egg and sperm join at fertilization. After outlining the course of the brain's formation, we will focus on how the genes that determine a person's sex affect brain and behavior—in particular, brain structures and behaviors that are not directly linked to sexual activities.

We have the least information about developmental changes during childhood and adulthood and thus cannot outline a sequence of changes like those during prenatal development; it is not clear that there is any such sequence. However, we do know that interactions with the environment produce changes in brain structures and that lack of certain interactions can alter normal developmental patterns.

Developmental changes in old age are the focus of much ongoing scientific study. What actually happens to the aging brain and why? What might be the agents of aging? The most recent theories and data are reported in the final section of this chapter.

Prenatal Development

In this section we look at prenatal brain development in two stages. First, we briefly outline the sequence of development of brain *structures*. Then we look at how individual neurons multiply, become differentiated from each other, find their way to their place of work, and join with each other to form structures and, finally, to form synapses and circuits.

Gross Anatomical Changes

Scientists know the general sequence of anatomical growth in the human fetus from examination of fetuses that did not survive until birth. The most indispensable body parts—the heart and brain—begin to form first, within the first weeks after fertilization.

The First Month By about the fifth day after fertilization, the original cell has divided until there are about a hundred embryonic cells, in the shape of a hollow ball (the blastocyst; see Figure 3.1). At about the

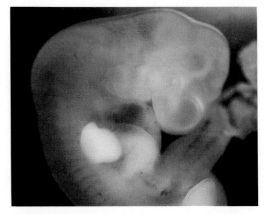

A fetus in the womb.

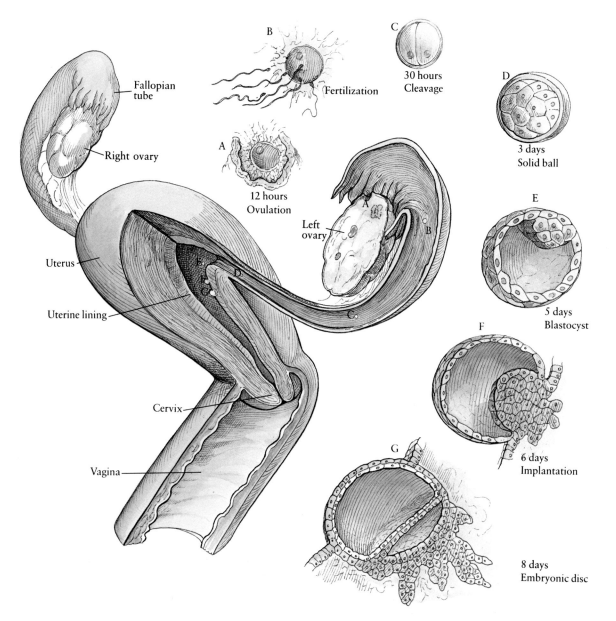

Figure 3.1

The first week of prenatal development. As the large drawing shows, most of the first week's development takes place in the Fallopian tube, as the organism makes its way to the uterus. (A) The egg is released from the ovary and begins its journey through the Fallopian tube toward the uterus. (B) If sperm have been deposited in the vagina during sexual intercourse, a few make their way to the far end of the Fallopian tube. As soon as one sperm penetrates the egg, chemical changes make it impossible for other sperm to enter. The sperm's genetic material combines with the egg's to form the zygote, a new cell with the full human complement of 46 chromosomes. (C) Cleavage, or cell division, first takes place about 30 hours after fertilization, as the zygote continues its passage through the Fallopian tube toward the uterus. Cell division continues until (D) a solid ball of cells has formed. This ball is no larger than the original egg. (E) As cell division continues, the spaces between the inner cells of the ball become larger until the ball becomes the blastocyst, a hollow sphere of cells with a small mass of cells adhering to one point in its inner surface. (F) Now within the uterus, the blastocyst makes contact with the uterine lining, where it implants itself. (G) By the eighth day, the thickened cell mass that was evident inside the blastocyst at five days has become the embryonic disc, from which the baby will develop.

Figure 3.2
Stages of development in the embryonic human brain. At 30 days, the major regions can be recognized in primitive form. By 2 months, most of the subcortical regions are fairly well along in their development. The cerebral and cerebellar cortices continue to develop throughout gestation and beyond the time of birth.

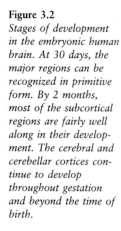
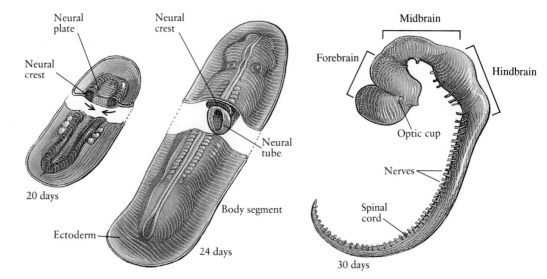

eighth day, cells on the inside of this ball detach themselves and form a flat plate across the inside—the *embryonic disc*. Within a week, some of the cells in this homogeneous cluster begin to lose their uniform character—that is, cell differentiation begins—and the disc is soon made up of two distinct layers, the ectoderm and endoderm. The *ectoderm* will become the nervous system (as well as skin, hair, and fingernails). The *endoderm* will go on to form the respiratory and digestive tracts and related organs. Later a third layer, the *mesoderm,* forms between the first two layers. Although the mesoderm does not become nervous tissue, it contributes to formation of the nervous system.

Shortly after the ectoderm has become differentiated, it thickens and builds up along its midline. At this point, it is identifiable as the primitive *neural plate*. (Figures 3.2 and 3.3 show details of these developmental processes.) Experiments have shown that even at this primitive point in development— three to four weeks after conception— specific segments of the plate are assigned to

form specific brain parts. Early in the formation of the neural plate, such assignments are still capable of being modified; that is, if some parts of the neural plate are removed, the remaining tissues can make up for the lost pieces, and a complete brain will still develop. However, only a few days further into the developmental program, missing pieces can no longer be replaced, and the brain formed will be incomplete.

As the neural plate continues its growth, parallel ridges begin to form across it, and within a few days of their development, these ridges fold over toward each other and fuse, to form the *neural tube*. The top of this hollow tube soon thickens and begins to show three bulges. These bulges become the hindbrain, the midbrain, and the forebrain. The remainder of the neural tube becomes the spinal cord.

As Figure 3.3 shows, a cluster of young neurons, or *neuroblasts,* remains outside the neural tube when it folds and fuses. This cluster, *the neural crest,* will give rise to the peripheral autonomic nervous system.

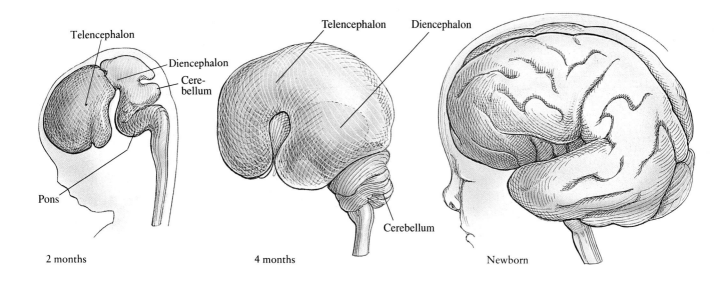

Telencephalon
Diencephalon
Cerebellum
Pons

2 months

Telencephalon   Diencephalon

Cerebellum

4 months

Newborn

The Second Month   Soon after the three primary bulges form, the first signs of eye development begin; what can now be called the brain begins to undergo the first of a series of folds and bends, which clearly differentiate its three major divisions and form its large internal cavities, the cerebral ventricles.

The next major developmental specialization occurs when the large forebrain bulge

Neural plate
Ectoderm

Neural groove

Neural tube
Neural crest

Figure 3.3
The earliest development of the nervous system, occurring during weeks three and four of prenatal life. Two views of each developmental stage are shown: at left an external view of the developing embryo and at right a cross-section as indicated by the dashed line. From the top down, you can see how the primitive ectoderm thickens and differentiates to form the neural plate, which folds to become the neural groove and, finally, the neural tube. Note, at bottom, the group of cells remaining outside the neural tube—the neural crest, from which the peripheral nervous system develops.

undergoes another division to become the *telencephalon,* which later forms all portions of the cortex, and the *diencephalon,* which forms all structures of the thalamus and hypothalamus.

It is the development of the telencephalon, highly specialized in mammals and most advanced in the primates, that accounts for the greater functional capacities of the human nervous system.

Development of the Telencephalon The telencephalon passes through three stages as it develops, although all parts of it are continuously developing. First, it gives rise to the olfactory portions of the brain, including the hippocampus and other connected regions that lie around the inside edge of the cortex. These border structures become the limbic system.

Second, the walls of the forebrain become thicker. The masses of growing cells that constitute this thickening are the basal ganglia. These cells will become structures such as the caudate nucleus, globus pallidus, and putamen, all of which are critically involved in the coordination of sensory and motor control systems, and the amygdala, which is critically involved in integrating sensory signals with internal adaptive responses.

Third, the cerebral cortex, and all of its specialized regions, develops. The product of this stage of development is often referred to as the "neocortex," or new cortex, since it is a more recent evolutionary development. It is distinguished from the "paleocortex," or old cortex, because the olfactory and limbic structures that develop in the preceding two stages can also be seen in the brains of very primitive vertebrate animals. (Even though the structures of these limbic brain parts are similar in human beings and other animals, the function of such structures is often somewhat different across species.)

The neocortex is unique to mammals, and it has grown so large in human beings that its surface becomes intricately folded as it develops. The infolding begins as the neocortex achieves its maximum growth rate, about 250,000 cells per minute. When development is complete, 70 percent of the billions of neurons that make up the brain are in the cerebral cortex.

Processes of Neuronal Development

The eight major processes that occur as neurons develop to form all parts of the brain are outlined in Table 3.1 and discussed in some detail in the following sections.

Induction How is it that some cells in the neural plate are induced to form the nervous system while other, seemingly identical cells go on to form skin, hair, and fingernails? Although no definitive answer can be given

Table 3.1   *Processes of Neuronal Development*

Process	Description
Induction	Process that allows some part of the ectoderm of the neural disc to become transformed into the neural plate.
Proliferation	The cell division that produces, from the few cells making up the neural plate and neural tube, the billions of cells of a complete brain.
Migration	Movement of newborn cells from the region in which they proliferated to their final destination in the brain.
Aggregation	Selective adhesion of cells of a similar kind as a first step in the formation of functional brain parts.
Differentiation	A neuron's commitment to a particular mode of transmitting messages—for example, excitatory vs. inhibitory, as well as size, shape, location, and connections.
Circuit formation	Establishment of synaptic connections with other neurons through growth of axons and dendrites.
Programmed cell death and synapse refinement	Elimination of redundant or extraneous cells and of some cell-to-cell connections.

yet, it is known that the crucial event in this induction is an interaction between the ectoderm and the mesoderm underlying it. Scientists believe that the mesoderm transfers specific chemical substances to the ectoderm and that these substances influence the genetic expression of the cells so that they become committed to the formation of neural tissue.

The mesoderm forms after the ectoderm, and the sequence of its formation determines which parts of the ectoderm will develop into each of the three major parts of the brain and the spinal cord. The first part of the mesoderm that forms under the ectoderm induces the development of forebrain structures. The next part cues the formation of midbrain and hindbrain. The final part causes the ectoderm associated with it to produce the spinal cord.

Even though neuroscientists are convinced that the mesoderm must transfer some chemical substances, called *trophic factors,* to the ectoderm to work its effects, no one has yet been able to isolate or identify such factors. This experimental work is extremely difficult: the amount of tissue involved is minuscule and the timing is crucial, because the ectoderm may be responsive to signals from the mesoderm for only a very short period of time.

Proliferation   Cells begin to rapidly divide and multiply, or *proliferate,* soon after the neural tube is closed off. As the cells proliferate, they move from the tube's outer surface— *the marginal zone*—to its inner surface—the *ventricular zone*—and back again. A newly divided cell synthesizes its DNA while close to the outer surface, then moves to the inner surface before dividing. Figure 3.4 shows how the cell reshapes itself to put forth what is called a *process,* a tentaclelike piece of itself. The mass of the cell then moves along the process until the cell reaches its destina-

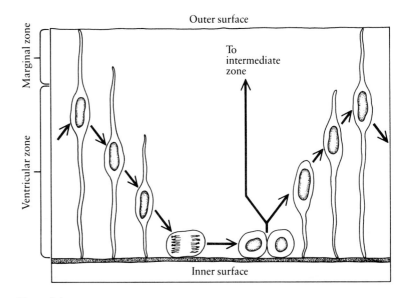

Figure 3.4
From left to right, how a cell behaves as it proliferates, to provide the building blocks of the central nervous system. Here in the neural tube, a cell synthesizes its DNA when near the outer surface of the tube; then, by putting forth a process, it moves its nucleus to the inner surface of the tube. There, it withdraws the process and divides. The daughter cells either repeat the process or begin their migration.

tion. Finally, the process is withdrawn. You can see in Figure 3.4 that after a cell moves to the inner surface of the neural tube, it becomes completely round before the next cell division, or *mitosis.*

After a cell divides, the daughter cells form processes, move up to the outer surface, synthesize DNA, and then move down again to divide. After a number of such cycles, some mechanism—the nature of which is unknown—turns off a cell's ability to synthesize DNA and, consequently, to proliferate. Some of the cells produced are neurons; some are glial-cell precursors. The young neurons never again divide.

The period of proliferation differs for different populations of cells, and each population appears to follow a rigid schedule for

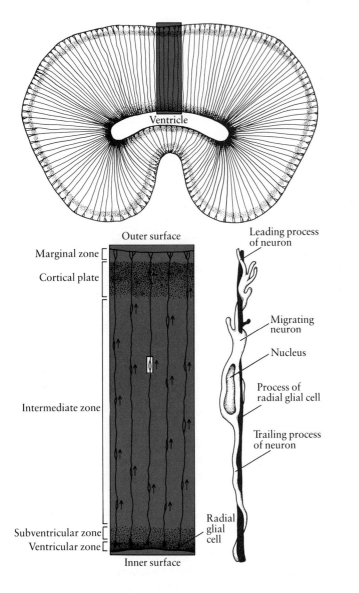

Ventricle

Outer surface

Marginal zone

Cortical plate

Leading process
of neuron

Migrating
neuron

Nucleus

Process of
radial glial cell

Intermediate zone

Trailing process
of neuron

Subventricular zone

Ventricular zone

Inner surface

Radial
glial
cell

Figure 3.5
Top, drawing of a Golgi-stained section through the wall of the cerebral hemisphere of a fetal monkey; the specialized supporting cells, the radial glial cells, can be seen clearly. Bottom left, the processes of these glia are very long, extending from the inner surface to the outer surface of the developing neural tube and its derivative structures. The arrows indicate that the cells migrate along the processes from the inner surface of the cerebral hemisphere to the marginal zone at the outer surface. Bottom right, from the close relation between the processes of the migrating neuron and the radial glial cell, it is clear that the migrating neuron depends on the glial substrate for guidance.

neural tube. When they stop dividing early in the brain's formation, they form a layer between these two zones—the *intermediate zone*—thereby thickening the developing brain.

In some parts of the brain, a layer of cells forms between the ventricular zone and the intermediate zone—the *subventricular zone* (Figure 3.5). In this region, cells continue to proliferate, giving rise to many of the neurons and glial cells that migrate to form the forebrain.

These glial cells appear to play a prominent role in directing the migration of many neurons to their ultimate destination. The cell bodies of these specialized glial cells lie inside the subventricular zone, but their cell processes radiate out to the surface of the developing brain. It seems that neurons use these long glial processes as a kind of scaffolding, in much the same way as the vine of a bean plant grows along a string the gardener sets out for it (see Figure 3.5; Rakic, 1974).

In one species of mouse, scientists have found that a mutant gene (a gene that has

ending division, relative to the other populations. A cell's withdrawal from the proliferative cycle seems to trigger its migration toward its final functional location.

Migration   During the proliferative phase, cells move up and down between the marginal zone and the ventricular zone of the been altered in some fundamental way) results in the virtual absence of these glia in the mouse's cerebellum. Absence of the glia results in impaired migration and thus the death of neurons that would normally have been part of the cerebellum. Because the cerebellum is grossly abnormal, the mouse's movements are impaired—it trembles constantly and is extremely weak; in fact, it is called the weaver mouse to describe its characteristic way of moving (Rakic & Sidman, 1973).

Given the number of cells that must find their way to their place of work and the great distance that many of them have to travel, it is not surprising that some should become misplaced. This happens even in normal development. Studies indicate that as many as 3 percent of cells may migrate to incorrect locations. Almost all of these, however, degenerate during the stage of programmed cell death (Oppenheim, 1981).

Aggregation After a neuron has migrated to its final location, it often adheres to cells of a similar kind. This aggregation produces functional units such as the thalamic nuclei and the layers of the cortex. In experiments in which individual cells from several different areas of the developing brain were removed and then mixed together in a nutrient medium in the laboratory, the cells that had been taken from a given area tended to find each other and aggregate (Garber & Moscona, 1972).

The mechanism that allows these cells to "recognize" each other and to "prefer" each other works by means of specific classes of large molecules on the cell's surface. This is similar to the mechanism that allows cells of the immune system to differentiate between "self" and "not-self" when they go about their task of destroying invading bacteria or other microorganisms. These cell-surface molecules not only serve the recognition function but also bind similar cells to each other.

One cell-surface molecule has recently been identified; it is called N CAM (which stands for neural cell adhesion molecule). The developmental program causes some cells to produce N CAM on their surface at discrete times, and the cells bearing N CAM molecules can then find and bind strongly to each other (Hoffman & Edelman, 1983).

Differentiation Cell differentiation begins early, when germinal cells in the neural tube become identifiable as young neurons or young glia. How and when neurons are triggered to stop dividing and differentiate into specific types is not yet known. It appears, however, that as soon as a neuron withdraws from the proliferative phase, much of its destiny is set. It not only begins its migration but also seems to head for a definite location. The pattern of connections it will ultimately make seems to be set at this early time.

As stated earlier, different populations of cells begin and end their proliferative cycles at different times. The timing of the cycle for a population of cells is tied closely to its ultimate placing and function. For example, the population of cells that forms the deepest layer of the cerebral cortex is always the first to stop proliferating; the next set to complete mitosis forms the layer above that; and so on. Thus, the wave of cortical maturation proceeds from "inside out." The sequence varies for different structures, but it appears that cells occupying similar positions are always generated at the same time. Thus, a neuron's "birth date," the time it undergoes its final cell division, seems to be a critical time for determination of many of its characteristics.

It is likely that the neurotransmitter a neuron will manufacture is also decided when proliferation stops, but some experiments have found that a cell's environment may influence that function. In one experiment, young neurons were transplanted to the developing brainstem from lower parts of the neural crest. Normally, they would have developed into parts of the autonomic nervous system and would have produced norepinephrine as their transmitter. Instead, they produced acetylcholine, like the other cells in that brainstem area (Le Douarin et al., 1975). It may be that some neurons have the potential to produce several transmitters and that the local environment stimulates the production of one or the other during differentiation.

Circuit Formation: Development of Axons and Dendrites   One of the most intriguing problems in neural embryology is how axons find their way to their destinations. Some axons are thousands of times as long as the cell body from which they spring, and some have to make right or left turns as they grow and find their appropriate target on the opposite side of the brain.

Almost all neurons begin to put forth their axons and dendrites only after the cells have migrated to their final destination. The initial growth of these cell extensions and their orientation appear to be genetically determined, since cells that have been experimentally moved or rotated nevertheless show growth patterns just like their sister cells in the developing nervous system.

After their initial growth, however, the axon and dendrites can be influenced by a number of aspects of their environment, primarily mechanical and chemical ones. It appears that the axons of young neurons require contact with a certain underlying surface, or *substrate*, to help guide their growth. As described earlier in this chapter, when the glial cells of the cerebellum are absent, as in the weaver mouse, the cerebellar neurons fail to migrate properly and important cell circuitry is never established. The growing, searching axons seem to require that glial substrate in order to develop and to find their targets.

It is likely that this mechanical interaction also involves some chemical interaction—an interaction between molecules on the surface of the growing neuron and molecules on the surface of the substrate.

At the growing end of most axons is a distinctive structure called a *growth cone* (see figure at left). The tip of the axon is slightly swollen, and attached to it is an undulating membrane with constantly moving, fingerlike extensions—*filopodia*. The filopodia seem to be constantly exploring their imme-

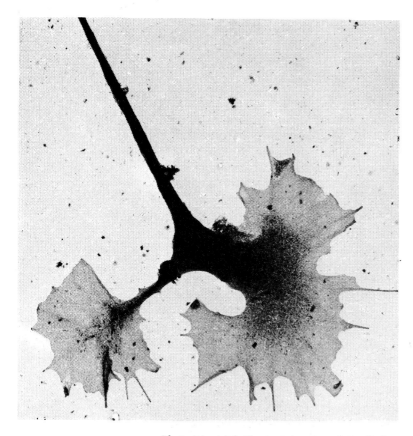

Photomicrograph of a growth cone at the end of an axon. Note the filopodia—the fingerlike extensions.

diate environment, expanding and contracting, as if searching for "the right" surface to adhere to. It is likely that the molecules on the substrate surface act as directional guides for the growth cones. This directional guidance may work in one of two ways.

The first mode of directional guidance is by attraction: the chemical that the growth cone "recognizes" may diffuse in such a way that it generates a *gradient,* with its concentration ranging from weaker to stronger, the stronger concentration being "upstream." The growth cone is then attracted to move toward the stronger concentration. The second mode may work by restriction: chemicals that are inhibitory to the neuron's growth may be arranged in such a way that they create a pathway that the growth cone has no option but to follow (Varon, 1985; see Figure 3.6).

Several substances have been identified as possibly playing a role in the directional guidance of growing axons. One of these is N CAM, discussed earlier as important in cell aggregation. Another guidance substance is *nerve-growth factor (NGF).* (Italian neuroscientist Rita Levi-Montalcini was awarded the 1986 Nobel Prize in Physiology or Medicine for this discovery.) Although NGF has not proved to affect most of the central nervous system, its role in guiding neuronal growth in the peripheral nervous system is clear. In one experiment, scientists injected NGF into the brain of young rats, and it caused the dorsal root ganglia—neurons lying alongside the spine—to send their axons into the spinal cord and up toward the brain, a completely abnormal pattern of growth. The axons just followed along the path of the injected NGF (Levi-Montalcini, 1952).

A number of studies have sought an understanding of "how axons find their way and make the right connections" by rearranging the anatomy of embryo frogs or

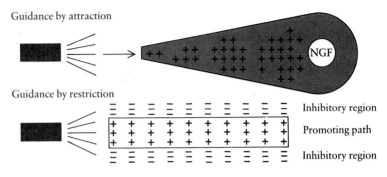

Figure 3.6
The drawing represents the two modes of directional guidance that have been suggested for leading the axon's growth cone to its correct location. In guidance by attraction, molecules on the surface of the axon's substrate may diffuse to form a gradient, with a stronger—and therefore more attractive—concentration in the direction the axon should take. In guidance by restriction, substrate molecules that are inhibitory to the neuron's growth may be arranged so as to form a pathway leading to the proper location for the neuron.

chicks and then examining either the innervation pattern that develops or the behavior of the animal. In one set of experiments, the developing eye of a frog was rotated 180 degrees. When this was done in an early stage of development, the image on the frog's retina was normal. A bit later, though, the resulting image on the retina was rotated just as the eye was. These results indicate that at the early stage, there is a great deal of plasticity in the developing system; that is, it has a great capacity for adjusting to change. After further development, however, that plasticity weakens or disappears. (Figure 3.7 shows how the scientists knew that the image on the frog's retina was rotated. They placed a tasty-looking fly in the frog's field of vision and observed where the frog directed its attack; Sperry, 1945).

The discovery that five proteins in the chick retina are developmentally regulated may explain such changes in plasticity. Two of these proteins are present during early

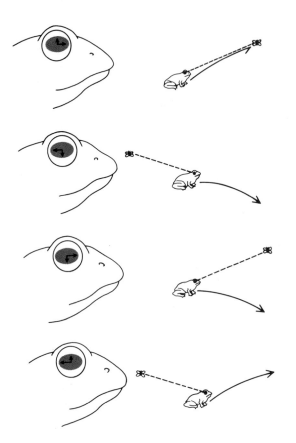

Figure 3.7
Scientists have many ways of studying how neurons make specific connections in the developing brain. One involves rotating or transplanting the eyes of frogs or of tadpoles at various stages of development and then seeing what effect the procedure has on the animals' visual behavior. The top drawing shows the behavior of a control frog, which had developed normally; the frog sees the insect ahead and above and strikes ahead and above. In the second drawing from the top, the frog's eye has been rotated 180 degrees; the frog strikes forward and down when the insect is behind and above. In the third drawing from top, the left eye has been substituted for the right eye and the dorsoventral axis reversed; the frog strikes down when the insect is above. In the bottom drawing, the left eye has again been substituted for the right, this time with the anteroventral axis reversed; the frog strikes up but in the wrong direction.

development but disappear later, and three are present in later stages of development but are absent earlier (Mintz & Glaser, 1978). This developmental program of gene expression could mean that the surface molecules in this area of the chick retina change, so axons seeking the "appropriate" connections can find them during the earlier stages but not later, after the early proteins disappear.

Circuit Formation: Formation of Synapses   The path that axons travel as they grow allows them to make their connections, either with other neurons or with the anatomical structures they will innervate and whose function they will regulate. As you know, the connections between neurons occur at the synapses, where one neuron releases a neurotransmitter that affects the activity of the receiving neuron. Each class of neuron in the central nervous system chooses to synapse with only a very limited repertoire of cell types.

Development of synapses is not confined to the prenatal period; in fact, the formation of most synapses in the human neocortex takes place after birth. In the cat, 98 percent of the synapses in the visual cortex start to appear only after birth (Cragg, 1972, 1975). Visual experience plays a big part in this postnatal development, as discussed later in this chapter.

Programmed Cell Death and Refinement of Synapses The developing nervous system produces many more neurons than exist in the final product. From this superabundance of cells (in some areas as much as 85 percent excess), a kind of sculpting action occurs as populations of neurons form synaptic connections with their targets. The process allows for the formation of required neural circuits, along with elimination of redundant or improperly connected cells, until the neural network is adjusted to match the size of the area it must innervate.

Whereas some superfluous neurons die early in their development, some may become mature before they are eliminated. They may differentiate, send forth an axon, and make contact with a target before they give up the ghost. One possible explanation for why some neurons survive and other, indistinguishable, neurons die is based on competition for the life-sustaining factors they can receive from their proper synaptic targets. That is, neurons that succeed in making a synaptic connection with a target—and thereby receive sufficient exposure to an appropriate growth factor—will survive. Those that make inappropriate connections or fail in the struggle for working connections are eliminated (Hamburger & Levi-Montalcini, 1949).

Experimental manipulations of embryos in which, for example, a third leg is grafted onto an animal show that under these circumstances there is much less cell death in the spinal cord than normally occurs. The extra limb offers more opportunity for the cells to develop working connections (Hollyday & Hamburger, 1976).

Besides competition, another mechanism that may act to eliminate some cells while strengthening others' connections is usage—whether a given set of cells actually functions before birth. When the limb of an embryo chick is treated with a paralyzing agent, cell death in that area is greatly reduced, and the limb ends up being innervated with an abnormally large number of neurons. It appears that in normal development of the limb, axons seek acetylcholine (ACh) receptors on muscles as their targets for synapse formation. The amount of physiological activity carried out by the limb *in utero* ordinarily regulates the number and distribution of these receptors on the muscle. Then axons compete for synaptic sites with these receptors. Since each receptor site can support only one synapse, neurons that are smaller or more immature lose out in competing for a connection. In the paralyzed limb, the cell membranes on the muscle do not undergo the changes stimulated by activity and therefore keep nonfunctional ACh receptor sites. The presence of these extra sites prevents the normal pruning of neurons in programmed cell death (Oppenheim, 1981).

Even though direct muscle-neuron connections are not part of the central nervous system, there is reason to believe that the organism's activity before birth also acts to hone and sharpen that system, at least at the level of spinal cord and subcortical brain connections. Human fetuses are very active before birth. They move their limbs against the tension of the amniotic fluid; they swallow; they perform breathing-like movements. This activity most likely serves to strengthen some neural connections and contributes to the death of cells that the system does not need.

Programmed cell death and refinement of synapses are developmental processes that continue after birth. In one study, for example, Rakic and his colleagues (1986) discovered a great overproduction of synapses during prenatal development and their paring down during the first four months of a monkey's postnatal life. The researchers suggest that functional or behavioral maturity results not from synapse formation but rather from elimination of excess connections and the increasing efficiency of those that remain and continue to operate.

The Genetic Plan

In prenatal development, then, the plans encoded in an individual's genes are unfolded. The fact that exact molecular mechanisms have not yet been worked out to explain most of these developmental phenomena should not obscure the more striking fact that, generation after generation, the brains of developing animals grow the right neurons in the right places.

Genetic specification determines a neuron's size and shape and the transmitter it will manufacture. (Even though the neuron's immediate environment may have some influence on what that transmitter will be, structural or secretory proteins produced by specific genes normally guide a neuron to a specified environment.) The neuron's *intracellular* operations (those within a given neuron) and its *intercellular* operations (those between two or more neurons) are also programmed by the proteins encoded by the genes it carries.

Even the general range of connections for most nerve cells seems to be highly specified in advance. The right connections are made in hierarchical circuits: neurons of the specialized visual receptor organ, the retina, always connect to the secondary relay neurons of the visual system and do not mingle with the auditory relays or the skin-sensing relays. The same sort of specificity of connection holds true for local circuits and single-source/divergent circuits—in fact, for every system in the brain.

A specific biochemical substrate may be important for growing neurons, factors that guide growth may be important for local sculpting, and local environments may influence which transmitter a neuron makes, but,

The cross-eyed look of the Siamese cat results from a miswiring in the cat's visual pathway.

in normal development, these controls are also supplied by the genetic program.

Sometimes, however, the genetic program is incomplete or scrambled in some way. For example, in the disorder known as Down syndrome, the affected individual inherits more than the normal complement of genes on a part of the twenty-first chromosome. The scrambled genetic program results in a number of physical abnormalities, some of which are reflected in the mental retardation that is part of the syndrome. Lack of a single gene or mutation of a single gene can profoundly affect development. The box on the facing page describes how such a single-gene mutation affects brain development and behavior of the Siamese cat—and produces the beautiful pattern of coloring that characterizes the breed.

In the section that follows, we look at how the genes that determine an individual's sex produce differences in brain development and how these physiological differences may be related to behavioral differences between the sexes.

The Siamese Cat: How a Single Gene Affects Brain Development

The distinctive markings of the beautiful Siamese cat and its characteristic cross-eyed look result from mutation of a single gene. This mutant gene also results in a serious miswiring of the cat's visual pathway.

How does this occur? A gene, as you probably know, specifies the manufacture of a given protein. (Genes also program the initial proliferation, differentiation, and migration of neurons, although the manner in which they do so remains a mystery.) In the case of the Siamese cat, the single gene that malfunctions normally produces an enzyme (tyrosinase) that is a necessary step in the synthesis of the dark pigment melanin. The result of this missing step is that melanin cannot be synthesized by the cat's body at its normal body temperature. Only the cooler areas of the body—the paws, the tips of the ears, the snout—are darkly pigmented.

This missing step in a metabolic pathway also disrupts development of the visual pathway—the normal neural connections between eye and brain (see figure at right). Some growing axons end up on the wrong side of the brain, and so the cats do not have a normal binocular field of vision. One type of miswiring produces cats that can see only objects appearing in the part of their visual field nearest their nose; another miswiring produces monocular rather than binocular vision.

Impaired development of the visual pathway is also present in albino mammals (such as some tigers, mice, or mink)—animals with a mutant gene that also prevents normal synthesis of the pigment melanin.

It is clear that the absence of the pigment somehow produces the aberrant growth pattern of visual path axons, even though the cells themselves do not normally contain melanin. Neuroscientists and geneticists do not yet know how this happens. Since another set of cells developing in the eye's retina do normally contain melanin, it could be that some interaction between the visual-path cells and the retinal cells is needed for normal development.

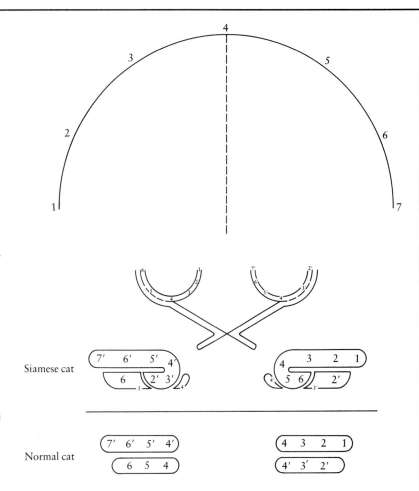

Siamese cat

Normal cat

The case of the Siamese cat offers a tantalizing insight to genetic mechanisms in the developing nervous system. It helps demonstrate the role genes play in development. Genes most likely do not contain a complete program for the laying down of all the brain's neural circuits; rather, they produce the elements that begin the orderly process of development. Many steps in the developmental process are governed by intracellular events and intercellular interactions; these events and interactions occur in a context that is almost always the same for members of a given species—except in cases like that of the Siamese cat, where one abnormal gene produces a number of unexpected developmental outcomes.

The map of the visual field on the lateral geniculate nucleus in Siamese cats (top) and normal cats (bottom).

Sex and the Brain

When egg and sperm unite at the moment of conception, a person's sex is determined. Each parent contributes a set of 23 chromosomes to the new cell, one of which is the chromosome that determines sex. Women always contribute an X chromosome, since a female's cells contain two X chromosomes; a male's cells contain one X chromosome and a smaller Y chromosome. If the impregnating sperm carries an X, the offspring will be female (XX); if it carries a Y, the embryo will develop into a male (XY).

Until the ninth week of prenatal development, there is no difference between the gonads (sex glands) of male and female embryos. During that week, genes on the Y chromosome cause the male gonads to develop into testes. These genes, it has been proposed, cause the production of a membrane protein called H-Y antigen (the H-Y histocompatability antigen), which attaches to the gonad and induces its change into testes (Jost, 1979). In the absence of this antigen, the gonads become ovaries and the fetus develops into a female.

As soon as the testes are formed, they begin to secrete hormones that masculinize the reproductive tract and the brain of male

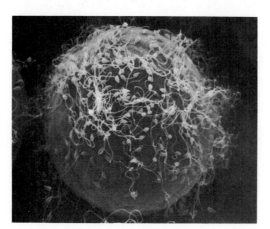

Sperm surrounding an egg.

fetuses. Females need not produce equivalent feminizing hormones, since the mother's body is replete with them. It seems that the basic model for development is a female one, and that masculinity must be imposed on the developing individual by the Y chromosome and the sequence of developmental events that it sets in motion.

Besides the difference in reproductive organs that the sex chromosomes produce, there are other characteristic physiological differences between the sexes. Men are, on the average, taller than women; they have a higher ratio of muscle to fat; and their chests are broader. Women are wider in the pelvis; their hip joints are formed a little differently; and their bodies use energy more efficiently. Though not as strong as men, women seem to have greater endurance. (Such differences reflect evolutionary patterns designed to help the human species survive. For most of its life on earth, the species *Homo sapiens* lived as hunting-gathering groups. Men hunted and so had need of stronger muscles and greater heart-lung capacity. Women gathered plants and plant products, and they bore children; they needed a greater capacity to store fat so that in times of scarcity they could call on those stores if they were pregnant or nursing.)

Given that the sex chromosomes produce such measurable physiological differences between male and female bodies, do they also produce any differences between male and female brains? They certainly do in many animals, and although the anatomical and physiological evidence for human beings is not abundant, significant differences have been found.

Genes, Hormones, and Brain Differences

Among canaries, it is the male that sings—a part of the courting ritual and claim for territory. The song is controlled by a nucleus of cells in the bird's left hemisphere, and this nucleus is much larger in males than in females. This difference between male and female anatomy and behavior is, without doubt, the result of hormonal influences. Early implantation of the male hormone testosterone in female birds, plus later treatment with androgens, causes them to sing and also enlarges the cortical nucleus, making it more nearly the size it has in males (Nottebohm & Arnold, 1976; Nottebohm, 1980). In the course of normal development, the male gene complement directs production of the testosterone.

In the canary, then, male and female brains are organized differently; the difference is anatomically obvious and is clearly linked to differences between male and female behaviors. How can a hormone work to produce such differences? To be precise, we will be discussing testosterone, since the male hormone is the one that produces the differentiation from the original female model.

When the male gonads begin to manufacture testosterone, it is secreted into the general circulation and reaches the brain. Certain target cells in the brain are able to recognize and react with the molecules of testosterone. These molecules have a unique shape, allowing them to become attached to the target cells. The receptors for these molecules are not on the cell membrane but are actually within the cell. The receptors accumulate and retain the hormone, which binds directly to specific sites in the cell's nucleus to regulate genetic mechanisms (see Figure 3.8). Testosterone can therefore increase the expression of selected gene products.

Such changes in genetic expression have at least two major effects. First, the testosterone-induced gene products (probably some structural proteins or some enzymes, not yet fully characterized) "sensitize" the cell, so that it responds later to the presence

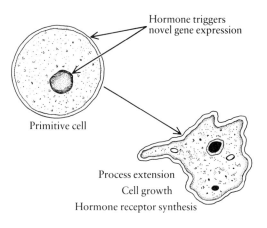

Figure 3.8
Ways in which testosterone, can alter the cell's development: by promoting or inhibiting growth; by inducing development or extension of axon branches or dendrites and their direction; by sensitizing receptors to respond later to presence of the hormone.

Hormone triggers novel gene expression

Primitive cell

Process extension
Cell growth
Hormone receptor synthesis

of the hormone (for example, at puberty). These prenatal effects of hormones on the brain are called *organizational* effects; the later effects, like those at puberty, are called *activational* effects. Second, these changes in genetic expression can produce the sort of anatomical differences we noted between the brains of male and female canaries. Similar *dimorphisms*, or male-female anatomical differences, have been found in the brains of hamsters and rats.

In studying the cellular basis of structural differences between male and female hamsters in an area of the brain called the suprachiasmatic nucleus, researchers noted that in the male brain, dendrites were more centrally concentrated, and in the female brain they were more peripherally distributed (Greenough et al., 1977). How might hormones effect such differences in neural growth? Greenough suggests four possibilities:

1. Hormones might affect the growth rate of axons and dendrites on neurons sensitive to them. The hormone-sensitive neurons would end up making different connections in male and female brains because the timing of their meeting up with other growing neurons would be different.

2. Hormones might trigger neurons sensitive to them to form synaptic connections. They might also serve to prevent sensitive cells from making the connections.

3. Hormones might alter the direction of growth of sensitive neurons, acting in the same manner as the nerve-growth factor.

4. Hormones might prevent cell death of sensitive neurons in competition with others, "stamping" in certain connections.

At present, no one can say for certain which, if any, of these mechanisms might be responsible for the sexual dimorphisms noted. However, relative to the first postulate, Norman Geschwind, in a paper published not long before his death in 1985, stated his belief that testosterone slows the growth of the left hemisphere in human males as compared to females and, in effect, favors relatively greater development of the right hemisphere in males. The delayed growth in the left hemisphere could explain why left-handedness, while relatively uncommon, is much more common in males. It might also account for developmental defects like dyslexia, which is four times as common in males and is often associated with left-handedness (Geschwind & Behan, 1982).

Geschwind also noted that left-handed people, usually males, are more vulnerable to certain diseases of the immune system. Testosterone has been shown to have suppressive effects on development of the immune system. Left-handedness, immune disorders, and learning disabilities tend to run in families, and thus it may be that some gene complexes responsible for immune responsiveness also regulate testosterone levels in certain people, who, therefore, secrete excess testosterone prenatally or are excessively sensitive to it.

The notion that prenatal testosterone delays left-hemisphere growth, if true, could explain some of the findings about male-female differences in brain and behavior.

Human Differences in Brain and Behavior

Psychologists have been able to agree that the following behaviors are, on the average, different for human males and females (Maccoby & Jacklin, 1974).

1. Males are more aggressive than females. This difference appears in all cultures and at an early age.

2. Females are more verbally fluent than males.

3. Males have more acute visual-spatial abilities than females.

In the discussion that follows, we will focus on the verbal and spatial-visual differences between the sexes. Aggression is discussed in Chapter 7.

Keep in mind that the male-female differences listed above are statistical (Figure 3.9); some individual males have more verbal fluency than most females and some individual females are better at visualizing objects in space than most males. Nevertheless, studies have found that, on the average, there are consistent differences between males and

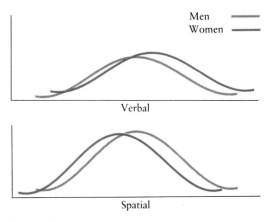

Figure 3.9
These idealized curves illustrate that while, on the average, females show higher verbal abilities and males show higher spatial abilities, the differences are quite small.

females in these characteristics. (Figure 3.10 gives examples of the types of problems females and males score better on.)

For the vast majority of people, the parts of the brain responsible for language lie in the left hemisphere. The right hemisphere is mainly responsible for the processing of visual-spatial information. Could there be some difference in the organization of the two hemispheres and their interconnections in males and females that would account for the differences in ability in these two areas?

On the basis of the known differences between the responsibilities of the two hemispheres—language, left; visual-spatial, right—we might well predict that left-hemisphere damage would produce verbal deficits and right-hemisphere damage would produce spatial deficits in adult patients. Her-

bert Lansdell (1962) predicted this very outcome when he began his study of the effects of partial removal of one temporal lobe in both males and females. (The subjects were patients who had undergone surgery to remove tumors or repair injuries.) The prediction held true for the males but not for the females. This surprising result caused Lansdell to speculate that the distribution of abilities may be different in male and female brains.

Subsequent studies lent some support to this conclusion. In one study, the researcher looked at 85 patients with damage to one or the other hemisphere (McGlone, 1978) and found that left-hemisphere damage produced aphasia in three times as many males as females and resulted in much greater impairment in the high-level verbal tasks tested by

NOW is to HERE as TIME is to:
A. DISTANCE   B. PLACE
C. PRESENT   D. THEN

RIGOROUS has the most nearly *opposite* meaning to:
A. STRINGENT   B. WEAK
C. LAX   D. FEVERISH

GIBBER has most nearly the *same* meaning as:
A. MONKEY   B. SPEAK
C. FEAR   D. CLARIFY

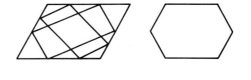

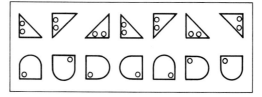

Figure 3.10
Verbal problems (top left) represent problems that females, on the average, solve more easily than males. Visual-spatial problems represent problems that males, on the average, solve more easily than females: top right, find in the figure at left the shape shown at right; middle right, the figures at left are models—from six choices to the right, pick the rotated figure identical to the model; bottom, does a, b, c, or d represent the sample figure when folded along the dashed lines?

the Wechsler Adult Intelligence Scale, one of the standard IQ tests. The Wechsler also has a set of tasks that require very little language for their solution; this performance scale includes several tests of visualization.

The results were that men with right-hemisphere damage showed greater impairment in the performance tasks relative to the verbal ones, and those with left-hemisphere damage performed worse on the verbal tasks than on the performance ones. For women, the side on which the damage had occurred seemed to make little difference. Their abilities were impaired, but the impairment did not correlate with right or left damage.

These and other such results (Wada et al., 1975) indicate that the male brain may be more specialized bilaterally than the female brain. Verbal and spatial functions appear to be more widely distributed in both hemispheres of the female brain, whereas these abilities appear to be more rigidly segregated in the male—verbal on the left, spatial on the right.

More recent work, especially that by Doreen Kimura (1982; Kimura & Harshman, 1984), suggests that the final story on male-female hemispheric differences may be much more complex than indicated by the earlier findings. Her studies with patients suffering brain damage indicate that males and females differ in the organization of speech functions *within* the left hemisphere. In females, speech appears to be critically dependent on areas toward the front of the brain; consequently, damage to the rear part of the left hemisphere rarely affects speech. In males, however, damage to either the front or back of the left hemisphere can impair the ability to speak.

In any case, the male-female differences in verbal and visual-spatial abilities are a statistical fact. Although we cannot point to specific anatomical differences between male and female brains as being responsible for

such differences, we can describe at least two known anatomical differences and suggest what roles they may play. First, there is a marked difference between male and female brains in the makeup of the corpus callosum, the large bundle of fibers that links the right and left hemispheres. The posterior part of the bundle is much wider and larger in women. This difference can be seen in the brains of fetuses as early as the twenty-sixth week of gestation (Lacoste-Utamsing & Holloway, 1982; Lacoste-Utamsing & Woodward, 1982). Perhaps the female corpus callosum permits more interhemispheric communication.

Another measurable anatomic difference is in the size of the planum temporale, the upper surface of the temporal lobe (Figure 3.11). In the left hemisphere, this area overlaps Wernicke's area, a major language center. In most brains, the left planum temporale is larger than the right, but when the right is found to be larger, it is almost exclusively in female brains (Wada et al., 1975). It may be that the relatively greater verbal fluency in females is related to the larger planum temporale, but this is pure conjecture.

One further source of information on the relationship between sex and the brain comes from studies of individuals who inherited an abnormal complement of sex-related genes.

Experiments of Nature

Although the occurrences are rare, genetic malfunctions or introduction of harmful substances to the prenatal environment sometimes interfere with normal sexual development. Studies of the way that individuals are affected can help give some insight into the part played by hormones in differentiating male and female brains and the behaviors we have been discussing.

Accidents can occur at the chromosomal level. During the process of *meiosis,* when

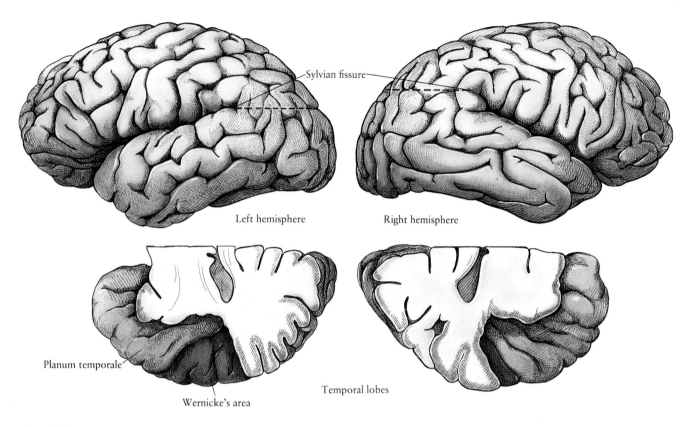

Left hemisphere   Right hemisphere

Sylvian fissure

Planum temporale

Wernicke's area   Temporal lobes

Figure 3.11
Anatomical asymmetries in the hemispheres of the brain. The Sylvian fissure, which defines the upper margin of the temporal lobe, slants upward more sharply in the right hemisphere. When the Sylvian fissure is opened and the cut completed along the dashed line, the planum temporale, which forms the upper surface of the temporal lobe, can be seen. It is usually much larger in the left hemisphere, and the enlarged region is part of Wernicke's area.

the chromosome pairs in the male or female cell separate to form sperm or egg, the process may go awry, leaving one daughter cell with too few or too many chromosomes at a given location. When one of these cells impregnates or is impregnated, the resulting individual will suffer some abnormality in his or her development.

Three abnormalities involving the sex chromosomes have been extensively studied. One is *Turner's syndrome*, in which individuals have only one X chromosome and no X or Y to make a pair—this configuration is designated as XO. These females are always unusually short and have short necks and widely spaced nipples. Their abnormality is sometimes not discovered until the age of puberty, when they fail to undergo the normal changes: they do not begin to menstruate and there is no breast development. Because they lack the additional X chromosome of normal females, they do not develop ovaries. A lack of ovaries means that, from the eighth week of prenatal life, they do not have available to them the sex hormones that the ovaries ordinarily manufacture and release into circulation. Besides the female hormone estrogen, the ovaries also normally produce small amounts of testosterone.

The most interesting behavioral deficit that Turner's syndrome women show, in light of our discussion of sexual dimorphism and the brain, is their poor performance on tests of visual-spatial ability. Their scores are generally much poorer than that of the average female, although their scores on the verbal tests are about average (Shaffer, 1962; Alexander et al. 1966). It may be that the total absence of male hormone in these women affected brain organization.

In another chromosomal aberration, *Klinefelter's syndrome,* the individual is born with an XXY genotype. These males show some feminization as adolescents and adults: they generally have little beard growth, they have a small penis and testes, their voices are unusually high, and they may show some breast development at puberty. However, their visual-spatial skills fall within the normal male range. Evidently, the hormones produced under direction of the Y chromosome were sufficient for masculinization of the brain in this area.

In contrast, some chromosomally normal XY males have a rare genetic deficiency (idiopathic hypogonadotropic hypogonadism) in which testosterone is not produced at puberty. These males score well below the average for men on tests of visual-spatial ability (Hier & Crowley, 1982). Perhaps the flow of hormones at puberty that activates parts of the brain involved in male sexual development is also responsible for activating the development of brain areas required for visual-spatial tasks.

Although the existing data allow few uncontestable assertions about human behaviors as developmental products of sex-linked genes, future studies will doubtless be able to verify or refute some of the proposed relationships between genes, brain physiology, and behavior. Since these relationships are easily demonstrated in a number of animal species, there is good reason to believe that they also exist in the human species.

Postnatal Development

At birth the human brain weighs, on average, about 25 percent of its adult weight. It reaches half its adult size by six months and almost 75 percent by age two. Since no new neurons are created after birth, the increase in brain size is accounted for by increase in the size of neurons and in the number of connections they make through axon growth and dendritic branching. New glial cells and the growth of myelin around many neurons accounts for some of the increase.

After birth, however, an individual's genetic program begins to interact with experience, so each individual brain will be a bit different from all others. Experience affects the course of brain development. The brain's processing of sensory and cognitive inputs determines the formation of synapses and the growth of dendrites. Experiments in which an animal is denied some sensory or cognitive input help show how this development takes place.

Sensory Inputs

A mouse's whiskers (or vibrissae) are very important sources of sensory input: they give the animal information about place and movement. Each whisker sends its input to a grouping of neurons—called a *barrel*—in the mouse's cerebral cortex, on the side opposite the whisker. The fibers that innervate the whiskers are linked to the barrels through at least two synaptic relays.

If one row of whiskers is removed shortly after birth, the cortical barrels that would

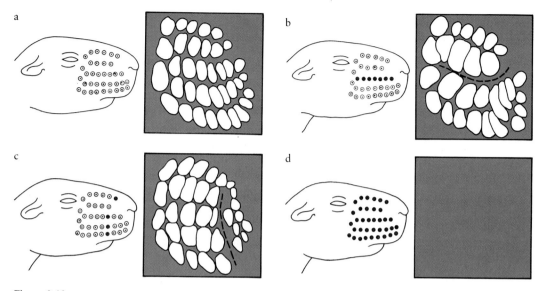

Figure 3.12

Experiments with mouse whiskers demonstrate the importance of sensory inputs to the brain's development, and also the brain's plasticity. The boxed drawings represent the groupings of neurons—or barrels—in the mouse's cerebral cortex that receive input from the whiskers; each barrel receives its input from a single whisker on the opposite side of the mouse's snout. A normal mouse and its barrels (a). When one row or column of whiskers was destroyed shortly after birth (b and c), the corresponding barrels failed to develop, but the adjoining barrels became enlarged, to compensate for the loss. When all the whiskers were destroyed (d), there was no cortical development.

have innervated those whiskers will fail to develop. The lack of normal sensory input to those cortical cells results in their shrinkage and loss of function. Also, the barrels of adjoining rows will be larger than normal, a development that demonstrates the system's plasticity—its ability to make up for the loss (Figure 3.12; Woolsey & Wann, 1976).

This plasticity can also be seen in rats raised in absolute darkness. In normal rat brains, each cortical relay neuron at level 3 of visual processing connects with about 50 cells at level 4. (You will read about these levels in detail in Chapter 4.) For the rats raised in the dark, each level-3 neuron synapses with only 5 or 10 at level 4. Yet, when

all level-4 neurons are examined under a microscope, there is no real deficit in the number of synapses on them. The reason for this is that the auditory and olfactory systems sent in neurons and took over the available synaptic space usually occupied by visual neurons. Since the rats could not use their sense of sight, a part of their visual system failed to develop normally. But lack of vision caused them to make greater use of their senses of smell and hearing in getting around and doing what rats do, so these information-processing systems increased their neural structure and functioning.

When one eye of a kitten is kept closed from soon after birth until it is several

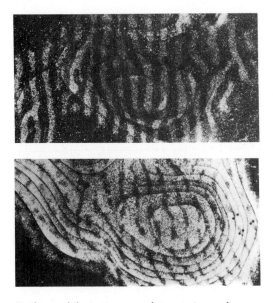

Evidence of the importance of sensory inputs for cortical development can be seen clearly when the two photos are compared. Shown are the ocular dominance columns—the columns of neurons that alternately receive input from right and left eye. Top, a relatively normal pattern (from a monkey whose right eye was closed in maturity). Below, the pattern in a monkey whose right eye was closed at two weeks of age and was kept closed for a year and a half; the columns for the functioning left eye obviously dominate.

months old, the kitten will no longer be able to see out of that eye, not because of deficits in any eye structure or in the retina, but because the visual cortex fails to develop. The same thing happens to young monkeys, whose visual system more closely resembles that of human beings (Hubel & Wiesel, 1962).

In Chapter 4, you will read about the columnar organization of the cortex. In layer 4 of the primary visual cortex, columns of cells receiving input from the left eye alternate with columns receiving information from the right eye. These are called *ocular dominance columns* (further discussed in Chapter 4). The effect on these columns of using only

one eye can be seen clearly in the photographs at left, prepared by T. Wiesel (1982). The top photograph shows the columnar organization of a monkey whose right eye was closed after it was 14 months old; it closely resembles the pattern one would see in normally reared monkeys. The lower photograph is the cortex of a monkey whose right eye was closed at 2 weeks of age and kept closed for 18 months. The columns representing the functioning left eye obviously dominate. Figure 3.13 diagrams the process.

It appears that during development the neurons from the two eyes compete for dendritic connections in layer 4, and the lack of visual stimulation for the right eye results in retarded growth of its axons. The left-eye neurons, which receive plenty of stimulation, then take over many more of the available synaptic connections that, under conditions of normal binocular vision, would have been connected to the right eye.

Human neural development undoubtedly has similar requirements for sensory input. One study of adults who were astigmatic as infants, and whose astigmatism had not been corrected by glasses, demonstrated abnormal cortical development. Astigmatism results from an abnormal curvature of the cornea (the clear outer covering of the eyeball), either in a vertical or horizontal dimension. It causes visual input to the eye to be blurred in the dimension affected. Using a viewing apparatus that compensates for the eye's abnormality, the researchers measured neural activity (evoked potentials) in the visual cortex as these subjects viewed patterns of lines at various orientations. Even though each of the subjects reported being able to see all the patterns through the viewing apparatus, there was less cortical response for the dimension that had always been blurred by the astigmatism (Freeman & Thibos, 1973).

Most normal environments provide the sensory stimuli necessary for normal human

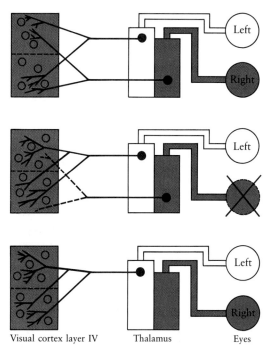

Visual cortex layer IV   Thalamus   Eyes

Figure 3.13
Effects of closing one eye on development of the visual cortex. The green boxes at left represent the visual cortex; the two boxes at right center represent the thalamus. Top, with both eyes open, neurons from the two eyes compete for connections in layer IV of the visual cortex; neither eye dominates. Middle, right eye is closed early in life; growth of that eye's axons, and therefore of cortical connections, is retarded. Bottom, axons from left eye then take over many of the available synaptic connections in layer IV.

development. In one classic study, the effects of a severely deprived environment were evident. Wayne Dennis (1960) studied infants in several orphanages in Iran. In two of these, infants spent virtually their entire first year of life just lying in their cribs. The babies were fed by means of bottles propped in their cribs. They were picked up only once every other day to be bathed. The sides of their cribs were covered with a cloth (to prevent drafts), so they could not see out. Whereas virtually all normally reared babies

can sit unaided by 9 months of age, some of these orphans still could not sit at 21 months. Fewer than 15 percent of them could walk at 3 years of age, whereas almost all normally reared children walk well before their second birthday.

When children are picked up, cuddled, and played with, they receive not only emotional and social stimulation but also stimulation of nerves and muscles. They learn to adjust their bodies to various ways of being held. Their sense organs and brains process the great variety of information they receive from looking at things from different perspectives and from feeling different skin pressures and muscle tensions. This kind of normal experience stimulates development of the brain.

Cognitive Inputs

Learning promotes brain development. This topic is discussed at length in Chapter 8, but a short, general description here will introduce some of the ways the brain changes to reflect learning and memory. Again, studies with animals give us the clearest indication of these developments.

When one group of rats was raised in an enriched laboratory environment—in a large cage containing many fellow rats and playthings that could be explored and manipulated—and another group was raised in small, isolated cages, the animals' brains differed markedly in a number of respects. The rats in the enriched environment had a thicker cerebral cortex, more dendritic spines on cortical neurons, greater dendritic branching, and more acetylcholine-secreting sites on their neurons (Rosenzweig, 1984).

The figure on page 80 gives dramatic evidence for the effects of learning on brain development. In this study, kittens were trained to lift a foreleg in order to avoid a mild electric shock. The kittens were suspended in a cloth sling, and when the paw was down, the

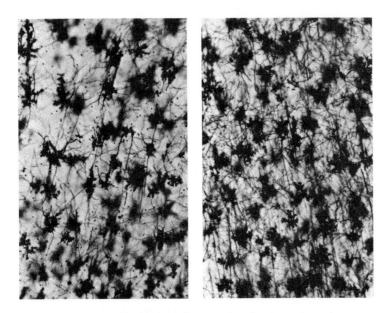

The effects of learning on the cortex can be seen when these two photomicrographs are compared. They are from the somatosensory cortex of kitten trained to raise a particular paw in response to a pattern of horizontal lines, a stimulus that signaled "danger" (application of a mild electric shock). A pattern of vertical lines signaled safety from shock. The "trained" area of the somatosensory cortex (on the right) shows a much greater number of a more complex dendritic branchings.

kitten received a shock and also saw a pattern of horizontal lines with one eye—the "danger" pattern. When the paw was lifted, they saw a pattern of vertical lines with the other eye—a pattern designating "safety." The kittens learned very quickly during their brief training sessions of 8 minutes a day and kept the foreleg up 95 percent of the time.

The figure at left shows the neural architecture in the region of the somatosensory cortex that had received input from the shocked paw; the figure at right is from the region connecting to the paw that required no training. The kitten's learning to avoid shock and to associate a given visual pattern with an event produced the greater number and complexity of dendritic branching that

can be seen clearly when the photomicrographs are compared (Spinelli et al., 1979, 1980).

Brain development after birth does not reveal an ordered sequence of changes like those during the brain's formation. It appears that much of the development during childhood and adulthood depends on an individual's interactions with his or her environment. It is clear, then, that brain development is a lifelong process. Although the brain grows less plastic with increasing age, it continues to be able to learn, and new learning changes it.

Aging and the Brain

All organisms age and die. Mayflies are born and die in the same day. Great tortoises can live for a century and a half. In mammals, a species' average life span is related to the size of the animal. Smaller animals, whose breathing rate and heartbeat are faster than those of larger animals, live a shorter chronological time. But in terms of biological time, all mammals, regardless of their size, tend to breathe about 200 million times during their lives, and their hearts beat about 800 million times (Gould, 1980). *Homo sapiens* is the one exception to this body size–lifespan ratio. Human beings live almost three times as long as mammals of our body size "should," even though our rate of breathing and heart rate are correctly scaled to our mammalian size.

The agents of aging remain as much of a mystery as do the agents directing development. Most hypotheses about why we age are rooted in genetic mechanisms. According to one hypothesis, the genetic program contains specific "aging" genes, which are switched on at a certain time of life just as the genes initiating puberty are. According to another hypothesis, in later life the organism simply runs out of genetic information and the biological changes of aging then follow. A third hypothesis states that the genetic program is subject to random damaging events over time and, therefore, essential proteins do not get produced; in their stead, cells produce proteins that are inactive or actually harmful. Other theories implicate the immune system, suggesting that it reacts adversely to the misspecified proteins produced as a result of damage to the genetic program—that is, the body reacts to its own products as if they were foreign substances. It produces antibodies in an autoimmune reaction, and increasing numbers of such autoimmune reactions would produce the changes seen in aging.

How is the aging process reflected in the structures and functioning of the brain? And how are these brain changes manifested in behavior?

Neurobiology of Aging

To date, scientists know more about "the aged brain" than they do about the aging one. Most of the changes discussed here have been found in the brains of very old organisms, and it is difficult to say when such changes might begin and at what rate they might proceed. Much of the data on human brains remains problematic because researchers were not able to discover the health status of the old people whose brain tissue was under study.

Still, a number of developments seem to be universal in the brain as it ages. The brain loses in size, weight, and volume. From a number of studies of human brains, it appears that there is a 5 percent loss in weight by age 70, 10 percent by 80, and 20 percent by 90 (Arendt, 1972; Ordy & Brizee, 1975). The cerebellum loses weight in proportion to the loss in the cerebrum.

This atrophy is a result of loss of neurons and their replacement by fibrous astrocytes.

Many, but not all, types of neurons seem to go through progressive changes as they age. The cells diminish in size. Their nuclei become smaller and more irregular in outline. The ribosomes in the cytoplasm become sparser. Some cells that are normally pigmented—such as the cells of the locus coeruleus and substantia nigra—lose some of their melanin. On the other hand, a fatty pigment, *lipofuscin,* is deposited in cells that do not ordinarily contain it. (Such age-linked pigments appear in the cells of many organs, including the skin, where they are known as "age spots.")

Some aged brains show neurofibrillary tangles and senile plaques. The tangles consist of skeins of microtubules that have proliferated inside a neuron and that eventually replace it, making the cell nonfunctional. The plaques are amorphous structures, made up of granules and filaments that are thought to be a sort of debris from degenerating neurons. There has been some controversy about whether these tangles and plaques are part of the normal aging process or, rather, reflect some sort of disease process. They appear in large numbers in brains of people who have died of Alzheimer's disease, a disease characterized by progressive mental deterioration. Alzheimer's disease is the leading form of senile dementia, a progressive loss of higher cognitive abilities (see Chapter 10).

In one study, brains of people who were known to be mentally competent at their death were compared with brains of individuals known to have suffered from senile dementia (Tomlinson et al., 1968). The mentally competent group ranged from 56 to 92 years of age at time of death. Although some plaques and tangles were found in the normal brains, the amounts were dramatically higher in the demented group. These researchers had assessed the mental competence of their subjects at regular intervals, up to just a few months before their deaths. In the aged subjects who were living an independent existence and who were fully able to cope with their environment until the time of death, abnormalities were minimal in the males and almost nonexistent in the females. The proliferation of these abnormal tissue clumps, then, seems to be correlated with a marked loss of mental function and should not be considered as part of the normal aging process.

One age-related change found in rats is a significant decline in the firing rate of the Purkinje cells, the primary output cells of the cerebellum (Rogers et al., 1981). The architecture of the cerebellum and its connections with other parts of the brain are well defined, and the Purkinje cells are large, so that measurement of the electrical activity of single cells is not too difficult. The researchers found that in very old rats, the firing rate of these cells was three to five times slower than the rate in young rats. Along with this slowing was a 25 percent loss in the number of cells and also a loss of dendrites.

In both rats and humans, the cerebellum is vital to controlled movement. If a degenerative process similar to that described above occurs in the human cerebellum, it could account for some behavioral and movement deficits noted in aged people.

Aging and Behavior

One universal finding about mental changes in old age may be related to the kinds of physiological changes just discussed: cognitive processes slow down in older people. In tests where speed of response is an important component, like some subtests in commonly used IQ tests, old people do not score as well as younger ones—or as well as they themselves scored when they were younger. Cerebellar contributions to this decrement might be a slowing in tracking of a visual target (Spooner et al., 1980) and slowing in the

ability to track a target by hand (Linnoila et al., 1980).

Besides this slowing, it is difficult to make many generalizations about age-related losses in intellectual functioning. The variability among older people seems to be greater than at any other part of the life span. Some 60-year-olds already show a noticeable decline in abilities, while some 90-year-olds are as sharp as they ever were, though a bit slower.

Several longitudinal studies (studies that test the same individuals repeatedly over a number of years) have shown that, on the average, scores on the verbal portions of IQ tests show little or no decline until the midseventies (Jarvik, 1983; Schaie, 1980; Eisdorfer & Wilkie, 1973). Vocabulary, comprehension, information, similarities, and arithmetic show almost no change from scores obtained earlier in life. There is some decline on tasks of the performance scale (a number of which are timed), and though the decline is statistically significant, it is not dramatic or disabling (see Figure 3.14).

Some part of this decline may be due to age-related changes in hearing and vision. In most people, visual and auditory acuity deteriorate as they age. The lens of the eye becomes more rigid and takes on a yellowish coloring; dark adaptation takes longer; there is some hearing loss and often an increased sensitivity to loud sounds and speech (Corso, 1975). Such sensory losses can decrease both the amount of information received and the rate at which the information can be processed.

The aging body is also subject to a number of diseases that can affect mental functioning. Foremost among these is *atherosclerosis*, hardening of the arteries, which affects the blood vessels that nourish the brain, along with the body's other vessels. Obstruction of circulation in the brain's vessels can produce *infarcts*, or injury of the brain tissue in the area of the obstruction—neurons are

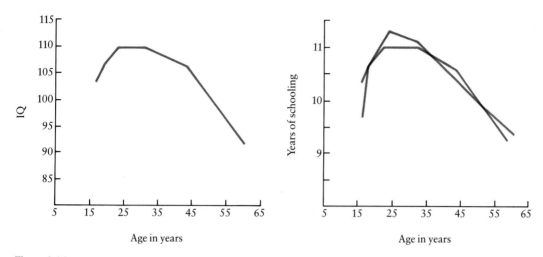

Figure 3.14
Left, cross-sectional data relating age and IQ. People in different age groups from 15 to 60 years old were given IQ tests at about the same time. (The data were collected by the developers of the widely used Wechsler Adult Intelligence Scale.) The curve connecting the data points seems to show that IQ declines after age 30— that people become less intelligent beginning at about their thirtieth birthday. Right, however, things change when the education level of each of the tested age groups is plotted and the curve at left is superimposed on the plot. Now it seems clear that the curve represents not a decline in IQ with age but an increase in amount of education received by different age groups over the years. (Adapted from Kimmel 1974)

destroyed. Atherosclerosis, in fact, is a major producer of *dementia* in the aged, the condition in which mental abilities deteriorate and even personality can change. Atherosclerotic dementia is the one type of dementia whose cause is well known.

In any case, less than 5 percent of the aged population—those 65 and over—suffer from any form of dementia, and only 1 to 2 percent are severely impaired (Kay & Bergmann, 1980). Even when faced with the body's increasing inadequacies as it ages, the brain finds ways to deal with the new problems. It comes up with alternative solutions for how to get the groceries home when you no longer have the strength to carry two big bags (pull a wheeled cart or find someone to drive you there). It devises intricate reminder systems (lists over the stove, calendars on the bathroom door, and lists of lists) for when the memory can no longer be counted on to recall upcoming events and appointments. One 82-year-old woman, in the hospital after a minor stroke, devised a clever strategy to get the neurologists to release her. Each day they would come in and ask her if she knew what day and date it was. She discovered that by shifting her eyes only slightly, she could read the day and date off the face of the clock facing her bed (she could not remember them). The parts of her brain that weren't injured were working to solve problems in her environment—in fact, to get her into a more desirable environment, home.

Stimulation of sense organs is a key element in normal development.

Development of Brain and Mind

The brain develops structurally during the nine months of prenatal life—and perhaps for a few months after that, since human beings seem to be born in a somewhat unfinished state. Certainly, brain development is a remarkable process: the proliferation, differentiation, and migration of those billions of cells, and their connections with each other in operational systems.

After birth, the mind develops. The brain at birth is prepared to take on a number of its functions, such as regulating heartbeat and breathing and body temperature. But development of a mind requires interaction of the organism with its physical, intellectual, emotional, and social environment. The human brain is well prepared to begin taking on this function. Experience molds it, strengthening some connections and some circuits. The brain is prepared to sense sights, sounds, textures, and smells, and it is prepared to remember them. As the brain develops, it is prepared to compare new sights and sounds with the ones in memory and to begin groupings of them on the basis of shared characteristics. Thus the brain learns and shapes a mind.

Summary

1. Formation of the nervous system begins about two weeks after fertilization, when cells in the embryonic disc differentiate into endoderm and ectoderm. Cells of the endoderm will form the respiratory and digestive systems. Cells of the ectoderm will form the nervous system, which begins as the neural plate, then thickens and folds over to form the neural tube. The top of the tube becomes the brain; the rest becomes the spinal cord. Cells remaining outside the tube as it forms, the neural crest, develop into the peripheral nervous system.

2. During the second month after fertilization, the three major divisions of the brain—hindbrain, midbrain, and forebrain—are formed, and the forebrain divides into the diencephalon and telencephalon. Development of telencephalon structures proceeds from the inside out, with the cerebral cortex, or neocortex, developing last. In human beings, the cortex comprises 70 percent of the brain's neurons.

3. The seven processes of neural development are described in Table 3.1. Although these processes are under genetic control, some environmental conditions seem necessary for normal development. For example, neurons that aggregate to form specific brain structures must express certain adhesion molecules on their surface (N CAM), and some migrating neurons require a particular biochemical substrate to guide them.

4. Males and females inherit different gene complements on the chromosomes that determine sex—XY for males and XX for females—and these differing sets of genes produce differences in anatomy and physiology of both body and brain. The agent of such differences is the male hormone testosterone, which male embryos begin secreting early in prenatal development.

5. Prenatally, hormones have an organizational effect on the brain. They change its anatomical development by entering cells and altering their genetic message, and they sensitize the cells so that they later respond to presence of the hormone. This later response is called an activational effect.

6. Human males and females have been shown to differ from each other, statistically, in three behaviors: males are more aggressive, females are more skilled verbally, and males have more acute visual-spatial skills. Since the two hemispheres of the brain are known to have different responsibilities in information processing in most people—the left hemisphere for language and the right for visual-spatial information—it has been suggested that the two hemispheres are organized differently in the sexes, with verbal and spatial functions more widely distributed in both hemispheres in females, and the male brain more specialized bilaterally.

7. The course of brain development after birth appears to depend crucially on an organism's interaction with its environment. Sensory and cognitive inputs promote dendritic growth and strengthen synapses. When certain inputs are denied an organism, as when one eye is covered in infancy, normal development of relevant brain areas fails to take place.

8. As organisms age, certain brain changes take place: the brain decreases in size, weight, and volume through loss of neurons and a decrease in the size of some types of neurons. Perhaps the most significant change is a decline in the firing rate of some neurons, since the most significant behavioral change in old age is a slowing down of information-processing abilities. This slowing down accounts almost entirely for the lower scores attained by old people on IQ tests.

Further Reading

Nauta, W. J. H., and Feirtag, M. 1986. *Fundamental Neuroanatomy.* New York: W. H. Freeman. See Section III, "Anatomy," Chapter 10, "Ontogeny; Spinal Cord."

Cowan, W. M. 1986. The development of the brain, In R. Thompson (ed.), *Progress in Neuroscience: Readings from Scientific American.* New York: W. H. Freeman. Current information on the processes of neuronal development and the formation of circuits in the embryo and fetus.

Varon, S. 1985. Factors promoting the growth of the nervous system. *Discussions in Neurosciences* (Foundation for the Study of the Nervous System), Vol. II, No. 3. This pamphlet discusses clearly how growth factors (such as nerve growth factor—NGF) function in the developing nervous system and describes the chemical factors now known to exist.

Science. 1981. Vol. 211, No. 4488. The entire March 20 issue is devoted to understanding the physiological bases of sex differences. It contains a number of articles by noted researchers on topics including sex differences in genes and chromosomes, the prenatal development of androgens, and sexual differentiation of the brain.

4

Sensing and Moving

4

Heat is everywhere now. I can't ignore it anymore. The air is like a furnace blast, so hot that my eyes under the goggles feel cool compared to the rest of my face. My hands are cool but the gloves have big black spots from perspiration on the back surrounded by white streaks of dried salt.

. . . On the horizon appears an image of buildings, shimmering slightly. I look down at the map and figure it must be Bowman. I think about ice water and air conditioning.

On the street and sidewalks of Bowman we see almost no one, even though plenty of parked cars show they're here. All inside. We swing the machines into an angled parking place. . . . A lone elderly person wearing a broad-brimmed hat watches us put the cycles on their stands and remove helmets and goggles.

"Hot enough for you?" he asks. His expression is blank.

John shakes his head and says, "Gawd!"

The expression, shaded by the hat, becomes almost a smile.

Robert Pirsig, *Zen and the Art of Motorcycle Maintenance*, 1974.

The intense heat of the desert, the severe thirst, the wary response to strangers dramatically mark the bike rider's entry into an uncertain new world. The flood of new sensations makes him acutely aware of his abilities to sense his surroundings and his body.

We all sense new "worlds" all the time, and our bodies and minds check continuously for external and internal changes. Our very lives depend on our success in sensing the worlds through which we move and on the accuracy with which our sensations guide our movements. We move away from threatening stimuli—extreme heat, the sight, sound, or smell of a predator—and toward food, comfort, and protection. These capacities to sense and to move, as we noted in Chapter 1, are two of the basic properties of all living animals, from the simplest to the most complex. Creatures with nervous systems, however, have sensing and moving abilities far beyond the capacities of simpler, nerveless ones.

The intricate cellular machinery of the sensing and moving systems relies on affiliations between many interconnected cells working together through a series of steps, like an assembly line. In this process, the brain continually interprets sensory information and directs the body to make the best response—to seek shade from the heat, or shelter from the rain, or to act on a decision that the emotionless stare of a stranger poses no threat. In order to understand some of the complexity that underlies sensation and movement, it may be helpful to look at a general model of how these systems work.

A General Model for the Sensing and Moving Systems

To communicate with each other, people through the ages have used "instruments" that range from the very simple flashes of reflected sunlight from one watch post to another to more complex systems—codes beaten on drums, complete sentences carried over telegraph wires, telephone or electronic waves bounced off communications satellites. All these systems have the same function, but the complex ones carry more information, faster, and with less interference. Achieving these improvements in communication required adding many new components to detect, filter, and amplify the signals.

The nerve cells in the sensory and motor systems must also communicate with each other for these systems to operate properly. And, as with the electronic communication systems used by people in the 1980s, sensory and motor systems have become quite complex, with many separate working elements having been added through the eons of evolution. These complex elements make it possible for some species to transmit information more effectively than others, which contributes to the survival abilities of those individuals.

As we examine what is known about the operations of the sensing and moving systems of the brain and spinal cord, keep in mind that we currently know enough to recognize that they are much more complexly organized than we can explain. These still-unexplained complexities almost certainly reflect undiscovered principles of sensory integration or motor coordination that somehow demand special biological components. In this chapter we examine the systems of neurons whose function is to sense the world around us and within us, and to control our movements. We shall point out numerous similarities in the structural organization of the sets of brain structures involved in these sensing and moving tasks. However, in order to address their unique properties properly, we begin with the organization and function of the sensing systems.

All the known parts of the sensing systems in simple and complex nervous systems seem to have at least the following components: (1) a *stimulus detector unit* consisting of a specialized sensory receptor neuron; (2) an *initial receiving center* where neurons receive convergent information from groups of detector units; and (3) one or more *secondary receiving and integrating centers* where neurons receive information from groups of ini-

Seeing, hearing, sensing, and complicated tasks depend on the complex integration of sensory and motor systems.

tial receiver neurons. In more complex nervous systems, the integrating centers are also linked to one another.

At some point in the sensory integration process, the brain begins to compare the incoming information about the elements in the world being examined with other objects and happenings that have been experienced previously. The combination of currently sensed information and recollections of previously experienced similar objects or entities allows the individual to *perceive* and infer the nature and meaning of what has just been sensed. (The mental process of *perception* is examined in greater detail in Chapter 8.)

The sensing system starts to operate when an environmental event, or *stimulus,* is detected by a sensory neuron, the primary sensory receptor. The stimulus detector converts the sensory event from its original physical form (light, sound, heat, pressure) into *action potentials*. These action potentials, or nerve impulses, now represent the sensory event in the form of cellular signals that can be further processed by the nervous system. The nerve impulses produced by the stimulus-detection receptors travel along the sensory neuron to the *receiving center* responsible for that form of sensing. Once the impulses are received in this primary processing area, information is abstracted from the qualities of the specific impulses. The mere arrival of the impulses reflects the occurrence of an event in that sensory information channel. The frequency of the impulses and the total number of sensory receptors transmitting them reflects the size of the object being sensed. From the stimulus events of your sensing a flower, for example, color, shape, size, fragrance, and distance are abstracted. This information and more is then transmitted from primary processing areas to secondary processing areas. In those areas further judgments about the flower—or whatever the sensory event happens to be—are made and sent on.

The later integrating centers in a sensory chain may also add in sensations from other sources, as well as available information about similar past experiences. At some point, the nature and importance of what has been detected is determined by the process of conscious identification that we call "perception." Finally, any required action is initiated.

All the systems specialized for sensing operate in this general way. To some extent, therefore, once we examine one sensory system, we can apply its operating principles to the other systems.

We can also analyze the operation of the motor system in terms of this model. The motor system has a similarly linked organization through which impulses travel, although in the reverse direction. Assemblies of hundreds of neurons in the portion of the cerebral cortex devoted to movement initia-

tion each direct the activity of a few tens of motor neurons in the spinal cord, each of which, in turn, directs the contraction of a single muscle fiber. While the sensory systems process information coming *into* the brain, the motor system processes information *going out* to the muscles. But the structural organizations of the two systems show similarities.

What Do We Sense?

Like other animals, we perceive the world around us through our sensing systems. Each system is named for the kind of sensory information that it is specialized to detect: sight, sound, touch, taste, smell, and gravity, for example. (Information about gravity gives us our so-called sense of *balance* or *equilibrium*.)

Other, less apparent senses allow us to detect limb position and joint angle. These senses, such as *proprioception*, the internal monitoring of body and limb positions, and *kinesthesis*, the continuous monitoring of movements, help us to guide our limbs as we carry out patterns of movement—walking without stumbling, or scratching our noses without poking our eyes, for example. Even less obvious "senses" track information from deeper sources in the body: temperature, blood chemistry and volume, and the chemical adjustments controlled by our endocrine organs. (These internal senses and the adjustments the body makes to them are considered in Chapter 5.)

Some animals have yet other sensory systems. Snakes sense objects by detecting infrared signals, and certain sea animals detect the electrical signals given off by their predators, their prey, and their local social groups.

All forms of sensing carry information about *time*—when the detection of the stimulus began and how long it has lasted. Sight, sound, smell, and touch also carry information about *location*, where in space the signal arose. By comparing the strengths of the signals detected by each of our two ears, or by determining the signal's location in our visual field, for example, the brain can determine the source of the signal in the environment.

Each of the sensory systems also distinguishes one or more *qualities* of the signal it detects. We see light in terms of color and brightness. We hear pitch and tone. We taste sweetness, sourness, and saltiness. We distinguish sensations on our body surface by the shape of the stimulus (sharp or dull), by its temperature (hot or cold), and by how it disturbs the skin (a steady pressure or a vibrating pressure). Each of the stimulus qualities distinguished by each of the senses indicates the existence of a cell (or cells) specialized to detect it, a *sensory receptor*.

Distinctions about *quantity* also require specialized receptor cells. The activity level of these quantity-detecting receptor cells reflects the intensity of the signal being detected—the brighter the light, the louder the tone, the sharper the sting, or the stronger the taste, the more the activity. The reverse is also true: less intense signals produce less receptor activity. Signals that are too weak for sensory detection are termed "subthreshold."

The intensity—or quantity—of a sensation also influences its interpretation. A playful tickle turns painful if it goes on too long or gets too rough. Although we commonly speak of "sensing pain," it would be more appropriate to say that we interpret "pain" from the quality and quantity—that is, the intensity and duration—of certain sensory signals that touch, sound, and even light can produce. Pain is therefore considered a "subjective" sensation—decisions about whether a stimulus is or is not painful require an interpretation by the person experiencing it. People also differ in their sensitivity to painful events. (The subject of pain and our reac-

tions to it are described at greater length in Chapter 7.)

Table 4.1 lists the six major human sensory systems, the specialized organs that detect the stimuli peculiar to each, the qualities detected, and the receptor cells in each that pick up the quality and quantity of the stimuli.

Oddly, smell and taste use only one kind of receptor cell, even though these two senses distinguish many different qualities, even at extremely low stimulus strengths. It is the location of these receptor cells on the surface of the tongue or the mucous membranes of the nose and throat, not the kind of cell, that determines the quality that each receptor detects. Presumably, it is the particular chemical being tasted or smelled that triggers different responses.

Fine-Tuning of the Receptive Process

Two aspects of the sensory response process—adaptation and information channeling—now deserve more attention.

As you have seen, the role of the stimulus detectors is to announce that changes in the external world have occurred. Some receptor cells respond most intensely when a stimulus begins, but as the stimulus continues, the response fades. This diminishing responsiveness is termed *adaptation*. The rate and degree of adaptation to a prolonged stimulus vary for each sense and with the conditions of the moment. We scarcely remember a tight shoe as we dash off to work or school. The sound of street traffic fades away until a siren or rumbling truck catches our notice. We can detect a persistent gas leak or the lingering scent of a pleasant perfume only when we breathe in deeply to see if it is still there.

In a way, the initial detection serves to bring the novel event into the pool of information we are using to interpret the current status of our world. The fading response al-

Table 4.1 *The fundamental properties of the six major sensing systems*

Sensation	Sensing system	Quality	Receptors
Vision	Retina	Brightness Contrast Motion Size Color	Rods Cones
Hearing	Cochlea	Pitch Tone	Hair cells
Equilibrium	Vestibular organ	Gravity Rotation	Macula cells Vestibular cells
Touch	Skin, internal organs	Pressure Temperature Vibration	Ruffini corpuscles Merkel discs Pacinian corpuscles

Taste	Tongue	Sweet, salty
		
		Bitter, sour
			Taste buds at
			  tip of tongue
			Taste buds at edge,
			  base of tongue

Smell	Olfactory nerves	Floral Fruity Musky Pungent	Olfactory receptor

lows us to update this interpretation as new sensory signals come through (see Figure 4.1). If the new and old signals were always equally strong, the flood of sensory information pouring in from all of our receptors would drown our ability to cope with any of it.

We use our capacity to gain refreshed information about the world in everything we do. If you close your eyes and try to identify an object placed in your hand, the task becomes much easier as you fondle it, turning it over and moving your fingers over its surface repeatedly. Each new touch provides a new angle of analysis, giving you new information to add onto the image you have been forming gradually from the first and subsequent touches. If you are awakened in a strange room, you quickly remap the location of the doors, windows, and major objects and use this information to interpret where you are.

Each activated sensory receptor feeds sensory information into a chain of synaptic relays specific to that sense. These relays carry the signal higher into the nervous system. During each leg of the relay, the signal receives additional processing. Once the actual physical stimulus—light waves, sound waves, odors, heat, cold—has been transduced by the receptor into nerve impulses, it no longer has any value in itself. From that point on, the physical event exists only in its coded patterns of nerve impulses within specific sensory channels in the nervous system.

The brain, then, reconstructs an image of the external world by piecing together all of the information it receives at any given time from every active sensory receptor. It is this collection of information that the brain interprets to make the mental construct that is our perception of our world at any given moment.

Table 4.2 names the major impulse-

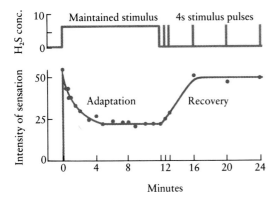

Figure 4.1
When a sensory event first occurs (square wave above represents onset and ending), the sensory receptor responds very vigorously. As the event continues, the receptor adapts to it, and activity in the nerve fiber diminishes to a lesser level of sustained activity. If stimuli are brief and periodic, the receptor responds fully each time without adaptation.

processing locations along the channels for each kind of sensory information. The table shows only the main features common to all sensory systems in level-by-level information

processing. Within each system, the information entering a given level may or may not get special handling. It may be heavily processed locally, as visual information is in the retina. (The retina contains not only the sensory receptors for light but also several linked initial processing neurons, the only specialized sensory organ that both detects and processes information in this way.) Or information may be sent as raw data for processing by several other systems that need it right away (equilibrium-sensing information goes directly to the brainstem for processing, for example).

Every synaptic connection offers an opportunity for the processing of sensory information. Simply put, information may be concentrated when receptors converge on common initial receiving neurons. Conversely, information may be diluted by the divergence of a few receptors onto many receiving neurons. At some synapses, more complex alterations are also likely to occur. To see how these modifications take place, you need to recall two of the basic neural-

Table 4.2 *Channels for specific forms of sensing*

	Relay level		
Sensation	Primary (level 1)	Secondary (level 2)	Tertiary (level 3)
Vision	Retina	Lateral geniculate Superior colliculus Hypothalamus	Primary visual cortex Secondary visual cortex
Hearing	Cochlear nuclei	Lemniscal, collicular, and medial geniculate nuclei	Primary auditory cortex
Equilibrium	Vestibular nuclei	Thalamus Spinal cord Oculomotor nuclei Brainstem Cerebellum	Somatosensory cortex
Touch	Spinal cord or brainstem	Thalamus	Somatosensory cortex
Smell	Olfactory bulb	Piriform cortex	Limbic system, hypothalamus
Taste	Medulla	Thalamus	Somatosensory cortex

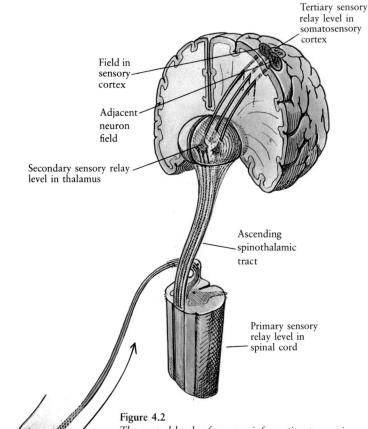

next and connect the various levels of a sensory system, and the *local circuits* that operate within each level to expand or restrict the number of integrating neurons.

Every receptor cell has a limited area over which it detects the external event to which it is sensitive. This area is called its *receptive field*. If we monitored one visual receptor in the retina, we would see that it is active only when light passing through the lens falls on that cell's receptive field. A sensory receptor in the skin detects events only in its receptive field, a bounded surface area of the skin above it. As you can see in Figure 4.2, each sensory receptor in the skin sends its main signal to one select subset of primary relay neurons at the initial receiving level in the spinal cord.

It should now be clear that information processing takes place during interactions between cells at each level. To gain a more detailed understanding of how a specific sensory system operates, we shall now examine some of the properties and principles of the visual system, the sense about which investigators currently know the most.

Figure 4.2
The several levels of sensory information processing from the receptive field at the tip of the index finger sensing a feather's touch, traveling to primary sensory neurons in the dorsal horn of the spinal cord. The second link carries the tactile information upward through the spinothalamic tract linking the dorsal horn to sensory centers in the thalamus, and the third link occurs when the thalamic neurons project their activity onto the somatic sensory region of the cerebral cortex, specifically to that area onto which is mapped the surface of the tip of the index finger. Adjacent fields in the sensory cortex will detect touch on adjacent parts of the index finger and on adjacent fingers. The receptive fields on the tips of the fingers are highly specialized so that one can experience tactile stimuli that are only millimeters apart as distinct. The receptive fields on the back of the shoulders are quite large, and normally one has much less power to discriminate closely grouped stimuli there as distinct.

Seeing: A Detailed Look at the Visual System

The visual system responds to stimulation by light. In a physical sense, light is electromagnetic radiation that has wavelengths ranging from very short (blue) to very long (red). We see objects because of the way they reflect light into our eyes. Which colors we see depends on which parts of the visible-light spectrum an object reflects or absorbs.

When the German medical physicist Hermann von Helmholtz examined animals' eyes in the last half of the nineteenth century, he discovered that visual information was displayed on the retina much as it is in any simple camera with a compound lens: upside

connection patterns described in Chapter 2: the *hierarchical circuits* that relay information from one level of a sensory system to the down and reduced in size. From these simple beginnings has grown a towering body of information on the visual system. In fact, we are closer to understanding how our visual image of the world is reconstructed than we are to understanding any other sensory interpretation.

In order to examine the structure and functions of the visual system, we first need to know what its individual components are and how they are organized into circuits. Then we shall see how external stimuli go through visual processing by neurons at different integrating levels. Finally, we consider some of the conclusions that psychologists have drawn about how we view the world.

The Structure of the Visual System

The major structural components of the visual system (see Figure 4.3) are (1) the *eye,* of which the elements for image focusing (the lens) and image detecting (the retina) are most relevant; (2) the *optic nerves,* which carry visual information from the output neurons of the retina to their initial relay targets in the thalamus and hypothalamus; (3) the second-level neuronal targets—the three pairs of nuclei known as the *lateral geniculate nuclei* and the *superior colliculi,* within the thalamus, and the *suprachiasmatic nuclei* in the hypothalamus; and (4) the *primary visual cortex,* which receives information from the thalamic nuclei. Information from the primary visual cortex is then distributed throughout a hierarchy of other visually related regions in the cerebral cortex.

The Eye   The eye is the only visual-response organ in mammals. It consists of a "cameralike" unit and an "image-recording" unit (see Figure 4.4). The parts of the cameralike unit are the *cornea,* a thin, curved, transparent membrane that starts the focusing process; the *lens,* an adjustable structure that completes the focusing process; and the *iris,*

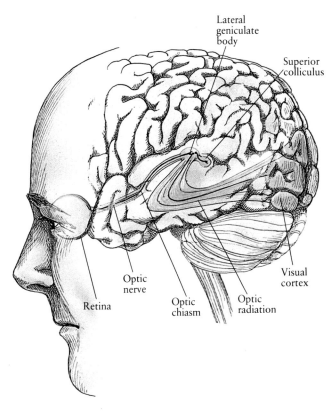

Figure 4.3
The component parts of the visual system beginning with the primary receptive component in the retina, the second level neurons in the lateral geniculate or superior colliculus, and the third level neurons in the visual cortex. The optic radiation consists of the fibers that connect the neurons of the lateral geniculate to the neurons in the visual cortex.

a circular muscle that alters the amount of light entering the eye by dilating or constricting the opening in its center, called the *pupil.*

The lens lies suspended like a hammock within a flexible lens capsule. When the muscles attached to the capsule contract or relax, the changed tension in the capsule changes the curvature of the lens. The focusing power of the lens arises from its ability to become thinner and flatter or thicker and more rounded, depending on the distance between an object and the viewer.

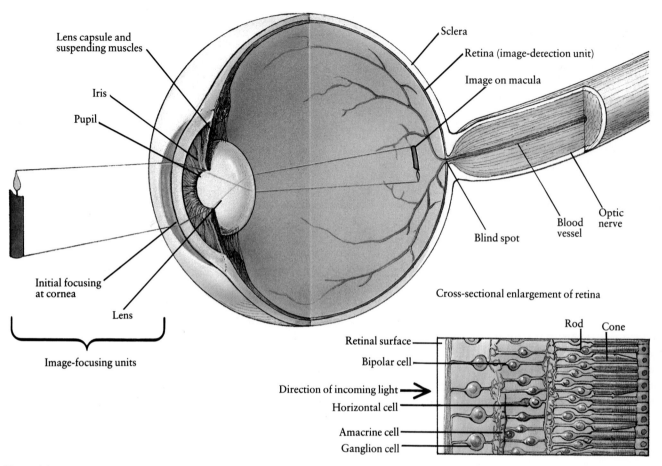

Lens capsule and
suspending muscles

Sclera

Retina (image-detection unit)

Image on macula

Iris

Pupil

Initial focusing
at cornea

Lens

Image-focusing units

Blind spot

Blood
vessel

Optic
nerve

Cross-sectional enlargement of retina

Rod   Cone

Retinal surface

Bipolar cell

Direction of incoming light

Horizontal cell

Amacrine cell

Ganglion cell

Figure 4.4
A cross-sectional drawing of the eye as seen from the side. The lens, its suspensory apparatus, and the iris are shown, as are the light-sensing detectors within the retina. The inset shows the cells of the retina in greater detail, with the initial detector cells, the rods and cones, facing away from the iris and the incoming light. The primary receptors converge on the bipolar cells, which converge on the ganglion cells. The axons of the ganglion cells converge on the optic disc, or blind spot, where there are no primary receptors. These axons form the optic nerve, which carries information into the visual system. The local-circuit horizontal and amacrine neurons expand or constrict the activity that arises from images detected by the primary receptors.

The size of the pupil—the opening in the iris—also influences what and how we see. Observe a friend inspecting something. If he or she brings the object closer, the size of the pupil shrinks. Smaller pupil size excludes the peripheral rays of light that are being re-

flected from the object and helps produce a sharper image (the lens will also change shape to focus on nearby objects). Now ask your friend to close his or her eyes for a half minute or so and then open them. From up close, you will see that the pupils are relatively dilated just after the eyes open, then rapidly close down to adjust to the room lighting. Autonomic nerve fibers in the involuntary muscles of the iris control these changes in pupil size automatically. These adjustments of the pupil (which you can observe) and of the lens (which your friend can experience) are termed *accommodation*.

The image-detecting part of the eye is the *retina*. On first examination, it may appear that the retina is constructed all wrong. The visual receptor cells, the rods and the cones, are not only as far as possible from the lens, but they also point away from the incoming light, with their light-sensitive tips poked down between darkly colored epithelial cells.

Exactly why the retina has evolved into this inverse layered structure is difficult to know. The neuronal layers between the incoming light and the receptor cells are essentially transparent. By detecting the light that reflects off the choroid pigment layer just beyond the tips of the rods and cones, each light receptor is essentially reading only a very small illuminated area. In some animals like dogs and cats, the choroid layers have highly reflective pigment that can increase their ability to detect dimly illuminated objects. Nevertheless, the reasons for this arrangement are still basically unknown.

Under the microscope, the retina displays a very highly organized layered structure (see detail, Figure 4.4). Five kinds of neurons can be observed, each located within its own layer: (1) the *rods* and *cones*—the primary light sensory receptors—connect with (2) the *bipolar neurons,* which connect with (3) the *ganglion cells,* which send their axons by way of the optic nerve to the initial relay neurons in the thalamus. Each rod and cone connects with several bipolar cells, and each bipolar cell can connect with several ganglion cells. This hierarchical pattern achieves a divergent processing of light that maximizes image detection. Also, two types of inhibitory local-circuit neurons within the retina, the *horizontal cells* and the *amacrine cells,* restrict the spread of the visual signal within the retina so that they converge onto the ganglion cells.

If we used fine electrodes to record the activity of single ganglion cells as light sweeps over the retina, we would find that each ganglion cell responds to light in a precisely bounded *receptive field*—a small region on the retina where light detected by rods and cones most intensely activates or inhibits the ganglion cell through convergence. A ganglion cell does not respond at all to light falling outside the perimeter of its receptive field. Some ganglion-cell receptive fields are "center-on," others are "center-off." A *center-on ganglion cell* is activated by light in the center of its receptive field but is inhibited by light at the perimeter. A *center-off ganglion cell* is turned off by activity in the center of its field but is activated by light at the borders. Such interactions between center-on and center-off ganglion cells make possible the contrast between the details of an image that is critical for sharp vision.

The distribution of the rods and cones on the inner layer of the retina is also organized in an orderly fashion. Cones are most dense on that part of the retina where images are most sharply focused by the cornea and the lens. This spot where visual acuity is the highest is called the *macula;* it is the point on the retina where images in the center of the field of visual focus will fall. No other retinal neurons are present in this small zone, so in cross section, the cone-enriched macula looks like a small pit (which is called the *fovea centralis*). Away from the fovea, a small number of cones are spread evenly over the retina. The cones respond to light of different colors, some being sensitive mainly to blue, some to red, and some to green light. (Recall that sunlight and electric lights appear white but actually contain the whole array of colors from blue to red. When moist clouds act as a prism to separate the various wavelengths of light, a rainbow is seen.)

Rods are sensitive to reflected brightness but not to color. They are densest around the

Figure 4.5
To discover the blind spot of your right optic disc, close your left eye and stare at the spot on the left as you move the figure closer. When the figure is about 12 inches from your eye, King Charles will "lose his head." (Adapted from Rushton.)

edges of the fovea, but more numerous than cones over the rest of the retina.

The normal layered cell structure of the retina picks up just outside the fovea. The layer facing the incoming light consists of the axons of the ganglion cells. These ganglion-cell axons from all over the retina converge on a point slightly below the fovea, where they comprise a bundle of axons—the *optic nerve*—which carries visual information to the brain. The convergence of the ganglion-cell axons, however, leaves no room for any receptors or other retinal neurons here. And light that falls on the retina at this point, therefore, is invisible. We are never aware of this hole, or "blind spot," because higher visual processing centers help us reconstruct a solid world. But Figure 4.5 will convince you that such a hole is there.

The Optic Nerve and the Optic Tract   The collected axons of the ganglion cells, bundled together in the optic nerve, travel to the base of the front of the hypothalamus, where

they come together in the *optic chiasm.* Here, a partial crossover of fibers, called the *optic decussation,* takes place. The continuation of these axon bundles, now again separated, is given a different name, the *optic tract.*

Imagine that you are looking up at the human visual system from below with a microscope that permits you to see each of the cellular levels—the primary, secondary, and tertiary levels, and the synapses that link them. From this vantage point, you can see that all of the ganglion cell axons on the half of the retina closest to the nose cross to the opposite side at the optic chiasm. As a result of this crossover, everything seen by the inside, or *nasal,* half of the retina of the left eye crosses over to the right optic tract, and everything seen by the nasal half of the retina of the right eye crosses to the left of the optic tract (see Figure 4.6). The information seen by the outside, or *temporal,* half of the retinal field remains uncrossed. From the optic chiasm on, all stimuli in the left side of the world you see are processed by the components of the visual system on the right side of the brain, and all stimuli in the right side of the world you see are processed by the components of the visual system on the left side of the brain.

Axons of the optic tract run to one of four second-level receiving and integrating centers. The *lateral geniculate nuclei* and the *superior colliculi* (see Figure 4.6) are the targets most critical to carrying out the function of seeing. The third target, the *suprachiasmatic nuclei* in the hypothalamus, uses information about light intensity to coordinate our internal rhythms (see Chapter 6). A fourth target, the *extraocular-muscle,* or *motor-nerve nuclei,* keep the movements of the eye coordinated as we shift our gaze.

The Lateral Geniculate Nucleus   The optic tract carries the ganglion cell axons to their secondary target neurons in the *lateral genic-*

ulate (see Figure 4.6), and these neurons, in turn, pass the information on to the tertiary target cells in the *primary visual cortex*. In addition to the specification of which ganglion-cell axons cross over at the optic chiasm, even further order within the early stages of the visual system's circuitry is apparent at the level of the lateral geniculate.

Recall that when you gaze straight ahead, a visual stimulus that is just off center will fall on the receptive fields of receptors in the nasal half of one visual field and on a corresponding receptive field in the temporal half of the other visual field. Both the nasal and temporal receptive fields are displaced by about the same angle from the center of the field. When the nasal-field axons cross over in the chiasm, these corresponding nasal-temporal field fibers come to lie near each other, and they travel to their secondary relay targets in tandem. Thus, the optic-nerve fibers carrying information about a particular point in space from ganglion cells that are close to each other also reach neurons near each other within the lateral geniculate. As the secondary target neurons in the lateral geniculate project onto the visual cortex, these maps of the retinal world are passed on to the cortex as well. This provides a *retinotopic* map of the visual field that has counterparts in the lateral geniculate as well as in the primary visual cortex.

These retinotopic maps have a diagnostic importance. They can help clinicians to map visual defects in the central portions of the visual system and determine the most likely locations of tumors or other damage that affects parts of the visual field.

The Superior Colliculus   We now come to a very interesting and important anatomic feature of the visual system. Many of the ganglion-cell axons branch before reaching the lateral geniculate. While one branch connects the retina to the lateral geniculate, the

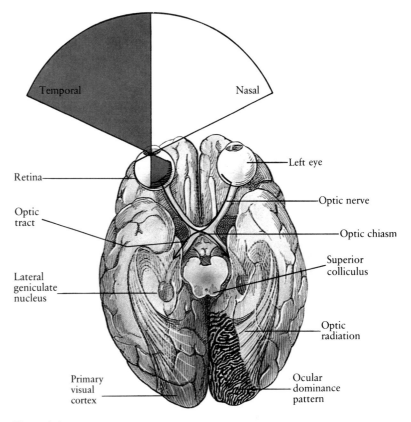

Figure 4.6
A view of the components of the visual system as viewed from beneath the brain which has been partially cut away to reveal the internal components. Images detected by the rods or cones in the nasal (inside) halves of each retina reach ganglion cells whose nerve fibers cross over at the optic chiasm to reach their level-two target neurons in the lateral geniculate and superior colliculus. The images detected by receptors in the temporal (outside) half of the retina connect to ganglion cells whose axons project to the level two neurons without crossing over. Thus, the right side of the visual system detects objects to the left of the midline and the left side of the visual system detects objects to the right of the midline.

other goes to another second-level relay target, the neurons in the superior colliculus (see Figure 4.6). This branching creates two "parallel" paths between retinal ganglion cells and separate thalamic receiving centers. Both branches retain the retinal map specifics—nasal, temporal, left, right, up, down, and so on. The fibers reaching the superior colliculus are thought to represent retinal receptive fields that are in the rod-rich peripheral zones where visual acuity is less but where detection of movement may be greater, while the fibers reaching the lateral geniculate represent cone-rich areas of high visual acuity.

The neurons of the superior colliculus also receive auditory information and vestibular information about head position, as well as visual information that has already been processed and fed back from the neurons of the primary visual cortex. Because it receives all this input, the colliculus is thought to serve as a subcortical center for integrating the information that we use to orient ourselves spatially in a moving world.

The target neurons of retinal input to the superior colliculus send their axons to a large nucleus in the thalamus called the *pulvinar*. In this path of visual transmittal, the pulvinar would be level 3. The size of the pulvinar increases as mammals become increasingly complex, and it is biggest of all in the human brain. Its large size suggests that it serves some peculiarly human visual function, but its actual role remains unknown.

Visual Areas of the Cerebral Cortex The retinotopic maps of the visual world from each lateral geniculate nucleus continue intact along the "optic radiation," the path taken by the level-2 lateral geniculate neurons to the primary visual cortex. At the cortical level, however, the retinotopic maps no longer represent that external world precisely. The volume of cortex dedicated to input from the macula, the region of highest visual acuity, is approximately 35 times larger than the area of cortex dedicated to an equal amount of retinal input from the periphery of the retina. This disparity in cortical representation of input from different parts of the retina gives information from the macula by far the greatest impact.

The primary visual cortex is also called "area 17," or the "striate cortex." The term

"striate" refers to a unique "stripe" seen in slices of this area that is produced by a wide zone of myelinated axons. The primary visual cortex displays a system of orderly layering that is unequaled anywhere else in the nervous system. The entire cerebral cortex has a general pattern of layering that normally includes about six layers, numbered I through VI, starting at the outer surface. The layers are distinguished by the number of their neurons. In the visual cortex of human beings and monkeys, however, the six layers are even more elaborately subdivided, especially in layers IV and V. Primate brains show more than 12 distinct layers of visual cortex, with layer IV, for example, subdivided into layers designated as IVA, IVB, and IVC, and then subdivided again as the sharp eyes of the microscopist note patterns within the patterns (see Figure 4.7).

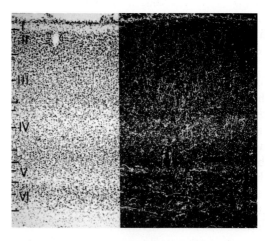

Figure 4.7
The most highly layered region of the primate cerebral cortex is the primary visual cortex. As seen in this micrograph, the six general layers are composed of cell-rich and cell-sparse populations; such layers are seen in almost all cortical regions. However, in the primary visual cortex, layer IV, the layer to which the level two neurons in the lateral geniculate make their connections is further subdivided into five distinct layers that are only seen in the visual cortex.

Cortical Representation of Vision

In examining this exquisitely delineated layering of cells and fibers, scientists have found important clues as to which reciprocally interconnected cortical areas are involved in the processing of visual information beyond the level of the primary visual cortex. These connections have, in turn, suggested some important principles of visual cortical organization.

Observations of patients with head injuries and experimental studies in animals have shown that the cortical areas where visual processing goes on extend well beyond the primary visual cortex. It is important to appreciate just how much of the cortex is involved in the process of vision, and how various aspects of visual information are handled by different specialized but interconnected areas of the overall visual system. Most of this information has come in the last few years, as scientists developed methods for specifying precisely which cells in which layers of each part of the cerebral cortex connect with one another.

Based on the patterns of cells within the six general layers of the cortex, scientists in the 1920s and 1930s recognized *cytoarchitectonic* properties that defined small regions of the cortex as specific cortical areas; lacking any functional means to characterize them, they gave each distinctive cytoarchitectonic area a numerical name. For this reason, the primary visual cortex is called area 17. As it now turns out, the area immediately adjacent to it, called area 18, receives much of the output of area 17. Area 18, in turn, connects with two still higher-level relay structures, which were originally numbered areas 19 and 20. With the new information on precise interconnectivity, scientists have recognized considerable degrees of mutual interconnection. Area 17 projects forward to area 18 and to 19, and 19 projects to 20; however, these areas also project

backward: 18 and 19 to 17, for example. The forward (or hierarchically upward) connections consistently link source neurons in layer III to targets in layer IV, while the backward (or downward) reverse connections link source neurons in layer V to targets in layers I and VI.

Taking these interconnection patterns as a reference, scientists have identified at least five more cortical levels where visual information is integrated in the cortex. Among them, the "highest" integrating level has been traced to visual fields within the frontal cortex. These cortical areas are adjacent to the so-called "association cortex," where several forms of sensory information are assembled. Relatively direct connections to the limbic system are also possible from this area of frontal cortex.

Analysis of such networks suggests that some increasing degree of abstraction of general features of the visual world probably occurs at each higher level of these reciprocally interconnected visual cortical regions. The question now is which features of the visual world are detected and analyzed by neurons of the primary visual cortical regions and which by the higher ones. Before we answer these questions, however, we need to consider some general features of cortical organization.

Signal-Processing Properties of Cortical Neurons

The impressive horizontally layered patterns of the cells and cell connections within the cortex seem to suggest that the main action within the brain occurs in horizontal planes. In the 1930s, however, the first close looks at the orientation of cortical neurons suggested to the Spanish cytologist Rafael Lorente de No that cortical events occurred locally within vertical assemblies, or columns—units that span the cortex from top to bottom. In the early 1960s, this view was dramatically confirmed. By observing the responses of cortical cells to sensory stimuli when fine electrodes were slowly moved across the thickness of the cortex, the American physiologist Vernon B. Mountcastle was able to compare response patterns within vertically related units. His original work was done on the cortical regions that map the body's surface, using information from receptors in and below the skin, but the conclusions about cortical structure that this work led to were later confirmed for the visual system. The basic finding was that sensory stimuli from the same general receptor site activate neurons that are *vertically* adjacent.

These vertically related columns of cells exist in roughly similar form throughout the cerebral cortex, although the sizes of the cells and the densities of their occurrence vary. Because of this, scientists believe that information processing in the cortex depends on how information reaches a cortical region and how the information received there is transformed by the connections among the cells within a given vertical column. The output of any one such column might be roughly compared to the result of a multistepped mathematical calculation in which the same operations are performed in the same order on whatever starting data are fed in: for example, to average your test scores, you add up all the scores and divide the total by the number of tests you took.

The information on which the cells within a cortical column operate—visual input for the visual cortex, somatic sensation for the sensory cortex, auditory data for the auditory cortex, and so on—has, of course, already been partially processed by initial receiving and integrating centers. The products of one cortical column's operations are then handed on, by means of specific intracortical synaptic relays, to another cortical column for yet another operation on the data.

Any given cortical column has about the same number of cells, roughly 100 or so, in a rat's brain, a cat's brain, a monkey's brain, or the brain of a human being. It is the greater number of columns in a cortex and the greater number of nerve fibers that link columns within cortical regions that make for the greater abilities of the species that have these cortical features.

With this concept of the vertical connections among the cells of a horizontally layered cortex in mind, we can now return to the specific cells of the visual system.

Neurons That Respond Selectively to Visual Features

Some retinal ganglion cells are activated by light in the center of their receptive field and turned off by light around their periphery; others show the opposite response. We might say that some retinal cells are excited by donuts and others by donut holes. In addition, and very critically, cells activated by donut-shaped light are also inhibited by hole-shaped light, and vice versa. Exposed to a solid circle of light, they might not be activated at all because the inhibiting force of light in the center balances out the activating light at the edges.

Experiments conducted by the American physiologist Steven Kuffler in the mid-1950s revealed why scientists could not analyze how the retina "sees" when they used diffuse light as a stimulus. Diffuse light stimulates many neighboring neurons that have differing receptive fields (center-on or center-off), and the homogenization that results weakens the response of the retinal ganglion cells under study. But, Kuffler found, very discrete light stimuli yield highly consistent patterns of individual ganglion-cell activation.

A few years later when David Hubel and Torsten Wiesel used the same discrete visual stimuli to activate lateral geniculate neurons of the cat and the monkey, they found response patterns very similar to those found in retinal ganglion-cell receptive fields. The geniculate also had cells with preferred receptive fields shaped like small donuts, in which either the center or the "surround" was the activating factor. Inhibitory effects of the surround on the center, or vice versa, were linked directly to the ganglion cell activating the target neuron in the geniculate. From these results, Hubel and Wiesel reasoned that the visual process begins with a comparison of the amount of light striking any small region of retina with the light level around it.

As they moved their electrode vertically down through the neuronal layers of the lateral geniculate, Hubel and Wiesel observed another consistent finding. The vertically adjacent neurons all seemed to be activated by light falling on the same specific region of the retinal field, with adjacent layers in the vertical array being maximally activated by the corresponding fields in the right eye or the left eye. This vertical layering of information from corresponding points in each retina further established the nature of the retinotopic maps at the level of the lateral geniculate.

Hubel and Wiesel then extended their analysis to layer-IV cells in the primary visual cortex (area 17), where the information arrives from the lateral geniculate. These cells also showed patterns of responsiveness similar to the patterns observed in the retina and geniculate cells. Cells above and below layer IV, however, appeared not to recognize the simple, small, donut-shaped retinal receptive fields at all. Visual stimuli consisting of black dots on white backgrounds, or vice versa, produced only weak or inconsistent responses. What accounted for the loss of similar visual responsiveness within the same vertical column?

The response of one cell, accidentally observed, began to clarify the mystery. The circle that had caused vigorous response in layer IV did little or nothing to stimulate cells in layer V, but the fine dark line at the edge of the stimulus field produced a brisk response in layer V. Soon the pattern became clear. Almost all cortical cells above and below layer IV preferred stimuli in the shape of slits, bars, or edges. Once this shape factor was evident, subsequent studies showed that different cells preferred edges at particular angles. Some specialized cells preferred that the edges be moving; some even preferred movement in a particular direction (see box). Particular cortical cells above and below layer IV also reacted to different-sized edgelines and to whether the edge was black-on-white or white-on-black.

Simple cortical cells respond only in a retinalike (or geniculatelike) center-on or center-off manner. "Complex" cells respond with preferences as to orientation, contour, and motion-related or field-ground features. Simple cells are almost certainly activated by the combined excitatory and inhibitory data coming to them from their sources in the geniculate. Complex cells are apparently able to extract other information from their sources about the size, shape, and movement of the signals.

How do the interactions between all these neurons yield the actual solid images that we see? If you looked at a photograph in your newspaper under a magnifying glass, you would "see" that the image there is made up of dots. In dark areas the dots are very close together, and in light areas they are farther apart. When you look only at the dots and the open spaces, you probably cannot tell what the picture shows. You lose the dots and see the picture only at a distance. In a very simple way, the responses of the ganglion cells in the retina, of their targets in the geniculate, and of the simple cells of the vis-

A Chance Discovery

By 1962, activity of retinal ganglion cells and cells in the lateral geniculate caused by the detection of images falling on the retina had been traced by electrical recording. Working with anesthetized cats, David Hubel and Torsten Wiesel began to study the response of cells in the primary visual cortex. Many of the cells in layer IV responded the same way as those in the retina and geniculate, showing intense activity when small spots of light fell on their receptive fields. Neurons above and below layer IV, however, seemed totally unresponsive until a chance observation gave the researchers a clue. As Hubel says,

At the beginning, we couldn't make the cells fire at all. We'd shine lights all over the screen and nothing seemed to work. And, rather by accident, one day we were shining small spots . . . onto the screen and we found that the black dot seemed to be working in a way that we couldn't understand until we found that it was the process of slipping the piece of glass into the projector, which swept the line, a very faint, precise, narrow line, across the retina. Every time we did that, we'd get a response. Even more than that, the line produced responses that swept across the screen in one direction, but not in the reverse direction. . . .

Thereafter, Hubel and Wiesel began to provoke the upper- and lower-layer cells of the visual cortex with images shaped like lines, bars, or rods. Not only did these cells respond preferentially to elongated images, they responded preferentially when the bars or lines were oriented at a particular angle.

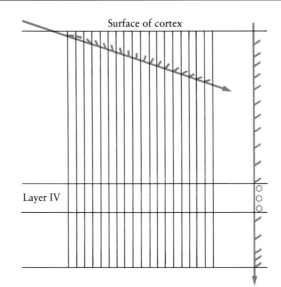

The orientation preferences, indicated by colored marks, of a group of visual-cortex neurons encountered by a microelectrode penetrating the cortex at a shallow angle in the zone above the layer IV.

Below, David Hubel and Torsten Wiesel.

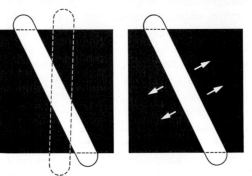

Far left and left center, a slide edge gave the first clue to response patterns of cells outside layer 4; the tracing of such a cell's response. Black rectangles, right, represent cells within columns at different cortical depths have different preferences as to line angle or direction of movement.

Figure 4.8
The pictures we see in print are composed entirely of dots. At high magnification (left), the picture cannot be "read." At progressively lower magnifications, the dots merge to form a legible image of the lower corner of the dog's right eye. Information may enter the visual system in this fashion.

ual cortex are the brain's dot-detection system (see Figure 4.8).

Bars and edges are handy images for describing what a complex neuron in the visual cortex detects. But those images still do not describe what our eyes see. To do that, we need to back up to some fundamental analysis.

It would be tempting to conclude that within a given cortical column, simple cells are "read out" by the complex cells. Upon close examination, however, the complex cells of area 17 seem to respond *before* the simple cells do. Perhaps a better concept for the dot-detecting neurons in the retina and the lateral geniculate is that they act as special "filters" for certain patterns of visual stimulation. When the cortical neurons receive this filtered data, the world may "look" much like a newspaper photo that is

seen from the distance at which the dots begin to merge but do not yet form a coherent image. The bars and edges could then simply be the shapes and other features of images in the form that can pass through the filters of the initial processing levels.

Two Eyes—One World

Many aspects of how we see can be described, but they have not been explained with biological precision. Indeed, many aspects may not yet even be identified. Much of the human brain is devoted to processing visual information, but scientists cannot yet say, even in general terms, how much.

We do know that we have two eyes, but we almost always see only one world. This ability to merge the information from both of our eyes rests on two underlying features of the visual system.

First, our eye movements are intricately coordinated as we scan our surroundings. If you gently push against the side of your eyeball while looking at the sharp edge of an object, you will briefly see the image that each eye contributes to the picture. The neurons in the superior colliculus are critical to the merger of these two images. The cells in these nuclei respond to moving stimuli preferentially. They too are arranged in vertical columns, the cells of which respond to stimuli in the same parts of the retina's visual field. It has been found that cells at the bottom of the column begin to fire just *before* a spontaneous eye movement. Let's suppose, for example, that while you are driving your car and looking straight ahead, you become aware of something flashing off to one side. The rods at the periphery of your vision field activate neurons in the superior colliculus that can drive the extraocular muscles to rotate the eyeball and shift your gaze precisely to the point in space where you detected the flashing object. Thus, you "turn your attention" by moving both eyes in tandem to the spot where a small flicker of light or motion occurred so that you can inspect it closely.

Cells in the deep layers of the colliculus also receive auditory information, and these cells respond to sound as well as to light stimuli. The combination of such information in these deep collicular cells provides signals to other cells lower in the midbrain that drive the muscles of the eyeball. These muscles are responsible for your shifting your gaze to the spot where you heard something happen.

Second, retinal maps of the world are transferred onto two identical maps in area 17. Intercortical connections later unite these maps in ways that are not yet fully understood. Investigators do know that at the level of the geniculate and area 17 in the visual cortex, at least, visual input from each eye is kept separate by some rather elaborate cir-

cuitry. In anesthetized experimental animals, cells in layer IV of area 17 respond to input from both eyes. More complex response patterns occur in cells above and below layer IV. Here, in general, some cells respond better to one eye than to the other—that is, in some cells input from one eye "dominates" input from the other.

In fact, the nerve fibers from a single part of the visual field of one eye can be traced across their geniculate connections all the way to the visual cortex. There they form alternating "ocular dominance" columns— that is, columns dominated by one eye or the other—of about 0.4 mm across throughout the thickness of the cortex. If we were to look down on the ocular-dominance columns in area 17, the columns dominated by one eye would merge together to form swirled ridges that look much like a fingerprint.

Animal experiments have revealed some surprising facts about cortical organization. If one eye is kept shut from birth, neither the neurons of the geniculate to which that eye's retinal ganglion cells connect nor the dominance columns in the cortex that would have been influenced by that eye will develop properly. Even though the retina of the closed eye is fully responsive when the eye is opened, the retinal connections never command their full measure of geniculate or cortical responsiveness. The cortical-dominance columns for the closed eye remain narrow. The eye left open from birth, however, influences cortical cells over an area that is much larger than normal. This work demonstrates that the degree of connectedness between sensory neurons and their cortical targets can be regulated by the level of activity in that sensory system.

The visual pathways from our right and left eyes provide a simple illustration of parallel circuitry (as do the aural pathways from our two ears). As you saw in Figure 4.6, visual input from receptor cells in each retina travels along virtually parallel routes from retina to visual cortex. Obviously, our two eyes, with their dual visual pathways, do more than balance our face and provide a "backup" system against blindness in one eye. They also work together to add something.

The slight differences in the horizontal position of the eyes in the skull result in very slightly different images of the same object being seen from either eye. To prove that this is so, hold your hand in front of you against a complex background. Using one of your fingers as a reference point, look at your fingertip first with one eye, and then with the other. As you do so, your finger will appear to jump back and forth across the objects in the background. With both eyes open, you will see that your finger clearly is closer to you than the objects in the background. The alternating one-eyed views of your finger reveal the difference, or visual disparity, between the way each of your two eyes views the same object. When the two eyes converge on the object, a depth difference is set up within your field of view.

The closer the object is, the greater the difference in each eye's view of it, and the greater the apparent depth between the object and its background, that is, the greater the depth of the field. As objects get farther away, the difference in each eye's view gets less, and so does your ability to tell exactly which objects are the farthest away. We make these judgments largely on the basis of what we infer about their relative sizes—for example, you might mistake a model airplane flying nearby for a commercial plane flying at a great distance.

Although it is not fully understood exactly how the brain combines, or fuses, the individual views of the two separate retinal images, it is clear that this happens well along the visual processing pathway—and cer-

tainly in the visual regions beyond the primary visual cortex, in which the points of view of the two eyes are still separate. When the right and the left retinal images are fused within the cortical visual system (wherever that takes place), we see one world in depth. People with only one good eye obviously can achieve only limited depth perception of nearby objects.

The workings of other parallel circuits also contribute to the richness of what we see. Within each visual pathway, different pieces of retinal information are channeled into three parallel subroutes. Specific image information (the detected "dots") goes through the lateral geniculate to the primary visual cortex. Information about motion is carried by different retinal axons to the colliculus and area 17 of the visual cortex. Information about diffuse light levels enters the suprachiasmatic pathway. This information, processed along these separate but parallel routes, is eventually recombined somewhere in the integrating circuitry of the cerebral cortex to provide the complete "picture."

This general scheme by which primary information is divided into separate processing channels for later recombination is, as we shall see, one that is also generally used by both the somatosensory and the motor systems.

Color: The Special Quality of Vision

Color is one of the qualities of vision that hardly seems to need description. Everyone knows the difference between a black-and-white movie and one in color. There is quite a bit to say about color detection, however.

We have briefly noted the existence of three types of cones, the specialized color receptors of the retina. The biological representation of color begins with these cells.

Light is usually considered in terms of the three primary colors—red, blue, and yellow.

However, the color responses of the cones, the retinal color sensors, is more limited. Each cone is specialized for reacting to only one color, or wavelength, of light, depending on which of the three known visual pigments (red, blue, and green) that cone contains. The data show that a cone responds only to the color of light for which its specific visual pigment is able to absorb light energy; thus, red cones respond only to red light, green cones to green light, and blue cones to blue light. However, when physiologists turned their attention to the color responses coming from the output cells of the retina, the ganglion cells, what they found was something not quite so simple. The retina, taken as a set of connected cells, responded to monochromatic light signals (that is, light signals composed of only one selected part of the color spectrum) as though it could detect *four* colors: red, blue, green, and yellow. Because no cone should be able to detect yellow light, the fact that yellow is detected requires some further understanding.

An early clue to the origin of yellow perception came from questioning people about the colors they could see under different testing conditions. If you stare at a gray shape surrounded by a bright green ring, the gray area will start to take on a reddish hue. If you stare at a bright red object and then close your eyes, you will see an "afterimage" of the shape in green. This chromatic *successive-contrast effect* is the source of the so-called "green flare" that can be seen when you stare intently at the setting sun. The afterimage of a blue object is yellow (you may need to put the blue object on a black background to see this).

It would seem, then, that blue and yellow are somehow linked, as are red and green. But these combinations may not seem correct to you. You know that to get green paint, for example, you mix blue and yellow

pigments. How does green reception come about?

One of the theoretical explanations best supported by the data is called the *opponent-process theory,* first proposed in the nineteenth century by the German physiologist Emil Hering. In Hering's view, certain colors were "opponents": yellow versus blue, red versus green, and black (no color) versus white (all colors). Single-cell recording experiments 100 years later gave the very results predicted by this concept. Cells with red center-on receptive fields have green center-off surrounds, and vice versa. Cells with yellow-sensitive center-ons are activated by blue center-off surrounds, and vice versa. The cones are activated by light of a specific color. Interactions of the horizontal cells combine these color-coded cone messages as they converge on the retinal ganglion cells, with significant modification by the integrating actions of the horizontal cells. As a result of the retinal circuitry and the on- and off-center color sensitivity of the cones, opponent colors are detected at the ganglion cells; green emerges as the opponent of red, yellow as the opponent of blue (see Figure 4.9).

Recent studies indicate that the color coding of input from the retina is retained in the visual cortex. Cells in the upper layers of the visual cortex have color-coded receptive fields and show opponent-color reactions, but they lack any preferred-edge orientation. David Hubel has suggested that the system for processing color information is separate from but parallel to the system for processing orientation.

Object Vision and Spatial Vision

We do not usually break down the process of seeing into whether it is one-eyed or two-eyed, color or black and white, until something goes wrong. In the main, we just see.

Other visual qualities go unnoticed as well. One such quality has to do with determining "where" something is in the space around us and "what" that something is. For a long time it was thought that the processing of these two visual qualities became separated at an early stage of the visual process. Spatial information functions were attributed to the superior colliculus as it signaled muscles to move the eyes around in order to gaze at objects. Feature-detection functions, it was thought, resulted from progressive analysis of the objects being viewed. Recent investigations suggest that neither of these explanations is correct. Rather, both kinds of visual analysis appear to depend on the input of the geniculate to area 17 and on the different systems to which area 17 then sends its information for further processing.

Feature Detection and Recognition

The most recent studies have explored the ability of monkeys to remember very sophisticated qualities of objects in order to get food pellets—they must choose a wooden square with stripes versus one without stripes, for example. Once experimental monkeys had learned these discriminations, they were subjected to experimental surgery to remove a small segment of one of the regions of the cerebral cortex to which circuits carrying visual information have been traced. When they recovered, the monkeys were retested. If a part of the temporal lobe receiving visual information were removed on both sides, the animal could still see—it would pick up the objects to try to get to the food pellets—but it was no longer able to discriminate the striped blocks from the solid ones. This surgical procedure, used in combination with circuit tracing and electrophysiological recording, places the visual function of "feature detection" in the temporal lobe area near the lower edge of the cortex.

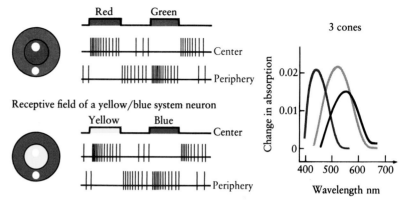

Figure 4.9
Probable patterns of color-coding within the retina. Above, a ganglion cell is activated by red center-on cones and green center-off cones. Below, activity of ganglion cells receiving input from yellow center-on and blue center-off cones. The center and periphery of these color-specific fields are organized in an opposing manner. (There are no yellow-sensitive cones. This quality arises from the convergence achieved by the horizontal, local-circuit neurons within the retina.)

The American neuropsychologist Mortimer Mishkin has suggested that cells in this visual temporal lobe area retain some "trace" of a previously seen object. This trace is then used as a pattern against which to compare the next object. A match gives one kind of response ("I know that object"), and a nonmatch gives another ("I've never seen that before"). Recordings of single cells in this area have detected cells that respond specifically to some monkey faces but not others, regardless of their angle of presentation. If the monkey's distinguishing facial features—its mouth, nose, or eyes—are masked, the incomplete face does not trigger any response in these cells.

Some researchers refer to a cell that has this number of specific requirements as a "grandmother" cell—that is, such a cell becomes active only when the sum of certain shapes, edges, and contours results in an identification of the object as "grand-

Disturbances of Vision

Given the number of parts to the visual system, the ability to see clearly, in color, with both eyes, to the limits of our visual fields, is susceptible to a number of disruptive conditions. The compromised ability to see well can be most easily understood in terms of problems at the periphery of the eye (i.e., problems of the parts within the eyeball) and central problems (problems within the optic nerve, optic tracts or projections, or the visual cortex). Visual problems in the eyeball are generally tended by an *ophthalmologist,* a medical doctor whose duties may include prescribing glasses or contact lenses, which are then constructed by an *optician,* a visual specialist who is not medically trained. An *optometrist* is also a non-medically trained vision specialist who measures visual acuity and prescribes corrective lenses but who does not deal with other problems of the eyeball apparatus.

Peripheral Disturbances of Vision

Visual problems of the eyeball may arise from abnormalities of eyeball shape, from the inability of the lens to accommodate, from the inability of the pupil to constrict or expand, or from problems with the neuronal elements within the retina. The most common disorders, nearsightedness (*myopia*) and farsightedness (*hyperopia*), arise from eyeballs that are too deep or too shallow, respectively, so that the image coming through the lens does not fall sharply on the retina. These problems can be corrected by lenses that refocus the image at the correct depth.

As we age, it is normal for growth of the facial bones to help overcome modest degrees of nearsightedness. Age brings another visual change that is less naturally remedied. The lens of the eye becomes harder and less malleable, and this change makes it difficult to focus on objects close to the face even though the eyeball itself does not undergo any change of shape. The progressive loss of near vision with age, *presbyopia,* is only correctable by wearing reading glasses or by having your arms stretched.

Astigmatism arises from irregularities in the surface of the cornea. These irregularities cause the images entering the eye from certain angles to be more distorted than images entering the eye from other angles. Astigmatism is readily corrected by contact lenses that essentially float on a shallow layer of tears and smooth out these irregularities. The surface of the cornea is also subject to physical damage, and, if infected, the resulting damage can significantly impair vision.

Abnormalities of color perception arise from a congenital absence of one or more of the genes that control the expression of the proteins that form the three different visual pigments and allow the cones to distinguish blue, green, or red light. The genetic defects of color blindness are recessive traits linked to the X chromosome. Since females have two X chromosomes, one from their mother and one from their father, they rarely express the defect. However, in the male (recall that males have the X-Y chromosome pair), there will

mother." A conclusion that there are too many different objects in the world for too few visual cells seems to miss the point. At this high level of visual detection, the final features being detected probably result from many lower-level interactions, each of which filters a lot of information out and lets only a little through. The visual-temporal cortex cells also receive other sorts of sensory input, including sounds and, perhaps, smells. These different inputs can also help to distinguish between the objects in the world outside the laboratory.

Thus the "grandmother" cell can be viewed as the target of a series of integrated detections and abstractions of a complex object. Once the full array of details defining an object of importance have been "learned," only a few of these details need to be detected subsequently in order to match the object being viewed now with one seen before. Thus, no cell that recognizes grandmother actually exists, only cells able to receive these higher-order details and to attempt matches with previously seen patterns of details. In this manner, the brain could register an almost infinite variety of objects.

Spatial Discrimination   The monkeys with the temporal lobe lesions may have lost their ability to distinguish objects according to what they looked like, but they did not lose their ability to discriminate among objects according to place. A monkey trained to only be one X chromosome, and if the defective gene is present, color blindness will result.

Other, less common, causes of visual disturbance arising within the eye include the development of *cataracts,* in which the lens capsule becomes opaque, usually as a result of aging. In *glaucoma,* the movement of fluid from the space behind the iris (the posterior chamber) to the space between the iris and the cornea (the anterior chamber) becomes obstructed, and the posterior chamber develops excessively high pressure. This high pressure compresses the retina and can destroy the ability of the rods and cones to function. Typically, the visual field loses function first at the periphery, and the field of view becomes progressively narrower as the disease progresses. In many cases, glaucoma can be treated by topical medications that ease the movement of the fluid between the chambers or reduce the rate of fluid production; surgical treatment is also possible to improve outflow.

The function of the retina can also be disturbed by direct trauma (producing the retinal separations that end the careers of promising athletes). Because of its high metabolic activity, the retina is very susceptible to the vascular problems that accompany the complications of *diabetes mellitus* and certain forms of *sickle-cell anemia.* When the optic nerve itself is damaged, as can occur with *multiple sclerosis*—a disease manifested by progressive disturbance of nerve fiber function throughout the central nervous system—vision may be patchy, with no signs of physical disturbance to the retina. Lastly, problems with the opposing strength of the extraocular muscles may cause double vision, as the eyes do not track in parallel. These muscles, as well as the eyelid opening muscle, are found to be weakened early in the course of *myasthenia gravis.*

Central Disturbances of Vision

When strokes, tumors, or trauma affect the visual pathways beyond the retina, the degree and location of the peripheral vision loss help to diagnose where the damage has occurred. Tumors that arise in the area of the pituitary frequently cause pressure on the optic chiasm, and the result includes a loss of the lateral (or temporal) visual half of the field (*bitemporal hemianopsia*), the half of the visual field where ganglion-cell axons cross over at the chiasm. When both eyes have lost vision on the same side of the body (*homonymous hemianopsia*), the problem must lie beyond the chiasm, either in the optic tract or the visual cortex, and, given the circuitry of the visual system, the problem must lie on the side opposite to that of the peripheral field lost. If the tumor is benign, the visual loss may be temporary. Finally, strokes or trauma to the visual cortex beyond the primary visual cortex may result in very subtle visual disturbances, as happened to the man who mistook his wife for a hat (see Chapter 8).

point at any movable object that is closest to any other fixed object performs quite well following the bilateral temporal lobe operation. Performance of location tasks, however, does suffer after removal of a different region of visually connected cortex, one at the upper edge of the parietal lobe just in front of area 17.

These results suggest that two parallel systems of visual analysis, one for spatial discrimination and another for object discrimination, do operate simultaneously higher up the processing ladder. Each system uses different routes and different combinations of cell circuitry. Each depends on the information received from earlier relays in the visual assembly line, and each uses that information in a slightly different way, combining it, in later processing, with inputs from other sensory systems. The end results of these parallel processes are combined later in the construction of the complete visual image of the world.

How General Is Parallel Processing?

Signs of parallel processing comparable to that noted in the visual system have been found in at least two other sensory systems, touch and hearing. Early studies attempting to trace peripheral sensory nerves from their body-surface locations to the cerebral cortex

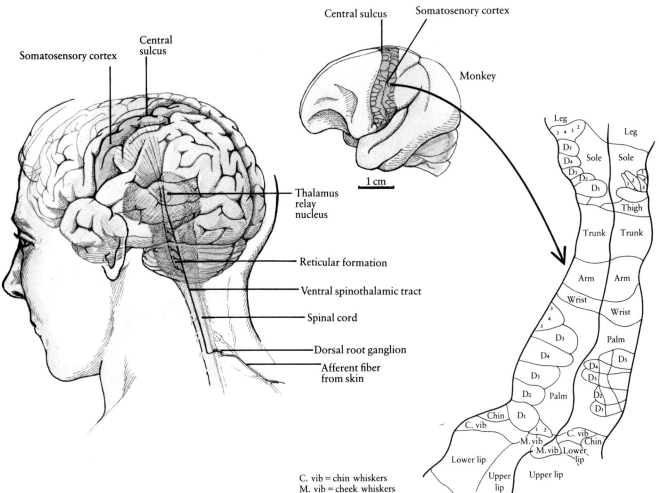

C. vib = chin whiskers
M. vib = cheek whiskers
D = fingers 1–5

Figure 4.10
The somatic sensory system in the human brain is shown at left as the components of the system. Sensory fibers arising from receptors in the skin enter the spinal cord through the dorsal root ganglia and synapse on neurons within the dorsal horn of the spinal cord. Those dorsal horn neurons send their axons through the spinothalamic tracts to synapse on neurons in the sensory nuclei in the thalamus. The thalamic neurons then project the map of the body's surface onto neurons within the so-called somatosensory region of the cerebral cortex, located just behind to a major surface landmark, the central sulcus. In all

mammals, the location of the somatosensory cortex relative to this "post-central" gyrus is similar. In experimental studies of the responses of neurons to discrete sensory activation of points on the body surface, it is possible to define a dual mapping of body points, as illustrated for the owl monkey's brain at right. Each bounded area defines the rough limits of responsivity of the cortical neurons to skin stimulation. Note that the amount of cortical volume devoted to the lips and digits of the hands is disproportionately large compared to the actual surface area of the proximal limbs and trunk.

produced distorted maps of the body surface on that region of cortex, known as the somatosensory cortex, that receives integrated information about touch. These "little man" maps, or "little monkey" maps (see Figure 4.10), devote much greater space to the face, lips, tongue, and fingers than to the legs, trunk, and back. Presumably the areas of skin with greater cortical representation have a greater ability to detect touch accurately.

More recent studies using finer techniques of recording and tracing suggest that, in fact, multiple body-surface maps do exist within the sensory cortex. These maps extend beyond the sensory-cortex zones originally thought to be reached by the thalamic sensory nuclei that receive and integrate pressure and touch stimuli (see Tables 4.1 and 4.2). The existence of these apparently redundant maps of the body's surface suggests that additional recombinations of tactile sensory abstractions may be possible within the cortex.

Had we been searching for simplicity in a sensing system, we would be most unhappy with so many "bells and whistles." But even these brief sketches of how we see, hear, or feel suggest that it is this very complexity that gives us the power to discriminate among sensory details, to recombine them, and, eventually, to decide whether we have encountered this or that sensory picture in the past.

When you answer the telephone, how many words does it take before you recognize the voice? A close friend may establish herself with a single word, while a more remote acquaintance may need to give you several clues before you recognize his identity. When you listen to a recording, you may not be able to pick out one voice from another. Yet in the recording studio, each voice and each instrument was probably recorded on a separate channel and then remixed by the director to create the full, balanced sound.

Our sources of primary sensory information are also kept separate, independently filtered, and available for final recombination. We depend on the rapidity of parallel processing operations to increase our capacity for analysis. A system designed to process information qualities "serially," or consecutively (image shapes, then color, then movement, then location, and so on) would be too slow to keep us current with a rapidly changing world.

These remarks on parallel processing in the visual and somatic sensory systems provide a general model for the basic understanding of how all the senses work. Now we will look briefly at three other senses: hearing, smell, and taste. As with vision and somatic sensation, we shall consider the receptors for each of these senses, their neural pathways from receptors to cortex, and the qualities we perceive through these systems.

Hearing: A Brief Look at the Auditory System

Although vision is usually considered the most important sense for human beings, hearing is the sense that allows members of our social species to communicate with each other—to hear and interpret speech. It is almost impossible for babies born deaf to learn to speak, even though their speech apparatus is completely intact. Such babies make the same speech sounds as hearing infants for the first few months of life, but because they cannot hear their own vocalizations, they soon stop producing those sounds. (Luckily, the language-processing areas of the brain are able to process visual symbols, so even those people who have never heard speech can communicate with

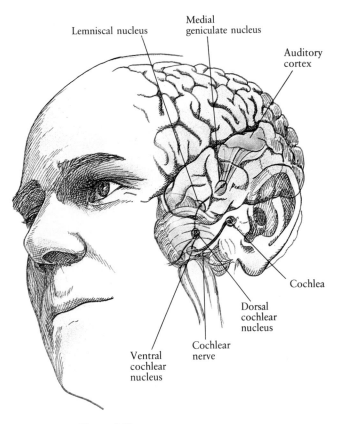

Lemniscal nucleus

Medial
geniculate nucleus

Auditory
cortex

Cochlea

Dorsal
cochlear
nucleus

Cochlear
nerve

Ventral
cochlear
nucleus

Figure 4.11
*The components of the brain that participate in the
function of hearing: the primary receptors are located
in the cochlea, in the inner ear. The cochlear nerve
conducts the auditory messages through intermediate
level neurons in the medial geniculate in the thalamus
and through the inferior colliculus. These second-level
neurons then transmit to third-level neurons in the
primary auditory cortex.*

others by sign language.) Besides its role in
communication, hearing, of course, gives us
information about the world that is vital to
our survival. Hearing is a multilevel system,
with primary sound receptors, intermediate
level relays, and a primary cortical representation, with many higher integrative areas
(see Figure 4.11).

What Sound Is

The stimulus that human beings perceive as
sound begins when some object in our environment vibrates. The vibration causes the
molecules making up the air to move, to alternately condense and rarefy (pull apart
from each other). This molecular movement
produces waves, or variations in air pressure,
which travel away from the vibrating object
at 700 miles per hour. When the frequency
of these air-pressure variations in a wave
ranges between 30 and 20,000 cycles per second, it stimulates the receptor cells in the
human auditory system and produces the
sensation of sound.

Just as the visual system does, our hearing
system distinguishes several qualities in the
signal it detects. We hear sounds that vary in
pitch, from high to low. The pitch we hear is
determined by the number of cycles per second of the sound wave: many cycles in high
sounds, fewer in low sounds. Pitch, or cycles
per second, is measured in units of *hertz
(Hz).* We also hear sounds that vary in *loudness,* a quality that results from the contrast
between the alternating maximum and mini-
mum air pressures that make up the wave.
Large contrasts we perceive as loud; smaller
ones, as soft. Loudness, a measure of the intensity of the stimulus, is noted in units of
decibels (dB).

Figure 4.12 depicts these differences for a
pure tone, as produced in a laboratory by a
tuning fork or an oboe. Such pure tones do
not represent the kinds of sound people hear
every day, however. We hear sounds with
timbre, that is, with a rich mixture of frequencies (see Figure 4.13). This mixture occurs because most sound-producing objects
have several vibrating parts. Even a single
violin string, when bowed or plucked, vibrates all along its length. The timbre lets us
distinguish between a violin and a cello and
between voices; often, the pitch and timbre

of just one word on the phone is enough to tell us who is calling.

In fact, we usually hear a rich mixture of complex sounds—an orchestra or a rock band; a voice on the telephone along with the jumble of sounds from a television program and the family dog barking in the background; the car radio, traffic sounds, and the voice of the person in the passenger seat. Our hearing system does not blend these different sounds, as our visual system does when two different wavelengths of light are mixed. We can usually follow the line of several instruments as we listen to a group play.

The Structure of the Ear

The outer parts of the ear—the external ear, or *pinna,* and the *external auditory canal*—serve mostly to funnel auditory stimuli to the middle ear. The sound waves travel through these structures to the *tympanic membrane* (or eardrum) and cause it to vibrate. These vibrations are passed on to the three tiny bones of the middle ear—the *ossicles:* first to the *malleus,* commonly called the hammer; then to the *incus,* or anvil; and then to the *stapes,* or stirrup (see Figure 4.14).

The bottom of the stapes (the part that looks like the footrest of a stirrup) passes the vibrations to the *cochlea,* the snail-shaped, fluid-filled organ that transduces the mechanical energy to neural energy. The cochlea is surrounded by bone, except where the stapes contacts it, at a membrane-covered opening, the *oval window,* and at another such opening, the *round window.* The fluid within the cochlea is set into motion by the pistonlike action of the stapes on the oval window.

The cochlea, when uncoiled and stretched straight, is seen to be a tapering cylinder, divided lengthwise into three fluid-filled sections (see page 116, upper right); two of these, the *vestibular canal* and the *tympanic canal,* are joined by a small hole at the nar-

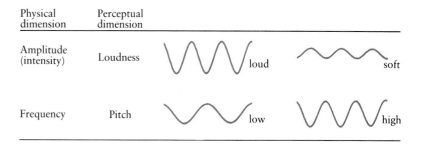

Physical dimension	Perceptual dimension		
Amplitude (intensity)	Loudness	loud	soft
Frequency	Pitch	low	high

Figure 4.12
The physical differences in sound waves that produce the different qualities of sounds, such as the pitch and loudness that we perceive.

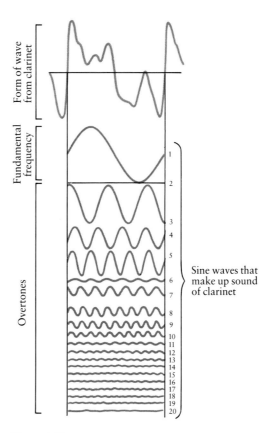

Figure 4.13
The "pure" timbre of a note played on a clarinet is actually composed of multiple frequencies as shown here. (Adapted from Stereo Review, *copyright © 1977 by Ziff-Davis Publishing Co.)*

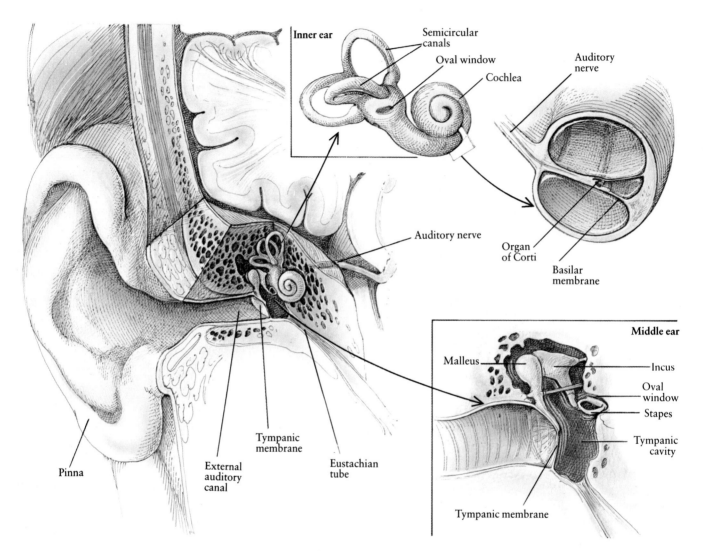

Figure 4.14

The structure of the ear, showing the relation of the external ear (pinna) to the middle and inner ear. The inset at the lower right shows the structure of the sound-detecting elements of the middle ear, indicating the physical connection between the ossicles and the detecting movements of the tympanic membrane which result from sound waves. Sound waves are transmitted to the hair cells of the cochlea through the oval window. The inset at the upper right shows a cross section through the cochlea revealing the inner structure of the organ of Corti. On the facing page, an enlargement of the cochlea. The primary receptor neurons, the hair cells, are embedded in the basilar membrane with their upper surfaces extending up to the tectorial membrane. When the basilar membrane vibrates as a result of the sound waves transmitted by the ossicles to the oval window, the hair cell upper surface is distorted, initiating activity within these neurons. This activity is then transmitted to level-two auditory neurons through the cochlear nerve.

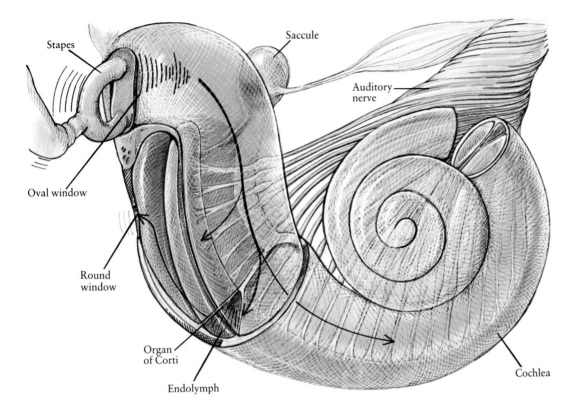

Stapes

Saccule

Auditory nerve

Oval window

Round window

Organ of Corti

Endolymph

Cochlea

row end of the cochlea, so the same fluid passes through both. Each inward push of the stapes on the oval window moves fluid down the vestibular canal, then up through the tympanic canal to the round window, whose membrane covering bulges to relieve the pressure. The middle fluid-filled section is the *cochlear canal*. The two membranes separating the three sections are the *basilar membrane* and *Reissner's membrane*.

The neurons that serve as receptor cells for sound are anchored in the basilar membrane within the cochlear canal. These neurons are called *hair cells* because cilia—fine hairlike filaments—project from their tops. These cilia attach to the *tectorial membrane,* a rigid flap of tissue that extends over the hair cells like a porch roof. (These structures—the basilar membrane, the hair cells, and the tectorial membrane—are often re-

ferred to collectively as the *organ of Corti.*) The motion of the liquid in the cochlea causes the basilar membrane to move relative to the tectorial membrane. This relative movement exerts a shearing force on the cilia, causing them to bend. It is these bending movements of the cilia that produce action potentials in the receptor neurons of the hearing system (see Figure 4.15).

We do not know exactly how the transduction of mechanical energy to electrical nerve energy takes place, but it appears that stimulation of the hair cell opens channels in its cell membrane that admit potassium ions from the fluid in the cochlear canal; the intake of potassium ions produces depolarization, and the nerve impulse begins its travels to the brain. If potassium ions are removed from the fluid in the cochlear canal, the hair cells can no longer fire (Valli et al., 1979).

Pathway from Ear to Cortex

The hair cells have no axons; the base of the cell synapses directly with processes of bipolar neurons (axons on both ends of the cell body) in a branch of the auditory nerve called the *cochlear nerve.*

Figure 4.15
Hair cells on the surface of the organ of Corti (see Figure 4.14). A single row of inner hair cells runs across the right side of the photograph; three rows of outer hair cells, arranged in V-shaped configurations, run across the left half of the photograph.

The cochlear nerve takes the complicated path sketched in Figure 4.16. In contrast to the optic nerve, which bifurcates only once on its way to the visual cortex, the cochlear nerve bifurcates several times at relays as it wends its way to the primary auditory cortex in the temporal lobe; this primary auditory target area is not on the surface of the temporal lobe but is enfolded deep within the Sylvian fissure. As a consequence of the branchings at these relays along the auditory pathway, every structure along the pathway receives input from both ears. This difference between visual and auditory pathways probably reflects the comparatively greater difficulty of locating a sound in space than of locating an object visually.

Neural Coding of Sound

Pitch   Lifelong studies by the American auditory physiologist Georg von Bekesy, of Harvard University, revealed that the basilar membrane within the cochlea reacts to the vibration it receives at the oval window by selective distortions. That is, the membrane

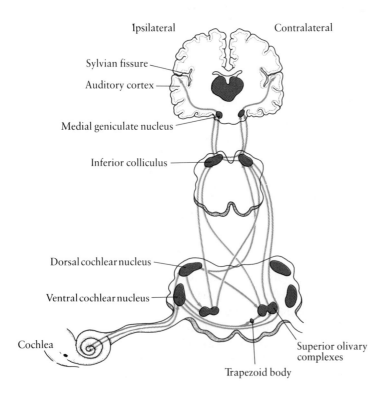

Ipsilateral   Contralateral

Sylvian fissure
Auditory cortex

Medial geniculate nucleus

Inferior colliculus

Dorsal cochlear nucleus

Ventral cochlear nucleus

Cochlea
                                          Superior olivary
                                          complexes
                        Trapezoid body

Figure 4.16
The pathway of the cochlear nerve. The first relay is at the cochlear nuclei. Here some of the cochlear nerve fibers branch and ascend to the dorsal cochlear nucleus, while the others descend within the hindbrain to the ventral cochlear nucleus.

The second auditory relay is at the superior olivary nuclei. Fibers from the ventral cochlear nucleus go to the dorsal cochlear nucleus and to both the right and left superior olivary nuclei; projections from the dorsal cochlear nucleus also go to both olivary nuclei and to other structures.

Subsequently, transmission passes to the next higher level relay, at the inferior colliculi in the midbrain; here another bifurcation takes place, with auditory information from each ear mixed and transferred to neurons on the opposite side. The last subcortical auditory station is the medial geniculate nucleus, in the thalamus. The medial geniculate then projects to the first cortical auditory level in the temporal lobe enfolded deep within the Sylvian fissure.

bulges, and the bulge travels, wavelike, some distance along the membrane. The point of maximum deflection of the bulge corresponds to the frequency of the sound stimulus: high-frequency sounds produce distortions of the membrane at the narrow end of the cochlea, near the oval window; low-frequency sounds produce distortions toward the other end (see Figure 4.15). Very low frequency sounds produce an almost uniform bulge along the entire membrane. The various displacements of the membrane stimulate various combinations of hair cells. These sensory receptors, then, firing from specific places on the basilar membrane, send the brain a specific message about the frequency of the auditory stimulus.

Location along the basilar membrane may not be the cue for coding sounds of very low frequency, since the entire membrane becomes distorted and vibrates. Rather, it may be the timing of neural firing that encodes the message about these low sounds; the rate at which the hair cells fire seems to be synchronized with the membrane's rate of vibration.

These neuronal messages follow an organizational pattern similar to the retinotopic design of the visual system. In this *tonotopic* system, adjacent neurons respond to tones that are only a note apart, and this relationship extends from the cochlea through all the relays to the cortex. Besides such neurons, which respond to only a small range of frequencies, there are also neurons that react to a wide range of frequencies. Others respond only to the beginning of a sound or only to the end of a sound or to both the start and end of a sound; in terms of the selectivity of their responses, these units seem to correspond to the center-on, center-off cells in the visual system.

Loudness   While the pitch of a sound is cued by place—that is, where the bulge on the basilar membrane is greatest—loudness is cued by how big and expansive the bulge is. Sound waves of larger amplitude (louder sounds) produce bigger bulges over a wider area, with more intense vibrations. The intensity of the vibrations causes the shearing force on the hair cells to be greater. This, in turn, presumably causes more neurotransmitter to be released. More neurotransmitter causes axons in the cochlear nerve to fire at a greater rate, and their rate of firing seems to determine our perception of loudness—at least for sounds of higher pitch.

Since rate of firing also determines pitch for low-frequency sounds, it cannot code for loudness of these sounds because a higher firing rate would make the pitch higher. Many scientists believe that low-frequency sounds are perceived as louder when a stimulus causes a greater number of neurons in the cochlear nerve to fire simultaneously.

Two small muscles attached to the ossicles in each ear can contract to protect the ear from very loud noises. The muscles displace the tiny bones, so the signal that the stapes transmits to the cochlea is less intense.

Location   The fact that we have two ears separated by the width of a head—and that we can easily swivel the head on its neck—accounts for our ability to locate a sound in space accurately. Most sounds arrive at one ear before the other, and the hair cells and higher-level relay neurons on each side respond selectively to these different arrival times. Besides this *time difference*, there is also a *phase difference* in what each ear hears; that is, different portions of a sound wave arrive at both ears simultaneously. With some neurons responding only during a particular phase of a sound wave, the two ears will detect the difference and pass it along the auditory pathways.

The time-difference cue works for locating an isolated sound, such as a click or footstep. The phase-difference cue helps us in locating the source of continuous sounds, such as a low-pitched hum. *Intensity differences* also help to locate the source of a sound, particularly with high-frequency sounds. Some of the high-frequency sound waves on the side where the sound originates are absorbed by the bones of the head and ear, casting a sort of "sonic shadow." The intensity of sound reaching the far ear will therefore be smaller.

With the several bifurcations and crossovers within the cochlear nerve and the secondary and tertiary levels of auditory processing, these codings for sound localization are carried through all the relay stations up to the cortex.

Feature Detection

The features of sound—its pitch, loudness, and location—are processed in parallel by specialized receptors and relay neurons. These sets of sensory data may undergo some processing at subcortical branchings and relay stations in the neuronal hierarchy of the auditory system. Still, when the auditory cortex of cats or monkeys is removed, the animals cannot locate a sound in space, cannot detect changes in a tone's duration, cannot discriminate between different sound patterns, and cannot detect changes in complex sounds. Although they can still detect differences in pitch and in loudness, their perception of sounds in their world obviously requires processing at the cortical level.

One question about primate auditory feature detection that remains open to discussion is whether human beings process speech sounds in some special way. Investigations on monkey auditory neurons found that some neurons in the auditory cortex are activated best by voices of other squirrel monkeys (Funkenstein et al., 1971). Most likely, our auditory system processes all the signals it receives in the same way, until—perhaps at the level of the primary auditory cortex— a sound is perceived as possibly a speech sound, at which time the neural signal is shunted to the left hemisphere for processing in the language centers there (these centers are discussed in Chapter 9).

At least one thing is certain: newborns can distinguish the sound of the human voice from other sounds. When researchers monitored changes in heart rate, respiration, and muscle activity of newborns while playing different sounds for them, they found the sound with the greatest effect to be a human voice (Hutt et al., 1968).

We have seen that the sense of hearing transmits the qualities of the sounds heard in separate but parallel pathways to higher subcortical centers, where they are processed and integrated as they are being passed on to the primary auditory cortex. Thus you can begin to see some of the remarkable similarities in the general methods of processing auditory, visual, and somatic sensory information.

Taste and Smell: A Brief Look

The stimuli that trigger sight and sound are physical energy in the form of light or motion. The stimuli for smell and taste are chemical. Substances that go into the mouth must be soluble in water, that is, in saliva, so the molecules can dissolve and their component chemicals can stimulate receptors on the tongue and palate. In order to produce the sensation of smell, substances must be in the form of a gas or vapor.

Taste

If you have ever had a bad head cold, you already know that smell and taste work closely together. When your nose is completely blocked, foods are virtually tasteless. With your nose in fine working order, however, the number of flavors available seems almost infinite.

Actually, the chemoreceptors in the mouth record only four qualities of taste:

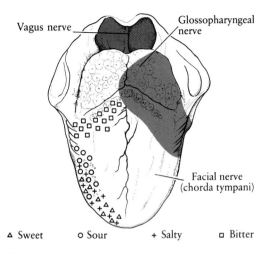

Vagus nerve

Glossopharyngeal nerve

Facial nerve (chorda tympani)

△ Sweet   ○ Sour   + Salty   □ Bitter

Figure 4.17
The location on the tongue's surface of the major qualities of taste detection for sweet, sour, salty, and bitter stimuli.

sweetness, sourness, saltiness, and bitterness. The many flavors we perceive come from various mixtures of these tastes and the smell of the food. The tip of the tongue is most sensitive to sweet and salty substances; the sides are most sensitive to sour things; and the back of the tongue, the throat, and the soft palate are most sensitive to bitterness (see Figure 4.17).

The chemoreceptors for taste are called the *taste buds*. Most people think that the small bumps on the tongue, the *papillae*, are the taste buds, but actually the taste buds lie buried around the papillae, in moatlike indentations that trap the saliva (see Figure 4.18). These receptor cells have hairlike processes that project into the moat. There, the chemical components of food stimulate the hairlike parts of the appropriate receptors (sweet, sour, salty, or bitter), and the chemical stimulus is transduced into neural energy. However, no obvious structural differences between the types of taste buds specialized for the four modalities of taste have been detected, even with use of high-resolution microscopes. Just how their location on the surface of the tongue allows them to detect these taste differences remains unclear. It is also not known exactly what properties of the tasted chemicals trigger the neurons' action potential.

The taste receptors toward the front of the

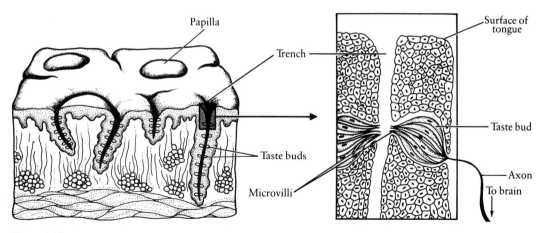

Papilla

Trench

Taste buds

Microvilli

Surface of tongue

Taste bud

Axon

To brain

Figure 4.18
A drawing of a microscopic view of the internal structure of the taste detecting receptors (the pappillae) and the special primary taste receptive cells (the taste buds) that line their surface. In the expanded drawing at right, the cells of the taste buds, buried within trenches on the sides of the pappillae, send their axons into one of the cranial nerves (facial, glossopharyngeal, and vagus) that carry gustatory information centrally.

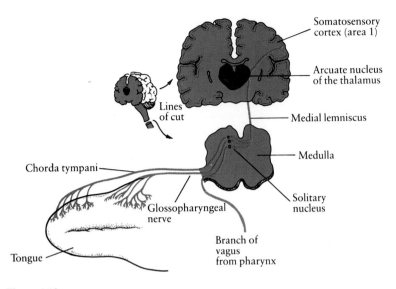

Figure 4.19
An overview of the neuronal components of the taste detection system, in which the primary receptors neurons are located in the tongue, the level 2 neurons are located within the medulla, in the nucleus of the solitary tract, and from which higher connections carry this information to the thalamus and ultimately to the cerebral cortex.

tongue are innervated by a branch of the facial nerve, the *chorda tympani,* so called because it travels through the middle ear just beneath the tympanic membrane. Receptors toward the back of the tongue are innervated by the *glossopharyngeal nerve.* Receptors on the palate and in the throat are innervated by the *vagus nerve* (see Figure 4.19). Sensory information traveling along these three nerves pass through one synaptic relay station in the medulla, the *nucleus of the solitary tract.* From there, they travel up through a thalamic nucleus, the *arcuate nucleus.* From the thalamus, they travel to the somatosensory cortex. Some fibers from the medulla also project to the lateral hypothalamus and to parts of the limbic system, pathways that might play a role in the pleasurable, or reinforcing, effects of sweet and salty foods.

Although the neural pathway for taste follows the general pattern of the routes for sight and sound, there is probably little interaction among these modalities below the cortical level. Because of the richness of cortical associations, however, we are able not only to savor the taste of an apple but also to delight in its shiny red color and to enjoy the crisp sound as we bite into it. In fact, some neurons in the taste pathways react to mechanical stimulation of the tongue and to temperature changes as well as to taste, an association that is not too surprising since the texture of food is such an important part of the taste experience. However, the routes by which these qualities are segregated and then processed within the gustatory system are not as obvious as those within the other major senses already described in this chapter.

The different taste qualities appear to be represented in different parts of the cortex. Sour and bitter substances stimulate neurons in adjacent areas at one end of the cortical taste area, whereas sweet substances stimulate neurons at the opposite end of the cortex. Salty substances trigger a reaction from neurons all over the cortical taste area (Yamamoto et al., 1981).

Smell

The anatomy of the olfactory sense differs importantly from that of the other senses in that no hierarchical thalamic relay system intervenes between the receptors for olfaction and the olfactory cortical levels of the brain. Rather, axons from the olfactory receptors, which lie in the *olfactory epithelium* at the top of the nasal cavity, terminate in the *olfactory bulbs,* which lie at the base of the brain at the ends of the stalklike *olfactory tracts.* In the olfactory bulbs, the receptor axons form synapses with dendrites from *mitral cells* in clusters, called glomeruli, that are made up of millions of axons. The axons of the mitral cells travel through the olfactory tracts directly to the *piriform cortex* and from there to various parts of the limbic system, primarily to the amygdala and the hypothalamus.

Whereas the neuronal pathways for all the other senses pass through the thalamus on their way to the cortex, in olfaction, neurons go first to the olfactory cortical areas and then project from there "down" to subcortical structures. This olfactory wiring diagram is not quite as perverse as it sounds, however. The olfactory cortical regions accessed by incoming olfactory messages are the most primitive levels of cortex. This cortex is not the specialized six-layered structure that we have been dealing with as we studied the other senses. This more primitive arrangement may underlie the close relationship between taste and smell.

The inclusion of the amygdala and hypothalamus in this pathway helps explain the association, for most animals, of smell and emotion-related behaviors such as sex and aggression. Many species of animals identify potential mates and possible predators or prey by smell. Mothers identify their young by smell. Your dog or cat marks out its territory at home by spraying urine or more specialized olfactory-laden secretions on objects around its boundary in hopes that other animals will smell its marker and keep out.

For human beings, smells seem to have the power of quickly calling up memories—often, emotion-laden ones—associated with those smells. Who can forget the smell of freshly mowed grass, or the recollection of that special person who wore roses in her hair? Much about the workings of olfaction remain a mystery. For example, no one knows how the molecules of the gases we inhale produce action potentials in the receptor neurons. It is presumed that the receptors have special sites to which only molecules of a certain shape may attach (Amoore et al., 1964), but this theory awaits proof. There also seems to be no satisfactory scheme for classifying odors and explaining the differences between them, as there is for classifying tastes, although a number of investigators have attempted to formulate such schemes.

Some scientists, notably the astronomer and science writer Robert Jastrow, believe that mammals' dependence on the sense of smell led to development of the cerebral cortex. About 100 million years ago, certain small shrewlike mammals roamed the earth beneath the greedy gaze of the dinosaurs. Their small eyes and long noses indicated that they were probably nocturnal animals and survived by smell rather than by sight. Jastrow suggests that when survival depends on smell, the survivor's brain must be capable of much more analysis than the brain of an animal whose survival depends mainly on sight. Response to a visual cue is immediate; for the dinosaur, it was essentially in the nature of "see a small moving object, eat it; see a large moving object, flee." In contrast, smell provides only a trace of an object. If it is the scent of prey, was the animal here recently? If so, it must be tracked with patience and skill. If it is the scent of a receptive female, what are her habits? Where would she be likely to go? Experience, memory, would be vital to animals navigating in the dark. They would do better if they memorized a map of their surroundings, with odors as their guide to the map. They would do still better if they could remember and plan. According to this hypothesis, a thin coating of gray matter gradually grew over and covered the "smell brain" of some of these little mammals, and this coating, which allowed the analysis necessary for survival, was the evolutionary ancestor of the cerebral cortex.

Perhaps the direct connection from nose to cortex in human beings reflects this ancient ancestry and accounts for the ability of aromas to evoke vivid memories of places and people.

Once the sensing systems have sent messages to the brain about what an object looks like, sounds like, smells like, feels like, and, in some cases, tastes like, the brain integrates these messages and comes up with a perception. If the object perceived matches one in memory and the perceiver can attach meaning to it—say, the object is a small four-legged creature, furry, colored almost entirely black but with a white stripe down its back—the brain might then begin its task of sending messages to certain muscle groups—probably to the effect of "run!"

Moving

Some thinkers prefer to analyze things in terms of the way they are put together; from the organization of parts, they try to reason out the rules that govern the operation of the whole assembly. Others prefer simply to remember which parts are thought to do what; they strive to get an overall impression of how a system might look or work without worrying about each individual part. In this book, we take the former course, striving for an appreciation of brain organization and the underlying principles by which the parts work together to achieve behavioral function. While hard facts and wiring diagrams have their place, so do living examples of the full range of human actions. With the motor system, however, we come directly up against the need for both kinds of understanding, as we consider how the brain makes the body move.

Very simply, we can view the assembly line for motor-system processing as running in a direction opposite to that of the sensory systems. In the sensory system, information arrives at sensory "detectors" on the periphery and moves up to the cortex. In the motor system, basic information originates in the motor cortex and ends at the periphery, with the actions of muscle units, or "effectors" (see Figure 4.20). The motor system also has its assembly-line hierarchies and its parallel processing components, and it too relies on sensory maps to work effectively. All of this is true whether the movement is a simple one, like scratching your nose, or as elegant and complex as an Olympic diver's performance from the high platform.

Muscles and Joints

Almost all the muscles in your body connect two bones across the joint they share in common. When a motor nerve activates a muscle to contract, the shortening of the muscle moves the end of the bone farthest away from the body closer to the body. Two exceptions to the "two-bone rule" are the extraocular muscles that move the eyeball and the muscles of the tongue. Even these excep-

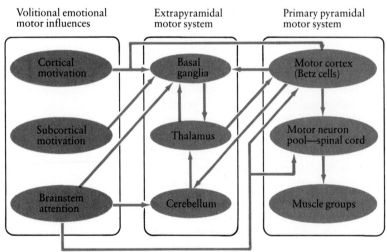

Figure 4.20
The several sets of structures that regulate movement can be broken down into three major groups: (1) the pyramidal motor system (right) that directly links the primary output neurons of the motor cortex (the Betz cells) to specific spinal motor neurons and to specific muscle groups; (2) the extrapyramidal motor system (center) that runs in parallel to monitor the ongoing results of the pyramidal systems commands to move specific joint angles and acts to coordinate the movement programs; and (3) the general "activating" systems (left) that separately bring arousal, and conscious and unconscious motivation to bear on the speed with which motor programs are initiated and executed.

A Perfect 10. Diving is one of three ways to enter the water from dry land. Executing a reverse one-and-a-half somersault with three-and-a-half twists from the 10-meter platform, however, exceeds all useful purposes. Such a dive is an exquisite, highly complex series of motions—motion for the sake of its own difficulty and beauty. In the struggle for perfection, Greg Louganis's body and brain must achieve a command and coordination that push human neurobiological capacities to their outer limits.

tions, however, do not escape another general rule; every muscle that pulls a bone (or an eyeball or a tongue) in one direction is opposed by another muscle whose contraction leads to the opposite movement. The action of opponent pairs of muscle is critical if human beings are to stand erect or maintain a steady position against the pull of gravity.

When the motor nerves are activated, they release a transmitter chemical, *acetylcholine,* that transmits the signal "contract" to targets in the muscle. (Many other neurons also use acetylcholine to send information to different target cells.) The sites on the muscle that respond to acetylcholine are rather specialized large molecules called *receptors,* but these are very different from the structures we have referred to as *receptor cells* in the sensory systems. The actions of acetylcholine at its muscle receptors can be mimicked by nicotine and totally blocked by the plant poison curare. (Curare is an effective hunting weapon because animals struck with a curare-dipped dart are paralyzed and cannot run away.) In the disease called *myasthenia gravis,* the muscles lose their ability to respond to acetylcholine because the acetylcholine receptors on the muscle cells are destroyed.

Most of the time, our muscles move only when we want them to. Therefore, we call such action *voluntary movement* (see Figure 4.21). Even when we make a movement we have chosen to make, we are usually unaware of the specific parts of our general motion. With few exceptions, we do not really know how to speak to one muscle at a time. Nevertheless, in a gross sense, the term "voluntary" distinguishes this class of movements from *reflex movement,* the kind that occurs, for example, if you inadvertently touch a hot stove and jerk your hand away before you experience any pain.

Regardless of the cause of the motor activity, a motor unit can only be activated by a command from its motor nerve. Therefore, we speak of the *motor neuron,* that is, the motor axon and the spinal nerve-cell body

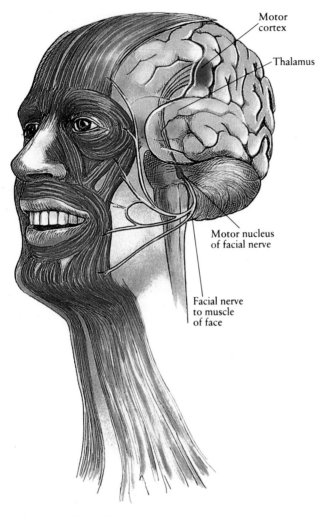

Motor
cortex

Thalamus

Motor nucleus
of facial nerve

Facial nerve
to muscle
of face

Figure 4.21
The voluntary muscles, such as those of the face, are activated when neurons in the facial zone of the motor cortex activate the motor neurons of the facial nerve. The beginning and final positions of the muscles are conveyed through internal muscle receptors to thalamic and other neurons that alter the movement program to achieve the desired final positions.

The number of muscles controlled by a given motor neuron varies, depending on how coarse or how fine the movements of those muscles need to be. The muscles that move the eyes have about one neuron for every three muscle fibers; the ones that move the thigh may have one neuron for every hundred muscle fibers.

The amount of strength that a single muscle can exert depends on the number of contractile fibers it contains. Motor neurons that control single large muscles, such as your biceps or your calf muscles, have many branches in their axons to serve all of the fibers in that muscle, and those axon branches are proportionately larger than those that control the small muscles of your fingers.

The Spinal Cord

The motor neurons and their axons, together with the muscles they control, are termed *motor units*. These motor units are roughly analogous to the first part of a sensory system in that their position is closest to the outside world.

The spinal cord, then, has a processing position similar to that of the retina in the visual system. The spinal cord and the retina are both ensembles of neurons one step removed from the periphery, and both perform substantial integrating and filtering functions using local-circuit neurons. The relatively simple kinds of integration possible at the spinal cord level, however, are just a preview of the more powerful and detailed motor acts the spinal cord can direct when it follows commands from motor centers in the cerebral cortex.

Spinal Reflexes   Muscle fibers also contain sensory nerves. The sense they represent is called *proprioception*, a term that means "self-detection," a sense that helps specify the position and tension of the muscle. These

from which it originates, as the *final common path* for movement. Any single muscle fiber is controlled by only one motor neuron, but one motor neuron may control many muscle fibers through branches in its axon.

sensory receptors lie buried either within the muscle, in a special complex called the "muscle spindle," or in the tendon, where the muscle attaches to a bone. These sensory detectors inform the spinal cord and other higher motor centers how much tension is being developed in the muscle. That information helps establish the current position of the joint angle, which provides a place to start from whenever a new movement must be performed.

When the doctor tests your reflexes during a physical examination, the tap to your kneecap stretches a tendon where the thigh muscle attaches to the top of the patella. This stretch activates the sensory fiber in the tendon, and that, in turn, excites spinal motor neurons that cause the thigh muscle to contract and the foot to fly up (see Figure 4.22). The whole reflex takes place very quickly, usually in less than a second, indicating how quickly these neurons conduct their local affairs.

Other local decisions are also made in the spinal cord—those that occur when a painful stimulus is encountered, for example. If you have ever received an electrical shock while prying a stubborn piece of bread out of your toaster, you probably found your arm "flying" away even before you experienced any pain. Under spinal cord control, a hurt extremity automatically withdraws by flexion of the joints in that limb. In the neurological disorders *multiple sclerosis* and *amyotrophic lateral sclerosis* (the latter is sometimes called Lou Gehrig's disease), one of the problems is that the sensory nerves do not properly activate flexion withdrawal reflexes. As a result, patients suffer from prolonged and frequent encounters with damaging objects.

Reciprocal Control of Opposing Muscles
If you step down on a tack while in a sitting position, you may not even notice that your

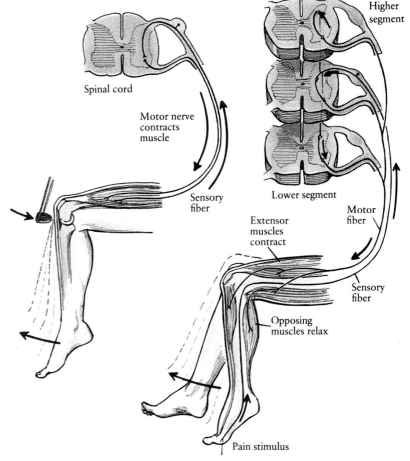

Figure 4.22
When a simple reflex action takes place, sensory stretch receptors of an extensor muscle directly activate the motor neurons of that muscle, causing extensor contraction. In crossed reflex action, the connections within a given segment of the spinal cord allow skin and stretch receptors in the periphery to produce coordinated muscle contractions with no added input from higher motor levels. Depending on the connection patterns, instructions to the motor neurons activate opposing flexors and extensors.

injured foot withdraws by flexion. You may well notice, however, that your other leg responds with the opposite movement, extension of the foot. This opposing movement of the limbs is called a "crossed extension."

The motor neurons that control this reflex are wired together in the spinal cord before birth. (Even a very young infant, if held up vertically with the legs free to move, can execute walking movements that are triggered mainly by the sensory receptors in the skin and the stretch receptors in the tendons.) Sensory nerve fibers in the sole of one foot directly activate spinal motor neurons which then cause the flexor muscles of the insulted leg to contract. Branches of these same sensory fibers also excite the spinal motor neurons that control the extensor muscles of the other leg.

These reciprocal muscle controls and cross innervation patterns in the spinal cord account for the counterbalancing movements of our arms and legs that we use when walking and during almost all our other activities.

What goes on, for instance, when you try to hold your arm out in front of you and point steadily at one fixed spot on the wall? The muscles holding your arm up are opposed by other muscles that keep it from flying up too far. Small reports from the proprioceptive nerves as to their muscle's relative tension and length constantly monitor this balancing act between opposing muscle groups. Sensory receptors within the contracted muscle are activated when that muscle is stretched by the opposing muscle. Tension receptors in the tendon are activated by the tension developed in the muscle as it pulls on the bone. If your shoulder muscles tire, the drooping of your arm stretches the shoulder muscle fibers and excites the motor neurons controlling the shoulder muscle. At the same time, the drop in tension decreases activity in the tendon receptors, and their constant inhibition on the opposing motor neuron is relaxed. The result is increased contraction of the shoulder muscle and a restoration of its pull on the arm.

The internally wired local systems of the spinal cord control all of these adjustments quite automatically once a movement program is selected. The decision to bring the arm up and point it at a spot on the wall, however, has to be initiated by a command from a higher center. The primary source of commands to the motor neurons of the spinal cord lies in the neurons of the motor cortex.

The Motor Cortex

The part of the cortex that initiates movements was first detected during investigations of paralysis in patients with localized brain injuries or strokes. One strip of cortex in each cerebral hemisphere is devoted to motor function. These two motor strips lie adjacent to the primary strips of cortex devoted to somatosensory maps of the body surface in each of the hemispheres. At one time, this cortical motor region was thought to be organized like the adjacent cortical sensory region—that is, according to a map that reflected the surface of the body. The notion seemed reasonable because when small regions of the motor cortex were stimulated, small muscle movements could be detected in certain parts of the body. This map, like that for touch (see figure on facing page), was also disproportionate to the surface of the body, with the lips, hands, and fingers taking up much more of the cortical area than the legs, trunk, and back muscles.

More recent microelectrode recordings from individual nerve cells in the motor region suggest another explanation for the apparent mapping of points that activate specific muscles. The neurons of the motor cortex, like those in the somatosensory cortex, seem to have a vertical, columnar organization. Fine-electrode recordings indicate that vertically related cells in the motor cortex, forming a functional motor column, do seem to control related muscle groups. Strange as it may seem, further studies show that adjacent neurons in a motor column behave differently during the performance of movements: some neurons are activated, some are inhibited, and some do not change at all.

It is currently believed that the important function of the cortical motor column is to achieve a specific joint position, not simply to activate specific related muscles. Depending upon the starting position of the joint, a given column might need to activate flexor muscles or extensor muscles in order to bring the joint to the desired angle. Viewed this way, a cortical motor column is a small ensemble of motor neurons that influence all the muscles acting on a particular joint. To extend this idea just a little, we can say that the cortex codes our movements, not by instructing a series of muscles to contract, but by giving a command to achieve a certain joint position.

The cortical neurons that communicate directly with the motor neurons of the spinal cord are called *Betz cells,* after the nineteenth-century Russian anatomist who first described them. Lying deep in the motor cortex, they are among the largest neurons in the brain, and their axons converge in a large nerve-fiber bundle called the *pyramidal tract.* As the Betz-cell axons descend to the spinal cord, this bundle crosses over from the side of the cortex in which its fibers originate to the other side of the spinal cord. That is why a stroke or lesion in the right motor cortex paralyzes the left side of the body.

Where does the excitation that drives the motor cortex units come from? The answer now appears to be that it arises from units of the somatosensory cortex at a very late stage in the processing of all forms of sensory information. Highly abstracted information about the position of the body's limbs and

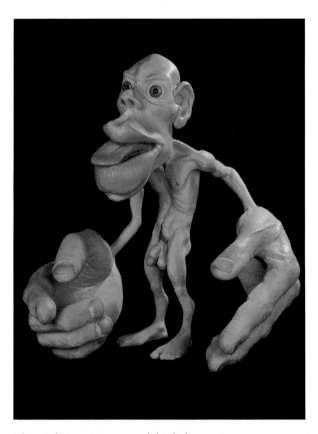

The misshapen appearance of this little man (a "homunculus") reflects the disproportionate areas of the somatic sensory cortex devoted to different surfaces of the body. Note that tongue, lips, face, and digits of the hands receive a far greater area within the cortex that would be represented by their proportion of the body's surface area.

the need to initiate movements rapidly is available at this stage, and this information, which includes a full awareness of current joint angles and muscle tension, guides the sensorimotor cortex in activating specific movements.

To complete our survey of the motor system, we need to look briefly at two other important structures that also regulate the

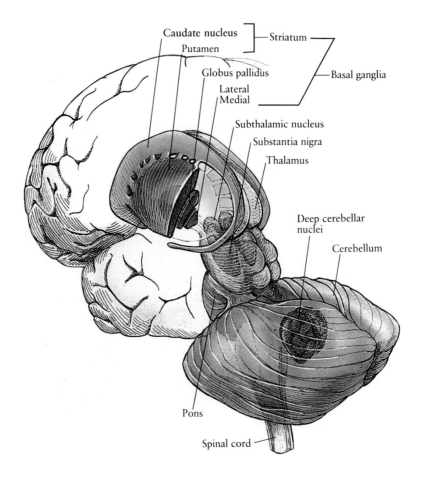

Caudate nucleus
Putamen
— Striatum
Globus pallidus
— Basal ganglia
Lateral
Medial
Subthalamic nucleus
Substantia nigra
Thalamus
Deep cerebellar nuclei
Cerebellum
Pons
Spinal cord

Figure 4.23
The basal ganglia, an alliance of brain places linked together within the extrapyramidal components of the motor system. The information flowing among the basal ganglia coordinates large muscular movements, initiating and terminating them.

performance of specific, directed voluntary movements: the *basal ganglia* and the *cerebellum.*

The Basal Ganglia

The term "basal ganglia" sounds more obscure than it is. The name simply refers to the location (at the *base* of the cortex) of certain collections of nerve cells (*ganglia*) that appear early in brain development (see Chapter 2). Within the basal ganglia are four separate units: the *striatum*, the *pallidum*, the *subthalamic nucleus*, and the *substantia nigra*

(see Figure 4.23). These names refer either to the location of the structure (*subthalamic*, "under the thalamus") or to its appearance (*striatum*, "striped"; *pallidum*, "pale"; *nigra*, "black").

The striatum receives information, including all forms of sensory information and information about the state of activity in the motor system, from almost all the regions of the cerebral cortex. Its "stripes" come from the heavily myelinated axons of the connections from the motor and sensory cerebral cortices. The striatum also receives raw sensory information from the thalamic nuclei before it is processed by the sensory cortex. A third source of input is a single-source/divergent neural connection from the substantia nigra. This last neural link is one of the few affecting the motor system whose neurotransmitter, *dopamine,* is known, and it therefore deserves further attention.

In patients with Parkinson's disease, the dopamine-transmitting neurons of the substantia nigra die. Early in the twentieth century, patients that succumbed to Parkinson's disease were found at post mortem to have lost the black pigment for which the substantia nigra is named. Once the neurotransmitter made by these dying neurons was identified as dopamine, this loss of color could be attributed to the loss of these neurons and of dopamine. This loss was then directly connected with the onset of symptoms: an inability to initiate voluntary movements, accompanied by tremulous motions of the head, hands, and arms when the patient sits quietly. Although the dopamine innervation is more dense in the striatum than in any other brain region, it still accounts for probably less than one-fifth of the synaptic connections there. Nevertheless, the loss of dopamine fibers and dopamine-mediated control is devastating to the smooth operation of the motor system. Patients can, however, be successfully treated for a while by bolstering their declining stores of dopamine with the drug L-DOPA (dihydroxyphenylalanine).

Recordings from neurons in the striatum show that their activity begins just before the initiation of a particular kind of movement, a slow, directed movement from one large region of space to another. When you close your eyes and try to touch the tip of your nose, for example, the largest part of the movement—bringing the hand from where it was to a position very close to your nose—is what draws upon activity in the basal ganglia. It is also the kind of movement lost by patients with Parkinson's disease.

Animals in which the dopamine neurons to the striatum are destroyed experimentally go through a critical period during which they seem unable to begin motor acts, even critical ones like eating and drinking. If they are offered strongly scented food, the increased sensory activation in part helps them overcome this deficiency. Human patients with Parkinson's disease can also temporarily overcome their motor defects if confronted with an emergency—a car coming toward them as they are about to step off the curb, for example. Patients with Parkinson's disease also show problems in initiating speech or eye movements, a fact suggesting that dopamine is also needed for proper function of motor control within other parts of the motor system, such as the motor cortex, spinal cord, or subcortical motivational systems (see Figure 4.20).

Parkinson's patients must take L-DOPA for the rest of their lives. An experimental dopamine-neuron transplant treatment now being tried in Sweden holds some promise for a more permanent treatment in the future.

The Cerebellum

As its name implies, the *cerebellum* (the word is a diminutive form of cerebrum and means "little cerebrum") is indeed a small brain. It has an extremely regular structure, the surface of which is greatly expanded relative to its volume by virtue of its many folds (see Figure 4.24). Sliced and viewed from the side, its individual small, folded lobes, which look something like leaves, are called "folia." An identical four-layered cellular structure curves through every folium. One of the two most prominent layers of this structure contains very large neurons, the

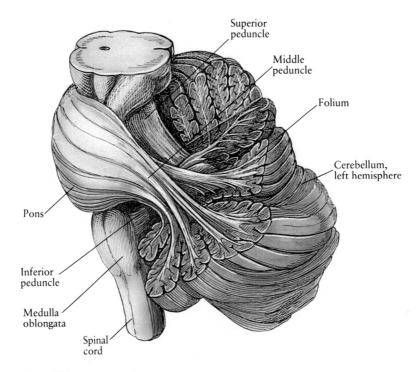

Superior
peduncle

Middle
peduncle

Folium

Cerebellum,
left hemisphere

Pons

Inferior
peduncle

Medulla
oblongata

Spinal
cord

Figure 4.24
The midline surface of the cerebellum as viewed from the left, showing the leaflike subdivisions, or folia. Within each folium, a highly redundant layered structure of fiber-rich and cell-rich zones are found. Each folium directs muscular activity within specific muscular groups and specific regions of the limbs and trunk. The superior, middle, and inferior peduncles are the routes by which axons from the pons and medulla enter the cerebellum, and by which cerebellar fibers exit.

Purkinje cells, which form a single layer. Another layer contains *granule-cell neurons* that cluster, several cells deep, just beneath the Purkinje neurons.

Information comes to the cerebellum from the cerebral cortex, from the brainstem, and from the spinal cord. The spinal cord carries up information about the position of the limbs, trunk, head, neck, and eyes, all of which is integrated by the Purkinje cells. Purkinje neurons seem to fire very rapidly and in bursts much of the time, perhaps indicating their constant surveillance of trunk, limb, and head location and position. The Purkinje

neurons then send their output to the *deep cerebellar nuclei* of large neurons buried deep within the cerebellum. Information from these nuclei modifies the activity of neurons in the motor cortex.

Despite its elegant structure and its very well-worked-out cellular circuitry, the exact role of the cerebellum in motor function is far from understood. Coarse experiments on subjects in whom the cerebellum is either injured or stimulated suggest the importance of this structure in controlling the muscle tone needed to hold a posture. Tests given to people suspected of drunkenness—walking a straight line and being able to stand still with their eyes shut—directly evaluate the cerebellum's success at this task.

In addition, during programs of fine movements the cerebellum determines where the parts of the body are at any given moment and compares the actual position of a body part to where it ought to be at that point. It is very much as though the cerebellum possesses a carbon copy of the pattern of activity that drives the neurons of the motor cortex during a movement. The cerebellum adjusts patterns of activity in the motor cortex and the spinal cord and smooths out their finer motions. When you move your finger to touch the end of your nose, the basal ganglia activate the large movement of your hand toward the general area of your nose, but it is the cerebellum that actually guides the final approach to an on-the-button landing.

The cerebellum is also critical for the performance of rapid, consecutive, simultaneous movements, such as the sophisticated movements of the trained typist or musician, or the somewhat coarser task of patting your head and rubbing your chest at the same time.

Review and Conclusions

When we began this chapter, it seemed sensible to categorize sensing and moving as two independent operations. Specific sensory systems, organized along roughly comparable lines, process each kind of sensory information. Specialized receptor cells in the skin or in one of the special sensory organs detect physical events occurring in the external world. These events are then transformed into neuronal activity that is processed by neurons connected in highly ordered circuits through which information flows sequentially. The several different qualities of visual information (such as movement, color, and form) are thus processed sequentially along separate but parallel channels, which eventually combine at the level of the cerebral cortex. Other forms of sensory information may also be handled along similar parallel lines.

The motor system also treats neural information sequentially. It operates in an ordered fashion, from initiation of movement in the motor cortex to activation of muscle fibers controlling joint position and stability by way of the spinal motor neurons. Parallel modifying systems in the cerebellum and basal ganglia provide coordinated and polished movement programs.

The sheer number of elements that the brain uses to discriminate among the qualities of a sensory stimulus and to move the parts of the body quickly, smoothly, and accurately in response may mask an important conclusion. The sensory and motor systems may be independent of each other, but very few sensory programs end without initiating or modifying movement. Sensing as an end in itself is rare, except, perhaps, when human beings try to analyze their own experience. Likewise, movement for movement's sake is usually undertaken only by athletes or dancers.

Globally, then, the brain maintains the organism by sensing its needs and initiating the actions necessary to satisfy them. But human brains also have an enormous capacity to compare the present with the past. From a very large number of sensory samples, we draw conclusions that almost immediately make clear which motor acts are necessary and which are not. Numerous parallel processing systems provide us with many overlapping versions of an immediate situation, filling in from past experience possible missing pieces, just as our visual systems fill in for us the small but significant hole in our visual image of the world.

In the next chapter, we turn to the ways in

which the brain also monitors the internal systems of the body, and how these internal systems modify the way we see the world and decide how to deal with it.

Summary

In this chapter, the following points stand out:

1. The systems responsible for sensing the external world and moving through it are composed of hierarchically organized, interacting neuronal groups.

2. For sensory systems, peripheral receptors exist to detect specific physical stimuli (light, sound, pressure, or temperature) or chemical stimuli (molecules making up, e.g., salt or sugar or vapors coming from car exhausts).

3. The receptor cells synapse on neurons that relay the information through modality-specific pathways that eventually reach the thalamic nuclei for each modality (except olfaction) and ultimately a primary cortical sensory area.

4. The component qualities of visual and auditory information that are recognized by the activity of different peripheral receptors are separated out, and sent along through separate, parallel thalamic and cortical structures.

5. Through the integrative actions of cortico-cortical connections, information processed by the primary sensory cortical areas is further processed and combined in visual, auditory, and other association fields. The recombined visual and auditory information then constitutes our information for perception of the events in the world around us.

6. Selected lesions of the association fields can produce partial losses of selected types of sensory information (e.g., the inability to recognize objects by touch).

7. The motor system also operates on a vertically oriented hierarchy, with commands to move arising in the motor cortex and stimulating selected neurons in the spinal cord and the muscles to which they are connected.

8. Parallel circuits arising from the spinal cord coordinate and monitor the position of body parts while they are in motion and coordinate the limbs and digits on their way to the intended new positions; this function is achieved through the extrapyramidal motor system, especially the cerebellum and basal ganglia.

9. Lesions to the primary motor system produce total paralysis of muscle groups. Lesions to the extrapyramidal motor system produce uncoordinated and often involuntary movements.

Further Reading

Hubel, D. H., and Wiesel, T. N. 1979. Brain mechanisms of vision. *Scientific American*, September 1979. An exploration of the architecture of the primary visual cortex in terms of how the various cells function—individually and in organized groups—as they process sensory information.

Evarts, Edward V. 1979. Brain mechanisms of movement. *Scientific American*, September 1979. The differences between the brain's role in reflex and in voluntary movement are revealed by studies using microelectrodes implanted in the brains of active monkeys. The importance of feedback signals from muscles to brain is explained.

Neisser, U. 1968. The processes of vision. *Scientific American*, September 1968. This article speculates about the constructive processes the brain uses when it processes visual information to arrive at perceptions.

Gibson, Eleanor J., and Spelke, E. S. 1983. The development of perception. In P. H. Mussen (ed.), *Handbook of Child Psychology,* Vol. III. New York: Wiley. Human beings are born with the intricate visual apparatus described in this chapter. They are able to process visual sensations, but how do they gain the capacity to perceive and to derive meaning from these sensations?

Kandel, E. and Schwartz, J., eds. 1985. *Principles of Neural Science,* 2nd edition. New York: Elsevier Scientific Publishing. Part V, Sensory Systems of the Brain: Sensation and Perception, pp. 285–426, and Part VI, Motor Systems of the Brain: Reflex and Voluntary Control of Movement, pp. 427–536. An advanced textbook coverage.

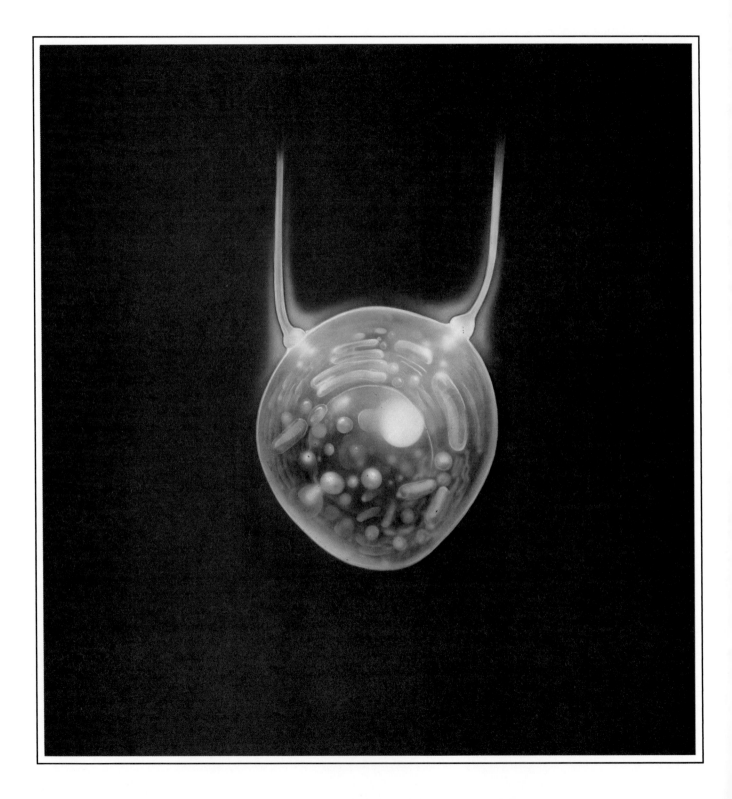

5

Homeostasis: Maintaining the Internal Environment

5

The world around us is constantly changing. Winter winds force us to wear heavy jackets and gloves. Central heating forces us to take them off. Summer sun reduces our need to preserve body heat until efficient air-conditioning turns the tables on us. Yet on any given day, whatever the temperature outside, the individual body temperatures of every healthy person you know would probably register within a tenth of a degree of each other. The bodies of human beings and other warm-blooded animals regulate their temperatures to a constant internal value of around 99°F, although that rises and falls a few tenths of a degree in a daily rhythm.

Most people differ in their eating habits. Some like a good breakfast, a light lunch, and a hearty dinner with dessert. Others skip meals throughout the day, or take a large lunch and a nap in the middle of the afternoon. Some people snack all the time; others seem scarcely to care about eating at all. Yet if you measured the blood-sugar levels of everybody in your English class, their individual measurements would probably all fall within a range of just around one-thousandth of a gram (1 mg) per milliliter of blood despite the wide ranges in diet and eating habits.

This precise regulation of body temperature and of blood-glucose levels are just two examples of the many crucial body functions that fall under the command of the nervous system. The fluids surrounding all our cells are also continuously monitored and regulated to an extraordinarily accurate level of near-constancy.

The process that keeps the internal environment constant is known as *homeostasis* (*homeo,* "same" or "similar"; *stasis,* "stabil-ity" or "balance"). The autonomic and diffuse enteric segments of the peripheral nervous system as well as the central nervous system, acting directly on the body through the pituitary gland and the endocrine organs, have primary responsibilities for homeostatic regulation. Together, these systems integrate the needs of the body with the demands of the external environment. (That statement should sound familiar. We have used just those words to describe the main responsibility of the brain. The central and peripheral nervous systems work together to sample and regulate our internal environment as well.)

The nineteenth-century French physiologist Claude Bernard, who spent his career studying the process of digestion and the regulation of blood flow, viewed the fluids of the body as the *milieu interne,* the "internal environment." In every individual organism, the concentration of specific salts and normal temperatures may be slightly different, but within a species, the internal environment of individuals conforms to the uniform standards for that species. Only momentary and modest deviations can be tolerated if the organism is to remain healthy and contribute to the survival of the species. Walter B. Cannon, a foremost American physiologist of the mid-twentieth century, expanded on Bernard's concept of the internal environment. He viewed the independence of an individual from continuous changes in the external world as arising from *homeostatic mechanisms* that work to maintain a uniform internal environment.

The capacity of an organism to overcome the demands imposed by its external environment varies considerably from species to species. Human beings, who can use more complex behaviors to complement their internal homeostatic mechanisms, appear to have the greatest freedom of all. Yet certain animals outstrip human beings in species-specific abilities: some, like the polar bear, withstand more cold; some, like desert spiders and lizards, withstand more heat; and some, like the dromedary, tolerate longer periods of water deprivation. In this chapter, we shall examine some of the structures responsible for endowing us with a measure of freedom from the changing physical demands of the world. We shall also look more closely at the regulatory mechanisms that maintain the constancy of our internal environment.

The Autonomic Nervous System

Certain organizational features of the sensory and motor systems make a good place to start our examination of the internal regulatory systems. All three divisions of the autonomic nervous sytem—the sympathetic division, the parasympathetic division, and the diffuse enteric division—have "sensory" and "motor" components. The sensory components monitor the internal world, while the motor components activate or inhibit the target structures that do the actual adjusting.

Intramuscular sensory receptors, along with sensory receptors in the tendon and elsewhere, detect pressure and stretch. Together they constitute a kind of internal sensing system that helps to guide our movements. Receptors of the sensory systems used in homeostasis work in a more general fashion: they detect chemical variations in blood composition or tension changes in the vascular system and in the "hollow organs"—the intestinal tract or the bladder, for example. These "sensory" limbs of the autonomic nervous system that pick up internal informa-

In the gravity-free, oxygen-free environment of outer space, astronauts wear special suits that contain heat loss, substitute for the pull of gravity, and maintain adequate oxygen pressure for brain function. On earth, these functions are achieved automatically by the brain and peripheral and autonomic nervous systems.

tion are organized very much like the sensory system that picks up information coming from the external surface of the body. Their incoming receptor neurons make their first synaptic relays within the spinal cord.

The "motor" limb of the autonomic nervous system carries outgoing impulses that dictate internal adjustments. This outgoing system begins with special autonomic preganglionic neurons in the spinal cord. Such an arrangement loosely resembles that of the spinal motor neurons in the motor system. Our major focus in this chapter is on these "motor" components of the autonomic system, which innervate the smooth muscles of the heart, blood vessels, and gut and cause them to constrict or relax. These same fibers also innervate glands and cause them to secrete hormones.

The autonomic nervous system has two large divisions: the *sympathetic* and the *parasympathetic*. Both divisions have an architectural feature that we have not encountered until now. The neurons that direct the internal muscles and glands are located entirely *outside* the central nervous system in small encapsulated clusters of cells called *ganglia*. In the autonomic nervous system, therefore, an additional structure exists between the spinal cord and the final target structure.

Autonomic neurons in the spinal cord integrate the sensory information from the viscera and from other sources. On this basis, they then regulate the activity of the neurons of the autonomic ganglia. The spinal-cord-to-ganglia axons are termed *preganglionic fibers*. The neurotransmitter for this link from the spinal cord to the autonomic ganglion neurons in both sympathetic and parasympathetic ganglia is almost always *acetylcholine*, the same transmitter used by the motor neurons in the spinal cord to exert direct control over the skeletal muscles. (When tobacco smokers inhale, part of their pleasurable response depends on nicotine stimulating those preganglionic acetylcholine neurons that activate the sympathetic nervous system.) The axons that emerge from the neurons of the autonomic ganglia, the *postganglionic fibers,* then run directly to their target organs, where they branch extensively and innervate their target tissues.

The sympathetic and parasympathetic divisions of the autonomic nervous system do differ, however, (1) in where their preganglionic fibers emerge from the spinal cord, (2) in how close their ganglia are to their target organs, (3) in the neurotransmitter that the postganglionic neurons use to regulate the activity of their targets, and (4) in their functions. It is to these points that we now turn.

The Sympathetic Nervous System

The sympathetic division receives its preganglionic control from neurons in the *thoracic* and *lumbar* areas of the spinal cord. Its ganglia lie relatively near the spinal cord, and its postganglionic fibers diverge over great distances to reach the cells in their appropriate target organs (see Figure 5.1). The major transmitter for the postganglionic sympathetic nerves is *norepinephrine,* one of the catecholamines that acts as a neurotransmitter in the central nervous system as well as in the peripheral nervous system.

A simple way to recall the targets of the sympathetic nervous system and its actions on them is to think of what happens to an aroused animal that must mobilize for "flight or fight." The pupils dilate to allow more light to enter. Heart rate picks up, and the increased contractile force of the heartbeat drives more blood. Vascular channels shift blood away from the skin and intestinal organs toward the muscles and the brain. Motility of the gastrointestinal system decreases and digestive processes slow down. The muscles along the air passages of the lungs relax, and respiratory rate increases, allowing more air to be moved in and out. Liver and fat cells are activated to furnish more glucose and fatty acids—the body's high-energy fuels—and the pancreas is instructed to release less insulin. This allows the brain to draw off a sizable fraction of the glucose entering the bloodstream because, unlike other organs, it does not require insulin to utilize blood glucose. The neurotransmitter that triggers these changes is norepinephrine.

An additional system also acts more generally to ensure that these changes take

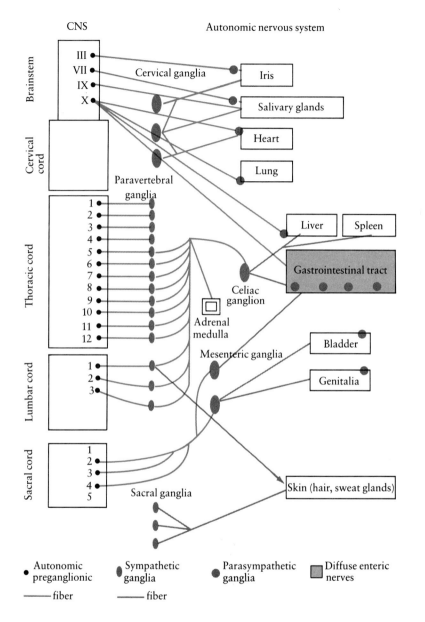

CNS   Autonomic nervous system

Figure 5.1

Basic elements of the autonomic nervous system. Preganglionic neurons, all of which use the transmitter acetylcholine, arise in two major divisions: the cranio-sacral preganglionic parasympathetic fibers from the cranial nerve nuclei (oculomotor [III], facial [VII], glossopharyngeal [IX] and vagus [X] neurons) and from the sacral spinal cord; and the thoracolumbar sympathetic fibers (from the indicated spinal segment levels). The length of these preganglionics is quite long for the parasympathetic fibers, whose target ganglia lie within or adjacent to their limited visceral targets (note that the vagus nerve innervates viscera from the heart to the lower gastrointestinal tract). The postganglionic parasympathetic fibers are also cholinergic, with coexisting neuropeptides in many cases. The preganglionic sympathetic fibers either connect with postganglionic neurons within the ganglia closest to the spinal cord (the paravertebral chain), or converge from several spinal levels on one of the more distantly placed ganglia (on the cervical, celiac, or mesenteric ganglia or on the adrenal medulla, a sympathetic ganglion that secretes its "postganglionic" catecholamine message directly into the bloodstream). The postganglionic sympathetic neurons and their very long postganglionic fibers all transmit signals with the transmitter norepinephrine and have coexisting peptides as well. For simplicity, the sympathetic innervation of the skin is shown only for the lumbar ganglia but occurs at all levels. The preganglionic parasympathetic fibers through their distal postganglionic neurons and the postganglionic sympathetic fibers also link directly to the diffuse enteric neurons of the gastrointestinal tract. The visceral afferent sensory fibers that bring information from the viscera back to the brain travel largely within the vagus nerve bundle but are not shown.

place: The two adrenals sit like small caps on the tops of the kidneys. In the middle, or medulla, of each adrenal is a separate group of cells innervated by preganglionic sympathetic fibers. The cells of the adrenal medulla are embryologically derived from the same neural-crest cells that produce the sympathetic ganglia, and thus the medulla is a component of the sympathetic nervous system. When activated by the preganglionic fibers, medullary cells secrete their own norepinephrine and epinephrine directly into the

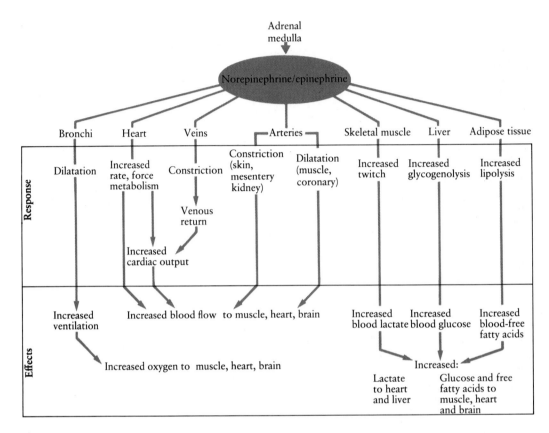

Figure 5.2
When autonomic nerve activity leads the adrenal medulla to secrete catechol-
amines, these messengers circulate through the bloodstream to influence the activity
of several different target tissues. These global signals assure a coordinated re-
sponse of widely separated organs. Glycogenolysis is the process by which glycogen
is broken down to glucose; lipolysis is the hydrolysis—decomposition by reaction
with water—of fat.

bloodstream, for broad distribution to sympathetic targets (see Figure 5.2).

Blood-borne chemical signals such as
these are referred to as *hormones* (literally,
"messengers"). Later in this chapter, we consider other hormone signals from other
glands. The collection of glands that secrete
their hormones into the bloodstream are referred to as the *endocrine glands,* or more
generally, the *endocrine system.*

The Parasympathetic Division of the Nervous System

The parasympathetic division receives its
preganglionic information from the *brainstem* (the "cranial component" of the system) and from the *lower,* or *sacral, segments*
of the spinal cord (see again Figure 5.1 on
page 141). Its preganglionic fibers include an
especially important nerve trunk called the

vagus nerve, the numerous branches of which supply all of the parasympathetic innervation of the heart, lungs, and intestinal tract. (The vagus nerve also carries sensory information coming in from these regions back to the preganglionic level.) The preganglionic parasympathetic axons are very long because their ganglia are generally located very close to or within the tissues they innervate.

Like the preganglionic fibers, the postganglionic fibers in this division also use the transmitter *acetylcholine.* But unlike the target responses of the other acetylcholine-producing fibers—the preganglionic fibers in both sympathetic and parasympathetic divisions—the targets of the postganglionic parasympathetic division are not sensitive to nicotine. They are activated by a different chemical—the drug muscarine—and blocked by another—the drug atropine. The important point here is that these differing target response patterns allow the use of drugs designed to act selectively to block or stimulate just the acetylcholine signals recognized by parasympathetically innervated glands or muscles.

Parasympathetic activity in the body sets the stage for "rest and recuperation." At its extreme, the overall effect of parasympathetic activity throughout our organ systems resembles the state of inactivity that follows a heavy meal. Stepped-up blood flow to the intestinal tract increases the movement of food through the gut and the secretion of digestive enzymes. Heart rate and the strength of heart contraction diminish, the pupils of the eyes constrict, and the airways narrow as their mucosal secretions increase. The urinary bladder also constricts. Taken together, these actions "restore" the body to the relaxed state it enjoyed before a period of "fight-or-flight" activity. (These phenomena are illustrated in Figure 5.1 and in Chapter 7).

Comparative Features of the Sympathetic and Parasympathetic Divisions

The sympathetic system, with its very long postganglionic fibers, presents a pattern of innervation that differs quite dramatically from that of the parasympathetic system, with its long preganglionic fibers and its ganglia located near or within its target organs. Many internal organs, such as the lungs, the heart, the salivary glands, the bladder, and the genital organs, receive innervation from both of the major divisions. (These organs are said to be "dually innervated.") Other tissues, such as some of the smaller arteries, receive only sympathetic innervation. In general, one might be tempted to say that the two divisions work alternatively: one or the other dominates, depending on the activities of the body and the commands of the higher autonomic centers.

This view is not completely correct, however. Both systems are active to some degree all the time. The fact that a target organ such as the heart or the iris can respond to both systems simply reflects the complementary aspects of the whole autonomic nervous system. For example, if you become very angry, your rising blood pressure activates the pressure receptors in your carotid arteries. The integrating center of the cardiovascular system in the lower medulla (see Figure 5.4) detects the signal. Output from this center then activates the preganglionic parasympathetic fibers of the vagus nerve to slow down the heart rate and decrease the force of heart contraction. At the same time, other output from this same vascular coordinating center depresses the activity of the sympathetic fibers and counteracts the rise in blood pressure through another channel.

To what degree is either division essential to adaptive response and, ultimately, to survival? Surprisingly, both animals and humans can tolerate an almost complete surgical removal of the sympathetic nervous system without any apparent ill effects, so long as the subjects are kept in carefully controlled environments. This form of surgical treatment has been advocated for certain forms of unremitting hypertension. However, outside the protective setting of the hospital or the laboratory, subjects who have undergone such surgery can tolerate very few environmental demands. They cannot regulate their body temperatures when exposed to heat or cold, they cannot regulate their blood pressure when they lose blood, and they are, in general, very prone to rapid fatigue when faced with any form of increased muscular workload.

The Diffuse Enteric Nervous System

Recent research has demonstrated the existence of a third major division of the autonomic nervous system. This division, the *diffuse enteric nervous system,* is responsible for gastrointestinal innervation and coordination, and it is independent of, but modifiable by, the sympathetic and parasympathetic systems. The diffuse enteric nervous system seems to be a third, separate, neural control unit between the autonomic postganglionic nerves and the glands and muscles of the gastrointestinal system.

The neural ganglia of the diffuse enteric system innervate the muscular walls of the gut. These neurons use acetylcholine and combine it with several of the neuropeptides as well. Axons from the cells in these ganglia directly activate the contractions of the circular and longitudinal muscles that propel food through the digestive system, a process called *peristalsis.* Thus these ganglia govern the pattern of the peristaltic movements locally. The presence of a food mass in the intestine, stretching the wall of the gut slightly, causes constriction of the segment immediately above the mass and relaxation of the segment immediately below. This results in

the mass of food being pushed lower. Activity of parasympathetic or sympathetic innervation in the gut, however, can modify enteric ganglionic activity. Parasympathetic activity increases peristalsis, while sympathetic activity decreases it.

The transmitter this system uses to excite the intestinal smooth muscle is *acetylcholine.* Inhibitory commands leading to relaxation, however, appear to be transmitted by several different substances, only a few of which have been identified. These neurotransmitters in the gut include at least three that also act independently in the central nervous system: the *endorphins* (see pages 223–225), *somatostatin* (see page 151), and *substance P* (see page 223).

Central Regulation of the Autonomic Nervous System

The degree of hierarchical control that the central nervous system exerts over the autonomic system is far looser than the control it exerts over the sensory and skeletal motor systems. The brain regions that connect most directly with autonomic function are the *hypothalamus* and the *brainstem,* especially that segment of the brainstem just above the spinal cord, the *medulla oblongata.* It is from these regions that we can trace the major input connections to the sympathetic and parasympathetic preganglionic autonomic neurons at the spinal level.

The Hypothalamus   The hypothalamus is one of the brain regions whose overall structure and organization appear to have remained fairly constant in the brains of vertebrates in many widely separated phyla.

In general, the hypothalamus is thought to be the principal location for visceral integrative functions. Neuronal systems in the hypothalamus feed directly into the circuits that activate the preganglionic limbs of the autonomic nerves. In addition, this same brain region takes direct control over the entire endocrine system through specific neurons in the hypothalamus that regulate the hormones secreted from the anterior lobe of the pituitary gland. The endocrine-regulating neurons of the hypothalamus send their axons to a highly vascular point on the lower surface of the hypothalamus called the *median eminence*. This point is directly adjacent to the stalk of the pituitary gland (see Figure 5.3). A special system of blood vessels, called the *pituitary portal circulation*, links the median eminence with the anterior pituitary. When endocrine-regulating neurons of the hypothalamus are active, their nerve terminals in the median eminence release their transmitter signals into this very limited circulatory system, to be carried directly and exclusively to the anterior pituitary.

The terminal axons of other hypothalamic neurons actually make up the posterior lobe of the pituitary. The transmitters from those axons are released from the posterior pituitary directly into the bloodstream as the hormones (1) *vasopressin*, which increases blood pressure during extreme emergencies when fluid or blood is lost and which also decreases urinary excretion of water (vasopressin has also been called the *antidiuretic* hormone), and (2) *oxytocin*, which activates the contraction of the uterus during the final stages of labor.

The hypothalamus performs myriad functions, some of them directly traceable to distinct clusters of neurons, or nuclei, within the structure. However, much of the hypothalamus is better considered as a collection of zones without clear-cut boundaries (see Figure 5.3). Three of these zones do appear to contain some definable nuclei, and we can talk about these structures in terms of their functions.

The *periventricular zone* is immediately adjacent to the third cerebral ventricle, which runs through the center of the hypo-

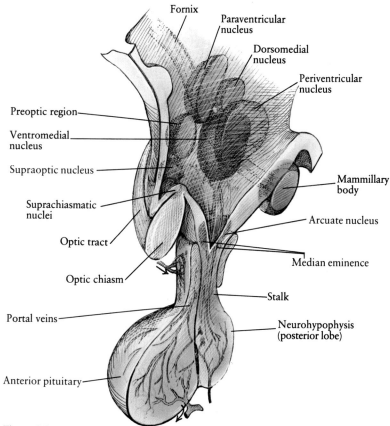

Figure 5.3
Structures of the hypothalamus and pituitary. The major functional zones of the hypothalamus are illustrated in simplified form. The various nuclei and other neuronal places within each zone are shown as if they were enclosed within a relatively narrow and oblong envelope running from front to back of an interior brain space.

thalamus. The cells lining the ventricles deliver information to cells in the periventricular zone about important internal properties that may require regulation: temperature, salt concentration, and levels of hormones being secreted by the thyroid, adrenals, or gonads upon instructions from the pituitary, for example.

The *medial zone* contains most of the neuronal nuclei that regulate the way the hypothalamus controls the endocrine system by means of pituitary output. In a crude sense, then, cells in the periventricular zone check on whether the commands issued to the pituitary by cells in the medial zone were, in fact, carried out.

Through diffusely placed neurons in the *lateral zone,* the hypothalamus receives higher-level control from the cerebral cortex and limbic system, as well as sensory information coming up from the centers in the medulla oblongata that coordinate respiratory and cardiovascular activity. The lateral zone provides a place where higher brain centers can consciously override the more-or-less automatic hypothalamic responses to variations detected in the internal environment. For example, sets of information from both the internal and external environment are compared in the cortex. If the cortex concludes that this is an inappropriate time and place for feeding, sensory information on low blood sugar and one's empty stomach will be filed away until a more opportune moment. Input from the limbic system is less likely to override the hypothalamus. More probably it adds emotional and motivational qualities to interpretations of external sensory signals or compares a current status report on the world with information from similar situations in the past.

Together with its cortical and limbic components, the hypothalamus also manages a variety of routine integrating activities, and it does so over much longer periods of time than its moment-by-moment monitoring activities take. The hypothalamus anticipates what the body will need on a normal daily schedule—it gets the endocrine system ready to be fully active just as we wake up, for example. It also monitors the hormones that the ovaries release as the reproductive cycle progresses, and issues the commands that prepare the uterus to receive a fertilized ovum. In migrating birds and hibernating mammals, the hypothalamus, which detects day length, coordinates activity over cycles lasting many months. (These aspects of the central control of internal functions are considered in greater detail in Chapters 6 and 7.)

The Medulla Oblongata   The entire hypothalamus makes up less than 5 percent of the mass of the brain. This small amount of tissue, however, contains centers that maintain virtually all the body's functions except for spontaneous respiratory movements, blood pressure, and cardiac rhythm. These last functions depend on the vitality of the medulla oblongata (see Figure 5.4). In patients with severe brain trauma, so-called "brain death" occurs when all signs of cortical electrical activity have disappeared and when hypothalamic and medullary controls have been lost—even though artificial respiration may maintain adequate oxygenation of spontaneously circulated blood.

The Endocrine System

An *endocrine organ* is one that secretes a substance directly into the bloodstream to regulate the cellular activity of certain other organs. (The term derives from *endo,* "within," and *krinein,* "to separate" or "secrete.") Endocrine organs are called *glands,* and the substances they secrete are called *hormones,* from the Greek word for "messenger." Each hormone adjusts the level of performance of its specific target-cell systems, usually increasing their rates of activity temporarily.

Hormones are very potent, so it takes very little of them to do the job. Cells that respond to hormones are genetically endowed with special surface molecules, or molecular "receptors," that detect even very low hormone concentrations. Once the cells receive the hormone, they initiate the series of internal adjustments that the hormone dictates.

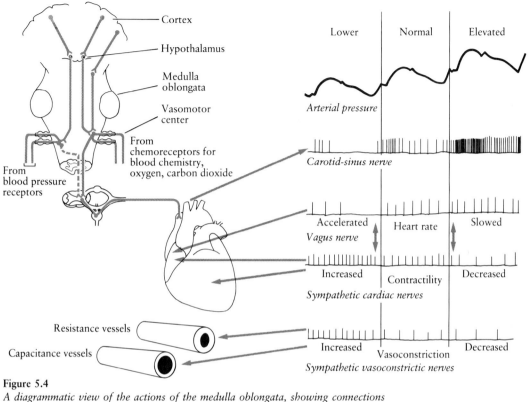

Figure 5.4
A diagrammatic view of the actions of the medulla oblongata, showing connections from various internal organs to the brainstem and reticular formation. Sensory signals from these visceral organs regulate the degree of arousal and attention that the brain focuses on external events. Such signals also initiate specific behavioral programs by which the organism adjusts for changes in the internal environment.

The Endocrine Organs and Their Hormones

Traditionally, the endocrine system has been viewed as separate but parallel to the nervous system in its regulating and integrating activities. Neurons secrete their chemical messengers, neurotransmitters, into the synaptic gap to regulate the activity of their synaptic target cells. Endocrine cells secrete their chemical messengers, hormones, into the bloodstream, which carries them to all the cells that have receptors for a particular hormone (see Figure 5.5). Some identical substances work in both systems, being hormones secreted by certain endocrine cells *and* transmitters secreted by certain neurons. Norepinephrine, somatostatin, vasopressin, and oxytocin all serve this dual purpose, as do some other messengers from the diffuse enteric nervous system, for example, cholecystokinin and vasoactive intestinal polypeptide (VIP).

The glands that make up the endocrine system are the *pituitary,* with its independently functioning *anterior* and *posterior lobes,* the *gonads,* the *thyroid,* the *parathyroid,* the *adrenal cortex* and the *adrenal*

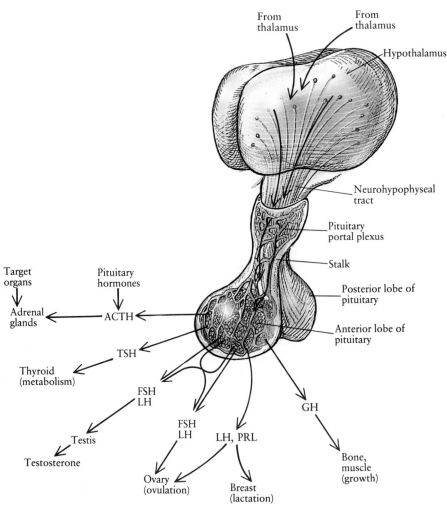

Figure 5.5
Surface view of the hypothalamus and the pituitary, showing the essential cell systems and the hormones they produce. Certain neurons of the hypothalamus secrete directly into the bloodstream through the posterior lobe of the pituitary. Others connect to the anterior lobe of the pituitary, triggering the release of hormones that travel to target organs throughout the body. Abbreviations: ACTH, adrenocorticotropic hormone; FSH, follicle-stimulating hormone; GH, growth hormone; LH, luteinizing hormone; TSH, thyroid-stimulating hormone; PRL, prolactin.

medulla, the *islet cells of the pancreas,* and the *secretory cells that line the intestinal tract.* Table 5.1 presents the fundamental features of the endocrine system.

The traditional view also held the pitui-

tary to be the "master gland" of the endocrine system. The growing recognition that anterior pituitary cells are themselves subject to control by hypothalamic neurons has forced a revision of this view, however. The an-

Table 5.1 *The endocrine system*

Tissue	Hormone	Target cells	Action
Pituitary, anterior lobe	Follicle-stimulating hormone	Gonads	Ovulation, spermatogenesis
	Luteinizing hormone	Gonads	Ovarian/spermatic maturation
	Thyrotropin	Thyroid	Thyroxin secretion
	Adrenocorticotropin	Adrenal cortex	Corticosteroid secretion
	Growth hormone	Liver	Somatomedin secretion
		All cells	Protein synthesis
	Prolactin	Breasts	Growth and milk secretion
Pituitary, posterior lobe	Vasopressin	Kidney tubules	Water retention
		Arterioles	Increase blood pressure
	Oxytocin	Uterus	Contraction
Gonads	Estrogen	Many	Secondary sexual characteristics, breast growth
	Testosterone	Many	Secondary sexual characteristics, muscle growth
Thyroid	Thyroxin	Many	Increases metabolic rate
Parathyroid	Calcitonin	Bone	Calcium retention
Adrenal cortex	Corticosteroids	Many	Mobilization of energy fuels
			Sensitization of vascular adrenergic receptors
			Inhibition of antibody formation and inflammation
	Aldosterone	Kidney	Sodium retention
Adrenal medulla	Epinephrine	Cardiovascular system, skin, muscle, liver, and others	Sympathetic activation
	Norepinephrine		
Pancreatic islets	Insulin	Many	Increases glucose uptake
	Glucagon	Liver, muscle	Increases glucose levels
	Somatostatin	Islets	Regulates insulin, glucagon secretion
Intestinal mucosa	Secretin	Exocrine pancreas	Digestive enzyme secretion
	Cholecystokinin	Gall bladder	Bile secretion
	Vasoactive intestinal polypeptide	Duodenum	Activates motility and secretion; increases blood flow
	Gastric inhibitory peptide	Duodenum	Inhibits motility and secretion
	Somatostatin	Duodenum	Inhibits motility and intestinal secretion

terior pituitary gland contains several different types of endocrine cells. Each type produces one of the pituitary hormones, and each type is directly regulated by a specific *hypophysiotropic* hormone from the hypothalamus. This hypothalamic-pituitary communication is routed through the very restricted network of blood vessels, or vascular bed, called the *pituitary-portal circulation,* which carries blood only between the base of the hypothalamus and the anterior lobe of the pituitary. Hypothalamic neurons secrete their hypophysiotropic hormones into this circulation, and their pituitary target cells react only to their particular hormones through specific surface receptors.

Thus far, six hypothalamic hormones, each secreted by a specific group of neurons located in the hypothalamus, have been identified as having selective actions on cells of the anterior pituitary (see Figure 5.6). Four of these hormones activate secretion and regulate synthesis rate of their target cells' hormones, and two inhibit secretion.

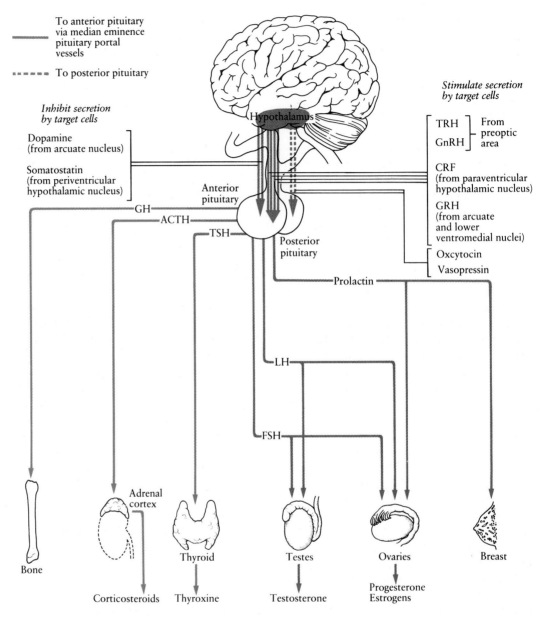

Figure 5.6
Each of the specific cell groups of the anterior pituitary controls specific endocrine organs throughout the body by means of its hormones. Each of these pituitary cell groups is under the command of activating or inhibiting factors secreted by hypothalamic neurons into the pituitary-portal circulation. Abbreviations: ACTH, adrenocorticotropic hormone; CRF, corticotropin-releasing hormone; FSH, follicle-stimulating hormone; GH, growth hormone; GnRH, gonadotropin-releasing hormone; GRH, growth hormone releasing hormone; LH, luteinizing hormone; TRH, thyrotropin-stimulating hormone; TSH, thyroid-stimulating hormone.

The fact that these specific neurons exert such potent control over the pituitary shows that the brain in general, and the hypothalamus in particular, is the real "master gland" of the endocrine system. Hypothalamic control over the endocrine system begins with hormonal messengers traveling across the pituitary-portal circulation. These same hypothalamic neurons may also make other synaptic connections in the brain, and there their secretory products function as neurotransmitters. The somatostatin neurons of the periventricular zone and the somatostatin neurons of the cerebral cortex and hippocampus, for example, use the same messenger substances, while somatostatin produced in the pancreatic islets acts as a "local hormone" to regulate insulin and glucagon secretion.

Thus, it may be more accurate to refer to the entire process by which the brain integrates the needs of the body with the demands of the environment as one of *neuroendocrine* functions. Some adjustments are made within local areas by autonomic neurons and coordinated through specific local hormone actions, while other adjustments are made more globally by hormone messengers secreted into the bloodstream.

On the molecular level, the traditional view has been that endocrine factors work by addressing distant targets globally through the bloodstream, with those cells capable of responding limited only by whether they do or do not have the proper hormone receptor molecules on their surfaces. This means that, in principle, there is no operational difference in the extracellular space between a nerve terminal or hormone-producing cell and its target cell except for the diffusion distance. And in fact, the diffusion distance is the only significant difference between a hormone and a synaptic transmitter. A messenger molecule, whether a transmitter or a hormone, is distinguished only by its ability to cause a response on a cell other than the one that made and released or secreted it and not by the route it traveled from the source to the target.

Certain other fundamental concepts of traditional endocrinology hold value with regard to homeostasis. Although the rate of secretion of some hormones, such as thyroxin, is very tightly controlled, most other endocrine hormones must fluctuate widely in their concentrations in order to maintain a constant level of cell performance in the face of changing moment-to-moment physiological demands on the organism. For example, insulin and glucagon secretions vary considerably in order to maintain blood glucose concentration within an acceptable range. Varying aldosterone (see Table 5.1) and vasopressin levels reflect the need to maintain constant plasma volume by regulating its salt and water concentrations. Epinephrine and norepinephrine levels vary with the level of overall activity, and within local vascular beds. This allows them to alter cardiac rate and force, and to adjust vascular channels selectively in order to keep the blood supply to specific organ systems appropriate to demand. The brain also regulates, through the pituitary, the output of corticosteroids through the adrenal cortex (see Figure 5.7).

Whether hormone levels vary or not, however, neuroendocrine operations can be considered in terms of *set-point values* around which the system strives for constancy.

Physiological Set-Points

Body temperature, blood glucose level, blood pressure, and salt concentration in the blood are some of the physiological properties that must be finely tuned in healthy people. The concept of the set-point helps us to understand how the central nervous system,

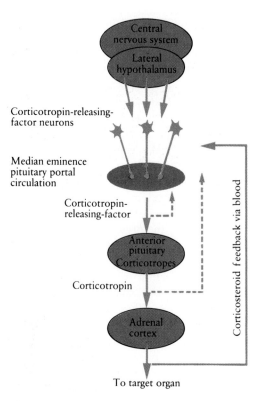

Figure 5.7
The coupling of the central nervous system and the endocrine system. Neurons in the hypothalamus produce a corticotropin-releasing factor that travels to the anterior pituitary via the pituitary-portal circulation. Certain cells, called corticotropes, in the pituitary then release corticotropin, which stimulates the secretion of corticosteroids by the adrenal cortex. Corticosteroids feeding back in the blood cause the pituitary and the central nervous system as a whole to continue or cease this process.

the autonomic nervous system, and the neuroendocrine components act in unison to regulate these and other factors.

Let us assume, then, that the body operates as though it works to maintain a constant value in temperature, blood glucose, salt, and oxygen, for example. Whenever deviations occur, sensors detect them and activate adaptive mechanisms in order to recover the normal set-point. Such systems operate by means of "negative feedback" from the peripheral sensors to a central controller. Examples from three physiological systems—temperature regulation, blood-pressure control, and appetite control—should help to illustrate the general features of such feedback arrangements.

Temperature Regulation

Body temperature is monitored by external thermoreceptors in the skin and by internal thermoreceptors on neurons in the periventricular zone of the hypothalamus. The internal sensing components measure the actual temperature of the blood and seem to be most critical for automatic adjustments of body temperature. Insertion of small thermal probes directly into the hypothalamus of experimental animals has revealed that neurons near the front of the periventricular hypothalamus can be activated by a drop or rise in the temperature of arterial blood. At the same time, commands from the hypothalamus to the autonomic nervous system activate heat-gain or heat-loss mechanisms.

When the hypothalamus senses a drop in body temperature, peripheral autonomic ganglia act to shunt blood away from the skin toward deeper structures and to erect fur or feathers in order to trap a layer of warm air next to the skin. The so-called "goose bumps" you get when you are chilled are a vestigial attempt to activate this mechanism. The heat-gain mechanisms also lead directly to shivering activity in the muscles to generate heat. When the hypothalamic detectors sense an elevation in arterial blood temperature, heat-loss mechanisms are activated and heat-gain operations are curtailed. To lose heat, the body shunts blood from its interior to the skin so that heat radiates out into the external environment. From here, it can also dissipate more efficiently by evaporative cooling during perspiration.

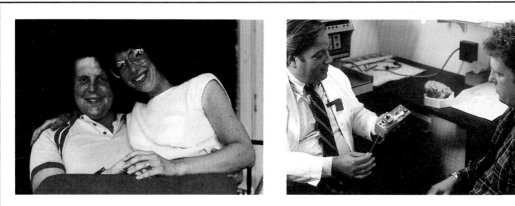

A Blow to the Head

I am a man, and I wanted to live as I viewed a normal man. . . .

Mitch Heller grew up normally—played hockey, graduated from college with a degree in engineering, got married. After an automobile accident in which he struck his head, however, everything began to change.

After about a month I realized I didn't have as much interest in sex. I couldn't perform as well. . . . It was very scary. . . . I knew something was going on inside my body and I didn't know what.

Not only was sex drive impaired. Mitch also began to lose secondary sexual characteristics—chest and facial hair, for example—and his sperm count dropped and continued to drop. All these signs indicated testosterone loss, but what could connect that to a bump on the head?

Dr. William Crowley at Massachusetts General Hospital had some tentative answers. Apparently the blow, taken on the side of the brain away from the impact, had traumatized those neurons in the hypothalamus that secrete gonadotropin-releasing hormones. With these signals to the pituitary lost, the testes no longer received their signals from the pituitary to secrete testosterone. Crowley prescribed a mechanical pump through which the hypothalamic hormone that starts this process, GnRH, could be administered automatically every two hours through a needle inserted subcutaneously in the abdomen.

With the pump in place, positive results followed. Sexual interest and chest hair gradually returned. Within six months, Mitch's sperm count was almost normal, and his wife became pregnant. In the future, his hypothalamus may regain normal function.

Top left, Mitch with his wife before treatment. Top right, Dr. Crowley explains the hormone pump. Above right, Mitch attaches the pump.

Even when you feel "emotional heat," inappropriate sweating responses may occur to "cool you off." During extreme anxiety, your hands and feet may grow "ice-cold," as though your body were retreating inward from the anxiety-producing stimulus. To date, however, speculations on the psychological "meaning" of physiological responses that accompany departures from emotional set-points remain just that—speculations.

The increase in activity of the sympathetic nervous system that occurs when you confront a tense situation provides a more-than-adequate explanation for your cold hands and feet, the increased rate and contractile force of your heartbeat, your dry mouth, and your fixed, wide-eyed stare.

When the body does exceed its normal upper temperature limit, as it does during an infection, for example, it means that heat-gain mechanisms have been overactivated. The white blood cells of an infected subject release an as-yet-uncharacterized substance, called *leucocyte pyrogen,* that activates heat-gain mechanisms and drives body temperature up. A rapid rise in body temperature is often paradoxically associated with the feeling that one is cold, hence the common "shaking chills" that accompany the onset of a fever.

The "purpose" of fever is unclear. Some, but by no means all, bacterial infections are actually conquered in part because the invading organisms are vulnerable to heat. (The spirochetes that cause syphilis are one example. The viruses that cause head colds, however, survive because air breathed in through the nose lowers the local temperature below 99°F.) Elevated body temperature also helps to activate certain antibody-producing cells, and this may increase the rate at which white blood cells move toward sites of infection, where they engulf the infectious agents.

The increased ability to activate heat-gain and heat-loss mechanisms when necessary involves a process of adaptation. As you probably know, your tolerance for cold weather increases during the winter, as does your tolerance for hot weather during the summer. Your body literally comes to anticipate the demands of the outside world. A person who exercises frequently also perspires more readily as the brain learns to put into action more and more quickly the co-ordinated programs associated with the "exercise" condition.

Control of Blood Pressure and Volume

Every level of the central and peripheral nervous system is to some extent involved in maintaining constant circulatory function. Pressure, or "baro-," receptors monitor the actual pressure of the blood within the large arteries above the heart, the carotid arteries, and the arch of the major artery, the aorta. When excess pressure activates neuronal receptors woven to the arterial walls, the fibers of these neurons carry that information to the primary relay nucleus in the medulla oblongata. From there, inhibitory commands are sent to vasomotor centers, and the activity of the peripheral sympathetic nervous system is depressed. At the same time, the parasympathetic system assumes control over the cardiovascular structures.

Normal blood pressure represents a continuous struggle for control of the cardiovascular system. The sympathetic nerves control the major blood vessels, and both sympathetic and parasympathetic divisions can regulate the rate and force of heart contractions. The pressure-detecting baroreceptors appear to be primarily responsible for setting the normal point around which the cardiovascular coordinating system operates. The baroreceptors show most sensitivity to changes from the point of normal blood pressure (that is, a pressure equal to that caused by a thin column of mercury 100 to 120 mm high).

In addition to the baroreceptors in the aorta and the carotid arteries, there are other stretch receptors sensitive to the pressure of the blood in the upper chambers, or *atria,* of the heart. Because the pressure of the blood entering the right atrium from the venous system reflects the blood's volume more accurately than its average pressure does, the atrial receptors use a different information base. When blood volume becomes excessive, as happens when salt is retained or under conditions of early "congestive heart failure," the atrial stretch receptors become activated. This activation causes cells in the walls of the atrium itself to release a hormone that acts on the kidney tubules and accelerates salt loss.

At higher levels of integration, the neurons of the hypothalamus monitor relative salt concentration in the plasma and activate water-gain or water-loss mechanisms. When salt concentration in the plasma rises above a certain set-point, large neurons in the medial zone of the hypothalamus secrete vasopressin from their axons directly into the venous blood of the posterior pituitary. Vasopressin carried through the bloodstream acts on the cells of the distal collecting ducts of the kidney, markedly increasing their permeability to water. This conserves fluid, and salt concentration decreases.

Another brain/kidney interaction also affects the process of water-volume regulation. Special cells in the kidneys, called *juxtaglomerular cells*, are activated when blood pressure goes down, as it does, for example, following substantial loss of blood, and especially in the presence of increased sympathetic nervous system activity. These kidney cells then secrete the enzyme *renin* into the bloodstream, where it acts upon a small protein made by the liver, *angiotensinogen*. This conversion process is continued through the action of other enzymes in the lungs and brain, and eventually produces a protein fragment called *angiotensin II*.

By causing the arterial muscles to constrict, angiotensin II induces a prompt, large rise in blood pressure. It also acts on certain vascular-volume receptor cells in the hypothalamus. Through cellular systems not fully understood, this action of angiotensin II causes the organism to drink excessively, and this, of course, raises the fluid level in the body. In fact, following direct injection of extremely small amounts (a millionth of a millionth of a gram) of angiotensin II into the cerebral ventricles, animals already sated on water begin to drink heavily, no matter what they are doing. This desire to drink is frequently observed among wounded soldiers and other trauma victims who have suffered large losses of blood.

Information is also relayed by other transmitters to cardiovascular centers in the lower medulla oblongata from vascular pressure receptors, as well as from vascular chemoreceptors that sense the levels of oxygen and carbon dioxide in the bloodstream. These centers then act to increase the firing rate of neurons in the respiratory and cardiovascular control systems. Activity in the centers on the side of the medulla leads to peripheral sympathetic activation and an elevation of blood pressure, while activity in the middle parts leads to parasympathetic activation and a fall in blood pressure.

The primary relay cells of the medulla also pass their information about blood pressure and flow to higher centers in the hypothalamus and the reticular activating system (see page 145), from which connections go to the cerebral and cerebellar cortices. These structures, in turn, exert considerable influence in coordinating blood flow to the muscles that require it.

Human subjects with chronically elevated blood pressure appear to have set-points that are set too high. The ultimate causes for this abnormality are difficult to determine in most cases. All levels of the vascular control system have been implicated. In some cases, kidney disease accounts for elevated pressure; in other cases, the sympathetic nervous system may be overactive. Depending on the probable site of the problem, the doctor selects the most appropriate treatment—surgery, diuretics for the kidneys, or other drugs.

Eating and Eating Behavior

Because the intake of nutrients is vital to all living creatures, the body must have physiological mechanisms that produce the motivation to eat—the motive we call *appetite,* or hunger. At the same time, there must exist mechanisms that tell the animal what to eat and when to stop eating. Since it is the job of the brain to guide the organism in its search for appropriate foodstuffs—whether they are tasty grasshoppers or Big Macs—the brain must be the ultimate recipient of these hunger or satiety signals. This signaling system works very well for most animals living in their natural habitats. Human beings may be the exception.

Although we cannot describe the entire process of digestion here, you need to know a few of the basic facts about these metabolic processes before you can understand the brain's role in eating.

1. All foods that pass through the digestive system are absorbed in one of three forms: glucose (derived from carbohydrates), amino acids (derived from proteins), and fats. Calories ingested in any of these forms that are not immediately expended for tissue needs will be converted to fat or to glycogen (an insoluble glucose polymer) and will be stored. The stored fat or the amino acids of muscle protein are later converted to glucose as required.

2. Glucose is the major source of energy for all tissue. The liver plays a vital part in converting stored fat and proteins to glucose.

3. In order for most cells to take up and use the glucose available in extracellular body fluids, insulin must also be present. Only the cells of the nervous system are able to take up and use glucose without insulin. Insulin is manufactured by the *islet cells* in the pancreas. These islet cells are sensitive to a variety of circulating hormones and other circulating neuroregulators, all of which, taken together, constitute a complex regulatory system.

Appetite Control: When to Eat What causes a person to say to himself or herself, "I'm hungry," or produces, in a rat, the equivalent experience? Not long ago, most textbooks answered this question by pointing to the hypothalamus. Experiments had shown that rats with lesions that destroyed the ventromedial nucleus of the hypothalamus ate much more than nonlesioned fellow rats and became extremely obese, often doubling their original weight. Such results were interpreted as demonstrating that the ventromedial nucleus acted as a "satiety center."

Other experiments destroyed the lateral hypothalamus and produced animals that would not eat or drink. This part of the brain was then dubbed the "hunger center." Thus it appeared, for a while, that the answer to hunger and satiety lay in the activities of these two centers in the hypothalamus.

As better techniques for brain study were developed and as knowledge of the brain's anatomy and chemistry grew, it became clear that the mechanisms controlling hunger and satiety were not simply located in single brain centers. The hypothalamic lesions in those early experiments had actually disrupted a number of important neural pathways and had produced widespread metabolic changes and behavioral deficits.

In 1955, the American nutritionist Jean Mayer proposed that glucose levels in the blood provided the hunger signal. Supposedly, low glucose levels were sensed by special neurons, called glucostats, which fired at a higher rate when glucose levels fell. Although glucose receptors were found in the lateral hypothalamus, researchers found that they did not play a crucial role in regulating eating. The liver also contains glucose receptors that monitor glucose levels in the blood passing through the hepatic portal vein. These appear to send information to the brain via a branch of the vagus nerve. However, it was found that cutting that branch of the vagus nerve in experimental animals had little effect on eating behavior. In fact, most of the time, glucose levels remain within a relatively narrow range, no matter what the timing and amount of food intake, because the metabolic system is so efficient at converting and storing excess nutrients and at calling up and reconverting those stores.

Recent research indicates that the motivation to eat involves a number of physiological mechanisms. The system is a complex one that is not yet well understood. The question of food intake actually has both short-term and long-term dimensions. The short-term question is "What starts a meal?" What mechanisms signal the imbalance in nutrient homeostasis so that an animal is motivated to begin eating? The long-term question is "What regulates body weight?" Recent research indicates that the same areas of the brain are involved in the signaling systems for both types of regulation and that neuropeptides play an important part in both.

A number of psychological factors also play a part in hunger, but let us first examine its physiological mechanisms.

The Set-Point Hypothesis of Eating   It has always been assumed that an animal's store of fat was the result of what it ate and of its metabolism—that is, that stored fat, or *adiposity,* was a secondary effect of some other primary regulators of feeding and digestion. It now appears that adiposity is the primary regulator of eating behaviors. The evidence now appears to show that the amount of an animal's fat store is somehow represented in its brain, and it is the brain that directs metabolic processes and eating behaviors to defend that store.

An experimental animal that has been starved and has lost weight will, when allowed to feed freely, overeat until it has gained back the fat it lost. An animal that has been force-fed until it has gained weight will, when allowed to feed freely again, undereat until it has lost the excess fat. It appears that total body adiposity is maintained at a relatively constant level in adult animals and that this maintenance is achieved through changes in food intake. Therefore, some representation of total body-fat level must exist in the brain, as well as some type of signaling system to alter eating behaviors and/or metabolic processes. The nature of this representation and the identity of the signals that allow the brain to read it are not yet known, but researchers are working on a number of likely explanations.

The signal appears more likely to be a circulating substance than one depending on neural-tract connections. The evidence for this comes from experiments in which two animals, an obese one and a normally lean one, are surgically joined, as if they were Siamese twins. Their nervous systems remain separate, but they share the same cardiovascular and extracellular fluid circulation. In this situation, the lean mouse begins to eat less than it did prior to the experiment, and it loses weight as if it had been overweight (Coleman & Hummel, 1969). Some circulating compound must pass between the two animals; it appears that the obese source dominates, since it influences the eating behavior of the lean animal.

A number of scientists believe that circulating insulin is the primary factor regulating both body weight and food intake. Although insulin does not pass easily through the blood-brain barrier (as you recall, the brain does not require insulin to use glucose), the hormone is present, for uncertain reasons, in

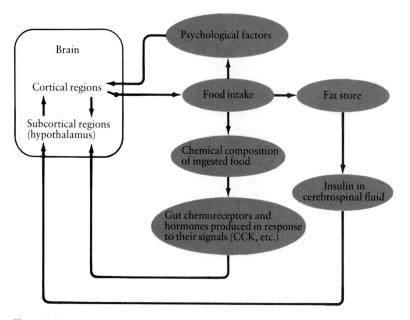

Figure 5.8
In this model representing the regulation of food intake and body weight, initiation of eating is influenced by psychological factors (the appearance and taste of food, learned associations with time and place of eating, etc.) as well as by signals from the hypothalamus to the cortex. The end of eating—the feeling of satiety—is influenced when gut chemoreceptors sense the chemical composition of the food consumed. These chemoreceptors stimulate the production of hormones, which feed back to the hypothalamus, which, in turn, influences the consumption decisions of the cortex. This process is ultimately regulated by the brain's monitoring of the body's fat stores, the monitoring signal presumably being insulin.

amphetamine, that release stored norepinephrine from axon terminals or prevent its reuptake can cause animals to stop eating. Several neural tracts carrying this transmitter enter and pass through the lateral hypothalamus.

One family of neuropeptides—the endorphins—has been found to increase the amount of food eaten during a meal. Whether these endogenous opiates initiate eating is not clear, but the finding that the level of these substances is elevated in the pituitary of genetically obese mice and rats suggests that they might be related to feeding behavior.

Long-term regulation of food intake, then, seems to be regulated by the brain's representation of the body's fat stores, with insulin as the primary agent signaling the state of those stores to the brain—whether they are being depleted or are getting too large relative to the brain's representation. On the other hand, short-term regulation—when to stop eating—seems to depend on several digestive hormones, or gut peptides. Figure 5.8 presents a simple model of the entire regulation process.

Appetite Control: When to Stop Eating
The stretch receptors in the stomach wall come into play when there is danger of an animal injuring itself by overfilling its stomach. But these receptors play only a minor role in the normal experience of satiety.

The major signals of satiation are digestive hormones secreted in the gut during a meal. There are a number of such hormones, and exactly which ones are secreted depends on the specific foods being consumed and their amounts. For obvious reasons, these substances are called *satiety factors*. Many of these gut peptides feed back indirectly to the brain to influence when a meal should end. Their efficacy was demonstrated when hungry rats were transfused with the blood of

the cerebrospinal fluid, which bathes the brain. Also, insulin-binding sites have been found in the brain, largely in the hypothalamus and in the olfactory lobe. Experiments in which insulin was applied directly onto neurons in the ventral hypothalamus revealed that these neurons changed their firing rate, much as they do in response to glucose. This firing appears to represent a signal to stop feeding: baboons that had insulin continually infused into their cerebrospinal fluid ate less and lost weight; in another such experiment, rats did the same.

The neurotransmitter norepinephrine appears to play a complex role in initiating and stopping the intake of food. Drugs, such as sated rats: the transfused rats ate much less than they normally would have (Davis et al., 1969).

As you saw in Chapter 2, a number of the peptides found in the digestive system are also found, in small amounts, in the brain, often in places that have no known role in eating or consuming. One of these gut peptides in the brain is *cholecystokinin (CCK)*; others are listed in Table 5.1 in the listing of hormones for "intestinal mucosa." All seem to serve two major functions: (1) they tailor the digestive process to the meal eaten, and (2) they interact with the nervous system to determine meal size. It may be that some gut hormones act by regulating the brain's responsiveness to insulin.

Appetite Control: Psychological Factors

For human beings—at least those lucky enough to live in a society where food is plentiful and readily available—a number of factors besides hunger lead people to eat. We are strongly influenced by learned associations having to do with time and place. For example, when the clock says it is lunchtime, we are apt to think that we're hungry, no matter what we may have eaten earlier in the day. We have learned that noon or one o'clock spells lunchtime. Certain places are also associated with food. Many of us find it almost impossible to sit through a movie without popcorn or a candy bar. As children, we learned to associate the movie theater with these snacks—it is a place where eating is done. (We don't munch through a play, however, because the legitimate theater tolerates eating and drinking only in the outer lobby.)

Socialization in the ways of our culture also plays a part in when and what we eat. Surrounded by others who are eating at a party, for example, we eat, no matter what our physiological status relative to food. But our culture has also given us certain food preferences. If the caterers at a party attended by Americans set out a buffet of squid cooked in its own ink (Spanish), fried grasshoppers (African), and sheep's eyes (Arabic), most of us would not feel that same "hunger." Such learned preferences soon lose force, however, when food is scarce and the physiological factors signaling hunger become urgent. People trapped by the Nazi blockade of Amsterdam and other cities in the Netherlands during World War II ate their pet cats and dogs and the famous tulip bulbs, which poisoned many of them.

Perhaps the interaction of psychological and physiological factors can be seen best in two types of human eating disorders: anorexia nervosa, which encompasses a disorder called bulimia, and obesity.

Eating Disorders

Most human beings, like most other animals, eat enough food to satisfy their energy needs and to maintain their fat store at a relatively stable level. Some, however, eat so little that their weight becomes dangerously low, and some eat so much that their weight becomes dangerously high.

Anorexia Nervosa and Bulimia

Anorexia means simply "loss of appetite," and *anorexia nervosa* is the name given to a clinical entity in which loss of appetite is presumably caused by psychological factors. The vast majority of anorectics are female, and they are usually young—between 12 and 18 years of age. An anorectic may eat so little food that her body weight drops to 70 or even 60 percent of what is considered normal for her height. One patient, 5 feet 2 inches tall, was admitted to a treatment program at a weight of 70 pounds and lost yet another 12 pounds before the therapists took over management of her eating (Goodsitt, 1985).

In a sense, "loss of appetite" does not truly describe the psychological state of these

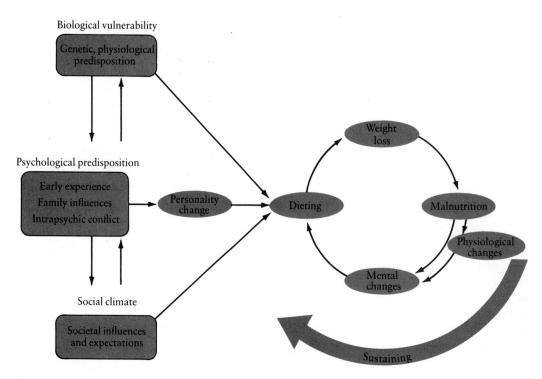

Figure 5.9
*A model depicting the interacting causes of anorexia nervosa and its self-perpetua-
tion in a "vicious cycle." That is, once the patient has undergone significant weight
loss, the physiological effects of malnutrition (e.g., slower emptying of the stomach)
and the psychological effects (e.g., increasing social isolation) help sustain the disorder.*

patients, since the symptoms that make up
this clinical syndrome include an obsession
with food. The appetite loss is actually the
pursuit of being thin, but the anorectic also
typically has such a severely distorted body
image that even when she is emaciated, she
sees herself as "too fat." Other symptoms
include depression and social isolation.

Some anorectics indulge in food binges on
occasion, eating prodigious amounts of
food—thousands of calories—within a short
period of time. Then they force themselves to
vomit, or they purge themselves with laxatives and diuretics, so that the calories will
not be absorbed. This binge-purge behavior
is called *bulimia.*

A number of physiological symptoms also
accompany anorexia nervosa. Body temperature drops below normal, menstruation
ceases, sleep is disturbed, depression is common, and metabolic abnormalities may include increased secretion of cortisol from the
adrenals and impaired production of vasopressin and norepinephrine. Whether these
changes are a cause or a result of the starvation is not yet known, but most doctors tend
to believe they reflect the malnutrition that
was brought on by psychological maladjust-
ment.

Figure 5.9 presents a model of the interacting causes and self-perpetuating effects of
anorexia nervosa. One contributing factor is

the social climate. In Western countries, for example, over the past two decades the "ideal" female figure—the one that appears in ads, movies, television programs—has been growing thinner. One need only compare the pin-up girls of the 1950s and 1960s with those of the 1980s to see the difference. This idealization of the boyish figure, with small breasts and narrow hips, is one force working on the psyche of anorectics. Of course, this ideal image is held up for all women, so there must be some predisposing factors in the psychological background of certain young women that makes them especially vulnerable to it.

Among the predisposing factors that have been identified are the girls' difficulties with autonomous functioning and with development of a sense of personal identity. Adolescence is a time when the body is changing from that of a child to that of an adult. The changes are so profound that they demand the focus of attention. They not only bring awareness of sexuality, they also serve as a warning that adult responsibilities lie not too far ahead in the future. The excessive weight loss of anorectic adolescents keeps the body more childlike and causes menstruation to stop, so girls can, from one point of view, put off the inner struggles of forming an identity and learning how to function autonomously, away from the family. Fear of growing up is thus viewed as being translated, by means of defense mechanisms, into fear of getting fat (Crisp, 1983).

Specific types of family interactions can help contribute to the onset of anorexia nervosa. If an infant's primary caretaker does not provide regular and consistently appropriate responses to her needs, particularly to the need for food, the child may not develop an accurate awareness of her own functions and may become deficient in her hunger awareness. If her mother continually says, "You can't be hungry yet, it's only 11 o'clock," perhaps she comes to believe that what she's feeling is something other than hunger.

One common characteristic of the families of anorectics is that they do not encourage expression of feelings. Another is that these girls are extremely obedient and overconforming during childhood. Some psychologists believe that the fierce control an anorectic maintains over what foods go into her body is a distorted expression of her need to gain some control over her life—to have one area of nonconformity vis-à-vis her family.

There may also be some predisposing physiological factors, perhaps genetic ones, that contribute to the disease. Several studies have found that in the families of anorectics, there seems to be an abnormally high incidence of depression, alcoholism, and psychosomatic disorders such as migraine. (See, for example, the case of Heidi, described on pages 162 and 163.) It has been suggested that some anorectics may behave as they do because of an abnormality in the brain mechanisms that control feeding and metabolism—changes, for example, in the activity of norepinephrine-producing neurons in the hypothalamus (Leibowitz, 1983). So far, however, there is little direct evidence for this.

Several psychological paths to anorexia nervosa appear to be possible. But whatever the cultural, psychological, and physiological disposing factors may be, once the weight loss has become significant and the young woman becomes malnourished, the disease becomes self-sustaining. The effect of the malnutrition on a number of physical functions tends to aggravate the disease. For example, emptying of the stomach is much slower in malnourished persons (Dubois et al., 1984). Furthermore, the social isolation that is common as the disorder progresses allows for less and less reality testing. In other words, there are fewer people to re-

Case History of an Anorectic

Heidi is a 17-year-old girl who lives with her parents and is a senior in high school. She was first referred for a diagnostic consultation six months after she began dieting in order to be more attractive. Heidi is 170 cm (5 feet 7 inches) tall and weighed 61 kg (135 pounds) before dieting. The lowest acceptable weight range for a woman at this height would be between 54.5 and 57 kg (120 and 128 pounds). Heidi gradually lost weight to a low of 40.5 kg (90 pounds), which she weighed two weeks prior to the consultation. She had never induced vomiting or abused laxatives, but she did exercise a great deal. She started menstruating at the age of 14, and her last period occurred just at the time she started dieting. She emphatically stated that she would like to weigh about 50 kg (110 pounds) and not one pound over that. At the time Heidi's dieting behavior began, she also began to have difficulties in school. She started to skip classes and go out with friends. After a few months, however, she began to have arguments and altercations with her friends. Then she began to stay at home; for several months prior to the consultation, she had isolated herself from her peer group and stayed in the house most of the day. She became very interested in cooking and started collecting recipes and cooking for her family. She admitted to feeling depressed and to having occasional crying spells. About two months before Heidi began to diet seriously, she broke up with her boyfriend, who had told her she was too fat and should lose weight.

Actual size   Constricted image   Expanded image
                         (−20%)   (+20%)

The perception of body shape and size can be evaluated through the use of special computer drawing programs that allow a subject to distort the width of an actual picture of a person's body by up to 20 percent larger or smaller. Both anorectics and normal subjects adjusted the figures of other people's bodies to normal dimension. However, anorectics consistently adjusted their own body picture to a size 20 percent larger than its true form, suggesting that they have a major problem with the perception of their own image.

Treatment

Heidi was mildly depressed and preoccupied with the fear of being fat. She stated that she had an obsession with counting calories and was not able to stop her dieting behavior. Heidi was referred to an experienced therapist in her area for outpatient therapy. Heidi was completely uninterested in treatment. An attempt was made to set up a variety of behavioral contracts, but Heidi refused to cooperate with any of them. After 10 sessions she refused to see the therapist, stating that she would gain her weight back alone. She then began a pattern of eating nothing during the day and then, late at night, eating 10 to 15 pieces of Kentucky Fried Chicken with an extensive amount of salt over about a two-hour period. Eventually she stayed up through the night, going to sleep at 5:30 A.M. and then sleeping until about 1 or 2 P.M. For a short period, Heidi tried to stop this pattern and attended school all day to make up credits; however, her eating difficulties prevailed, and she eventually stopped going to school entirely.

One year after the initial consultation, Heidi reluctantly came into the hospital for treatment. After the hospitalization, it became obvious that Heidi's mother had a severe problem with alcohol abuse and that there was a strong history of alcoholism and depression in her mother's family. During the first few days after hospitalization, Heidi was very upset and wanted to leave the hospital; however, when her parents supported the continued hospitalization, she became less agitated and more cooperative. Her weight on admission was 40.5 kg (90 pounds). She was placed on a liquid formula, Sustacal, with enough calories to maintain her weight plus 50% for activity. She was given this in six equal feedings throughout the day. The amount of calories was increased every 5 days until she reached her target weight.

Heidi needed a great deal of encouragement to interact with her peers. One week after hospital admission, she started attending the hospital school. Because of her desire to isolate herself, a program was put into effect that allowed Heidi access to her room for several hours each day if she gained weight on that day. She gradually became more involved with her peers and her school program, and by the time she reached her target weight was able to eat fairly normally.

Pop singer Karen Carpenter died in 1983 of the effects of anorexia.

During individual sessions, it became obvious that the patient had to stay at home to take care of her alcoholic mother. The mother's alcoholism was discussed in the family therapy sessions, and the mother entered a treatment program. Heidi eventually requested to be removed from her single room into a four-bed girls' dorm room on the unit. After a series of visits to her family, Heidi was discharged from the hospital program and transferred to an outpatient therapy program. Heidi also signed a behavioral contract, which she helped design with her outpatient therapist. In this contract she agreed to go to her family doctor's office to be weighed once a week. She agreed to eat three meals a day and not to eat at night. Every week that she had been able to maintain her weight within a normal weight range, she would reward herself by buying some new painting or drawing materials. The family agreed that Heidi could not be responsible for her mother's care. Alternative care programs were set up for the mother.

mark that "you're nothing but skin and bones."

Various psychotherapeutic approaches are used in treating the disorder, but all of them involve some management of the patient's food intake in order to provide adequate nourishment and so break the vicious circle (shown in Figure 5.8). When anorectics are given enough calories and nutrients so that they regain some of the lost weight, their sleep disturbances are eased and the depression often lifts, so psychotherapy is more likely to be effective.

Obesity Both psychological and physiological factors contribute to obesity. One of the important physiological factors is a difference in metabolic rate, the rate of conversion of available nutrients (sugars, fats, and proteins) into energy that is either used immediately for cell operations or is converted into body fat for later use. In a study in which food intake was measured in subjects matched for age, weight, height, and activity, some subjects were found to eat twice as much as their counterparts (Rose & Williams, 1961). With all other factors equal, it was clear that those subjects who ate less and maintained their weight had metabolisms that converted calories into tissue very efficiently. In view of the fact that activity rates did not vary, those who ate a great deal more to maintain the same weight must have been losing heat to the environment. People who gain excess weight, then, are likely to be efficient converters; to keep slim, they would have to eat a lot less than someone whose metabolic rate was higher.

A single fat cell is called an *adipocyte,* and obese people generally have larger adipocytes and more of them than thin people. In light of our discussion of the set-point hypothesis, we might well ask what role, if any, these cells play in the signaling system be-

tween brain and fat tissue. One theory suggests that what the brain ultimately regulates is the volume of individual fat cells and that fat cells emit some signal about their volume (Faust et al., 1978). In an obese person, these cells have been well filled. When they lose volume as the person diets, they would signal the brain, calling for more food to bring their volume back up. This might explain why losing weight and keeping it off is so difficult.

There is also evidence that one of the more important variables in controlling obesity is the level in adipose tissue of the enzyme *lipoprotein lipase (LPL).* LPL is responsible for the removal of fats from the blood and for the ability to store them in adipocytes. Obese people and animals have an elevated level of LPL, which is commensurate with their elevated level of stored fat. Moreover, when these people or animals restrict their food intake and lose weight, their LPL levels appear to go even higher. If increased LPL tends to favor fat storage, this might account for the plateaus that dieters hit, where food intake remains low but the needle on the scale stays in one place for days or weeks on end. LPL levels in adipose tissue may well be part of the signaling and control system for regulation of body fat.

Are obese people born with these numerous, voracious adipocytes? Perhaps. Strains of mice certainly show differences in their potential for accumulating fat (Schemmel et al., 1970). However, recent animal studies suggest that overfeeding in early life may cause the proliferation of these cells (West et al., 1982).

A number of psychological reactions to food and eating seem to differentiate obese from normal-weight people. Obese people are finickier about food. They will drink less of a doubtful-tasting milkshake, for example, than a normal-weight hungry person will, and more of one that tastes good. The obese seem to be more susceptible to cues relating to food—the odor from a bakery or the textures and colors of a pyramid of fruit outside a greengrocer's. Yet they appear unwilling to work hard for food. When normal-weight and obese subjects in one study were left alone in a room with a bowl of nuts in their shells, only 1 of 20 obese people used the nutcracker and ate a few, whereas 10 of 20 normal-weight subjects did. Parallels have been drawn between the food-related behavior of obese people and that of mice with lesions in the ventromedial hypothalamus (Schachter, 1971), but there is no evidence that obese human beings have ventromedial abnormalities. Other researchers suggest that these behavioral idiosyncracies simply reflect the fact that although obese people feel chronically hungry because of elevated LPL levels, social pressures usually frustrate them and prevent them from satisfying their hunger.

Learning undoubtedly also plays a large part in the development of obesity. If you grow up in a family where small portions are served, you are likely to come to believe that small meals are the norm and to want small meals. If, on the other hand, your family serves huge meals followed by huge desserts, you will come to consider this normal and to want generous portions. If your parents are obese and eat large meals to feed their hunger, you too may become obese.

Obesity, of course, is not only a socially disapproved condition. It is a health hazard. And for most obese adults, weight loss over time is a tremendously difficult—almost impossible—undertaking. The recidivism rate—the number of people who regain lost weight—is well over 90 percent in almost all forms of treatment. A regular exercise program along with regulation of food intake seems to offer the best chance for weight loss. With progress in research, there may be, in the not-too-distant future, a chemical means of dealing with obesity.

Other Set-Point Systems

Other internal regulatory systems make use of control systems every bit as intricate as the blood pressure, adrenal, endocrine, and appetite systems described above. Within the *reproductive system,* for example, an intricate series of endocrine feedback signals, along with direct influences from the central and peripheral nervous systems, enable one to prepare for, select a mate for, and consummate reproductive relationships.

Other intricate control systems allow for the elevation of corticosteroid secretion during periods of stress and for the prompt suppression of its secretion once the stressful period has passed (stress is described more fully in Chapter 7). Because extracellular calcium ions participate in so many intracellular events, their levels are also extensively regulated. Cells in the parathyroid glands that secrete calcitonin and parathormone, and cells in the kidneys, the liver, the bones, and even the skin, which synthesizes the vitamin D necessary for dietary calcium absorption, all participate in this almost, but not completely, nonneural regulation.

Maintenance of the Internal Milieu

In this chapter we have looked at the two major systems the brain uses to integrate the needs of the body with the moment-to-moment demands of the external environment.

The *autonomic nervous system* does its regulating through small shifts in predominance between two of its generally balanced divisions, the *sympathetic* and the *parasympathetic* nervous systems. Each of these divisions has a *sensing* component that monitors specific internal physical or chemical factors and an *effector* component that produces the changes necessary to maintain a constant internal environment. Within the *endocrine system,* the *hypothalamus* regulates a variety of internal organs through intermediate hormones secreted by the *pituitary.* Under the active control of neurons in the hypothalamus, the anterior lobe of the pituitary controls the endocrine glands throughout the body. The posterior lobe of the pituitary allows other hypothalamic neurons to secrete their hormones directly into the bloodstream. The activity of both sets of hypothalamic neurons can also be modified by current and recalled sensory information that has been processed by cortical and subcortical systems.

Both the autonomic and endocrine systems function as though they were monitoring a specific physical or chemical "setpoint" for every component of the internal environment. These systems activate or inhibit internal activity to keep each of those components within a very narrow range, despite wide variations in the external environment. For example, blood pressure is normally set to fixed standards, as is our utilization of calories.

In the next chapters, we turn our attention to the interplay between these global systems and the patterns of daily living. By considering the organized oscillations—or rhythms—of the operations of our internal regulatory systems, we can begin to see how the brain anticipates the cyclical demands of our daily and seasonal activities.

Summary

1. The brain executes its responsibility over the internal environment of the body through the autonomic nervous system and the endocrine system.

2. The autonomic nervous system has two major arms that serve the entire body, and a third division that offers additional regulation of the gastrointestinal system. The parasympathetic division of the autonomic nervous system is, in general, balanced by the activity of the sympathetic division of the autonomic nervous system. To change from one dynamic state to another (such as changing from the excited state of taking an examination to the more placid state that follows a good meal) requires turning one system up and concomitantly turning the other system down.

3. Through the anterior pituitary and its hormones, the brain can also speak to selected target cells throughout the body via the secretion of blood-borne messenger molecules, the hormones.

4. The several different hormones regulate overall metabolism, the activity of the gonads, the liver, and the adrenal glands, and in some stages of our lives the rate at which we grow.

5. The regulation of these hormone messages from the pituitary is also tightly monitored by the brain to match the activity of the messages with the demands of the body in whatever environment we are forced to exist.

6. Through the combined action of the autonomic nerves and the endocrine system, we are able to make short-term and long-term adjustments to alterations in our environment—for example, to remain cool when it is hot and vice versa.

7. The brain also regulates the degree to which we need to replenish our energy supplies by eating, although as human beings we are able to override these internal controls and eat at times not driven simply by hunger but because we enjoy it or find it relaxing.

8. Similarly, the brain is able to regulate

every one of the major visceral systems, including heart rate, blood pressure, and salt and water balance.

9. By establishing a normal value, the dynamically opposed systems regulated by the brain are able to maintain us in exact balance over a wide variety of normal chemical and physical standards.

Further Reading

Schachter, S. 1971. Some extraordinary facts about obese humans and rats. *American Psychologist,* 26:129–144. Some behaviors of obese rats and obese human beings show definite similarities, as compared to their normal-weight fellows.

Stunkard, A. J., and Stellar, E., eds. 1984. *Eating and its disorders.* New York: Raven. A collection of papers presenting recent research on obesity, anorexia nervosa, and other eating disorders.

Kandel, E., and Schwartz, J., eds. 1985. *Principles of Neural Science,* 2d edition. New York: Elsevier Scientific Publishing. Part VIII, Chapter 46 "Hypothalamus, Limbic System, and Cerebral Cortex: Homeostasis and Arousal," pp. 609–625. An advanced textbook coverage.

Pirke, K. M., and Ploog, D., eds., 1983. *The Psychobiology of Anorexia Nervosa.* New York: Springer-Verlag. A collection of current research papers on probable causes and effects of anorexia nervosa and bulimia.

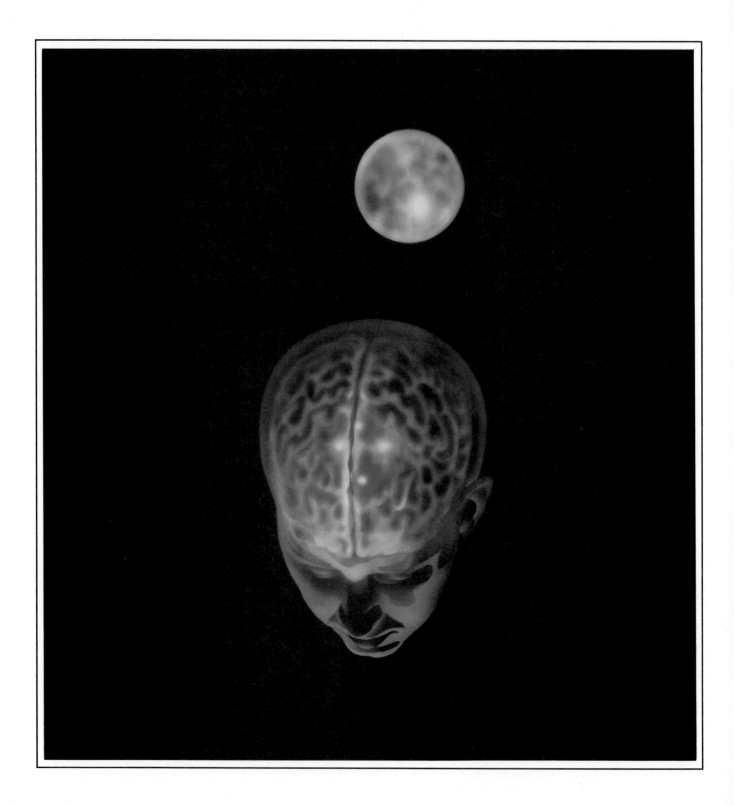

6

Rhythms
of the Brain

6

It is easy for us to perceive the rhythms in the world around us: spring, summer, fall, and winter follow their familiar cycle; the sun rises every day, moves across the sky, and sets; the moon waxes and wanes; the tides ebb and flow. Long before anyone knew anything about the turning of the earth and the movement of the planets around the sun, people witnessed these changes, speculated on their meanings, created rites and festivals to mark them, and planned their activities according to them. In medieval Europe, "books of the hours" depicted different seasonal and daily activities, and offered the faithful special prayers for each of the different occasions.

The body also has its rhythms, and many of them appear to be adapted to the earth's cycles. Most of these rhythms go on without our ever being aware of them: ebbs and flows of hormonal tides, cycles of fast and slow brain activity, cycles of high and low body temperature. Although we know very little about the performers, the conductor of these biological rhythms is, in human beings, the brain.

But rhythms exist in animals with less elaborate brains, and even in animals with no brain at all. Living in the sands of a beach on Cape Cod is a species of golden-brown algae. During the high tide, these single-celled organisms stay under the sand. But as the waters begin to recede during each daylight outgoing tide, the algae move up between the grains of sand and bask in the sunlight, recharging their photosynthesis machinery (see Figure 6.1). Moments before the returning tide reaches them, they burrow back down into the safety of the sand.

Tides, of course, do not occur at the same

Long before scientists found that many biological rhythms are adaptations to earth's seasonal rhythms and light-dark cycles, human beings marked the significance of seasonal changes with rites and celebrations. This illustration of such rites is from a medieval book of hours, Les Très Riches Heures *of Jean, duc de Berry (ca. 1413).*

clock time every day. Our clocks reflect the 24-hour solar day, but tides ebb and flow according to the lunar day, which is 24.8 hours long. On Monday, therefore, the algae on the Atlantic coast of the northeastern

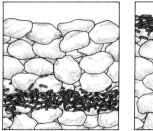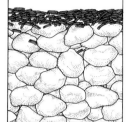

Figure 6.1
These golden-brown algae remain about 1 mm below the surface of the sand during high tide. Each day, they propel themselves upward to the surface when the tide ebbs, bask in the sun, and burrow again just before the tide returns (Palmer, 1975).

United States must rush to their burrows at 2:01 P.M., on Tuesday at 2:57 P.M., on Wednesday at 3:55 P.M., and so on.

Do these single-celled plants respond to environmental cues in keeping their intricate schedule? Samples of this population were scooped up in their beach sand, taken to the laboratory, and put in a tub kept in continuous light, with no simulated tides. Without environmental cues—no days, nights, or tidal changes—the algae still climbed to the surface of the sand just as the tide receded at their old beach, and burrowed just before the tide returned. They were so punctual that the experimenters could assess the level of the tide at a beach that was 27 miles away. Clearly, some biological clock, set on lunar time, directs this activity.

Types of Rhythms

The golden-brown algae show a daily activity rhythm, even though that day is 24.8 hours long. Such rhythms are called *circadian* (Latin *circa,* "about," and *dies,* "a day"). The human sleep/waking cycle is a circadian rhythm, as are rhythms in body temperature, hormone levels, urine produc-

tion, and levels of cognitive and motor performance.

Rhythms that occur over a period longer than a day are called *infradian (infra,* "below") because their frequency is lower than once a day. Some squirrels, for example, hibernate every year; their body temperature drops, and they become completely inactive for several months. This annual pattern is an infradian rhythm. So is the monthly cycle of ovulation and menstruation in human females.

Rhythms that repeat more than once a day are called *ultradian (ultra,* "beyond") because their frequency is higher than once a day. The cycle of stages that takes place within the normal 6- to 8-hour period that human beings sleep is one example, and there are many more.

Interest in these rhythms goes beyond the desire to know how living things function. Knowledge of the ebb and flow of the chemicals that the body produces may dictate, for example, that certain medications are more effective when taken at a given time of day. Experiments with mice have shown that their susceptibility to toxic agents varies dramatically with the time. Mice are active at night, and during that time they can tolerate a drug dosage perfectly well that might kill or incapacitate them during the day. In one experiment, 80 percent of mice given a bacterial toxin early in the evening died, but only 20 percent died when given the identical dose in the middle of the night (Halberg et al., 1960). Then, too, the diagnosis of many illnesses depends on measurement of certain substance levels in the blood or urine. Knowing how the levels of these substances fluctuate during the day can aid in accurate diagnosis.

Much of the research on biological rhythms has been carried out with plants, birds, and nonhuman animals. (Research with human beings is possible only when no damage could possibly occur, and even then experimental conditions are severely limited.) Researchers hope to discover: (1) how a rhythm is functionally organized; (2) where the pacemaker that drives the rhythm is located anatomically and how it operates physiologically; and (3) what the cellular and biochemical mechanisms are that cause the pacemaker to generate the rhythm.

Studies of Rhythms in Nonhuman Organisms

Over 250 years ago, the French astronomer Jean Jacques d'Ortous de Mairan, having noted that his heliotrope plant spread its leaves open during the day and closed them at night, decided to see whether this unfold-ing and folding was a response to light and dark. He put the plant in a dark closet and observed it. Not only did the plant continue to open and close in the absence of light, its cycle of opening and closing corresponded to the day/night cycle outside. The plant's rhythms, he concluded, must be governed by an inner mechanism.

Flowers show such regularity in unfolding and folding their petals each day that the great biologist Linnaeus created a garden plan for a flower clock. Each species of flower opens and closes in its turn, starting at 6 A.M. and ending at 6 P.M.

Simple Organisms

The algae that perform with such clocklike regularity in the Cape Cod sands consist of

The opening of the morning glory over a four-hour period is timed by a circadian biological clock.

A photograph of Aplysia californica, *whose large neurons make it an excellent subject of study. Neurons in the outer rim of its eye act as pacemakers, keeping the sea slug's feeding and resting cycles attuned to cycles of light and dark.*

only one cell, so the mechanism that produces their circadian rhythm of activity *must* exist within that cell. So far, however, attempts to pinpoint the pacemaker or any of its parts, anatomically or functionally, have been unsuccessful. Researchers have exposed these organisms to high temperatures and a number of potentially disruptive chemicals, but their rhythms continue, undisrupted.

Another single-celled organism, *Gonyaulax,* has four different circadian rhythms, each relating to one of four different functions: photosynthesis, luminescence, irritability, and cell division. Are these different rhythms driven by a single pacemaker or four different ones? The answer has not yet been found. Even when the cell's nucleus is removed by microsurgery, the rhythms continue.

One well-studied multicelled organism is *Aplysia californica,* a sluglike animal that adjusts its activities to the tides of the Pacific beaches. *Aplysia* makes a good subject because the connections and functions of its large neurons are relatively easy to discover. Felix Strumwasser noted that certain neurons in the outer rim of the eye showed a rhythm in the frequency of their firing, firing

faster in the light and slower in the dark. When these neurons were removed, placed in a special bath of sea water in the laboratory, and kept in complete darkness, they fired in just the same patterns observed in the living animal.

The rhythm of these pacemaker neurons, which help to keep the daily feeding and resting cycles of *Aplysia* in tune with the cycles of dark and light and of tidal comings and goings, is evidently set by some process within the cells. This process, like that in the single-celled algae, has not yet been discovered, although scientists believe that a link may exist between the rate of protein synthesis in a cell and its rhythm.

Birds and Mammals

Every fall, the willow warblers migrate from central and northern Europe, where they have bred, to the warm climate of central and southern Africa. Many species of birds follow such migration patterns: the Atlantic golden plover flies from as far south as Argentina to breed in the Yukon, a trip of about 7000 miles; the Arctic tern breeds in northern Europe, Asia, and North America, and migrates to the Antarctic. What triggers migration? Do these birds sense the days getting shorter or the temperature gradually dropping?

To answer such questions, scientists took fledgling warblers from their European nests in the spring and divided them into four groups. One group was left in its natural environment. The second was kept in a laboratory near its home territory, but at a constant temperature of 53°F and a constant cycle of 12-hour alternating periods of light and darkness. The other two groups were flown by airplane to their usual wintering quarters in Africa. One of these groups was kept under the same laboratory conditions as the second group in Europe, while the other lived outdoors in natural conditions. All four

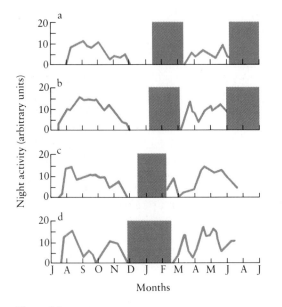

Figure 6.2
Night activity in experimental groups of willow warblers: in a lab in Germany (a) and in Africa (c), in a natural setting in Germany (b) and in Africa (d). Colored bars represent periods of feather molting (Gwinner, 1968).

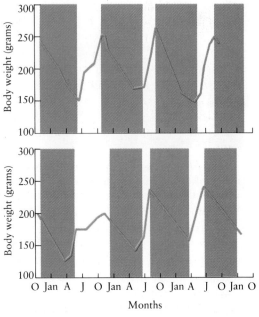

Figure 6.3
As the golden-mantled ground squirrel comes out of hibernation during a 2-hour period (facing page), its body temperature rises from near freezing to normal. Above, evidence that ambient temperature does not affect hibernation patterns. The 4-year-record at top shows patterns of weight gain and loss at room temperature of 53°F; bottom, at just above freezing. Brown areas show hibernation periods (Pengelley & Asmundson, 1971).

groups of birds, it turned out, went through the same yearly cycle of behaviors. No matter where they were, they tended to show a migratory urge, manifested by night activity not seen at other times, in the spring and fall and to shed their feathers in the intervening periods (see Figure 6.2). This basic infradian rhythm appears to be determined primarily by an inner mechanism.

Another infradian cycle of behavior, seen in many species of mammals, is hibernation. The golden-mantled ground squirrel, a native of the Rocky Mountains, hibernates during the hard winters there. When kept in a laboratory under constant temperature (some at 32°F, some at normal room temperature) and alternating 12-hour periods of light and dark, the squirrels nonetheless increased their food consumption and gained weight in September and October, then went

into hibernation, their temperatures and weights dropping (see Figure 6.3). They awakened to feeding and activity in the spring. This annual cycle seems to be genetically programmed in the golden-mantled squirrel. In fact, squirrels raised from birth in the laboratory under light and temperature conditions that were held constant showed the same cyclical behavior over three years.

The Role of Environmental Cues

The genetic heritage that causes willow warblers to prepare for migration and golden-mantled squirrels to prepare for hibernation at almost the same time each year no doubt reflects a long evolutionary history. If the

Onset of arousal

3°C

4°C

14.5°C

17.5°C

20°C

26°C

35°C

Arousal complete

animals waited for certain environmental events before preparing their bodies for these activities, their survival would not be so certain. A prolonged Indian summer in the Rockies, for instance, might lead a squirrel to put off fattening up, and a sudden blizzard would be disastrous for it. Therefore, the squirrel's biological time clock must override most environmental cues.

This time clock does not remain unaffected by all environmental conditions, however. When the experimenters kept the squirrels at a temperature of 95°F, close to the animals' normal body temperature, hibernation did not take place, although the squirrels did show the same annual cycle of weight gain and loss. So at least one environmental condition, *temperature,* can affect some genetically programmed rhythms.

Another environmental condition that may be vital to the timing of some rhythms is *light.* The heliotrope plant brought indoors and kept in total darkness showed the same cycle of leaf folding and unfolding that it did outdoors. But later experiments have shown that certain plant seedlings raised in darkness show no rhythmic pattern at all until they receive a single exposure to light. That single exposure is enough to set into action the genetic mechanism for opening and closing in response to light and dark (Bünning, 1973).

The rhythms displayed by some species of birds are also influenced by the amount and intensity of light. Like most birds, finches are normally active during the daylight hours and rest at night. If they are kept in constant dim light with only 15 minutes of bright light a day, the timing of the bright light influences their activity cycle. When the period of bright light comes early in their waking period, the birds become active earlier, accelerating their cycle. If it comes later, their period of most intense activity is delayed (Aschoff et al., 1971).

Scientists use the German word *Zeitgeber,* which literally means "time-giver," as the general term for environmental cues that affect biological rhythms. How might Zeitgebers affect an organism's biological clock? And what physiological mechanisms might constitute the clock itself?

The Pineal Gland

Any biological clock that is influenced by light must have three elements: (1) an input pathway through which light energy gets to the pacemaker and stimulates it; (2) a pacemaker that generates and regulates the rhythm; and (3) an output pathway through which signals that activate the rhythmic activity are sent. In a number of nonhuman animals, the *pineal gland* seems to serve as just such a light-influenced biological clock.

Input Pathways   The light input pathways to the pineal gland appear to vary in different animals. In rats, the pathway is part of the optic tract, but a branch unnecessary for vision. Birds sense light directly through their skulls, as well as through their eyes. Chick pineal glands, removed and kept in culture, respond to changes in lighting conditions, which suggests that in chicks, at least, the pineal has its own photoreceptors.

Pacemaking Activities   Within the pineal gland, the transmitter serotonin is converted into the hormone melatonin, which is secreted into the bloodstream. Melatonin appears to be the agent for several functions of the pineal gland that relate to time and lighting cycles. For example, in some lizards, melatonin seems to cause the lightening of skin color every time darkness falls. In sparrows and chickens, the level of melatonin circulating in the blood appears to cause the normal circadian rhythm of daytime activity and nighttime rest and the cycle of body temperature changes. (When melatonin is injected into sparrows, for example, they go to sleep.)

Two enzymes produced within the pineal gland accomplish this conversion of melatonin in a two-step process. One of these enzymes is N-*acetyltransferase.* The activity of N-acetyltransferase determines the amount of melatonin released by the pineal gland into the bloodstream, and the amount of melatonin circulating in the blood controls such physiological rhythms as the cycle of body temperature changes and such behavioral rhythms as the sleep/waking cycle. Therefore, some scientists believe that N-acetyltransferase acts as a timer for these functions.

In many species of animals, both diurnal (active during the day) and nocturnal (active during the night), N-acetyltransferase activity is always highest when it is dark. In chickens, the activity of N-acetyltransferase is 27 times higher at night than during the day, while the amount of melatonin is 10 times higher, peaking at about the same time as the amount of enzyme peaks. The increased melatonin causes the chicken to roost (sleep) and lowers its body temperature.

Because the number of hours of light and darkness varies during the year, light must somehow influence the activity of the N-acetyltransferase clock. Studies with chicks showed how this influence works (Binkley, 1979). In chicks kept in constant darkness, the 24-hour rhythm of N-acetyltransferase persisted. In chicks kept in constant light, the amount of N-acetyltransferase was reduced. Even more interesting, when chicks raised in alternating 12-hour periods of light and dark were suddenly exposed to light during a dark period, their enzyme activity dropped rapidly (see Figure 6.4). This response reveals the sensitivity of the pineal gland to light. No such effect was observed when chicks were plunged into a sudden "lights out" during a regular light period, however. This lack of

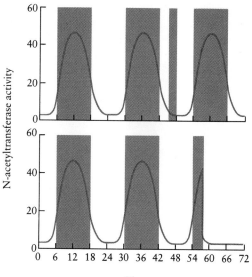

Figure 6.4
When chicks raised in alternating 12-hour periods of light and dark were exposed to darkness early in a light period (top), there was no increase in N-acetyltransferase activity. But when light was introduced during a dark period (bottom), enzyme activity decreased dramatically (Binkley, 1979).

response apparently indicates that the gland is not always sensitive to changes in light—there are times each day when its rhythm cannot be altered by environmental changes.

The gland *is* sensitive to changes in light during the dark periods—nighttime in the barnyard—and it may somehow provide the means by which chickens measure the different lengths of successive nights. The morning light reaches the pineal gland, causing the activity of N-acetyltransferase to be reduced; this reduction reduces the amount of melatonin released. With less melatonin in circulation, the chicken's body temperature rises, and it begins its daily activity of feeding and scratching. Because dawn may arrive at 4:30 A.M. in the summer and 6:30 A.M. in the winter, the chicken's pineal biological clock

The chicken's pineal gland senses light directly through the skull, and this may explain why the cock's crow is the first sound in the barnyard every morning.

must be reset every day while still maintaining its 24-hour period.

The mechanisms of this biological clock in chickens are clear. No such timekeeping function of the pineal gland in human beings can be established, however. Great differences exist even between rats and chickens in the way light reaches the gland, in the neural mechanism of enzyme regulation, and in the chemical processes that govern the activity of *N*-acetyltransferase. In rats, for example, norepinephrine released from the sympathetic nerves innervating the pineal stimulates activation of the enzyme; in chickens, it inhibits it. Some clocks that time human physiological rhythms may operate in ways that resemble the pineal's rhythmic production of *N*-acetyltransferase, but human experimentation is out of the question, and no one can, as yet, say for sure.

Human Circadian Rhythms

Everyone is aware of one daily rhythm: the human cycle of sleep and wakefulness. The human body actually has more than a hundred such rhythms, although many of them appear to be coordinated with the sleep/ waking cycle. Body temperature, for example, fluctuates about 3°F during a 24-hour day. It is higher during the day, peaking in the afternoon, and reaches its lowest point between 2 and 5 A.M. You may recall times when you stayed up particularly late, studying for an exam or taking a late plane. If you felt chilled, it was not only because you were more tired than usual, it was also because your body temperature was at its lowest point.

Urine flow is also rhythmic, being lowest at night during sleep. This is an important conservation mechanism. Because we spend about eight hours of every day lying flat and ingesting nothing, we would run the risk of depleting blood volume and bone mass if we excreted fluid during the night. The rate of urine excretion is probably determined by the rhythmic output of different hormones in the body. For example, scientists have found a pronounced circadian rhythm in concentrations of vasopressin, the antidiuretic hormone produced by the posterior pituitary, in the blood of normal people.

One hormone manufactured by the adrenal cortex, *cortisol*, is secreted in its greatest quantity just before dawn, readying the body for the activities of the coming day. In nocturnal animals, these adrenal hormones peak in the early evening.

All of these rhythms are obviously in synchrony with the sleep/waking rhythm.

Sleep/Wakefulness

Sleep is a specific state of the nervous system, with its own characteristics and cycles of brain activity. A person does not fall asleep gradually; the changeover from the waking state to the sleeping state is instantaneous. This was demonstrated in an experiment by William Dement in which the subject, lying down and ready for sleep with eyelids taped open, was shown a light that flashed every second or two and was asked to press a button each time he saw the flash. The button-pushing response showed no gradual slowing down. The action, and therefore perception, stopped abruptly when the subject fell asleep, although his eyes were wide open.

Scientists do not yet know what the purpose of sleep is, but it obviously is a biological requirement for our species. It has been said that sleep exists "to prevent us from wandering around in the dark and bumping into things," and if you have ever camped out in the wilds, as our primitive ancestors lived, you may find more sense than humor in this.

Sleep seems to be regulated by the interaction among clusters of neurons at several sites within the brain, including the reticular formation, the raphe nuclei, and the locus coeruleus. These mechanisms are discussed later in this chapter, when we describe the cycles of sleep, an ultradian rhythm.

Not every human being requires 8 hours of sleep every night. The amount of sleep people need, or feel they need, varies widely: some operate perfectly well on 4 or 5 hours a night, while others do not feel rested with less than 8 or 9. But whether its duration is long or short, a person tends to follow the same sleep pattern, or cycle.

Most of us also arrange our lives on the basis of certain patterns. We find, or create, many timing cues, or Zeitgebers, in our environment besides the cycle of dark and light. We eat our meals at certain times; we go to work or school at certain times; and we go home at certain times. Our social activities, too, are patterned: we usually go to parties or the movies in the evening and almost never in the morning. Most of us, of course, wear a watch or keep an eye on the clock in order "to keep track of time." What effect do these outside timing cues have on our biological rhythms? What would our days and nights be like if we had no access to such cues?

A number of experiments have been carried out with subjects who volunteered to spend long periods of time in isolation, apart not only from other people but also from all time-giving cues. Most strikingly, all such subjects isolated for only a few weeks tended to go onto cycles close to that of the 24.8-hour lunar day.

When a person's time is entirely freed from time-giving cues, it is said to be "free running." Michel Siffre's sleep/waking cycles during a part of his two-month stay underground show that many of his "days" were much longer than 24 or 25 hours and very few were shorter (see box on page 180).

Another subject, David Lafferty, remained in a cave for 127 days. Lafferty's cycles were entirely erratic at first. His "day" was sometimes 19 hours, during which he was active for 10 and asleep for 9; sometimes it was 53 hours, during which he was awake for 18 and asleep for 35. Toward the end of his stay, he settled down and lived a "day" of about 25 hours.

In the total absence of time-giving cues, then, human sleep/activity cycles are not regular. The importance of social time-giving cues is clear in places like the Artic, where darkness is virtually continuous during the winter and daylight is continuous in the summer. The Eskimos who live there nevertheless keep regular sleep/activity cycles.

Some circumstances of modern life, however, introduce irregularities of sleep/waking cycles into our lives: jet travel, changing work shifts, insomnia. Do these changes have any effect on the body's other rhythms? Do they cause loss of synchrony, and if so, what are the physical or psychological effects of such a loss?

A STAY BEYOND TIME

In the spring of 1972, French cave-explorer Michel Siffre lived deep in a Texas cave for six months while researchers observed his brain rhythms.

You live following your mind . . . it's all your brain, your functions. It's black—you have not the alternance of day and night. The cave where I was, it's a semitropical cave, you know, no sound, nothing . . . darkness completely.

Siffre lived in a carefully prepared cave that no light could enter. He ate whenever he was hungry. He slept when he wished, attaching electrodes to his scalp so that his sleep cycles could be recorded. He took his temperature several times a day, and sent urine samples to the surface for analysis. He phoned up to report when he retired for sleep, and the researchers turned off his lights. When he awoke, he phoned, and they turned his lights back on. Siffre called each of his sleep/waking cycles one day.

During Siffre's stay in the cave, his "days" lengthened so that his cycle 151 was actually the 179th day—the last day—below ground. He had "lost" a month of solar time. Here is his diary entry.

Cycle 151: Sullenly, mechanically, I stumble through my battery of tests. Just as I finish my laps on the hated bicycle, the telephone rings. Gerard tells me that it is August 10, a stormy day, and the experiment has concluded; I am confused; I believed it to be mid-July. Then, as the truth sinks in, comes a flood of relief.

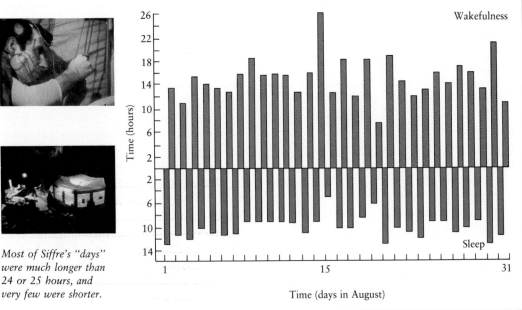

Most of Siffre's "days" were much longer than 24 or 25 hours, and very few were shorter.

When Rhythms Fall Out of Phase

In the long-term cave experiments, the subjects on free-running time lengthened their "days" well beyond the usual 24-hour cycle, and this departure did indeed break the synchrony between the rhythm of body temperature and the sleep/activity cycle. Ordinarily, you recall, the body temperature reaches its highest point in the afternoon, when most people are very active. The lowest temperature occurs between 2 and 5 A.M., when most of us are asleep. One cave-dweller's "days" lengthened to an average of 33 hours, but his temperature cycle remained in a 24.8-hour pattern (see Figure 6.5). Therefore, he sometimes experienced both a high and a low temperature during the active part of his "day"; on day 12, in fact, he experienced two highs and two lows during one "day."

Body temperature dramatically affected the length of the sleeping period in isolated subjects on free-running schedules. When a subject's retirement time coincided with his lowest body temperature, the subject slept for a relatively short time—around 8 hours. In contrast, if he retired when his body temperature was at its high point, he slept as long as 14 hours. People on a 24-hour cycle of daytime activity and nighttime sleep normally fall asleep when their body temperature begins to drop and awaken when it has started to rise. Evidently, the daily rhythm of body temperature affects how long a person sleeps, but most of us, because our lives are carefully scheduled, do not perceive that influence. If we occasionally happen to sleep for 12 hours, we generally ascribe it to being overtired or to that extra glass of wine. But perhaps the long sleep simply results from falling asleep when our body temperature is at its high point.

Jet Lag   One very common circumstance in the modern world that disrupts the schedules of many people is long-distance airplane

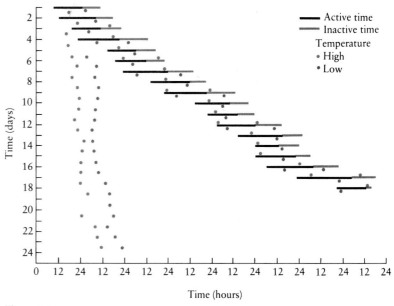

Figure 6.5
Desynchronization of body rhythms in an isolated cave dweller. Black bars represent the hours the subject was awake and active. Green bars represent sleep. High body temperatures are dots above the line; low body temperatures are below. The vertical rows (left) indicate regular temperature rhythm relative to erratic activity rhythm (Aschoff, 1969).

travel. We fly from coast to coast in the United States in about 5 hours, jumping over several time zones. If you fly from San Francisco to London, the flight takes about 10 hours, and you step off the plane into a day that is 8 hours ahead of your circadian clock. If your plane left at noon, you arrive at 10 P.M. your time, but 6 A.M. London time.

Most of us have experienced at least the jet lag that comes from a coast-to-coast flight. For a while, we feel tired and irritable; we have trouble sleeping; our digestive systems may bother us; we feel a little dull—not quite mentally or physically fit. These feelings result from the *desynchronization* of our body rhythms, the uncoupling of two or more rhythms that ordinarily work in harmony. Desynchronization occurs because of a *phase shift,* that is, a change in the timing of our biological clocks with respect to clock

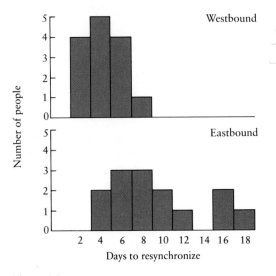

Figure 6.6
Resynchronization of body rhythms after jet lag resulting from flight over six time zones. Fourteen subjects flew westbound (above), and fourteen flew eastbound (below). Although there are wide individual differences in resynchronization, it generally takes less time to readjust after westbound flights (Kline & Wegmann, 1979).

time. Whereas ordinarily we go to bed when our body temperature starts to drop, we may be trying to go to sleep in our new location when body temperature is rising. Whereas normally our adrenal glands pour out cortisol just before we awaken, that wave of cortisol may be rushing through us in the middle of the day or just as we go to bed. For a few days after the flight we may wake up feeling sluggish and find ourselves wide-eyed at bedtime.

Eventually these rhythms return to normal and become resynchronized. But because some rhythms adjust more quickly than others, it takes a while for full rhythm synchrony to return. How long that takes depends on several things. For one, speed of readjustment depends on whether you have lost or gained time. After westbound flights, in which biological clocks lose time relative

to the 24-hour day, rhythms must *phase-delay* in order to adjust to schedules in the new locale. After eastbound flights, they must *phase-advance*. Phase-delay is evidently easier for the body than phase-advance: it takes less time for people flying westward to synchronize (see Figure 6.6). For another, the time it takes to adjust to a new time frame depends on one's physiology. People vary widely in their adaptive abilities.

The best way to deal with jet lag is to adjust your schedule to that of your locale as soon as possible, so that its time-giving cues—its Zeitgebers—will begin to work on your rhythms right away. In one study, subjects were flown across six time zones. Some had to stay in their hotel rooms, and some went out and joined in the life around them. Those who stayed inside adjusted to the new schedule much more slowly (Klein & Wegmann, 1974). If you arrive in London at 6 A.M. London time, you should try not to go to bed, even though it is 10 P.M. for you. You should have breakfast and stay out in the daylight. If you go to bed about the same time as Londoners do that night, you stand a better chance of waking up feeling like a Londoner than like a sleepless San Franciscan.

One factor in examining the effect of Zeitgebers on human beings is unique to our species. That factor is an individual person's motivation. The effectiveness of one strident Zeitgeber—the alarm clock—depends on the day of the week and what the consequences may be of ignoring the alarm. People almost always follow the clock's dictate to get out of bed during the week, but on the weekend they can, and usually do, go back to sleep. In fact, "Monday morning blues" may be a kind of jet lag resulting from going to bed and getting up progressively later on Friday, Saturday, and Sunday. By Monday morning, our circadian system may have become phase-shifted with respect to environmental time, so we must get up much ear-

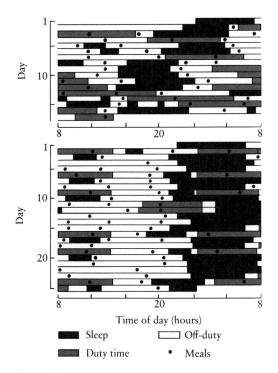

Sleep   **Off-duty**

Duty time   **•** Meals

Figure 6.7
Plots of two pilots' sleep time, duty time, and meals show little correspondence with circadian time. The airlines schedule pilots' off time solely on the basis of work time (Fuller, Sulzman & Moore-Ede, 1981).

lier relative to subjective body time (Moore-Ede et al., 1983).

Shift work Some industries and organizations run 24 hours a day. Airlines, for instance, often have pilots and flight attendants on different, staggered shifts (Figure 6.7). Hospitals and airports must have personnel on duty at all times, and many factories operate with three 8-hour shifts a day. Because many workers dislike permanent swing-shift work (4 P.M. to midnight) or graveyard-shift work (midnight to 8 A.M.), they often rotate shifts, working one week on swing shift, one on graveyard, one on days—then back to graveyard.

Changes in work schedules, of course, require shifts in sleep schedules, so the results of shift rotation are often just like those of jet lag. They bring about desynchronization of biological rhythms, with a consequent decrease in efficiency. Because some people require five or six days to readjust their body rhythms and get them back into phase after an 8-hour change in the sleep/waking schedule, some shift workers on one-week rotations never have a chance to readjust.

Air-traffic controllers usually rotate shifts—every few days in some towers, every two weeks in others. Certain shifts always handle peak traffic, with takeoffs and landings every few seconds, and rotation means that this nerve-wracking burden is shared all around. The controllers are prime candidates for the disease processes caused by prolonged stress—stomach ulcers and hypertension, for example (see Chapter 7). Although it is difficult to say which features of the job contribute most to their problems, shift rotation, with its rhythm desynchronization, undoubtedly plays its part.

A number of near-accidents have been traced to the lowered efficiency of pilots who had not adapted to their new shifts. One Boeing 707 that had filed a flight plan to land at Los Angeles International Airport appeared on the tower's radar but just kept going, at 32,000 feet, heading west over the Pacific. Confused and worried, the air-traffic controllers were able to trigger some alarms in the cockpit. The entire crew, it turns out, had fallen asleep, and the plane was cruising on automatic pilot. Luckily, the plane carried enough fuel to return to Los Angeles.

The effects of shift rotation may have been one factor behind the near-disaster at the Three Mile Island nuclear plant. The control-room crew failed to notice several signs warning of imminent danger. It turns out that this crew had just been placed on the

The same work goes on round the clock at this salt-flats plant near Ogden, Utah.

night shift after a 6-week period of constant shift rotation (Moore-Ede, 1982).

Increasing knowledge about the human circadian system and greater appreciation for the potential health hazards of rotating shift-work schedules have encouraged industry to take biological rhythms into account in designing work schedules. During a recent study at the round-the-clock plant of the Great Salt Lake Minerals and Chemicals Corporation in Ogden, Utah, Charles Czeisler and his colleagues documented the health and sleep complaints of employees and reports of their falling asleep on the job. The plant's normal shift schedule required crews to work an 8-hour shift for 7 days, then move back one shift, working graveyard, swing, and day shifts, then repeat the cycle.

Not only was one week too short a period for full rhythm resynchronization, the researchers suspected, but the workers had to phase-advance, with an especially big time advance from day to graveyard shift. A new shift pattern was designed using phase-delay: the crews moved from graveyard, to day, to swing shift. In addition, the crews spent three times as long—21 days—on each shift before rotating. After nine months, the workers on the new schedule said they felt more satisfied, and the plant's records revealed reduced job turnover and increased productivity levels.

As with jet lag, individual workers differ greatly in their speed of adjustment to and tolerance for shift work. Some people suffer persistent fatigue, sleeping problems, irritability, decreased efficiency, and digestive problems after only a few months, or even after many years, of shift work. Others adjust with apparent ease. One physiological factor may differentiate these groups: researchers have found that workers with high tolerance for shifting schedules have a greater range of body temperature in their circadian changes than workers with low tolerance (Reinberg et al., 1983).

The physiological problems that result from jet lag and shift work highlight the fact that our lives are normally adapted to our planet's cycle of light and dark. Even though we have the capacity to turn night into day with electricity—as is done so dramatically in places like Las Vegas—or to add hours to a day—by jet travel, for instance—violating the earth's circadian rhythm takes its toll. By desynchronizing our own biological rhythms, we make ourselves miserable for a while.

Human Ultradian Rhythms

Several hormones, such as luteinizing hormone and follicle-stimulating hormone, are secreted into the bloodstream in an ultradian rhythm. Careful measuring techniques can chart the episodic release of these hormones.

Some of the other ultradian rhythms that punctuate our days, however, are difficult to discern and even more difficult to explain. One subtle ultradian rhythm recurs approximately every hour and a half, whether we are awake or asleep. Day in, day out, as EEGs show, human adults experience a cycle in brain activity every 90 minutes or so, a rhythm so subtle that we are not aware of it. However, special tests involving verbal and spatial matching tasks also reveal that human alertness and cognitive performance appear to run in 90- to 100-minute cycles. Research into such shifts in daytime brain function has only recently begun, even though the nighttime portion of this ultradian rhythm has been known almost since sleep research began.

Sleep Cycles

In human beings, five stages, or levels, of sleep can be identified by electroencephalography (see Figure 6.8). People sitting or lying down quietly show *alpha rhythms,* in which activity oscillates with a frequency of 8 to 12 cycles per second (stage 1). As the sleep period begins, the basic rhythms slow, and the amplitude of the individual peaks of electrical activity decreases (stage 2). Sleep researchers interpret this as more or less random neuronal activity. Deeper stages of sleep are marked by the appearance of more synchronous events that interrupt the low-voltage, slow activity (stage 3). These events are called *sleep spindles,* bursts of activity synchronized at about 12 to 14 cycles per second but lasting for less than 1 second at a time. Still deeper stages of sleep show even more marked slowing of activity and the appearance of *delta waves,* in which oscillations occur at about 4 cycles per second (stage 4). Finally, as the deepest stage of

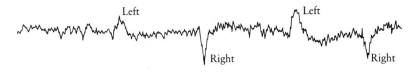

Awake, eyes open, looking left, right, left, right

Stage 1, 8–12 cycles per second, alpha waves

Stage 2, 3–7 cycles per second, theta waves

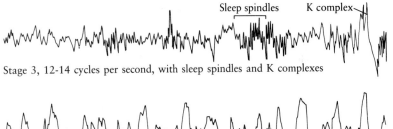

Stage 3, 12-14 cycles per second, with sleep spindles and K complexes

Stage 4, $\frac{1}{2}$–2 cycles per second, delta waves

REM sleep (stage 5), low voltage, random activity

Figure 6.8
The various levels of arousal, somnolence, and sleep are indicated by changing patterns and amplitudes of brain activity as recorded by electrodes placed on the scalp. The electroencephalogram, or EEG, reflects the activity of large numbers of neurons within the brain region closest to the surface electrodes. REM sleep resembles waking activity, except that electrodes record no muscular activity other than that of the eye muscles.

sleep is entered, electroencephalographic activity changes to a pattern of faster, low-amplitude activity punctuated by occasional bursts of phasic events during which the eye muscles show rapid movement. This fifth stage, called rapid-eye-movement or REM sleep, is also accompanied by almost total relaxation of the skeletal muscles. People

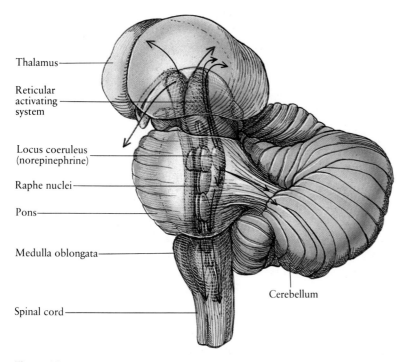

Thalamus

Reticular
activating
system

Locus coeruleus
(norepinephrine)

Raphe nuclei

Pons

Medulla oblongata

Cerebellum

Spinal cord

Figure 6.9
The major brain places implicated in sleep stages and waking: the reticular activating system, the raphe nuclei (transmitter, serotonin), and the locus coeruleus (transmitter, norepinephrine).

awakened during REM sleep say that they had been dreaming, and therefore REM sleep has been regarded as synonymous with dream sleep. Other studies have suggested that dreaming can also occur during deep slow-wave sleep, like that of the delta-wave stage.

Some studies attempting to determine which brain systems lead to the generation of sleep and its stages have used stimulation or lesions of specific brain regions, the standard strategies of brain research.

In the early 1950s, work done by the Italian physiologist Giuseppi Moruzzi and the American physiologist Horace Magoun pointed to the core of the pons and brainstem as a critical region (see Figure 6.9). Anatomical studies had indicated that fibers

ascend from this area to the cortically directed nuclei of the thalamus. Such circuitry means that this reticular core is in an efficient position to influence the cerebral cortex. Electrical stimulation of the reticular formation in the pons did indeed lead to activity that could be seen in the cortical electroencephalogram. In addition, lesions of the pons led to permanently comatose animals.

Recordings of the activity of specific neurons of the pons within the reticular formation have subsequently established that some of these neurons make specific shifts in their activity just before the transitions between sleep stages. Some of these pontine cells increase their discharge rate dramatically just before deep REM sleep begins, at that point firing some 50 to 100 times as rapidly as they did during the quiet waking stage. The fact that these cells begin to increase their rates of discharge well before the EEG shifts from slow-wave to REM sleep certainly suggests that these cells participate in the events leading to the transition to REM sleep.

Two other groups of pontine neurons tend to show opposite patterns of discharge with sleep-stage transitions. Interest in these neurons stemmed originally only from the fact that scientists knew something about the identity of the neurotransmitters of these neurons and, thus, about the possible role of those transmitters in sleep-stage regulation. The two groups of cells are: (1) the cluster of *norepinephrine-containing neurons* in the *nucleus locus coeruleus* and (2) the cluster of *serotonin-containing neurons* in the *dorsal raphe nucleus* (see Figure 6.9). Recordings from single neurons in these nuclei show maximal activity during waking, progressive slowing through the earlier stages of slow-wave sleep, almost complete silence before the end of slow-wave sleep, and persistent silence throughout REM sleep.

The pontine neurons that become active during REM sleep and the neurons of the locus coeruleus and the raphe nuclei that become silent during REM sleep are, in fact, now thought to be connected to each other. A simple explanation would suggest that early activity in the REM-on cells turns down the activity in the REM-off cells. But this hypothetical explanation does not explain what makes the REM-on cells pause near the end of a REM episode or what eventually restores their activity once they have gone "off." It is also possible that many other, as yet unrecorded neurons in the pons show similar patterns and that these patterns of activity fit even more closely with the timing of sleep/waking stages.

These studies did serve to suggest that the transmitters serotonin and norepinephrine play a role in the regulation of sleep and waking, since lesions of the locus coeruleus and of the dorsal raphe nuclei can severely disrupt normal sleep stages, depressing REM sleep especially. They also suggested a role for these transmitters in human attentiveness, since certain tranquilizing drugs that affect behavior by making the person drowsy and unresponsive also deplete the brain's stores of serotonin and norepinephrine.

The circuits of both norepinephrine- and serotonin-secreting neurons are of the single-source/divergent pattern (see Chapter 2). The cells in each nucleus send their axons to many regions of the brain and thus appear to be in a position to influence a large number of other neurons. Therefore, they are potentially able to play a role in generating global behaviors like sleeping and attentiveness.

Detailed observations of the activity patterns of neurons in the locus coeruleus add support to these suggestions. In animals that are awake and interacting with their environment, the neurons of the locus coeruleus show brief periods of increased activity while they process novel sensory events in the external environment, whether touch, light, sound, or smell. Since these data suggest that activation of the locus coeruleus is linked to the onset of brief states of heightened responsiveness, or attentiveness, it seems reasonable to suppose that slowing in the activity of the locus coeruleus could allow sleep to begin.

Other single-source/divergent systems probably also participate in the regulation of transitions between sleep and wakefulness and between stages of sleep. The dopamine neurons of the pons form one such system, and the acetylcholine neurons, some in the pontine reticular formation and some in the diencephalon, are another. Both neuronal systems project to many target locations in the brain and could serve to integrate the activity of these different targets.

REM Sleep

According to some measures, including the EEG pattern of brain activity, REM sleep resembles the waking state more than a sleeping one. Several other measures of physiological activity during REM sleep also resemble those of the waking state: increases and irregularities in heart and respiration rate, elevation in blood pressure, and erection of the penis. The eyes move quickly back and forth, as if the sleeper were watching things.

At the same time, REM sleep is a very deep sleep. In fact, most major body muscles become virtually paralyzed. Yet it is during REM sleep that vivid dreams occur. When sleep researchers awaken people in the midst of a REM period, almost all report that they were dreaming and can describe in detail the dream they were in the midst of. Only about 20 percent of the time do sleepers report they were dreaming when awakened from non-REM sleep.

The first REM period lasts about 10 minutes, but as the night wears on, REM periods become longer and are interrupted only by

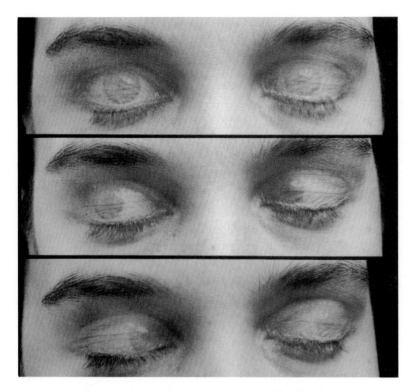

During REM sleep, our eyes move busily as if we were watching the images we see moving in our dreams.

descent into stage 2 (Figure 6.10). In other words, sleep becomes lighter after the first few hours. An adult who sleeps 7½ hours each night generally spends 1½ to 2 hours in REM sleep.

All mammals appear to have REM sleep. You may have seen your cat's or dog's eyes moving in its sleep, along with twitches of its whiskers and paws. Reptiles do not have it, but birds do have occasional, very brief episodes of something resembling REM sleep. This difference might suggest that REM sleep is a characteristic of more highly developed brains and that the more complex the brain, the more REM sleep there is. But among mammals, the amount of time spent in REM sleep seems to follow no rule. Opossums have more REM sleep than human beings. Newborn human beings spend 50 percent of their sleeping time in REM periods, while infants born prematurely spend about 75 percent.

So the purpose of this paradoxical kind of sleep—an aroused, alert brain but a paralyzed body—is hard to pin down. Some investigators have suggested that REM sleep facilitates neural growth in young organisms (Roffwarg et al., 1968), and findings that the rate of protein synthesis in the brain is at its highest during REM sleep help support this hypothesis (Drucker-Colin & Spanis, 1976).

Human Infradian Rhythms

Rhythms that span long time periods are generally more difficult to characterize and study than are daily rhythms or those with cycles of less than 24 hours. In many animals, seasonal swings in hormone levels are signaled by clusters of behavioral events and physical changes. The stag, for example, grows antlers in the spring and summer, which subsequently turn to horn. It uses these antlers to challenge other stags as it

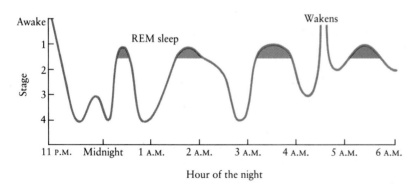

Figure 6.10
Pattern of a night's sleep. Sleep increases and decreases in depth, and periods of REM sleep get longer as the night progresses.

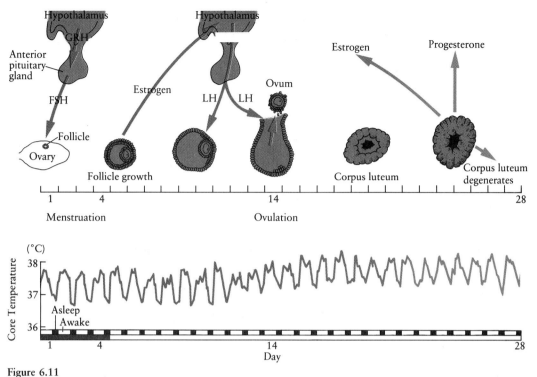

Figure 6.11
*The hormonal events of the human female reproductive cycle, an infradian rhythm.
At bottom, temperature is elevated during ovulation, an example of a circadian
rhythm apparently linked to an infradian rhythm.*

fights for a harem during rutting season, then loses its antlers when rutting is over. Clear signs like these tell researchers when to study the male animal's cyclical testosterone levels.

Human beings do not grow horns, and monthly or quarterly or annual patterns of small changes in human hormonal levels or in localized neuronal activity may go on undetected. That is why we have less information about these rhythms.

The Human Female Reproductive Cycle

The period of the human female reproductive rhythm is about 28 days. Each cycle begins when certain neurons in the preoptic area of the hypothalamus begin to secrete *gonadotropin-releasing hormone* (GnRH).

GnRH travels directly to the anterior pituitary through blood vessels connecting the two structures, and it stimulates the pituitary to produce and release two hormones into the bloodstream at appropriate times: *follicle-stimulating hormone* (FSH) and *luteinizing hormone* (LH) (see Figure 6.11).

FSH acts on the ovary to stimulate the growth of the *follicle,* the hollow ball of tissue containing the *ovum,* or egg. (All the eggs a woman will produce are present in her ovaries at the beginning of her fertile years; the eggs mature there, and one is released each month.) As the follicle grows, it secretes increasing amounts of *estrogen.* This estrogen, in turn, feeds back to the pituitary, inhibiting it from sending out more FSH. Estrogen also stimulates the pituitary to release

LH, which, in turn, causes the walls of the follicle to break and release the mature ovum. This whole process, called *ovulation*, takes about 10 to 14 days.

After the release of the egg, the remaining follicular tissue undergoes changes and becomes the *corpus luteum*. Luteinizing hormone causes the corpus luteum to secrete large quantities of the hormone *progesterone*. Progesterone increases blood supply to the uterus wall, preparing it for the egg's implantation in case fertilization takes place. Progesterone also feeds back to the pituitary and signals it to inhibit the secretion of LH. If fertilization does not occur, the level of progesterone decreases, the corpus luteum shrinks, and the uterine lining that had been built up to receive the egg is expelled in menstruation.

The mechanism that controls the infradian reproductive cycle in human females is not well understood. In some animals, the estrous cycle is tied to circadian rhythms. (The female reproductive cycle is called "estrous" when the uterine lining is absorbed; when it is expelled, it is called "menstrual.") Female hamsters, for example, normally ovulate every 96 hours. But if they are kept in constant dim lighting, their circadian sleep/waking cycles lengthen from 24 to 25 hours, and their estrous cycles lengthen to 100 hours. The lengthening of the circadian rhythm, then, results in a longer estrous cycle.

Some relationship between circadian rhythms of body temperature and the infradian reproductive cycle in women does exist, as any woman who has tried to conceive a child or who has used the rhythm method of birth control knows (see Figure 6.11). An increase in body temperature, taken upon awakening, of 0.4°F or more above the average temperature of the five preceding days indicates that ovulation is taking place.

Seasonal Rhythms

The seasonal rhythms observed in migrating birds and hibernating squirrels are now quite well understood. As we saw, these rhythms are genetically set, but in some cases, they can be influenced by environmental factors such as light and temperature.

Although they do not migrate or hibernate, some human beings do seem to experience a seasonal rhythmic depression. During the summer months, their moods are good and their energy levels high, they are productive, and their outlook on life is positive. When winter comes, however, their mood plummets, they become extremely depressed, lethargic, and pessimistic, and they feel unable to cope with life.

Thomas Wehr and his colleagues at the National Institute of Mental Health, who have been studying this form of depression, strongly suspect that a disturbance in seasonal rhythmicity may be involved (1979). They speculate that something prevents these patients with seasonal mood swings from adjusting properly to seasonal changes as the days grow shorter.

The researchers conjecture that the human pineal gland and related brain structures may be responsible for these winter depressions. In human beings, the brain structures responsible for sensing light and dark are thought to be the suprachiasmatic nuclei, which lie within the hypothalamus (see the discussion on page 198). Neurons from these structures project through several relays in the spinal cord and sympathetic nervous system to the pineal gland, where serotonin is converted to melatonin. (Remember that, in some animals, high levels of melatonin occur, in a circadian rhythm, only after darkness falls.) Experimental treatment for seasonal depression exposes the patient to a bank of high-intensity full-spectrum lights for several hours before day breaks.

Some scientists believe that a number of people undergo seasonal depression, the symptoms coming on during the short days of winter. Such patients may find relief from their symptoms when treated by exposure to day-lengthening full-spectrum lights.

Although it is not clear that melatonin has anything to do with the depression or its lifting, this artificial extension of the day seems to have helped some patients overcome their depression.

Scientific work on these problems is very speculative and experimental because the mechanisms that govern human biological rhythms are so hard to discover. Sexual behavior, for example, is clearly cyclic in many species of animals, and a number of the mechanisms governing its cycles are well known. Such cycles hardly seem to exist in human beings. Nevertheless, we will look at sexual behavior here, partly for its own sake and partly to search for any mechanisms that might govern its rhythms.

Sexual Behavior: Rhythms and Cycles

For all animals except the human one, sexual behavior has one purpose—to produce offspring. For many animals including the human one, nature seems to have cleverly arranged things so that sexual behaviors are pleasurable, and therefore motivation to engage in them is abundant. But the motivation and the behaviors have to be appropriate to the animal's environment. That is, offspring have to be born into circumstances that will favor their survival. They should not be born, for example, at a time of year when food supplies are low or when extreme temperatures could endanger them or when short days may curtail their parents' food-hunting time. For most animals, then, the motivation to engage in sexual behaviors occurs in cycles, which are tied to the earth's rhythms—the cycle of seasons, the lengthening and shortening of days, the rise and fall of temperature.

What physiological mechanisms produce the motivation and the behaviors? For some animals and some behaviors, scientists are now able to provide complete models—to describe most of the neural mechanisms and hormonal actions involved. One such model explains why and how female rats perform the postural behavior called *lordosis,* the crouching, rump-raised position that not only facilitates intercourse but is necessary for fertilization to occur (Pfaff, 1980).

Lordosis in Female Rats

The lordosis behavior involves many neural circuits in the rat, including touch receptors in the skin; neurons driving the muscles required for assuming the sexually receptive posture; and many neurons in the brainstem, the midbrain, the hypothalamus, and even the forebrain. Rats whose forebrain has been disconnected from the lower brainstem and spinal cord do not perform lordosis, so this behavior cannot be a simple spinal reflex, triggered by touch in the proper place. The actions of certain hormones—estrogen, progesterone, and luteinizing hormone releasing hormone (LHRH), which is released by the pituitary—are also necessary.

Environmental inputs—the presence of a

male and the stimulation provided by his mounting behaviors—are also necessary. Let us begin describing lordosis with the male providing this stimulation.

During the natural course of mating behavior in rats and mice, the male repeatedly grasps the flanks of the female and mounts her while thrusting his lower body against her rump, tailbase, and perineum. Stimulation of the skin in these regions causes a barrage of action potentials in most of the primary sensory neurons in the area, but only certain pressure-sensitive neurons give the sustained responses that can initiate lordosis. If enough of these neurons fire, the sequence that initiates lordosis begins.

Input from these primary sensory neurons converges on pressure-sensitive interneurons in the lumbar area of the rat's spinal cord. If the sum of the stimuli is large enough, the message to induce lordosis will be passed on through fibers that carry the message to structures in the brainstem. These brainstem places may be able to exert some control over the postural changes in lordosis, but they cannot do so over a long period of time; that is, they cannot sustain the behavior for the time required for the sexual act. The control necessary to achieve this part of the behavior comes through fibers *descending* to the spinal cord from cells in and around the ventromedial nucleus of the hypothalamus. When these cells are destroyed in experimental animals, lordosis does not take place.

These ventromedial hypothalamic neurons, however, must be primed by prior exposure to estrogen to work their effects. Estrogen is required for lordosis to occur. In fact, to facilitate the behavior, estrogen blood levels in the female must have been raised for at least 20 hours prior to stimulation by the male.

In all vertebrate species, specific groups of neurons in the medial hypothalamus (as well as in other brain regions) respond to estrogen. Estrogen can increase the electrical activity of these cells and can also cause them to manufacture and secrete more of their own transmitter (although the specific transmitter has not yet been identified). This heightened output travels down to the midbrain and facilitates lordosis. Also, these medial hypothalamic cells integrate the behavioral responses of lordosis with other aspects of the animal's physiology; for example, they coordinate the behaviors with controls exerted by the autonomic nervous system, controls having to do with rate of respiration, heartbeat, and so on (see Chapter 5).

Progesterone enhances the action of estrogen. It does so by inhibiting activity in a group of serotonin-containing neurons that ordinarily act to inhibit responses to touch stimuli. The effect of the progesterone inhibition, then, is to enhance the animal's response to touch stimulation and thus to facilitate lordosis.

Several groups of axons descend from the medial hypothalamic and preoptic area to the midbrain (see Figure 6.12). Then axons from cells in the midbrain descend through the reticular formation to the spinal cord. These descending neural tracts constitute the pathways to the spinal motor neurons, the final common pathway controlling the muscles that must flex or stretch to produce lordosis.

Even though the primary stimulus for lordosis is the male's pressure on the female's rump, a female rat engages in courtship behaviors before ever being touched by the male. She does some characteristic hopping and darting about, and displays some irresistible ear wiggling. When she goes through such routines, it is clear to all onlookers, whether rodent suitors or human researchers, that the rat is in an excited state. This excitability depends upon the actions of estrogen and progesterone and prepares her to

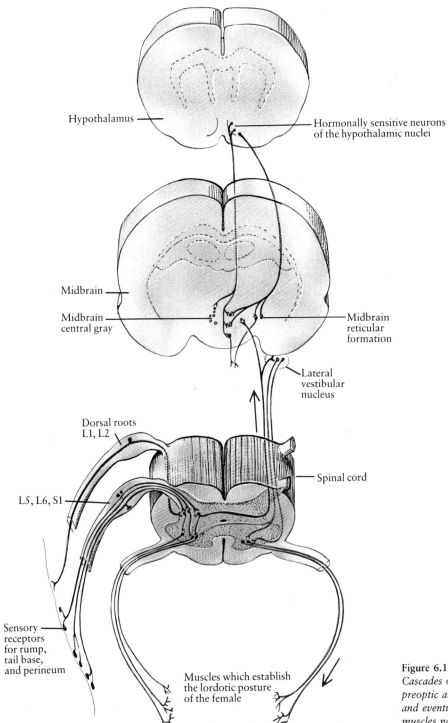

Hypothalamus

Hormonally sensitive neurons
of the hypothalamic nuclei

Midbrain

Midbrain
central gray

Midbrain
reticular
formation

Lateral
vestibular
nucleus

Dorsal roots
L1, L2

Spinal cord

L5, L6, S1

Sensory
receptors
for rump,
tail base,
and perineum

Muscles which establish
the lordotic posture
of the female

Figure 6.12
*Cascades of axons descending from hypothalamic and
preoptic areas to midbrain, to reticular formation,
and eventually to spinal motoneurons that control the
muscles necessary for lordosis.*

perform the specific lordosis behavior in response to the pressure stimulus from the male rat. In other words, the hormones have a preparative role, as well as a reactive neural and behavioral one.

To ensure that offspring have the best chance of survival, preparation for mating must be carefully timed. The female's peak of excitability and receptivity should coincide with ovulation, and ovulation should be timed for propitious birth seasons. This involves the integration of at least six chemical messengers—the neurotransmitters, estrogen, progesterone, luteinizing hormone releasing hormone, luteinizing hormone, and follicle stimulating hormone—and at least five types of tissue—in sense organs, the central nervous system (including the hypothalamus), the pituitary, the ovary, and the uterus. In the rat, hypothalamic nerve cells receive information about day length through the suprachiasmatic nuclei, and day length influences timing of ovulation. In fact, when rats are raised under conditions of constant illumination, the timing of ovulatory cycles is affected. Specialized thermoreceptors in the preoptic area of the hypothalamus also receive information about changes in body temperature. Neurons in the ventromedial nucleus of the hypothalamus direct feeding behavior and so process information about food supply. Information relative to stress or pain also converges on the hypothalamus. Thus, the hypothalamus receives much of the information needed to regulate reproduction and reproductive behavior according to environmental rhythms.

The hypothalamus does its job of regulation both through the release of hormones and by controlling behavior. In the female, the hypothalamus sends LHRH to the pituitary, which, in turn, sends LH and FSH to the ovaries. The ovaries then manufacture and release estrogen and progesterone, which travel to the hypothalamus and pre-pare the animal for mating. These hormones also feed back to the brain and pituitary to regulate further hormone release. At the same time, LH and FSH carry the message to begin ovulation. The job of LHRH is to integrate these happenings so that ovulation will occur at the same time the rats mate, since fertilization is the goal.

Hormones and Sexual Behavior

In Chapter 3, we discussed the origin of sex differences in the brain. We described how hormones have both an organizational effect—producing anatomical changes during development and priming cells so that they will later respond to the hormone—and an activational effect—the primed cells responding later in life to the presence of the hormone by initiating certain behavioral or biochemical processes (see pp. 70–72). The clearest evidence of these hormonal roles can be seen in sexual behavior, and especially in the alterations in such behavior that are produced by experiments with animals.

The organizational effects of hormones take place during a sensitive period for development of the structures involved—the areas in and around the hypothalamus discussed in the preceding section. In the rat, this sensitive period starts a few days before birth and ends about ten days after birth. The outcomes of various experimental manipulations show this to be so. If a male rat is castrated immediately after birth and then, later in life, is injected with testosterone, he will not be able to perform male sexual behaviors. The testosterone has no effect because the absence of hormones during the sensitive period prevented the organizational changes necessary for masculine sexuality. Such a rat is said to have undergone *demasculinization*. If this demasculinized rat is injected with estrogen as an adult, it will, in fact, display lordosis behavior and will produce LHRH;

in this case, it is said to have undergone *feminization*.

A female rat treated with testosterone during the sensitive period will permanently lose the capacity to release LHRH in response to estrogen stimulation and will not engage in lordosis behavior. It has undergone *defeminization*. And if treated with testosterone in adulthood, it will show the characteristic masculine sexual behavior of mounting; it will have been *masculinized*.

The importance of the organizational effects during development is underscored in experiments where demasculinized rats were injected with testosterone in later life. These rats did not show masculine sexual behaviors; rather, they showed an increase in the feminine ones (Sodersten & Larsson, 1974).

Given this basic picture of how hormones organize the sexual "identity" of mice and rats and how hormones interact with given neural tracts to produce sexual behaviors in these animals, what, if anything, can this tell us about human sexual behavior and sexual identity? Can we extrapolate from rat to human and, if so, how far?

Human Sexual Behavior

The hormones that influence sex-related physiological events and behaviors seem to be much the same in all vertebrates. For example, the mechanisms governing ovulation in human females, described earlier in this chapter, do not differ markedly from the process in mice. Estrogens and androgens are present and circulate in all vertebrates, and they seem to be accumulated by, and influence the activity of, certain medial hypothalamic and limbic nerve cells in every animal "from fish to philosopher" (Pfaff, 1980). The principles of feedback from hormone-producing cells to neurons to hormone-producing cells also seem to be much the same.

Since, in general, neuroanatomy has been conservative during the course of vertebrate evolution—that is, passage from smaller to bigger brains has been accomplished not by losing tracts and structures but by retaining them and adding new ones—we can expect that the principles governing neural control of behavior will be generally similar across species. But beyond these principles, the specifics of human sexual behavior are very different from those of mouse behavior.

Of Mice and Men One outstanding difference between human beings and other animals is that human females do not have cycles consisting of periods of high sexual receptivity alternating with periods of total nonresponsiveness. That is, sexual responsiveness in humans does not seem to be strongly tied to hormonal levels. Removal of the ovaries, for example, has little or no effect on females' sexual activity.

For males, on the other hand, mouse and man seem to have in common the need for testosterone. In order to be potent and fertile, they both need normal levels of it. (The body's production of this hormone is not cyclic; a constant feedback system monitors the level and produces gonad-stimulating hormones—FSH and LH—as needed to maintain normal secretion of testosterone. The hypothalamus does the monitoring, and the anterior pituitary produces the gonad-stimulating hormones; see Figure 5.6, p. 150.) Without testosterone, there is no sperm production, and eventually the male becomes unable to achieve penile erection. In many adult men deprived of testosterone, the decline in sexual activity is gradual, over a number of years. If castration should take place before puberty, however, there will be no sexual development, and sexual responsiveness will never occur. In Italy, during the eighteenth century, talented boy sopranos were purposely castrated so that testosterone production in adolescence would not lower their voices.

Androgens and estrogens are present in both males and females, although the relative amounts of them differ, of course. Some evidence suggests that the small amount of androgens in females may be responsible for sexual arousal levels. Women who are treated with androgens for medical reasons often report an increase in sexual desire, and women who have undergone removal of the adrenal glands (which manufacture androgen) experience a lessening of sex drive (Money, 1961; Michael, 1980).

Sex and the Cerebral Cortex   Even though the principles of neural control of behavior apply across species, the sheer size and complexity of the human cerebral cortex means that sexual behavior, like many other behaviors, will be the object of thought and the subject of learning. Even in other vertebrates, the cortex appears to play a profound role in sexual behavior. For example, dogs whose spinal cord has been cut so that the cortex plays no part in the behavior will have erections of the penis and will ejaculate if their penis is mechanically stimulated. But a normal, intact dog will not have such a reaction to mechanical stimulation unless a receptive female dog is present. The dog's cortex, then, inhibits the sexual reaction to mechanical stimulation (Hart, 1967). It decides what is or is not sexually arousing.

The human cortex can be endlessly inventive in its decisions about sexual arousal and in its search for and enjoyment of sexual activity. For some people, at least some of the time, simply imagining—fantasizing about—a sexual encounter can bring about sexual arousal and even orgasm. Human males can send sexual signals to human females in the form of fast sportscars, poetry, or athletic prowess. Females can send signals to males

in a single meaningful glance, a long philosophical conversation, or athletic prowess. Each male or female will react to such signals individually, depending on his or her society's mores, social class, family upbringing, and individual psychological and biological characteristics—that is, depending on his or her experiential history.

Homosexuality   Some men and women are sexually attracted to members of their own sex; they are homosexual rather than heterosexual. It is estimated that 2 to 4 percent of the male population and 0.5 to 1 percent of the female population engage in exclusively homosexual behavior (Katchadourian & Lunde, 1980). A number of psychological theories have attempted to account for this sexual orientation by pointing to various childhood experiences. Some psychologists have postulated that a certain family constellation, involving a weak or absent father and a strong, domineering mother, is the common background for many homosexuals. Others have concluded that early learning experiences—homosexual episodes that produced reward in the form of sexual pleasure—are responsible.

A large-scale study of hundreds of male and female homosexuals, however, failed to support either of these premises (Bell et al., 1981). Statistical analysis of events in the life histories of these subjects revealed that the best predictor of homosexuality in adulthood was a self-report of homosexual feelings, which preceded any homosexual activity by an average of three years. The researchers concluded that their results suggest a biological basis for homosexuality, at least in part.

Many studies over the years have attempted to find some such biological basis, but none was successful—until recently. In one study of homosexual males (Gladue et al., 1984), the reactions of homosexual men, heterosexual men, and women were studied in response to injected estrogen. In women, as you know, elevated estrogen levels trigger the release of luteinizing hormone (LH) from the anterior pituitary. After the estrogen injections, the researchers measured blood levels of LH in these three groups. As expected, the levels in women showed a dramatic rise. The amount in heterosexual men remained pretty much at preinjection levels. In homosexual men, however, there was a statistically significant increase in blood levels of LH—not as great an increase as in women but markedly greater than in heterosexual men.

One may not conclude, on the basis of results from this one study, that homosexuality is biologically based, but, given what we know about the organizational effects of androgen on the developing brain, it does seem possible that the brains of homosexual men (the pituitary-hypothalamus complex, at least) received less than the normal male amount of exposure to androgens during a sensitive period of prenatal development.

Human Sexual Response   No matter what one's sexual orientation, one's means of attracting potential partners, or the sexual techniques one employs, the sexual act produces a sequence of predictable physiological reactions, which are very similar in males and females. Table 6.1 describes these phases of the human sexual response.

Since human sexual behavior does not appear to be governed by rhythms, we will have to look at experiments with other mammals to discover what structures may serve to coordinate an animal's activities with events in its environment. We already have a good idea, from our earlier description of sexual behavior in rats, that the structure must be part of or close to the hypothala-mus. In many mammals, the suprachiasmatic nuclei act as pacemakers.

Pacemakers in the Mammalian Brain: The Suprachiasmatic Nuclei

In the late 1960s, the physiologist Curt Richter performed a series of experiments on rats in an attempt to find those brain sites responsible for rhythmicity. Richter destroyed portions of hundreds of animal brains—over 200 different sites—and then looked for disturbances in each animal's circadian eating, drinking, and activity patterns. As a result of this lengthy series of trials, Richter discovered that he could disrupt rats' daily rhythms by destroying a portion of the hypothalamus.

During those same years, related research presented an intriguing puzzle. Rats with circadian rhythms timed to a light/dark cycle in the laboratory showed no disruption in their rhythms even when the visual pathways between their retinas and their brains were destroyed. Clearly, the rats' biological clock mechanism, which Richter had located in the hypothalamus, was not getting its information about light and darkness through the normal visual pathways.

The puzzle was soon solved by anatomical studies that revealed a separate neural pathway linking each retina to the hypothalamus. These pathways lead directly from the eyes to a pair of relatively small cell clusters in the hypothalamus, called the *suprachiasmatic nuclei* (*supra,* "above"). These nuclei lie just above the optic chiasm, where half the nerve fibers from each eye cross to the other side. Armed with this clue, two research groups soon proved that the suprachiasmatic nuclei are the critical hypothalamic structures nec-

Table 6.1   *The human sexual response*

| Phase | Reactions of the sex organs | | General body reactions | |
	Male	Female	Male	Female
Excitement	Penile erection	Vaginal lubrication	Nipple erection	Nipple erection
	As phase is continued:	As phase is continued:		Sex-tension flush
	Thickening, flattening, and elevation of scrotal sac	Thickening of vaginal walls and labia		
	Partial testicular elevation and size increase	Expansion of inner ⅔ of vagina and cervix		
		Tumescence of clitoris		
Plateau	Increased size of penis head and testicular tumescence	Outer ⅓ of vagina narrows	Sex-tension flush	Sex-tension flush
	Full testicular elevation and rotation	Congestion of blood vessels	Muscle spasms in hands and feet	Muscle spasms in hands and feet
	Purple hue on penis head	Full expansion of inner ⅔ of vagina; full elevation of cervix; darkening of labia	Generalized tension of skeletal muscles	Generalized tension of skeletal muscles
	Mucoid secretion	Mucoid secretion; clitoral withdrawal	Hyperventilation	Hyperventilation
			Increased heart rate	Increased heart rate
Orgasmic	**Ejaculation**	**Pelvic response**	Specific skeletal muscle contractions	Specific skeletal muscle contractions
	Contractions of accessory organs of reproduction	Contractions of uterus	Hyperventilation	Hyperventilation
	Relaxation of external bladder function	Minimal relaxation of external cervical opening	Increased heart rate	Increased heart rate
	Contraction of penile urethra	Contractions of outer ⅓ of vagina, external rectal sphincter, and external urethral sphincter		
	Contractions of anal sphincter			
Resolution	Refractory period with rapid loss of penile congestion	Retarded loss of vasocongestion; ready return to orgasm	Sweating reaction	Sweating reaction
	Loss of penile erection	Loss of clitoral tumescence	Hyperventilation	Hyperventilation
		Loss of skin color	Increased heart rate	Increased heart rate

essary for normal circadian rhythmicity in rats.

Structures analogous to the suprachiasmatic nuclei have been found in all nonhuman mammalian species subsequently studied, from platypus to chimpanzee. And the human hypothalamus, too, contains suprachiasmatic nuclei (see Figure 6.13).

Each suprachiasmatic nucleus—there is one in each side of the hypothalamus—is composed of about 10,000 small, densely packed neural cell bodies whose dendrites branch sparsely. Many closely neighboring neurons synapse on one another in a mesh of local circuitry. Such mutual synapsing among close neurons is unusual in the brain, but many scientists have conjectured that our neural clocks might be composed of just such closely packed interacting neurons. It appears that several different neurotransmitters might be secreted by neurons in these nuclei, but serotonin, which comes from the raphe nuclei via single-source/divergent circuits, is the only established neurotransmitter found there in high concentrations.

The neuronal pathways in and out of the suprachiasmatic nuclei are difficult to trace because of the dense packing of the neurons. The tract coming in from the retina is known, and some neurons also come in from a portion of the thalamus and from the raphe nuclei in the brainstem. The raphe nuclei contain neurons that produce serotonin, and these are the source of the high concentration of serotonin found in the suprachiasmatic nuclei.

Neurons with their cell bodies in the suprachiasmatic nuclei send axons to other nuclei in the hypothalamus (which may also be pacemakers). They also send fibers to the pituitary and, through a multisynaptic circuit, to the pineal gland and to portions of the brainstem known to be involved in the timing of sleep.

Evidence that the suprachiasmatic nuclei actually generate rhythms themselves comes from experiments in rats. Electrical recordings of nerve cell activity in the suprachiasmatic nuclei and at other sites in the brains of normal animals by S. T. Inouye and H. Kawamura established that all sites showed spontaneous firing rhythms that paralleled the animals' circadian sleep/waking cycles. When all of the neuronal connections between the suprachiasmatic nuclei and the rest of the brain were surgically severed, nerve-cell firing persisted in a circadian rhythm within the suprachiasmatic nuclei but disappeared elsewhere in the brain. This evidence points strongly to the role of these nuclei as pacemakers in rats, at least.

The only evidence that exists for human beings is based on post-mortem examination. Tumors that caused behavioral disorders were found to have damaged the area of the suprachiasmatic nuclei. Patients found to have had tumors that damaged the ante-

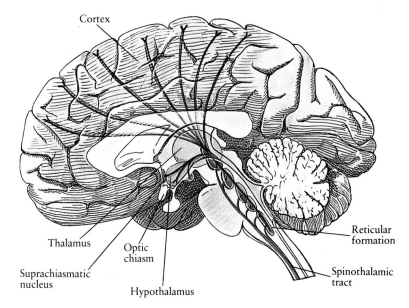

Figure 6.13
The suprachiasmatic nucleus appears just above the optic chiasm in the base of the hypothalamus in this midline view of the right hemibrain. The highly divergent axons of neurons arising from single sources in the reticular formation can also be seen.

rior tip of the third ventricle and optic chiasm (the location of the suprachiasmatic nuclei) were reported as having had serious sleep/waking disorders (Fulton & Bailey, 1929).

Multiple Pacemakers

Although the suprachiasmatic nuclei clearly are important components in controlling circadian timing systems in mammals, evidence suggests that other mammalian pacemakers also exist. A squirrel monkey subjected to lesions in the suprachiasmatic nuclei, for instance, loses its feeding, drinking, and activity rhythms, but its daily body temperature cycle remains unaltered. This indicates that some other pacemaker might be guiding its fluctuations in temperature.

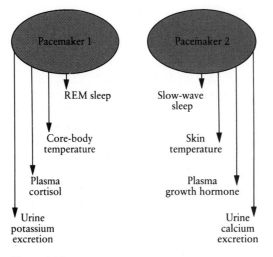

Figure 6.14
The rhythms within each of these clusters do not uncouple under free-running conditions; therefore, each cluster appears to be driven by a separate pacemaker (Moore-Ede, Sulzman, & Fuller, 1982).

Additional evidence suggesting that more than one circadian pacemaker operates in mammals comes from the studies of people, like Michel Siffre (see page 180), living in isolation. The fact that these subjects spontaneously undergo desynchronization—that their circadian temperature rhythm does not stay synchronized with their sleep/waking cycles, for example—suggests the existence of more than one pacemaker. Certain clusters of rhythms in these isolates never desynchronize, and this suggests that they might be driven by one pacemaker.

One such cluster includes rhythms of sleep/waking activity, skin temperature, and levels of certain chemicals, such as blood levels of growth hormone and urine levels of calcium (see Figure 6.14). In fact, it is thought (but by no means proved) that the pacemaker controlling this cluster is the suprachiasmatic nuclei. Another cluster of functions that seem always to vary together, even when other body functions fall out of

synchrony, includes the cycles of REM sleep, internal body temperature, level of cortisol in the blood, and level of potassium in the urine (also shown in Figure 6.14). The pacemaker that controls these rhythms appears to be more stable than the one controlling the sleep/waking rhythm. In case studies where rhythms are allowed to free-run—where the environment offers no Zeitgebers—this cluster rarely breaks away from its 24.8-hour cycle (Moore-Ede et al., 1982).

Many questions about biological clocks in human beings and other mammals remain unanswered—how many there are, how they interact, and whether the body contains a "master pacemaker" that sets and controls the timing of all the others. More knowledge is needed, for example, to aid in the diagnosis and treatment of disorders that may be caused by rhythm desynchronization.

Rhythms and Psychological Disturbance

New findings about biological rhythms have suggested that desynchronization may play a role in causing some psychological disturbances. Two of these, depression and insomnia, have been the most successfully studied.

Depression

Depression is almost invariably cyclic in human patients, although cycles vary considerably with the person. (Chapter 10 discusses depression and manic-depressive disorder more fully.) When investigators monitored the sleep cycles of depressed patients, they found a significant variation from the normal pattern in their EEGs. Many depressed patients enter REM sleep much earlier in their sleep cycles than normal people do. The REM/nonREM rhythm and the sleep/waking rhythm seem to have fallen out of their normal phase relationship. (Recall that these two rhythms appear to be governed by two different pacemakers.)

With this information in hand, researchers Frederick Goodwin, Thomas Wehr, and their colleagues decided to see whether they could restore these rhythms to normal synchrony, and, if so, whether the depression would lift. They had the depressed patients go to bed 6 hours earlier than normal to get their REM/non-REM and sleep/wake cycles back in synchrony. In a number of patients, the strategy worked. For about two weeks after the early bedtime was established, depression did lift—but only temporarily. The rhythms soon drifted out of phase again, and depression returned.

Although sleep deprivation is by no means a perfected treatment for depression, the fact that it works at all suggests that disturbances in the brain clock controlling the sleep/waking rhythm may play some part in depressive illness. Of course, it is equally possible that the sleep disturbance results from some other disease process, which is also causing the depression. For instance, another current hypothesis about the cause of depression suggests that abnormalities at those brain synapses that use the neurotransmitter norepinephrine are responsible for the condition (see Chapter 10). As you read earlier in this chapter, norepinephrine has been proposed as one of the major neurotransmitters controlling the REM/non-REM sleep cycle. If this hypothesis proves true, it could explain the abnormality in REM/non-REM cycling often observed in depressed patients.

Treatment based on knowledge of biological rhythms, however, has had more success in helping people who suffer with a specific type of insomnia.

Delayed Sleep-Phase Insomnia

The following case was described in the attending doctor's initial report of delayed sleep-phase insomnia.

A 24-year-old male student had had difficulty falling asleep since childhood. He was rarely able to doze off before 1:30 A.M., and he awakened only with great difficulty in the morning, despite an alarm clock and his mother's assistance. When he entered college, he was unable to fall asleep until 5:30 or 6 A.M. even though he consistently turned out the lights by 1 or 2 A.M. On weekends and holidays he often slept until 3 in the afternoon. At age 23, because of extreme sleepiness and fatigue during the day, he finally interrupted his education to seek medical help.

Unlike people with other types of insomnia, these sufferers can sleep soundly for a full eight-hour period and awaken refreshed if their sleep periods are not confined to a strict schedule. They just cannot move their late bedtimes any earlier, and they suffer constant insomnia and fatigue in trying to conform to a socially acceptable schedule.

Charles Czeisler, who did the earlier-mentioned study of shift-workers in Utah, has suggested a novel form of treatment. If patients could not adjust their sleep/waking schedules to an earlier bedtime, perhaps they could move their bedtimes later and later, all the way around the clock through the daytime and on to a normal bedtime. He prescribes moving bedtime three hours later each day for a week until patients reach an hour near the desired bedtime. Then they must adhere strictly to the new time in order to set the clock permanently.

The young man just described was admitted to the hospital for four weeks. His specific treatment involved progressive delay of the sleep period later and later until its beginning coincided with a clock time of 10 P.M. He was awakened at 6 A.M. This new schedule was then maintained for seven more nights before his discharge. At home, the patient kept a log of his sleep/wake schedule for two months and adhered to the new

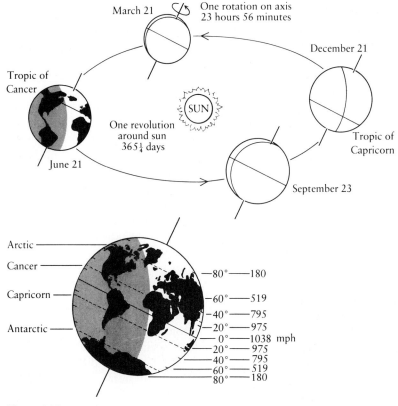

Figure 6.15
The earth's light-dark cycle, which drives most human rhythms, occurs as a result of the earth's revolution around the sun and its daily rotation on its axis.

schedule with excellent results. When he went back to college, he no longer suffered from sleepy periods during the day. He was able to get up for morning classes and developed normal new social patterns.

Characteristics of Biological Clocks

The biological clocks that we have examined here have the same function as any clock—they measure time. Although the number and location of these timekeepers in human beings is still something of a mystery, the best candidates for this function so far—the suprachiasmatic nuclei—are located in the hypothalamus. It is likely that before too long, scientists will be able to explain in detail how the components of this pacemaker—its neural circuitry, its connections with other structures, and the neurotransmitters that it secretes or receives—function in keeping the body's time.

Biological clocks measure time in such a way that the nervous system of an organism can integrate the needs of the body with the demands of the environment. For organisms that live on our planet, the most salient environmental event is the daily cycle of light and dark (see Figure 6.15). Almost all the rhythms we have examined relate directly or indirectly to the earth's circadian cycle of day and night. Even seasonal rhythms, such as migration and hibernation, appear to be driven by daily rhythms.

All rhythms are genetically programmed, products of evolution that enable organisms to adapt to their environments. The program is, however, a flexible one, allowing organisms to respond to certain changes in their environment, particularly to changes in the amount of light as days shorten and lengthen during the year. Even in human beings, the light/dark cycle is an effective agent for maintaining biological rhythms in customary set patterns. When people are isolated from lighting cues—and from social cues—their biological clocks start to free-run and their rhythms become desynchronized.

Social cues may be as important as any other Zeitgebers for human beings, who are, after all, "social animals," as Elliot Aronson calls them. In one study conducted at NASA, two four-member groups of volunteers were kept in constant illumination so that their circadian rhythms could free-run. All members of each group maintained synchrony with each other, one group keeping to a 24.4-hour schedule, and the other to one of 24.1 hours. When a subject was moved from one group to another, he showed a progressive phase shift and resynchronization with the new group. Just the presence of other people produced this synchrony (Vernikos-Danellis & Winget, 1979).

The cave-dwelling volunteers who spent months in total isolation not only underwent desynchronization of their biological rhythms, which caused them physical discomfort, they also suffered great emotional upset from being alone for such long periods. Michel Siffre kept a journal during his six-month period of complete solitude. On the 77th day of his stay (which he thought was his 63rd), he recalled emerging from his earlier two-month stay "in acute physical and emotional distress." He writes that, at this point, he is not suffering such distress, but he notices "a fragility of memory; I recall nothing from yesterday. Even events of the morning are lost. If I do not write things down immediately, I forget them. . . ." On his 94th day alone, he writes, "I am living through the nadir of my life. This long loneliness is beyond all bearing."

His solitude, then, affected both his emotional state and his thinking and memory, two aspects of human brain activity that are closely interrelated. Those relationships are discussed in both Chapters 7 and 8.

Summary

1. All organisms appear to undergo physiological processes that occur in regular cycles, adapted to the earth's cycles. These rhythms may be circadian, occurring daily; infradian, occurring less often than once a day—monthly, for example; or ultradian, occurring more than once a day.

2. Simple organisms, even those consisting of just one cell, display biological rhythms. The mechanism that controls the rhythm —the pacemaker—has not yet been discovered.

3. The seasonal hibernation patterns of animals like squirrels and the migrations of birds are genetically set, but these rhythms may be affected by extremes of temperature and by the amount and intensity of light that the animal experiences.

4. The pineal gland appears to act as a biological clock in some animals. Within the pineal, the transmitter serotonin is converted into the hormone melatonin by two enzymes, one of which is *N*-acetyltransferase. Some scientists consider this enzyme to be the pacemaker for birds' circadian rhythms since its activity is much higher at

night, producing ten times as much melatonin as during the day. Melatonin, as has been shown experimentally, causes birds to roost and lowers their body temperature. N-acetyltransferase activity is influenced by the amount of light, which the pineal of birds seems to sense directly, through the skull.

5. Human beings display a number of biological rhythms—for example, the circadian sleep/waking and body temperature rhythms. Usually, these rhythms are in phase, with the body's lowest daily temperature occurring during night sleep. Some events, such as jet lag or staggered shift work, can cause the rhythms to fall out of phase. The result may be minor health problems and decreased behavioral and cognitive efficiency.

6. One human ultradian rhythm is the cycles in brain activity that go on during sleep. There are five stages of sleep, each characterized by a particular type of brain wave, as measured by electroencephalograph. During the fifth stage, called REM sleep, or rapid-eye-movement sleep, most vivid dreams occur. Also, the wave pattern of REM sleep closely resembles the pattern of the waking state, but skeletal muscles are virtually paralyzed.

7. Scientists have identified brain structures and transmitters that participate in the transition from sleep to wakefulness and between sleep stages. Some neurons in the reticular formation in the pons greatly increase their firing rate just before REM sleep begins. Two other groups of pontine neurons and their transmitters also play a role in the regulation of sleep and attentiveness: the locus coeruleus, whose neurons secrete norepinephrine, and the raphe nucleus, whose neurons secrete serotonin.

8. The menstrual cycle is a human infradian rhythm; it is related to the circadian rhythm of body temperature.

9. In many animals—but not in human beings—the female reproductive cycle is tied to the cycle of seasons so that infants will be born at times of year when their chance of survival is best. In the female rat, estrogen and progesterone acting in the medial hypothalamus prepare the animal for sexual activity, timed to coincide with ovulation. In all, six chemical messengers—transmitters and hormones—and five types of tissue are integrated to assure propitious timing of sexual activity. A vital behavioral element of this activity is the female receptive posture, called lordosis.

10. Mature sexual behavior depends in large part on hormonal actions during sensitive periods in early development—prenatally in human beings, the first two weeks of life in rats. These early hormones have an organizational effect on the brain, priming cells in the hypothalamus so that they are sensitive to the hormone during maturity.

11. In animals higher on the evolutionary scale, especially in human beings, the cerebral cortex plays an important role in sexual behavior.

12. The suprachiasmatic nuclei, in the hypothalamus, have been identified as a biological clock governing circadian rhythmicity in rats. It is likely that these nuclei serve such a function in other mammals. It is also likely that more than one circadian pacemaker operates in mammals.

13. Some psychological disturbances—depression and certain types of insomnia—may result from a desynchronization of biological rhythms.

Further Readings

Moore-Ede, M. C., Sulzman, F. M., and Fuller, C. A. 1982. *The Clocks That Time Us*. Cambridge, Mass.: Harvard University Press. A readable explication of current knowledge about biological clocks. Complete coverage.

Hobson, J. A. 1988. *The Dreaming Brain*. New York: Basic Books. A noted neuroscientist discusses how dreams originate in the brain itself.

Binkley, S. 1979. A timekeeping enzyme in the pineal gland. *Scientific American,* April, 1979. The biochemistry of some biological rhythms in animals has been delineated. This article supplies necessary background and explains exactly how the brain and body of these animals keep their behavior in phase with the earth's cycles.

Silver, R., and Feder, H., eds. 1979. *Hormones and Reproductive Behavior—Readings from Scientific American*. San Francisco, W. H. Freeman. Reprints of articles pertinent to circadian and reproductive cycles.

Pfaff, D. 1980. *Estrogens and Brain Function*. New York: Springer-Verlag. A well-done monograph that examines the interactions between the multiple sites at which gonadal steroids can regulate female reproductive behaviors.

7

Emotions: The Highs and Lows of the Brain

7

It had started the night before when he had wakened and heard the lion roaring somewhere up along the river. It was a deep sound and at the end there were sort of coughing grunts that made him seem just outside the tent, and when Francis Macomber woke in the night to hear it he was afraid. He could hear his wife breathing quietly, asleep. There was no one to tell he was afraid, nor to be afraid with him. . . . Then while they were eating breakfast by lantern light out in the dining tent, before the sun was up, the lion roared again . . . .

They were driving slowly along the high bank of the stream. . . . The car stopped. "There he is," he heard the whisper. "Ahead and to the right. Get out and take him. He's a marvellous lion."

Macomber sat there, sweating under his arms, his mouth dry, his stomach hollow feeling . . . . He stepped out . . . and down onto the ground . . . . His . . . hands were shaking and as he walked away from the car it was almost impossi-

ble for him to make his legs move. They were stiff in the thighs, but he could feel the muscles fluttering.

Thirty-five yards into the grass the big lion lay flattened out along the ground. His ears were back and his only movement was a slight twitching up and down of his long black-tufted tail. . . . Macomber heard the coughing grunt, and saw the swishing rush in the grass. The next thing he knew he was running, running wildly, in panic in the open, running toward the stream.

In "The Short Happy Life of Francis Macomber," from which the excerpt above is taken, Ernest Hemingway portrays an emotion all of us have felt at one time or another—fear. Few of us, of course, face a lion about to charge. But soldiers face battle, women face childbirth, children face bullies on their way to school. Even sitting in the dentist's waiting room or hearing the coughing grunt of a plane's engine in midair can produce the dry mouth, the hollow gut, the racing heart, the shaking hands, and the experience, "I'm afraid."

We all recognize the physiological changes that accompany strong emotion—Macomber's parched mouth, pounding heart, and shaking legs. Most of these physiological changes are mediated by our brains and can be measured and verified. "Lie detectors" record just such alterations in blood pressure, skin moisture, and breathing rate. Milder emotions—appreciation, affection, irritation—are accompanied by less apparent changes, but changes nonetheless occur. Every time one performs some act or has a thought, a feeling, or a memory, some physiological change occurs in the brain and nervous system. Impulses race from neuron to neuron.

Strong emotions may include pleasure or pain and arise from the numerous interactions of daily life.

But a catalog of all the known cellular and mechanical events in the language of neurobiology does not equate with a description of what we feel. No one-to-one correspondence exists between neural events and the states we experience and describe to ourselves as "emotions." We do, however, feel afraid or elated or sad because of neural events and processes that take place within the dynamic systems of the brain that regulate emotion. Here we use the common vocabulary of emotion to describe how we feel, and we use the language of neurobiology to describe *how it is* that we have the experiences that we call "emotion."

Emotion and Motivation

Even though we can discuss emotions and feel fairly certain that we understand each other when we describe being afraid or being overjoyed, scientists have not yet been able to agree on a clear definition of emotion— one that avoids subjective terms and does not rely on a list of examples. Therefore, we shall not attempt a definition but instead shall proceed on the basis of a shared understanding of what human beings experience when they say things like I felt very angry, or very sad, or very happy.

William James, an American psychologist who created one of the first theories of emotion that attempted to relate the experience of emotion to physiological functions, described the powerful role that emotions play in human experience.

Conceive yourself, if possible, suddenly stripped of all the emotion with which your world now inspires you, and try to imagine it *as it exists,* purely by itself, without your favorable or unfavorable, hopeful or apprehensive comment. It will be almost impossible for you to realize such a condition of negativity and deadness. No one portion of the universe would then have importance beyond another; and the whole collection of its things and series of its events would be without significance, character, expression, or perspective. Whatever of value, interest, or meaning our respective worlds may appear imbued with are thus pure gifts of the spectator's mind.

Emotion and motivation are closely linked. Psychologists generally define *motivation*—which is not an observable process and therefore cannot be measured directly— as a hypothetical state that is inferred from goal-directed behavior. If an animal directs its behavior toward obtaining water, we can infer that it is motivated by thirst. If the animal works hard to obtain the goal, ignoring tempting food and, if a male, bypassing attractive females along the way, we can infer that its motivation is strong.

Emotional behavior is a means for one animal to communicate its motivational state to another of its species. Squirrel monkeys, for example, make specific vocal calls to seek contact with another animal, to indicate that they are in a state of high excitement, to regulate the distance between animals, and to express aggression (Ploog, 1981).

Many goal-directed behaviors, especially those performed by human beings, are performed because the goal has an incentive value for the person—in other words, because he or she expects that attainment of the goal will produce some positive emotion, or at least reduce some negative emotion. You study hard for a test because getting a good mark will make you happy; also, the act of studying and preparing for the test allays your anxiety about passing the course and getting a degree.

If we assume that even the fulfillment of such basic needs as drinking when we are thirsty produces a positive feeling—call this mild emotion satisfaction—then it is clear, as James says, that emotion is all-pervasive in our lives. Emotion gives value and interest

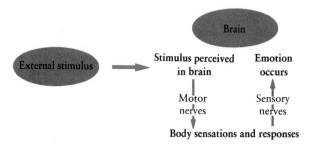

Figure 7.1
The James-Lange theory of emotion holds that the psychological experience of emotion follows the perception of one's own physiological reactions.

to our immediate actions and motivates us to undertake actions in the future.

Theories of Emotion

People have always been aware of the visceral changes that accompany emotional arousal—changes in heart rate, breathing, stomach and intestine contractions, and the rest. For at least the past 100 years, scientists have known that such changes are commanded by the brain. But how the brain functions to produce these changes and how the changes relate to the emotions that a person experiences have been, and remain, a matter of controversy.

The James-Lange Theory

In the late 1800s, William James, drawing on the ideas of Carl Lange, a Danish psychologist, spelled out what came to be known as the James-Lange theory of emotion (see Figure 7.1).

Common sense tells us that someone staring into the open jaws of a lion first says to himself "I'm scared," then experiences the autonomic arousal that accompanies fear. But have you ever sat alone at home reading in the evening and suddenly had a sense that something nearby had moved? You probably were unsure about what you saw or, indeed, that you had seen anything. But your heart speeded up and your mouth went a little dry. The James-Lange theory proposed that a person sitting very still after such a puzzling event would take note of his or her racing heart and dry mouth and then conclude, "Wow, that scared me!" In essence, the theory proposes that after the initial perception, the experience of emotion results from the perception of one's own physiological changes. In other words, the physical sensations *are* the emotion. As James said, "We feel sorry because we cry, angry because we strike, afraid because we tremble" (James, 1884).

Although his theory attempted to ground the emotions in physiological functions, James could not produce evidence to support it. However, more recent experimental evidence, described later in this chapter, supports some of this theory.

The Cannon-Bard Theory

In 1929, the physiologist Walter Cannon pointed out that the James-Lange theory erred in its assumption that each emotional experience has its own particular set of physiological changes. Cannon's studies gave evidence that the same pattern of physiological arousal accompanies a number of emotions. Even a simple physical experience, scalp tingles, for example, can occur while listening to a beautiful piece of music or while watching an autopsy. Thus, emotions have to be more than just the sensations of arousal. More recent studies seem to support Cannon's contention. The states of arousal that accompany strong emotional reactions do appear to be much the same, and they do come upon us relatively slowly.

Cannon constructed a theory, later modified by Phillip Bard, saying, in essence, that when a person faces an emotion-arousing event, nerve impulses first pass through the thalamus. There, the theory goes, the message splits: half goes to the cerebral cortex, where it produces the subjective experience of fear or anger or happiness; the other half goes to the hypothalamus, which commands the body's physiological changes. According to the Cannon-Bard theory, then, the psychological experience of emotion and the physiological reactions are simultaneous (see Figure 7.2).

The physiology of the Cannon-Bard theory was not correct in its particulars. But it did bring the origination of emotion back into the brain from the peripheral organs, where the James-Lange theory had located it.

The Papez Circuit

The Cannon-Bard theory focused on the role of the thalamus as a "center" for emotional experience. We know today, thanks largely to the direction set by anatomist James W. Papez in 1937, that emotion is a function not of specific brain "centers" but of circuitry (see Figure 7.3). The structures in Papez's "circuit" constitute much of what is now called the limbic system (see Figure 7.4).

Papez called this circuit the "stream of feeling." He also proposed a "stream of movement," which relays sensations through the thalamus to the corpus striatum, and a "stream of thought," which relays sensations through the thalamus to the major portions of the cerebral cortex. In the merging of these streams, Papez said, "sensory excitations . . . receive their emotional coloring." Papez's contribution stands, even today, as a basic outline for what scientists know about the neuroanatomy of the emotions, although the anatomy and physiology of these structures is now known to be much more complex than envisioned by Papez.

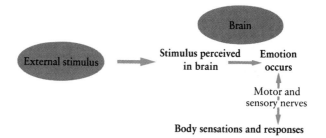

Figure 7.2
The Cannon-Bard theory, in contrast to the James-Lange theory, says that the psychological experience of emotion and the physiological reactions are simultaneous.

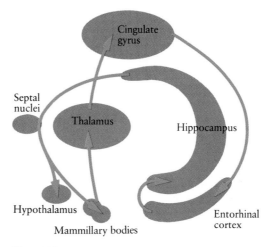

Figure 7.3
Much of what is now known to be the limbic system is called out in the Papez circuit.

Brain Structures that Mediate Emotion

Many of the structures responsible for the homeostasis and rhythms of the body (see Chapters 5 and 6) also produce emotion. This is not too surprising. In order to support the requirements of its internal systems, for example, a hungry animal stalks and attacks a smaller animal in order to eat it (aggression). At the same time, it must be constantly alert

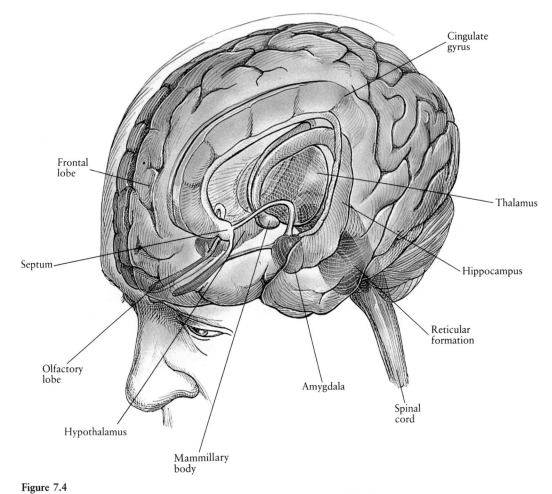

Figure 7.4
The major brain structures forming the limbic system. From this view, their locations around the border, or limbus, of the brain can be appreciated.

to danger and ready to defend itself against attack by larger predators (fear).

The most important of the brain's structures that produce emotion are, taken together, called the *limbic system*. This system is also known as the "animal brain" because its parts and functions appear to be essentially alike in all mammals. The limbic system sits above the brainstem but under the cortex. A number of structures in the brainstem and parts of the cortex also participate in producing emotion. All these limbic, cortical, and brainstem structures are connected by neural pathways.

The Limbic System

The limbic system includes a number of interconnected structures (see Figure 7.4). Certain nuclei in the *anterior thalamus* participate in the limbic alliance. Under that gland lies the small but potent *hypothalamus*, whose neurons specifically effect changes in the autonomic nervous system—heart rate, respiration, and so on—that accompany strong emotion. Deep in the lateral forebrain lies the *amygdala,* a walnut-sized mass of gray cells. Animal experiments have shown that the amygdala is active in the production of aggressive behavior or fear reactions. Adjacent to the amygdala is the *hippocampus.* The role of the hippocampus in producing emotion is not yet clear.

Encircling the hippocampus and the other structures of the limbic system is the *cingulate gyrus* ("cingulate" means "girdling" or "encircling"). A two-way fiber system, the *fornix,* follows the curve of the cingulate gyrus and connects the hippocampus to the hypothalamus. Another structure, the *septum,* receives neural input through the fornix from the hippocampus and sends neural output to the hypothalamus.

When we look at the course of the neural pathways in the brain, we can see why all our interactions with our environment have an emotional quality of some sort. Incoming neural messages from all the senses, after traveling through pathways in the brainstem, the various processing levels in the cortex, or both, pass through one or more of the limbic structures: the amygdala, the hippocampus, or part of the hypothalamus. Outgoing messages down from the cortex also pass through these structures.

Structures in the Brainstem

Within the brainstem, the *reticular formation* plays an important role in emotion (see Figure 7.5). It receives sensory information through various neural pathways and acts as a kind of filter (in fact, "reticulum" means "little net," which the structure resembles), passing on only information that is novel or persistent. Its fibers project widely to areas of the cerebral cortex, some by way of the thalamus. Most neurons in the reticular formation are thought to be "nonspecific." This

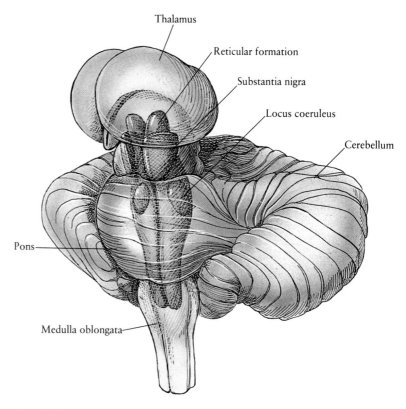

Figure 7.5
Structures in the brainstem that play a role in emotion. Dopamine fibers from the substantia nigra and norepinephrine fibers from the locus coeruleus arise to innervate the entire forebrain. Both of these neuron groups and several others form discrete parts contributing to the reticular activating system.

means that, unlike neurons in a primary sensory pathway—visual, auditory, or motor, for example (see Chapter 4)—which respond to only one type of stimulus, neurons in the reticular formation can respond to information from many sources. These neurons pass along messages from the eyes, the skin, and the viscera, among other organs and structures, to the limbic system and the cortex.

Some structures within the pons and some midbrain components of the reticular formation have particular functions. The *locus coeruleus,* or "blue area," in the pons is a concentrated collection of cell bodies of neurons with single-source/divergent circuitry that secrete the neurotransmitter *norepine-phrine*. As you saw in Chapter 6 in connection with REM sleep, some neural pathways from the locus coeruleus travel up into parts of the thalamus and hypothalamus and many parts of the cortex. Other pathways travel down to the cerebellum and into the spinal cord. The product of these specialized neurons, the transmitter norepinephrine (also secreted as a hormone by the adrenal medulla), triggers emotional arousal. It has been suggested that too little norepinephrine action in the brain results in depression; too much norepinephrine action over too long a time is implicated in severe stress reactions. Norepinephrine may also play a part in producing feelings that an organism experiences as pleasure.

The *substantia nigra,* or "black area," in the midbrain is a concentration of cell bodies of neurons, again of the single-source/divergent type of circuit, that secrete the neurotransmitter *dopamine.* Among other things, dopamine appears to facilitate some pleasurable sensations, and it is known to mediate the exhilaration that people seek in taking cocaine and amphetamines. Patients with Parkinson's disease show deterioration of the neurons in the substantia nigra, with a resultant insufficiency of dopamine. L-dopa, the drug given to these patients, aids in dopamine production, but it can also produce schizophrenialike symptoms. These reactions suggest that an excess of dopamine plays some part in schizophrenia itself (see Chapter 10).

The Cerebral Cortex

The parts of the cerebral cortex thought to be most active in emotion are the *frontal lobes,* which receive direct neural projections from the thalamus. Because emotion colors thought, the temporal lobes are likely to figure in emotion too, but little is yet

Phineas Gage's accident took place on September 13, 1848.

known about how the mechanisms linking thought and emotion interact.

The importance of the frontal lobes to temper and personality has been known at least since 1848. In that year, an explosion blew a 3-foot-long, 13-pound metal rod up through the skull of Phineas Gage, a 25-year-old railroad construction foreman. The accident removed his left frontal lobe. Miraculously, the man survived, but he was profoundly changed. Before the accident, Gage had been dependable, industrious, and well liked. When he recovered, he was restless, loud, profane, and impulsive. His doctor described him as "manifesting but little deference for his fellows, impatient of restraint or advice when it conflicts with his desires, at times pertinaciously obstinate, yet capricious and vacillating, devising many plans of future operations, which are no sooner arranged than they are abandoned . . . " (Harlow, 1868).

It is impossible to reconstruct an exact clinical picture of this case after the fact. Part of Gage's character change may have been an emotional reaction to his damaged looks. Indeed, he did travel around for a while with P. T. Barnum, carrying his rod and displaying himself as a freak. But subsequent scientific evidence has shown that the frontal lobes, perhaps because of their associations with the thalamus, play an important part in emotional experience and expression.

Much is known about the anatomy of these limbic, brainstem, and cortical structures and the neural pathways that connect them to each other and to other parts of the brain and nervous system. But exactly *how* they function in emotion—especially human emotion—is still largely a matter of inference.

The Role of the Autonomic Nervous System in Emotion

The brain, of course, does its work through its control of the body's systems. The arousal that you experience with fear or rage is triggered by your brain, but it is implemented by your *autonomic nervous system* (ANS).

The autonomic nervous system has two anatomically distinct divisions (see Chapter 5, Figure 5.1, page 141). The *sympathetic division* mobilizes the body's resources and energy—the "fight-or-flight" response. In general, the *parasympathetic division* works to conserve bodily energy and resources. As you have seen, the two divisions do work together, even though their functions may seem antagonistic. The balance among their various activities at any given moment depends on an interaction between the demands of the external situation and the body's internal condition.

To illustrate how the two divisions work in emotion, suppose that you have just finished a big meal. The parasympathetic nerves slow your heart rate and enhance your digestive activity. But if a man with a gun suddenly breaks into your dining room— or if you only hear a noise outside the window—your sympathetic nerves take over. Your digestion processes slow down; your heart rate increases; blood is diverted from arteries in the skin and digestive organs

to provide more to muscles and brain; your lungs expand to use more oxygen; the pupils of your eyes dilate to let more light in; and your sweat glands become active, preparing to cool your body during its coming exertion. Activation of the sympathetic nervous system also causes your adrenal medulla to secrete epinephrine (sometimes called adrenalin) and causes other sympathetic nerves to send transmitter norepinephrine, which acts directly on the heart and blood vessels. Together, these chemical signals tell the circulatory system to increase blood pressure. Epinephrine circulating through the blood increases heart rate and heart output directly. Norepinephrine released from the sympathetic nerves constricts certain blood vessels, decreasing the volume of blood going to areas not essential for quick response—the gut, skin, and kidneys—and increasing blood flow to areas that must be prepared—the brain and the muscles.

When a person is faced with an event that calls for mobilization, the ANS responds within 1 to 2 seconds. This seems very fast. But consider what happens when you see a car in front of you on the highway come to a sudden stop. In less than half a second you automatically step on your brake, and you have probably also checked your rearview mirror to see how close the car behind you is. The experience of arousal—the pounding heart, shaking hands, and so on—comes *after* the emergency is over. Your brain apparently dealt with the situation without help from its elaborate but relatively slow backup equipment.

This timing delay happens because the hierarchical neural pathways from the sensory receptors to the cortex and back are fairly direct. The messages go through the reticular system, through the thalamus, and up to the cortex. Within a split second you take appropriate action. In this case, you step on the brake. Meanwhile, the same messages are also going through neural pathways connecting the thalamus and hypothalamus, and those connecting the hypothalamus and the frontal region of the cortex by way of the amygdala and hippocampus. If these systems all agree that danger has been perceived, the hypothalamus sets off the ANS arousal mechanisms, which go into effect after a second or so. The hormonal messages from the now-alerted pituitary are blood-borne, however, and they travel more slowly than messages speeding along neural pathways. Hence the delay in physiological response. In terms of species adaptation, of course, you were ready to fight, to flee, or to take other action had the danger been an attack. That may explain why so many fender-benders are followed by vociferous arguments about who was to blame.

Of course, the emotional reaction that follows a fender-bender has an obvious cause. But it sometimes happens that we feel anxious or uneasy or exalted without having had, in the immediate past, some experience that we can point to as the cause of that feeling. The James-Lange theory says that we examine our physiological reactions and decide from them what emotion we feel. The studies described in the following section examine the role of cognition in the experience of emotion.

Cognition and Emotion

In 1924, Gregorio Marañon published an important but essentially anecdotal study bearing on emotions. When he injected patients with epinephrine, Marañon wrote, about one-third of them said they experienced something like an emotional state. The rest said they felt no emotion but described a physiological state of arousal. The people who reported feeling emotional, however, carefully specified that they felt *"as if"* they were afraid, or *"as if"* something exciting were about to happen. When Marañon happened to talk with a few of these people about some important life event in their recent past—a death in the family or an upcoming wedding—their feeling lost its "as if" status and became full emotion—whether grief or joy.

On the basis of Marañon's report and other evidence, Stanley Schachter theorized that in order to experience an emotion, both physiological arousal and a cognitive evaluation must be necessary. Neither one alone could produce a true emotional state.

In the best known of his experiments testing this hypothesis (Schachter & Singer, 1962), some subjects received an injection of epinephrine which they were told contained vitamins that would have an effect on visual skills. Control subjects received only a placebo, a saline injection, which they too were told contained vitamins. After the injection, subjects from both these groups were treated in one of three ways: (1) Some were told about the physiological effects of epinephrine. That is, without naming epinephrine, the researchers warned them that they might feel palpitations, tremors, and the like. (2) Some were given no information. And (3) some were misinformed. They were told that their hands and feet might feel numb, for example, or that they might have a slight itch or a headache.

After the injection and the explanation, each subject waited in a room with someone who said he was also a subject but who was actually a "stooge," part of the experimental setup. Some stooges behaved euphorically, chuckling to themselves, playing basketball with the wastebasket, and so on. Others were highly irritable and insulting, becoming angrier and angrier until they left the room in a rage.

The experimenters observed the pairs

through a one-way mirror, and later they questioned the subjects about their feelings. The epinephrine-injected subjects who had been informed correctly about the drug's effects showed and reported the least reaction to the stooges' behavior. Those who had been misinformed, who had physiological symptoms different from those they had been told to expect, were most influenced. They acted like the stooge in the waiting room and reported that they felt very happy or very angry, depending on which stooge they had been paired with. Those who received no information after injection reacted in a manner between that of the other two sets.

These results appear to confirm Schachter's thesis. If physiological arousal is induced (by injection or by an event) in someone who has no immediate explanation for it, the person will give an emotional label to that state based on his or her knowledge of what is going on at the time.

George W. Hohmann's study (1966) of patients who had suffered spinal-cord injuries lends support to Schachter's thesis. Hohmann divided his subjects into five groups according to how high on the spinal cord their injury was. (The higher the damage, the less visceral sensation a person can feel.) Then he asked these patients to compare the emotional reactions they had before and after their injuries. He found that the people with injuries high on the spinal cord reported the greatest difference in their before-and-after emotional experience, whether it was grief, fear, or joy. In fact, these descriptions of emotional states after injury resembled those given by Marañon's subjects: the subjects reported feeling "as if" they were afraid or "as if" they were joyful. Marañon's subjects had had these "almost" feelings when they had no appropriate cognitive cues to help them interpret their physiological arousal. Hohmann's patients had the feelings

when the right cues were there, but they could not feel any physiological arousal.

In human beings, the thinking and learning areas of the brain interact with the limbic system. George Mandler (1975) makes the point that even events that would seem to trigger "wired-in" autonomic responses in human beings—a sudden loss of support for one's weight, for example—can be modified by one's meaning analysis of the event. Some people react euphorically to the feeling of the ground falling out from under them on a roller coaster. These same people, experiencing the same feeling of release from gravity when an airplane suddenly drops in an air pocket, would probably be terrified. One difference between these reactions lies in our sense of whether or not we are in control of the situation. If you choose to ride on the roller coaster, you expect the sensations, and you have some sense of control. As an airplane passenger, you are—and feel—helpless if the plane drops.

This cognitive factor—the sense that one has some control of a situation—turns out to be significant not only in emotional arousal but also in the experience of pain and stress, as discussed in later sections of this chapter. First, however, we look briefly at an emotional behavior that has been the focus of much research—aggression.

Aggression

Animal studies performed over the past four or five decades have given rise to a vast body of literature on what has been called "aggression." Like emotion, aggression is difficult to define. Some earlier theories assumed that aggression was a unitary concept—that there was an aggressive drive or instinct and that it operated pretty much the same way in all individuals of a species and under all circumstances. Experiments eventually showed that, even in mice and rats, "aggression" differs from individual to individual and from one situation to another.

The different types of aggressive behaviors found in animals include:

1. Predatory aggression—a hungry animal stalks and kills the prey it feeds on.

2. Competitive aggression—males of a species threaten or attack each other for position in a dominance hierarchy, for females, or for food.

3. Defensive aggression—an animal faced with an inescapable threat responds with fear-motivated threat or attack.

4. Irritative aggression—a laboratory animal threatens or attacks in response to some aversive stimulus, such as an electric shock.

5. Territorial aggression—an animal actively responds to an intruder violating the boundaries of the group's or its own established living area.

6. Maternal protective aggression—a female threatens or attacks another animal perceived as endangering her infants.

7. Female social aggression—a female attacks a juvenile or a strange female.

8. Sex-related aggression—a male whose normal sexual advances have been rebuffed turns and attacks the female who rebuffed him.

9. Instrumental aggression—an animal repeats threat or attack behavior that has worked in the past to achieve a similar outcome; for example, the dominant monkey in a hierarchy might use threats to affirm and consolidate his position even when no other animal is being provocative or competitive.

Electrode Studies

Some early research using implanted electrodes pointed to the hypothalamus as the brain site responsible for aggression.

In the early 1950s, W. R. Hess, a Swiss neuroscientist and Nobel Prize winner, conducted the pioneering studies using electrode placement. Hess found that when he stimulated a specific area of a cat's hypothalamus, it showed behaviors typical of aggression in the face of threat: it spat and growled, it lashed its tail, it extended its claws, its fur stood on end (Figure 7.6). The subject showed all the behavior any cat shows when confronted by a barking dog—but in the absence of a dog or any other environmental cues. Neural activities alone, arising from the hypothalamus, appeared to produce this expression of fear-provoked aggression.

Undoubtedly the most dramatic exhibi-

Figure 7.6
With an electrode implanted in one area of its hypothalamus, this cat postures aggressively when electrical stimulation is applied (Hess, 1957).

tion of electrical stimulation apparently affecting emotional behavior was staged by Jose Delgado. He implanted an electrode in the hypothalamus of a bull bred specifically to fight aggressively in the ring. Delgado claimed that stimulation would turn off the bull's aggression. Standing in the bullring himself at the moment of the bull's charge, Delgado pushed the button that fired the electrode. The bull stopped in its tracks. Of course, a one-time study with just one subject offers drama, but little in the way of scientific verification.

Later electrode studies have indicated that stimulation of several areas of the hypothalamus and parts of the amygdala can elicit behaviors typical of one or more of the nine types of aggression described above. In fact, one part of the amygdala has been shown to inhibit predatory aggression (Vergnes, 1975). Nevertheless, the interactions of these structures are quite complex, and no complete picture has yet emerged of how the parts interact in stimulating or inhibiting aggressive behaviors in animals, especially as animals behave in their natural environments.

Hormones

Hormones also appear to play a part in aggressive activity. In most species, males are more aggressive than females, a characteristic that seems a consequence of the organizational effect of prenatal androgen on the developing brain (see Chapter 3). Female animals injected prenatally with androgen become more aggressive than other females when they are given androgens later in life. Later androgen injections in females with no prenatal exposure to the hormone have no effect on aggressive behavior (Brain, 1980).

Relative levels of circulating androgens in adult males do not seem to correlate with levels of aggression, although castration, which severely curtails hormone production, does, over time, reduce the amount of social conflict an animal will engage in.

Neurotransmitters

Neuroscientists have been able to breed mice for high levels of aggressive behavior. They selected a strain of mice notable for its willingness to attack a strange but docile neutral mouse and then bred the most aggressive of these individuals so that the trait grew stronger generation after generation.

When compared with mice from the original generation, the later, more aggressive mice were found to have a somewhat lower brain concentration of the neurotransmitter serotonin (one of the transmitters implicated in human depression; see Chapter 10). This finding is supported by studies in which experimental animals are given drugs that deplete the brain's ability to make serotonin; these animals become more likely to attack neutral targets. In other experiments, when certain serotonin-rich tracts in the brains of cats were electrically stimulated, the cats showed intense rage during the stimulation period.

Although it appears that serotonin plays some part in aggression, many other transmitter systems and circuits are probably involved. For example, rats bred for their willingness to attack mice are found to have increased blood levels of the enzymes that produce norepinephrine and epinephrine the circulating hormones produced by the adrenal medulla. In contrast, when norepinephrine in the brain is measured after the brain stimulation that produced aggression, its level is lower than before the stimulation. Aggressive behavior is also more likely after normal animals are treated with some of the drugs used to treat human depression, which

Jose Delgado stops the charge of a fighting bull by sending a pulse through the electrode implanted in the bull's hypothalamus.

work in part by prolonging the effects of norepinephrine in the brain.

Animal Studies and Human Aggression

Aggression is a widely variable phenomenon in animals below humans on the phylogenetic scale. In human beings, the behaviors that might be classified as aggressive are so various that no classification is likely to prove particularly precise. In fact, some scientists feel that aggression in human beings should be considered separately from aggression in other animals (Brain, 1979; Moyer, 1976).

When you consider that the most damaging sorts of human aggression—the Nazi policy of exterminating whole population groups, for example, which depended on an entire bureaucracy, carefully filling out the forms to order poison-gas dispensers and to keep the trains full of victims running on time—it does appear somewhat fruitless to try to find animal models for human behavior in this area. In fact, as Nobel Prize—winning philosopher and writer Arthur Koestler (1969) suggests, "The trouble with our species is not an overdose of self-asserting *aggression* but an excess of self-transcending devotion, which manifests itself in blind obedience and loyalty to the king, country, or cause. . . . One of the central features of the human predicament is this overwhelming capacity and need for identification with a social group and/or system of beliefs, which is indifferent to reason, indifferent to self-interest, and even to the claim of self-preservation."

Pain

Pain is not an emotion, but painful sensations can undoubtedly elicit emotions. Like emotion, pain usually energizes an organism into action. Just as fear prepares you to fight or flee, pain signals you, in no uncertain terms, to do something in order to break contact with a potentially damaging agent and to begin restoring the injured part.

A very small number of people are insensitive to pain, and they often suffer severe tissue damage from cuts and burns. One such woman eventually died because she did not receive the normal discomfort signals from her joints telling her to change her posture—she never moved in her sleep, for example. The woman died at an early age of spine damage.

How Pain Is Sensed

Pain receptors in human beings are present in the skin, in sheath tissue surrounding muscles, in internal organs, and in the membranes around bone. These receptors in animals are called *nociceptors* (from the same root word as "noxious," meaning harmful or destructive) because neuroscientists cannot, with certainty, establish that what an animal feels is pain. Animals, after all, cannot say what they feel. Human beings can report pain reliably, so the nerve endings that sense pain are called simply "pain receptors." These receptors have a much higher threshold for firing than those for temperature and touch and react mainly to physical stimuli that distort them or to chemical stimuli that, in essence, "irritate" them into activity. Inflamed joints or sore, torn muscles form natural substances called prostaglandins, which irritate the receptors and cause the experience of traumatic pain. Drugs like aspirin and other drugstore pain treatments seem to have the ability to fight pain because they act to stop the body's synthesis of prostaglandins.

The simplest response patterns to noxious stimuli take place reflexively—that is, the impulses travel only to the spinal cord, which commands a quick response. If you step on a thorn while walking barefoot, impulses from receptors at the injury site activate the flexion withdrawal reflex, and you lift your foot. (Meanwhile, the crossed extension reflex causes you to straighten the other leg, taking your weight off the injured foot.) Other branches of the sensory neuron from the pain receptors synapse on an intermediate neuron, which sends the message up the pathways to your brain for processing. But you will have lifted your foot before your brain registers any pain message.

Pain receptors in the skin are excited by cuts and scrapes, heat, chemical substances released when tissue is damaged, and lack of proper blood circulation to an area. Most of these receptors are not specific: they can respond to several noxious stimuli. It also appears that they can signal not only the presence of a stimulus but also its location and its intensity.

The action of most pain receptors within the body is less well charted. The workings of a few are known, such as lung-irritant receptors which signal, for instance, pulmonary congestion or the presence of dust particles.

Pain Pathways to the Brain

Two different neural pathways transmit pain messages to the brain (see Figure 7.7). One is a system of myelinated, fast-conducting, thin fibers that give the experience of a fast, bright pain sensation. The other is a system of unmyelinated, slow-conducting fibers that produce diffuse, nagging pain.

The fibers of the *fast pathway* make direct connection with the thalamus, where they make synaptic connections with fibers that project to motor and sensory areas of the cortex. It appears that this system allows the organism to discriminate exactly where the injury is, how serious the damage is, and how long the pain has been going on.

The fibers of the *slow pathway* project to the reticular formation, the medulla, the

pons, the midbrain, the hypothalamus, and the thalamus. Some fibers contact neurons that connect with the hypothalamus and amygdala in the limbic system, while other fibers connect with diffuse neural networks to many other parts of the brain. The many synapses in this system, the lack of myelination of its neurons, and the narrow diameter of its conducting pathways make it the slower of the two.

The fast system may function as a warning system, providing immediate information about the presence of injury, its extent, and its location. The unpleasant, nagging pain characteristic of the slower system may act as a reminder to the brain that an injury has occurred, that normal activity should be restricted, and that attention must be paid.

In a way, the fast system is "free of emotion," whereas the timing of the slower one allows the injured person to attribute qualities to the damage report. Actually, it appears that both the limbic system and prefrontal cortex mediate the emotional coloration of pain. Our *perception* of pain seems to include both the sensation of pain and our emotional reaction to that sensation. Patients who have undergone a frontal lobotomy, an operation that severs the connections between the frontal lobes and the thalamus, rarely complain about severe pain or ask for medication. In fact, they typically report after the operation that they still have pain but that it does not "bother" them. Phineas Gage, you recall, appeared to suffer little pain after the accident that blew away his frontal lobe, despite the enormous physical damage he sustained.

Chemical Transmission and Inhibition of Pain

One important synaptic relay in the transmission of pain impulses to the brain takes place in a part of the spinal cord called the *dorsal horns.* Many fibers from pain recep-

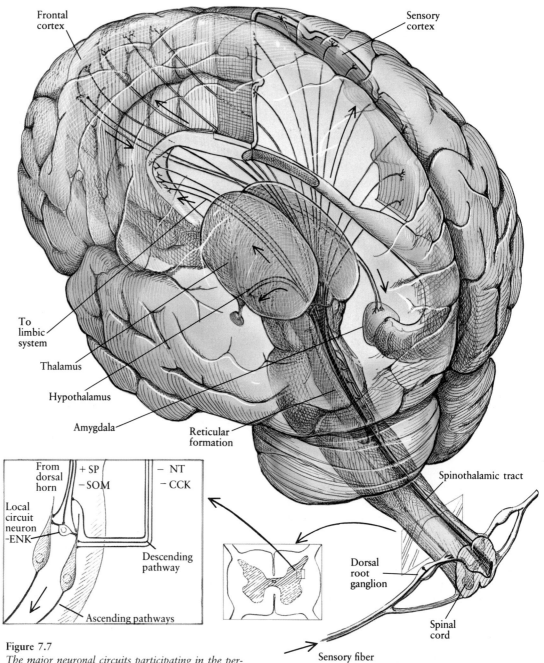

Frontal
cortex

Sensory
cortex

To
limbic
system

Thalamus

Hypothalamus

Amygdala

Reticular
formation

Spinothalamic tract

From
dorsal
horn

+ SP
− SOM

− NT
− CCK

Local
circuit
neuron
-ENK

Descending
pathway

Ascending pathways

Dorsal
root
ganglion

Spinal
cord

Sensory fiber

Figure 7.7
*The major neuronal circuits participating in the per-
ception of sensory stimuli underlying the experience
of pain are shown extending from sensory receptors
in the skin through synaptic relays in the spinal cord,
thalamus, sensory cortex, and limbic system. The arrows indicate the paths taken by sensory information*
*moving along the fast, or specific, pathway. Informa-
tion moving along the slow, or nonspecific, pathway
is disseminated largely through fibers in the reticular
formation.*

tors synapse there with other ascending neurons. Discharges of these spinal neurons can be 10 times greater than the discharge of a single pain receptor, indicating that the dorsal horns provide a place where many of the fibers from receptors of the slow pathway converge. These spinal fibers also display a buildup of responsiveness during painful stimulation, and this high level of activity can continue as long as 100 seconds after the painful stimulus has been removed.

This buildup, along with the continuation of firing after removal of the stimulus, indicated to some researchers that a neurotransmitter must be involved, one that is released and inactivated relatively slowly. In fact, the transmitter, a neuropeptide called *substance P*, found in neurons on each side of the spinal cord, has been isolated. Substance P appears to be a specialized transmitter of pain-related information from peripheral pain receptors to the central system. It has also been found widely distributed in neurons in the brain, so it probably has functions besides the transmission of pain impulses.

Luckily for us, the human nervous system not only manufactures a substance that transmits pain sensations, it also provides us with painkillers. In 1972, researchers studying the biological basis of drug addiction began to locate more precisely the receptor sites in animal and human brains where opium and its derivatives, morphine and heroin, produce their specific effects. What were these receptors doing in the body? Surely there could be no evolutionary advantage in a mammalian addiction to drugs. The most likely explanation for the existence of such receptors was that opiatelike substances are produced by the body itself and that they work through receptors that morphine only borrows. In fact, a number of such natural opiates have now been identified. They are called *opioid peptides* or *endorphins*, a word

coined from the phrase "endogenous morphine."

Early in the 1960s, Ronald Melzack and Patrick Wall observed that acupuncture could be carried out with the subject reporting little pain or discomfort from the insertion of the needles. The two scientists conjectured that the kind of stimulation caused by insertion of the needles triggers impulses in the reticular formation that travel down the spinal cord and, in essence, close a spinal "gate," shutting down the perception of pain. Their elaboration of this work led to what is called the gate-control theory of pain. We now know that the closing of these "gates" is a chemical process—the work of endorphins.

Both endorphins and opiates such as heroin are believed to work in the following way to regulate the perception of pain. A pain signal starts impulses up the spinal cord, through the slow pain pathway just described. These neurons contain substance P, and they synapse onto neurons in the dorsal horns within the spinal cord, the upper parts of the gray matter forming a butterflylike outline within the cord's white matter (see Figure 7.7). At these synapses, the neurons secrete substance P, which excites those neurons sensitive to it. These neurons then proceed to send the pain message to the brain. However, the dorsal horns also house endorphin-containing neurons, which synapse onto the pain-transmitting neurons. When these neurons release endorphin, it binds to the pain-transmitting neuron and inhibits the release of substance P. The receiving neuron at the synapse gets less stimulation because it responds less well to the substance P, and fewer pain impulses go to the brain.

Endorphin-containing neurons and opiate receptor sites exist in many other areas of the nervous system as well. One such area, which also lies along the slow pain pathway,

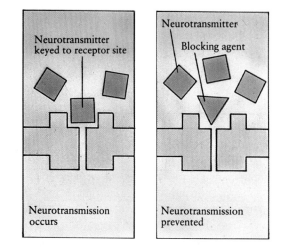

Figure 7.8
Neurotransmitters and their antagonist drugs act through the same receptors. Left, the neurotransmitter molecule fits the receptor-recognition site precisely. At right, in the presence of an antagonist drug, the neurotransmitter molecules cannot gain recognition by the receptor. In practice, antagonist drugs often bind more tightly to the receptor than do transmitter molecules, thus preventing transmission for long periods of time.

is the *periaqueductal gray* area, a cluster of neurons lying in the thalamus and the pons. Injection of morphine directly into the periaqueductal gray reduces pain. Electrical stimulation there causes endorphins to be released and also produces relief. In fact, stimulation by means of implanted electrodes has been used experimentally to treat people suffering from pain that does not respond to any other treatment.

Scientists have been able to study the action and location of both manufactured and natural opiates using the antagonist drug naloxone. The shape of naloxone molecules allows them to bind to opiate-receptor sites, although the drug itself has no pain-killing properties. When naloxone occupies those sites, neither the opiates nor the endorphins can get in to activate the receptor (see Figure 7.8). No inhibition of the release *or of*

the effects of transmitters of pain sensations can therefore take place. (Naloxone is given to heroin addicts who have overdosed.)

Researchers looking into the pain-killing properties of cells in the periaqueductal gray first electrically stimulated that area in laboratory mice. They saw that mice so stimulated became relatively insensitive to the pain of being placed on a hot surface; at least they did not run away. When naloxone was administered before the electrical stimulation, the mice were more sensitive than normal to the heat-produced pain. Use of naloxone thus revealed that electrical stimulation of the periaqueductal gray had caused endorphins to be released: the naloxone occupied the receptor sites that endorphins would otherwise have found. Later studies have confirmed that cells containing high amounts of endogenous opioid are contained in the periaqueductal gray.

Studies using radioactively labeled opiate drugs have shown that opiate receptors populate the limbic system in high concentrations. Because the perception of pain involves both the sensation of pain and an emotional reaction to the sensation, the discovery of these receptors in the limbic system amounts to a physical confirmation of a psychological hypothesis. The euphoria so desired by heroin users probably arises from the binding of the drug to limbic system sites. The fact that heroin and endorphins bind to the same sites suggests that endorphins also play a role in aspects of emotion not directly related to pain.

The Role of Endorphins in Emotion

The role of endorphins in modulating pain seems clear. While the perception of pain is necessary to warn us of danger to flesh and bone, constant intense pain would incapacitate us. Endorphins regulate the degree of pain we feel, enabling us to remove ourselves from the pain inducer and to begin nursing any wounds. Endorphins seem to play a similar modulating role in emotions. The arousal that occurs during fear or rage can be so intense that an animal or a person cannot behave in ways that would save it from injury or loss. Endorphins seem to modulate the arousal so that an organism, while experiencing the emotion, can adapt its behavior to the situation.

Research into the use of endorphins by the nervous system is in its infancy, and evidence concerning their role in emotion is scarce. It does appear that fear can call endorphins into action. Mice given electric shocks in a training procedure that included a warning signal before the shock evidently released endorphins at the sound of the signal, even when no shock followed. Fear of the pain seemed to be sufficient to make the mice prepare for it. Perhaps human beings do the same sort of thing. It would be nice to think that the sight of a dentist's drill, for instance, could cause streams of endorphins to rush to our aid.

Some forms of fear are so extreme that they are considered symptomatic of mental disorder. These anxiety disorders include the phobias—extreme, irrational fears of particular objects or situations. People who suffer from claustrophobia, fear of enclosed spaces, cannot get on elevators, for instance, without suffering severe anxiety. Just thinking about the objects of such fears causes victims to experience arousal of the autonomic nervous system—racing heart, sweating, dry mouth. Some researchers believe that these people may not experience the normal regulation of arousal provided by endorphins.

A number of studies have shown that stress and anxiety can cause the release of endorphins from neural circuits in experimental animals. Their "perception of pain," as measured by their movement away from a pain-inducing stimulus, went down after stress caused them to secrete endorphins. In one study using human subjects, pain was induced by electric shocks to the foot. The resulting pain was evaluated not by subjective means—by people recounting how much it hurt—but by measuring the reflex actions of leg muscles, the muscles that react when you step on a thorn, for example. The experimenters induced stress by sounding a warning signal two minutes before a shock might or might not be delivered. The subjects were tested under three conditions: (1) no injection (control); (2) injection of a painkiller; and (3) injection of naloxone. The initial pain-reflex sensitivity was identical in all three conditions. But repeated stress—hearing the warning signal several times—caused sensitivity to decrease in both the no-injection and painkiller-injection conditions. This indicated that the subjects had indeed produced endorphins under stress. Proof of endorphin action came from the finding that, with the naloxone injection, pain-reflex sensitivity immediately increased by 30 percent. In other words, when naloxone occupied the endorphin receptor sites, no modulation of the pain by stress-induced endorphins was possible.

Individual Perception of Pain

Pain perception, like most aspects of brain science, is a complex matter. It differs from person to person—and within any single person—from time to time. The pain experience depends partly on physiology. Sensitivity to pain probably stretches over a wide range, with those rare people who never feel any pain at one end and, at the other end, people (perhaps deficient, for some reason, in endorphin production) who feel extreme pain from even minor bumps or scrapes. Physiological differences aside, however, the way one experiences pain depends on one's past experience—on what one has learned from the surrounding culture and its representatives, one's family. It depends on the

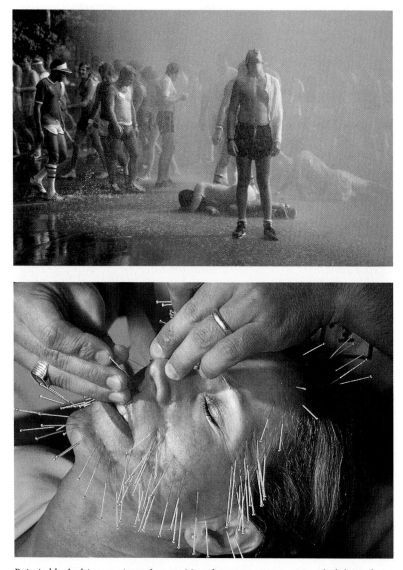

Pain is blocked in a variety of ways. Marathon runners may gain relief through a pathway that does not involve endorphins but is integrated at the highest levels of the nervous system. Evidence shows that pain relief provided by acupuncture comes from endorphins that the body produces in response to the punctures.

Cultural learning, or socialization, clearly shapes human perception of pain. In some societies, women do not dread childbirth; they go about their business until shortly before a baby is born, have the baby, and go back to their tasks a few hours later. In other societies, women have learned to expect terrible pain and so they have it, as if childbirth were a severe illness. The Lamaze method of training for "natural childbirth" starts with the premise that women in most Western cultures have been conditioned to expect and fear the pain of childbirth. The fear produces changes in their muscle tone and breathing patterns that hamper the process and make it more painful. The Lamaze methods teach breathing control and provide exercises to strengthen pelvic muscles. They also explain the entire process of birth, so women know what to expect. Thus, learning, which takes place in the higher cortical regions, can modify the experience of pain, just as it modifies the experience of emotion.

In nonhuman animals it also appears that learning modulates the experience of pain. In one of a series of conditioning experiments begun around the turn of the century, Ivan Pavlov discovered that when dogs were consistently given food immediately after an electric shock to the foot—a shock strong enough to cause the dogs to react violently before conditioning—the animals stopped showing any signs of pain. Instead, they salivated and wagged their tails after the shock.

In World War II studies of pain perception, the physician H. K. Beecher noted that significantly fewer soldiers injured on the battlefield requested morphine than did civilians recuperating from surgery. The soldier's response to injury, Beecher said, "was relief, thankfulness at his escape alive from the battlefield, even euphoria; to the civilian, major surgery was a depressing, calamitous event." The meaning that one assigns to a wound,

meaning that one assigns to a pain-inducing event. And it depends on such moment-to-moment psychological factors as attentiveness, anxiety, and suggestion.

then, can profoundly influence the amount of pain one feels.

Even mere suggestion can alter pain perception. When placebos—nonactive sugar or salt pills or injections—are given to experimental subjects as a painkiller, some people actually experience pain relief. Just the expectation of relief appears to cause the release of endorphins.

Some currently accumulating evidence points to the existence of pain-relief systems within the body that are separate from the endorphin system. The first work suggesting the existence of nonendorphin pain-relief systems was done recently by D. S. Mayer. He tested the pain-relief and anesthetic effects of acupuncture and found (1) that acupuncture does produce such effects, and (2) that because these effects can be blocked by naloxone, its effects are the work of endorphins. But when Mayer tested the effects of hypnosis, a powerful form of suggestion, he found (1) that it does produce protection from pain, and (2) that naloxone does not block its effects. Mayer suggests that hypnosis works through another pain-relief pathway, integrated at the highest levels of the nervous system and involving cognitive and memory factors.

Perhaps this pain-relief pathway is put to use by people, such as long-distance runners or football players, whose intense concentration on their goals enables them to ignore or subdue pain. Ballet dancers, too, can execute triumphant performances on bloody feet. But research into this pathway has only begun.

Pleasure

Just as with pain, pleasure in animals can only be inferred from their behavior. If a stimulus is rewarding, animals will quickly learn whatever tasks are required to give

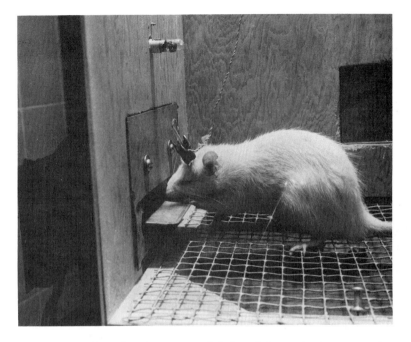

With an electrode implanted in an area of the hypothalamus that has come to be known as a "pleasure center," this rat pushes a lever to apply electrical stimulation to its own brain (Olds, 1953).

them access to that reward. (Pain also produces quick learning; animals need very few trials to learn how to avoid aversive, pain-giving stimuli.)

In 1953, James Olds and his colleagues implanted electrodes in an area of a rat's hypothalamus. The animal not only quickly learned to press a lever to receive the stimulation but, once having learned, continued to press the lever—as many as several thousand times per hour for 10 hours. Because the rat worked so hard to produce the experience, this behavior has been taken to mean that the rat "liked" the feeling. Certain areas of the hypothalamus therefore came to be called "pleasure centers."

Many subsequent studies of pleasure centers in animals have identified a number of areas that cause animals to give themselves self-stimulation. This "reward-pathway" follows virtually the same route as the dopamine-transmitting neurons from the substantia nigra and the norepinephrine-transmitting neurons from the locus coeruleus. Because stimulation by electrodes does increase the synthesis and release of these two neurotransmitters, it may be fair to infer that one or both of them are activated by the electrical stimuli that produce the rewarding sensations. However, it is not possible to conclude that these circuits actually "produce" the sensation.

Endorphins have also been suggested as playing a role in the experience of pleasure. A number of studies have used naloxone to see whether normal people, enjoying normal activities that they consider pleasurable, owed any of this pleasure to endorphins. Subjects are placed in laboratory settings and are asked to engage in activities they like. Some eat good food; some listen to their favorite passages of music; runners run on treadmills to the point of getting the runner's "high"; some are asked to masturbate. The subjects are asked to undergo the same experience on more than one occasion; before beginning the activity, each receives an injection, sometimes of naloxone and sometimes of a placebo. The subjects do not, of course, know which is which.

Later, the subjects are asked to rate their pleasurable sensations. If endorphins played a major role in their pleasurable reactions, their reported enjoyment under naloxone should have been less intense. But the subjects' reports did not differentiate between the naloxone and placebo conditions. Evidently, endorphins are not a major contributor to everyday pleasures.

For a number of reasons, much less has been learned about the positive emotions—the highs—than about the negative ones—the lows. In recent years, much study has been focused on stress—its causes and con-sequences—and, as a result, we now have quite a bit of information about it.

Stress and Anxiety

"Stress" is a word currently used—and often incorrectly—in many popular magazines and books. Thousands of self-help books promise to teach their readers how to avoid or manage it. But stress, according to Hans Selye, a foremost researcher in this area, is "the nonspecific response of the body to any demand." You *want* your brain and body to respond in ways that help you meet the demands made by disease or by events such as a final exam, an at-bat in the ninth inning of a tie ballgame, or an important job interview. Stress, in other words, is not always bad; it is an important part of everyone's life. Challenges and changes, which often engender stress, provide the opportunities for adaptation to new life circumstances.

Stress itself, then, is not harmful. In fact, one study found that young mice exposed from time to time to mild stresses—handling, or weak electric shocks—became better able to handle stressful events than their unstressed littermates (Levine, 1960). As adults, they were also stronger and larger—and their adrenal glands were larger.

What is potentially harmful to animals, including human beings, is a prolonged period of stress or a combination of stressful events—called "stressors"—that make it very difficult, or impossible, to adapt to the demands of the situation.

Selye's General Adaptation Syndrome
Selye (1956) proposed three phases in an animal's stress reaction, which he called the "general adaptation syndrome": (1) alarm, (2) resistance, and (3) exhaustion.

In the alarm reaction, the sympathetic nervous system is aroused, just as described on p. 215. The hypothalamus sends a chemical signal to the pituitary, causing it to increase its release of adrenocorticotropic hormone (ACTH). ACTH, in turn, travels in the bloodstream to the adrenal glands and causes them to secrete hormones, corticosteroids, which prepare organs all over the body to engage in action and to deal with potential injury. Sympathetic nerves and the adrenal medulla secrete norepinephrine into the bloodstream. Increased levels of norepinephrine, of ACTH, or of corticosteroids are the signs that researchers use to measure stress arousal.

In the resistance stage, the body mobilizes its resources to overcome the stress-producing event. In most diseases and injuries, antibodies rush to the affected site. In psychological stress, the sympathetic system prepares one for fight or flight.

Everybody goes through the alarm and resistance stages many, many times during his or her life. When resistance is successful, the body returns to normal. But if a stressor continues, the body may reach a stage of exhaustion. In the mice Selye originally studied, for example, exposure to extreme cold first caused the adrenal glands to discharge all their microscopic fat granules, which contain the corticosteroids (alarm). The glands then became laden with an unusually large number of fat droplets containing more corticosteroids (resistance). Finally, all those droplets were discharged, and the mice could produce no more. They died (exhaustion). In psychological terms, exhaustion equals breakdown; sometimes the breakdown takes the form of mental illness, sometimes of psychosomatic disease.

Stress, Disease, and the Feeling of Control

In a song from the musical *Guys and Dolls*, Adelaide, sneezing and coughing, laments her lover's many delays in marrying her. Just from waiting around for a plain little band of gold, a person, she says, "can develop a cold." Many psychological and physiological studies have corroborated this connection between emotion and disease.

In one large-scale study, 5000 patients spoke about the events in their lives that preceded their physical illnesses. The researchers found that dramatic life changes had preceded illness in a large number of cases. The patients reported events in their lives like death of a spouse, divorce, marriage, change of residence, being fired from a job, or retirement that occurred within two years before they became ill. In a subsequent study of a group of physicians, researchers quantified such life changes by point ratings and, on the basis of the subjects' recent histories, predicted those at high risk for illness. Of those rated at high risk, 49 percent reported having contracted some sort of illness during the eight months of the study; only 9 percent of those judged as low-risk reported being ill. The psychologists concluded that the struggle of coping with life crises, especially when a person's coping techniques are faulty, can lower resistance to disease (Holmes & Masuda, 1972). Although unsubstantiated by physiological evidence, this conclusion fits Selye's description of the stages of resistance and exhaustion.

Many scientists believe that stomach ulceration, for example, is caused by psychological factors. Ulcers can be induced not only in people but also in rats and monkeys. A series of studies with rats as subjects, conducted by Jay Weiss, demonstrated such a psychological dimension to the effects of environmental stress. These rats were put in an experimental apparatus that controlled all movement (see Figure 7.9). All shocks were of the same intensity. One control rat received no shocks; the other two rats received simultaneous electric shocks to their tails. One of the shocked rats consistently

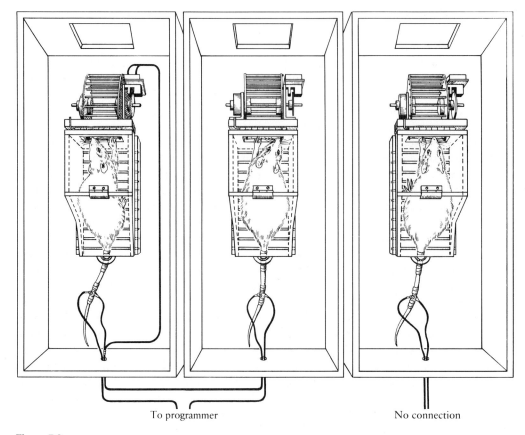

To programmer   No connection

Figure 7.9
*In this experimental setup, the control rat received no shocks. The other two rats
got identical shocks, but one heard a warning tone 10 seconds before each shock.
The ability to predict shock resulted in fewer stomach ulcers than did random
shock (Weiss, 1980).*

heard a beeping tone 10 seconds before the shock, while the other heard beeps, but random ones with no predictive meaning. The rat that heard the warning beep, and so could predict the arrival of the shocks, showed very little ulceration. The shocked rat who had no way to predict the arrival of the shocks developed rather severe ulcers.

With the original experiment complete, Weiss then arranged the setup so that one of the rats could avoid the shock for itself and its partner by jumping onto a platform dur-

ing the warning signal (or, if it had been a bit slow, it could terminate the shock for them both by jumping onto the platform after it began). The rats that were able to cope with shock by avoiding it or escaping from it showed much less ulceration than their helpless partners, even though both groups had received identical amounts of shock.

Even for rats, then, the predictability of events in their environment, feedback from that environment about the outcome of their actions, and the consequent sense of being able to cope help prevent stress and its effects.

Studies using human subjects (Champion, 1950; Geer et al., 1970) indicate that some of these principles govern our behavior too. When volunteer subjects are given inescapable shocks, those who have been told by the experimenters that they can stop (not prevent) the shock by clenching a fist or pressing a button show less emotional arousal (measured by amount of skin moisture) than subjects who know they have no control. The shocks were brief, so the subjects who pressed the button believed that their actions were responsible for ending the shock. Because they got feedback in the form of termination of the shock, they felt that they had a means of coping with the situation.

What happens to a lone animal given a series of shocks that it has no power to escape? Martin Seligman (1975) gave a series of shocks to two group of dogs. One control group of dogs was permitted to learn how to escape; they could jump a hurdle into the other side of the box in which they were placed, where no shocks were delivered. The other group was first given a series of inescapable shocks, then given the opportunity to learn the escape mechanism. They could not. They did not even try. Seligman calls this phenomenon "learned helplessness."

Jay Weiss's research may have shed some light on Seligman's findings. When Weiss sacrificed a number of rats used in his experiment and studied their brains, he found that the helpless rats, even though they had received fewer shocks, had decreased levels of norepinephrine in their brains. Weiss believes that the helplessness of Seligman's dogs—their inability to learn an escape mechanism when it was finally made available to them—resulted from a temporary depletion of norepinephrine in their brains. The "executive rats," those that had been able to jump on the platform and avoid or escape the shock, had normal brain levels of norepinephrine.

Brain Function and Everyday Stress

It may seem far-fetched to generalize from laboratory situations involving electric shock to situations that generate stress in ordinary human lives. But a recent study by Jay R. Kaplan and his colleagues with monkeys comes a bit closer. In this study, which showed that social stress can contribute to atherosclerosis, or hardening of the arteries, all the monkeys had been fed from birth with a "prudent" diet, one low in saturated fats, containing almost no cholesterol. Over a two-year period, some of the monkeys were subjected to a number of stressful conditions arising from the usual social organization of monkey life. For instance, individual monkeys were repeatedly taken from their own social group and put into a new one, where they had no rank in the dominance hierarchy and had to fight for position. Groups of the male monkeys were also visited for two-week periods by one female in heat, and so were subjected to the stress of fighting for her favors. The stressed monkeys ended up having significantly more numerous and more severe arterial lesions (the signs of atherosclerosis) than the monkeys whose social life was stable.

Is it too far-fetched to draw an analogy between the stresses of these monkeys' social lives and the stresses encountered by, say, a middle-management executive or a single working mother? The executive receives directives from her superiors that she must carry out, yet she probably had no control over the decision-making that produced them. Most of the time she is acutely aware of being in competition with others for promotion—and of those below her competing for her job. Most of her social life involves other employees of the corporation, so work tensions carry over into her private life. Add to this the frustration of rush-hour commuter traffic and the necessity for travel, with attendant jet lag, and you have a formula for stress.

The single working mother's life often requires her to balance at least three conflicting claims: the requirements of her job, the psychological and social needs of her children, and her desires for personal fulfillment. How serious does a child's cold have to be for the mother to stay home from work? What does she do when she has to work late on the same evening that her son has a Little League game? In a way, she loses the feeling of control whatever she decides. Something important always remains undone.

Prolonged stress of this kind produces the psychological state that we commonly call anxiety. In a modern, complex culture, many people experience it. Our limbic system, our "animal brain," does its job in producing emotional arousal, and our cortex monitors and modulates that arousal. It is a fine balance. But if we feel that things have slipped out of our control, if stressors seem to pile up endlessly, the fine balance may be disturbed. Anxiety may represent tensions between limbic and cortical impulses.

One widespread means that people use to allay anxiety is to take tranquilizers. The one most often used is Valium, a benzodiazepine thought to work by promoting the effectiveness of the neurotransmitter GABA (gamma-amino butyric acid), whose primary function is to inhibit the firing of neurons (Costa & Guidotti, 1979; McGeer & McGeer, 1981). GABA has its own receptors, and Valium receptors are very close to them; when the drug is present, it actually aids in GABA's binding to its own receptors. The more GABA bound to a neuron, the less likely it is to fire. (The discovery of opiate binding sites led to the discovery of endorphins, so the finding of tranquilizer binding sites has led to a search for the body's own tranquilizers.

The first related factor identified is an 18–amino acid peptide that acts like a "reverse" Valium, producing anxiety. If valid, this finding would suggest that Valium works by opposing the effects of the still unidentified natural factor, a bit like the way that naloxone blocks the opioid peptide responses.)

The limbic system contains many neurons that GABA acts upon. It seems likely, then, that tranquilizers do their job by inhibiting the flow of messages through the limbic system, thereby dampening emotional arousal.

One psychopharmacological study produced findings in rats that seem relevant to human anxiety. Rats were trained to run a maze for food rewards. One group was rewarded every time they correctly negotiated the maze; another group found the food reward only some of the time. Then, for both groups, all reward ceased. The rats that had been rewarded each time they ran the maze soon stopped searching. In the language of classical conditioning, the behavior was extinguished. But the rats that had found the food reward only occasionally—that is, who had received only partial reinforcement—took much longer to stop their searching. The uncertainty of reward during training was thought to create an anxiety state, which was revealed by their persistent running of the maze long after the reward had been withdrawn and long after the other group of rats had given up the search.

The researcher (Gray, 1977), using implanted electrodes, had noted that in the "anxious" rats, a certain level of electrical activity occurred in the hippocampus. When these rats were given barbiturates, alcohol, or tranquilizers, the frequency of electrical activity in the hippocampus decreased, and the animals stopped their fruitless, anxious searches for the reward, their anxiety apparently reduced. Such findings suggest why so many people elect to use alcohol and tranquilizing drugs despite their potential dan-

The monkey shows a "fear grin," a submissive gesture. The human smile, shown even by very young infants, may have its origins in such a gesture.

gers, since these substances temporarily reduce anxiety levels and modulate the stresses of living in a complex modern society.

After all this discussion of the brain's lows, one might be tempted to ask why human beings have evolved in a way that makes them subject to such emotional storms. Why have we inherited this capacity to feel so awful? Perhaps fish are better off. The poet T. S. Eliot once said as much: "I should have been a pair of ragged claws, scuttling across the floors of silent seas." Luckily, we have also inherited the capacity for feeling wonderful—for experiencing emotions like joy, tenderness, affection, exultation. There appear to be some logical reasons for our emotional lives being more variegated than that of fish or crustaceans.

The Development of Emotions: An Evolutionary Perspective

Animals low on the evolutionary scale—fish and crustaceans, for example—have only an elaborated brainstem. The limbic system evolved only in higher species. The cortex becomes larger, relative to body size, up the phylogenetic scale to human beings and bottle-nose dolphins.

The brainstem and other hindbrain structures are the sources of the rigidly programmed—or "hard-wired"—behaviors necessary to survival. All lizards of a certain species, for example, turn sideways and display their dewlap in threat. Among human behaviors, smiling in greeting seems to be a genetically wired-in expression. Newborns in all cultures show a smilelike expression, and infants only two or three months old smile at nearby faces. Even infants born with extreme microcephaly, that is, very little cortex, may exhibit the smilelike expression. This smile may have had the same origin as the "fear grin" that other primates use as a protective response or a gesture of submission. At the very least, it may have been (and, in a way, still is) a gesture indicating that one is not intending to attack. In human infants, this smilelike expression helps elicit the caregiving that these helpless creatures require for survival.

The Limbic System and Care of the Young

Many mammals other than human beings have well-developed limbic systems, whereas reptiles and amphibians do not. Clearly, mammals show more emotional behavior than reptiles or amphibians. Your turtle, for example, is unlikely to let you know that he's happy to see you coming home after work in the same way that your dog or cat does, and, when threatened, he will freeze, not flee, unless he is underwater. In fact, the higher up the evolutionary scale an animal is, the more emotion it can display (Hebb & Thompson, 1968). Human beings are the most emotional creatures of all, with many highly differentiated emotional expressions and, at least according to subjective reports, a wide variety of emotional experiences.

It is because the human limbic system interacts with the cortex and because the frontal association cortex is so highly developed in humans that our emotional life is so variegated. Because of this relatively high cortical development, human beings have the ability to abstract and to remember. Therefore, we can feel intense anger over an idea, such as injustice, or shame at not living up to some cultural notion of how we should behave.

Another important evolutionary development accompanied development of the limbic system, and the two may have a common origin. Mammals and birds are, with rare exceptions, the only organisms to devote a relatively long time and a great deal of attention to the care of their young. These behaviors, which we term "affectionate," are necessary if the relatively helpless young are to survive, and when the limbic system evolved, the capacity for such behaviors and whatever feelings we attribute to them became possible.

An experiment conducted by Paul MacLean and his colleagues neatly demonstrates the relationship between parts of the brain and affectionate behaviors in hamsters. Removal of the hamsters' cerebral cortices at birth caused no observable impairment of their instinctual behavior patterns—the decorticated hamsters found food, played, mated, took care of their young, and showed

appropriate aggression. Later, the researchers surgically removed parts of the limbic system that were not essential to life from some of these hamsters. The animals immediately stopped playing, and no longer showed any maternal behaviors.

The Limbic System and Social Communication

The naturalist Charles Darwin also studied emotion. His studies, as summarized in *The Expression of the Emotions in Man and Animals* (1872), led him to believe that many facial and gestural expressions of emotion are the result of the evolutionary process. A number of our expressions bear a strong resemblance to those of our distant primate kin, and Darwin saw these expressions as remnants of attack and defense sequences from earlier times. Ethologist Niko Tinbergen calls them "intention movements"—fragments from the phases during which an animal prepared for action. As social animals evolved, these expressions, which had earlier only heralded actual behaviors, developed functions of their own. These new functions made a system of social communication possible. An animal could convey information to others about its own internal state or about certain events in the environment, a highly useful ability that enables a social species to build increasingly complex society.

There is good evidence that a number of fundamental human emotions have an evolutionary basis—that is, they are "wired" into our genes by way of the limbic system. Researchers showed the photographs reproduced in Table 7.1 to people in a number of different cultures and asked them to identify the emotion being expressed. Even though their cultures varied widely, the great majority of people recognized most of the basic emotions: fear, anger, surprise, happiness.

Table 7.1 *Agreement on judgments of emotion in five literate cultures*

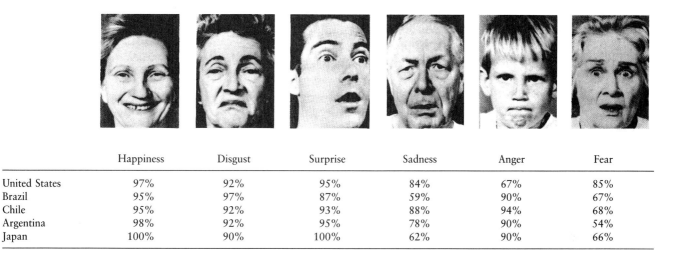

	Happiness	Disgust	Surprise	Sadness	Anger	Fear
United States	97%	92%	95%	84%	67%	85%
Brazil	95%	97%	87%	59%	90%	67%
Chile	95%	92%	93%	88%	94%	68%
Argentina	98%	92%	95%	78%	90%	54%
Japan	100%	90%	100%	62%	90%	66%

Summary

1. Since scientists have been unable to come up with a satisfactory definition of emotion, it is not defined here. Instead, we assume that all readers can agree on what constitutes discrete emotions, such as happiness, anger, sadness.

2. Motivation, which is closely linked to emotion, is inferred from an organism's goal-directed behavior. If the organism works hard to attain a specific goal, we assume that it is motivated. For human beings, we can make the further assumption that goal-directed behaviors are performed because the goal has an incentive value for the performer and that attainment of the goal will therefore produce a positive emotion.

3. Early theories attempting to relate physiological change to the experience of emotion include: (1) the James-Lange theory, which suggested that the experience of emotion results from perception of one's own, preceding, physiological reactions; (2) the Cannon-Bard theory, which inferred a neural pathway through which nerve impulses simultaneously would give the cerebral cortex the experience of emotion and would command, through the thalamus, the body's physiological changes; (3) the Papez circuit, which suggested that a number of linked brain structures were responsible for emotion.

4. A number of brain structures are now known to be responsible for emotion. One is the limbic system, which consists of a number of interconnected structures (see Figure 7.4). In the brainstem are the reticular formation; the locus coeruleus and its widely disseminated transmitter norepinephrine; and the substantia nigra and its widely disseminated transmitter dopamine. Of the parts of the cerebral cortex, the frontal lobes appear to be most important in the experience of emotion. The autonomic nervous system, especially the sympathetic division, mobilizes the body's re-

sources for emergency actions—the "fight-or-flight" response.

5. If the physiological changes of "fight or flight" occur in a human being who has no immediate explanation for them, the person will label his or her emotional state on the basis of environmental evidence, which indicates how the thinking brain interacts with the limbic system in human beings.

6. Aggression in animals is of various types, some of which can be invoked by electrical stimulation of several areas of the hypothalamus and parts of the amygdala. Animals bred for aggressiveness have lower brain concentrations of the neurotransmitter serotonin. Human aggression remains largely a puzzle.

7. Pain is sensed through receptors in the skin, in sheath tissue surrounding muscle, in internal organs, and in the membranes around bone. These receptors react mainly to physical stimuli that distort them or to chemical stimuli that irritate them, such as the prostaglandins released by sore muscles.

8. Pain messages from the receptors travel to the brain via two different pathways: the fast pathway, whose fibers make direct connection with the thalamus, then synapse with fibers going to motor and sensory areas of the cortex; and the slow pathway, whose fibers project to the reticular formation, the medulla, the pons, the midbrain, the hypothalamus, and the thalamus. The fast system permits immediate action to withdraw from further danger, and the slow system, along with the limbic system and prefrontal cortex, mediate the emotional reaction to the pain.

9. A neurotransmitter, substance P, is a specialized transmitter of pain-related information from peripheral pain receptors to the brain. It is secreted by fibers in the dorsal horns of the spinal cord. The effect of substance P can be modulated by endorphins, which bind to pain-transmitting neurons and inhibit its release. Endorphin-containing neurons exist in many areas of the nervous system.

10. Endorphins also appear to play a role in modulating the arousal that accompanies fear, rage, or stress.

11. Studies using implanted electrodes detected "pleasure centers" in several brain areas of animals, who would press levers to give themselves long periods of electrical stimulation there. Since these areas coincide with pathways followed by the dopamine-transmitting neurons from the substantia nigra and the norepinephrine-secreting neurons from the locus coeruleus, it is likely that release of these transmitters plays a part in the pleasurable sensations.

12. A stress reaction, according to Selye's general adaptation syndrome, includes the three phases of alarm, resistance, and exhaustion. In the alarm phase, the sympathetic nervous system is aroused. In the resistance phase, the body mobilizes its resources to return to its prestress state. If stress continues despite resistance, exhaustion can occur, either physiological or psychological, in the form of mental illness or psychosomatic disease.

13. Predictability of environmental events and feedback from the environment, allowing an animal a sense of having control over what happens to it, are important to stress prevention.

14. The limbic system is not very elaborate in animals below mammals on the evolutionary scale. Development of the limbic system may have accompanied the bearing of helpless young that require much care for a relatively long period of time.

Further Reading

Zajonc, R. B. 1980. Feeling and thinking. *American Psychologist*, 35:151–175. A noted psychologist explores the relation between emotion and cognition.

Miller, Jonathan. 1983. *States of Mind*. New York: Pantheon. Chapter 8, Dialogue with George Mandler, The nature of emotion. Mandler, a noted psychologist and researcher, in dialogue with physician and writer Miller, presents a wide-ranging discussion of human emotional experience.

Weiss, J. M. 1972. Psychological factors in stress and disease. *Scientific American*, June, 1972. Experiments with rats were able to separate the physical and psychological factors in stressful conditions and to show that the psychological factors were the main cause of stomach ulcers and other disorders.

Cooper, J. R., Bloom, F. E., and Roth, R. H. 1986. *The Biochemical Basis of Neuropharmacology*, 5th ed. New York: Oxford University Press. Chapter 12, The peptides, pp. 352–394. An easy-to-read account of the opioid and other peptide systems that act within the central nervous system.

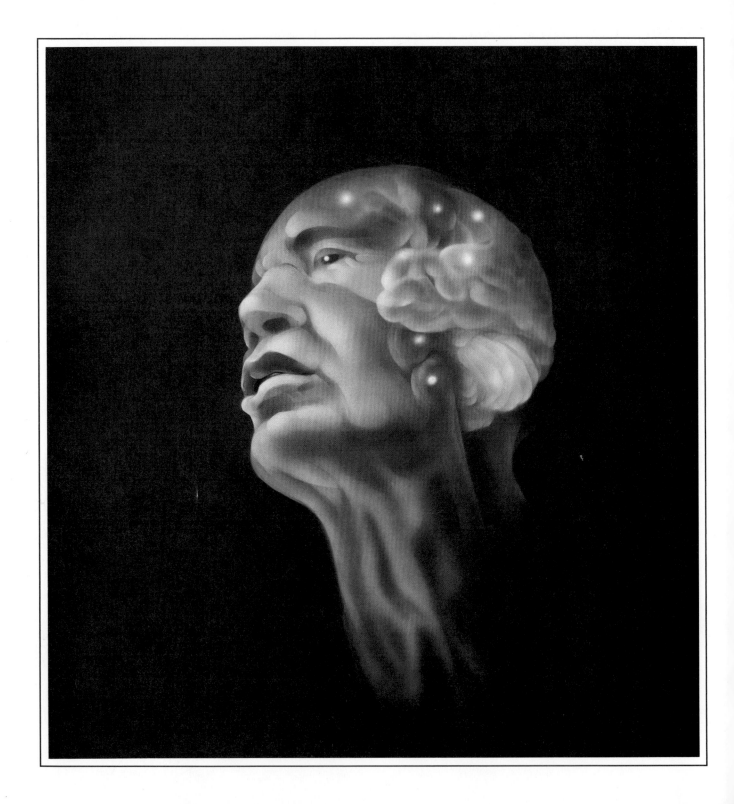

8
Learning and Memory

8

From the moment of birth—and probably for some time before—we experience things. We see shapes and colors, hear a variety of sounds, feel substance and texture, smell odors wafting through the air, taste things that are sweet, sour, or salty. We feel parts of our body move in space, against the pull of Earth's gravity. These experiences can modify the nervous system directly.

When researchers deprive certain target structures in the brain of environmental stimuli—by sealing shut a newborn kitten's eye, for example—those neurons show fewer dendrite branchings, fewer dendrite spines, and fewer synapses (see Chapter 3). Indeed, they show less development in every particular than the neurons receiving normal stimulation. Thus, visual experience—as well as other types of sensory experience—drives neural development.

Other experiments, including those of Mark Rosenzweig and his associates, have shown that rats raised in "enriched" laboratory environments—with plenty of rat company, a large cage, and numerous objects to play with—developed larger cerebral cortices than rats raised in isolation, in small, empty cages (see Figure 8.1). For the rats, expanded social and physical experience produced more extensive neural development, an advantage reflected in the rats' ability to learn tasks like maze-running faster and more reliably than rats raised in isolation. Experience, then, can cause physical modifications in the brain, and these changes, in turn, can modify subsequent behavior. In other words, experience produces learning. In fact, most psychologists define *learning* as a relatively permanent change in behavior as a result of experience.

Learning and remembering are, for all practical purposes, two sides of the same coin, although learning refers to the information acquisition process and memory to the storage process. Even the simplest kinds of learning imply that something has been remembered. Cats that repeatedly hear the sound of the can opener followed soon after by the sight and smell of their food *learn* that the sound of the can opener means that food is on the way. They *remember* that particular sound and its usual consequences. Six-month-old human babies come to differentiate between their mother's face and other faces. At about this age babies have *learned* the particular contours and expressions that characterize mother's face. They *remember* that face, and keep a representation of it well

Virtually everything we human beings know about the world, we know through learning. Babies even have to learn to recognize the particular combination of features that constitutes their mother's face.

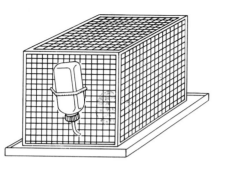
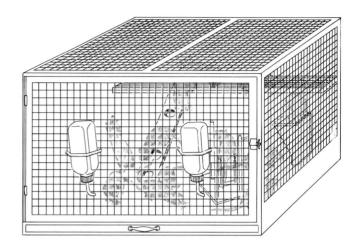

Figure 8.1
One rat in its small, isolated laboratory environment, and a company of 12 rats in their enriched environment, where playthings were changed daily. Rats from the enriched environment were able to learn tasks faster and had thicker, better-developed cerebral cortices than rats raised in isolation (Rosenzweig, 1972).

enough in mind to compare its image with the images of other faces that present themselves at close range during the day. Your study of this book will result in your learning and remembering a great deal of structured information about the brain. These three examples illustrate what a wide range of experience can constitute learning—from the simplest kinds of learning in simple animals to the complex frameworks of knowledge that the human brain is capable of constructing.

In this chapter we shall look first at learning in animals with very simple nervous systems. In the neurons of these animals, researchers have been able to pinpoint and describe some physical and chemical changes that represent the learning. In animals whose nervous systems include a brain, and whose learning capacity is therefore greater and more flexible, research becomes much more complex. The second section of the chapter takes up various brain systems and processes that are known to contribute to learning and memory in many mammals, from the rat to

the human. Finally, because the human brain is the most complex of all, it has characteristics not shared with other animals. Some of those characteristics are discussed in the last sections of the chapter.

Simple Learning and Neural Changes

Neuroscientists have so far studied three kinds of simple learning: (1) habituation, (2) sensitization, and (3) classical, or Pavlovian, conditioning. These forms of learning are called "simple" to differentiate them from those kinds of human learning that are voluntary and that require, for example, the formation of concepts or the use of classification skills. Simple learning occurs without the subject's awareness of a change in behavior. Most animals, and even animals with only ganglia for brains, can learn in these elementary ways.

Another type of simple learning is operant conditioning, in which a behavior naturally performed by an organism is modified as a result of its consequences—reward or punishment. Because this type of learning plays an important role in human behavior, it is discussed later in the chapter.

Habituation and Sensitization

Habituation takes place when a stimulus that an organism originally responded to is presented so often that the organism stops responding to it. In *sensitization*, the opposite of habituation, an animal learns to respond vigorously to a previously neutral stimulus. Both habituation and sensitization have survival value. In sensitization, an animal generally experiences some noxious or irritating stimulus, learns to regard it as dangerous, and consequently attempts to avoid it. In habituation, a stimulus that originally aroused the animal is subsequently experienced several times without irritation or harm; the animal learns to ignore the stimulus, leaving it free to attend to other stimuli. (Because habituation and sensitization are reciprocal, we deal specifically only with the former in this discussion.)

Human adults show habituation all the time. Suppose that you are from a small town and you visit friends in, say, Manhattan. The sound of heavy traffic under your window keeps you awake all night. If you ask your friends how they manage to fall asleep with all that noise, they are likely to answer, "What noise? I don't even hear it any more." They have habituated to the sound of the traffic.

Human newborns are capable of habituation from birth. In studying the hearing capacities of infants, for instance, experimenters attached a sensing device to a 4-hour-old baby's pacifier and played a tone that the baby could hear. When the tone was first played, the baby stopped sucking for a few seconds, presumably to listen (see Figure 8.2). After the tone had been repeated several times, the baby went back to sucking. When a tone only one note different from the first was played, the baby again stopped sucking to listen. This revived attention showed that the baby had indeed habituated to the first tone. Just as interesting, it also revealed how remarkably acute hearing capacities are in the newborn.

What neural changes might account for the process of habituation? It is not yet possible to answer this question for the human brain, but studies by Eric Kandel and his colleagues of *Aplysia californica*, a marine snail, have demonstrated that changes at the cellular level do accompany habituation. *Aplysia's* nervous system is made up of about 18,000 neurons, some of them so large they can be seen by the naked eye.

Aplysia has a reflex behavior vital to its survival: the gill-withdrawal reflex (see Figure 8.3). When waters are calm, *Aplysia* extends its gill to breathe. In rough waters, or if its siphon is touched by a piece of floating debris—or by experimenters in the laboratory shooting it with a jet of water—it withdraws the gill to protect it. This gill with-

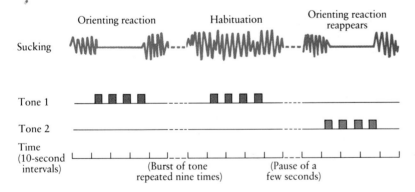

Figure 8.2
A sensing device in a pacifier, sucked on by a baby only 4 hours old, produced the tracing at the top. The baby stopped sucking when the tone was first played but habituated to it—that is, resumed sucking—after hearing the tone 9 or 10 times. Sucking stopped again when the second tone was sounded (Bronshtein & Petrova, 1967).

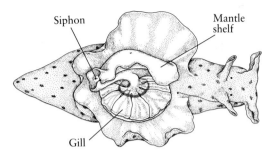

Siphon

Mantle
shelf

Gill

Figure 8.3
After brief stimulation, Aplysia *normally retracts its gill into the position shown in blue. Prolonged stimulation can produce habituation, so the gill-withdrawal response weakens or actually ceases (Kandel, 1979).*

drawal is controlled by one ganglion containing 6 motor neurons and 24 sensory neurons, the latter making direct contact with the former via excitatory synapses, and indirect contact via interneurons.

After repeated stimulation of the gill in laboratory training, *Aplysia* withdraws the gill less vigorously or not at all, and after 10 stimulations, habituation may last as long as a few hours. The researchers discovered that this short-term learning depends on a change at the synapses between the sensory and motor neurons. Specifically, as stimulation continues, less neurotransmitter is released from the sensory neurons across the synapses to the motor neurons. The motor neurons thus receive a lower level of activation, and the behavior they generate—gill withdrawal—is less vigorously performed. In *Aplysia,* then, short-term habituation results when excitation at the synapses in an already existing neural pathway decreases. With no stimulation, after a few hours the amount of transmitter released returns to normal, and the gill-withdrawal reflex is again vigorous.

Habituation and sensitization are the simplest kinds of learning because the organism need not learn any association between

events or stimuli. In classical conditioning, the animal does have to learn such an association.

Classical Conditioning

In the early 1900s, Ivan Pavlov conducted the experiments that demonstrated what has come to be called classical conditioning. While studying dogs' digestive systems, he discovered that the animals began to salivate at the sight of the white-coated attendants who usually brought them food, well before the dogs actually had the food in front of them. Pavlov went on to find that the sound of a bell or a flash of light, if presented consistently before the arrival of food, also caused the dogs to salivate.

Classical conditioning, then, occurs when a stimulus that naturally produces a certain reaction, as food produces salivation, is paired a number of times with another stimulus, such as the ringing of a bell, so that the neutral stimulus comes to elicit the same reaction as the primary stimulus. For conditioning to take place, the two stimuli must be presented very close to each other in time, with the sound of the bell immediately preceding the presentation of food. In this example, the food is called the *unconditioned stimulus* (US); the bell, a previously neutral stimulus, is the *conditioned stimulus* (CS); salivation when food is presented is the *unconditioned response* (UR); salivation upon hearing the bell is the *conditioned response* (CR). (Pavlov himself used the terms "unconditional stimulus"—the stimulus with no conditions attached—and "conditional stimulus"—the stimulus that requires the condition of being paired with a primary stimulus.) In other words, an animal learns the association between an unconditioned stimulus (food) and a conditioned stimulus (bell) so that its behavior in response to the previously neutral stimulus (bell) changes. The cat that comes running to the kitchen when it

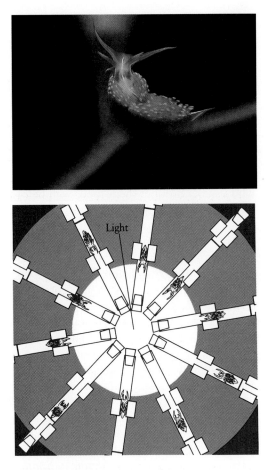

Light

Figure 8.4
Top, the sea snail Hermissenda crassicornis. *Below, the experimental set-up used to condition Hermissenda. Each snail was kept in a fluid-filled glass tube attached to the turntable, which had at its center a photoelectric cell to produce the flashes of light. As a control, the scientists first recorded how long it took each snail to move from the end of its tube to the light, with no turbulence. Then the snails were confined to the end of their tubes and the turntable was rotated. The snails were released and their rate of progress toward the light was recorded after the turbulence. The preconditioning and postconditioning rates were then compared.*

hears the can opener has been conditioned to associate that sound with the presentation of food.

Human beings can be classically conditioned, and emotional responses—fear, in particular—are likely to be learned that way. Before children are old enough to understand why they are poked, prodded, and generally manipulated against their will by doctors and nurses, they often cry at the sight of any white-coated person. They have learned to associate cold instruments, astringent smells, and hypodermic injections (US) with a white coat (CS) and so show the conditioned response, fear, to the previously neutral stimulus (the white coat).

A recent series of experiments has succeeded not only in conditioning a marine snail, *Hermissenda crassicornis,* to associate light with a specific movement, it has also traced the neural changes that mediate this learning (Alkon, 1983). The organisms that *Hermissenda* feeds on cluster in well-lighted water near the surface, so the snail naturally moves toward light. But because its body is vulnerable to injury in rough waters, the snail also naturally responds to turbulence by reflexively contracting its foot and thus slowing its movement toward surface light. When the waters are turbulent, *Hermissenda* seeks a hard surface to cling to deeper, where it is calm and where the animal can go for weeks without feeding.

The experimenters first measured the time that a group of snails took to move toward light (UR). They then subjected some of these snails to turbulence (US) by rotating a turntable (see Figure 8.4), and the rotation was always preceded by a light signal (CS). The pairing of light and turbulence trained the snails to associate light with the onset of turbulence. They slowed their rate of movement toward light (CR), a response that often lasted for many weeks. In fact, the feet of the trained snails contracted when they saw a light. Finally, the researchers analyzed the neural mechanisms mediating this response on three levels: the anatomical, the biophysical, and the biochemical.

Neuroanatomical Changes The researchers had mapped the snail's nervous system, pinpointing the pathways involved in the sensing of light and in the response to turbulence. Light generates electrical signals in two types of photoreceptor cells in the animal's eyes, and these signals are transmitted, in sequence, to interneurons, motor neurons, and groups of muscles. Turbulence, sensed by hair cells in earlike organs, causes electrical signals to be transmitted, in sequence, to another set of interneurons, motor neurons, and muscle groups. Some axons of the hair cells also have synapses with light-receptor axons, and in this way the two sensory systems interact.

One type of photoreceptor cell in the eye, the A cell, is excitatory. The second type, the B cell, is inhibitory—that is, when activated, it inhibits impulses along the chain of neurons that drive the muscle contractions the animal uses to move toward light. The more active the B cells become, the greater the inhibition they produce.

The hair cells normally send inhibitory messages to the B cells, keeping them in the resting state (negatively charged). During the turbulence caused by rotation, that inhibition is increased. But when the rotation stops—after the light has flashed—the hair cell releases its inhibitory hold on the B cell. The B cell becomes excited and exercises its inhibitory role on the muscles that move the snail toward light. After conditioning, just the light alone will cause the B cells to perform their inhibitory role.

Associative learning in this marine snail, then, directly results from changes in the excitability of particular, identified neurons. Because excitability is largely a property of

the nerve-cell membrane, the next question was what happens to the membrane of the B cell in the course of conditioning?

Biophysical Changes in the Cell Membrane In Chapter 2 you saw that a neuron at rest is polarized—the inside of the cell is negative with respect to the outside. At rest, the concentration of potassium is higher inside the cell, and the concentration of sodium is higher outside. In response to a sensory stimulus or to the effect of a chemical transmitter, channels in the cell membrane open, and sodium and calcium ions flow into the cell, depolarizing it. Depolarization also causes potassium channels to open and, because of its high concentration within the cell, potassium flows out. The membrane is studded with channels that are specific for different ions. When the changes in membrane potential depolarize the neuron sufficiently, the wave of activity can spread along the length of the axon. This wave of activity is the nerve impulse.

Conditioning in *Hermissenda* appears to take the following course:

1. Before conditioning, the B cell receives inhibitory messages from the hair cell; these keep it in the negatively charged resting state by allowing potassium ions to flow out.

2. The light flashes, exciting the B cell: sodium ions rush into the cell, followed by calcium ions.

3. At this moment, the turntable begins to move, producing turbulence. With this movement, the hair cell increases its inhibition of the B cell.

4. The turntable stops, and the hair cell relaxes its inhibitory hold on the B cell. The B cell becomes more positive as more of its calcium channels open.

5. The concentration of calcium ions

within the B cell cytoplasm increases dramatically.

6. The gates on certain membrane channels close, preventing potassium ions from flowing out of the cell.

7. The cell is depolarized and fires its message, inhibiting the snail from moving.

8. The cell's excited state may last for days, and during this time the cell will always react to a flash of light alone in the same way.

Biochemical Mechanisms Although the level of calcium within the photoreceptor cells increases during training, it returns to normal after training ends. Yet the learned behavior persists for weeks: the B cell continues to be excitable and to inhibit the action of the muscles that would move the snail toward light. What biochemical mechanism might account for this persistent response?

The high level of calcium during training activates certain enzymes. These enzymes have a specific biochemical task, to attach phosphate molecules to proteins—a process called *phosphorylation*. Phosphorylation often changes the character of the protein, and since the ion channels in the cell membrane are themselves proteins, these channels could become phosphorylated, changing their specificity. (Recall that some channels are specific for sodium ions, some for potassium ions, some for calcium ions.) This change could directly reduce potassium outflow.

Furthermore, it appears that once these phosphorylating enzymes are activated, they keep on working, changing cell membrane proteins for a long time after calcium levels have decreased to normal.

The analysis of neural changes in invertebrate learning is one of the most complete to date, even though some parts of the analysis still rest on conjecture. Whether similar changes occur in higher animals is not known. It seems likely, however, that the cellular mechanisms of learning and memory used by simpler organisms might be preserved in evolution, even though additional brain mechanisms and systems for memory storage are undoubtedly present in complicated vertebrate nervous systems.

Brain Systems and Memory

For animals with brains, we want to know more than which cellular changes may constitute memory storage; we want to know how memory is organized in the brain. Which regions of the brain are important? Which brain systems participate in learning and memory? Recent research has been able to provide some important clues.

The Cerebellum

The cerebellum (see Figure 8.5) functions in the control of all kinds of movement. It "programs" the coordination of the many individual movements that go to make up the action of, say, lifting an apple to your mouth to bite into it. Patients who have sustained injuries to the cerebellum report that they must consciously perform each step of a complex movement that they had performed "automatically" before their injury—bringing the apple up and stopping its movement before it makes contact with their lips, for example.

Recent work (McCormick et al., 1982) suggests that a wide variety of classically conditioned learned responses may be stored in the cerebellum. For example, in one experiment, rabbits were conditioned to blink an eyelid in response to a tone. A puff of air directed at the rabbit's eye (US) was repeatedly associated with the sound of a tone (CS). Like people, rabbits show the reflex response of blinking (UR) when an irritating stimulus, such as a puff of air, hits the eye.

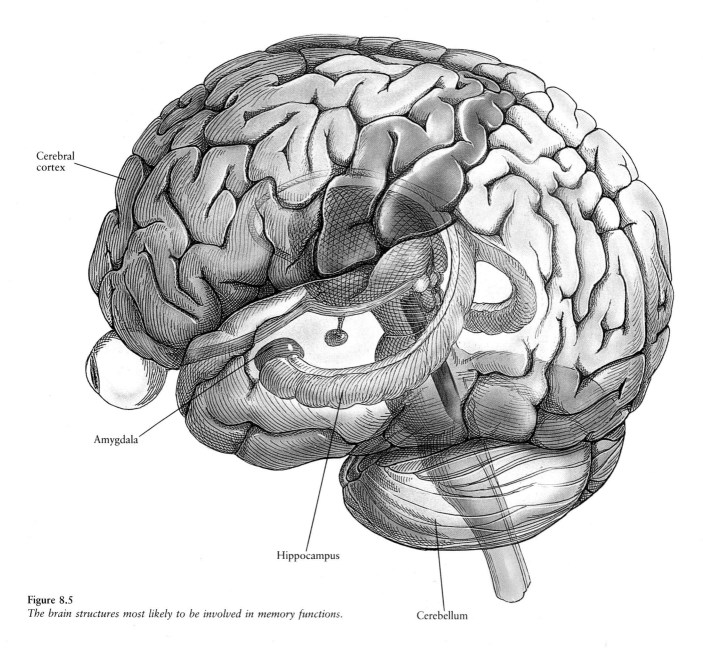

Cerebral
cortex

Amygdala

Hippocampus

Cerebellum

Figure 8.5
The brain structures most likely to be involved in memory functions.

After a number of pairings of air puffs with the tone, the rabbits learned to blink at the sound alone (CR).

With the conditioning process complete, the researchers removed a very small part of the rabbits' cerebellum on the left side, the same side as the eye that had been trained. The conditioned response completely disappeared, but the unconditioned response—blinking in response to a puff of air—remained normal. In addition, the right eyelid could subsequently be conditioned to the tone, but the left eyelid could never re-learn the response. The memory trace for eyelid conditioning seems to develop in this one particular region of the cerebellum—the deep cerebellar nuclei—and destruction of that region also destroys that trace. Other neural changes may also contribute to the learned response, but the changes in the cerebellum are obviously essential.

The Hippocampus

The hippocampus (see Figure 8.5) has been the subject of much research over the past three decades, but we still cannot say precisely what functions it performs in learning and memory. Studies conducted from various points of departure have discovered several roles that it may play. The few human patients who are known to have suffered severe damage to both left and right hippocampi show serious learning problems. After the damage occurs, they are unable to store memories of anything they learn; they cannot even remember the name or the face of someone they encountered only minutes before. Their memory of events that occurred before their brain damage, however, appears to be unimpaired. (See pages 254–255 and 262–265 for a discussion of these human patients and their problems.)

By implanting electrodes in single neurons of rats' brains, researchers have learned that some neurons in the hippocampus seem to respond only when the animal is at a certain place in a familiar environment (O'Keefe & Nadel, 1978). The monitored cell remains quiet until the animal reaches a certain point. At that point, and only at that point, the neuron begins firing rapidly. As soon as the rat moves past this place, the neuron quiets down (see Figure 8.6). In rats, at least, the hippocampus apparently plays an important role in the learning of a "spatial map."

This spatial map is not analogous to a road map, however. Rather, it is a kind of filter for sensory events that have already been processed by the cerebral cortex. The rat's hippocampus is, in a sense, "recognizing" a space that the rat has traveled before. If the hippocampus is damaged, the rat's ability to learn a maze at all is severely damaged.

Another study (Olton et al., 1980) used a maze modeled after the way rats forage in the wild (see Figure 8.7). Every arm of the maze had food at its end, as would many routes in a natural setting. The rat's problem was to remember where it had already been in order to run to a place where it had not yet eaten the food. After only a few runs, normal rats learned the maze so well that they never retraced their steps. When these rats' hippocampi were removed, however, they often retraced their paths, apparently unable to remember where they had been and where they had not. It was as though the rat had lost its "working memory."

That the hippocampus operates somehow in "working memory," or short-term memory, is indicated by its differing levels of activity during classical conditioning. Little, if any, neuronal activity goes on in the hippocampus during conditioning of the eyelid blink in rabbits, for example. Even rabbits without a hippocampus can be conditioned to blink an eyelid. But if a rabbit's hippocampus is subjected to enough electrical stimulation to produce the abnormal neuronal activity of epileptic-like seizures, the rabbit is unable to learn the response, as Richard Thompson and his colleagues have found. (In this matter, at least, an abnormal hippocampus is worse than no hippocampus at all.) If a pause is introduced between presentation of the tone and the puff of air, neurons in the hippocampus start to fire during that pause, as if the hippocampus kept the tone in working memory until the puff of air arrived. When Thompson made training tasks more complex, reversing the rules on an animal trained to respond to one stimulus and not to respond to another, he recorded massive neuronal activity in the hippocampus. The added complexity seemed to require more neural activity. Nevertheless, the role of the hippocampus in simple eyelid conditioning and its role as a "spatial mapmaker," or "working memory," are two very different things.

Recent research has revealed that cells in the hippocampus, when stimulated repeatedly by electrodes, continue firing for as long as weeks after the stimulation stops. This technique, called *long-term potentiation,* produces neuronal firing resembling that found in an animal going about the ordinary business of learning something.

You will recall that many neurons, after repeated stimulation, become less active—as in the case of *Aplysia's* habituation. Researchers believe that the increased excitability of hippocampal neurons after repeated stimulation may represent long-lasting changes taking place at the synapses there, changes that underlie learning. And it does appear that after long-term potentiation, the neurons involved do show structural changes. Some researchers have provided evidence that the heads of dendritic spines swell. Others have shown that the number of synapses onto dendritic shafts increases. Such changes in neuron structure and in the quality and quantity of connectivity between them might be the neural basis for certain kinds of learning and memory. No conclusions are possible yet, but research is continuing.

The hippocampus receives very indirect neural input from all the senses (see Chapter 7). Messages traveling along neural pathways from the brainstem and cortex undergo considerable sensory processing, but eventually they reach the hippocampus, the amygdala, or the hypothalamus, or all of these structures. Pathways down from the cortex

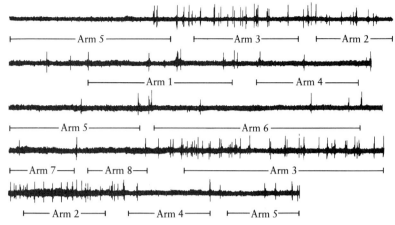

Figure 8.6
Activity recorded from an electrode implanted in one neuron of a rat's hippocampus in the O'Keefe and Nadel (1978) experiment. The neuron fires rapidly only when the rat is in arms 2 or 3 of the maze, places that evidently have some special spatial meaning to the rat.

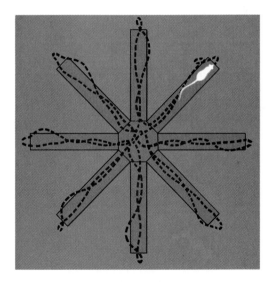

Figure 8.7
The radial arm maze created by Olton to test rats' memory. Food was placed at the end of every arm, and, just as in the wild, the rat's problem was to find all the food without retracing its steps, wasting time running to places it had already visited. The pattern shown here reflects the perfect learning of normal rats: This rat visited each arm of the maze only once, eating whatever it found there; it did not go back to an empty arm even one time.

also pass through these structures. A study using monkeys as subjects showed that both the hippocampus and the amygdala had to be removed to destroy previous learning and prevent new learning. Before the operation, the monkeys learned relatively quickly to choose the novel object of a pair—one that they had not seen before. After their operations, monkeys minus only amygdala or those minus only hippocampus relearned the novelty task only a little less successfully than normal monkeys did: 91 percent versus 97 percent correct. The monkeys who had lost both their hippocampus and their amygdala, however, had only a 60 percent success rate, almost the level of chance. Either they could not learn the criterion for making a choice, or they could not remember and recognize objects they had already seen.

It is clear that the hippocampus plays a role in learning and memory, even if its exact function cannot yet be described. Now let us

A monkey at Harry Harlow's primate laboratory at the University of Wisconsin solves an oddity problem.

look at a structure even more certainly responsible for learning but whose functions are even less well understood.

The Cortex

There is no doubt that the cerebral cortex in the human brain is vital to learning and memory, but its complexity makes it difficult to study. Because human thinking and problem-solving usually employ language, animal experiments can offer only the roughest analogies. The simple learning involved in habituation and classical conditioning does not seem to require higher cortical functions.

Monkeys can learn to solve several kinds of problems that involve complex learning. The animals are trained on a number of discrimination problems, and if, as a result of the earlier training, they are able to learn later problems more quickly, they are said to have formed a *learning set*. For example, in the *oddity problem* devised by Harry Harlow, the primate psychologist, monkeys are shown a set of three objects, two of which are identical—two toy cars and a truck, for example. They are rewarded for picking the odd object. After a monkey picks the truck in a number of trials, it is shown three entirely different objects—two oranges and an apple, for example. Eventually, the monkey apparently forms the concept of "oddness" and picks the odd object of a set every time on the first trial. Loss of large parts of the temporal lobes of the cortex destroys the ability to form such concepts.

The fact that animals raised in enriched environments have slightly thicker cortical layers and more elaborated neuronal structures than animals raised in deprived environments shows that experience— learning—causes changes in an animal's cortex. It must be that in human beings, in whom the cortex is so prominent, the same sorts of changes occur. In conjunction with the other brain structures that help us process information, the human cortex stores our experience, and it must change as we learn and remember. But it is not yet possible to say precisely what those changes are.

Transmitter Systems

An animal's survival depends on its remembering which events predict pleasure and which predict pain. Therefore the value of information to an animal—that is, whether or not a piece of information should be stored in memory—depends in part on what occurs after the animal has initially registered the information. Several hormones and neurotransmitters have been suggested as the agents that influence, or modulate, this initial learning.

A prime candidate for this role is the hormone *norepinephrine,* secreted by the adrenal medulla during states of emotional arousal. If pain is used as punishment in training animals to perform a behavior—a strong electrical shock to the foot, for example—and the animals are then given a small dose of norepinephrine, they later show much better memory for the correct behavior than animals not given the chemical (McGaugh, 1983). A weak electrical shock does not mobilize as much of the body's natural norepinephrine, and animals so trained require much more injected norepinephrine to produce the same improvement in memory. Amphetamine, a stimulant drug known to facilitate memory, also works by activating the body's norepinephrine and dopamine systems. (The possible role of norepinephrine in consolidating human memory is discussed on page 261). But circulating norepinephrine cannot cross the blood/brain barrier, so the precise physiological mechanism that might mediate its role in learning is not known.

Protein Synthesis

All the molecules that make up our bodies are continuously being broken down and reformed. In the brain, too, 90 percent of its proteins are broken down and replaced within no more than two weeks. The structures made up of proteins do not change, of course: the process is more like that of individual bricks in a brick house being replaced here and there.

The template on which protein is made in the cell is RNA. A number of studies have suggested that the rate of RNA production of protein seems to increase in animals during learning. The problem with such findings is that everything a neuron does involves protein synthesis, so there is really no way to know exactly what the increased rate reflects.

In one series of experiments on baby chicks, Steven Rose and his colleagues (1973) made every effort to control outside influences. All chicks show the natural species-specific learning behavior of *imprinting.* They become attached to and follow—that is, they learn to recognize—the first moving object they encounter as soon after hatching as they can walk, usually in about 16 hours. The moving object is usually their mother, although some researchers of animal behavior have had chicks following balls, mechanical toys, and even themselves.

Increased production of protein can be detected in the chick's brain within 2 hours of its exposure to an imprinting stimulus. To rule out any possible effects not related to this learning, researchers cut the pathway that transfers visual information between the two halves of the chick's brain. In effect, they used one-half of the chick's brain as a control for the other (experimental) half. When they covered one eye so that the chick saw the imprinting stimulus with just one eye, the rate of protein synthesis was greater in the

These ducklings imprinted on Nobel-prize-winning ethologist Konrad Lorenz because he was the first moving object they saw after hatching.

biochemical mechanisms of nerve-impulse transmission are very similar for all neurons in all animals. If these mechanisms have been preserved in evolution, it seems reasonable to assume that the cellular mechanisms of learning and memory used by simple organisms are also so preserved.

In several recent experiments, scientists injected the phosphorylating enzyme responsible for *Aplysia's* and *Hermissenda's* learning into neurons in brains of many different types of mammals. The enzyme produced excitability much like that exhibited in the snails' cell membranes. Whether this cellular reaction has the same function in the cat and the snail is not yet known. But knowledge of biochemical principles of learning in simple animals gives scientists a base from which to study more complicated nervous systems.

Studies at the cellular level alone, however, would hardly unlock the secrets of how the human brain remembers the score of a Beethoven symphony or even the trivia needed to do a crossword puzzle. That study must go on at the level of brain systems, where the tens of billions of neurons in the human brain are connected with one another according to a complicated but specific design. In higher nonhuman animals, scientists use learning experiments and brain manipulation. In human beings, psychological studies of normal people, and sometimes of those who are mentally retarded, offer insight into how human beings process and store information. And studies of people who display amnesia after brain damage provide particularly important evidence about the organization of memory functions in the brain.

half of the brain that learned to recognize the imprinting stimulus.

The role of these newly manufactured proteins in memory, it is conjectured, would be to travel down the axon to the synapse and change the synapse structure in ways that would, at least temporarily, make it more effective. This modification, then, would be the physical basis of the learning.

Simple Learning and the Human Brain

How can cellular events in the sea snail or protein synthesis in a chick's brain shed light on human learning and memory? The basic

The Human Memory System

Almost four decades ago, psychologist Karl Lashley, a pioneer in experimental studies of brain and behavior, attempted to answer the question of how memory is organized in the brain. He taught animals a specific task, then removed different pieces of cerebral cortex, one by one, to find where the memory was stored. No matter how much cortex he removed, however, he could not find a specific location where the memory trace, or the "engram," as he called it, was stored. In 1950 he wrote:

This series of experiments . . . has discovered nothing directly of the real nature of the engram. I sometimes feel, in reviewing the evidence on the localization of the memory trace, that the necessary conclusion is that learning just is not possible.

Subsequent research made the reasons for Lashley's failure clear: many regions and structures in the brain in addition to the cerebral cortex are critical to learning and memory. Memories also appear to be stored in a distributed and redundant way in the cortex.

One of Lashley's students, Donald Hebb (1949), went on to construct a theory of memory processes that has guided subsequent research for over three decades. Hebb distinguished between short-term and long-term memory. Short-term memory, he said, was an active process of limited duration, leaving no traces, while long-term memory was produced by structural changes in the nervous system.

Hebb thought that these structural changes resulted from repeated activation of a loop of neurons. The loop might run from the cortex to the thalamus or the hippocampus and back to the cortex. Repeated activation of the neurons composing the loop would cause the synapses between them to become functionally connected. Once connected, these neurons would constitute a *cell assembly,* and any excitation of neurons in the assembly would activate the entire assembly. Thus a memory could be stored and retrieved by any sensation, thought, or emotion that activated some of the neurons in the

cell assembly. The structural changes, Hebb believed, probably occurred at synapses and took the form of some growth process or of some metabolic change that increased each neuron's effect on the next.

The idea of cell assemblies emphasizes that memories are not static "records," not simply products of a change in the structure of a single nerve cell or molecule in the brain. This focus on memory as a process involving the interaction of many nerve cells seems the best way to explain neurologically what psychologists have discovered about how people normally process information.

Information-Processing Aspects of Memory

In order to remember something, a person must do three things successfully: acquire a piece of information, retain it, and retrieve it. If you fail to remember something, the problem may lie in any of these three processes.

But memory is not quite this simple. We do not learn and remember discrete pieces of information; we construct frameworks of knowledge, and the organization of these frameworks guides our learning, storing, and retrieving of knowledge. And memory is an active process—existing knowledge is always changing and always being examined and reformulated by our thinking brains—so its properties are not easy to capture.

As Jerome Bruner, the noted American psychologist, has said, human beings have the capacity—and the tendency—"to convert encounters with the particular into instances of the general." This capacity seems to be part of our species-specific heritage. Most English-speaking 3- or 4-year-olds, for example, go through a period of using words like "goed" and "breaked," even though they never hear such words spoken and have previously used the correct forms "went" and "broke." They do this because their encounters with many particular verbs have led them to formulate on their own (in some still mysterious way) the general language rule that "you form the past tense of a verb by adding *-ed* to the end of it." They cannot, of course, state the rule, but developmental psycholinguists have shown that they inevitably act upon this tendency to generalize (Slobin, 1979; Platt & MacWhinney, 1983).

Short-Term and Long-Term Memory

Memory seems to have several phases. One is extremely short-term, *immediate memory*, in which items are stored for only a few seconds. As you ride in a car watching the scenery go by, you may be able to recall some objects you saw a second or two earlier, but not much longer. Some items from immediate memory—the items to which you attend—get transferred to short-term memory.

Items may be held in *short-term memory* for several minutes. Consider what happens when someone gives you a phone number and you have no pencil. You can probably remember the number by rehearsing it in your mind until you get to the phone, but if your attention is distracted—if someone speaks to you or you drop the coin you were about to put in the pay phone—you will probably forget the number or get it confused. We seem to be able to keep five to nine separate items in short-term memory—seven plus or minus two, in information-processing terms. Another information-processing term, "chunking," explains why it sometimes seems that we can keep more than that in mind. The phone number 481-3965 is seven items, but the phone number 234-5678 is only one item if we see it as a chunk, that is, as the item "digits 2 through 8." The word "fox" is one item, but so is the phrase "the quick brown fox" to people who have learned touch typing.

Some items from short-term memory get transferred to *long-term memory,* where

storage may last for hours or for a lifetime. We know that one brain system necessary for making this transfer is the hippocampus. This function of the hippocampus was discovered when a patient, referred to as H. M. in the literature about his postoperative capacities, underwent brain surgery. There is one hippocampus in each of the brain's temporal lobes, and, in H. M.'s case, both hippocampi were removed in an attempt to ease his violent epileptic seizures. (After the discovery of H. M.'s subsequent incapacity, this procedure was never again performed.)

As a consequence of his surgery, H. M. lives entirely in the present. He can remember events—objects or people—only for the time they remain in his short-term memory. If you chat with him and then leave the room for a few minutes, when you return he will have no recollection of ever having seen you before. The following observations come from the clinical report prepared by Dr. Brenda Milner (1972).

> There has been little change in . . . [H. M.'s] clinical picture during the years which have elapsed since the operation. . . . There [is no] evidence of general intellectual loss, in fact, his intelligence as measured by standard tests is actually a little higher now than before the operation. . . . Yet the remarkable memory defect persists, and it is clear that H. M. can remember little of the experiences of the last years. . . .

> Ten months after the operation, the family moved to a new house which was situated only a few blocks away from their old one, on the same street. When examined . . . nearly a year later, H. M. had not yet learned the new address, nor could he be trusted to find his way home alone, because he would go to the old house. Six years ago, the family moved again, and H. M. is still unsure of his present address, although he does seem to know that he has moved. [The patient] will do the same jigsaw puzzles day after day without showing any practice effect, and read the same magazines over and over again without finding their contents familiar. . . .

I'll Always Remember

Most of us remember our graduation day—even the middle-aged Beach Boys sing about it. Most of us, in fact, remember a surprising number of things about high school, once our memories are jogged. Such recall is very long-term memory.

Investigations of memory in the laboratory usually give subjects limited learning tasks that assure comparable experimental conditions and, therefore, meaningful measurements of short-term memory. In 1974, a research team (Bahrick, Bahrick & Wittlinger) set out to test long-term memory about events that most people share. Working with a sample population of 392 high-school graduates, who had had at least four years to acquire and use a fairly constant body of information, the investigators tested their subjects with recall and recognition tasks, using names and photographs from high-school yearbooks.

Not surprisingly, they found that people recognize better than they recall. Those who had graduated as long as 35 years ago could recognize the pictures of 9 out of 10 classmates. More recent graduates did just as well recognizing names alone, but after 30 years or more, the success rate dropped slightly to 70 or 80 percent. For at least 10 to 15 years, the subjects could match 90 percent of names to faces, but this rate dropped to 60 percent after 20 to 25 years—still, a fair success rate.

Women did better than men on all of these tests, with one notable exception. Men out of school 20 years or more exceeded their female classmates on all but one recall test. Men remember significantly more boys, while women remember only slightly more girls than boys. Both men and women remembered best the people they had dated or their close friends.

A look at your own high-school yearbook will probably confirm these observations. The study reiterated what most of us already know: the human brain stores more than most of us want or need to remember. It is access and retrieval that cause our problems.

In 1949, they were going to be married after college. In 1969, he remembered her well enough to ask her to his second wedding to somebody else.

Even such profound amnesias as these are, however, compatible with a normal attention span. . . . On one occasion, he was asked to remember the number 584 and was then allowed to sit quietly with no interruption for 15 minutes, at which point he was able to recall the number correctly without hesitation. When asked how he had been able to do this, he replied,

"It's easy. You just remember 8. You see 5, 8, and 4 add to 17. You remember 8, subtract it from 17 and it leaves 9. Divide 9 in half and you get 5 and 4, and there you are: 584. Easy."

In spite of H. M.'s elaborate mnemonic scheme he was unable, a minute or so later, to remember either the number 584 or any of the associated complex train of thought; in fact, he did not know that he had been given a number to remember. . . .

One gets some idea of what such an amnesic state must be like from H. M.'s own comments. . . . Between tests, he would suddenly look up and say, rather anxiously,

"Right now, I'm wondering. Have I done or said anything amiss? You see, at this moment everything looks clear to me, but what happened just before? That's what worries me. It's like waking from a dream. I just don't remember."

H. M. has a good memory of events in his life that preceded the operation. The memories already in his long-term storage—at least those that were stored one to three years before his surgery—were not lost. The fact that H. M. suffered some amnesia for events that preceded his surgery by a year or two but not for previous events suggests that memory may undergo changes—consolidation—for some time after learning.

Memory Consolidation

The hippocampus lies within the temporal lobe of the brain, and some evidence suggests that it and the medial part of the temporal lobe—that is, the part lying closest to the midline of the body—play a role in the process of memory consolidation. *Memory consolidation* refers to the changes, physical and psychological, that go on as the brain organizes and restructures information that may become a part of permanent memory. Even after some of the information has passed into long-term memory, parts of it may still undergo transformation, and parts may be forgotten before the reorganized material becomes permanently stored.

As a simple example of reorganization, think back to when, as a child, you learned to read. At first you had to be able to recall that the difference between d and b was that "the loop on the b goes on the right." Once you had mastered letter recognition, your reorganized memory permitted you to recognize the letters without retrieving such cues. Once you learned to read with ease, your memory for the sounds, shapes, and combinations of letters became a coherent and stable whole. Skilled readers never read letter-by-letter or even word-by-word; they process chunks of words at a time.

The hippocampus and the medial temporal area appear to act in the formation and development of memory rather than being sites of permanent storage. The fact that H. M., in whom this area was destroyed, retained intact memories for events that preceded his surgery by more than three years is evidence that the temporal area is not the site of permanent storage. That he lost his memory for many events that occurred during the three years before his surgery, however, is evidence that this area plays a role in the formation of memory. (It is also possible, of course, that H. M.'s epilepsy may also have interfered with memory consolidation.)

Other evidence comes from patients who undergo electroconvulsive shock therapy (ECT) for severe depression. Electric shock is known to be especially disruptive to the hippocampus, and ECT patients typically suffer amnesia for events that occurred during the few years prior to treatment. Their memory of earlier events is not affected.

Larry Squire (1984) speculates that at the time something is learned, the temporal region establishes a relationship with memory storage sites elsewhere in the brain, primarily in other parts of the cortex. Interaction between these areas may be required for as long as several years while reorganization of memory goes on. The reorganization involves a physical remodeling of neural circuitry in some way, Squire believes. At some point, then, when reorganization and remodeling are complete—when the memory is permanently stored in the cortex—the temporal region is no longer required to support that memory's retention or retrieval.

Besides the phases of short-term and long-term memory that characterize human remembering and failing to remember, it appears that we have two distinct ways of learning and remembering things, depending on what is being learned.

Procedural and Declarative Memory

Even though they cannot remember facts about the world, H. M. and other patients with tissue damage like his can learn and remember *how to do* things. For example, groups of such patients have been taught the skill of mirror reading (see Figure 8.8). They took three days to become skillful at the task, about the same number of days that normal people take, and they retained a high level of skill for the three months during which they were tested. Yet when tested, many of the patients did not remember ever having worked at the task before, and none of them could later remember the words that they had read (Cohen & Squire, 1980).

Having noted that many normal people who learned to solve the Tower of Hanoi problem (see page 258) had difficulty describing what they had learned, Neal Cohen decided that solving the puzzle might involve a kind of procedural learning that patient H. M. could tackle. In fact, H. M., over sev-

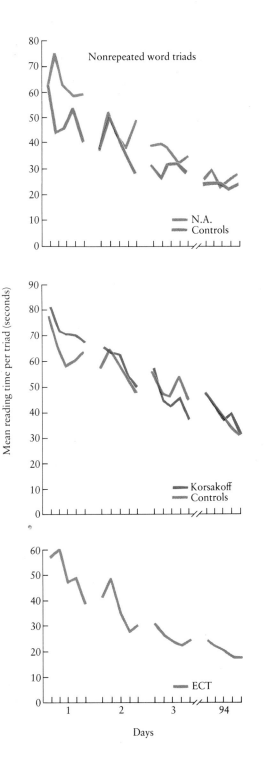

Figure 8.8
The procedural skill of mirror reading of groups of words, like the three words shown above, was acquired at a normal rate by amnesiac patients and was retained at a normal level for 3 months after learning (Cohen & Squire, 1980). N. A. is patient N. A.; Korsakoff, patients with Korsakoff's syndrome; ECT, patients who had undergone electroconvulsive therapy.

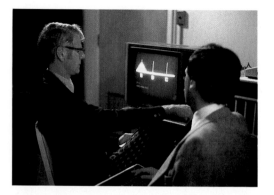

In the Tower of Hanoi puzzle, the person solving the problem is presented with five different-sized disks stacked on one of three pegs, with the largest disk on the bottom. The disks must be transferred from the first peg to the third one at a time in the same configuration, though no disk may go on top of a smaller disk and no disk under another disk may be moved. The puzzle can be solved in 31 moves. Above, Neal Cohen used a computerized version to test an amnesiac patient.

eral daily sessions, did learn to solve the puzzle and could successfully repeat his correct solution, even though at the beginning of each session he appeared not to remember having worked on it and claimed not to know exactly what was expected of him. To some, this behavior suggests that H. M.'s amnesia might represent a problem in retrieval from memory rather than a storage problem. Larry Squire and Neal Cohen, however, think it is more likely that H. M., and others like him, just do not store all the information stored by normal people who learn to solve such problems.

All of this suggests to investigators that the brain processes two kinds of information in separate ways and that each kind of information is stored differently. *Procedural knowledge* is knowledge of how to do something. *Declarative knowledge,* in Squire's words, "provides an explicit, accessible record of individual previous experiences, a sense of familiarity about those experiences." The latter requires processing in the temporal region and parts of the thalamus while the former apparently does not.

Procedural learning probably developed earlier in evolution than declarative learning. In fact, habituation and classical conditioning, which take place without awareness that learning has occurred, are examples of procedural learning. Experimental proof is not yet available, but another distinction may be that procedural memory occurs as biochemical or biophysical changes only in the neural circuits directly involved in the procedure learned. (We examined such changes in connection with *Aplysia*'s habituation and *Hermissenda*'s classical conditioning.) This type of change differs from the *remodeling* of neural circuitry that declarative memory is thought to require.

The distinction between these two kinds of learning may help explain why adult human beings are almost completely unable to recall people and events from their infancy and very early childhood. The noted developmental theorist Jean Piaget called the first two years of life the *sensorimotor period* of cognitive development. In essence, the infant spends these first two years of life learning the uses of the body—how to use the hand in grasping different objects, how to coordinate the muscles used in crawling and walking, how to deal with gravity, how to judge the relative size of objects near and far away, how to connect physical causes (shaking the hand) and effects (hearing the rattle make noise). In fact, Piaget said, the infant's knowledge of things is limited to what he or she can do to them. People and objects have no existence of their own, independent of the sensorimotor actions the infant performs on them, until the child is about 2. This scenario corresponds almost perfectly to that of procedural learning.

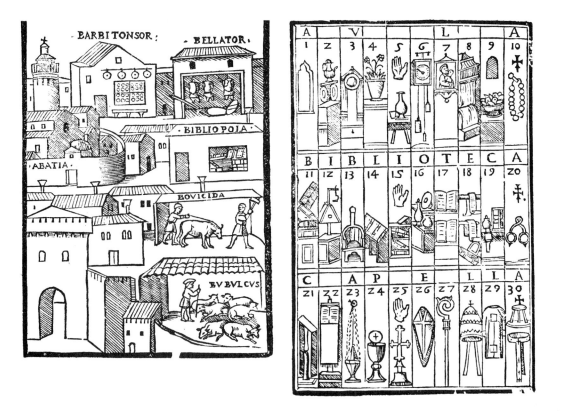

The "method of loci," or "places," as an aid to memory goes back to the Greeks and Romans. This guide was written and illustrated by Dominican friars in the sixteenth century. At left are the abbey and its outbuildings—the courtyard, the library, the chapel. Each object in each row at the right (every fifth item is a hand or a cross so the speaker can keep track of items on each hand) is associated with an idea in the speech, then "placed" along the route through the abbey. When the speaker needs to recall the speech, he retraces the route through the abbey, finding each object (or idea) in the order he wishes to use it (Johannes Romberch, Congestorium Artificia Memoriae, *Venice, 1553*).

Because the infant cannot hold in mind representations of objects or events much before age 2, it would seem that no declarative memories are possible. When 2-year-olds come to understand that objects have an existence of their own, they come to a corollary understanding—that they too have an existence of their own, a self. Toddlers are capable of holding things in mind, of remembering, but the prelogical quality of their thought (Piaget says they are incapable of "connected relational reasoning") helps to explain why declarative storage from this early phase may be so different from that of adults that its content is later lost.

The distinction between procedural and declarative memory may also help to explain why some *mnemonic devices*—schemes to aid in storing and recalling memories—work so well. One of the most commonly used of

No one knows why, but Joey jumps on the fire hydrant every time he passes it and stays there as long as he is allowed to. Joey's behavior has somehow been operantly conditioned by the promise of a reward that only Joey knows about.

such devices, the *method of loci* (or places), was invented by the Greek orators, and it has worked well ever since. The technique consists of visualizing a familiar location and then, in your mind's eye, placing things to be remembered—the points you want to make in a speech, for example—at prominent places along the route. When the time comes, you mentally revisit the place, retrace your path, and find at each location the item you placed there. This device uses a procedural context for organizing declarative information.

Besides the functional differences among these various aspects of memory, there is one other important qualitative factor in human learning that influences what information is stored in memory and can be retrieved from it: whether or not the action is followed by rewarding or punishing consequences.

Reward and Punishment in Learning and Remembering

Operant conditioning is the name of the learning theory that attempts to explain how behavior is shaped by its consequences. It differs from classical conditioning in a number of important respects, but probably the most important is that it deals not with reflexes but with what B. F. Skinner, its major theorist, calls *operant behaviors*—that is, behaviors that an animal or person voluntarily and naturally performs.

In essence, the theory says that an operant behavior that results in the attainment of something the organism likes tends to be repeated, and a behavior that results in something the organism dislikes tends not to be repeated. This basic principle is extremely important in determining what behaviors an animal or a person will learn and remember.

The survival of an animal depends, of course, on its doing things that are rewarding. Behaviors that produce food, for example, are rewarded by something to eat, and if the animal remembers the behaviors that produced the reward and repeats them, it can enhance its chances of survival. The animal also learns to avoid behaviors that result in its being hurt or frightened. To say that an animal tends to repeat a behavior that results in attaining something it likes is to say that learning and emotion interact. We learn to repeat behaviors that are accompanied by positive emotional qualities, and we learn to avoid repeating behaviors that are accompanied by fear or discomfort (even though we may have learned how to perform the behavior). But what brain mechanisms might account for this interaction?

Recent research by James L. McGaugh suggests possible physiological bases for the effects of operant conditioning. Many studies have shown that an animal's memory of a behavior it was trained for in the laboratory (usually through classical conditioning) can be disrupted by a number of different treatments administered soon after the training—electrical stimulation of various parts of the brain, for example, or the injection of various hormones. The fact that these post-training treatments altered memory retention so readily suggested to McGaugh and his colleagues that memory consolidation could be subject to the physiological effects of everyday experiences.

If the physiological consequences of an experience are considerable, the organism would best retain that experience for long periods of time. If the consequences are trivial, the experience is best forgotten quickly. Thus, time-dependent memory processes may be the result of the development of a mechanism with which organisms select from recent experiences those that should be permanently stored (Gold & McGaugh, 1975, p. 375).

In a more recent series of experiments, McGaugh trained rats in a variety of learning tasks. Then he subjected the animals to several treatments in order to examine the interactive influences of the amygdala and circulating norepinephrine (produced by the adrenal medulla) on how well the rats remembered the tasks.

The results of these experiments suggest that influences of the amygdala on other parts of the brain, in combination with influences from circulating hormones (primarily adrenal norepinephrine), may indeed affect memory consolidation. (The mechanism for the hormonal process remains unclear, however, because these hormones do not pass through the blood/brain barrier.) McGaugh does not suggest that the amygdala stores memories. Rather, the research suggests that a sequence of physiological processes underlies memory storage, and one of these is carried out by the amygdala, which somehow modulates the activity of "memory cells." In addition, the amygdala's activity could be indirectly influenced by norepinephrine and other circulating hormones. Such a mechanism would help explain the role of reward and motivation in learning.

These studies help us to see some of the structures and processes involved in memory and how they might operate together. They do not, by any means, offer a complete blueprint for the workings of the human memory system. Another set of studies that looked at the specific deficits of damaged brains adds some details to the picture.

What Can We Learn from Damaged Brains?

People who have amnesia in the movies usually wake up in hospital beds without a single recollection of their past lives. Will he recognize his wife when she walks into the

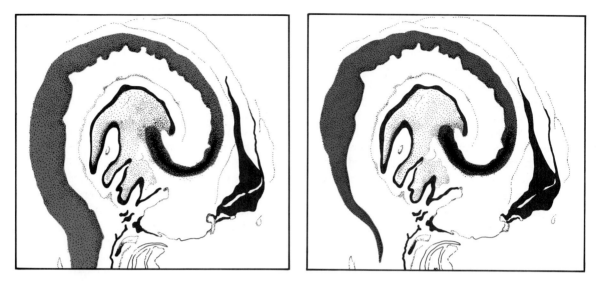

Two schematic views of the hippocampus. Left, normal hippocampus; note the thick band (light brown) of pyramidal cells. Right, hippocampus of patient with memory loss; note the colossal loss of pyramidal cells at left.

room? Will he remember that he has witnessed a murder? Such depictions are quite inaccurate. Amnesia can take many forms, but rarely, if ever, are all memories erased.

Four Types of Amnesia

Patient H. M.   H. M., the epileptic patient mentioned earlier, is an amnesiac. H. M.'s memories for events that preceded his surgery by three years are intact. His amnesia is really a problem of transferring declarative memories from short-term to long-term memory. He cannot remember facts about the world, but he can learn how to do things. H. M.'s amnesia resulted from surgery that removed most of both hippocampi and amygdalas.

Another patient with the same clinical signs of memory impairment as patient H. M. died recently, and a detailed examination of his brain at autopsy showed bilateral damage to the hippocampus—but only to a very small area of it (Zola-Morgan et al.,

1986). (The damage might have been a result of insufficient blood flow during a stroke.) Yet loss of these relatively few cells produced the same sort of amnesia suffered by patient H. M.

Patient N. A.   Another famous clinical case of amnesia is that of N. A., who suffered a penetrating brain injury when a fencing foil went up his nose. N. A.'s long-term memory for events preceding his accident also appears to be unimpaired. N. A.'s amnesia, like H. M.'s, takes the form of an inability to learn new material, but his inability is much more obvious when the material to be learned is verbal. He quickly forgets lists of words and connected prose but seems to be able to remember faces and spatial locations more readily. N. A.'s injury occurred in the left dorsomedial nucleus of the thalamus.

Korsakoff's Syndrome   Amnesia also occurs in patients with *Korsakoff's syndrome*, a disease of chronic alcoholics, who often go for long periods of time without eating. It results from a deficiency of vitamin B$_1$ (thiamine) and is usually progressive. (If discovered early enough, it can be treated with massive doses of vitamin B$_1$.) Patients with Korsakoff's syndrome not only have trouble forming new memories but they also suffer amnesia for events that took place earlier in their lives, before the disease process set in.

Unlike H. M. or N. A., these patients show other deficiencies in thinking and problem solving. Given a series of problems in which the solution requires switching strategies, Korsakoff patients persevere in using a strategy long after it becomes apparent that it is wrong.

For example, one type of problem used in testing patients offers them an array of cards showing geometrical shapes. Not told which of the shapes is the correct solution, the patients pick shapes one at a time until they happen to pick, say, the triangle, at which point they are told "yes, the triangle is correct." One simple test of thinking abilities is to see whether a subject will pick the triangle on the next few trials. A more complex test occurs when the experimenter then changes the solution to a circle, for instance. After picking a triangle and being told that it is the wrong answer, normal people—and H. M. and N. A.—try other shapes until they pick the circle. A Korsakoff patient keeps on choosing the triangle.

Another problem-solving characteristic that normal people display is *proactive inhibition*—that is, when learning successive groups of words that belong to the same category (animal names, for example) the content of lists learned earlier interferes with the learning of later ones. When later word groups are changed to a different category (vegetable names, for example), proactive interference disappears and learning improves. Korsakoff patients show no improved learning when a new category of words is presented.

The brain damage in Korsakoff's syndrome appears to be widespread. Damage to the same thalamic nucleus that N. A. lost seems to occur in most Korsakoff patients. But neuronal loss also occurs in the cerebellum and cerebral cortex, often in the frontal lobe. In fact, studies have shown that patients without amnesia but who have sustained injuries to the frontal lobes persevere in their mistakes during problem solving, just as Korsakoff patients do (Moscovitch, 1981). This kind of failure, then, may not be directly related to the amnesia. It may just be an additional cognitive dysfunction caused by other brain damage. Alcoholics frequently fall down, for example, and trauma to the head may do some of the damage.

Electroconvulsive Shock Therapy A fourth kind of amnesia that is clearly identifiable and easily studied (the patient can, in fact, be studied both before and after treatment) is the amnesia that follows electroconvulsive shock therapy (ECT). When ECT is used to treat severe cases of depression (see Chapter 10), treatments are usually scheduled every other day in a series of 6 to 12 treatments. The amnesia caused by each shock recovers to some extent after each treatment but accumulates during the series.

Memory of recent events is disrupted by ECT, but long-term memory remains intact. It is not possible to say precisely which brain structures are most affected, but it is likely that insult to the temporal area and the hippocampus, which is very sensitive to seizures, produces the amnesia.

Knowledge of the specific characteristics of each of these amnesias (see, for example, Figure 8.9) and the specific brain areas implicated in each has contributed to the view of brain researchers that two regions of the

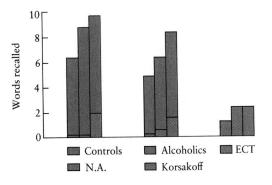

Figure 8.9
In this study, 10 word pairs were presented three times to amnesiacs and controls. After each presentation, the subjects saw the first word of each pair and tried to recall the second. These results show how severely handicapped amnesiacs are in terms of new learning (Cohen & Squire, 1980).

brain have separate functions in the operation of normal memory.

Two Brain Regions and Their Functions

Amnesia is not only not remembering, it is forgetting. Two studies of the rate of forgetting in patients with amnesia (with normal subjects used as controls) indicate that the two different brain regions identified as injured in these patients contribute in two different ways to memory function.

In the first study, normal people, patient H. M., and patients with Korsakoff's syndrome were shown 120 slides, one at a time.

Normal subjects saw each picture for 1 second; amnesiacs viewed each one for as long as 16 seconds. When they were shown some of these pictures along with some new ones 10 minutes, 1 day, and 1 week later, they indicated whether they recognized each picture. At 10 minutes after viewing, patients with Korsakoff's syndrome forgot at a normal rate, but H. M. forgot at an abnormally rapid rate. Another similar study found that Korsakoff patients forgot at a normal rate, but that patients receiving ECT forgot at a very rapid rate. Yet other studies showed that patient N. A. forgot at a normal rate.

N. A. and the Korsakoff patients, whose rate of forgetting new material was relatively normal, have injuries in the thalamic region. H. M. and patients receiving ECT, who forgot at an unusually rapid rate, have suffered injuries or disruption of the hippocampus and the temporal stem. These two different regions therefore appear to make essential but fundamentally different contributions to normal memory functions (Squire, 1984). Experiments with monkeys as subjects support this distinction. Monkeys whose thalamus has been operated on do not show rapid memory loss, whereas monkeys whose hippocampus and amygdala were bilaterally removed do.

The hippocampus, amygdala, and related structures are apparently necessary in memory consolidation, the transfer of declarative material to long-term memory. The thalamic region, on the other hand, appears to be necessary to the initial coding of certain kinds of declarative information. N. A., for example, has trouble coding verbal material, but he can learn skills—procedural material.

The Korsakoff patients are the only amnesiacs in the group to suffer impairment in their memory of events that long preceded their illness. They are also deficient in a number of thinking abilities, and these deficiencies may keep them from reconstructing

Table 8.1 *Rates of forgetting in brain-damaged subjects*

Forget at a normal rate (Primary injury site: medial dorsal thalamic nucleus)	Forget at a rapid rate (Primary injury site: hippocampus and temporal stem)
Patient N. A.	Patient H. M.
Patients with Korsakoff's syndrome	Patients receiving bilateral ECT
Monkeys with medial thalamic lesions	Monkeys with amygdala and hippocampus lesions

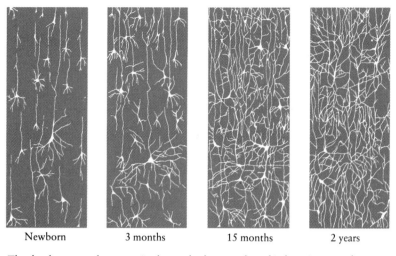

| Newborn | 3 months | 15 months | 2 years |

The development of neurons in the cerebral cortex from birth to 2 years of age. The neurons grow both in size and in number of connections between them (Conel, 1939, 1959).

past memories: they do not form concepts well, they cannot come up with techniques for problem solving, and they persevere in incorrect solutions. The Korsakoff patients are also the only ones with lesions of the cerebral cortex.

Studies of damaged brains, then, do offer insights into the working of normal brains (see Table 8.1). Another approach is to examine how environment facilitates or hinders the development of normal brains.

The Brain's Plasticity: Environmental Effects

The brain of a newborn human being is about 25 percent of its adult size. The size of the neurons in the brain and the complexity of neural connections and networks develop as one grows and interacts with people and objects in the world. The basic blueprint for

neural development and patterning is undoubtedly laid down by the genes. But experience affects those patterns.

You have seen that the anatomy of animals' brains is affected by their environment. Rosenzweig's rats raised in their enriched environment had a greater weight and thickness of cerebral cortex than the ones raised in isolation. The study was replicated 16 times, and in all the experiments the result was the same. The researchers found more spines, which often serve as receivers in synaptic contacts, on the dendrites of cortical neurons in rats from enriched environments (Globus et al., 1973). Synaptic junctions in rats from enriched environments averaged about 50 percent larger than those in rats raised in isolation (Møllgaard et al., 1971), and synaptic contacts were more frequent in the rats from enriched environments (Greenough et al., 1978). Neuroscientists believe that these kinds of changes may represent learning and memory storage in the brain.

Experiments that involve isolation are, of course, impossible with human subjects, and no one can say for certain what kinds of brain changes in human beings may depend on environmental stimulation. Nevertheless, some psychological studies indicate that stimulating environments may not only promote intellectual growth but may also make up for early physiological damage. One such study reported on all children born on the island of Kauai in 1955 and followed these children through age 10 (Werner et al., 1971). The goal was to investigate the later development of babies who suffered some sort of birth complication, such as premature birth, low birth weight, or lack of oxygen during labor, conditions often presumed to put children at risk for brain damage. The follow-up at age 10 showed that although 34 percent of the children born in 1955 were having some kind of learning or emotional problems, only a small proportion of these difficulties could be attributed to birth complications. The researchers concluded that "ten times more children had problems related to the effects of poor environment than to the effects of [birth-related] stress."

A similar large study in Great Britain produced the same results: few prematurely born children from privileged environments were retarded at age 7, but among children of similarly low birth weights in poor environments, there was "a marked excess of retarded and very dull children" (Drillien, 1964). A "poor environment" might include malnourishment, lack of medical care, abuse, and physical neglect—not keeping a child clean and safe and decently clothed— or psychological neglect—not talking to the child and not offering affection, attention, or stimulation.

No researcher would consider rearing a human child in isolation. But occasionally, bizarre circumstances occur where, in effect, it does happen.

Such is the case of Genie, found in California in 1970 (Curtiss, 1977). Genie was 13 when she came to the attention of authorities. From the age of 20 months she was kept in a small room in her parents' house. She had never been out of the room; she was kept naked and restrained to a kind of potty chair by a harness her father had designed. She could move only her hands and feet. The psychotic father, who apparently hated children, forbade the almost blind mother to speak to the child. (He had put one child born earlier in the garage to avoid hearing her cry, and she died there of pneumonia at 2 months of age.) Genie was fed only milk and baby food during her 13 years.

When the girl was found, she weighed only 59 pounds. She could not straighten her arms or legs. She did not know how to chew. She could not control her bladder or bowels. She could not recognize words or speak at all. According to the mother's report (the father killed himself soon after Genie was discovered), Genie appeared to have been a normal baby.

Over the following six years, Genie had plenty of interactions with the world, as well as training and testing by psychologists. She gained some language comprehension and learned to speak at about the level of a 2- to 3-year-old: "want milk," "two hand." She learned to use tools, to draw, and to connect cause-and-effect in some situations. And she could get from one place to another—to a candy counter in the supermarket, for example—proving that she could construct mental maps of space. Her IQ score on non-verbal tests was a low-normal 74 in 1977. But her language did not develop further, and, in fact, she made types of language errors that even normal 2-year-olds never make. When Genie's EEG patterns were monitored as she listened to words or watched pictures, it became clear that she was using the right hemisphere of her brain for both language and nonlanguage functions, whereas normally the left hemisphere is specialized for language.

Susan Curtiss, the psycholinguist who worked with Genie, suggests that the acquisition of language is what triggers the normal pattern of hemispheric specialization: if language is not acquired at the appropriate time, "the cortical tissue normally committed for language and related abilities may functionally atrophy."

No human environment, it seems, could be more deprived than the one in which Genie spent her formative years, and her lack of experience affected her brain development in ways that could be measured by an EEG. We know nothing about the development of her cortex or neural patterns and synapses, but from her behavior when she was found, it seems reasonable to conclude that the human nervous systems must grow up human in order to generate "human" behavior.

The plasticity of the human nervous system extends from our being subject to simple learning like habituation to our ability to learn, remember, manipulate, and create. The enormous number of facts and procedures that we use are organized and reorganized into interlocking frameworks so that we can retrieve a piece of data from memory along many different pathways.

Take the word "book." One memory path leads us to think of a bound set of printed pages meant to be read. But we can also think of getting a booking, of booking a hotel room, of booking bridge tricks, or of a bookie making book. We can think of the books an accountant keeps, or of a judge throwing the book at a criminal, or of the Good Book. Each time we learn a new meaning for the letters *b-o-o-k*, a reorganization takes place.

The human memory and the information-processing capacities of the brain are so extraordinary that no computer can yet approach their complexity. Perhaps the most extraordinary characteristic of this human memory and cognitive system is our capacity to think, and to think about ourselves thinking—our capacity for consciousness. It is to these "higher order" functions that we shall turn in the next chapter.

Summary

1. Simple forms of learning, that is, learning that occurs without the subject's awareness of a change in behavior, can take place even in organisms without a brain. Habituation occurs when a stimulus that initially aroused an organism is presented repeatedly without causing the organism irritation or harm; eventually, the organism learns to ignore the stimulus—it becomes habituated to it.

2. In classical conditioning, an organism learns to associate a previously neutral stimulus with a stimulus that naturally evokes a reflexive response, and the animal ends up responding to the initially neutral stimulus just as it had always responded to the primary stimulus. In the classical Pavlovian example, a dog repeatedly hears a bell (conditioned stimulus) immediately before it is given food (unconditioned stimulus). The dog, which naturally salivates at the presentation of food (unconditioned response), learns to salivate at the sound of the bell (conditioned response).

3. When the neuroanatomical and biophysical changes underlying a conditioned

response were examined in a sea snail, researchers found that particular neurons—the B photoreceptor cells in the eye—become excited and increase their activity. This postconditioning excitation—depolarization resulting from increased concentrations of calcium and potassium ions in the cell—may last for days. Additionally, the high level of calcium activates certain enzymes, which are thought to change the character of the proteins making up the ion channels in the cell membrane, so that potassium outflow is reduced. These enzymes appear to keep on working long after calcium levels have returned to normal in the cell, and this long-term change could reflect the fact that the conditioned response may persist for weeks.

4. Regions of the brain that appear to be important in learning and memory are: the cerebellum, which may store some classically conditioned responses; the hippocampus, which appears to be vital in short-term memory, or "working memory"; and the cerebral cortex.

5. Memory appears to have several phases. One is immediate memory, where items are stored for only a few seconds. Items that were the focus of attention may get transferred to short-term memory, where storage may last for several minutes. Some items from short-term memory may be transferred to long-term memory, which means they may be held for hours or for a lifetime. The hippocampus is necessary for making the transfer from short-term to long-term memory; its bilateral destruction has been proved to prevent the formation of long-term memories.

6. The human brain seems to process and store different kinds of information in separate ways. Procedural knowledge, which is knowledge of how to do something, and declarative knowledge, which has cultural content and may have a linguistic basis, are two distinct kinds of learning. Declarative learning is processed in the temporal lobe and parts of the thalamus, whereas procedural learning apparently is not.

7. Learning and emotion interact. Such interaction is the basis for the theory of operant conditioning. An operant behavior is any behavior an animal naturally performs. The theory says that performance of a behavior that produces a rewarding experience for the animal tends to be repeated, and performance of a behavior that results in punishment tends not to be repeated. One mechanism that might operate in such memory consolidation is the circulating hormones that are called up during emotion-arousing circumstances, especially adrenal norepinephrine. These hormones could affect the activity of the amygdala, in a sequence of physiological processes that underlie memory storage.

8. Studies of victims of various types of amnesias indicate that at least two regions of the brain operate in memory storage and have separate functions. The hippocampus, amygdala, and related structures seem to be necessary in the transfer of declarative knowledge to long-term memory. The thalamic region, in contrast, appears necessary to the initial coding of certain kinds of declarative information.

Further Reading

Squire, Larry R. 1987. *Memory and Brain*. New York: Oxford University Press. A lucid and comprehensive account of research done over the past two decades in the attempt to discover how memory is represented in the brain. Biochemical, clinical-pathological, and information-processing approaches are covered.

Kandel, E. R. 1979. Cellular insights into behavior and learning. *Harvey Lectures,* Series 73, pp. 29–92. A noted researcher presents, for a general audience, what he has learned about activity and changes in nerve cells as animals learn.

Norman, D. A. 1982. *Learning and Memory.* New York: W. H. Freeman. A brief but thorough survey of the information-processing approach to human learning and memory.

9

Thinking and Consciousness

9

△ ○ △ ○ △ —

You probably solved this problem—you put a circle in the blank—even before you consciously saw this row of symbols as a problem. During the second or so that this response took, you were *thinking*—engaging in structured mental actions. But how much of that thinking were you aware of?

Thinking, or mental action, is sometimes conscious and often not conscious. The concept of consciousness itself is so rich and complex that it has no simple definition. We all know what we mean by the phrase "state of consciousness": the condition that is turned off when we go to sleep or is lost when we suffer a severe blow to the head. But state of consciousness is not our subject here. Rather, we shall examine *active consciousness,* the state of being aware of our thoughts and behaviors. As a working definition, let us say that *consciousness* is awareness of one's own mental and/or physical actions.

Not all scientists agree with this definition. Because neuroscientists cannot yet blueprint the brain mechanisms responsible for this focused awareness, the nature of human consciousness remains at the center of an ancient and ongoing debate. Participants in the debate include physiologists, philosophers, theologians, and computer scientists in the field of artificial intelligence, as well as neuroscientists of all stripes. One point of controversy is whether consciousness is an integral, material process of the brain or a separate, nonmaterial function—a spirit, or soul. Our position has already been stated. Just as sensing, moving, adapting, learning, and feeling can ultimately be explained in terms of the structure and workings of the brain, so will consciousness ultimately be explained. We know that certain drugs can alter consciousness by altering brain chemistry. (Some of these drugs are discussed on page 273.)

Another point of controversy is whether or not consciousness is the exclusive province of human beings. Are other animals capable of consciousness? Some argue that their behavior indicates that they do engage in conscious thinking. The behavior of the monkeys that wash sand off corn kernels given to them by anthropologists on the beaches of northern Japan is often cited as an example of animal thought. So is that of the "creative" crows that drop shellfish onto the rocks to break them open while other crows look on and learn from them. These monkeys and crows are capable of procedural learning—they can learn and remember *how to do* some things without being aware of the fact that they have learned; Jerome Bruner characterizes procedural learning as "memory without record." But such animal behavior does not indicate conscious thinking.

As you saw in Chapter 8, declarative learning requires both storage of previous experience in memory frameworks and access to those data when a situation reminds one that they are on tap. Declarative knowledge includes a record of one's previous experiences, a sense of familiarity with those experiences, information about the time and place that they occurred, and facts about the world derived from those experiences. To make all this knowledge accessible, human beings use language. We even use words to classify objects and events that we have never experienced, or been conscious of, before. Once we name new experiences, we can

Altered Consciousness

Human beings in all known cultures throughout recorded history have chosen to ingest substances that alter brain chemistry and, thus, alter consciousness. Many medicines prescribed by doctors into the 1950s contained some form of opium. Laudanum, a sleeping aid and potion "for the nerves" favored during the Victorian era, is a mixture of alcohol and morphine. The popularity of the first cola drinks owed something to the presence of cocaine in the formula. Common substances that alter consciousness range from the caffeine in coffee, to alcohol—perhaps the drug of choice in Western cultures—to potent hallucinogens like LSD.

Human beings seem to have two compelling but contradictory needs: we like things to stay the same, to be familiar, and we also crave novelty. We search for substances that will get us out of our rut—drug abusers often report that they take drugs to relieve boredom—and substances that calm our anxiety when things become too unpredictable. The two drugs that have recently become increasingly common as boredom relievers are cocaine and marijuana.

The Indians of the Andes mountains have for centuries chewed the leaves of the coca bush. When ingested, cocaine acts as a stimulant to the central nervous system. It acts to inhibit the reuptake of norepinephrine in the central nervous system and peripheral nervous system and of dopamine in the central nervous system after the release of those neurotransmitters into their synapses. Thus, more of these transmitters remain available to receiving cells for longer periods of time, and this excess produces the stimulation and energy that users feel. This effect is also produced by drugs used for the treatment of depression (see Chapter 10). Amphetamine, another stimulant, accomplishes the same result by forcing the release of norepinephrine and dopamine into their synapses.

The hallucinogens include mescaline, which comes from the peyote cactus; psilocybin and psilocine, which occur in certain mushrooms; and LSD, which is derived in the laboratory. Marijuana is also called a hallucinogen, but its

effects are far less potent than those of the other drugs.

Marijuana, which comes from the hemp plant *Cannabis sativa,* is used extensively throughout the world. The principal active materials in marijuana are called tetrahydrocannabinols, or THCs, but very little is known of how these substances act on the central nervous system. Marijuana users report initial feelings of euphoria and heightened sensitivities to sights, sounds, and tastes. They often experience a splitting of consciousness, simultaneously feeling their intoxication and observing themselves having the experience. A pleasant lethargy follows the euphoria.

The long-term effects of these drugs on the central nervous system are not yet clear, but there is plenty of evidence that their abuse can, at the least, result in severe psychological dependency. Warnings against use of the drugs abound—on television, in magazines, in newspapers. Nevertheless, in a species whose members choose recreation in the form of jumping out of airplanes, climbing sheer rock precipices, or racing automobiles at incredible speeds, it is not surprising that a significant number of human beings choose to use such "recreational" drugs.

file them in their appropriate frameworks. All of this is to say that we use *language* to name and describe the things that appear in consciousness. Language is the basic means by which human beings structure their experience, and therefore consciousness most often depends on language. (A few aspects of conscious thought, such as the mental representation and rotation of objects in space, do not depend upon language.)

If consciousness does depend on language, human consciousness is obviously not present at birth. It develops as we gain experience in the world and as we build up a "vocabulary" that allows us to think about things and the relationships among things, to plan and decide, to select and act. Having the capacity for conscious awareness does not mean that we are aware all the time, of course. We often act—or even think and solve problems like the one that opened this chapter—without our consciousness being engaged. It is only later, when we think back on what we did, when we focus our conscious mind on our action, that, by some imaginative reconstruction of the behavior or the event, we fit the action into a rational or at least a plausible pattern that emerges from our consciously held goals, self-image, and values.

We can perform some actions without conscious planning because, as the psychologist Julian Jaynes says, "Our minds often work much faster than consciousness can keep up." *Mind,* as we use the term, is not synonymous with consciousness but with the working of the brain as a whole—mind is a product of what the brain does. Those brain events that we experience as *conscious* are only those events that are processed through the brain's language system.

You have seen how the brain carries out its responsibilities for directing specific behaviors—how we move, how we sense, how we learn and remember, how we regulate our internal systems, how we feel. We do some or all of these things simultaneously, and our brains integrate and organize all of them. These same high integrative abilities also make thinking and consciousness possible. Although we are far from a thorough understanding of how such integration occurs, in a gross sense we do at least know something about where much of this integration takes place. That place is the cerebral cortex.

Anatomy and Mind

What we call thinking and consciousness appears to depend on the quarter-inch thickness of the cerebral cortex that covers the four lobes of the brain. Its intricate and highly ordered architecture contains about 75 percent of the brain's approximately 50 billion neurons. You are already familiar with some regions of the cortex that are dedicated to specific functions. The primary visual cortex, located in the occipital lobe, for example, processes visual stimuli and is instrumental in producing our sense of sight. Many areas of the cortex, however, do not have such specific, wired-in functions.

Association Cortex

These large "uncommitted" areas have been called *association cortex* (see Figure 9.1). Traditional brain science has held that associations between specialized areas are formed here, integrating data from those areas. Here, too, it is believed, current information is integrated with emotions and memories, making it possible for human beings to think, decide, and plan.

Association areas in the parietal lobe, for example, are thought to synthesize information from the somatosensory cortex— messages from the skin, muscles, tendons, and joints about the body's position and

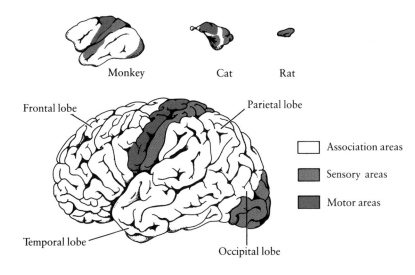

Frontal lobe — Parietal lobe

Temporal lobe — Occipital lobe

☐ Association areas

■ Sensory areas

■ Motor areas

Figure 9.1
The uncolored areas represent the association areas of the human cerebral cortex. You can see that the association areas are larger than the parts of the cortex known to be responsible for specific sensory or motor functions. This ratio of association areas to other areas is largest in human beings and increases as one ascends the evolutionary scale: rats apparently have no association areas; cats have a small area; and monkeys have quite a bit, but not as much as human beings have.

movement—with information about sight and sound transmitted from the visual and auditory cortices in the occipital and temporal lobes. This integrated information helps us to form an accurate sense of our physical selves as we move through our environment. The blending of sensory impressions with input from our memory stores allows us to assign meaning to specific sights, sounds, smells, and touches. The sensation of something moving and furry touching your arm means one thing if you hear a purr and see your cat, but quite another if you hear a growl and see a bear.

Association areas in the frontal cortex are thought to mediate decisions about what action to take in the presence of a cat or a bear, for example. An integrated sensory picture of the event is transmitted to the frontal cortex. Through extensive reciprocal connections with the limbic system, emotional tone is added, along with input from memory. Other connections contribute information that enables the frontal cortex to assess the current demands of the body and the environment and to assign priorities—to judge what is better or worse for the self in a given situation. The frontal cortex also

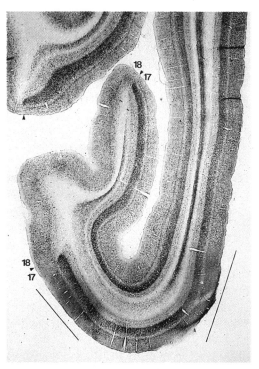

Very low-power view of a slice through the occipital lobe of the cerebral cortex of a monkey. The tissue section has been stained to reveal the layers of cells. One of those layers is interrupted at the boundary indicated by the arrows separating the primary visual cortex (area 17) and the secondary visual cortex (area 18).

seems to be responsible for generating our long-range goals and our judgments in light of those goals.

Accounts of people with damaged frontal lobes (a number of which were presented in Chapter 7) do attest to the critical role of the frontal cortex in judging and planning. These victims have great difficulty reconciling life's conflicting and shifting demands. Like Phineas Gage, they become irresponsible, unable to act appropriately or to carry out any consistent life plan.

The frontal cortex appears to cooperate, through massive nerve connections, with the temporal cortex in carrying on some of the brain's highest functions. The unique human ability to use language, for example, involves association areas in the temporal and frontal lobes, along with the occipital lobe. The temporal cortex is active in memory, both in decisions about what will be stored, and in the storage and retrieval, not only of the memories themselves, but also of whether the remembered events were evaluated as pleasant or unpleasant. Extensive damage in this area can produce loss of long-term memory (or, at least, an inability to retrieve such memories). Obviously, the plan-making tasks of the frontal lobes must depend greatly on relevant experiences from the past, and this data may be transmitted from the temporal cortex.

This traditional account of how association areas of the cortex operate is only hypothetical, since there are very few data to corroborate or deny it. It is based on observation of the brain's gross anatomy—its hierarchical circuitry and observable division into lobes. Besides there being little experimental verification for its hypotheses, the theory is limited by offering only a piece-by-piece account of the brain's higher functions. At least one more step seems to be required to explain the feeling that an "I" is perceiving and evaluating its environment and is choosing when and how to act. More recent discoveries about the detailed architecture and functioning of the brain have led to a theory of consciousness based on the cortex's columnar organization, a theory that promises to provide scientifically testable hypotheses (Mountcastle, 1978).

Columns of Neurons and Consciousness

In earlier chapters, you read about the columnar organization of the cortex: in Chapter 3, we described how, in the developing brain, neurons migrate along a glial cell to assume a regular vertical patterning, which forms a sort of grid with the horizontal layering of the cortex (see Figure 9.2). In Chapter 4, we explained that these vertical columns are integral to the organization and information-processing capacities of the visual cortex, auditory cortex, and so on.

In fact, all parts of the cortex, including the so-called association areas, are organized in columns. The basic unit, or *minicolumn,* consists of 100 or so vertically interrelated neurons that span the layers of the cortex. These minicolumns are virtually identical in size in all parts of the cortex. They consist of: (1) target neurons that receive their major input from subcortical structures—the specific sensory and motor nuclei of the thalamus, for instance; (2) target neurons that receive their major input from other regions of the cortex; (3) local-circuit neurons that connect the cells making up the minicolumn; and (4) output neurons that send messages from the minicolumn back to the thalamus or to other cortical regions or to targets in the limbic system.

Several of these minicolumns may have connections with each other and form a *column.* Although the shape of columns in different parts of the cortex may vary, according to the number of constituent minicolumns and their mode of packing,

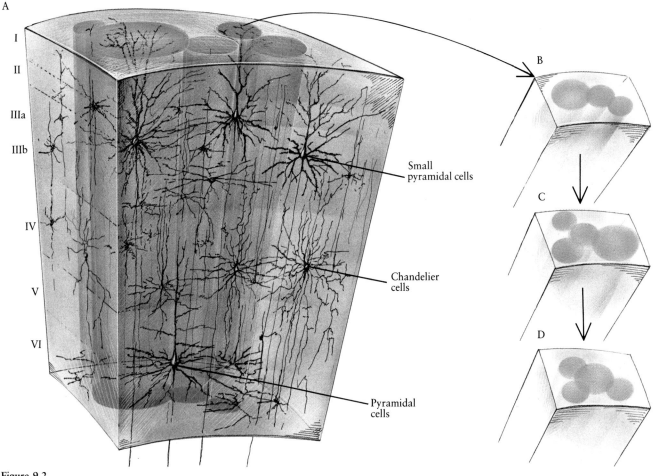

Figure 9.2
*Diagrammatic representation of the columnar organization of the cortex. The
larger, variously shaped, overlapping columns (A) are made up of minicolumns,
vertically connected sets of single cells. The details at right (B, C, and D) show
the shifting locations of vertically connected cells active at a given time.*

these columns constitute the fundamental
information-processing units of the cortex,
according to Vernon Mountcastle (see Figure
9.2). To get some idea of how such columns
work, refer again to p. 78, which shows,
through a special staining technique, the
ocular dominance columns of the monkey's
visual cortex. Alternating columns in the visual cortex process information from the left

eye and right eye. Of course, cortical processing of visual information is very complex, involving much more than binocular
processing, as you know from having read
Chapter 4.

Some small idea of the complexity of information processing can be had by examining some of Mountcastle's experimental
findings. He has determined, through use of

microelectrodes in a functioning monkey's brain, that cells in two areas of the parietal cortex are active when the animal performs actions on and within his immediate environment. Different sets of columns are active during: (1) projection of the arm toward an object of interest; (2) manipulation of an object; (3) fixation of gaze and thus of visual attention; (4) movement of the eyes as a result of visual stimulation; (5) movement of the eyes in slow pursuit tracking of an object; and (6) the sudden appearance of an object in the periphery of the visual field.

Now, a given column might be active during several of these actions. In other words, the columnar organization is what Mountcastle calls a *distributed system.* The most important characteristic of a distributed system is that information flow through it may follow a number of different pathways and that the dominance of one path or another is a dynamic and changing property of the system.

The pathways include not only ones processing information coming from the outside world but also ones carrying information from other parts of the brain; this internally generated information—memories, emotions, cognitive skills, for example—Mountcastle calls *reentrant* information. The internally generated neural activity may pass, in cycles, through a number of pathways—first those handling primary sensory data but then moving successively to more general and abstract processing units of the cortex. The consequence of this distributed system simultaneously handling both reentrant information and current information about external conditions is that a person can continuously update perceptual images of his or her self and self-in-the-world and can match that image against external conditions. The match between internal readout and external world is the proposed mechanism for conscious awareness.

One other mechanism of this distributed system is that it has access to outflow systems of the brain at many levels and therefore has many possible command levels— levels where an "I" may evaluate the environment and choose to act. This command function is likely to take over in that part of the system that possesses the most urgent and necessary information. Pain and danger, for example, usually focus one's consciousness quickly on ways to escape or avoid them, no matter what one was focusing on when the pain or danger occurred.

Mountcastle's explanation of the workings of consciousness is, of course, far from proven. Given the human brain's complexity and the impossibility of human experimentation, scientists may never be able to validate the hypotheses. Still, animal experiments, like the test with monkeys mentioned earlier, in which sets of neurons are monitored in an animal that is moving about and performing certain tasks, offer some data as a basis for the conjectures. For example, in such a study of neurons in the parietal association area in monkeys, Mountcastle and his colleagues (1975) found that certain sets of neurons function to command the operation of the limbs, hands, and eyes to perform certain acts in the animals' immediate environment. These sets of cells are not activated by sensory stimuli alone, and they do not discharge when the hands or limbs are moved aimlessly. They discharge only when the animal is motivated to obtain a certain nearby object it sees (food or drink, in these experiments). These sets of neurons, then, represent a general command function that is exercised in a holistic fashion—perhaps something approaching monkey consciousness.

One other aspect of brain anatomy vital to our understanding of consciousness and language is the hemispheric organization of the cerebrum.

The Cerebral Hemispheres

The two hemispheres that compose the forebrain are connected at several points by cables of neurons, often called *commissures*. The largest and most important of these is the *corpus callosum* (see Figure 9.3). The right hemisphere controls sensing and moving on the body's left side, and the left hemisphere controls those functions on the body's right side. For hearing and vision, hemispheric control is a bit more complex. As you saw in Chapter 4, each eye has a left visual field and a right visual field. Information in the right visual field goes only to the left hemisphere, and information in the left visual field goes only to the right hemisphere (see Figure 9.4). These visual areas of the left and right hemispheres normally communicate through the corpus callosum. In contrast to these contralateral functions, human language is usually localized in only one hemisphere of the brain.

The most promising insights into the physiological bases of mind and consciousness have been reached through clinical studies of people whose brains have been damaged as a result of accident or illness, or who have undergone brain surgery—in particular, the operation that separates the brain's two hemispheres from each other.

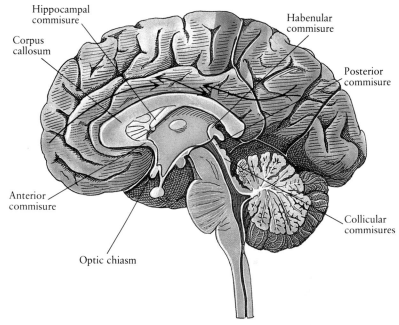

Figure 9.3
The major commissures connecting the brain's two hemispheres. The large size of the corpus callosum relative to the other connectors stands out. Here the brain has been sectioned at the midline.

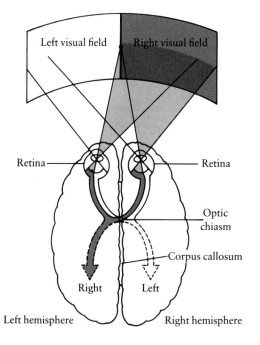

Figure 9.4
The visual pathways and visual fields. When the optic nerves travel from the retina on their way to the brain, they first come together at the optic chiasm. Here, a partial crossover of fibers takes place. The fibers coming from the half of the retina closest to the nose cross over to the opposite side; the fibers coming from the outside, or temporal, half of the retina do not cross over. Consequently, when a person fixates his gaze on a point, information from the right visual field goes only to the left hemisphere, and information from the left visual field goes only to the right hemisphere. Normally, the visual areas of the two hemispheres communicate through the corpus callosum. If that commissure is cut and if the eyes and head are kept still, each hemisphere can see only half the visual world.

The Bisected Brain

During an epileptic seizure, abnormal and progressively wilder neural firing spreads from the site of a brain lesion to other parts of the brain. When this wild firing passes through the corpus callosum, the entire brain becomes involved in the seizure. In some life-threatening cases of epilepsy that do not respond to any other type of treatment, neurosurgeons cut the corpus callosum in order to contain the neural storm. The procedure succeeds very well, and patients appear to be virtually unchanged in personality, intelligence, and behavior after the operation. But ingenious tests, conducted by neurologists and psychologists, indicate that the brain bisection does indeed change the consciousness and thought patterns of these patients in profound but seldom noticed ways.

In one specially designed test, patient N. G., a California woman whose corpus callosum had been severed, sits in front of a screen with a small black dot at its center (see Figure 9.5). The experimenter asks her

to look continuously at the dot. Then a picture of a cup is flashed to the right of the dot using a *tachistoscope*, a special device that allows the experimenter to control precisely how long a picture stays on the screen. Such presentations are very brief—about one-tenth of a second—so that subjects do not have time to move their eyes away from the dot. The experimenter wants only one hemisphere to view the picture, and eye movement could result in its being perceived by both hemispheres.

When patient N. G. is asked what she saw, she reports that she saw the cup. Again she is asked to look at the dot, and a picture of a spoon is flashed to its left. Asked now what she saw, she says, "Nothing." Then the researcher asks her to reach under the screen, where several small objects are scattered, and to choose, by touch only, an object resembling the picture that had just been flashed. With her left hand, she handles several of the objects and brings out a spoon. Asked what she is holding, she says "a pencil."

In another such test, a picture of a nude woman is flashed to the left of the dot. N. G. blushes and begins to giggle. Asked what she saw, she says, "Nothing, just a flash of light." "Then why are you laughing?" asks the experimenter. "Oh, doctor, you have some machine!" N. G. replies.

When N. G. saw the picture of the cup in her right visual field, which was processed in the left hemisphere, she had no trouble naming the item. When she was shown the spoon in her left visual field, processed in her right hemisphere, she said she had seen nothing. Yet she had obviously processed that information because she was able to pick the spoon from an array of objects. In N. G., as in most people, the left hemisphere is responsible for language and speech. With the corpus callosum intact, the left hemisphere and right hemisphere work together in perceiving

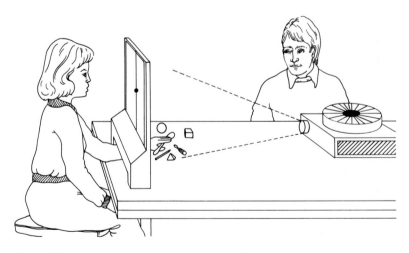

Figure 9.5
The experimental setup for tachistoscope studies. Images are projected through the screen either to the right or to the left of the central black dot that the subject fixates his or her gaze on.

Figure 9.6
The composite-picture study. The subject becomes familiar with the faces in the photographs, then a composite picture is flashed by tachistoscope so that the left hemisphere (right visual field) sees the child's half-face and the right (left visual field) sees the half-face of the young woman with sunglasses. When asked to say what she saw, the subject reports having seen the child. When asked to point to what she saw, she chooses the young woman.

and naming things. But each side of N. G.'s bisected brain is essentially blind to what the other side sees. Because her right hemisphere is mute, it recognized the spoon but could not name it.

N. G.'s reaction to the nude picture, which appeared to the left of the center of the screen, is especially interesting. Her right hemisphere had obviously processed the image because she blushed and giggled when the picture was flashed. But because her left, verbal, hemisphere did not know what had happened, it tried to make sense of her general state of embarrassment by rationalizing that the machine must somehow have sparked her response.

In another tachistoscope study the subject is first shown the four photographs seen in Figure 9.6. Then she sits in front of the screen, onto which is flashed a composite picture, half of one face (a woman wearing glasses) on the left side of the dot and half of another (a child) on the right. When asked what she saw, the patient answers, "a child," the half-face she saw with her left, speaking, hemisphere. Later, the same composite picture is flashed, and she is asked to select the picture she saw by pointing to it. This time she points to the woman, seen by her right, nonspeaking, hemisphere.

One interesting aspect of this study is that patients denied that there had been anything unusual about the pictures they had seen. They perceived the half-face as a whole—that is, their brain *completed* the picture. This constructive aspect of perception helps explain why split-brain patients normally function well in their everyday lives. Another aid they use, in both experimental and day-to-day situations, is *cross-cuing*. One hemisphere uses clues available to it to detect information supposedly only accessible to the other hemisphere. For example, if the left hand (controlled by the right hemisphere) is given a set of keys to identify, the left hemisphere might recognize the clinking sound and be able to say "keys," even though neither sight nor touch of the keys had been available to the left hemisphere.

In spite of the split brain's constructive and cunning ways, it appears that, as Roger W. Sperry (1974), a pioneer in split-brain surgery and Nobel laureate, has noted,

Each hemisphere . . . has its own . . . private sensations, perceptions, thoughts, and ideas, all of which are cut off from the corresponding experiences in the opposite hemisphere. Each left and right hemisphere has its own private chain of memories and learning experiences that are inaccessible to recall by the other hemisphere. In many respects each disconnected hemisphere appears to have a separate "mind of its own."

Hemispheric Specialization and Dominance

Split-brain studies indicate that, in general, the left hemisphere is responsible for language and speech, and the right hemisphere directs skills related to visual and spatial processing. Other research indicates more subtle differences in the way the two hemispheres process information. The left hemisphere is believed to process information analytically and sequentially. The right appears to process information simultaneously and as a whole. It tends to perceive an array like that in the figure at the top of the next column as a total construct rather than as the separate parts that go to make it up.

Each hemisphere, then, appears to have particular strengths and weaknesses, and

Figures like these are quickly and easily perceived as wholes by the right hemisphere. (From the Street Gestalt Completion Test.)

each appears to contribute in its own way to thinking and consciousness. In examining these different attributes, we shall look first at some more specific evidence for left- and right-brain characteristics, then turn to some of the ways in which the two hemispheres may work together in thinking and consciousness when the corpus callosum remains intact.

The Left Hemisphere and Language

A patient, fully conscious, lies on the table, a small tube inserted into the carotid artery on one side of his neck. The physician asks him to raise both arms and to begin counting backward from 100 by 3s. Sodium amytal, an anesthetic, is then injected into the artery, which carries it to the hemisphere of the brain bathed by the blood carried through that artery. Within seconds, the arm opposite to the side of the injection falls limp. Then the patient stops counting. If the hemisphere anesthetized is the one controlling speech, the patient will remain speechless for several minutes. If not, he will start counting again within a few seconds and be able to carry on a conversation, even though half his brain is anesthetized. This procedure, the *Wada test,* enables neurosurgeons to determine which hemisphere controls the speech of a patient scheduled to undergo brain surgery. With this information, the surgeon can try to avoid trauma to that area.

Results of the Wada test show that in over 95 percent of all right-handed people with no history of early brain damage, the left hemisphere controls speech and language. In the remaining 5 percent, speech is controlled in the right hemisphere. A majority of left-handers—about 70 percent—also have left-hemisphere control of language. About 15 percent of left-handers have speech in the right hemisphere, and 15 percent show evidence of bilateral speech control.

When the Wada test was administered to patients known to have suffered damage to the left hemisphere in early life, it showed that the right hemisphere either controls or participates in control of speech in 70 percent of the left-handers and 19 percent of the right-handers. In these patients, the right hemisphere evidently developed language capacities to compensate for the early left-hemisphere damage. Shifts such as these give clear evidence of the plasticity of the brain in infancy and early childhood.

Brain Sites That Function in Language

Scientists have known for over a century that, for most people, speech is controlled by the left hemisphere. In 1836, an obscure French physician, Marc Dax, presented a short paper at a medical society meeting in Montpellier in which he described 40 of his patients who had suffered speech disturbances. All, without exception, showed signs of damage to the left hemisphere. As significant as these findings were, Dax's report went unremarked by contemporary scientists, perhaps because it came from someone practicing outside of Paris. Twenty-five years later, Paul Broca presented to the Anthropological Society in Paris a case study of a patient who had lost the ability to talk but who could nevertheless read and write normally and could comprehend everything said to

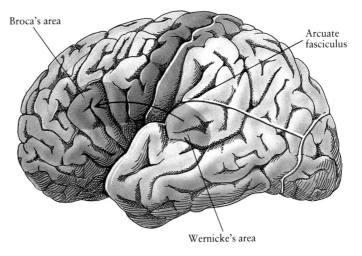

Figure 9.7
Areas of the left hemisphere known to be active in speech and language. Wernicke's area and Broca's area are connected by a collection of nerve fibers called the arcuate fasciculus, indicated by an arrow because it cannot be visualized from this angle.

him. Broca pointed to a lesion in the frontal lobe of the left hemisphere as the cause of the patient's speech problem. That specific area, adjacent to the area of the motor cortex that controls the muscles of the face, tongue, jaw, and throat, has come to be called *Broca's area* (see Figure 9.7). The specific impairment in producing the sounds of speech, even though language ability remains normal, is called *Broca's aphasia.*

Victims of another kind of aphasia produce well-formed speech sounds in essentially correct grammatical sequences, but they make meaningless sounds: "I think that there's an awful lot of mung, but I think I've a lot of net and tunged in a little wheat duh-vayden" (Buckingham & Kertesz, 1974). Damage to the upper, posterior part of the left temporal lobe, named *Wernicke's area* after Carl Wernicke who located it in 1874 (see Figure 9.7), produces this aphasia, called *Wernicke's aphasia.*

Aphasia is simply a disturbance of language, and these disturbances can take many forms, some of which are described in Table

Table 9.1   *Aphasias*

Name	Symptoms	Location of brain lesion
Broca's aphasia	Difficulty in the motor act of producing language; comprehension unimpaired; reading and writing unimpaired; patient aware of disability.	Frontal region of left hemisphere, especially Broca's area
Wernicke's aphasia	Comprehension of speech very impaired; production of speech fluent but odd or meaningless, full of nonexistent words; rhythm and intonation of speech and grammatical form preserved; reading and writing impaired; patients seem unaware of meaningless speech.	Posterior region of first temporal gyrus, or Wernicke's area
Conduction aphasia	Speech is fluent but somewhat meaningless; may show some comprehension and reading ability; unable to repeat phrases correctly.	Damage to fiber tracts connecting Wernicke's area to Broca's area
Word deafness	Comprehension of spoken language impaired; comprehension of written language normal; production of verbal and written language normal.	Lesion in the area connecting Wernicke's area to auditory inputs
Anomic aphasia	Inability to think of a specific word or the name of a person or an object; comprehension and conversation virtually normal.	Angular gyrus (junction of the temporal, parietal, and occipital lobes), left hemisphere
Global aphasia	Severe impairment of all language-related function.	Widespread damage to left hemisphere

SOURCE: Adapted from Springer & Deutsch, 1981.

9.1. Aphasia can present itself as difficulty in producing speech sounds, as inability to produce meaningful speech even while the sounds are correct, or as a breakdown in comprehension of speech sounds. Study of well-defined aphasias has helped to pinpoint brain areas with specific responsibilities for parts of the language process. As a result of this mapping of Broca's area, Wernicke's area, and the other brain parts indicated in Table 9.1, neuroscientists have been able to construct a model of how the brain produces and processes language.

According to this model, the underlying structure of an utterance—its form and meaning—arises in Wernicke's area. It then passes through a collection of nerve fibers, called the *arcuate fasciculus* (see Figure 9.7), to Broca's area. There, the impulses evoke a detailed and coordinated program for vocalization—a program for how each lip, tongue, and throat muscle must move. The program is then transmitted to the adjacent area of the motor cortex that controls the face, and the appropriate muscles are activated.

Wernicke's area is also important in language comprehension. The sound of a word is received in the primary auditory cortex, but the processed message must pass through the adjacent Wernicke's area if the sound is to be understood as language.

When words are read rather than heard,

the information is thought to be transmitted from the primary visual cortex to the angular gyrus, where the visual input is somehow matched with the sounds that the words have when spoken. The auditory form of the word is then processed for comprehension in Wernicke's area, as it would be if the words had been heard. Because spoken language long preceded written language in human evolution, and because all human young learn to speak and to comprehend spoken language before they learn to read or write, the hypothesis that the processing of written language is sound-based seems to make sense.

Although this general model of how the brain generates and processes speech is consistent with the symptoms characteristic of Broca's and Wernicke's aphasias, it is not universally accepted among neuroscientists as reflecting the normal workings of the brain in producing language. Many neuroscientists believe that at least the entire left hemisphere and perhaps many other portions of the brain function in language. As Hughlings Jackson warned long ago, "to locate the damage which destroys speech and to locate speech are two different things" (Taylor, 1958).

Recent studies using direct electrical stimulation of the brains of surgical patients support the idea that language capacity is widely distributed in the brain. Stimulation of many sites in the language region of the cortex interferes with reading ability, and stimulation at sites in the frontal, temporal, and parietal lobes disrupts both the ability to speak and to understand speech sounds.

Among patients with command of two languages, stimulation at sites in the center of the language area of the cortex disrupts speech in both languages, but stimulation at some sites outside this central region disrupts only one or the other of the two languages. Because bilingual speakers who develop aphasia usually experience difficulties in both languages, it appears that the basic brain organization of the two languages is the same. An exception may occur in cases where one of the languages is based on an alphabet and the other is based on ideographs, symbols that represent objects or ideas rather than sounds. Chinese is an ideographic language, for instance. Differences in reading ability after brain damage suggest that these different kinds of language are organized differently in the brain.

Greater understanding of how the brain processes language may shed light on a problem that exists only in literate cultures, the learning disability called *dyslexia*.

Dyslexia *Developmental dyslexia* is a disturbance in the ability to read that is not caused by mental retardation or physical injury. Dyslexics have normal intelligence, and their comprehension and production of spoken language is unimpaired. Their reading problems take several forms and may, in fact, be caused by a number of different factors. In some, the disturbance appears to be primarily visual and spatial. These dyslexics have difficulty in perceiving words as wholes and in knowing what words look like—they cannot differentiate between "lap" and "pal," for example. Other dyslexics are unable to match letter combinations with the sounds of those letters. They are at a loss when asked to pronounce unfamiliar words— they may recognize and pronounce the word "stone" correctly, for example, but they cannot read the word "notes."

One explanation of the visual-spatial problem encountered in some dyslexics attributes the difficulty to unstable eye dominance (Stein & Fowler, 1981). Most people have a dominant eye, just as they have a dominant hand. Unstable eye dominance would lead to disordered eye movements, which would make it difficult for a person to

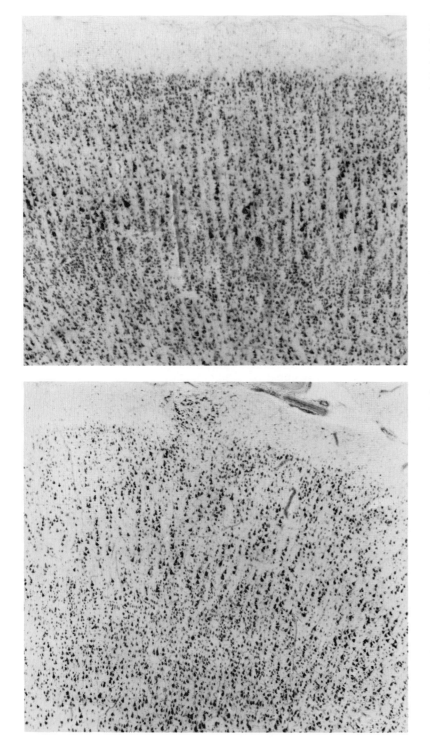

follow the sequence of letters and words on a page. Unstable eye dominance may, itself, reflect unstable cerebral control—that is, neither hemisphere assumes dominant control over eye movements.

Some dyslexias may reflect developmental abnormalities in the language area of the cortex. The brain of a 20-year-old known dyslexic was analyzed after he suffered a fatal accident (with no trauma to the brain). Examination of the sectioned brain revealed striking disorganization in the architecture of the language areas in the left hemisphere (Galaburda & Kemper, 1979). The normal layering of cells was disrupted, and large, primitive cells, not normally present in this area, were found scattered here and there. Misshapen clumps of convoluted tissue, called polymicrogyria, were also found. One or more of the developmental processes described in Chapter 3 must have gone awry while the brain was forming. It appears that, at least, the orderly process of cell migration was disrupted. (The photographs at left illustrate this young man's case.)

This is the first piece of evidence linking dyslexia to anatomical abnormalities (such tissue aberrations do not show up on brain scans). But it is only one case. Furthermore, because the term "dyslexia" is currently used to cover a number of different language disabilities, it is impossible to conclude that disordered brain anatomy causes dyslexia.

Some evidence suggests that the development and incidence of dyslexia may depend on the kind of language a person learns to

Above, normal architecture of cells in the language area of the left hemisphere. Several distinct layers can be discerned, and the cells have a characteristic columnar organization. Below, the same area in the young dyslexic whose brain was examined by Galaburda. The arrangement of cells is disrupted throughout, and nerve cell bodies appear in the topmost layer where they are normally never seen.

read. Although 1 to 3 percent of the population in Western countries is dyslexic, the incidence in Japan is just one-tenth of that. Japan has two types of written language (see Figure 9.8). One is *kana,* which, like our alphabet, uses symbols that represent sounds. (In kana, each symbol stands for a syllable, or combination of sounds.) The other is *kanji,* where the written symbols are ideographs, each symbol representing a thing or an idea rather than a sound. It may be that the kanji ideographs are processed in a visual-spatial mode on the right side of the brain. Evidence from Japanese stroke victims suggests that this is indeed what happens. Japanese with stroke damage in the left hemisphere may lose their ability to read words written in kana, but they retain their ability to read kanji. In fact, some dyslexic American children have successfully learned to read English represented by Chinese characters in a special system devised by researchers (Kozin et al., 1971).

Another form of language that makes use of visual-spatial skills is the sign language used by the deaf.

Sign Language Many deaf persons, especially those born deaf, find that a gestural language—American Sign Language (ASL) in the United States—is their most effective vehicle for communication. ASL is a formal language with a complex vocabulary of 4,000 signs and a well-defined grammatical structure, even though it is based on spatial relationships. Each sign represents a word. The word order is different from that of English, with the most concrete or vivid element in each sentence coming first, followed by signs that explain or describe the situation (adjectives, adverbs, or verbs), followed by the result, outcome, or end product of the situation.

Which half of the brain would be responsible for the comprehension of this nonver-

Figure 9.8
Two alphabets are written, and sometimes mixed, in Japanese. Kanji, at the left, uses symbols that are almost pictorial. Kana, at the right, uses symbols that stand for sound combinations, or syllables.

bal language? Evidence reveals that signers who suffer aphasia—in this case, disruption of the ability to produce or comprehend ASL—have damage in the left hemisphere, in the same language areas that process vocal language in people who can hear. But it appears that in signers who began using ASL as very young children, the left hemisphere is also superior to the right in visual and spatial tasks. This reversal of the usual right-hemisphere superiority in these tasks seems to make good sense for a language whose comprehension depends on perceiving subtle dif-

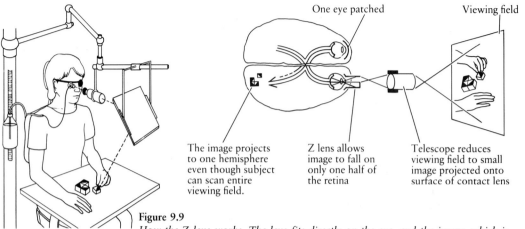

One eye patched

Viewing field

The image projects
to one hemisphere
even though subject
can scan entire
viewing field.

Z lens allows
image to fall on
only one half of
the retina

Telescope reduces
viewing field to small
image projected onto
surface of contact lens

Figure 9.9
*How the Z lens works. The lens fits directly on the eye, and the image, which is
projected to only one-half of the retina, is fed directly through the lens. The other
eye is patched, so there is no possibility of both hemispheres viewing the material.
Subjects can view images for much longer than the tachistoscope permits.*

ferences in the positions of the arms and
hands in space.

It is of interest to note also that most readers of Braille, the system of written language
used by the blind in which symbols are read
through touch, prefer to use their left hand
to identify the symbols. This usage implies
another interesting type of coordination between the superior language skills of the left
hemisphere and the normally superior spatial skills of the right.

The Right Hemisphere

Because of the left hemisphere's importance
in producing and comprehending language
and in performing language-ruled movements, it has been designated the "dominant" hemisphere. The right hemisphere,
then, became the "minor" hemisphere.
Many people still use this designation, even
though more recent studies have shown that
the right hemisphere has its own special
functions and that it can even process language.

Tachistoscope studies had indicated that

the right hemisphere was woefully deficient
in, if not totally ignorant of, language comprehension. Subsequently, however, Eran
Zaidel (1975) created an instrument called
the Z lens, which serves the same function as
the tachistoscope but is superior to it in several respects. The Z lens permits prolonged
viewing of stimuli, whereas the tachistoscope
flashes for only one- or two-tenths of a second because any slight eye movement away
from the center dot presents the stimulus to
both visual fields. The Z lens also ensures,
with complete certainty, that only one hemisphere of a person's brain receives the visual
information used for the test (see Figure
9.9).

Zaidel worked with two split-brain patients whose left hemispheres were dominant
for language. In one test, the patients heard a
word spoken by the experimenter, saw three
pictures through the Z lens in the left visual
field (right hemisphere), and were asked to
select the picture corresponding to the word.
Another test required them to follow spoken
instructions, such as "Put the yellow square

on the red circle" while viewing the blocks in the left visual field.

Zaidel found that the right hemisphere could comprehend more words and more about words than had been thought. Earlier tachistoscope results had indicated that the right hemisphere could comprehend nouns but not verbs. Using the Z lens, which gives patients more than a fraction of a second to view words, Zaidel found that the noun-verb distinction was invalid: verbs took a bit longer to be processed, but they were understood. On the vocabulary tests, the right hemisphere's comprehension vocabulary was roughly equivalent to that of a 10-year-old. Its processing of the sequential strings of words that made up the spoken instructions was somewhat poorer than its comprehension of single words.

Even though the right hemisphere has these rough comprehension abilities, it cannot produce speech. Evidently, the specialized brain regions, such as Broca's area and Wernicke's area, are required for language production.

Visual and Spatial Processes   In a number of ways, the right hemisphere has proved superior to the left in perception of spatial relationships and in manipulating objects to reflect those perceptions. To test this, split-brain patients were shown cut-up drawings of shapes, then asked to choose, by touch alone, using one hand or the other, the solid shape that the drawing represented (see Figure 9.10). Choices by the left hand (right hemisphere) ranged between 75 and 90 percent correct; the right hand (left hemisphere) scored at around 50 percent, about the level of chance, in six of seven patients (Nebes, 1972).

In other studies, researchers have asked patients to arrange patterned blocks to match a design shown on a card (see Figure 9.11). Results for one patient over a series of

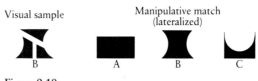

Visual sample   Manipulative match
                                      (lateralized)

Figure 9.10
Objects used to test spatial judgment. Split-brain patients manipulated the solid objects with one hand or the other and attempted to judge which was represented in the fragmented sample picture. Left-hand scores were much higher (Nebes, 1972).

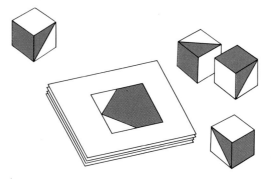

Figure 9.11
In the block-design task, subjects are asked to arrange the patterned blocks to match a specific design. Split-brain patients are asked to use one hand or the other. Performance by the left hand is far superior, as the table below shows.

Performance of left and right hands on block-design task

| Design | Time (in seconds) | |
	Left hand	Right hand
1	11	18
2	[a]	74[b]
3	13	36
4	12	69
5	15	95[b]
6	25	74[c]

[a] Design not completed within time limit (120 seconds).
[b] Subject gave up before end of time limit.
[c] Correct design was constructed but in wrong orientation.

trials are shown in Figure 9.11. The hand controlled by the right hemisphere was far superior to the hand controlled by the left, although the latter was not totally incompetent.

Michael Gazzaniga, a noted American psychologist and researcher, suggests that the right hemisphere has only a slight relative advantage in perception of spatial relations. Its true superiority lies in its ability to map those perceptions physically onto objects by manipulating them. That is, the right hemisphere is superior in producing the physical actions that arrange or construct items so that the resulting relationship of the parts fairly represents one's perception of them.

Musical Processes   At the age of 57, the French composer Maurice Ravel suffered severe damage to his left hemisphere in an automobile accident. The report of his subsequent condition stated that, although he could "still listen to music, attend a concert, and express criticism on it or describe the musical pleasure he felt, he never again was able to compose the pieces he heard in his head" (Alajouanini, 1948). Ravel suffered from Wernicke's aphasia and was unable to play the piano again or sing in tune, and he could no longer read or write musical notation.

There is no doubt that the right hemisphere also plays a role in the processing of music. In cases such as that of Ravel, left hemisphere damage does not eliminate the appreciation of hearing music and the ability to perceive discordant notes or rhythmic anomalies. There have been numerous reports of people who, with massive left hemisphere damage and aphasia, could nonetheless still correctly carry the melody and sing the lyrics of a song.

Neither studies of musical abilities after brain damage nor studies of music perception in persons with normal brains have established the localization of musical ability in one or the other hemisphere, however. The components of music are numerous and complex in themselves—melody, pitch, timbre, harmony, and rhythm. These are combined in an incalculable number of ways to produce music from Bach to rock. In addition, music listeners range from those who are highly trained to those who do not know what a musical phrase or a chord is. Consequently, most reviewers of the relevant research conclude that it is impossible to ascribe primary responsibility for music function to one hemisphere or the other (Gates & Bradshaw, 1977; Brust, 1980).

Two Hemispheres: One Brain

The study of specific hemispheric functions in patients with bisected brains offers insights into what each hemisphere might contribute in the intact brain. In addition, researchers use experimental means to study hemispheric function in normal brains.

In tachistoscope studies of people with normal brains, for example, experimenters assume that faster responses from the left visual field reveal that the right hemisphere is best equipped to deal with the material presented, and faster ones from the right visual field are evidence of left hemisphere superiority. Another test often used with normal subjects is the dichotic listening test: different auditory stimuli are presented simultaneously to each ear, and subjects are asked to report what they heard. If they report more accurately what was presented to the left ear, the response is interpreted as indicating right hemispheric superiority in processing the stimuli, and vice versa. The results of such studies seem to show a left hemisphere advantage for language-related sounds—even for language played backwards. The evidence for any right hemisphere advantage is less clear-cut.

The two hemispheres of the brain do have

specialized functions, but in an intact brain, the hemispheres work together, giving human beings flexibility and extraordinary problem-solving prowess. Interest in different hemispheric functions has led some neuroscientists to wonder if there might be anatomical or physiological differences between the hemispheres that could account for such specialization. Until recently, it was assumed that the brain's two hemispheres were anatomically identical. Research during the past two decades, however, has proved otherwise.

The Anatomy and Physiology of Hemispheric Differences

In 1968, after detailed post-mortem examination of 100 brains, Norman Geschwind and Walter Levitsky reported marked anatomical differences between the hemispheres. In 65 percent of those brains, the upper sur- face of the temporal lobe, a region overlap- ping Wernicke's area, called the *planum tem- porale,* was significantly larger in the left hemisphere. In 11 percent of the brains, the planum temporale was larger in the right hemisphere. The remaining 24 percent showed no difference between the hemi- spheres.

Since this original study, hundreds of other brains have been measured, and the findings are generally consistent: about 70 percent of all the brains studied have a larger planum temporale in the left hemi- sphere (see Figure 9.12). This difference most likely reflects the fact that the control of speech and language is, for most people, located in the left hemisphere.

Other studies have produced findings of additional hemispheric asymmetries, many of which are related to handedness. (The asymmetries are listed in Table 9.2, and the topic of handedness is discussed on pages 294 and 295.) Such differences might provide

Table 9.2　*Percentages of anatomical asymmetries among right-handers and among left- and mixed-handers*

Asymmetry	Right-handers			Left- and mixed-handers		
	Yes	Equal	Reverse	Yes	Equal	Reverse
Sylvian fissure higher on right (Galaburda, LeMay, Kemper & Geschwind, 1978)	67	25	8	20	70	10
Occipital horn of lateral ventrical longer on left (McRae, Branch & Milner, 1968)	60	30	10	38	31	31
Frontal lobe wider on right (LeMay, 1977)	61	20	19	40	33	27
Occipital lobe wider on left (LeMay, 1977)	66	24	10	36	48	26
Frontal lobe protrudes on right (LeMay, 1977)	66	20	14	35	30	35
Occipital lobe protrudes on left (LeMay, 1977)	77	10.5	12.5	35	30	35

SOURCE: M. C. Corballis, *Human Laterality* (Academic Press, 1983), p. 72.

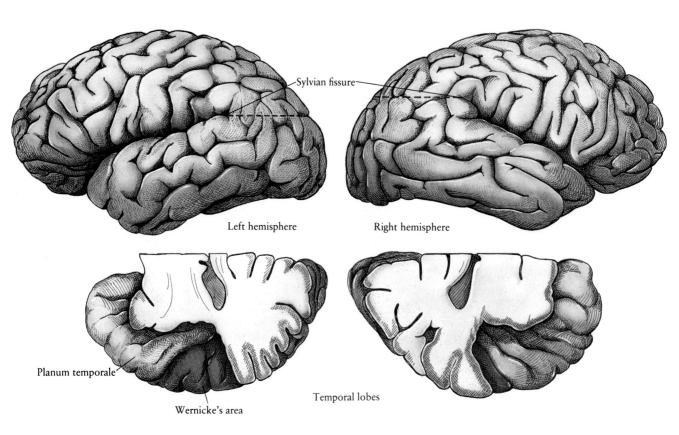

Left hemisphere   **Right hemisphere**

Sylvian fissure

Planum temporale

Wernicke's area   Temporal lobes

Figure 9.12
Anatomical asymmetries in the hemispheres of the brain. The Sylvian fissure, which defines the upper margin of the temporal lobe, slants upward more sharply in the right hemisphere. When the Sylvian fissure is opened and the cut completed along the dotted line, the planum temporale, which forms the upper surface of the temporal lobe, can be seen. It is usually much larger in the left hemisphere, and the enlarged region is part of Wernicke's area.

a physical basis for the different functions of the two hemispheres. When the evidence of hemispheric asymmetry first became known, some scientists suggested that the asymmetry in the language area could be an effect of language learning, but such asymmetries have also been detected in the human fetus. Thus, the anatomical difference is more likely a cause than an effect. Another asymmetry was discovered in the course of carotid angiography, x-ray examination of the brain by means of dyes injected into the carotid artery (Galaburda et al., 1978). The fact that the paths of large blood vessels in the brain reflect the anatomy of surrounding tissue has enabled researchers to discover that the Sylvian fissure (sometimes called the lateral fissure), the large groove in the cortex that divides the temporal lobe from the rest of the cortex, is longer and straighter in the left hemisphere. It slants more sharply upward in the right hemisphere. Fossil skulls of Neanderthal man show evidence of this asymmetry, which suggests that hemispheric

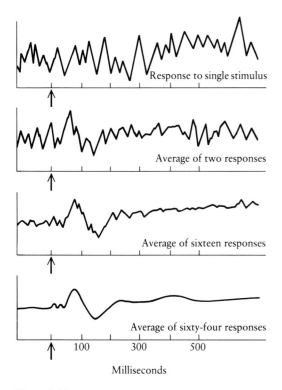

Figure 9.13
The evoked-potential records the brain's response to visual or auditory stimuli. The computer averages responses to a repeated stimulus so that the evoked response emerges from the background EEG "noise." The average of 64 responses produces a clear tracing.

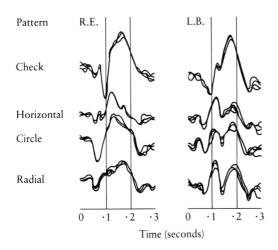

asymmetry may be part of the genetic heritage of *Homo sapiens*.

Evidence that anatomical asymmetries in the brains of newborn infants reflect functional differences comes from studies of *evoked potentials* produced by speech sounds in infants as young as one week old. This technique measures the brain's response to stimuli. When a person perceives a flash of light, for example, a large number of neurons in the visual area of the cortex fire almost simultaneously, changing the membrane potentials of millions of neurons. This evoked potential is often significant enough to be recorded through electrodes placed on the scalp. Because electrodes also pick up random brain activity, the measurement of an evoked potential requires that the stimulus be presented a number of times and that the evoked-potential signals be fed through a computer, which averages the responses (Figure 9.13) and produces records like those shown in Figure 9.14.

In the tests of infants, records of electrical activity in the brain in response to speech sounds showed that in 9 of 10 infants, the responses from the left hemisphere were of markedly greater amplitude. When nonspeech sounds were played—a burst of noise or a musical chord—all 10 infants showed evoked potentials of greater amplitude in the right hemisphere (Molfese et al., 1975).

Our brains, then, seem anatomically and physiologically prepared to process language as part of our species inheritance. In most of us, the cortex of the left hemisphere is the part of the brain programmed for this function. Unlike most sensory and motor functions, however, the development of the lan-

Figure 9.14
The evoked-potential responses of individual people to the same stimulus usually differ. Each column represents one person's response to four different visual patterns.

Handedness, Stuttering, and the Hemispheres

The vast majority of human beings write with their right hand and use it almost exclusively for tasks requiring skillful manipulation of objects. This is true of all cultures, and archeological evidence points to it having been true since prehistoric times. The paintings on the walls of Egyptian tombs often depicted people engaged in everyday activities, and most are seen performing those activities with the right hand—eating, pouring, counting. Even drawings of hunters found on cave walls show the weapons being wielded by the right hand. And the paleolithic weapons and tools that have been found appear to have been made for the right hand. No such overwhelming preference is found in the rest of the animal kingdom.

Why, then, are some 10 percent of human beings left-handed? And what relationship exists between hand preference and the two hemispheres of the brain?

Cultural Influences

Not many modern writers attribute the right-hand preference to cultural influences alone. Although it is true that some cultures—the Taiwanese, for example—put pressure on children to perform important activities with the right hand, one must move one step back and ask why that culture formulated such a strong right-hand bias. And why no single culture has ever been found in which a similar left-hand bias predominated.

In earlier decades in this century, American educators and parents did push young people to write with the right hand, no matter what their hand preference. Now that the pressure is off, the number of left-handed writers has risen from 2 to about 10 percent, which seems to represent the proportion of natural left-handers in human populations. About 2 percent of Taiwanese currently write with the left hand, a number that seems to represent the proportion

of left-handers who are resistant to change (Corballis, 1983).

Biology and Pathology

On the nature side of the argument, there are many approaches. One school of thought holds that right-handedness is a universal human trait and that all left-handedness is a result of some prenatal or perinatal damage to the brain, most likely caused by a lack of oxygen (Bakan and Reed, 1973). Since the incidence of left-handedness in twins is twice as high as that in the rest of the population—20 percent—and since twins are more vulnerable to damage from intrauterine crowding and from difficult birth processes, these data are sometimes cited as evidence for the damage hypothesis.

Other biological approaches posit genetic models of handedness. The probability of being left-handed is greater if your parent or parents are left-handed, but even if both your parents are left-handed, it doesn't necessarily mean that you will be left-handed. No simple genetic model seems able to fit all the data, including the fact that the incidence of left-handedness is about the same in both identical and fraternal twins. Since identical twins share 100 percent of their genes in common and fraternal twins, 50 percent, the incidence should not be the same. Of the many genetic models available, (see, for example, Rife, 1950; Trankell, 1955; Levy & Nagylaki, 1972), we shall briefly describe only one here, that of Marion Annett (1981).

Genetics of the Right-Shift

Annett suggests that most people inherit a gene that she calls the "right-shift factor." Most, but not all, of these people will become right-handers. Those who do not inherit this gene may become right-handers or left-handers or be ambidextrous, depending on chance factors—training or injury, for example. Evidence to support this hypothesis comes from the fact that left-handers show much less consistency than right-handers in other measures of laterality. Right-handers usually have dominant right eyes, ears, and feet, and they gesture almost exclusively with their right hands. Left-handers tend to gesture, while speaking, about equally with both hands (Kimura, 1973), and they show mixed patterns of eye, ear, and foot dominance.

In one test of her theory, Annett had a group of children of two left-handed parents perform a peg-sorting task and timed their performance with each hand. About half did better with their right hand, and about half did better with their left. The results upheld her prediction that hand preference in this group would be determined by chance (since presumably none had inherited the right-shift factor). The parents were interviewed to determine whether any of them had suffered trauma during their own births. Those who reported such traumas had significantly more right-handed children. These left-handed parents may, then, have inherited the right-shift gene but were forced, because of the birth-trauma injury, to use the left hand. Nonetheless, they were able to pass along the right-shift gene to their children.

Hand, Brain, and Speech

You know that control of the right hand resides in the left hemisphere and vice versa. You also know that, for most people, the left hemisphere controls speech. But these numbers differ for right- and left-handers: 15 percent of left-handers have speech represented in both hemispheres.

One proposed explanation of why people stutter points to bilateral representation of speech and competition between the hemispheres in its control (Orton, 1937). In one study, four stutterers were given the Wada test (they were being tested for neurological problems unrelated to their stuttering). All four of the subjects, three left-handers and one right-hander, showed evidence of bilateral control of speech. During the test, persons with speech control on one side or the other (usually the left) have a brief period of aphasia when the anesthetic reaches the hemisphere in which speech is represented and no effect when the other hemisphere is anesthetized. The stutterers showed impairment in their speech with anesthesia to either side (Jones, 1966).

Subsequent studies tend to confirm that a significant proportion of stutterers have speech represented bilaterally and that at least some stuttering does come from conflict between the cerebral hemispheres, particularly in the control of *speech production*. When cerebral blood flow was examined in two stutterers, it was found that while the subjects were stuttering, activity in Broca's area was greater in the right than in the left hemisphere, whereas activity in Wernicke's area was greater in the left. When the subjects were given a drug that controlled their stuttering, the greater activity in Broca's area shifted to the left hemisphere. These data suggest a conflict in cerebral control of speech between Broca's areas on the left and right (Wood et al., 1980).

Speaking requires precise and intricate programming of the muscles involved and of the larynx. The requirement for such precise, sequentially ordered actions, like that necessary for tool use, may, according to Michael Corballis (1983), have led to the evolution of human cerebral lateralization. The brain can operate more efficiently when only one hemisphere manages these detailed sequences. But, as he also points out, lack of consistent lateralization has little to do with the deeper issues of language or cognition. Left-handers or stutterers as a group are no less intelligent, accomplished, or creative than right-handers. In fact, both Michelangelo and Leonardo da Vinci were left-handed.

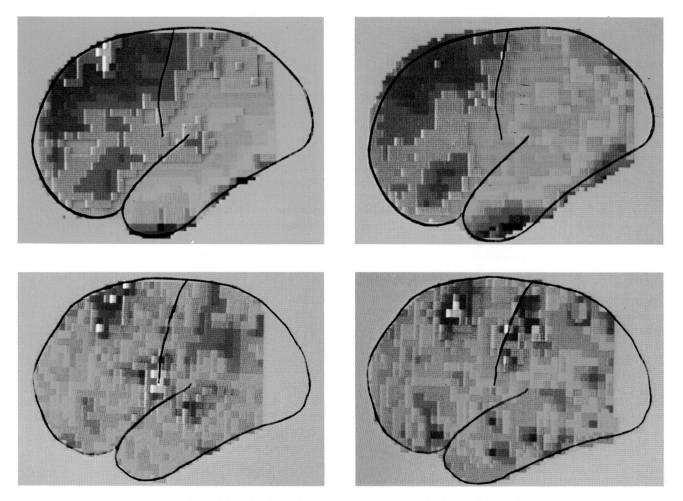

One method of detecting hemispheric differences measures blood flow through the brain during different activities. Radioactive isotopes are injected, and their passage is detected by a computer, which generates pictures like these. The average rate of blood flow shows up as green; rates below average are shades of blue, and rates above average are shades of red. Top, the left and right hemispheres of a patient resting with eyes closed. The frontal lobes of both hemispheres are active, as if the person were thinking and planning. Bottom, the left and right hemispheres as the person is speaking. Although both hemispheres are activated, the mouth-tongue-larynx area in the left hemisphere is less distinct, and it coalesces with the auditory cortex.

guage function shows plasticity. That is, if the language areas in the left cortex are damaged early in life, areas in the right cortex are able to take over their responsibilities.

On rare occasions, when a cancerous tumor has spread throughout a hemisphere of the brain, for example, surgeons must remove the cortical covering of the entire hemisphere in a procedure called a *hemispherectomy*. Adults whose right hemisphere is removed show little language impairment. Those whose left hemisphere is operated on suffer severe aphasia, which seldom shows improvement.

When infants undergo this procedure, however, the outcome is very different. The language development of children whose left hemispheres were removed in infancy shows almost no deficits. Standard tests of verbal intelligence reveal no differences between these children and normal children—and no difference between children having had left or right hemispherectomies.

Only extremely subtle tests can discover any shortcomings. In one of these tests, three 9- to 10-year-olds who had undergone hemispherectomies before 5 months of age were asked to judge whether the following three sentences were meaningful and acceptable English:

1. I paid the money by the man.
2. I was paid the money to the lady.
3. I was paid the money by the boy.

Two of these children had undergone removal of the left hemisphere; the other had had a right hemispherectomy. The child whose left hemisphere was intact correctly said that sentences 1 and 2 were grammatically incorrect and that sentence 3 was acceptable. The two children whose left hemispheres had been operated on could not make these distinctions, although normal children of this age can easily do so (Dennis & Whitaker, 1976).

Brain plasticity seems to be responsible for the children's relatively unimpaired capacities. Early in life the brain seems to show a tremendous capacity for reorganizing itself to compensate for damage to its parts. This plasticity, however, decreases with age. Older children who undergo left hemispherectomy generally learn to speak, but their language comprehension is impaired and their grammar imperfect.

Even in the absence of brain damage, the brain's plasticity may come into play. When Genie, the girl reared in isolation was found at age 13 (see pages 266–267), she could not speak or comprehend speech. After she had learned some language, psychologists used evoked-potential studies to see which part of her brain was processing that language. They found that she was using her right hemisphere for both language and nonlanguage functions.

Susan Curtiss, the psycholinguist who worked with Genie, suggests that it is acquisition of language that triggers the normal pattern of hemispheric specialization; if language is not acquired at the appropriate time, "the cortical tissue normally committed for language and related abilities may functionally atrophy." This interpretation is based on the findings of David Hubel and Torsten Weisel, which show that neurons not exposed to normal visual input fail to develop the normal number of connections with other cells and so become functionally inactive. No evidence exists for the failure of neurons in the language areas to develop connections, however, because animal experiments, like those used by Hubel and Weisel, are not possible for investigating human language.

Patient P. S.: Language and Cognitive Dissonance

One case, patient P. S., stands out as apparently unique among all the patients with bisected brains. Early in life, epileptic lesions had evidently caused damage to P. S.'s left hemisphere, and the brain's plasticity had allowed the development of some language-processing ability in his right hemisphere. After a routine brain bisection, an unusual thing happened: researchers could communicate with both the patient's left and right hemispheres. This communication has led to some valuable insights into the nature of consciousness and the role language plays in it.

P. S.'s right hemisphere not only possessed the ability to understand single words, but it could also understand complex verbal instructions and could direct his left hand to spell out responses to questions by using the letters of a Scrabble game. Testing of P. S.'s separated hemispheres produced an amazing result: two discrete spheres of consciousness seemed to be operating side by side within him. When Michael Gazzaniga asked P. S.'s left hemisphere "What do you want to be?" he responded, "Draftsman." When the same question was posed to the right hemisphere, he spelled out, "Automobile racer." Gazzaniga describes the moment when he and his associates discovered P. S.'s two "selves":

We stared at each other for what seemed an eternity. A half-brain had told us about its own feelings and opinions, and the other half-brain, the talkative left, temporarily put aside its dominant ways and watched its silent partner express its views. . . . Paul's right side told us about his favorite TV star, girlfriend, food, and other preferences. After each question, which we had carefully lateralized to the right hemisphere through our testing techniques, we asked Paul what the question was. He (that is, his left brain) shot back, "I didn't see anything." Then his left hand, controlled by the right hemisphere, would . . . proceed to write out the answer to our question. . . . Here was a separate mental system that could express mood, feeling, opinion.

P. S. was able to act in response to verbal commands presented exclusively to one hemisphere or the other. Most interesting were his left hemisphere's verbal explanations for actions he carried out in response to commands presented to his right hemisphere. When, for example, the command "rub" was flashed to his right hemisphere,

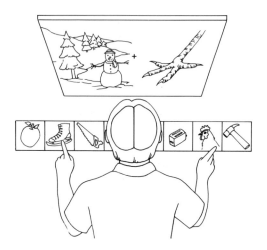

Figure 9.15
Simultaneous tachistoscope presentation of differing stimuli to P. S.'s right and left hemispheres. When he chose matching stimuli with each hand, his choices were appropriate to each hemisphere's stimulus. But his left hemisphere's verbal explanation of its choice consistently included a rationale for the right hemisphere's choice, even though the left hemisphere had no idea what, if anything, the right hemisphere had seen.

he began to rub the back of his head with his left hand. Asked what the command had been, his left hemisphere said "itch." Apparently, his left hemisphere observed the right hemisphere's response and guessed what the command might have been.

The results of one series of tests, a sample of which is depicted in Figure 9.15, were particularly revealing. With the tachistoscope, each of P. S.'s hemispheres was simultaneously presented with a different pictured object. Also before him were pictures of other objects, and he was asked to pick, for each flashed stimulus, the one pictured object that was most closely related to the stimulus. Each hand responded for its own hemisphere.

When shown a chicken claw in the left hemisphere and a snow scene in the right, P. S. quickly responded correctly by choosing a picture of a chicken with his right hand. Then he chose a picture of a shovel with his left. When asked "What did you see?" he said, "I saw a claw and I picked the chicken, and you have to clean out the chicken shed with a shovel."

During an entire series of such choices, the left hemisphere consistently identified why it had made its choice, then went on to incorporate the right hemisphere's choice into the framework of its response, even though it had not been asked to do so. And although the left hemisphere could only construct a plausible guess, its answers had an unquestionable ring of certainty.

The behavior of P. S.'s left, verbal hemisphere in justifying his right hemisphere's actions and in trying to make the actions of both consonant illustrates a well-known psychological theory, that of *cognitive dissonance* (Festinger, 1957). According to this theory, all human beings feel a strong need to avoid disharmony between their actions and their beliefs. If a man, for instance, believes himself to be prudent and conservative yet is persuaded to invest in high-risk stocks, the cognitive dissonance between his beliefs and his actions will make him extremely uncomfortable. He will try to erase the dissonance either by changing his behavior, selling the speculative stocks and buying blue chips, or by changing his conception of himself, protesting that although he may appear prudent and conservative in his personal life, he can be quite adventuresome in business.

Many experiments have confirmed the operation of this psychological principle in people with normal, intact brains. Its operation in P. S., with his separated hemispheres, reveals something about the role of language in human consciousness. As Michael Gazzaniga concludes, "The environment has ways of planting hooks in our minds, and while the verbal system may not know the why or what of it all, part of its job is to make sense out of the emotional and other mental systems and, in so doing, allow man, with his mental complexity, the illusion of a unified self."

Conscious and Nonconscious Information Processing

Virtually everyone who drives a car has had the experience at least once of arriving at some destination and having no recollection of the last 10 or 15 minutes on the road. You might have been talking with a passenger or listening to music or just thinking about something else. In any case, you were probably a bit surprised to find yourself home safely, with so little attention having been paid to the surrounding traffic and the route.

Nevertheless, you must have been processing the necessary information at some level to have escaped accident and ended up where you wanted to be. You must have perceived the cars around you and the road signs or landmarks along your route to have safely navigated. And you must have acted on those perceptions—without having engaged the language-using, conscious, part of your mind.

There are ample experimental data demonstrating this kind of perception and processing below the level of consciousness. One interesting outcome of specific brain damage—the neglect syndrome—helps to throw light on the topic.

The Neglect Syndrome

Some patients with fairly extensive damage to the posterior area of the right hemisphere (parieto-occipital cortex) behave as if the left side of space, and even the left side of their bodies, had ceased to exist (see Figure 9.16). A man may stand in front of a mirror to shave and yet shave only the right side of his face. A woman may eat all the food on the

Model   Patient's copy

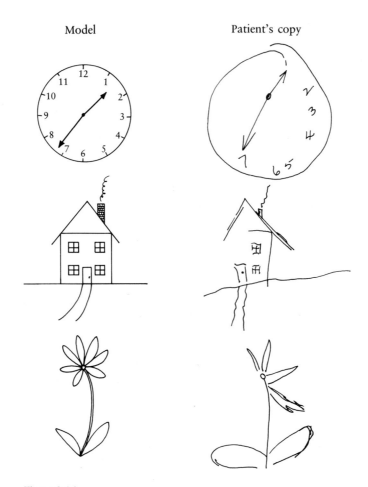

Figure 9.16
Drawings copied by a patient with the neglect syndrome demonstrate the profound neglect of the left side of space.

right side of her plate and ask for a second helping until someone points out that all the food on the left side of the plate remains un-eaten. Such patients reproduce drawings like those in Figure 9.16. Patients with equivalent damage to the left hemisphere generally do not show this *neglect syndrome*.

Patients with this right-hemisphere dam-age do not suffer from blindness. In testing situations where pictures of objects are flashed to the left visual field, they can iden-tify the object. Interestingly, however, when two stimuli are simultaneously flashed to both left and right visual fields, the patients will report seeing the picture in the right field and claim that was all they saw (Volpe et al., 1979). The patients evidently have no aware-ness of having seen anything in their left vis-ual field. Did they, in fact, see the picture or not?

To answer this question, the task was changed slightly. Instead of being asked to name what they saw in their left visual field, the patients were asked to say whether the two pictures flashed to the right and left visual fields were the same or different. Patients answered this question with a great deal of accuracy. Obviously, then, they had perceived the object in the left visual field and they remembered it, but they were not conscious of processing the information.

One study made the same point with normal subjects by flashing them pictures of nonsense shapes at speeds so fast that later recognition of these shapes was impossible (Zajonc, 1980). Later, when these subjects were given a number of nonsense shapes— some that had been flashed and some they had never seen before—and were asked to indicate which shapes they preferred, many chose the shapes that had been flashed. They had gained familiarity with these shapes, even though they had never consciously "seen" them.

Another such study involved patients whose left hemisphere had been anesthetized for medical purposes (Risse & Gazzaniga, 1978). With the anesthetic at work, these subjects were given an object to feel with the left hand. After the anesthetic wore off, they were asked to name the object. They could not. But when shown an array of objects and asked to identify the object by pointing to it, they could do so accurately. The information had obviously registered, though not in verbal codes. Information coded in the absence of language proved to be inaccessible to consciousness, although it was readily accessible through behavior. In a sense, these subjects had "neglected" that incoming information.

One explanation of the neglect syndrome says that it occurs with right-hemisphere damage and not left because of the language-processing skills of the left. That is, the dominant left hemisphere, which uses language to rationalize the person's experience (as you saw in the case of patient P. S.), assumes that what it sees is all there is to see. Many patients with the neglect syndrome insist that

there is nothing wrong with how they perceive and act in the world.

Other explanations of the neglect syndrome propose that the right-hemisphere damage has produced deficits in the mechanisms controlling perception. The following anecdote indicates, however, that the phenomenon does not depend on sensory processing. Physicians asked a patient with the neglect syndrome to *imagine* and describe a plaza in Milan (see page 302) that the patient had known well before his illness. They asked him to imagine himself arriving from the north end of the plaza and to describe what he saw. The patient went on to describe the buildings one by one on the west side— that is, to the right of where he pictured himself entering. He did not mention any of the buildings on the left. Then he was asked to imagine himself entering from the south. This time he described all the buildings on the east side. The neglect syndrome appears to affect even the recall of images from memory (Bisiach & Luzzatti, 1978).

Consciousness and Emotion

Joseph LeDoux (1985) believes that the nonconscious systems of information processing that we human beings use in comprehending external events—in judging how far away from us a large dog is, for example, or in deciding whether a cup of coffee is too hot to drink—are "direct descendants of comparable systems of our evolutionary ancestors . . . and reflect our biological heritage as vertebrates." One subset of these systems may be characterized as an emotional system. LeDoux makes the point that we find it much easier to consciously control our emotional *behavior* than our emotions. Some event may make us furious, and even though we have the impulse to punch someone in the nose, we refrain from doing so most of the time. Yet the feeling of anger may persist for hours or even days.

The Piazza del Duomo in Milan.

LeDoux believes that the neural pathways between the mechanisms of emotion and the mechanisms of consciousness, which are based on linguistic encoding, are limited, so that many emotional reactions take place without being consciously encoded. It is only after the fact, when we examine our feelings and our behavior, that we decide the significance of an event. These speculations resemble those of the James-Lange theory of emotion and coincide with the experimental findings of Stanley Schachter, discussed in Chapter 7. His subjects, unaware that they had received an injection of adrenaline, felt an emotional arousal for which they had no explanation. Faced with this puzzle, they ascribed meaning to their feeling by observing the angry or euphoric behavior of those around them and deciding that they, too, were feeling the same thing. The behavior of patient P. S., when his left, verbal, hemisphere justified his right hemisphere's actions, also lends some support to this hypothesis.

Cortex, Consciousness, and Self

We have seen that the brain's two hemispheres are not identical, either anatomically or functionally. For most people, the right hemisphere seems to process information as a whole, whereas the left hemisphere processes information in a sequential manner. The most important sequential processing in the left hemisphere is the processing of language—a species-specific behavior unique to *Homo sapiens*.

Most of the evidence for hemispheric functions comes from brain-damaged individuals. In all normal people, however, the two hemispheres constantly interact, with neural impulses running through the several commissures connecting them. Specifically, the cortices of both hemispheres are linked by many fibers passing through the corpus callosum.

It is our cerebral cortex—what has been called the "enchanted loom"—that is responsible for the characteristics that set human beings apart from other animals. It has given us the power to create tools—from the stone axe to the nuclear reactor—and to invent vehicles that move us faster than the cheetah and fly us higher and farther than the eagle. And human language allows us to preserve and pass on information about such creations to future generations, something no other animal can do.

The human cortex is probably more intricate in structure and more complex in functioning than anything else known to us. Its mechanisms, according to Vernon Mountcastle's model, are alike in all of us. Yet the operations of these ensembles of neurons creates in each of us a unique consciousness, a self unlike any other. Mountcastle himself best describes this process (1975):

Sensory stimuli reaching us are transfused at peripheral nerve endings, and neural replicas dispatched brainward, to the great grey mantle of the cerebral cortex. We use them to form dynamic and continually updated neural maps of the external world, and of our place and orientation, and of events, within it. At the level of sensation, your images and my images are virtually the same, and readily identified one to another by verbal description, or common reaction.

Beyond that, each image is conjoined with genetic and stored experiential information that makes each of us uniquely private. From that complex integral each of us constructs at a higher level of perceptual experience his own, very personal, view from within.

Summary

1. Consciousness is defined as awareness of one's own mental and/or physical actions. Usually, language is the vehicle that makes thought and action available to conscious awareness.

2. The large areas of the cerebral cortex not committed to processing specific sensory or motor information are called association cortex. It is in these areas, according to some scientists, that primary information from all the senses is integrated, then further integrated with emotions and memories, creating consciousness.

3. Another approach, that of Vernon Mountcastle, says that consciousness is ultimately a function of the columnar organization of the cerebral cortex, which he characterizes as a distributed system. That is, the columns' intrinsic and extrinsic connections allow for dynamic and changing information flow through the system, with different pathways used according to the organism's needs. Through such pathways come not only information from the outside world but also reentrant information—memories, emotions, cognitive skills. This simultaneous processing of external and internally generated information allows a continuous updating of perceptual images of oneself, which, when matched against external conditions, is the proposed mechanism for consciousness.

4. Much insight into the workings of consciousness has been obtained from patients who, for medical reasons, have had the two hemispheres of their brains disconnected by surgery that cuts through the corpus callosum. Specially designed studies that allow only one hemisphere or the other to see objects reveal that each hemisphere processes information somewhat differently: the left analytically and sequentially; the right, simultaneously and as a whole.

5. In over 95 percent of right-handers and 70 percent of left-handers, the left hemisphere controls speech and language. Specific brain areas involved are: Broca's area, responsible for producing the sounds of speech; Wernicke's area, responsible for production and comprehension of meaningful language; and the arcuate fasciculus, a tract of nerve fibers connecting Broca's and Wernicke's areas. If the left hemisphere sustains damage early in life, control of language is developed in the right hemisphere, in corresponding areas of the brain.

6. The right hemisphere appears to be superior for the perception of spatial relations. It plays a role in the processing of music. And it has, even in people whose left hemisphere is dominant for language, some slight ability to comprehend language.

7. A number of anatomical differences between the hemispheres have been noted. In about 70 percent of people, the planum temporale, the upper surface of the temporal lobe, is larger in the left hemisphere; this asymmetry in the language area has also been seen in human fetuses. The Sylvian fissure, which defines the upper limit of the temporal lobe, slants upward more sharply in the right hemisphere in most right-handers. A number of asymmetries are related to handedness (see Table 9.2 and box on pages 294–295).

8. Studies conducted with one split-brain patient, P. S., whose right hemisphere had developed enough facility in language so that it could communicate with the researchers by spelling out answers to questions with Scrabble tiles, revealed that each hemisphere may have its own consciousness. The hemispheres differed in their preferences for careers, foods, and favorite television stars. Studies with P. S. also showed that if the left, language-dominant, hemisphere became aware of discrepancies in such replies, it somehow incorporated the right hemisphere's choice into its response, constructing a rationale for its presence, thus avoiding cognitive dissonance.

9. Some people with damage to the posterior area of the right hemisphere display the neglect syndrome, behaving as if the left side of space had ceased to exist. It initially appeared that they do not process information presented to their left visual field, but when researchers probed, it became clear that these patients have processed the left-field information, but at a nonconscious level. Much information processed by normal persons is processed at a nonconscious level.

Further Reading

Le Doux, J. E. 1985. Brain, mind, and language. In D. A. Oakley (ed.), *Brain and Mind*. New York: Methuen. An exploration of the role of language in the mind's operations, with accounts of classical and current research that sheds light on the topic.

Springer, S. P., and Deutsch, G. 1985. *Left Brain, Right Brain,* revised edition. New York: W. H. Freeman. A short, well-presented compilation of research and theory into all aspects of the brain's two hemispheres.

Gazzaniga, M. S. 1985. *The Social Brain: Discovering the Networks of the Mind.* New York: Basic Books. An easy-to-read coverage of the frontiers of research on hemisphere specialization and the higher intellectual processes.

Corballis, M. C. 1983. *Human Laterality.* New York: Academic. Exhaustive coverage of theory and research about handedness and topics related to it.

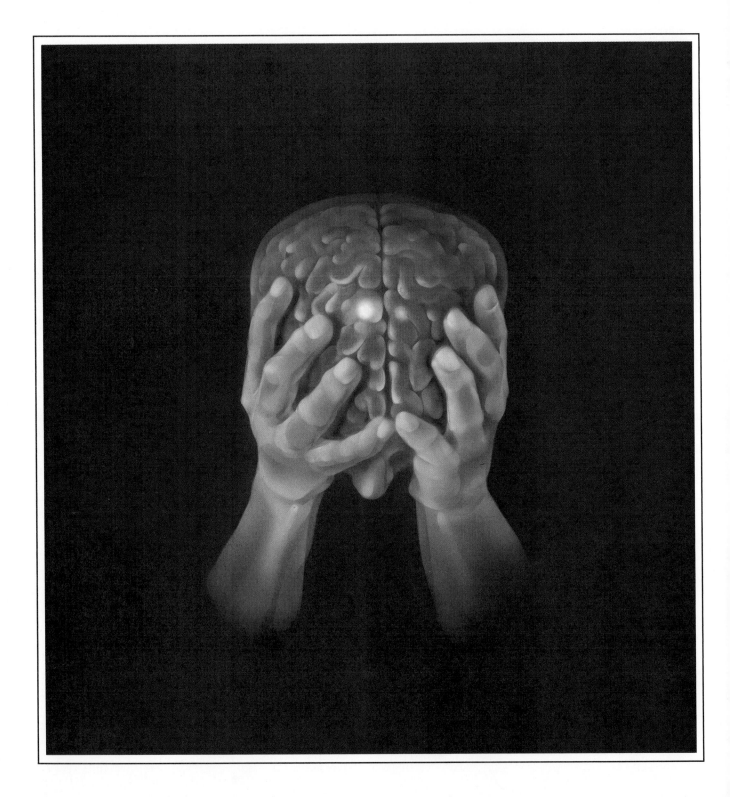

10

The Malfunctioning Mind

10

Doctor: How are you doing?

Gerry: I'm not doing so hot. I think and feel as though people have called me here to electrocute me, judge me, put me in jail . . . or kill me, electrocute me, because of some of the sins I've been in.

Doctor: It must be very frightening for you, if it feels like you're about to get killed?

Gerry: . . . It's so scary, I could tell you that picture's got a headache.

Doctor: Can you tell me more about that—the picture . . . has a headache?

Gerry: Okay, when a sperm and an egg go together to make a baby, only one sperm goes up in the . . . egg, and when they touch, there's two contact points that touch before the other two, and . . . then it's carried up into the air. And . . . when they fuse, it's like nuclear fusion, except it's human fusion . . . there's a mass loss of the proton . . . one heat abstraction spins around, comes back down into the proton to form the mind, and the mind could be reduced to one atom.

Doctor: At this point, what would you like us to do for you?

Gerry: I'd like you to get me off of cigarettes, get me dried out, cleaned up, so I can go home and get a job in a bakery and go to medical school.

Doctor: If you had to pick one or two things that you'd like us to help you with, what would they be?

Gerry: Schizophrenia.

Doctor: Schizophrenia. What does that mean? Different people use the word different ways.

Gerry: Schizophrenia is when you . . . you hear voices inside your head. You know? Like, inside your head, but I'm psychosomatic . . . I can . . . pantomime with people. Psychosomatic. That's what that means.

You may have only rarely, or never, encountered people who express abnormal thinking like this in their conversations. Gerry suffers from a severe mental disease, *schizophrenia,* which is characterized by disordered thinking and behaving, perceptual distortions, and gross delusions. He is, as his doctor says, a "textbook case."

Depending on how old you are and how long it has been since you were last cooped up indoors with small children, you may or may not smile at the line "insanity is hereditary—you get it from your children." The constant clamor, physical activity, and unending interruptions practically "drive you crazy." You probably did not need to read about stress in Chapter 7 to realize that modern living can make you feel like you too are "going crazy." But what does it really mean to be insane, or to "go crazy," and how different is a serious mental illness from a temper tantrum or a day of being "depressed"? How does Gerry's conversation differ from that of someone who is temporarily "not himself" or "not herself"?

The view taken in this book is that the biological science of the brain can give us a better and deeper understanding of the nature and causes of mental illness than any other approach available now. Everything the brain does is becoming explainable in terms of specific nerve cells, their neurotransmitters, and their responsive cells. Given this bias, we cannot examine abnormal psychology or psychiatry comprehensively. These are vast fields with their own categories of dysfunction and conceptual frameworks. Instead, we shall look at biological discoveries that might explain disorders of thinking and behaving.

Looking at the roles of certain brain cells, their chemical signals, and their mechanisms in the diseased mind can lead us to a new understanding of how the normal brain works. It may also help us to see what goes wrong with the brain, and these insights should lead to ways of predicting who may be most susceptible to mental problems. Current medical research on these problems seeks not only to develop better understanding of their different causes and to provide more effective treatment, it also seeks to find ways to prevent these problems in the future. Historically, however, the approaches to mental illness were often far less constructive.

Historical Views of Behavior Disorders

Early descriptions

Like most phenomena in medical history, abnormal states of behavior were recorded in the Bible as well as by ancient Greek and Chinese observers. All early cultures treated behavioral problems as though evil spirits had taken possession of people, and punishment was the only proper course of action. In addition to abandoning or beating such people, many cultures designed elaborate religious rituals to cast out the demons. One treatment strategy included drilling holes in the skull to allow the evil spirits to escape. The Old Testament also shares this general view. Deuteronomy reports that God punishes those who disobey Him with "madness, blindness and astonishment of the heart," mental states possibly equivalent to mania, dementia, and stupor.

Hippocrates accurately described the depression that follows childbirth. He also gave the name "hysteria" to a disorder in women caused, he said, by "wandering of the uterus." We currently refer to these physical symptoms without apparent organic cause that show up, in both women and men, after some life event has caused great

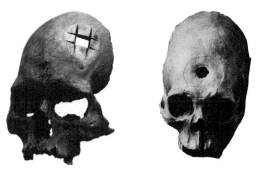

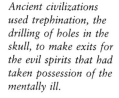

Ancient civilizations used trephination, the drilling of holes in the skull, to make exits for the evil spirits that had taken possession of the mentally ill.

anxiety and conflict as "conversion reactions." Hippocrates also gave more accurate descriptions of epileptic seizures than his predecessors. Unknown even to the Greeks were the earlier Chinese writings in *The Yellow Emperor's Classic of Internal Medicine*, which also describe insanity, dementia, and convulsions relatively accurately.

Near the end of the eighth century A.D., Arab physicians, who had rediscovered earlier Greek medical writings, developed what

Trephination, or cutting the stone of folly, continued into early modern times. Jan Saunders van Hemessen painted The Surgeon *around 1530.*

TEMPERANCE *enjoying a Frugal Meal.*

Contemporary cartoonists mercilessly caricatured the peculiar behavior of King George III (above, left). Because the royal physicians kept such detailed notes of everything the king did, modern reexaminations of his case have been possible. The evidence suggests that the king was not in fact "mad," but rather that he suffered from a rare form of metabolic disease known today as acute intermittent porphyria. In this disease, the body is unable to construct properly the hemoglobin molecules that allow red blood cells to transport oxygen. Large amounts of unassembled hemoglobin components are then excreted in the urine. The deep red urine (center test tube; its color resembles that of port wine, shown in the right test tube, more than the color of normal urine, shown in the left test tube) that characterized the king's episodes was described by contemporary physicians, without its significance being understood. To this day, however, medical investigators do not know how this very specific metabolic disease produces the pain and, in some cases, the mental problems that are its characteristics.

we can call the first humane treatment centers for the mentally ill. They established "asylums" where the ill, mainly "melancholic" patients, were cared for with special diets, rest, and music. In line with the traditions of many cultures that a supernatural power spoke through the insane, Moslems

supported the view that Allah had chosen these people to speak the truth.

With some rare exceptions, no further lasting changes in concept or treatment occurred until well into the Renaissance. Western thought perpetuated the view that the mentally ill, being possessed of evil spirits,

Sigmund Freud
1856–1939

Emil Kraepelin
1855–1925

Eugen Bleuler
1857–1939

John Hughlings Jackson
1835–1911

Ivan Petrovich Pavlov
1849–1936

could be treated by exorcism, beating, or burning. Throughout the Inquisition and the era of witchcraft, madnesses and delusions were viewed as epidemics, and those who survived more formal social punishments were kept in dungeons. Such views held sway until the middle of the sixteenth century, when the Swiss physicians Weyer and Paracelsus expressed the view that abnormal mental conditions were really medical problems.

However, during the birth pains of medical science in the sixteenth and seventeenth centuries, understanding of these diseases was still constrained by the weight of religious thought. Medical diseases might affect the body, but the soul—the world of the mind and spirit—was deemed to be the property of God. Nevertheless, both the power of the church and the emerging influence of Protestantism encouraged royal sovereigns to accept responsibility for their subjects. This led to the creation of large institutions for the mentally ill. Still more or less imprisoned, the mentally ill were ignored in hopes that they and their problems would disappear.

A major turning point in this rather dismal state of affairs came with the tragic illness of George III of England. Beginning in 1788, the king, whose reign included the years of the American Revolution, suffered a recurring illness characterized by periods of intense abdominal pain, insomnia, and extreme restlessness, accompanied by confusion and irrational behaviors. At times George's behavior was so bizarre that a straitjacket was required. After the third or fourth recurrence, Parliament made his son regent in 1810. For the rest of his life, George III remained the "mad king."

The king's prominence and the severity of his illness, however, led to the first systematic attempts by medical investigators to deal with such problems. Two of the king's sons set up the first research fund for mental disorders. The king's episodic disease, with its fluctuating cycles of apparent insanity and normalcy, was later identified as a rare form of the metabolic disorder called *porphyria*. (See illustration on page 310.)

The eighteenth and nineteenth centuries were halcyon days for general scientific discovery. The plight of the mentally ill, however, changed little, except that the standard of care became slightly better. Large general asylums for the insane, pioneered by the French superintendent Philippe Pinel in the late eighteenth century, improved their facilities, but these places remained common hiding grounds for the mentally ill throughout the Western world. This period did see the beginnings of a scientific understanding of the brain, and this enabled some of the most prophetic scholars of the brain, the mind, and behavior to do their most important work: Sigmund Freud, John Hughlings Jackson, Emil Kraepelin, Eugene Bleuler, and Ivan Pavlov.

The Last Fifty Years

By the 1920s and 1930s, medical science had eliminated two diseases that accounted for a sizable number of the patients imprisoned in asylums.

First to go was *pellagra,* a disease caused by dietary insufficiency of the B vitamin niacin. (The specific B vitamins had first to be discovered before the foods containing them could be identified.) The foods richest in niacin were, it turned out, missing from the diets of many poverty-stricken and protein-deficient communities. Pellagra was once estimated to account for 10 percent of the admissions to state asylums in the southern United States, where corn was a major dietary staple. (Corn niacin is especially hard to digest.) The delirium, confusion, and general disorientation of the pellagra victim were often accompanied by periods of "mania": extremely excited behavior, loud and incessant talking, and constant movement. High fevers often appeared to precipitate these mental derangements, supporting the belief that some "germs," the common name for unknown infectious agents, were propagated among the squalor of the poor and caused "insanity." It never occurred to most people that the "insanity germ" did not spread to those who guarded the inmates. The prompt remission of pellagra with adequate nutrition and niacin supplements can be viewed as a total cure for this "madness."

Another now-curable mental illness, is, in fact, caused by a germ. This disorder is known as *general paresis,* a late stage in the infection of the brain by syphilis. Before antibiotics provided an effective treatment for the primary infectious episode of syphilis, all patients went effectively untreated. After a delay of 10 or so years, up to one-third of those afflicted underwent an increasingly pronounced loss of memory and capacity for concentration, progressing to chronic fatigue and lethargy, accompanied by emotional instability ranging between depression and illusions of grandeur. Pathologic findings abounded as large parts of the brain were destroyed by the invading syphilis bacteria.

Shortly before the end of World War I, the Austrian physician Julius von Wagner-Jauregg devised a fever therapy. Syphilis-infected patients were given secondary malaria infections, and the high fevers from the malaria killed the heat-sensitive syphilis bacteria. Later, the patients had to be given quinine drugs to treat the malaria, but this seemed a small price to avoid the progressive mental deterioration of neurosyphilis. In 1927, Wagner-Jauregg received the Nobel Prize for this cure. Today, of course, syphilis is fully cured by treatment in its early stages with antibiotics such as penicillin, so general paresis is virtually eliminated.

Porphyria, pellagra, and general paresis are now known to be "organic" forms of mental illness. In other words, enough observable, verifiable signs of chemical or structural pathology were found to attribute the cause of the patient's abnormal behavior to specific cellular changes within the brain. These successes suggest that the causes of other serious mental illnesses for which there are no obvious "organic" signs may also eventually yield to detection and attack. In such an effort, the primary point of departure is more accurate diagnosis.

Diseases of the Brain and Disorders of Behavior

It is critical that we understand the terms "disease" and "disorder" in considering specific abnormalities of the brain and the ways they affect the mind and behavior. At first glance, a disease might seem to be the more "serious" condition, but that depends on what we mean by "serious." A disease is a specific set of conditions that occur together in a particular illness, the conditions that cause heart failure or kidney failure, for example. Such diseases may arise from a variety of inherited, infectious, or toxic causes. Diseases manifest themselves in more-or-less repeatable forms, the pattern of symptoms or complaints that patients or their families notice, along with other signs that the doctor recognizes when examining the patient. Diseases can affect the whole body, or parts of it. In practical terms, then, a disease is a disease when enough doctors agree that a particular cluster of signs and symptoms constitute a reproducible set of findings, with a more or less consistent time course, to which they then give a name—whether or not they understand its cause and whether or not they know how to treat it.

The degree of illness in a disorder may be no less serious than that in some diseases. Diseases and disorders both involve malfunction. But whatever its cause, a disorder only becomes a disease when its manifestations are recognized as having a truly consistent form. Many disorders of thinking and behaving take highly variable forms, and their manifestations have no recognizable common foundation. Like being left-handed or having red hair, these conditions are defined as abnormal only because of what most people—or in the case of thinking and behaving, most doctors—are willing to accept as normal.

In a gross sense, all diseases are disorders, but not all disorders are diseases. This discussion reserves the term "disease" for the most consistent, repeating forms of abnormal brain conditions, and uses the term "disorder" (or its more common synonym "illness," the opposite of wellness) for various abnormal conditions that are still incompletely defined.

There are several reasons why it is important to understand the difference between a disease and a disorder, insofar as abnormal behavior goes. In the first place, this text takes the view that biological explanations await discovery for everything that the brain does, when it is working correctly and when it is not. Therefore, how we define the condition "when it is not working correctly" becomes critical for being able to identify the biological and behavioral differences in the same individual at various times in the course of his or her disease, and then to see if similar correlations can be made in others with the same disease. Second, in order to gain better insight into the nature of the major psychiatric diseases, we must be able to determine whether we can categorize groups of mentally affected patients into separate clusters of findings that might then constitute the basis for a starting definition of a specific disease. If we were to try to lump everyone who falls outside of what we deem today as normal into one large category, we would be unable to find any consistent meaningful differences, even if we knew what to measure.

Finally, from the medical point of view, diseases are characterized by some degree of pathological change that demands a treatment or prevention strategy aimed at it, whether that be a medication, a vaccine, or long, thoughtful conversations. Behavior that is disordered to a lesser degree, like being unable to fall asleep when one is nervous the night before a test or being unable to pass up chocolate candy, may require action on the part of the person who has it, but such "abnormal" behaviors probably will not require drugs or vaccines. Furthermore, not all behavioral problems can be readily reduced to a chemical or biological explanation now, nor are they likely to be in the near future. As students of the brain and behavior, we need to recognize that and con-

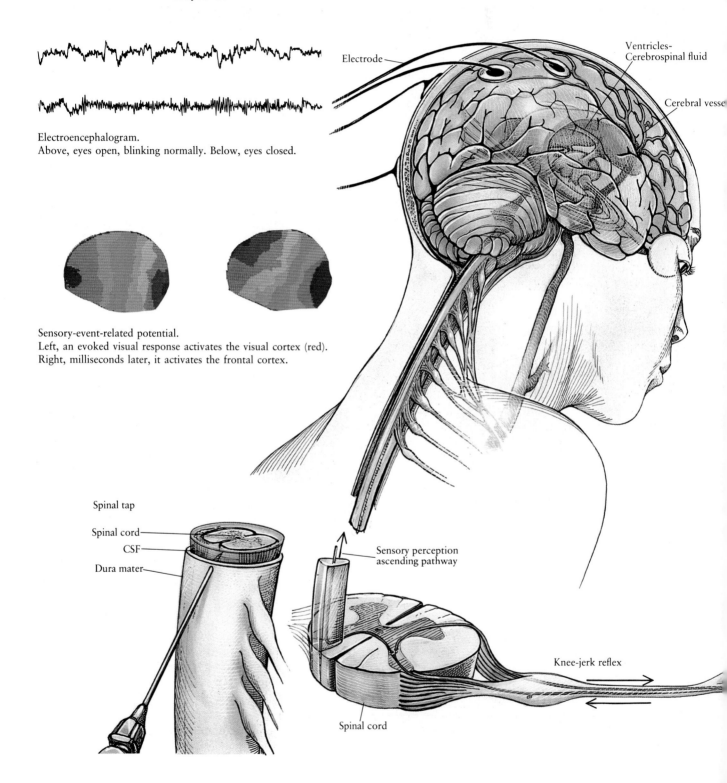

Electrode

Ventricles-
Cerebrospinal fluid

Cerebral vessel

Electroencephalogram.
Above, eyes open, blinking normally. Below, eyes closed.

Sensory-event-related potential.
Left, an evoked visual response activates the visual cortex (red).
Right, milliseconds later, it activates the frontal cortex.

Spinal tap

Spinal cord

CSF

Dura mater

Sensory perception
ascending pathway

Knee-jerk reflex

Spinal cord

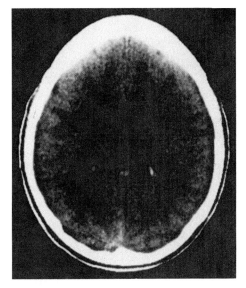

X-ray of a normal brain.

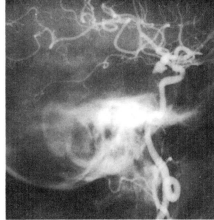

Angiogram.

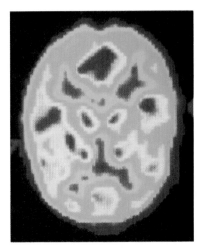

PETT scan, showing activation of the auditory cortices as the subject listens to a Sherlock Holmes mystery.

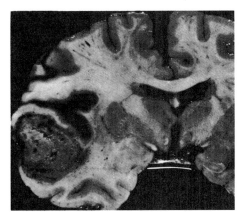

Post-mortem photo of an astrocytoma in the cerebral cortex.

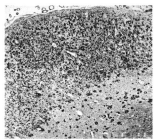

Post-mortem slide of the cerebral cortex of an Alzheimer's patient. The cortex is loaded with plaques, which show here as black spots.

Figure 10.1

In addition to an interview with the patient to determine the history of the illness, and after performing a physical examination to test nerve function, the neurologist may request additional tests. These tests could include analysis of the electrical signs of the brain's activity, such as an electroencephalogram (EEG) or a Sensory Event Related Potential (both, far left). Such tests detect evidence of a local or generalized dysfunction in the brain's activity. Additional tests could then involve examination of the brain's shape and size by conventional x-ray or by one of the more sophisticated imaging instruments. The x-ray of a normal brain shows mainly the skull, since the brain itself does not have any density that will block the passage of the x-rays, unless special "soft tissue" imaging is done. These other imaging devices can produce pictures of the brain's structure in relation to its specific patterns of blood flow, termed an angiogram, or in relation to its patterns of glucose utilization, termed a Positron Emission Transaxial Tomogram (PETT scan). Such studies help to distinguish between various disorders that can affect the same parts of the brain.

In some cases, chemical and microscopic analysis of the cerebrospinal fluid (CSF) (far left, below) may provide helpful information regarding the presence or absence of infection or the nature of an injury.

Ultimately, when no diagnosis can be reached, an eventual postmortem examination may be the only way to verify the actual disease process.

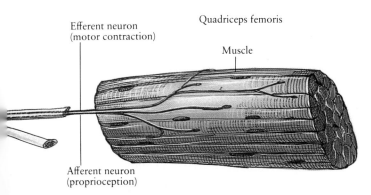

Efferent neuron (motor contraction)

Quadriceps femoris

Muscle

Afferent neuron (proprioception)

315

centrate our efforts now on those problems for which some solutions may be possible.

Brain-Cell Dysfunction

How is a state of "unhealth" in the brain identified and studied? Explanations of virtually all the diseases of other organ systems—the lungs, the kidneys, or the skin, for example—center on problems with the structure or function of the cells in those organs. Diseases of the brain also arise from problems in the brain-cell function. The study of the cellular dysfunctions that cause disease is known as *pathology*. Pathologists find that the brain is susceptible to the same *organic* sources of disease as the other major body systems: abnormalities of development, inherited metabolic problems, infections, allergies, tumors, inadequate blood supply, injury, and the scars that persist after recovery. (The term "organic" simply means that the disease is "real" to the extent that it shows up in an organ.) The study of the organic diseases of the brain and the rest of the central nervous system is known as *neurology*, and organic problems in sensing the world around us—blindness, deafness, or other loss of sensing or moving ability—are the province of the neurologist.

At times, however, no obvious organic pathology can be found to explain brain malfunction, particularly when the symptoms appear largely in the patient's mood, thinking, or social interactions. To distinguish them from organic disorders, such problems are often termed *functional disorders*—that is, the person's abnormal behavior clearly interferes with his or her normal function, but no organic cause can be discerned. Functional disorders are treated by the psychiatrist or the clinical psychologist. It is worth noting here, however, that failure to recognize the organic nature of a brain problem may not mean that it is *only* functional; rather, it may be due to an inability to find or measure the right index of the problem.

Diagnostic Tests to Identify Brain Diseases

The examination of a patient with symptoms of disordered brain function by a medical doctor, generally a neurologist, occurs in several phases. First comes a careful verbal interview of the patient, and sometimes of those with whom the patient lives, in order to determine when and how the problem began and how it manifests itself. Next, the patient receives a thorough physical examination to test the function of the sensory and motor systems. At this point, some tentative understanding of the nature of the problem, and whether or not it is treatable, may be possible. In some cases, an accurate diagnosis requires additional tests (see Figure 10.1 on pages 314 and 315).

By ruling out various causes of the pathology, the neurologist attempts to determine the best therapy. For example, a patient may consult a neurologist with a sudden "speaking" problem. Examinations reveal that the patient can understand speech but cannot initiate it. Further examination shows no deficits in tongue and lip movements or in vocal cord movement. The electroencephalogram is normal. However, x-ray analysis reveals a problem over the left temporal cortex: the density of the brain mass is reduced. Injection of a dye into the carotid arteries normally provides an x-ray image of the entire vascular structure supplying the brain. In this case, the vascular-dye x-ray image, termed an *angiogram*, reveals that blood vessels in the left cerebral cortex are closed. The diagnosis is then made: a limited stroke in that portion of the left cerebral cortex responsible for speech.

Had the tests revealed increased brain mass and increased blood flow, the diagnosis might have been a tumor, either of the blood vessels or of the supporting cells. The treatment for that condition might be surgical removal of the tumor followed by radiation or chemotherapy rather than the supportive measures required in the case of stroke. Had the patient's problem been widespread tumors with invasion of the central nervous system, surgical removal would not be feasible. In patients with degenerative disorders, in which the disease process destroys neurons, no treatment is currently possible. Given our present state of knowledge, only preventive strategies are available to provide relief for future generations.

Examination of the nervous system after death, the "postmortem examination," provides direct physical evidence of the nature and extent of a disease. The postmortem examination helps establish the relative importance of particular diagnostic signs and tests after the fact. This is especially instructive in cases where diagnosis was difficult or impossible while the patient was alive. Postmortem information, in turn, helps in the evaluation of future patients who present similar problems.

Normal versus Abnormal Variations in Mood and Thought

Virtually all of us have occasional strange thoughts or impulses. Usually, however, we maintain our normal behavioral patterns by overcoming impulses that we recognize in ourselves as abnormal. Most of us also have peculiarities, which we call eccentricities when we observe them in someone else—moods, fixations, suspicions, odd habits, giggling, nervous tics. Such eccentricities are, in a sense, learned behaviors. Most people have found that such behavioral devices have a reinforcing, or self-strengthening, value. Repeating the behavior, no matter how strange or annoy-

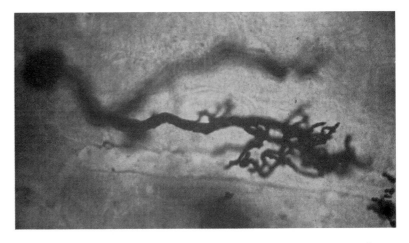

Post-mortem examination of nondiseased brain allows neuroscientists to see the changes effected by disease. This Purkinje cell of an aged rat looks very different from the normal cell shown on page 18, but the difference is due to age, not to disease. This type of change is a normal effect of age in rats, as discovered by doing many such examinations.

ing, has a positive value for the performer. It attracts the attention or achieves the stress reduction that the person craves, and in this context, the behavior makes sense.

Everyone also has fluctuations in mood. One is occasionally elated by some unexpected good fortune and occasionally saddened by loss or disappointment. Our general state of health, our work habits, and our degree of exposure to stress or fatigue an all modify our responses to such events. Seasonal transitions, the anniversaries of tragic losses, even "jet lag" can all trigger fluctuations in normal moods and affect behavior by altering emotional state—increasing or decreasing appetite, self-perceived vigor, sleep satisfaction, and sexual awareness.

These normal fluctuations in mood and occasional intrusions of "strange thoughts" differ substantially in quality and quantity from the severe problems that occur in those patients whose behavior requires psychiatric attention in a clinical setting. (Table 10.1 lists the categories of psychiatric disorders

Table 10.1 *Summary of official diagnostic categories of the major psychiatric disorders**

I. Disorders of Infancy, Childhood, or Adolescence

These diseases include inheritable disorders leading to mental retardation such as *trisomy 21* (previously called Down syndrome, or mongolism); *phenylketonuria* and related diseases, in which essential enzymes are missing; and the *Lesch-Nyhan syndrome,* one of several untreatable, severe behavioral problems which include self-mutilation, bizarre movements, and mental retardation. In these cases, a single, particular genetic error has been found, but in no case is it clear how the specific metabolic abnormalities lead to the highly abnormal behavior and retarded mental development.

II. Organic Brain Syndromes

These diseases exhibit a progressive and irreversible loss of mental capacity as the brain is being destroyed by infection, vascular insufficiency, or toxicity. Some of the most common organic brain syndromes are *repeated cerebrovascular accidents,* or "strokes," in which brain tissue dies from inadequate arterial blood supply; *Alzheimer's disease,* a progressive and untreatable degenerative disorder of adults, involving primarily the neocortex and hippocampal brain regions; *acute* or *chronic toxicity* (literally, poisoning) caused by exposure to alcohol, or other toxic chemicals, such as insecticides and poisonous metals (arsenic, bismuth, or lead, for example). *Pellagra, porphyria,* and *general paresis,* produced by definable organic causes, belong to this general category.

III. Disorders of Drug Dependence

The severe behavioral problems produced by the disorders of drug dependency stem from the direct toxic effects of using the drugs, ranging from poisonous additives to the use of nonsterile needles; the variable degrees of potency that lead to inadvertent overdosing; and the criminality associated with acquiring the money to buy drugs and with the penalties for drug possession.

The most common chemical dependency disorder is *alcoholism.* Aside from its direct toxic effects on the brain, liver, and heart, excessive use of alcohol is also a major cause of fatal automobile accidents, aggressive assaults, homicides, and many suicides. *Specific* chemical dependencies have been described for several classes of drugs: *opiates* (heroin, morphine, methadone, codeine, demerol); *barbiturates; marijuana* and related products of the cannabis plant; *cocaine; amphetamines; hallucinogenic drugs* (LSD, psilocin, phencyclidine [PCP, or angle dust]); and *volatile chemicals* (glue solvents and amyl nitrate).

IV. Psychosomatic (or Psychophysiological) Disorders

These disorders involve medical illnesses, the precipitating causes of which can be directly related to behavioral or social factors in the patient's environment. A combination of biological, behavioral, and social factors triggers the onset of recurrent episodes of a particular complex of medical symptoms: *dysfunction of the gastrointestinal tract,* some forms of *arthritis,* some *chronic skin irritations,* some forms of *asthma,* and some forms of *high blood pressure.* In these problems, one sees an exaggerated response of the body mediated largely by signals within the autonomic nervous system.

V. Situational Disorders

These are the extreme individual reactions to conditions of severe environmental stress, such as *battlefield shock,* termed "combat fatigue," or the *depression* that may accompany grieving over the death of a close friend or relative. The transient nature of the disorder and the striking relationship in time to the

* Based on American Psychiatric Association, *Diagnostic and Statistical Manual* (3d ed.), Washington D.C., 1979.

currently accepted by American psychiatrists.) Many patients are highly disturbed over their inability to control their fears, delusions, mood fluctuations, or frank losses of contact with reality. The inability to control their own thought content threatens to destroy the very qualities of high-order brain function that distinguish us as human beings. The doctor whom such a disturbed patient may eventually consult must decide whether or not the emotional or intellectual fluctuation is different enough from the normal range of fluctuations to deserve some special intervention. To do this, the doctor must stressful life-event distinguish it from more severe behavioral problems that require treatment.

VI. Character and Personality Disorders

These behavioral problems of varying severity range from mild forms of *antisocial behaviors* to *obsessions, compulsions,* and *overt antisocial acts* including aggressiveness, kleptomania (compulsive stealing), pyromania (compulsive setting of fires), and more serious criminality. In general, the onset of such behaviors occurs in late adolescence, after which the behaviors generally fall into a lifelong pattern; the abnormal behaviors are rarely noticed by the subject as being any sort of problem.

VII. Neuroses

The neuroses are behavioral disorders characterized either by *anxiety* (unrealistic apprehension and nervousness) and *fears* (phobias) or by *overpowering drives to perform apparently irrational activities* (obsessive-compulsive acts, such as repeated handwashing). These disorders are estimated to affect perhaps 5 percent of the population, so they are not uncommon. With some exceptions, they are rarely incapacitating, and they may respond well to treatment with tranquilizing drugs or psychotherapy directed at uncovering the unrecognized conflicts that create the problem.

In general, the neurotic patient finds the symptoms of the neurosis—the panic attacks, for example, or the fears or irrational repeated behaviors—very distressing and seeks treatment to eliminate them. This quality distinguishes a neurotic disorder from the same sorts of behavioral problems found in patients with so-called *character* or *personality disorders*. In the latter case, subjects believe that their behaviors, which others find odd or objectionable, are totally justified. Such eccentric behaviors may, in fact, be learned adaptations to conditions of anticipated stress—perhaps an extreme form is the rituals that professional athletes perform when peak ability is required.

In general, patients with neuroses do not show disturbances in reality testing or thought processes, or in the perception of sensory events. This category of mental disorder also includes *dissociative disorders,* in which sufferers disassociate themselves from conflicts in their present situations, real or perceived. The major forms of dissociation are those in which the patient's concept of self undergoes severe alterations: forgetting about large periods of one's life (*psychogenic amnesia);* ignoring the existence of one's own personality (*depersonalization*); and exhibiting more than one personality, each of which predominates at different times, totally altering the subject's behavior patterns and social relationships (*multiple personality disorder*).

VII. Psychoses

The term "disease" is most convincingly applied to these severe mental disorders. There are two forms of psychosis: the *affective disorders* and the *schizophrenias.* Each major form includes several patterns and subclasses of behavioral abnormality. Both of these sets of diseases are severely incapacitating and often chronic, and they virtually always demand therapy. In each case, an accurate diagnosis based on structured interviews and behavioral observations, supplemented by chemical, functional, and structural tests, is the best guide to an informed selection of the best therapy. The partial success of selective drug treatments for the schizophrenias and the affective disorders has helped investigators to deduce possible mechanisms of the underlying physiological malfunction.

analyze the behavioral problem in a more specific manner.

We now come to an important fork in our path to understanding the several different forms of disease that can affect mental capacities. In light of the historical evidence available, we can draw the following, admittedly oversimplified, conclusion about the interpretation of mental disturbances: if the disturbance that brought the patient to the doctor's attention was characterized by a progressive loss of sensory, motor, and mental function, and if at death a postmortem examination was able to reveal, either with

The artist Vincent van Gogh (1853–1890) did this drawing, "Wooded Landscape with Houses," in the village of Auvers shortly before his suicide. Art historians interpret the atypical presentation of natural forms, trees, and cottages as a reflection of his progressive mental disturbance.

or without a microscope, significant and reproducible changes in the structure of the brain, those "neurodegenerative" disorders became the province of the neurologist and were taken as diseases. On the other hand, if the pathologist was unable to observe consistent changes in the brain, despite the continued emotional or intellectual problems of the patient before death, the diagnostic categories constructed of those findings became the province of the psychiatrist. Although there are many exceptions to this generalization, it serves to illustrate an important attitudinal difference that historically has colored the interpretation of abnormal behavior: if it could be seen that there was physically something abnormal about the brain to go with the abnormal behavior, then

the disease was regarded as real; however, in the absence of such objective changes to account for the behavioral problems, the problems were somehow regarded as less real, perhaps even an act played out by the patient to gain attention.

We next examine in some detail three of the most serious neurodegenerative disorders, not only to understand their nature and to contrast them with the psychiatric diseases discussed later in the chapter, but also to recognize their behavioral components and the implications of those behavioral findings for psychiatric diseases, for which the objective signs of chemical or structural pathology are still minimal.

Degenerative Diseases of the Brain

As people live longer by taking advantage of improved treatments for the infectious and cardiovascular diseases that were once unavoidably fatal, the incidence of degenerative disorders of the brain has increased. A degenerative disorder is one in which the disease process is progressive (that is, once the disease starts, it grows unremittingly more severe). Three of the most frequent and devastating degenerative disorders, each named for the physician who first described it, are Parkinson's disease, Huntington's disease, and Alzheimer's disease, and each disease involves the destruction of specific sets of neurons in rather distinctive ways.

Parkinson's Disease

In the early nineteenth century, Dr. James Parkinson, a London physician, observed patients who displayed a rhythmic trembling of the hands and arms while otherwise inactive. When he himself tried to move their arms and legs, he noted an underlying stiffness to the muscle tone that would yield intermittently to continued pulling, producing a cogwheel feeling. These patients had trouble starting movements (like walking or writing) and once started had trouble terminating them. After his description of these findings, other doctors soon reported that they had patients with very similar problems. For almost 150 years, the degenerative disease that Dr. Parkinson had identified was diagnosed, yet physicians had no clues as to what the cause might be and no way to treat it. One of the few signs of the disease in postmortem examinations of the brain was a loss of the pigmented neurons that give the substantia nigra and locus coeruleus their color-descriptive names.

In the late 1950s, after the discovery of the neurotransmitters norepinephrine and dopamine, and the establishment of their presence in normal brains, an Austrian neuropathologist, Dr. Oleh Hornykiewicz, was able to correlate the loss of these black and blue pigmented neurons in Parkinson's disease patients with a dramatic loss of the transmitter dopamine from the brain regions in the basal ganglia. (As discussed in Chapter 4, the basal ganglia initiate programs of movement and monitor them for accuracy of performance while they are going on.) Hornykiewicz also detected losses of norepinephrine and of serotonin. Having found the substantially decreased dopamine and knowing the chemical pathways by which substantia nigra neurons can synthesize dopamine, Hornykiewicz and his colleagues reasoned that it might be possible to force the synthesis of dopamine by dosing the Parkinson's patients with large amounts of its precursor, the amino acid dihydroxyphenylalanine (known by its initials DOPA), which, fortunately, is able to cross the blood/brain barrier. The treatment worked, and now in oral form, DOPA treatment is able to diminish greatly the signs and symptoms of the missing dopamine. (Sometimes DOPA is referred to as L-DOPA; the L has chemical significance to amino acid chemists, since mammals only use the L forms of amino acids, and bacteria use the D forms. Early treatment of Parkinson's with DOPA used mixtures of the L and D forms, but as soon as chemists learned how to get the L out of there, its purification made the drug twice as effective.)

Despite its initial effectiveness in most patients, DOPA treatment does not really slow down the underlying degeneration. After variable periods, from months to years, the disease ceases to respond to the treatment. The reasons for the loss of DOPA effectiveness are not known, but it may be that other systems of degenerating neurons, such as those that produce norepinephrine and serotonin, eventually become more prominently affected. (One other fact is worth noting, for a later section of this chapter: when they are trying to find the right dose of DOPA for a patient, physicians sometimes set the dosage too high. As a result, the patient's symptoms change; they exhibit mania and confusion, symptoms associated with acute schizophrenia.)

The cause of Parkinson's disease is not precisely known. At one time virus infections that affected the brain were held to be the cause. The worldwide epidemic of severe influenza that occurred just at the end of World War I, for example, was thought to be a significant cause of the disease until investigators began to notice that people who were born after that epidemic began to show the disease in their late 50s and 60s too. A recent source of the disease, detected in young people who were drug abusers, was traced to a contaminant of the underground synthesis of heroinlike drugs, producing a toxin that selectively destroys the substantia nigra neurons. Because this toxin is closely related in its chemical structure to certain herbicides, and because the incidence of Parkinson's disease worldwide is related to the degree of industrialization of the area, some epidemiologists (scientists who map the distribution of diseases geographically and demographically, looking for correlative evidence) have suggested that such environmental toxins may be a more frequent cause of Parkinson's disease than has been recognized.

Although there is no way to reverse the disease process once it has begun, scientists continue to look for new ways to restore the person's functioning. One highly innovative method that has cured experimental Parkinson's disease in laboratory animals has recently found some success in human beings. Bits of the center of the adrenal gland (where cells normally make and secrete norepinephrine and epinephrine) have been transplanted into the brains of patients with Parkinson's disease. Once transplanted, the adrenal medullary cells seem to function in part like the lost substantia nigra neurons; in any case, in at least two patients who were unresponsive to DOPA treatment before surgery, significant and long-lasting improvement has been reported. Just how useful and effective this surgical approach may be remains to be determined.

Huntington's Disease

The basal ganglia are also implicated in another serious neurologic disease, described in the late nineteenth century by the American physician George Huntington, on the basis of cases that he, his father, and his grandfather had observed in their practices. This disease generally began in the patients' late 30s and early 40s with mild mental problems, especially forgetfulness and outbursts of temperamental behavior, along with depression. Such behavioral symptoms were sooner or later accompanied by awkward movements, sudden collapses, and uncontrollable flailing movements of the arms and upper body. These movement problems, as

well as slurred speech and worsening mental faculties became progressive, leading to total disability and death.

The most striking feature of this disease, however, was not its dramatic movement disorder and rapid progression of symptoms. The doctors Huntington observed that the disease occurred in clusters within families and followed certain patterns of inheritance, which are termed *autosomal dominant*. To understand this term, recall that every physical trait—hair and skin color, height, and body build—that is inheritable is represented by specific chemical molecules called genes that encode this information in an individual's chromosomes. Human beings have 23 pairs of chromosomes; 22 of these pairs are referred to as autosomes, and one pair, the X and the Y, are called the sex chromosomes. Some diseases, like color blindness and hemophilia, are carried by genes on the sex chromosomes, and these inherited diseases are termed *sex-linked*. Diseases that are inherited from genes on one of the other 22 pairs of chromosomes are called autosomal disorders. When the disease-producing gene is dominant, it needs only to be present in one parent to produce the disease if the child lives long enough.

By following generation after generation of families with Huntington's disease and carefully tabulating the results of the offspring marriages, the Huntington doctors established that the children of any parent whose mother or father had the disease had a 50 percent chance of having the disease too. In those third-generation children who were free of the disease, none of their children or anyone in the following generations would show it, unless a new intermarriage with a mate who carried the disease occurred. Because most Americans in the nineteenth and twentieth centuries had their children during their late teens and early 20s, the disease frequently did not show up in the grandparents until two generations had come into the world. As a result, even the best-intentioned parent had no way of controlling the disease.

Although no treatment exists for victims of Huntington's disease, some progress in detecting its inheritance has been made. By studying the patterns of the disease in a remote South American village where there was extensive inbreeding and a very high incidence of the disease, scientists have determined that the gene for Huntington's disease is carried on a specific part of chromosome 4. A test may soon enable investigators to pinpoint which children of a Huntington's-disease parent have not inherited the gene. (Because there are some cases in which the mental problems appear early and well separated from the later progressive motor problems, some researchers believe that the eventual determination of the nature of this abnormal gene may also help throw light on the inheritable factors involved in such psychiatric diseases as schizophrenia.)

Residents of the village in Northern Venezuala with the high incidence of Huntington's disease.

Alzheimer's Disease

The German physician Alois Alzheimer was the first to describe a case of progressive forgetfulness leading to loss of all mental faculties within a few years in a previously healthy woman in her late 40s. Studying the patient's brain at postmortem, Alzheimer observed major wasting of the cerebral cortex. Using stains that deposited silver salts in the nerve cells and examining thin slices of the stained brain under the microscope, Alzheimer saw that the brain was filled with large collections of fibrils tangled in collections within the nerve cell bodies of the cortex. The progressive loss of mental abilities seen in this patient, and later in other relatively young patients whose brains at autopsy revealed the dramatic nature of the degenerative process, became known as Alzheimer's dementia, or, because it was first described in relatively young people, as pre-

senile dementia. After many cases were studied, age of onset became less important as a distinguishing characteristic, and the progressive loss of mental abilities became more important. Because the disease does not generally appear until a person's late 60s, and because the early symptoms of forgetfulness may be very subtle, a solid diagnosis prior to advanced signs and symptoms is very difficult.

Alzheimer's disease has some of the general features of both Parkinson's disease and Huntington's disease. As in Parkinson's disease, specific changes occur in the brain chemistry. Several neurotransmitters are lost, especially within the cerebral cortex. A number of treatments have been attempted; however, no drug that replenishes those missing transmitters has been more than transiently helpful. In any case, the underlying progressive nature of the disease is not affected by this sort of treatment. As with Huntington's disease, some signs have indicated that inheritability is higher in certain families, but Alzheimer's families have, until recently, been too rare to study in detail. However, very recent international research strongly suggests that in some families Alzheimer's disease is inheritable, and that the gene for the disease is located on chromosome 21, very close to one of the genes that is duplicated in Down syndrome (see Chapter 3). This new information ties in with an older observation that the only other disease in which the brains of the patients show tangles like those of Alzheimer's is Down syndrome. These recent data linking Alzheimer's disease to a specific genetic location keeps alive the possibility of a predictive test for the disease.

An estimated 10 percent of all Americans over age 65 show mild to moderate dementia, of which Alzheimer's is by far the most frequent cause. Alzheimer's disease increases with age up through age 80, and as our population lives longer and longer, the incidence of Alzheimer's disease is anticipated to grow substantially. With more and more people surviving into their 70s, by the end of this century more than 20 percent of the population may be subject to Alzheimer's disease. Since Alzheimer's patients may often survive 10 or more years, with progressive loss of mental function, the high demand their care places on hospital and nursing resources means catastrophic costs for our health care system unless some solution to this problem can be found.

Imagine living at the time when Dr. Alzheimer described his first case of progressive forgetfulness followed by bizarre outbursts of wild behavior and then degeneration in a few short years to the point of total unresponsiveness. When he presented this case to the German Psychiatric Society, he was al-

most booed from the room, as physicians in that era were unprepared to believe that the brain could be the cause of this sort of behavior. Suppose further that he had not stumbled on the right stain to reveal the loss of neurons and the accumulation of the fibril tangles and that nothing obvious had been seen in those brains. What sort of theories might have been raised to explain the disease? In the next section, we examine some other serious diseases of behavior in which the physical findings remain almost, but not completely, invisible.

Diagnosis by Analysis of Behavior

Medical understanding of functional brain disorders accompanied by behavioral problems lags far behind that of most organic brain disorders. A major difference between the two categories lies in whether or not "objective" tests of brain function can successfully detect a source for the disorder. Often patients with problems in cognitive or emotional performance show no abnormality in general medical, sensory, or motor function, in EEGs, brain x-rays, or tests of the cerebrospinal fluid. Even postmortem examination may fail to reveal any source of the problem. Nevertheless, it is standard practice in evaluating a patient with behavior disorder of unknown cause to apply all these diagnostic tests (except, of course, the postmortem) in order to eliminate possible organic causes before starting clinical psychiatric treatment.

But many psychiatrists, led in part by the St. Louis school under Eli Robins, believe that the diagnosis of a psychiatric condition should be based on more than simply the exclusion of organic illness. Considerable disagreement often existed after different psychiatrists had evaluated the same patient, and standard diagnostic tools were clearly needed.

Psychiatrists have therefore begun to adopt generally accepted criteria for diagnosing psychiatric "disease states." On the basis of comparisons of groups of patients with different symptoms and behaviors of specified duration and intensity, doctors have established the criteria that must exist in order for a specific psychiatric diagnosis to be reached. With these criteria being constantly tested and revised, more and more doctors can use consistent diagnostic categories to identify psychiatric diseases rather than relying on their impressions of what the problem might be.

Some of these criteria point to relatively obvious features. How old was the patient when the problems first arose? How long have the problems persisted? Does the patient have associated problems in appetite, sleep, or movement? Are there problems in interacting with other family members or with a peer group? Is there any family history of similar problems? Has the patient suffered any particular stress recently?

The present-day psychiatric interview begins with a brief, uniform doctor-patient exchange called the Mental Status Examination. Generally, the clinician probes the patient's mental and emotional condition within a carefully structured format. Similar questions are asked of all patients. Initial answers are compared with later results as the patient's treatment proceeds. This allows clinicians to track the patient's progress, to gain knowledge about the natural or treated course of the disease itself, and to compare results across different patient populations.

The interview probes seven major areas of mental and emotional functioning.

1. *Consciousness.* Is the patient alert and responsive to the interviewer? Is the patient aware of where, when, and why the interview is taking place?

2. *Affect and emotional tone.* Is the patient's emotional state appropriate for the circumstances? Does the patient exhibit or describe signs that could be interpreted as depression, euphoria, anxiety, fear, aggression, or rage?

3. *Motor behavior.* Is the patient dressed appropriately and able to remain at ease while being interviewed? Does the patient exhibit prolonged posturing or repeat purposeless motor acts (twirling the hair or rubbing the ears or nose, for example)? Does the patient make unusual, abrupt, or purposeless spontaneous movements?

4. *Thinking.* Does the patient express any specific inappropriate ideas or preoccupations about himself or herself ("I am Adolf Hitler!" "Aliens have chosen me to destroy the world.")? Are answers to questions delivered at a normal speed? Does the patient express fears of real or imagined conditions?

5. *Perception.* Does the patient describe an inappropriate awareness of sensations? Does the patient describe nonexistent events (hearing voices or feeling attacks of pain)?

6. *Memory.* Can the patient describe recent and more distant current events correctly? Can the patient perform mental acts requiring memory and concentration?

7. *Intelligence.* Can the patient express a logical flow of ideas or associations in response to a thought problem ("What does this statement mean: A rolling stone gathers no moss?") and arrive at a logical conclusion? Is ability appropriate to educational achievements and occupational history?

Even more structured ways to interview patients have evolved in recent years. These interview formats permit psychiatrists and psychologists to probe for the same general sorts of information. With these common

HAMILTON RATING SCALE

PATIENT _____   DATE _____ TIME _____

RATER _____   SCORE _____

1 DEPRESSED MOOD
(Sadness, hopeless,
helpless, worthless)

0 Absent
1 These feeling states indicated only on questioning
2 These feeling states spontaneously reported verbally
3 Communicates feeling states non-verbally—i.e., through facial expression, posture, voice, and tendency to weep
4 Patient reports VIRTUALLY ONLY these feeling states in his spontaneous verbal and non-verbal communication

2 FEELINGS OF GUILT

0 Absent
1 Self-reproach, feels he has let people down
2 Ideas of guilt or rumination over past errors or sinful deeds
3 Present illness is a punishment. Delusions of guilt
4 Hears accusatory or denunciatory voices and/or experiences threatening visual hallucinations

3 SUICIDE

0 Absent
1 Feels life is not worth living
2 Wishes he were dead or any thoughts of possible death to self
3 Suicide ideas or gesture
4 Attempts at suicide (any serious attempt rates 4)

4 INSOMNIA (EARLY)

0 No difficulty falling asleep
1 Complaints of occasional difficulty falling aleep—i.e., more than $1/2$ hour
2 Complains of nightly difficulty falling asleep

5 INSOMNIA (MIDDLE)

0 No difficulty
1 Patient complaints of being restless and disturbed during the night
2 Waking during the night—any getting out of bed rates 2 (except for purposes of voiding)

6 INSOMNIA (LATE)

0 No difficulty
1 Waking in early hours of the morning but goes back to sleep
2 Unable to fall asleep again if gets out of bed

7 WORK AND ACTIVITITES

0 No difficulty
1 Thoughts and feelings of incapacity, fatigue or weakness related to activities, work or hobbies
2 Loss of interest in activity, hobbies or work—either directly reported by patient, or indirect in listlessness, indecision and vacillation (feels he has to push self to work or join activities)
3 Decrease in actual time spent in activities or decrease in productivity. In hospital, rate 3 if patient does not spend at least three hours a day in activities (hospital job or hobbies) exclusive of ward chores
4 Stopped working because of present illness. In hospital, rate 4 if patient engages in no activities except ward chores, or if patient fails to perform ward chores unassisted

8 RETARDATION
(Slowness of thought and
speech; impaired ability to
concentrate; decreased
motor activity)

0 Normal speech and thought
1 Slight retardation at interview
2 Obvious retardation at inteview
3 Interview difficult
4 Complete stupor

9 AGITATION

0 None
1 Fidgetiness
2 "Playing with" hands, hair, etc.
3 Moving about, can't sit still
4 Hand-wringing, nail-biting, hair-pulling, biting of lips

The first page of the Hamilton Rating Scale.

formats they can evaluate mental function and the stability, fluctuation, or progression of the symptoms. They can also evaluate descriptions by family and friends of events leading up to the patient's problems. Structured interviews focus on precise symptoms and signs as the patient expresses them and provide results roughly equivalent to those of a physical examination in a patient with a neurological problem. While some interview results may lead to specific diagnoses, others do not. In cases where the interview produces no specific diagnosis, clues that need follow-up are pursued in more definitive verbal tests of intellectual function (so-called intelligence testing) and emotional status (personality profiles and affect or self-rating scales), and in tests of language, logic, mathematical, and abstract psychological abilities. (See facing page for an example.)

Along with the ongoing progress in describing specific, reproducible forms of behavior problems and in analyzing a patient's behavior in terms of responses to uniform interviews, an additional strategy has evolved. Objective tests of the brain's chemistry, structure, and function can be combined with psychological findings, to help medical scientists refine the bases for psychiatric diagnosis and select the most appropriate form of treatment.

The Biological Basis of Psychosis

Support for the belief in a biological basis for the major psychiatric diseases comes largely from two sources. Clinical studies on family members related by blood point to the likelihood of genetic factors in susceptibility. In addition, human and animal studies on the effects of drugs that mimic or antagonize brain transmitters strongly suggest that a biological "explanation" exists for many behavioral conditions.

Clinical Studies

Family-pedigree studies show that an unusually high incidence of depression or schizophrenia in a family can sometimes be traced through several generations. Scientists look for a very high "penetrance" of inheritable factors—that is, they look to see how many members of a family have the disease. If the number exceeds that in the general population, the factor is presumed to be inherited. Such patterns exist in some forms of acute intermittent porphyria, in Huntington's disease, and perhaps in Alzheimer's disease, as we have just seen.

Risk studies survey the blood-related family members of a psychotic patient for incidence of psychosis. Scientists then determine whether or not this incidence rate exceeds that for members of a comparable "control" population. In both affective psychosis and in schizophrenia, such studies show that the risk of exhibiting one of these diseases increases directly with the closeness of the genetic relationship to someone with that disease. Evidence that strongly supports inheritable factors emerges from studies of the incidence of psychosis among half siblings, who share only one common biologic parent. The increased incidence of depression or schizophrenia among such siblings over that of the general population indicates the importance in mental illness of shared genetic information.

Twin and *adopted-twin studies* put the link between genetic relatedness and mental disease to an even stricter test. If a genetic link exists, twins should have similar outcomes because they have similar genetic backgrounds. Identical twins, who develop from the same fertilized egg and who share totally identical genetic information, should show the most concordance (that is, if one has the disease, the other twin would also eventually have it). Fraternal twins, who result from the impregnation of two different

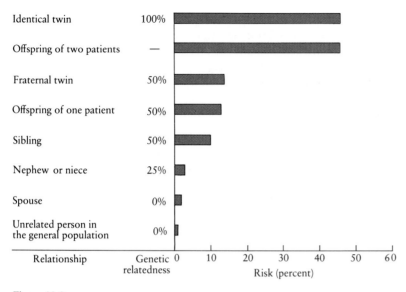

Relationship	Genetic relatedness	
Identical twin	100%	
Offspring of two patients	—	
Fraternal twin	50%	
Offspring of one patient	50%	
Sibling	50%	
Nephew or niece	25%	
Spouse	0%	
Unrelated person in the general population	0%	

Figure 10.2
The risk of developing schizophrenia during one's lifetime is largely a function of genetic relatedness to a schizophrenic rather than of environmental or experiential factors. (Data from Gottesman & Shields, 1982).

ova by different sperm and who share less common genetic background, should be less concordant than identical twins but more concordant than half-brothers or half-sisters. In fact, in schizophrenia, in affective psychosis, and in alcoholism, twin studies do document the very high degree of inheritability predicted by such logic (see Figure 10.2). Even if a twin does not exhibit the disease, the healthy twin's children are just as likely as the children of the psychotic twin to express the susceptibility.

In adopted-twin studies, investigators examine the outcome for twins when one or both are reared by adoptive parents. In this way, one has a means for a "natural" experiment: the genetic backgrounds of the individuals may be identical or at least highly similar but their life environments and experiences will differ. Again the question is, in what proportion of the twin pairs will both show the psychiatric disorder. Adopted-twin studies undertaken in countries like Denmark and Sweden, where medical records are very complete, show that in some 50 percent of such twin pairs, both twins develop the same psychiatric disease. This rate is almost as high as it is when the children grow up with their biological parents, and it strongly suggests that child-rearing practices per se have very little to do with the manifestation of the inheritable trait that makes these children susceptible to the psychiatric disease.

However, it is no simple matter to separate genetic and environmental factors. While such twin and adoption findings document the existence of an inheritable factor, the rate of concordance is never 100 percent in any twin study, even though identical twins share 100 percent of their genes in common. This discrepancy both reveals the difficulties involved in isolating the genetic factor responsible for psychiatric disease and indicates the degree to which environmental influences can affect its expression.

Chemical Studies

Biochemical and physiological tests that precisely measure specific aspects of brain function have already led some researchers to formulate theories about the cellular abnormalities that underlie mental disorders. Perfected to a high degree of accuracy, tests that detect the presence of these abnormalities could eventually be employed in "screening." Such tests, applied objectively to large numbers of people, would make diagnosis possible long before a potential patient developed clear behavioral symptoms.

Psychopharmacology, the study of the effects of drugs on behavior, has led to drug treatments for both schizophrenia and affective psychoses. The success of these treatments strongly suggests that some preexisting chemical abnormality is "treated" by the drugs, and the drugs often do reestablish normal mental function. But the fact that they are not consistently successful in all cases of schizophrenia or affective psychosis suggests that the same symptoms may arise from different biological causes. If the same clusters of signs and symptoms do arise from more than one pathological change, that would help to explain the incomplete patterns of inheritance as well as the failures of drug therapies.

Animal responses to drugs provide another biological model for what may be abnormal in mental diseases. Although the effects of drugs on the behavior of animals do not exactly match those in humans, the fact that an animal can be "depressed" by certain sedatives and "excited" by other drugs suggests that "behavior" can be manipulated by chemical alterations in the brain. When these drugs are found to operate on the same neurotransmitter systems in animals and humans, and when depression and excitement represent opposing effects on that same transmitter system, the assumption of a link between brain chemistry, cell function, and abnormal behavior becomes even more reasonable.

None of these methods alone can establish with certainty that any mental disease of unknown causes can actually be laid to a specific biological factor. But when many lines of evidence lead to the same general conclusion, the case becomes very compelling. Because the case for real but incompletely defined biological bases for affective psychosis and for the schizophrenias is most solid at this time, let us now turn to an examination of those prevalent psychoses.

Affective Psychosis

The Nature of Affective Psychosis

Everyone is occasionally depressed, and this emotional state can almost always be attributed to some cause: a tragedy (the death of a mate, a child, or a parent), or a disappointment (getting a low grade or losing a championship game). The effects of these events may last a few days to a few weeks. A person with psychotic depression has the same general feelings, but they are far more intense and far longer-lasting. Consider the following interview with a depressed patient.

Doctor: I know that you have been feeling depressed, and I think that all of us have ups and downs and the blues sometimes. Is the depression you've been having different from the "ordinary blues"?

Katie: Yes, definitely.

Doctor: What seems so different about it to you?

Katie: Well, you are just so down that you can't manipulate.

Doctor: So when you're depressed you have a lot of trouble functioning?

Katie: Right, uh huh.

Doctor: Is the type of depression you're feeling a kind of sadness or more than that?

Katie: It's more the hopelessness. . . . I can't talk about this.

Doctor: You're really having a hard time talking about these topics?

Katie: Uh huh.

Doctor: When you are depressed do you think it's hard even to think about being depressed?

Katie: Uh huh, and that gets me more upset.

Doctor: Do you think your sleep is affected when you are depressed in this way?

Katie: For several months I don't think I've slept at all.

Doctor: How do you deal with these feelings— being sad and uncomfortable with people?

Katie: To be honest with you, lately, I've just given up. I'm not coping with it very well at all.

Doctor: . . . Does that make you feel that sometimes life is not worth living?

Katie: Yes.

Doctor: Does it help to realize that the guilt and the sadness are really symptoms of an illness and not necessarily the way you have to feel?

Katie: Well, I guess if I could believe that.

Doctor: But you are tending not to believe that?

Katie: I'm having some trouble with my spiritual beliefs right now.

"Affect" is a term scientists use for an overall emotional state, or mood. Thus, "affective psychosis" refers to the psychiatric disease that is expressed in abnormally extreme, long-lasting emotions. Clinically, then, *affective psychosis* is a severe mood disturbance in which prolonged periods of inappropriate depression alternate either with periods of normal mood or with periods of excessive, inappropriate euphoria and mania.

The biblical description of King Saul's behavior—remember that Saul eventually "fell on his own sword"—bears a strong resemblance to present-day manic-depressive disease. First dejected when unable to find his father's mules, then elated when Samuel anointed him ("God gave him another heart"), Saul became inspired to raise an army to challenge the Philistines. Rejected for failing to obey God's will completely ("But the spirit of the Lord departed from Saul and an evil spirit from the Lord troubled him"), he was restored again by the music therapy of his successor-to-be.

In this disease, the sadness, grief, and hopelessness, or the elation and euphoria, are so intense that these emotions persist well beyond the event that may have triggered them. In fact, many times these intense feelings seem to arise with no specific triggering event. Along with the changes in normal mood, patients often describe many other physical and mental complaints: an extreme lack of self-confidence, poor ability to concentrate on anything other than their sadness, intense feelings of hopelessness, despair for the future, and, often, recurrent thoughts of death and suicide. Problems with sleeping and eating are prominent. Some depressed patients experience difficulty falling asleep, awaken early, and lose substantial amounts of weight from lack of appetite. Others sleep and eat excessively.

Affective psychosis takes three major forms. In *unipolar depression,* the patient shows only episodic depressive problems with otherwise normal mood level in between. In *mania,* at the opposite end of the spectrum, the patient has episodes of being inappropriately elated, unconcerned about important problems, overconfident, and hyperactive in both motor and speech patterns, with thoughts jumping quickly from one subject to another. Bursting with apparently endless energy, the manic patient has little need for sleep. The most common form of this disease, *bipolar,* or *manic-depressive, psychosis* is characterized by alternating periods of depression and mania, sometimes with very brief periods of normal emotional behavior in between. In the discussion that follows, we consider affective disease as one general phenomenon because many psychiatrists view the different expressions of the disease as variations on the same underlying, but unknown, thematic biological problem.

Incidence of Affective Psychosis

Many people with severe depressions never report their problems to a doctor or a hospital, so figures on how many people have the disorder must be imprecise. Several different estimates in many countries, however, show that depression is clearly the most prevalent psychiatric disease. Affective psychosis may account for up to 70 percent of the psychiatric diagnoses in a general medical practice. Statistics based on U.S. population figures indicate that about 1 out of 4 adults will experience some form of severe affective disturbance at some time in their lives. Twelve of every 100 adult men and 18 of every 100 adult women will see a psychiatrist, a clinical psychologist, or a general physician and be diagnosed as having affective psychosis. In the United States, 3 to 4 percent of adults may be receiving treatment for their depres-

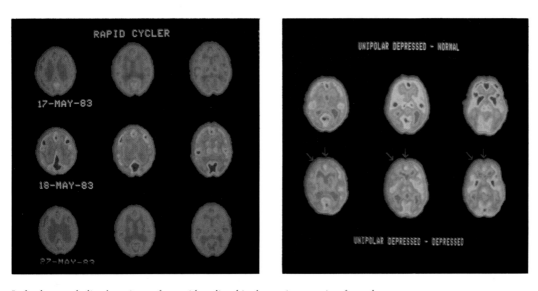

Left, the metabolic alterations of a rapid-cycling bipolar patient moving from depression to mania. Each row of the PETT scans displays three different sections of the brain. The center row illustrates a hypomanic phase, while the top and bottom rows illustrate two different states of depression. Right, metabolic alteration in a unipolar depression patient. In the top row, the patient is in a normal good mood. In the bottom row, the patient is depressed. During the depression, metabolic activity is reduced most prominently in the frontal cortex and anterior cingulate.

sion at any given time. Suicide, which many psychiatrists and psychologists attribute directly to affective psychosis, may account for more than 25,000 deaths per year, making it a leading cause of death.

A direct relationship exists between the patient's age and frequency of different kinds of affective problems. Bipolar disorder may begin in one's 20s and 30s, while unipolar depressions are most frequent in later life, especially during one's 40s to 60s.

Diagnosis of Affective Psychosis

When a doctor receives a patient complaining of problems with affect, the first interview questions may focus on how long the symptoms have been present, whether the person has ever had such problems before, and whether there are associated sleep and appetite disturbances or other physical symptoms. Next, the doctor determines whether the patient has any of the diseases found in other organs that sometimes produce severe emotional problems: certain infections; disorders of the thyroid or adrenal glands; the so-called "autoimmune" diseases, such as systemic lupus erythematosis, which lead to inflammation of connective tissues and joints; and certain degenerative disorders of the nervous system, such as Alzheimer's disease and Parkinson's disease. If the doctor rules out all of these diseases and if the affective symptoms have been present for more than two weeks, a diagnosis of affective psychosis can be strongly considered. (Table 10.2 distinguishes the symptoms of psychotic depression from those of neurotic depression.)

In addition to describing the patient's complaints and their duration, frequency,

Table 10.2 *Diagnostic distinctions between forms of depression*

Feature	Psychotic	Neurotic
Precipitating events	Absent, rare	Frequent
Thought and motor problems	Frequent	Rare
Daily pattern	Worse in A.M.	Worse in P.M.
Sleep problems	Early awakening	Onset problems
Weight loss	Often	Rare
Self-regard	Self-reproach, guilt	Self-pity
Course	More acute	More chronic
Previous personality	Normal	Usually normal
Dexamethasone suppression test	Frequently abnormal	Usually normal
REM latency	Short	Normal

and variations, the clinician might use additional procedures in reaching a diagnosis. Two such tests have recently been found to provide objective information that distinguishes many subjects with affective psychosis from the temporary or chronic neurotic forms of depression. One test focuses on sleep problems, while the other isolates disturbances in the way the brain regulates the endocrine system (see pages 334 and 335).

Although sleep disturbances are a frequent complaint of the depressed patient, only within the past three decades have researchers employed electroencephalographic (EEG) recordings to analyze the brain's activity during sleep. Today computers are used to examine the sleep EEG records of large numbers of patients and to measure more precisely the duration of the several different stages of sleep (see Chapter 6). Recently, emphasis has been focused on how long it takes the patient to fall asleep and reach the stage of rapid-eye-movement (REM) sleep. Such studies appear to show that psychotically depressed patients take less time—about 55 minutes on the average after falling asleep—to enter into their first REM sleep episode. This is slightly less than half the time required by normal subjects, or

those with neurotic depressions. Depressed patients who enter REM quickly often show very favorable responses to antidepressant drugs.

Is sleep abnormality a cause or a side-effect of an underlying brain disease that leads to depression? Are altered sleep-stage durations an expression of this brain problem? No one as yet has a biological explanation of how psychotic depression influences the neuronal circuits that regulate sleep.

The Possible Biological Basis of Affective Psychosis

Much of what passes for a biological explanation of affective disease stems from chance observations of the behavioral effects of certain drugs used on humans and on animals for other purposes. Observation of these changes in behavior has led to biochemical studies of what those drugs did to certain neurotransmitters in the brains of animals. A few examples illustrate this roundabout way of developing drugs and their role in the search for the bases of mental illnesses.

In the early 1950s, the essential component of an Indian-root medication was developed in the United States as a sedative to treat schizophrenia and, in lesser doses, high blood pressure. Animals given this drug, known as *reserpine*, showed sedation and loss of spontaneous motion. Human subjects given the drug for high blood pressure also became depressed, and frequently suicidal. Apparently reserpine induced a "chemical depression." Later, this drug was shown to deplete the brain's contents of three transmitters: norepinephrine, serotonin, and dopamine. This suggested that the loss of these three transmitters was a cause for the behavioral depression.

At about this time, tuberculosis patients given a new drug, which was thought to help the effectiveness of certain antibiotics, became hyperactive, exhibiting mania-like symptoms. This effect depended on the ability of the new drug to block a brain and liver enzyme, *monoamine oxidase* (or MAO), which normally breaks down the same three transmitters that are depleted by reserpine. This evidence, combined with the reserpine effects, was interpreted to mean that inhibition of MAO might prolong the actions of these neurotransmitters and produce mania. In addition, *amphetamine,* a stimulant drug, was found to activate release of the catecholamines dopamine and norepinephrine. These and other findings led the American psychiatrists Joseph Schildkraut and Seymour Kety to propose a *catecholamine hypothesis of depression,* in which they conceived of depression as caused by a loss of transmission at the catecholamine synapses in the brain.

Later, antidepressant drugs were also found to produce their effects specifically on these transmitters. Normally, the catecholamines, serotonin, and certain other neurotransmitters are reaccumulated by the nerve terminals that secrete them. But the antidepressant drugs were found to block this reuptake process specifically at norepinephrine, dopamine, and serotonin terminals. This action was seen as prolonging the presence of the amines on the synapses of the receiving cells. Thus, the hypothesis went, the drugs worked because they helped restore an underlying deficiency in the process of catecholamine transmission.

Once a testable statement of this clarity is put forward, researchers can run tests that strengthen or weaken the initial hypothesis. Some of these tests have yielded results that are difficult to reconcile with the original idea. For example, less than 10 percent of people treated with reserpine actually get depressed, yet all of them show catecholamine and serotonin depletion. Recall that the catecholamines and serotonin can be chemically grouped under the more general term monoamine (see Chapter 2). In addition, many other effective antidepressants have no obvious effects on monoamine reuptake. Furthermore, the drugs often take several days to begin to improve the patient's affect, even though the effects on reuptake are present immediately. Lastly, mania and the manic phase of manic-depressive psychosis both respond very well to long-term treatment with small doses of the salts of lithium, even though this treatment has no specific effect on the catecholamine systems. These extended tests, therefore, have not in general confirmed the catecholamine hypothesis.

In the past decade, scientists have turned their attention to the longer-term effects of drug treatments, and particularly to explanations for the lag between treatment and improvement. Many of the studies have focused on measuring the effectiveness of synaptic transmission by norepinephrine or serotonin. Cellular responsiveness to these transmitters was found to shift in concert with changing intensities of synaptic transmission. Responsiveness increases when amine supplies are depleted and decreases when amine supplies are augmented (see Figure 10.3). The time required to undergo these "up" or "down" regulations of responsiveness is generally 3 to 7 days. Some scientists believe that this delay accounts for the delay in clinical response, and that the regulation of synaptic responsiveness is the primary event being treated. If transmitter chemistry correlates with affect on the level of synaptic responsiveness, then the catecholamine hypothesis could well require further revision.

In any case, much more work is required to sort out differences between individual patients and their responses to specific drugs. For example, some measurements of transmitter metabolism made on spinal fluid have detected two separate subgroups of psychotically depressed patients. Those with lower

Chemical Tests of Psychosis

In the case of the neurodegenerative disorders, we saw how useful it was for understanding the nature of the diseases to have an objective physical test that revealed something of the abnormality—loss of pigmented cells in Parkinson's disease; loss of neurons in Huntington's; and the accumulation of neuronal tangles, loss of cerebral cortex mass, and loss of neurotransmitters in Alzheimer's disease. Furthermore, the establishment of the precise patterns of inheritance in Huntington's disease, and in at least some forms of Alzheimer's disease, led to the identification of chromosomal abnormalities which may soon shed light on exactly what is missing or extra in these chromosomes and which brain cells have the broken gene.

However, as we have also seen, despite the application of a lot of effort, little similar objective evidence of pathology has turned up thus far in schizophrenia or in depression. One test that has received some attention in this

way emerged from the studies on abnormalities in the sleep cycles of depressed patients and attempts to understand the endocrine system's role in the abnormal sleep.

Evaluating the regulatory effectiveness of the endocrine system in depressed patients depends on an experimental procedure known as the *dexamethasone suppression test* (DST). The drug dexamethasone suppresses the signals coming from the brain and pituitary that drive the adrenal cortex to secrete natural cortisone. Normally, when the adrenal glands release cortisone into the bloodstream, the brain and the pituitary recognize the presence of the adrenal

The dexamethasone suppression test provides a means to assess the relative status of the brain's control over the pituitary/adrenal axis. In a typical program, the patient receives a small oral dose of dexamethasone, a powerful synthetic version of the cortisone normally made and secreted by the cells of the adrenal cortex. Under usual conditions, this small dose of the powerful steroid would signal the brain to suppress further secretion of the hypothalamic corticotropin-releasing factor and of the pituitary adrenocorticotropin-releasing hormone (ACTH). In response, urinary excretion of natural adrenal steroids would greatly diminish for the next 12 to 18 hours. In patients with adrenal tumors, and in other patients undergoing extreme stress, like that which occurs in some forms of affective psychosis, dexamethasone fails to suppress the brain and pituitary hormone signals, and adrenal steroids continue to be excreted in the urine in normal or excess amounts. This failure to suppress adrenal steroid production has been employed as a research tool to discover the presence of some forms of depression.

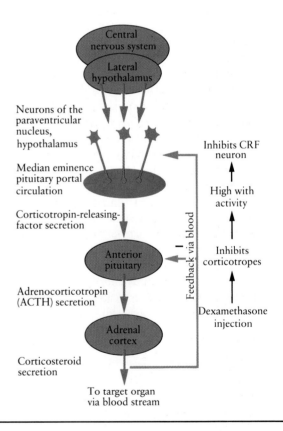

steroid and stop activating further secretion. Dexamethasone, a powerful synthetic version of natural cortisone used to treat allergic and inflammatory diseases, overrides a normal person's own cortisone secretions. In the presence of the drug, the responses of the brain and pituitary to the feedback signal can be tested.

Chronic abnormal hyperactivity of the adrenal cortex, such as that caused by tumors of the adrenal gland, is reflected in a loss of this feedback. In the presence of continuous hyperactivity, dexamethasone cannot suppress the brain and pituitary signals that cause the adrenal glands to secrete steroids. (A number of other medical conditions, such as diabetes mellitus, also cause failure to suppress steroid secretion.) Psychotically depressed patients do fail to suppress their steroid secretion, although they have no detectable problems with either the adrenal or the pituitary glands. In the neurotic forms of depression, steroid secretion is suppressed more effectively by dexamethasone.

Despite initial enthusiastic reception, the success of the dexamethasone test as a diagnostic procedure to discriminate chemically between psychotically depressed patients and neurotically depressed patients still has a long way to go. This does not mean that the idea of such a test is silly. More likely it means that scientists have not yet recognized all the variables that need to be evaluated in the interpretation of suppression and nonsuppression.

A potential diagnostic procedure that is receiving more limited attention is the use of Positron Emission Tomography (see Figure 10.1). Positrons are emitted from certain unstable isotopes of oxygen and fluorine; scientists make use of these isotopes to label molecules like glucose, and they employ positron detectors around the patient's head, connected to powerful computers that determine the source of the positron-emitting compounds within the brain. Normally, the results of this test are expressed as colors across a spectrum, the most heavily labeled brain areas being white-red, and the least heavily labeled being blue. In individual patients examined while depressed and during recovery, selective decreases in brain metabolism, especially over the frontal lobe areas, have been observed. However, the test is still only a research tool; it is quite expensive to use, and has not yet been repeated in a large enough series of subjects to determine whether the brain's decreased use of glucose causes the depression or reflects the depression and whether metabolic conditions besides depression might show similar changes.

While such endocrine work continues, very recent studies have suggested another avenue, which could eventually provide a means of chemical diagnosis. That avenue is the search for genetic markers. The new tests come from attempts to identify the nature of the transmission of depression across generations within communities that: (1) are geographically well-defined; (2) keep excellent family records; (3) permit limited access to the outside world; and (4) are treated by psychiatrists who use diagnostic criteria that are comparable to those in common scientific use. Recent studies suggest that there may be multiple genetic markers capable of predicting which offspring of a family may inherit factors that increase their risk of developing depression. In a study of manic-depressive illness in the Amish population of southeastern Pennsylvania, a linked genetic marker on chromosome 11 showed a high degree of correlation across three generations over four different families. In an unrelated study of depression among the non-Askenazi Jews in Israel, the genetic marker seemed to be linked to the X chromosome.

Although all these studies will require validation through replication by other groups of researchers, biological underpinnings for the psychoses are beginning to emerge.

levels of the metabolic by-products, or *metabolites,* of norepinephrine show better responses to a norepinephrine-directed antidepressant than to other antidepressants.

Those with very low levels of serotonin metabolites form a group with a much higher incidence of suicide. However, much has been learned about neurotransmitters since these simple theories were generated more than 30 years ago. Today, many researchers would avoid the conclusion that such diseases are built on one single specific chemical transmitter system.

Other Forms of Treatment

Aside from drug treatments, two other forms of therapy for affective psychosis are in active use. A 4- to 8-day series of electroconvulsive (or shock) treatments (ECT) can be very helpful. In these treatments the patient is given a very short-acting general anesthetic and a muscle relaxant, and then a generalized convulsion is induced by applying electrical stimulation to the brain through electrodes on the scalp. These treatments are

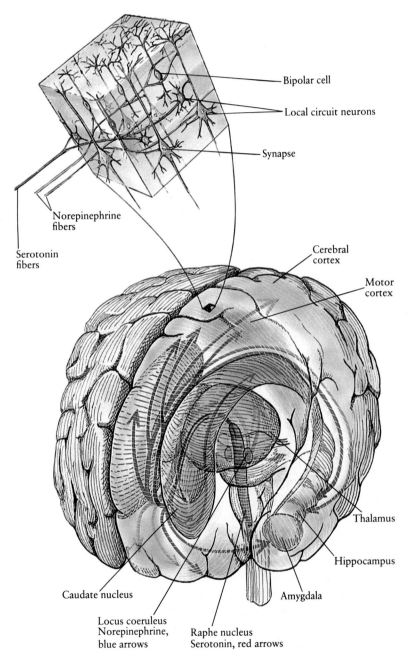

Bipolar cell

Local circuit neurons

Synapse

Norepinephrine fibers

Serotonin fibers

Cerebral cortex

Motor cortex

Thalamus

Hippocampus

Amygdala

Caudate nucleus

Locus coeruleus Norepinephrine, blue arrows

Raphe nucleus Serotonin, red arrows

Figure 10.3
A schematic representation, based on experimental work with animal brains, of the possible circuitry in the human brain of two monoamine neurotransmitters that may be implicated in affective disorder.

Serotonin (red arrows): The raphe nuclei of the pons and brainstem extend their divergent axons toward selected target neurons throughout the central nervous system. These thin axons act to modify the activity of neurons in many brain regions, and, in some cases of affective psychosis, these neurons may be underactive. Antidepressants can supplement the amount of synaptically released serotonin by decreasing active reuptake of the serotonin being released from synaptic locations.

Norepinephrine (blue arrows): The locus coeruleus extends a highly divergent, branched circuitry toward selected target neurons in almost all areas of the forebrain, midbrain, and cerebellum. According to some hypotheses, norepinephrine-mediated transmission may be overactive in mania and underactive in depression. Thus, antidepressant drugs would act to supplement this underactive transmission. Although serotonin and norepinephrine fibers take similar general routes, their circuits appear to involve different target neurons.

always given in the hospital under vigilant medical care.

ECT often provides a dramatic and rapid improvement in mood. Indeed, ECT apparently leads to permanent remission of the depressive episode over the next several days in nearly two-thirds of the patients. The bases for the therapeutic action of ECT are unknown, and continued treatment with other forms of antidepressant medication may also be necessary

Although an objective description of shock therapy may sound a bit barbaric, the rapid positive effects on patient mood are dramatic. Except for short-term amnesia, which may be critical for the therapeutic effect, no other serious side-effects are found. Therefore, the use of ECT has much to recommend it.

In certain cases of depression, one treatment that is still experimental directly confronts alterations in the patient's sleep patterns. Cyclically depressed patients show insomnia the night before their mood switches from depression to mania. Extending this observation, researchers have found that depressed patients with severe sleep disturbances show brief (2- to 5-day) improvements when kept awake and active all night. The resetting of daily rhythms by the one night of enforced wakefulness may help resynchronize the patient's rhythms and lead to more balanced affect. Support for this therapeutic procedure, still to come, might provide insight into the nature of the relationship between the rhythm-regulating brain centers (described in Chapters 6 and 7).

Some patients who show so-called "winter depression" have benefited from exposure to full-spectrum indoor lighting that stimulates the sun's light during the long winter (see Chapter 6). One basis for this effect, seen in a few patients, could be that seasonal variations superimpose their ultradian rhythms on the patient's daily rhythms.

The Schizophrenias

The group of psychiatric disorders known as the schizophrenias are perhaps the most devastating, puzzling, and frustrating of all mental illnesses. The schizophrenias are defined medically as a group of severe and generally chronic disturbances of mental function, characterized by disturbed thinking, feeling, and behaving. They are referred to as a *group* of diseases, and have been ever since the Swiss psychiatrist Eugen Bleuler coined the term "schizophrenia" in 1908.

The Nature of the Schizophrenias

A simple—perhaps overly simple—summary of the symptoms of schizophrenia includes: (1) disorders of perception (hearing voices or smelling "poison" gas); (2) disorders of emotion (laughing or crying at completely inappropriate times, often with rapid shifts from one extreme response to the other); and (3) disorders of thinking, especially very loose associations (the appearance of a car may lead to thoughts of a face, and the face, to the faces of those who are chasing one or trying to control one's brain). Many of Gerry Smith's peculiar-sounding statements quoted at the beginning of the chapter fit these general categories of the schizophrenic disease picture.

The overall behavior of schizophrenic patients is primarily characterized by abnormally distorted perceptions of what is real and what is not. Some patients hear voices, or sense extreme threat from everyday images—the face of their mother or their husband, for instance. They believe that their ideas of the world are imposed on their minds by outside forces, and thus overcome, they are unable to separate fact from fantasy. The specific course in individual patients can be highly varied, however. Sometimes a specific stressful life event seems to precipitate the onset of thought and behavioral prob-

Gerry Smith is diagnosed as schizophrenic. His family allowed him to be interviewed on television and offered some photographs of his childhood. About allowing a camera crew to film his schizophrenic son, the father of Gerry Smith says; "It's awful bad when you only got one kid too because . . . we loved the boy and we done everything we could for him. I just hope the people, and the public can understand what . . . we're doing. I hope it helps the public. It may not help us, it may not help Gerald. I certainly hope it helps somebody. It certainly won't do them no harm, would it? That's the way we feel about it."

When Gerry talks about himself, he displays the disordered thinking characteristic of the schizophrenic. "I'm a very sensitive person and I pick up . . . I pick up a lot of . . . I pick up very sensitive things. The least little bit of aggression of a person's face freaks me out . . . I'm afraid I will be killed . . . by a Martin Luther King . . . type of thing."

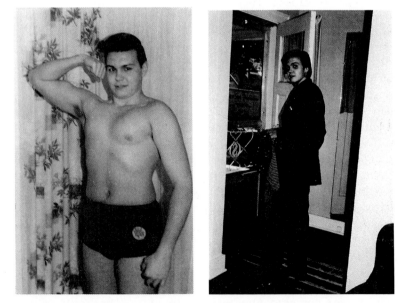

His mother looks through the family album. "When this one here was made, we had moved to a different location and at that point his allergies had started real bad. And this one was made on a Sunday, we might have been getting ready to go to church, I don't remember, and they decided they'd make the picture. He always had to clown with his face."

"Then he decided that he'd gained too much weight so he'd go on a crash diet. And he did. And he went from looking like that to looking like this. Which wasn't to me a healthy look. And that was when he started going downhill, or what you would say, but that's when his sickness probably started coming to a head."

lems. More often, no such specific casual event can be identified. Some patients improve quickly, while others remain disturbed, with episodes of extremely aberrant behavior persisting for years.

Many patients show a loss of the ability to concentrate, to relate one set of observations to another in a logical way. Others retain highly logical or effective thinking in some parts of their lives but lose it with minimal provocation. At the same time, schizophrenic patients are unable to generalize, to find the common features in, for example, a table and a chair, an apple and an orange. This inability to make general abstractions is said to arise from an extremely "concrete" way of looking at the world.

Some patients giggle incessantly, despite the situation at hand. Others sit mute and motionless for hours. Still others show periods of extremely disruptive aggressive behavior and require restraint to avoid hurting themselves or others. These few patterns only hint at the wide variation in schizophrenic presentations that caused Bleuler to call them "the schizophrenias."

It seems clear that a disturbance of the thinking process occurs in all of these patients. But it is not at all clear that the same, unknown cause is the source of the problem in all cases, or that these extremely varied clinical problems can have the same fundamental biological basis. Another perplexing point about this group of thinking abnormalities is their episodic nature. Some schizophrenic patients can behave and function quite normally for long periods of time, with only occasional lapses into severe states of disorientation and delusions.

Incidence of the Schizophrenias

The schizophrenias are a major health problem, accounting for a very high proportion, perhaps more than 50 percent, of the admissions to psychiatric hospitals. Looked at in another way, this group of diseases represents more than one-fourth of all the patients in any hospital at any given time. In the United States, more than 300,000 new cases of schizophrenia are diagnosed every year.

The incidence of schizophrenia can be estimated in very personal terms. If you survive to age 55, you have a 1 in 100 chance of being diagnosed as a schizophrenic. More than half of those diagnosed are under 30, and the peak period for showing the signs of the disease fall between ages 20 and 30. Men tend to express their disease at younger ages than women. Because schizophrenia can be a lifelong illness and because it often begins early in adult life, the disease accounts for a substantial loss of potential productivity. Obviously, it represents a major human tragedy when it strikes.

Basic Types of Schizophrenia

Clinical studies of patients with schizophrenia over the past several decades have suggested a split in this diagnostic category. Each of the two basic forms of the disease has a characteristic course, and each responds in a partially predictable way to the major forms of treatment. Psychiatrists had long found it difficult to understand the relationship between the "positive symptoms" that are suffered by some schizophrenics—hallucinations, thought disorders, and delusions—and the "negative symptoms" expressed by others—loss of emotional responses, inanimate postures, loss of spontaneous speech, and general lack of motivation. These two categories of symptoms had been described in the early 1900s by Bleuler and by his contemporary, the German psychiatrist Emil Kraepelin. In the early 1980s, the English psychiatrist Tim Crow suggested that each set of symptoms might, in fact, represent a different disease process. Those with the positive symptoms he refers to as type I, those with the negative symptoms, as type II.

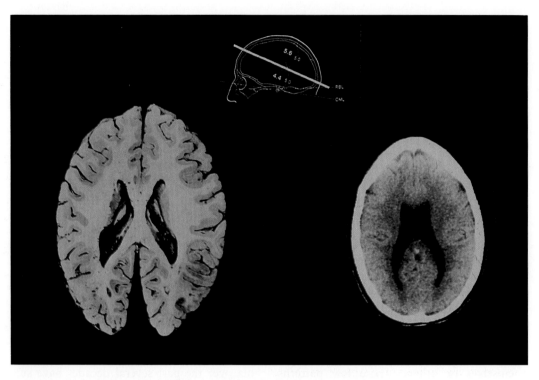

A Computerized Axial Tomogram (CAT) scan allows the psychiatrist to see the surface of the brain and the outlines of the ventricles. In comparison to the normal brain (left), the brain of the schizophrenic (right) shows greatly enlarged ventricles, indicating a wasting process in the cerebral cortex.

Other psychiatrists take issue with this split because sometimes the same patient can show type-I and type-II symptoms at different times or even simultaneously. The distinction, however, seems to have some value in predicting responsiveness to antipsychotic medications. Such drugs are generally most useful in type-I patients and least useful in type IIs. Furthermore, type-I patients show little or no brain abnormality, while those with type-II disease often show loss of brain size, with shrinkage of the cerebellum and of the cerebral ventricles (see figure above).

The two basic subtypes also show substantial differences in the long-term course of the disease. In a study of several hundred schizophrenics in Germany, those patients

who presented with complaints of acute onset of hallucinations (almost always the delusion of voices speaking to them) had the best outcomes. Most of these patients also showed delusions and paranoia—that is, they based their behavior on an unreal but organized series of conclusions. Such patients, for example, may believe that they are Jesus Christ or Napoleon, or that there is a plot to assassinate them. An optimistic outcome was especially likely if the abnormalities in thinking and behaving developed suddenly (in less than 6 months) in patients who had previously shown a fairly normal life pattern, including normal interactions with other people. The most pessimistic outcomes were found in subjects who had long histories of personality or behavior problems, who did not do well in school or social interactions, and in whom the onset of florid symptoms was more gradual. Except for those who first expressed their abnormal thought patterns immediately after delivering a child, precipitating events had no obvious value in predicting outcome.

When well-studied groups of schizophrenic patients are followed for long periods of time, some interesting findings emerge. About one-fourth of all the patients may be expected to have a complete recovery and to have no obvious residual signs of having had the disease. More than half of the remainder also show substantial improvement but nevertheless show some residual signs, such as occasional memory or sleep problems, or not feeling exactly "right," or just not being able to tolerate tension and stress very well. This group of schizophrenic patients does especially poorly when they return to disruptive family situations. Some psychiatrists view this as an indication that the disruptive family life actually led to the disease.

About three-fourths of those who do improve do so within the first 3 years after the diagnosis is made. Those given antipsychotic drugs show greater improvement, faster. Those who do not respond during their first 3 years after diagnosis, however, do not actually show the progressive decline in function that was once the expected outcome. In fact, many cases of complete recovery 20 or 30 years after the initial appearance of the disease have been documented.

Biological Clues to the Nature of the Schizophrenias

Converging lines of research have led to the modern view that the schizophrenic diseases have a biological basis.

1. A *strong genetic factor* would seem to account for the fact that there is a higher

The chances of four identical quadruplets being diagnosed as schizophrenic are 1 in 2 billion, and the Genain sisters, shown here at their 51st birthday party, are that case. Problems for Nora, Iris, Myra, and Hester began in high school, and the women have been in and out of hospitals since then. Inasmuch as they share identical genetic material, doctors at the National Institute of Mental Health believe that the variations in the degree of their illnesses stem from differential family treatment.

incidence of schizophrenia in people who are related to a known schizophrenic than there is in the general population.

2. *Psychosis-inducing* (or *psychotogenic*) drugs, whose mechanisms of action can be related to specific brain transmitter systems, can produce some signs and symptoms that resemble certain kinds of symptoms in schizophrenic subjects.

3. *Antipsychotic drugs* help many schizophrenic patients to achieve a positive therapeutic response, which can be directly related to the drug's ability to interfere with certain specific chemical transmitter systems.

These fundamental observations suggest that specific brain parts and specific chemical systems may be disturbed by the underlying disease process. Further work will help to put these parts of the schizophrenic puzzle

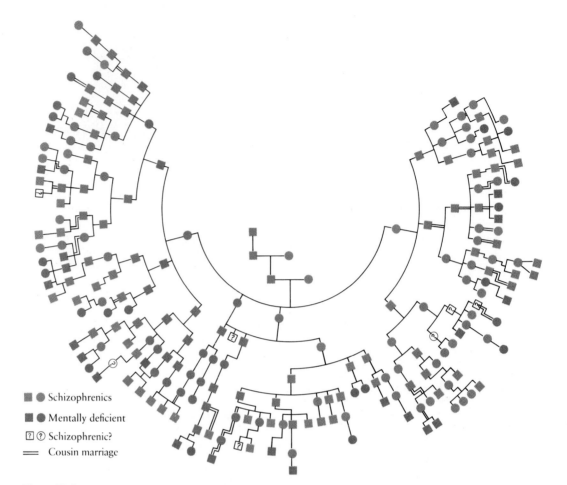

Figure 10.4
The diagrams here and on the facing page illustrate the incidence of schizophrenia and of mental retardation within two very large families living in an isolated community in far northern Sweden. Excellent medical records were available to the investigators. Marriage partnerships among the earliest ancestors are linked by horizontal lines, and the offspring of a marriage by vertical lines. For the four most recent generations, the four outermost rings in each family, colors encode the most probable diagnosis as schizophrenia (in green), mental retardation (in blue), or presumed normal (in pink). While there has been some inbreeding, as shown when double lines indicate marriages between cousins, there is an extraordinarily high propagation of severe disease in almost all children, indicating that the end result cannot be attributed solely to "inbreeding" (from Wetterberg et al., 1981).

into a more logical framework. However, before we discuss this evidence in detail, it is proper to point out that no specific causes of schizophrenia have yet been directly identified.

The Genetics of Schizophrenia   Many psychiatrists have noted that the chances of having schizophrenia increase with the degree to which a person is directly related to someone already known to have schizophrenia. In

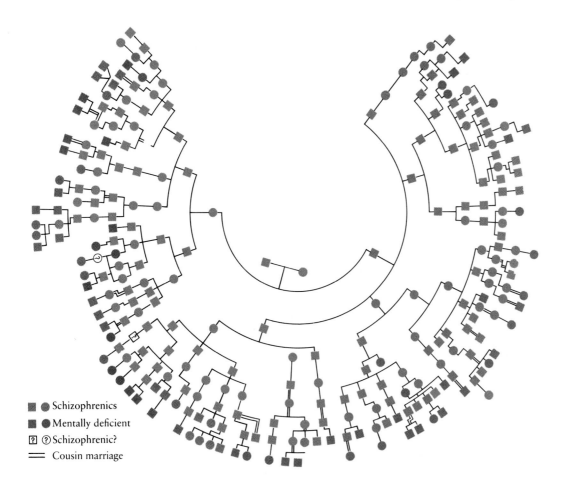

■● Schizophrenics
■● Mentally deficient
? ? Schizophrenic?
══ Cousin marriage

some parts of the world, certain remote parts of Sweden, for example, the incidence of schizophrenia within certain family pedigrees is very high (see Figure 10.4).

We said earlier that for those who survive to age 55, the chances of being diagnosed as a schizophrenic are about 1 out of 100. However, for those who are identical twins of a schizophrenic, the odds increase to nearly 1 in 2. The reasons for this are the same as those that account for the familial patterns in affective psychosis. A fraternal twin of a schizophrenic has about one-third the chance of developing schizophrenia as an identical twin, but that is still 14 times more

likely than for a person who is unrelated to a schizophrenic. Children born to two schizophrenic parents have almost as great a chance of becoming schizophrenic as identical twins—about 1 in 2. Other close relatives of schizophrenics, first cousins, brothers, sisters, or even half-brothers and half-sisters, also show, on average, an increased incidence of schizophrenia over the general public.

Given these genetic tendencies, it is tempting to conclude that the brain conditions that cause schizophrenia must have some biological basis. This conclusion might misinterpret the facts, however. After all, if identical twins are truly identical in all their inherited biological properties, why is the incidence of schizophrenia not 100 percent in both twins? This incomplete expression strongly suggests that environmental factors—perhaps the supports of family or friends and the stresses of growing up—must also have a lot to do with "becoming schizophrenic." Some clinicians, in fact, take the position that an abnormal parent behaves in a way that transmits the behavioral disorder to the children, and that twins or other close relatives might simply share this similar environment.

Adopted-twin studies provide a partial answer to such views. Identical twins born of schizophrenic parents who are brought up in different family settings still share the same high incidence of becoming schizophrenic as they would if their own parents reared them. Even related children of schizophrenics who are not twins and who are reared by adopted families that are not schizophrenic show the expected high incidences. The adopted-out children of nonschizophrenic parents raised in those families show no increase in incidence. One other interesting possibility raised early on by critics of the twin studies was that perhaps just being a twin was enough to increase the incidence of schizophrenia. This question is relatively easy to answer. Twins as a group do not show any higher incidence of schizophrenia than the average population.

The genetics of schizophrenia is relatively complicated, but it still speaks a clear message. Some inheritable predisposing "factor" can lead to the development of schizophrenia. What might such a factor be, and how might it "produce" a disease?

Let us hypothesize a *schizogenic*, that is, a "schizophrenia-producing," bacterium or virus. Such an infection might be "caught" in early childhood from a close sibling or parent and remain latent in the brain until later in life. Brain-infecting viruses with such long latencies are now recognized, and an inheritable factor might make some people more susceptible than others. The spinal fluid of chronic, or type-II schizophrenics may, indeed, show signs of infection with viruses, such as cytomegalovirus, that can be harbored in cells and destroy them slowly over many years. The structural atrophy seen in the brains of type-II patients (see figures on page 345) could be viewed as loss of brain tissue from a progressive virus infection. Behavioral changes, then, might not be unlike the dementia that came with long-term syphilis.

Local environmental factors, such as contaminated food or water supplies in a particular geographical region, could also be imagined. For example, the west coast of Ireland, the northwestern coast of Yugoslavia, and the northern part of Sweden have much higher incidences of schizophrenia than other parts of the world. Due to their relative social isolation, those areas may also offer greater frequencies for some inbreeding to enlarge the susceptible population. Similarly, there are about two-and-a-half times as many admissions per person for schizophrenia in the New England states as in the Middle West. The explanations for such high-incidence pockets of schizophrenia have yet to be discovered.

Biochemical Hypotheses of Schizophrenia

Other views of the underlying causes of schizophrenia have focused on biochemical models. Such views hold that enzymes in the brain of the schizophrenic may produce some abnormal chemical that causes the signs and symptoms. The discovery that the drug LSD could produce vivid visual hallucinations encourages this idea, but research on LSD has produced no significant insight into the nature of actual schizophrenia, in which LSD-type hallucinations (colorful, amorphous, and visual) are extremely rare. Researchers have suggested several possible psychosis-producing chemicals, but when other workers look for them, they cannot confirm their existence.

The endorphin transmitters have also been considered. An abnormal version of this transmitter might directly cause the signs and symptoms of schizophrenia. Or failure to produce enough of the right endorphin, in combination with genetic and enviornmental influences, might be a destabilizing factor. But attempts to measure abnormalities of specific transmitter systems in the brains of schizophrenics have not been very illuminating as yet, either.

Another approach to deciphering the puzzle of schizophrenia has been taken in studies that focus on one transmitter system in the brain, a system discussed earlier in connection with the regulation of movement and the movement deficits of Parkinson's disease. That neurotransmitter is dopamine.

Dopamine and Schizophrenia Two lines of research and chance observation have led to an increased interest in the hypothesis that abnormalities in dopamine transmission in the brain may play an important part in the expression of schizophrenia.

One line of evidence comes from the abuse of amphetamine, a drug whose chemical structure is very similar to that of dopamine. Much hard research work suggests that the dopamine system is critical to the excitatory hyperactivity that amphetamine produces. Human beings who dose themselves with large amounts of amphetamine crave the ecstatic, excited feeling that the drug produces. Continued use of the drug leads to tolerance, requiring the drug abuser to take ever-increasing doses. Those who continue to take high doses for many days can go through a series of behavioral changes very much like some aspects of the acute paranoid hallucinations exhibited by

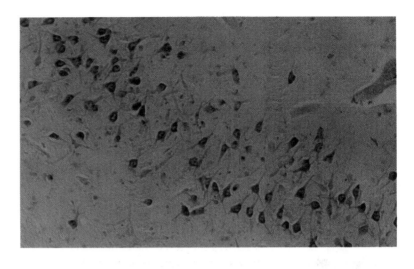

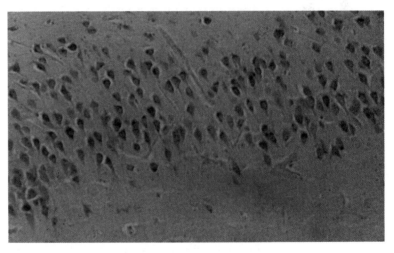

Some cases of schizophrenia reveal abnormal cellular structure in postmortem examination. In this illustration, the hippocampal neurons stained purple-brown (above) show abnormal shape and position, as well as reduced frequency, when compared to those from a normal subject of the same age who died from a nonneurological cause (below).

some type-I schizophrenics. Animals given large doses of amphetamine first show extreme hyperactivity, then bizarre repetitive movements that, in a very general way, resemble some of the bizarre postures and motor behaviors seen in the schizophrenic patient. Furthermore, some victims of Parkinson's disease who receive too much L-DOPA (see page 321 of this chapter) may undergo an acute psychotic episode, with hallucinations, delusions, and paranoias that pass when the L-DOPA dosage is reduced or stopped. These observations have suggested that schizophrenia may arise from excessive dopamine transmission.

What makes this hypothesis even more compelling is that the same drugs, called "antipsychotic" or "neuroleptic" (*neuro*, "nerve"; *lepsis*, "to take hold of," or "seize") drugs, that treat the acute paranoid hallucinatory states of the schizophrenic also relieve paranoia in the amphetamine abuser, the amphetamine overdosed animal, and the Parkinson's patient. Indeed, too much treatment with antipsychotic drugs leads to drug-induced Parkinsonism. These drugs—the phenothiazines and haloperidol are two examples—appear to produce their main antipsychotic effect by antagonizing dopamine transmission.

The other line of evidence stems from postmortem analysis, and it, too, supports the idea that some sort of problem in the dopamine-transmitting sites results in excessive dopamine transmission (see Figure 10.5). Postmortem examination shows that schizophrenic patients have slightly elevated amounts of dopamine in the dopamine-rich areas of their brains. These areas also show changes indicating that their responsiveness to dopamine had inappropriately increased along with the increase in dopamine content. Chronic use of antipsychotic drugs may have caused some of these changes, but the increases are still noteworthy after drug use has been adjusted for. Dopamine changes are much more marked in those schizophrenics who died at younger ages. And, in general, antidopamine antipsychotic drugs also produce their most effective actions in younger type-I schizophrenics.

Like all partially acceptable hypotheses, however, this one also has its holes. Dopamine changes, while reproducible in some studies, have not been seen in all such studies. Furthermore, dopamine transmits information in many parts of the brain, and it is difficult to explain how primary effects that

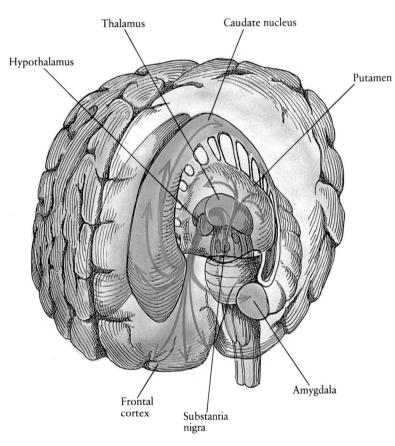

Figure 10.5

A schematic representation of the possible circuitry in the human brain of dopamine, a neurotransmitter possibly implicated in schizophrenia. The source of the dopamine fibers in the forebrain and midbrain are two single-source nuclei, one in the substantia nigra, the other nearby in the midbrain. Dopamine fibers arising in these two nuclei innervate extrapyramidal targets in the basal ganglia, and limbic system targets in the amygdala, septum, thalamus, and frontal cortex. In schizophrenia, this system may be overactive, and this overactivity may be regulated by antipsychotic drugs that antagonize the actions of dopamine.

In Parkinson's disease, this system is destroyed by the disease process, and dopamine transmission is achieved by treating the patient with L-DOPA, which surviving neurons can convert into dopamine.

Labels in figure: Thalamus, Caudate nucleus, Hypothalamus, Putamen, Frontal cortex, Substantia nigra, Amygdala result in perceptual, cognitive, or emotional problems would not result in more obvious sensory or motor problems as well. Although antipsychotic drugs cause patients to improve in direct correlation with the drug's ability to antagonize dopamine, other "atypical" antipsychotic drugs that have no observable interaction at all with dopamine also work well. Furthermore, many type-II schizophrenics do not readily improve with any of the existing medications. Apparently, many systems in the brain influence the behavioral problems of schizophrenia, and whether or not the dopamine-transmitter system per se is the culprit remains to be shown.

Brain, Mind, and Behavioral Disorders: Future Directions

Our journey through the history and the vagaries of humanity's approach to mental illness pauses here. We have seen that serious mental diseases are beginning to be characterized by specific hypotheses. Even though verification of these hypotheses has yet to be concluded, treatment procedures and diagnostic tests based on the suggested causative mechanisms hold great promise for more sharply focused future research. Perhaps small subsets of the major psychoses will submit to definition by these hypotheses, adding to the ranks of those behavioral diseases found to have organic causes.

The behavior disorders that lie beyond our present knowledge represent as much our failure to understand the biology of the cognitive and emotional operations of the brain as they do our inability to characterize the mechanisms underlying its disorders. It is quite clear from current research activity that the brain makes thousands of molecules exclusively important for the vitality of the brain. These molecules, whose identities are yet to be established, will undoubtedly cast new light on the specific properties of neurons and glia and suggest new methods of communication between brain cells, as well as new modes of synapse and circuit modifiability. Behavioral events will become far better understood through the new, noninvasive research methods; these methods are capable of resolving which particular brain structures participate in phenomena that remain vague, such as attention, calculation, and abstract analysis. Eventually, we will have enough data in hand to determine how far we can carry the view that everything the normal as well as the disordered brain does, no matter how complex, can be explained in terms of the interactions among its operational units.

Summary

1. A central view of this text is that everything that the brain does, both when it is healthy and when it is ill, can ultimately be represented in terms of the cells and chemicals of the brain.

2. Neurological and psychiatric diseases illustrate our understanding of how these states of ill health can be produced and how they are analyzed so that others can be protected from them in the future.

3. Historically, people suffering from diseases that affected their behavior, especially thinking and moving behaviors, were regarded as either evil or possessed by spirits. Modern humane treatments for the mentally ill were rare until well into the nineteenth century.

4. Scientific analysis and understanding of major causes for institutionalization of patients with abnormal behavior resulted from the discovery of the brain's dependence on vitamin B_1 (niacin) and of crude but effective fever therapy for neurosyph-

ilis. Elimination of these minor causes of serious mental illness allowed psychiatrists to focus on the untreatables.

5. Neurological diseases are characterized in general by consistent clusters of objective pathologic findings in brain structure, function, and chemistry. Each symptom and pathologic cluster establishes the nature of the disease and separates that disease from others, even though there may be no solid understanding of the nature of the problem, nor a treatment for it.

6. Three of the better understood degenerative neurologic diseases are Parkinson's disease (a temporarily treatable movement disorder in which dopamine-containing circuits die), Huntington's disease (an untreatable, inheritable movement disorder with different chemical and structural deficits), and Alzheimer's disease (an untreatable progressive loss of intellectual function with still different chemical and structural deficits).

7. Psychiatric disorders are characterized by abnormal behavior in emotion, thought, and social interactions, but they have few objective signs based on structural, chemical, or functional tests of the brain. Clusters of these emotional and thought problems allow discrimination of different forms of psychiatric disease, each with different natural histories, treatment outcomes, and future expectations, and each with different hypothetical explanations upon which the treatments are in part based.

8. The two major forms of mental illness are schizophrenia (a potentially treatable, but serious disorder of thought and analytical abilities, that has been related to overactivity within some of the brain's dopamine circuits) and affective disorder (a generally treatable disorder of extreme

highs and lows of emotion that has been related to underutilization of signals mediated by norepinephrine and serotonin circuits).

9. Some neurologic and psychiatric diseases have a strong genetic component, and have been linked to specific gene areas on specific chromosomes. In the future, the diagnosis, treatment, and prevention of these diseases may be based upon a true molecular understanding of the cause of the pathology. Nevertheless, environmental factors, from toxins to nutrition to emotion, can build upon the inherited and uncharacterized genetic susceptibilities to produce or resist expression of the disease.

Further Reading

Sacks, O. 1985. *The Man Who Mistook His Wife for a Hat and Other Clinical Tales*. New York: Summit. A famous neurologist recounts some of the cases he has seen—people whose neurological disease or injury produced extraordinary effects.

Andreasen, N. C., ed. 1986. *Can Schizophrenia Be Localized in the Brain?* Washington D.C.: American Psychiatric Press. A thoroughly readable and up-to-date coverage of the information by which psychiatrists and neuroscientists may be able to link up their respective points of view.

Diagnostic and Statistical Manual III-R. 1987. Washington D.C.: American Psychiatric Association Press. A small volume that details the diagnostic criteria that are to be considered the standards of reference.

Robertson, M. 1987. Molecular genetics of the mind—news and views. *Nature 352: 755*. A brief but insightful coverage of the recent, but not yet easily interpretable, evidence that there may be different molecular linkages between certain forms of affective disorder and its chromosomal locations in different racial groups.

Breakefield, X.O., and Cambi, F. 1987. Molecular genetic insights into neurologic diseases. *Annual Review of Neuroscience 10:* 535–594. An excellent and up-to-date summary of the basis for the recent insights into the inheritable and possibly inheritable neurological disorders of humans and other animals.

Gottesman, I. I., and Shields, J. 1982. *Schizophrenia: The Epigenetic Disorder.* Cambridge: Cambridge University Press. A monograph that covers the historical and recent findings on the schizophrenias as diseases that may be genetically transmitted in part.

Glossary

accommodation In visual processing, the adjustments of the pupil and lens in focusing.

acetylcholine A prevalent neurotransmitter in both the brain, where it may help regulate memory, and in the peripheral nervous system, where it controls the actions of skeletal and smooth muscle.

action potential A nerve impulse; temporary reversal of the interior membrane's electrical state from negative to positive. An action potential results from a brief change in the neuron membrane's permeability to sodium and potassium ions. Also referred to as depolarization.

activational effects Effects of hormones on brain cells that, during prenatal development, were subject to the organizational effects of those hormones; the early hormones, in effect, "prime" the cells to be activated at a later time. See also **organizational effects.**

acupuncture A method developed in Chinese medicine for pain suppression through stimulation of skin and muscle by means of insertion of needles at specified points of the body.

adaptation Diminishing responsiveness of a sensory receptor to prolonged presentation of a stimulus.

addiction The compulsive desire to take drugs, such as opiates, cocaine, amphetamine, alcohol, and nicotine.

adipocyte A single fat cell.

adiposity Stored fat; now believed to be the primary regulator of feeding and digestion.

adrenal cortex Endocrine organ that secretes corticosteroids for metabolic functions, aldosterone for sodium retention in the kidneys, androgens for male sexual development, and estrogens for female sexual development.

adrenal medulla Endocrine organ that secretes epinephrine and norepinephrine for the activation of the sympathetic nervous system.

affective psychosis Psychiatric disease in which prolonged periods of deep depression, unrelated to events in the life of the patient, alternate either with periods of normal mood or with periods of excessive, inappropriate euphoria, and mania.

aggregation See Table 3.1, Processes of Neural Development.

alpha rhythms Patterns of brain wave activity with rhythms of 8 to 12 waves per second; associated with a state of relaxation while awake.

Alzheimer's disease A degenerative, and eventually fatal, brain disorder with symptoms including deterioration of mental capacities, memory loss, disorientation, and motor deficits; may be familial in some cases.

amacrine cells Local-circuit neurons that regulate the spread of the visual signal within the retina.

amino acid transmitters The most prevalent transmitters within the brain. These neurotransmitters include glutamate and aspartate, which are excitatory, and glycine and gamma-amino butyric acid (GABA), which are inhibitory.

amphetamine A stimulant drug that activates the release of the catecholamines dopamine and norepinephrine.

amygdala A forebrain structure and important component of the limbic system. Sometimes called the amygdaloid complex because it is composed of a number of nuclei.

amyotrophic lateral sclerosis A fatal neurological disorder of unknown etiology; symptoms include gradual paralysis due to loss of motor neurons in the spinal cord and loss of input to the spinal cord form the brain; also known as Lou Gehrig's disease.

androgens Group of sex steroid hormones, including testosterone, found more abundantly in males than females; responsible for male sexual maturation.

angiography X-ray examination of the brain by means of dyes injected into the carotid artery; used for the detection of irregularities in the vascular system, such as blocked arteries.

angiotensin II A protein fragment produced by the actions of renin and other enzymes on angiotensinogen; causes arterial muscles to constrict, inducing a prompt, large rise in blood pressure.

angiotensinogen Small protein made by the liver and converted into angiotensin II, through the actions of renal and plasma enzymes, to increase blood pressure.

anorexia nervosa Disorder in which severe loss of appetite is presumably caused by psychological factors; most frequently affects young females and can lead to starvation. Anorectics are obsessed with food, have a severely distorted body image, and often suffer from depression and social isolation.

anoxia Severe deficit of oxygen reaching the body tissues.

anxiety Unrealistic apprehension and nervousness.

aphasia Disturbance in language comprehension or production. See Table 9.1.

arcuate fasciculus A collection of intracortical nerve fibers connecting Wernicke's area and Broca's area; critical for speech and speech perception.

association cortex The large areas of the cerebral cortex thought to receive and integrate information from more specialized areas—sensory, motor, and limbic areas and memory stores—allowing humans to think, decide, and plan.

astigmatism An irregularity on the surface of the cornea causing the images entering the eye from certain angles to be distorted.

astrocyte The most common type of glial cell. Thought to scavenge excess neurotransmitter and ions from the spaces between neurons. May also contribute glucose to very active neurons and redirect blood flow to especially active regions.

atherosclerosis Disease caused by deposition of fatty substances on the inside of artery walls and hardening of the arteries, so that blood flow is diminished or blocked. Obstruction in the brain's blood vessels can result in tissue damage (stroke); if damage is extensive, dementia can result.

audition The sense of hearing.

auditory nerve A bundle of nerve fibers extending from the cochlea to the brain and containing two branches: the cochlear nerve for the transmission of auditory information and the vestibular nerve for the relaying of information related to balance.

autonomic nervous system The division of the peripheral nervous system responsible for regulating the activity of the internal organs; includes the sympathetic and parasympathetic nervous systems.

autoreceptor Presynaptic receptor that monitors the amount of a neuron's own neurotransmitter and so helps regulate the production and release of the chemical.

autosomal dominant disorders Diseases that are inherited from a dominant gene on one of the twenty-two pairs of non-sex chromosomes.

axon The fiberlike extension of a neuron through which the cell sends information to target cells.

axonal transport An energy-requiring intracellular transport system by which the neuron maintains the viability of its dendritic branchings and its synaptic terminals.

basal ganglia A cluster of ganglia located at the base of the cortex composed of the caudate nucleus, globus pallidus, and the putamen; play an important part in the motor system.

basilar membrane In the inner ear, this membrane separates the cochlear canal and the tympanic canal. Its movement in relation to the tectorial membrane forces the cilia of the receptor cells to bend, producing the sensation of sound.

Betz cells Cortical neurons that communicate directly with the motor neurons of the spinal cord.

bipolar depression See **manic-depressive psychosis**.

bipolar neurons In the retina, a neuron that transmits information from the rods and cones to the ganglion cells within the eye.

blastocyst Embryo about the fifth day after fertilization, being a hollow sphere of cells with a small mass of cells adhering to one point on its inner surface.

blood/brain barrier   Diffusional barrier created by astrocytes and cells in the walls of the blood vessels within the brain; prevents most blood-borne substances from passing from the blood-stream into the brain.

brainstem   The major route by which the fore-brain sends information to and receives information from the spinal cord and peripheral nervous system and which is therefore vital to survival; controls, among other functions, respiration and heart rhythms.

Broca's area   Brain region located in the frontal lobe of the left hemisphere and responsible for the production of the sounds of speech. Damage to this area results in Broca's aphasia, a disorder that is characterized by impaired speech production, although comprehension of language is unimpaired.

bulimia   Eating disorder in which the person eats excessive amounts of food and then induces vomiting or takes laxatives to force the food out of the body before calories can be absorbed; often associated with anorexia nervosa.

Cannon-Bard theory   Theory of emotion formulated by Walter Cannon and modified by Phillip Bard, postulating that the psychological experience of emotion and the associated physiological reactions are simultaneous.

cataract   A visual disturbance, often a result of aging, in which the lens of the eye becomes clouded.

catecholamines   The neurotransmitters dopamine, epinephrine, and norepinephrine; these function both in the brain and in the sympathetic nervous system.

catecholamine hypothesis of depression   Proposal that depression is caused by a loss of transmission at the catecholamine synapses in the brain.

CAT scan   See **computerized axial tomography.**

central nervous system   The brain and spinal cord.

cerebellum   A relatively large structure attached to the roof of the hindbrain. Its intricate, regular cellular architecture helps control movement by connections to the pons, medulla, spinal cord, and thalamus. Also may serve to store some responses learned through classical conditioning.

cerebral cortex   The outermost layer of the cerebral hemispheres of the brain; responsible for all forms of conscious activity.

cerebrospinal fluid   Liquid found within the ventricles of the brain and the central canal of the spinal cord; acts in conjunction with the meninges as a shock absorber for the brain and spinal cord.

cholecystokinin   Hormone released from the lining of the stomach during the early stages of digestion; acts as a powerful suppressant of normal eating. Also found in the brain in small amounts.

chorda tympani   A branch of the facial nerve innervating taste receptors of the tongue; relays information from the front portion of the tongue to the brain.

choroid plexus   A group of specialized blood vessels, located in the ventricles, that produce the cerebrospinal fluid.

cingulate gyrus   A component of the limbic system, encircling the hippocampus and other limbic structures.

circadian rhythm   A cycle of behavior or physiological change lasting approximately 24 hours.

classical conditioning   Learning in which a stimulus that naturally produces a specific response (unconditioned stimulus) is repeatedly paired with a neutral stimulus (conditioned stimulus), with the result that the conditioned stimulus eventually comes to evoke the same response as the unconditioned stimulus; also known as Pavlovian conditioning.

cochlea   Snail-shaped, fluid-filled organ of the inner ear responsible for transducing mechanical energy to neural energy to produce auditory sensation.

cochlear canal   One of three sections of the cochlea.

cochlear nerve   A branch of the auditory nerve responsible for transmitting auditory information from the cochlea to the brain.

cognition   The process or processes by which an organism gains knowledge of or becomes aware of events or objects in its environment, especially as regards the organism's relationship to that environment.

cognitive dissonance   Leon Festinger's theory that people are motivated to avoid disharmony and achieve consistency between their actions and their beliefs.

computerized axial tomography (CAT) scan An imaging method using a computer and X-rays to produce a sequence of two-dimensional "slices" through the brain; allows neurologists to diagnose and localize lesions within the brain.

conditioned response In classical conditioning, the learned response to a previously neutral stimulus.

conditioned stimulus In classical conditioning, a previously neutral stimulus that has come to evoke the same response as an unconditioned stimulus with which it has repeatedly been paired.

cone A primary receptor neuron for vision located in the retina and most densely in the fovea; sensitive to light of color and used primarily for daytime vision.

consciousness Awareness of one's own mental and/or physical actions.

convergent circuit Neural-connection pattern in which a target cell receives simultaneous incoming messages from a number of transmitting cells.

cornea A thin, curved, transparent membrane on the surface of the front of the eye; begins the focusing process for vision.

corpus callosum The large bundle of nerve fibers linking the left and right cerebral hemispheres.

corpus luteum The follicular tissue remaining after the release of the ovum during ovulation; under the influence of luteinizing hormone, it secretes large quantities of progesterone.

cortisol Hormone manufactured by the adrenal cortex; secreted in its greatest quantity before dawn in human beings, readying the body for the activities of the coming day.

cross cuing In split-brain patients, the use by one hemisphere of cues available to it to detect information supposedly only accessible to the other hemisphere. Use of sounds, for example, to identify an object that cannot be seen.

cytoplasm All material enclosed by the plasma membrane of a cell.

cytoplasmic organelles See **organelles**.

declarative knowledge Memory of facts and experiences; tends to be knowledge that can be

verbally communicated. See also **procedural knowledge**.

delta waves Brain wave activity, at approximately four cycles per second, associated with relatively deep sleep (stage 4).

delirium A condition of extreme mental confusion, often accompanied by excess activity; generally due to metabolic problems; usually reversible.

dementia A sustained, multidimensional loss of cognitive ability due to brain damage; generally irreversible.

dendrite Treelike protrusion from the soma of a neuron; along with the soma, constitutes the receiving zone for messages from other cells.

depolarization See **action potential**.

desynchronization The uncoupling of two or more physiological rhythms that ordinarily work together.

dexamethasone suppression test A diagnostic procedure used to evaluate the regulatory effectiveness of the endocrine system in depressed patients.

diencephalon The portion of the forebrain composed of the thalamus and hypothalamus.

differentiation See Table 3.1, Processes of Neural Development.

diffuse enteric nervous system A subdivision of the peripheral nervous system; regulates the digestive tract.

dimorphism Male-female anatomical difference.

divergent circuit Neural-connection pattern in which an individual neuron sends simultaneous messages to a number of other neurons.

dopamine Neurotransmitter; a catecholamine. Known to function in the control of complex movements, since dopamine-transmitting neurons are destroyed in victims of Parkinson's disease. Also thought to function in regulating emotional responses and to play a role in the expression of schizophrenia.

dorsal horn Area of the spinal cord where many nerve fibers from peripheral pain receptors synapse with other ascending nerve fibers.

dorsal raphe nucleus Group of serotonin-containing neurons in the pons that play a role in the regulation of sleep and waking.

Down syndrome A disorder in human beings caused by nondisjunction and therefore the presence of an extra copy of chromosome 21; characterized by severe mental retardation and various physical abnormalities. Formerly known as mongolism.

dyslexia Disturbance in the ability to read not caused by mental retardation or physical injury.

ectoderm One of three distinct layers of cells differentiating from the embryonic disc very early in embryonic development; develops into the nervous system, as well as the skin, hair, and fingernails.

electroencephalogram (EEG) Recording of the electrical activity of the brain, achieved by placing electrodes on the surface of the skull.

embryonic disc The flat plate of cells that forms across the inside of the blastocyst during the eighth day of prenatal development; from it the embryo will develop.

endocrine organ Organ that secretes a substance (hormone) directly into the bloodstream to regulate the cellular activity of certain other organs; also known as a gland.

endoplasmic reticulum The network of intracellular membrane channels by which substances are distributed to different parts of the cell. In neurons, rough endoplasmic reticulum is studded with ribosomes and is very active in the production of products for outside secretion, namely neurotransmitters; smooth endoplasmic reticulum, also known as the Golgi apparatus, forms the membrane packages for these cellular products.

endorphins Neurotransmitters in the brain that can produce cellular and behavioral effects like those of morphine.

epinephrine Hormone released by the adrenal medulla; acts with norepinephrine to activate the sympathetic division of the autonomic nervous system (see Figures 4.1 and 4.2); also has limited functions within the pons and medulla. Sometimes called adrenalin.

estrogen A group of sex steroid hormones found more abundantly in females than males; responsible for female sexual maturation.

evoked potentials A measure of the brain's electrical activity in response to sensory stimuli; achieved by placing electrodes on the surface of the skull, repeatedly presenting a given stimulus, then using a computer to average the results.

excitation Synaptic message in which one cell commands another to activity.

exocrine gland Gland whose hormones do not enter the bloodstream but reach their target cells through ducts.

external auditory canal A part of the outer ear responsible, along with the pinna, for focusing and funneling auditory stimuli to the structures of the middle ear.

filopodia Fingerlike extensions of the growth cone; a temporary structure at the growing ends of developing axons.

follicle Hollow ball of tissue containing the ovum.

follicle-stimulating hormone (FSH) Hormone released by the anterior pituitary gland; its release is triggered by the hypothalamus. It stimulates the production of sperm in the male and growth of the follicle in females.

forebrain Largest major division of the brain; its subdivisions are the diencephalon and telencephalon. The forebrain is credited with the highest intellectual functions.

fornix The two-way fiber system of axons connecting the hypothalamus and the hippocampus.

fovea A small area of the retina that contains only cones and where visual acuity is highest.

frontal lobe One of the four subdivisions of each hemisphere of the cerebral cortex. The frontal lobe has a role in controlling motor functions and associating the functions of other cortical areas.

gamma-amino butyric acid (GABA) Amino acid transmitter in the brain whose primary function is to inhibit the firing of neurons.

ganglia Small encapsulated clusters of neural cells that direct internal muscles and glands; located entirely outside the central nervous system.

ganglion cells A layer of retinal neurons whose axons form the optic nerve.

general adaptation syndrome Theory by Hans Selye explaining animals' physiological reaction to stress; consists of three phases: (1) alarm, (2) resistance, and (3) exhaustion.

gland See **endocrine organ**.

glaucoma   A disease of the eye marked by high pressure within the eyeball, which compresses the retina and destroys the ability of the rods and cones to function.

glia   Specialized cells that serve a supporting role in the nervous system. See also **astrocyte: oligodendrocyte.**

glossopharyngeal nerve   Cranial nerve that conveys taste information from the posterior portion of the tongue to the brain.

Golgi method   An early and successful staining method to reveal the complete form of a nerve cell for microscopic analysis.

gonad   Primary sex gland: testis in males and ovary in females.

gonadotropin-releasing hormone (GRH)   Hormone secreted by the hypothalamus initiating the female reproductive cycle; stimulates the pituitary gland to produce and secrete follicle-stimulating hormone and luteinizing hormone.

granule-cell neurons   Nerve cells within the cerebellum that form a thick layer beneath the Purkinje cells; believed to play a role in motor coordination and balance.

growth cone   A distinctive structure at the growing end of most axons; site where most new material is added to the axon.

gustation   The sense of taste.

habituation   Simple learning in which a stimulus that an organism originally responded to is presented so often that the organism stops responding to it.

hair cells   Auditory receptor cells, having cilia that project from their tops. The cilia bend from the relative actions of the basilar membrane, in which the cells are anchored, and the tectorial membrane, producing the nerve impulses that start on their path to the brain.

hemispherectomy   Surgical removal of the cortical covering of an entire hemisphere.

hierarchical circuit   Neural-connection pattern in which cells are linked as in a chain, with information ascending or descending from one level of the circuit to the next. Pattern common to the sensory systems.

hindbrain   Region of the brain responsible for controlling internal body states and motor coordination, and also serving as a relay region between the spinal cord and other areas of the brain; composed of the pons, medulla oblongata, and cerebellum.

hippocampus   Seahorse-shaped structure located within the telencephalon and considered an important part of the limbic system; functions in learning, memory, and emotion.

homeostasis   The process by which the body maintains a uniform internal environment.

horizontal cells   Inhibitory local-circuit neurons that restrict the spread of the visual signal within the retina.

hormones   Chemical messengers secreted by endocrine and exocrine glands to regulate the cellular activity of target cells.

Huntington's disease   A hereditary neurologic disease characterized by motor movement disorders, slurred speech, and progressively worsening mental capacities. Symptoms do not begin to appear until patient is about 40 years of age.

hyperopia   Also known as far-sightedness; inability to focus well on close objects. This common vision problem arises from the retina being too close to the lens so that the image of nearby objects fails to fall sharply on the retina.

hypophysiotropic hormones   Hormones secreted by the hypothalamus via the pituitary-portal circulatory system for the regulation of the pituitary gland.

hypothalamus   A complex brain structure composed of many nuclei with various functions; functions include regulating visceral integrative functions, monitoring information from the autonomic nervous system, and controlling the functions of the pituitary gland. Located under the thalamus in the diencephalon.

idiopathic hypogonadotropic hypogonadism   Rare genetic deficiency in which there is no production of testosterone at puberty, even though the male has the normal XY genotype.

immediate memory   A phase of memory that is extremely short-term, with information stored for only a few seconds.

imprinting   A species-specific learning behavior in certain birds whereby the young become attached to and follow the first moving object they encounter after hatching.

incus   A component of the ossicles, the incus receives auditory vibrations from the malleus and, in turn, passes on these vibrations to the stapes; commonly called the anvil.

induction See Table 3.1, Processes of Neural Development.

infarct Damage to brain tissue produced by circulatory obstruction of the brain's blood vessels and resultant lack of circulation.

inferior colliculi Collections of neurons and their connections, protruding from the upper surface of the midbrain, that relay auditory information to the brain.

infradian rhythm Cycle of behavioral or physiological change occurring over a period longer than 24 hours (e.g., hibernation of some animals).

inhibition In reference to neurons, a synaptic message that prevents the recipient cell from firing.

intercellular Referring to activity between two or more cells.

intermediate zone Layer of cells formed between the ventricular and marginal zones of the neural tube during the proliferative phase of neural development.

intracellular Referring to activity within a given cell.

ions Electrically charged atoms.

iris A circular muscle that alters the amount of light entering the eye by dilating or constricting the pupil, the opening in its center.

islet cells of the pancreas Endocrine organ that secretes insulin to increase glucose uptake, glucagon to increase glucose levels, and somatostatin for the regulation of insulin and glucagon secretion.

James-Lange theory William James's theory of emotion, based on the ideas of Carl Lange, proposing that the experience of emotion results from an individual's perception of his or her own physiological changes, such as increased heart rate.

juxtaglomerular cell Specialized kidney cell that, when blood pressure drops, secretes the enzyme renin into the bloodstream; renin converts angiotensinogen to angiotensin II in a process to elevate blood pressure to normal levels.

Klinefelter's syndrome Chromosomal abnormality in which the individual has an XXY genotype instead of the normal male XY. These males show some feminization as adolescents and adults, having little beard growth, small penis and testis, and unusually high voices; many show some breast development during puberty.

Korsakoff's syndrome A disease associated with chronic alcoholism, resulting from a deficiency of vitamin B_1. Patients sustain damage to the left dorsomedial nucleus of the thalamus and loss of neurons in the cerebellum and frontal cortex. Consequently, they suffer severe cognitive deficits.

lateral geniculate nucleus Thalamic nucleus specialized for the processing and relaying of visual information.

lens An adjustable structure of the eye that completes the focusing process initiated by the cornea.

leucocyte pyrogen An uncharacterized substance released by the white blood cells of a person with an infection; activates heat-gain mechanisms and drives body temperature up.

limbic system A group of brain structures, including the amygdala, hippocampus, septum, and basal ganglia, that work in alliance to help regulate emotion, memory, and certain aspects of movement.

lipofuscin A fatty pigment deposited in the cells of many organs during the aging process; known as "age spots" when the pigment appears in the skin.

lipoprotein lipase (LPL) Enzyme responsible for the removal of fats from the blood and for the ability to store them in adipocytes; LPL levels may be part of the signaling and control system for the regulation of body fat.

local circuit Simple neural-connection pattern with limited range of influence; operates as a filter within one or more levels of a hierarchical circuit to broaden or narrow the flow of information as it moves through the hierarchy. May be excitatory or inhibitory.

locus coeruleus Within the pons, a concentrated set of neural cell bodies whose axons secrete the neurotransmitter norepinephrine.

long-term memory The final phase of memory in which information storage may last from hours to a lifetime.

lordosis Receptive sexual posture of some female mammals, facilitating intercourse and necessary for fertilization to occur.

luteinizing hormone Hormone secreted by the pituitary gland; during the human female reproductive cycle, causes the wall of the follicle within the ovary to break and release the mature ovum and stimulates the production of progesterone by the corpus lutem. In males, stimulates the production of testosterone.

malleus A component of the ossicles, the malleus receives the vibrations of the tympanic membrane and passes them on to the incus; commonly called the hammer.

mania An affective psychosis in which the patient displays inappropriate elation, unconcern for important problems, overconfidence, and hyperactivity in both motor and speech patterns.

manic-depressive psychosis A severe affective disorder characterized by alternating episodes of mania and depression; also known as bipolar depression.

marginal zone The outer surface of the embryonic neural tube.

medulla oblongata The brain region between the pons and spinal cord that operates as a control center for respiration, blood pressure, and heart rhythm.

meiosis The process whereby chromosome pairs in the male and female reproductive cells separate to form sperm and egg.

melatonin A hormone, converted from serotonin in the pineal gland and released by it into the bloodstream; in many animals, melatonin effects physiological changes related to time and lighting cycles.

memory consolidation The changes, physical and psychological, that take place as the brain organizes and restructures information that may become a permanent part of memory.

meninges The membranes that encase the central nervous system.

mesoderm Layer of cells that develops between the ectoderm and endoderm in embryonic development.

method of loci A mnemonic device in which a person visualizes a familiar place and then imagines placing things to be remembered at prominent points along the route. When recall is per-

formed, the person mentally revisits the place, retracing the path and finding the items placed at each location.

microtubule Organelle that acts as a fine "strut" to help maintain a cell's structure and, in neurons, guides the transport of substances to the axon or dendrites from the soma and back to the soma from these protrusions.

midbrain Smallest major region of the brain, between the pons and diencephalon; it has few distinctive features, among them being the inferior and superior colliculi.

migration See Table 3.1, Processes of Neural Development.

minicolumn Basic organizational unit of the cortex consisting of vertically connected neurons that span the layers of the cortex.

mitochondria Organelles that provide energy for the cell by converting sugar and oxygen into special energy molecules.

mitosis Cell division and duplication resulting in two daughter cells.

monoamine oxidase (MAO) The brain and liver enzyme that normally breaks down the monoamines norepinephrine, serotonin, and dopamine.

motivation In psychology, a hypothetical state inferred from an organism's goal-directed behavior.

motor neuron Neuron that carries information from the central nervous system to the muscle.

mnemonic devices Techniques to aid in storing and recalling memories.

multiple sclerosis Neurological disorder in which the myelin covering of some neurons is destroyed; patient suffers various neural and muscular dysfunctions, depending on the nerves involved.

myasthenia gravis Disease in which the acetylcholine receptors on the muscle cells are destroyed, so that muscles can no longer receive the signal to contract.

myelin Compact wrapping material that surrounds and insulates axons of some neurons; produced by oligodendrocytes in the central nervous system and Schwann cells in the peripheral nervous system.

myopia Also known as near-sightedness; inability to focus well on far objects. This common vision problem is caused by the eyeball being too deep, so that the retina is too far from the lens and the image of distant objects fails to fall sharply on the retina.

N-acetyltransferase (5-hydroxy-N-acetyltransferase) Enzyme produced within the pineal gland of some animals and functioning in the conversion of serotonin to melatonin; determines the amount of melatonin released by the pineal gland into the bloodstream.

neglect syndrome Condition found in some patients with extensive damage to the posterior area of the right cerebral hemisphere; patient acts as if the left side of his or her perceived space has ceased to exist.

neocortex The cerebral cortex.

neostriatum The caudate nucleus, a structure within the basal ganglia that receives information from all areas of the cerebral cortex, including all forms of sensory information and information regarding the motor system.

nerve-growth factor (NGF) Substance whose role is to guide neuronal growth during embryonic development, especially in the peripheral nervous system.

neural crest Cluster of young neurons remaining outside the neural tube after its formation; develops into the peripheral autonomic nervous system.

neural plate Embryonic structure that develops from the ectoderm and from which the neural tube develops.

neural tube Hollow tube formed early in embryonic development, from the fusing of parallel ridges that form across the neural plate; the top of the tube becomes the brain, and the remainder becomes the spinal cord.

neuroblast In embryonic development, a cell destined to develop into a neuron.

neurofibrillary tangles Skeins of microtubules that have proliferated inside a brain neuron and eventually replace the neuron, making the cell nonfunctional. Diagnostic criterion for Alzheimer's disease.

neuroglia See **astrocyte; oligodendrocyte.**

neurology The branch of medicine concerned with the study of the diseases of the brain.

neuron Nerve cell; specialized for the transmission of information.

neurosis Behavioral disorder in which patient suffers anxiety or phobia or performs obsessive-compulsive acts.

neurotransmitter Chemical released by nerve cells at a synapse for the purpose of relaying information.

nociceptors In animals, nerve endings that signal the sensation of pain; in human beings called "pain receptors."

norepinephrine Neurotransmitter, a catecholamine, produced both in the brain (notably, in the locus coeruleus) and in the peripheral nervous system (the sympathetic division of the autonomic nervous system). Has diverse behavioral effects.

nucleus In the brain, an aggregation of neurons that is anatomically distinct from surrounding matter; cells making up a nucleus usually function as a unit.

nucleus locus coeruleus See **locus coeruleus.**

nucleus of the solitary tract Synaptic relay station in the medulla; receives information regarding taste from the chorda tympani, glossopharyngeal nerve, and the vagus nerve and passes it on to the thalamic arcuate nucleus.

obsessive-compulsive behavior Overpowering drive to perform apparently irrational activities; symptom of neurosis.

occipital lobe One of the four subdivisions of each hemisphere of the cerebral cortex; specialized for visual perception.

ocular dominance columns In layer 4 of the primary visual cortex, the columns of cells that alternately receive input from the left and right eye.

oddity problem A learning procedure in which animals are shown two identical objects and one odd one and are rewarded for picking the odd object. After a number of successful trials with the same three objects, the objects are changed. The goal is to have the subjects form a concept of oddness.

olfaction The sense of smell.

oligodendrocyte Specialized glial cell found in the central nervous system; responsible for myelination of neurons.

operant conditioning Learning theory stating that behavior is shaped by its consequences: a behavior that brings reward will be learned and repeated; one that brings punishment is unlikely to be repeated.

opponent-process theory The theory proposing that color vision is possible by the nature of the "opposing" characteristics of certain color pairs and the nature of the receptive fields of the retina's ganglion cells interacting with the horizontal cells.

ophthalmologist Medical doctor specializing in visual problems and whose duties may include prescribing glasses or contact lens.

optic chiasm Area where the optic nerves from each eye come together and some fibers cross over to the opposite hemisphere of the brain; at the base of the front of the hypothalamus.

optic nerve Bundle of nerve fibers (the collected axons of the retina's ganglion cells) that carries visual information from the retina of each eye to the optic chiasm, where it becomes the optic tract.

optic tract The continuation of the axon bundles after the cross-over at the optic chiasm; axons of the optic tract run to one of four second-level receiving centers.

organelles Small structures within a cell that maintain the cells and do their work: for example, mitochondria, microtubules, and endoplasmic reticulum.

organizational effects Prenatal effects of hormones on cells of the brain to sensitize the cells so that they will later respond to the presence of the hormone; the hormones probably change a cell's anatomical development by altering its genetic messages.

organ of Corti The auditory receptor organ found within the cochlea; composed of the hair cells, basilar membrane, and tectorial membrane.

ossicles The three tiny bones that compose the middle ear; includes the malleus, incus, and stapes.

oval window A membrane-covered opening in the bone surrounding the cochlea; it receives auditory vibrations from the stapes and transmits them into the fluid-filled cochlea.

ovulation The process by which an ovum matures and is released from the ovary.

ovum The female egg cell.

oxytocin A peptide hormone released by the axons that comprise the posterior pituitary; causes contraction of the uterus during the final stages of labor. Its function in males, where it is equally abundant, is unknown.

Papez circuit A set of interconnected brain structures that James W. Papez proposed functions in the experience of emotion. This set of structures constitutes much of what is now known as the limbic system.

papillae The small bumps on the surface of the tongue around which the taste buds lie.

parasympathetic nervous system A branch of the autonomic nervous system concerned with the conservation of the body's energy and resources during relaxed states.

parathyroid Endocrine organ that secretes calcitonin and functions in maintaining normal calcium balance in the body.

parietal lobe One of the four subdivisions of each hemisphere of the cerebral cortex; plays a role in sensory processes and in language.

Parkinson's disease A neurological disease whose symptoms include fine tremor, rigidity of movement, and difficulty in initiating movements and in terminating movements once started; caused by deficient amounts of the neurotransmitter dopamine due to destruction of dopamine-producing neurons in the substantia nigra and the ventral tegmentum.

pathology The branch of medicine concerned with study of the cellular dysfunctions that cause disease.

Pavlovian conditioning See classical conditioning.

pellagra A disease caused by dietary insufficiency of niacin, resulting in delirium, confusion, and general disorientation often accompanied by periods of mania.

peptides Chains of amino acids that function as neurotransmitters, neuromodulators, or hormones.

perception Awareness of objects and events in the environment attained through the brain's interpretation of sensory data.

periaqueductal gray area A cluster of neurons lying in the thalamus and pons; contains endorphin-producing neurons and opiate receptor sites and thus can modulate the sensation of pain.

peripheral nervous system A division of the nervous system consisting of all the nerves not part of the brain or spinal cord.

peristalsis Contractions of the circular and longitudinal muscles of stomach and intestines that propel food through the digestive system; innervated by the diffuse enteric system.

phase-advance The adjustment of a biological clock after it gains time relative to the 24-hour day; occurs after eastbound air travel.

phase-delay The adjustment of a biological clock after it loses time relative to the 24-hour day; occurs after westbound air travel.

phase shift A change in the timing of one's biological clock with respect to clock time. See **phase-advance; phase-delay.**

phenylketonuria (PKU) A hereditary abnormality caused by absence of an enzyme needed to metabolize the amino acid phenylalanine, which is present in many common foods. If untreated (treatment is a diet low in phenylalin), phenylalanine accumulates, and severe retardation results.

phobia Unrealistic and persistent fear of particular things or events; a symptom of neurosis.

phosphorylation The attachment of phosphate molecules to another substance, often altering the character of the substance involved. In the cell membrane of neurons, the substances believed to become phosphorylated are proteins—specifically, the proteins composing the ion channels. Such chemical change could alter a channel's specificity (e.g., from sodium to potassium).

pineal gland An endocrine organ found in the brain; in some animals, it seems to serve as a light-influenced biological clock.

pinna The external part of the ear, serving, along with the external auditory canal, to focus and funnel auditory stimuli to the structures of the middle ear.

pitch Auditory sensation determined by the number of cycles per second of the sound wave; many cycles per second corresponds with sounds of high pitch, and fewer cycles per second corresponds with sounds of low pitch.

pituitary gland Endocrine organ closely linked with the hypothalamus; composed of two lobes, the anterior and posterior. It secretes a number of hormones that regulate the activity of other endocrine organs in the body.

pituitary-portal circulation A restricted network of blood vessels that carry blood only between the base of the hypothalamus and the anterior lobe of the pituitary gland.

planum temporale The upper surface of the temporal lobe; enlarged on the side of the dominant hemisphere.

plaque An amorphous collection of amyloid protein in the cortical gray matter of patients with Alzheimer's disease.

plasma membrane Cell membrane; the thin layer of tissue that surrounds a cell and forms a boundary between the cell's interior and its environment.

plasticity Capacity for adjusting to change; characteristic of early neural development.

pons A component of the hindbrain that works in conjunction with the medulla and diencephalon to control respiration and heart rhythms. The pons is a major route by which the forebrain sends information to and receives information from the spinal cord and peripheral nervous system.

porphyria Inherited metabolic disease in which the body is unable properly to construct the hemoglobin molecules that allow red blood cells to transport oxygen; results in an organic mental disorder characterized by periods of normalcy fluctuating with episodes of agitation, depression, and disturbance of memory.

positron emission transaxial tomography (PETT) scan A diagnostic imaging procedure enabling scientists to map activity (e.g., glucose utilization) within the living brain by recording the emission of positrons from injected molecules (e.g., glucose) labeled with positron-emitting compounds.

postganglionic fibers Within the autonomic nervous system, the axons that emerge from the neurons of the autonomic ganglia and connect directly with target organs.

postsynaptic neuron Neuron receiving information across the synapse from a presynaptic neuron.

preganglionic fibers Within the autonomic nervous system, the axons that connect spinal nerves with autonomic ganglia.

presbyopia The progressive loss of near vision associated with increasing age.

presynaptic neuron Neuron sending information across the synapse to a postsynaptic neuron.

primary visual cortex Major structural component of the visual system, responsible for processing of visual information received from the thalamic nuclei. Information from the primary visual cortex, also known as area 17 or the striate cortex, is then distributed throughout a hierarchy of other vision-related regions of the cerebral cortex.

proactive inhibition A process in which previously learned information interferes with the learning of new information because the contents of both sets of information are similar.

procedural knowledge In contrast to declarative knowledge, knowledge of how to do something—skills. Generally, procedural knowledge is difficult to express verbally.

process A tentaclelike extension of a cell.

progesterone During the female reproductive cycle, hormone secreted by the corpus luteum that increases the blood supply to the uterine wall, preparing it for the egg's implantation should fertilization occur.

programmed cell death/synapse refinement See Table 3.1, Processes of Neural Development.

proliferation See Table 3.1, Processes of Neural Development.

proprioception The ability to sense limb position and muscle tension; monitored by sensory receptors in muscles and tendons.

psychopharmacology The study of the effects of drugs on behavior.

psychoses Severe mental disorders including the affective disorders and schizophrenia; often chronic and severely incapacitating.

pupil The opening in the iris; responsible for regulating the amount of light entering the eye.

pulvinar A large nucleus in the thalamus receiving visual input from the superior colliculus and, ultimately, from the retina.

Purkinje cells The primary output cells of the cerebellar cortex, they integrate information from the cerebral cortex, thalamus, medulla, and spinal cord regarding location and position of the head, limbs, and trunk.

pyramidal tract The large nerve-fiber bundle composed of the axons of Betz cells and other cells of the motor cortex. One tract originates in each hemisphere, and they cross over from the side of origin to the other side of the spinal cord; thus, damage to one side of the motor cortex produces motor disabilities on the opposite side of the body.

rapid eye movement (REM) sleep The fifth and deepest stage of sleep; although there is rapid movement of the eye muscles, there is total relaxation of the skeletal muscles. Most vivid dreams occur during REM sleep.

receptive field A receptor cell's region of sensitivity.

Reissner's membrane Membrane within the cochlea separating the vestibular canal and the cochlear canal.

renin Enzyme secreted by juxtaglomerular cells of the kidneys when blood pressure drops; converts angiotensinogen into angiotensin II in a process to restore blood pressure levels to normal.

resting potential The electrical potential across the membrane of an unstimulated neuron, with the inside of the cell negative relative to the outside.

reticular formation A zone of extended nonnuclear structures within the midbrain, pons, and medulla that plays an important role in arousal (sleep and wakefulness) and attention; its nonspecific neurons receive sensory information from various neural sources and act as a filter, passing on only information that is novel or persistent.

retina The light-sensitive, image-recording part of the eye; has a highly organized, layered structure composed of primary receptor neurons (rods and cones), bipolar neurons, amacrine cells, and ganglion cells.

retinotopic organization The correspondence between points in space and comparable points in each retina; despite the crossing over of some nerve fibers of each optic nerve at the optic chiasm. This organization is maintained throughout the organization of the nervous system.

reuptake The process by which some presynaptic neurons draw back excessive neurotransmitter into its vesicles.

ribosomes Organelles for protein synthesis, both for products to be secreted outside the cell (attached to rough endoplasmic reticulum) and for products (enzymes, structural proteins) used within the cell ("free" ribosomes).

rod A sensory neuron located in the periphery of

the retina; sensitive to light of low intensity and specialized for nighttime vision.

rough endoplasmic reticulum   See **endoplasmic reticulum.**

round window   A membrane-covered opening in the cochlea which allows the fluid within the cochlea to move back and forth upon stimulation from the stapes.

sacral segments   Lower area of the spinal cord; along with the brainstem, receives preganglionic information for the parasympathetic nervous system.

satiety factors   Digestive hormones secreted into the gut during a meal, influencing when a meal should end.

schizophrenia   A group of severe and generally chronic disorders of mental functioning characterized by disturbed thinking, feelings, and behaviors.

Schwann cell   Specialized glial cell found in the peripheral nervous system; responsible for the production of myelin.

sensitization   A behavior in which an organism learns to respond vigorously to a previously neutral stimulus.

septum   A structure of the telencephalon and part of the limbic system; forms the wall between the fluid-filled lateral ventricles.

serotonin   A monoamine neurotransmitter believed to function in temperature regulation, sensory perception, and the onset of sleep. Neurons using serotonin as a transmitter are found in the brain and in the gut.

short-term memory   A phase of memory in which a limited amount of information may be held for several minutes.

sleep spindles   Bursts of brain wave activity synchronized at about 12 to 15 cycles per second but lasting less than one second at a time; interrupts low-voltage, slow activity during stage-3 sleep.

smooth endoplasmic reticulum   See **endoplasmic reticulum.**

soma   The cell body of a neuron.

somatic sensation   Relating to the sense of touch.

somatostatin   A ubiquitous peptide hormone produced by the pancreatic islets (acting to regulate insulin and glucagon secretion), by cells in the lining of the gut (acting to slow peristalsis during nutrient transport), and by neurons in the brain and autonomic nervous system.

stapes   A component of the ossicles, the stapes has a footplate that transmits auditory vibrations to the inner ear via the oval window; commonly known as the stirrup.

stimulus   An environmental event capable of being detected by sensory receptors.

stimulus detector unit   Component of the nervous system consisting of specialized sensory receptor neurons.

striatum   See **neostriatum.**

substance P   Neuropeptide that, among other possible functions, appears to be a specialized transmitter of pain-related information from peripheral nerves to the central system.

substantia nigra   Within the midbrain, a concentrated set of neural cell bodies that secrete the neurotransmitter dopamine.

subventricular zone   Layer of cells forming between the ventricular and intermediate zones of the neural tube; region where many neurons and glial cells form and migrate to form the forebrain.

sulci   The deep grooves in the cerebral hemispheres of primates and certain other mammals (singular **sulcus**).

summation   The aggregation of neurotransmitter and its subsequent action potential on a single nerve cell due either to (1) a presynaptic neuron firing a number of times in rapid succession or (2) numerous presynaptic neurons firing simultaneously.

superior colliculi   Nuclei protruding from the top of the midbrain; functions as a relay station in the visual system, along with the integration of information used in spatial orientation.

suprachiasmatic nuclei   Hypothalamic structures considered the chief pacemaker of the brain, synchronizing many of the circadian rhythms of the body.

sylvian fissure   The large groove in the cortex dividing the temporal lobe from the rest of the cortex; longer and straighter in the left hemisphere.

sympathetic nervous system   A branch of the autonomic nervous system responsible for mobilizing the body's energy and resources during times of stress and arousal.

synapse   The area of contact between the axon

of a presynaptic neuron and the dendrite or soma of a postsynaptic neuron; site of information transfer between nerve cells.

synaptic transmission   The process of information transfer at the synapse.

synaptic gap   The small space separating the presynaptic and postsynaptic cells.

synaptic vesicles   The tiny storage organelles ("bladders") within an axon where a neuron's neurotransmitter is stored; each vesicle contains thousands of copies of the transmitter molecules.

tachistoscope   An instrument that flashes visual stimuli for short, regular intervals onto the visual field, used for the testing of hemispheric dominance.

tectorial membrane   Component of the organ of Corti, this rigid flap of tissue extends over the hair cells and works in conjunction with the basilar membrane in the sensation of auditory stimuli.

telencephalon   Portion of the forebrain containing the cerebral cortex.

temporal lobe   One of the four major subdivisions of each hemisphere of the cerebral cortex; functions in auditory perception, speech, and complex visual perceptions.

thalamus   Portion of the diencephalon, serving as a relay station for almost all sensory information coming into and out of the forebrian.

thyroid   An endocrine organ that secretes thyroxin and acts in the regulation of body growth and rate of metabolism.

timbre   Auditory sensation that is rich mixture of frequencies and allows for discriminations between similar sound sources.

trophic factors   Chemical substances thought to be transferred from the mesoderm to the ectoderm to influence embryonic development.

Turner's syndrome   Chromosomal abnormality in which individuals have only one X chromosome and no X or Y to make a pair. These females, designated as XO, are characterized as being sterile, short, and immature looking, along with having poor visual-spatial abilities.

tympanic canal   One of the three sections of the cochlea through which fluid passes during the sensation of auditory stimuli.

tympanic membrane   Commonly known as the eardrum, this thin, fibrous membrane vibrates in proportion to the intensity of sound waves, passing on the vibrations to the structures of the middle ear.

unconditioned response   In classical conditioning, a response that naturally follows the presentation of an unconditioned stimulus.

unconditioned stimulus   In classical conditioning, a stimulus that naturally evokes a specific response without training.

ultradian rhythm   Cycle of behavioral and physiological change that is repeated more than once a day (e.g., human sleep cycle).

unipolar depression   An affective disorder typified by episodic depressive problems alternating with an otherwise normal mood level.

vagus nerve   The largest of the cranial nerves, the vagus nerve has numerous branches that supply all the parasympathetic innervation of the heart, lungs, and intestinal tract; also carries sensory information coming in from these regions back to the preganglionic level and relays information from the receptors located in the palate and throat to the brain.

valium   Benzodiazepine thought to work by promoting the effectiveness of the inhibitory functions of GABA; tranquilizer commonly used to alleviate stress and anxiety.

vasopressin   A peptide hormone released by the nerve fibers comprising the posterior pituitary gland; acts in the body to increase blood pressure during extreme emergencies when fluid or blood are lost; acts to decrease urinary excretion of water, for which it has also been called the antidiuretic hormone. In the brain, other neurons use the peptide for synaptic regulation.

ventricular zone   The inner surface of the embryonic neural tube.

vestibular apparatus   A complex of organs located at the sides of the skull and beneath the ear; provides the sense of balance and is used in monitoring head and posture movements, along with spatial orientation.

vestibular canal   One of the three sections of the cochlea through which fluid passes during sensation of auditory stimuli.

Wada test   A diagnostic test used for the localization of hemispheric functioning; involves the injection of sodium amytal, an anesthetic, into the carotid artery supplying blood to one hemisphere of the brain.

Wernicke's area   Brain region located in the temporal lobe and responsible for the comprehension of language and the production of meaningful speech. Damage to this area results in Wernicke's aphasia, a disorder characterized by fluent but meaningless speech.

Zeitgeber   German term that refers to the environmental cues affecting biological rhythms.

Z lens   Device that projects a visual image directly onto one half of the retina of one eye, ensuring that only one hemisphere receives visual information; used in the testing of hemispheric dominance.

References

Adams, R. A. 1980. The morphological aspects of aging in the human nervous system. In J. E. Birren and K. Bergmann (eds.), *Handbook of Mental Health and Aging.* Englewood Cliffs, N.J.: Prentice-Hall.

Alajouanine, T. 1948. Aphasia and artistic realization. *Brain, 71:*229–241.

Alexander, D., A. A. Ehrhardt, and J. Money. 1966. Defective figure drawing, geometric and human, in Turner's syndrome. *Journal of Nervous and Mental Diseases, 142:*161–167.

Alkon, D. L. 1983. Learning in a marine snail. *Scientific American, 249:*70–84.

Amiel-Tyson, C. 1982. Neurological signs, etiology, and implications. In P. Straton (ed.) *Psychobiology of the Human Newborn.* New York: Wiley.

Anand, B. K., and J. R. Brobeck. 1951. Hypothalamic control of food intake in rats and cats. *Yale Journal of Biological Medicine, 24:*123–133.

Annett, M. 1964. A model of the inheritance of handedness and cerebral dominance. *Nature, 204:*59–60.

Annett, M. 1974. Handedness in the children of two left-handed parents. *Quarterly Journal of Psychology, 65:*129–131.

Annett, M. 1981. The genetics of handedness. *Trends in Neurosciences, 3:*256–258.

Arendt, A. 1972. Altern des "Zentral nerven Systems." In *Handbuch der Allgemeiner Pathologie.* Berlin: Springer-Verlag.

Aschoff, J., ed. 1980. *Biological Rhythms,* vol. 4, *Handbook of Behavioral Neurobiology.* New York: Plenum.

Aschoff, J. 1981. Circadian rhythms: Interference with and dependence on work-rest schedules. In L. C. Johnson et al. (eds.), *Biological Rhythms, Sleep and Shift Work.* New York: SP Medical and Scientific Books.

Aschoff, J., U. Gerecke, A. Kureck, H. Pohl, P. Rieger, U. von Saint-Paul, and R. Wever. 1971. Interdependent parameters of circadian activity rhythms in birds and man. In M. Menaker (ed.), *Biochronometry,* vol. 3. Washington, D.C.: National Academy of Sciences.

Aschoff, J., and R. Wever. 1965. Circadian rhythms of finches in light-dark circles with interposed twilights. *Comparative Biochemistry and Physiology, 16:*507–514.

Bahrick, H. P., P. O. Bahrick, & R. P. Wittlinger. 1974. Those unforgettable high-school days. *Psychology Today,* December:50–56.

Bakan, P. 1978. Why left-handedness? *Behavioral and Brain Sciences, 2:*279–280.

Bakan, P. G. Dibb, and P. Reed. 1973. Handedness and birth stress. *Neuropsychologia, 11:*363–366.

Bard, P. 1934. On emotional expression after decortication with some remarks of certain theoretical views. Part I, *Psychological Review, 4:*309–329; Part II, 4:424–449.

Barnes, D. M. 1986. Nervous and immune systems linked in a variety of diseases. *Science, 232:*160–161.

Bauman, M. L., and T. L. Kemper. 1982. Morphologic and histoanatomic observations of the brain in the untreated human phenylketonuria. *Acta Neuropathologica (Berlin), 58:*55–63.

Beecher, H. K. 1959. *Measurement of Subjective Responses: Quantitative Effects of Drugs.* New York: Oxford University Press.

Bell, A. P., Weinberg, M. S., and Hammersmith, S. E. 1981. *Sexual Preference: Its Development in Men and Women.* Bloomington: Indiana University Press.

Berry, H. K. 1969. Phenylketonuria: diagnosis, treatment, and long-term management. In G. Farrell (ed.), *Congenital Mental Retardation.* Austin: University of Texas Press.

Binkley. S. 1979. A timekeeping enzyme in the pineal gland. *Scientific American, 240:*66–71.

Birren, J. E., and R. B. Sloane (eds.). 1980. *Handbook of Mental Health and Aging.* Englewood Cliffs, N.J.: Prentice-Hall.

Bishop, M. P., S. T. Elder, and R. G. Heath. 1963. Intracranial self-stimulation in man. *Science, 140:*393–396.

Bisiach, E., and C. Luzzatti. 1978. Unilateral neglect of representational space. *Cortex, 14:*129–133.

Body, H. 1976. An examination of cerebral cortex and brainstem aging. In R. D. Terry and S. Gershon (eds.), *Neurobiology of Aging.* New York: Raven.

Bondareff, W. 1980. Neurobiology of aging. In J. E. Birren and K. Bergmann (eds.), *Handbook of Mental Health and Aging.* Englewood Cliffs, N.J.: Prentice-Hall.

Botwinick, J. 1977. Intellectual abilities. In J. E. Birren

and K. W. Schaie (eds.), *Handbook of the Psychology of Aging*. New York: Van Nostrand Reinhold.

Bower, G. 1981. Mood and memory. *American Psychologist, 36*:128–148.

Brain, P. F. 1979. *Hormones, Drugs, and Aggression*, vol. 3. Annual Research Reviews. Montreal: Eden Press.

Brain, P. F. 1980. Diverse action of hormones on "aggression" in animals and man. In L. Valzelli and L. Morgese (eds.), *Aggression and Violence: A Psychobiological and Clinical Approach*. Milan: Edizioni Saint Vincent.

Brewton, C. B., K. C. Liang, and J. L. McGaugh. 1981. Adrenal demedullation alters the effect of amygdala stimulation on retention of avoidance tasks. *Neuroscience Abstracts, 7*:870.

Brody, H. 1955. Organization of the cerebral cortex. III. A study of aging in the human cerebral cortex. *Journal of Comparative Neurology, 102*:511–556.

Bronshtein, A. I., and E. P. Petrova. 1967. The auditory analyzer in young infants. In Y. Brackbill and G. Thompson (eds.), *Behavior in Infancy and Early Childhood*. New York: Free Press.

Broughton, R. 1975. Biorhythmic variations in consciousness and psychological functions. *Canadian Psychological Review, 16*:217–239.

Bruner, J. S. 1969. Foreword to *The Mind of a Mnemonist*, by A. R. Luria. New York: Avon Books.

Brust, J. C. M. 1980. Music and language: Musical alexia and agraphia. *Brain, 103*:367–392.

Buckingham, H. W., Jr., and A. Kertesz. 1974. A linguistic analysis of fluent aphasics. *Brain and Language, 1*:29–42.

Bünning, E. 1973. *The Physiological Clock: Circadian Rhythms and Biological Chronometry*. New York: Springer-Verlag.

Cannon, W. B. 1927. The James-Lange theory of emotion: A critical examination and an alternative theory. *American Journal of Psychology, 39*:106–124.

Cannon, W. B. 1929. *Bodily Changes in Pain, Hunger, Fear, and Rage*. New York: Appleton-Century-Crofts.

Caplan, D., and J. C. Marshall. 1972. Generative grammar and aphasic disorders: A theory of language representation in the human brain. *Foundations of Language, 12*:583–596.

Champion, R. A. 1950. Studies of experimentally induced disturbance. *Australian Journal of Psychology, 2*:90–99.

Chase, M. H. 1973. Somatic reflex activity during sleep and wakefulness. In O. Petre-Quadens and J. Schlag (eds.), *Basic Sleep Mechanisms*. New York: Academic Press.

Cohen, J. 1967. *Psychological Time in Health and Disease*. Springfield, Ill.: Charles C Thomas.

Cohen, N. J. 1981. Neuropsychological evidence for a distinction between procedural and declarative knowledge in human memory and amnesia. Ph.D. thesis, University of California, San Diego.

Cohen, N. J. and L. R. Squire. 1980. Preserved learning and retention of pattern analyzing skill in amnesia: Dissociation of knowing how and knowing that. *Science, 210*:207–209.

Cohen, N. J., and L. R. Squire. 1981. Retrograde amnesia and remote memory impairment. *Neuropsychologia, 19*:337–356.

Coleman, D. L., and K. P. Hummel. 1969. Effects of parabiosis of normal with genetically diabetic mice. *American Journal of Physiology, 217*:1298–1304.

Conel, J. L. 1939–1963. *The Postnatal Development of the Human Cerebral Cortex* (7 vols.). Cambridge, Mass.: Harvard University Press.

Corballis, M. C. 1983. *Human Laterality*. New York: Academic.

Coren, S., and C. Porac. 1977. Fifty centuries of right-handedness: The historical record. *Science, 198*:631–632.

Corso, J. F. 1975. Sensory processes in man during maturity and senescence. In J. M. Ordy and K. R. Brizzee (eds.), *Neurobiology of Aging*. New York: Plenum.

Costa, E., and A. Guidotti. 1979. Molecular mechanisms in the receptor action of benzodiazepines. *American Review of Pharmacology and Toxicology, 19*:531–545.

Cotman, C. W., and J. McGaugh. 1980. *Behavioral Neuroscience: An Introduction*. New York: Academic Press.

Cowan, W. M. 1981. *Studies in Developmental Neurobiology*. New York: Oxford University Press.

Cragg, B. G. 1975. The development of synapses in the visual system of the cat. *Journal of Comparative Neurology, 160*:147–166.

Crisp, A. H. 1983. Treatment of anorexia nervosa: What can be the role of psychopharmacological agents? In K. M. Pirke and D. Ploog (eds.), *The Psychobiology of Anorexia Nervosa*. New York: Springer-Verlag.

Curtiss, S. 1977. *Genie: A Psycholinguistic Study of a Modern-Day "Wild Child."* New York: Academic Press.

Czeisler, C., G. S. Richardson, R. M. Coleman, J. C. Zimmerman, M. C. Moore-Ede, W. C. Dement, and E. D. Weitzman. 1981. Chronotherapy: Resetting the circadian clocks of patients with delayed sleep phase insomnia. *Sleep, 4*:1–21.

Czeisler, C. A., E. D. Weitzman, M. C. Moore-Ede, J. C. Zimmerman, and R. S. Knauer. 1980. Human sleep:

Its duration and organization depend on its circadian phase. *Science, 210*:1264–1267.

Darwin, C. 1965. *The Expression of the Emotions in Man and Animals*. Originally published in 1872. Chicago: The University of Chicago Press.

Davis, J. D., and D. J. Brief. 1981. Chronic intraventricular insulin infusions reduce food intake and body weight in rats, *Soc. Neurosci. Abstr. 7:655*.

Davis, J. D., R. J. Gallagher, R. F. Ladove, and A. J. Turansky. 1969. Inhibition of food intake by a humoral factor. *Journal of Comparative Physiological Psychology*, 67:407–417.

Delgado, J. M. R. 1969. *Physical Control of the Mind: Toward a Psychocivilized Society*. New York: Harper & Row.

Dement, W. C. 1972. *Some Must Watch While Some Must Sleep*. New York: W. H. Freeman.

Dennis, M., and H. Whitaker. 1976. Language acquisition following hemi-decortication: Linguistic superiority of the left over the right hemisphere. *Brain and Language*, 3:404–433.

Dennis, W. 1960. Causes of retardation among institutional children: Iran. *Journal of Genetic Psychology*, 96:46–60.

Deutsch, J. A. 1973. The cholinergic synapse and the site of memory. In J. A. Deutsch (ed.), *The Physiological Basis of Memory*. New York: Academic Press.

Dickerson, J. W. T., and H. McGurk (eds.). 1982. *Brain and Behavioural Development; Interdisciplinary Perspectives on Structure and Function*. London: Surrey University Press.

Dorner, G. 1976. *Hormones and Brain Differentiation*. New York: Elsevier.

Drillien, C. M. 1964. *The Growth and Development of the Prematurely Born Infant*. Edinburgh, Scotland: Livingstone.

Drucker-Colin, R. R., and C. W. Spanis. 1976. Is there a sleep transmitter? *Progress in Neurobiology*, 6:1–22.

Dubois, A., H. A. Gross, and M. H. Ebert. 1984. Gastric function in primary anorexia nervosa. In K. M. Pirke and D. Ploog (eds.), *The Psychobiology of Anorexia Nervosa*. New York: Springer-Verlag.

Durden-Smith, J., and D. deSimone. 1983. *Sex and the Brain*. New York: Arbor House.

Dyer, R. G., N. K. MacLeod, and F. Ellendorf. 1976. Electrophysiological evidence for sexual dimorphism and synaptic convergence in the preoptic and anterior hypothalamic areas of the rat. *Proceedings of the Royal Society, London. B 193*:421–440.

Ebert, P. D. 1983. Selection for aggression in a natural population. In E. C. Simmel et al. (eds.), *Aggressive Behavior: Genetic and Neural Approaches*. Hillsdale, N.J.: Lawrence Erlbaum.

Edelman, G. M. 1976. Surface modulation in cell recognition and cell growth. *Science, 192*:218–226.

Edelman, G. M., and V. B. Mountcastle. 1978. *The Mindful Brain*. Cambridge, Mass.: MIT Press.

Eisdorfer, C., and F. Wilkie. 1973. Intellectual changes with advancing age. In L. F. Jarvik, C. Eisdorfer, and J. E. Blum (eds.) *Intellectual Functioning in Adults*, pp. 21–29. New York: Springer-Verlag.

Elliott, J. 1979. Finally: Some details on *in vitro* fertilization. *Journal of the American Medical Association*, 241:868–869.

Emde, R. W., J. J. Gaensbauer, and R. J. Harmon. 1976. *Emotional Expression in Infancy*. New York: International Universities Press.

Epstein, C. J. 1986. *The Neurobiology of Down Syndrome*. New York: Raven.

Faust, I. M., P. R. Johnson, J. S. Stern, and J. Hirsch. 1978. Diet-induced adipocyte number increase in adult rats: a new model of obesity. *American Journal of Physiology, 235*:E279–E286.

Festinger, L. 1957. *A Theory of Cognitive Dissonance*. Stanford Cal.: Stanford University Press.

Finch, C. 1973. Catecholamine metabolism in the brains of aging male mice. *Brain Research, 52*:261–276.

Frankenhaeuser, M. 1971. Behavior and circulating catecholamines. *Brain Research, 31*:241–262.

Frankenhaeuser, M. 1975. Experimental approaches to the study of catecholamines and emotion. In L. Levi (ed.), *Emotions: Their Parameters and Measurement*. New York: Raven Press.

Freeman, R. D., and L. N. Thibos. 1973. Electrophysiological evidence that abnormal early visual experience can modify the human brain. *Science, 180*:876–878.

Fuller, C., F. Sulzman, and M. Moore-Ede. 1981. Shift work and the jet lag syndrome: Conflicts between environmental and body time. In L. C. Johnson et al. (eds.), *Biological Rhythms, Sleep, and Shift Work*. New York: SP Medical and Scientific Books.

Fulton, J. F., and P. Bailey. 1929. Tumors in the region of the third ventricle: Their diagnosis and relation to pathological sleep. *Journal of Nervous and Mental Disorders, 69*:1–25.

Funkenstein, H. H., P. G. Nelson, P. Winter, Z. Wollberg, and J. D. Newman. 1971. Unit responses in the auditory cortex of awake squirrel monkeys to vocal stimulation. In M. B. Sachs (ed.), *Physiology of the Auditory System*. Baltimore: National Educational Consultants.

Galaburda, A. M., and T. M. Kemper. 1979. Cytoarchitectonic abnormalities in developmental dyslexia: A case study. *Annals of Neurology 6*:94–100.

Galaburda, A. M., M. Le May, T. L. Kemper, and N.

Geschwind. 1978. Right-left asymmetries in the brain. *Science, 199*:852–856.

Garber, B. B., and A. A. Moscona. 1972. Reconstruction of brain tissue from cell suspensions. I. Aggregation patterns of cells dissociated from different regions of the developing brain. *Developmental Biology, 27*:217–234.

Gates, A., and J. Bradshaw. 1977. The role of the cerebral hemispheres in music. *Brain and Language, 4*:403–431.

Gazzaniga, M. S. 1970. *The Bisected Brain*. New York: Appleton-Century-Crofts.

Gazzaniga, M. S., and J. E. Le Doux. 1978. *The Integrated Mind*. New York: Plenum.

Geer, J. H., G. C. Davison, and R. I. Gatchel. 1970. Reduction of stress in humans through nonveridical perceived control of aversive stimulation. *Journal of Personality and Social Psychology, 16*:731–738.

Geinisman, Y., and W. Bondareff. 1976. Decrease in the number of synapses in the senescent brain: A quantitative electron microscopic analysis of the dentate gyrus molecular layer in the rat. *Mechanisms of Aging and Development, 5*:11–23.

Geschwind, N. 1979. Specializations of the human brain. *Scientific American, 241*:158–168.

Geschwind, N., and P. Behan. 1982. Left-handedness: Association with immune disease, migraine, and developmental learning disorder. *Proceedings of the National Academy of Science USA, 79*:5097–5100.

Geschwind, N., and W. Levitsky. 1968. Human brain: Left-right asymmetries in temporal speech region. *Science, 161*:186–187.

Gispen, W. H., and J. Traber (eds.). 1983. *Aging of the Brain*, Developments in Neurology, vol. 7. New York: Elsevier.

Gladue, B. A., R. Green, and R. E. Hellman. 1984. Neuroendocrine response to estrogen and sexual orientation. *Science, 225*:1496–1499.

Globus, A., M. R. Rosenzweig, E. Bennett, and M. C. Diamond. 1973. Effects of differential experience on dendritic spine counts in rat cerebral cortex. *Journal of Comparative Physiology and Psychology, 82*:175–181.

Gold, P., and J. L. McGaugh. 1975. *Short-Term Memory*. New York: Academic Press.

Goldschneider, I., and A. A. Moscona. 1972. Tissue-specific cell-surface antigens in embryonic cells. *Journal of Cell Biology, 53*:435–449.

Goodglass, H., and N. Geschwind. 1976. Language disorders (aphasia). In *Handbook of Perception*, vol. 7, *Language and Speech*. New York: Academic Press.

Goodsit, A. 1985. Self psychology and the treatment of anorexia nervosa. In D. M. Garner and P. E. Garfinkel (eds.), *Handbook of Psychotherapy for Ano-*

rexia Nervosa and Bulimia. New York: Guilford Press.

Gordon, H. W., and A. Galatzer. 1980. Cerebral organization in patients with gonadal dysgenesis. *Psychoneuroendocrinology, 5*:235–244.

Gorski, R. A., J. H. Gordon, J. E. Shryne, and A. M. Southam. 1978. Evidence for a morphological sex difference within the medial preoptic area of the rat brain. *Brain Research, 148*:333–346.

Gottlieb, D. I., and Glaser, L. 1981. Cellular recognition during neural development. In D. I. Gottlieb and L. Glaser, *Studies in Developmental Neurobiology*. New York: Oxford University Press.

Gould, S. J. 1977. *Ontogeny and Phylogeny*. Cambridge, Mass.: Harvard University Press.

Gould, S. J. 1980. *The Panda's Thumb: More Reflections in Natural History*. New York: Norton.

Goy, R. W., and B. S. McEwen. 1980. *Sexual Differentiation of the Brain*. Cambridge, Mass.: MIT Press.

Goy, R. W. 1968. Organizing effects of androgen on the behavior of rhesus monkeys. In R. P. Michael (ed.), *Endocrinology and Human Behavior*, New York: Oxford University Press.

Gray, J. A. 1977. Drug effects on fear and frustration: Possible limbic site of action of minor tranquilizers. In L. L. Iversen et al. (eds.), *Handbook of Psychopharmacology*, vol. 8, pp. 433–529. New York: Plenum.

Greenough, W. T., C. S. Carter, C. Steerman, and T. J. DeVoogd. 1977. Sex differences in dendritic patterns in hamster preoptic area. *Brain Research, 126*:63–72.

Greenough, W. T., and F. F. Chang. 1984. Anatomically detectable correlates of information storage in the nervous system of animals. In C. W. Cotman (ed.) *Neuronal Plasticity*, 2d ed. New York: Raven.

Greenough, W. T., R. W. West, and T. J. DeVoogd. 1978. Subsynaptic plate perforations: Changes with age and experience in the rat. *Science, 202*:1096–1098.

Greenwood, P., D. H. Wilson, and M. S. Gazzaniga. 1977. Dream report following commissurotomy. *Cortex, 13*:311–316.

Griffin, D. R. 1976. *The Question of Animal Awareness*. New York: Rockefeller University Press.

Griffin, D. R. 1984. *Animal Thinking*. Cambridge, Mass.: Harvard University Press.

Griffiths, J. D., and P. R. Payne. 1976. Energy expenditure in small children of obese and non-obese mothers. *Nature, 260*:698–700.

Grossman, S. 1967. *A Textbook of Physiological Psychology*. New York: Wiley.

Guillery, R. W., V. A. Casagrande, and M. D. Uberdorfer. 1974. Congenitally abnormal vision in Siamese cats. *Nature* (London), *252*:195–199.

Gwinner, E. 1968. Circannuale Periodik als Grundlage

des Jahreszeitlichen Funktionswandels bei Zugvögeln. *Journal für Ornithologie,* 109:70–95.

Halberg, F., E. A. Johnson, B. W. Brown, and J. J. Bittner. 1960. Susceptibility rhythm to *E. Coli* endotoxin and bioassay. *Proceedings of the Society for Experimental Biology and Medicine,* 103:142–144.

Halmi, K. A. 1985. Behavioral management for anorexia nervosa. In D. M. Garner and P. E. Garfinkel (eds.), *Handbook of Psychotherapy for Anorexia Nervosa and Bulimia.* New York: Guilford Press.

Hamburger, V., and R. Levi-Montalcini. 1949. Proliferation, differentiation, and degeneration in the spinal ganglia of the chick embryo under normal and experimental conditions. *Journal of Experimental Zoology,* 111:457–501.

Harlow, H. F. 1949. The formation of learning sets. *Psychological Review,* 56:51–56.

Harlow, J. M. 1848. Passage of an iron rod through the head. *Boston Medical and Surgical Journal,* 39:389–393.

Harris, L. J. 1980. Which hand is the "eye" of the blind? A new look at an old question. In J. Herron (ed.), *Neuropsychology of Left Handedness.* New York: Academic Press.

Hart, B. 1967. Sexual reflexes and mating behavior in the male dog. *Journal of Comparative and Physiological Psychology,* 66:388–399.

Hebb, D. O. 1949. *The Organization of Behavior.* New York: Wiley.

Hebb, D. O., and W. R. Thompson. 1968. The social significance of animal studies. In G. Lindzey (ed.), *Handbook of Social Psychology,* Cambridge, Mass.: Addison-Wesley.

Hess, W. R. 1957. *The Functional Organization of the Diencephalon.* New York: Grune & Stratton.

Hetherington, A. W., and S. W. Ranson. 1939. Experimental hypothalamicohypophyseal obesity in the rat. *Proceedings of the Society for Experimental Biology and Medicine,* 41:465–466.

Hier, D., and W. Crowley. 1982. Spatial ability in androgen-deficient men. *New England Journal of Medicine,* May 20, 1982.

Hoffman, S., and G. M. Edelman. 1983. Kinetics of homophilic binding by embryonic and adult forms of the neural cell. *Proceedings of the National Academy of Sciences,* 80:5762–5766.

Hollyday, M., and V. Hamburger. 1975. Reduction of normally occurring motor neuron depletion following supernumerary limb transplantation in chick embryo. *Neuroscience Abstracts,* 1:779.

Hohmann, G. W. 1966. Some effects of spinal cord lesions on experienced emotional feelings. *Psychophysiology,* 3:143–156.

Holmes, T. H., and M. Masuda. 1972. Psychosomatic syndrome: When mothers-in-law or other disasters visit, a person can develop a bad, bad cold. Or worse. *Psychology Today,* April.

Hubel, D. H., and T. N. Wiesel. 1962. Receptive fields, binocular interaction, and functional architecture in the cat's visual cortex. *Journal of Physiology,* 160:106–154.

Hubel, D. H., and T. N. Wiesel. 1979. Brain mechanisms of vision. *Scientific American,* 241:150–162.

Hughes, M. 1982. Sex differences in brain development: Process and effects. In J. W. T. Dickerson and H. McGurk (eds.), *Brain and Behavioural Development.* London: Surrey University Press.

Hunt, R. K., and M. Jacobson. 1972. Development and stability of positional information in Xenopus retinal ganglion cells. *Proceedings of the National Academy of Sciences,* 69:780–783.

Hutt, S. J., C. Hutt, H. G. Lehard, H. von Bernuth, and W. J. Muntjewerff. 1968. Auditory responsivity in the human neonate. *Nature,* 218:888–890.

Ibuka, N., S. T. Inouye, and H. Kawamura. 1977. Analysis of sleep-wakefulness rhythms in male rats after suprachiasmatic nucleus lesions and ocular enucleation. *Brain Research,* 122:33–47.

Inouye, S. T., and H. Kawamura. 1979. Persistence of circadian rhythmicity in mammalian hypothalamic "island" containing the suprachiasmatic nucleus. *Proceedings of the National Academy of Science USA,* 76:5961–5966.

Jacobson, M. 1978. *Developmental Neurobiology.* New York: Holt.

James, W. 1884. What is emotion? *Mind,* 9:188-204.

James, W. 1890. *The Principles of Psychology,* Vol. 2. New York: Holt.

Jarvik, J. F. 1983. Age is in—is the wit out? In D. Samuel et al. (eds.), *Aging of the Brain.* New York: Raven.

Jaynes, J. 1976. *The Origin of Consciousness in the Breakdown of the Bicameral Mind.* Boston: Houghton-Miflin.

Jaynes, J. 1977. Reflections on the dawn of consciousness. *Psychology Today,* 11:58.

Jencks, C., M. Smith, H. Acland, M. J. Bane, D. Cohen, H. Gintis, B. Heyns, and S. Michelson. 1972. *Inequality: A Reassessment of the Effect of Family and Schooling in America.* New York: Basic Books.

Johnson, L. C., W. P. Colquhoun, D. I. Tepas, and M. J. Colligan (eds.). 1981. *Biological Rhythms, Sleep, and Shift Work.* New York: SP Medical and Scientific Books.

Jolly, A. 1972. *The Evolution of Primate Behavior.* New York: MacMillan.

Jonec, V., and C. Finch. 1975. Aging and dopamine uptake by subcellular fractions of the C57 B1/6J male mouse brain. *Brain Research, 91*:197–215.

Jones, R. K. 1966. Observations on stammering after localized cerebral injury. *Journal of Neurology, Neurosurgery, and Psychiatry, 29*:192–195.

Jost, A. D. 1979. Basic sexual trends in the development of vertebrates. In *Human Reproduction.* London: Paladin.

Jouvet, M. 1977. Neuropharmacology of the sleep-waking cycle. In L. L. Iversen *et al.* (eds.), *Handbook of Psychopharmacology,* vol. 8, pp. 233–293. New York: Plenum.

Kandel, E. R. 1976. *Cellular Basis of Behavior: An Introduction to Behavioral Neurobiology.* New York: W. H. Freeman.

Kandel, E. R. 1979. Small systems of neurons. *Scientific American, 241*:61–70.

Kandel, E. R., and J. H. Schwartz. 1982. Molecular biology of learning: Modulation of transmitter release. *Science, 218*:433–442.

Kaplan, J. R., S. B. Manuck, T. B. Clarkson, F. M. Lusso, D. M. Taub, and E. W. Miller. 1983. Social stress and atherosclerosis in normocholesterolemic monkeys. *Science, 200*:733–735.

Katchadourian, H. A., and D. T. Lunde. 1980. *Fundamentals of Human Sexuality,* 3d ed. New York: Holt.

Kay, D. W. K., and K. Bergmann. 1980. Epidemiology of mental disorders among the aged in the community. In J. E. Birren and K. Bergmann (eds.), *Handbook of Mental Health and Aging.* Englewood Cliffs, N.J.: Prentice-Hall.

Kimura, D. 1973. Manual activity during speaking. II. Left-handers. *Neuropsychologia, 11*:45–50.

Kimura, D. 1979. Neuromotor mechanisms in the evolution of human communication. In H. D. Steklis and M. J. Raleigh (eds.), *Neurobiology of Social Communication in Primates.* New York: Academic Press.

Kimura, D., and Y. Archibald. 1974. Motor functions of the left hemisphere. *Brain, 97*:337–350.

Klein, K. E., and H. M. Wegmann. 1974. The resynchronization of human circadian rhythms after transmeridian flights as a result of flight direction and mode of activity. In L. E. Scheving et al. (eds.), *Chronobiology.* Tokyo: Igaku.

Koestler, A. 1969. The urge to self-destruction. In *The Place of Value in a World of Facts.* Proceedings of the 14th Nobel Symposium, Stockholm.

Kolers, P. A. 1976. Pattern-analyzing memory. *Science, 191*:1280–1281.

Kolers, P. A. 1979. A pattern-analyzing basis of recognition. In L. S. Cermak and F. I. M. Craik (eds.), *Level of Processing in Human Memory.* pp. 363–384. Hillsdale, N.J.: Lawrence Erlbaum.

Kuhl, P. K., and J. D. Miller. 1975. Speech perception by the chinchilla: voiced-voiceless distinction in alveolar plosive consonants. *Science, 190*:69–72.

Lacoste-Utamsing, C. de, and R. Holloway. 1982. Sexual dimorphism in the human corpus callosum. *Science, 216*:1431–1432.

Lacoste-Utamsing, C. de, and D. J. Woodward. 1982. Sexual dimorphism in human fetal corpora callosa. Abstracts of the 1982 meeting of the Society for Neuroscience.

Landfield, P. W. 1983. Mechanisms of altered neural function during aging. In W. H. Gispen and J. Traber (eds.), *Aging of the Brain.* New York: Elsevier.

Landfield, P. W., J. L. McGaugh, and G. Lynch. 1978. Impaired synaptic potentiation processes in the hippocampus of aged, memory-deficient rats. *Brain Research, 150*:85–101.

Landmesser, L. 1981. Pathway selection by embryonic neurons. In W. M. Cowan (ed.), *Studies in Developmental Neurobiology.* New York: Oxford University Press.

Lange, C. G., and W. James. 1922. *The Emotions.* Baltimore: Williams & Wilkins.

Lansdell, H. 1962. A sex difference in effect of temporal lobe neurosurgery on design preference. *Nature, 194*: 852–854.

Lashley, K. S. 1950. *In Search of the Engram.* Society of Experimental Biology Symposium. No. 4: Physiological Mechanisms in Animal Behavior. Cambridge: Cambridge University Press.

Lassen, N. A., D. H. Ingvar, and E. Skinhoj. 1978. Brain function and blood flow. *Scientific American, 239*:62–71.

Lavie, P., and D. F. Kripke. 1975. Ultradian rhythms: The 90-minute clock inside us. *Psychology Today, 8*:54–65.

Ledbetter, D. H., J. T. Mascarello, V. M. Riccard, et al. 1982. Chromosome 15 abnormalities and the Prader-Willi syndrome: A follow-up report of 40 cases. *American Journal of Human Genetics, 34*:278–285.

LeDouarin, N. M., D. Renaud, M. A. Teillet, and G. H. LeDouarin. 1975. Cholinergic differentiation of presumptive adrenergic neuroblasts in interspecific chimeras after heterotopic transplantations. *Proceedings of the National Academy of Science, 72*:728–732.

LeDoux, J. E. 1985. Brain, mind, and language. In D. A. Oakley (ed.), *Brain and Mind.* New York: Methuen.

LeDoux, J. E., D. H. Wilson, and M. S. Gazzaniga. 1977. A divided mind: Observations on the conscious properties of the separated hemispheres. *Annals of*

Neurology, 2:417–421.

LeMay, M. 1977. Assymetries of the skull and handedness: Phrenology revisited. *Journal of Neurological Sciences* 32:243–253.

Leibowitz, S. F. 1983. Noradrenergic function in the medial hypothalamus: Potential relation to anorexia nervosa and bulimia. In K. M. Pirke and D. Ploog (eds.), *The Psychobiology of Anorexia Nervosa.* New York: Springer-Verlag.

Levi-Montalcini, R., and V. Hamburger. 1953. A diffusable agent of mouse sarcoma producing hyperplasia of sympathetic ganglia and hyperneurotization of the chick embryo. *Journal of Experimental Zoology,* 123:233–288.

Levi-Montalcini, R. 1952. Effects of mouse tumor transplantation on the nervous system. *Annals of the New York Academy of Science,* 55:330–343.

Levi-Montalcini, R. 1966. The nerve growth factor: Its mode of action on sensory and sympathetic nerve cells. *Harvey Lectures,* 60:217–259.

Levine, S. 1960. Stimulation in infancy. *Scientific American,* 202:80–86.

Levy, J. 1978. Lateral differences in the human brain in cognition and behavioral control. In P. Buser (ed.) *Cerebral Correlates of Human Experience.* New York: North Holland.

Levy, J., and T. Nagylaki. 1972. A model for the genetics of handedness. *Genetics,* 72:117–128.

Lim, R., D. E. Turriff, S. S. Troy, B. W. Moore, and L. F. Eng. 1977. Glial maturation factor: Effect on chemical differentiation of glioblasts in culture. *Science,* 195:195–196.

Lindsay, P. H., and D. A. Norman. 1977. *Human Information Processing,* 2d ed. New York: Academic Press.

Linnoila, M., C. W. Erwin, D. Ramm, and W. P. Cleveland. 1980. Effects of age and alcohol on psychomotor performance of men. *Journal of Studies in Alcohol,* 41:488–495.

Loo, Y. H., T. Fulton, K. Miller, and H. Wisniewski. 1980. Phenylacetate and brain dysfunction in experimental phenylketonuria: Synaptic development. *Life Sciences* 27:1283–1290.

Lorenz, K. Z. 1971. *Studies in Animal and Human Behaviors* (Robert Martin, translator). Cambridge, Mass.: Harvard University Press.

Lucas, A. R. 1981. Towards the understanding of anorexia nervosa as a disease entity. *Mayo Clinic Proceedings,* 56:254–264.

Luce, G. G. 1971. *Biological Rhythms in Human and Animal Physiology.* New York: Dover.

Lund, R. D. 1978. *Development and Plasticity of the Brain: An Introduction.* New York: Oxford University Press.

Maccoby, E., and C. Jacklin. 1974. *The Psychology of Sex Differences.* Palo Alto, Cal.: Stanford University Press.

MacLean, P. D. 1980. Sensory and perceptive factors in emotional functions of the brain. In A. O. Porty (ed.), *Explaining Emotions.* Berkeley: University of California Press.

Mandler, G. 1975. *Mind and Emotion.* New York: Wiley.

Marañon, G. 1924. Contribution à l'étude de l'action émotive de l'adrenaline. *Revue Française d'Endocrinologie,* 2:301–325.

Margules, D. L., B. Moiset, M. J. Lewis, H. Shibuya, and C. B. Pert. 1978. β-Endorphin is associated with overeating in genetically obese mice (*ob/ob*) and rats (*fa/fa*). *Science* 202:988–991.

Marx. J. L. 1982. Autoimmunity in left-handers. *Science,* 217:141–144.

Mayer, D. J. 1979. Endogenous analgesia systems: Neural and behavioral mechanisms. In J. J. Bonica et al. (eds.), *Advances in Pain Research and Therapy,* Vol. 3. New York: Raven.

Mayer, J. 1955. Regulation of energy intake and the body weight: the glucostatic theory and the lipostatic hypothesis. *Annals of the New York Academy of Science,* 63:15–42.

McCormick, D. A., G. A. Clark, D. G. Lavord, and R. F. Thompson. 1982. Initial localization of the memory trace for a basic form of learning. *Proceedings of the National Academy of Science USA,* 79:2731–2735.

McGaugh, J. J. 1982. *Memory Consolidation.* Hillsdale, N.J.: Lawrence Erlbaum.

McGaugh, J. L. 1983. Hormonal influences on memory storage. *American Psychologist,* 38:161–174.

McGeer, E. G., N. B. Boyce, J. O'Kosky, J. Suzuki, and P. L. McGeer. 1985. Acetylcholine and aromatic amine systems in postmortem brain of an infant with Down's syndrome. *Experimental Neurology,* 87:557–570.

McGeer, P. L., and E. G. McGeer. 1981. Amino acid transmitters. In G. J. Siegel et al. (eds.), *Basic Neurochemistry,* 3d ed., pp. 233–254. Boston: Little-Brown.

McGlone, J. 1978. Sex difference in functional brain asymmetry. *Cortex,* 14:122–128.

McGlone, J. 1980. Sex differences in human brain asymmetry: A critical survey. *Behavior and Brain Science,* 3:215–263.

McGlone, J., and A. Kertesz. 1973. Sex differences in cerebral processing of visuo-spatial tasks. *Cortex,* 9:313–320.

McRae, D. L., Branch, C. L., and Milner, B. 1968. The occipital horns and cerebral dominance. *Neurology* 18:95–98.

Melzak, R., and P. D. Wall. 1965. Pain mechanisms: A new theory. *Science, 150*:971–979.

Meyer, D. R. 1958. Some psychological determinants of sparing and loss following damage to the brain. In H. F. Harlow and C. N. Woolsey (eds.), *Biological and Biochemical Bases of Behavior*. Madison: University of Wisconsin Press.

Michael, R. P. 1980. Hormones and sexual behavior in the female. In D. T. Krieger and J. C. Hughes (eds.), *Neuroendocrinology*. Sunderland, Mass.: Sinauer Assoc.

Milner. B. 1972. Disorders of learning and memory after temporal lobe lesions in man. *Clinical Neurosurgery, 19*:421–446.

Mintz, G., and L. Glaser. 1978. Specific glycoprotein changes during development of the chick neural retina. *Journal of Cell Biology, 79*:132–137.

Mishkin, M. 1978. Memory in monkeys severely impaired by combined but not by separate removal of amygdala and hippocampus. *Nature, 273*:297–298.

Molfese, D. L., R. B. Freeman, Jr., and D. S. Palermo. 1975. The ontogeny of brain lateralization for speech and nonspeech stimuli. *Brain and Language, 2*:356–368.

Møllgaard, K., M. C. Diamond, E. L. Bennett, M. R. Rosenzweig, and B. Lindner. 1971. Quantitative synaptic changes with differential experience in rat brain. *International Journal of Neuroscience, 2*:113–128.

Money, J. 1961. Sex hormones and other variables in human eroticism. In W. C. Young (ed.), *Sex Internal Secretions*, vol. 2. Baltimore: Williams & Wilkins.

Money, J., and A. A. Ehrhardt. 1972. *Man & Woman, Boy & Girl*. Baltimore: Johns Hopkins University Press.

Moore-Ede, M. C., F. M. Sulzman, and C. A. Fuller, 1982. *The Clocks that Time Us*. Cambridge, Mass.: Harvard University Press.

Moscona, A. A., and R. E. Hausman. 1977. Biological and biochemical studies on embryonic cell recognition. In J. W. Lash and M. M. Burger (eds.), *Cell and Tissue Interactions*. New York: Raven.

Moscovitch, M. 1981. Multiple dissociations of function in the amnesic syndrome. In L. S. Cermak (ed.), *Human Memory and Amnesia*. Hillsdale, N.J.: Lawrence Erlbaum.

Mountcastle, V. B. 1975. The view from within: Pathways to the study of perception. *Johns Hopkins Medical Journal, 136*:109–131.

Mountcastle, V. B., 1978. An organizing principle for cerebral function: The unit module and the distributed system. In G. M. Edelman and V. B. Mountcastle, *The Mindful Brain*. Cambridge, Mass.: MIT Press.

Moyer, K. E. 1976. *The Psychobiology of Aggression*. New York: Harper and Row.

Murphy, M. R., P. D. MacLean, and S. C. Hamilton. 1981. Species-typical behavior of hamsters deprived from birth of the neocortex. *Science, 213*:459–461.

Nauta, W. J. H. 1972. Neural associations of the frontal cortex. *Acta Neurobiologiae Experimentalis, 32*:125–140.

Nauta, W. J. H. and V. B. Domesick. 1980. Neural associations of the limbic system. In A. Beckman (ed.), *Neural Substrates of Behavior*. New York: Spectrum.

Nauta, W. J. H., and M. Feirtag. 1979. The organization of the brain. *Scientific American, 41*:78–105.

Nebes, R. 1972. Dominance of the minor hemisphere in commissurotomized man in a test of figural unification. *Brain, 95*:633–638.

Nisbett, R. E. 1972. Hunger, obesity, and the ventromedial hypothalamus. *Psychological Review, 79*:433–453.

Norman, D. A. 1982. *Learning and Memory*. New York: W. H. Freeman.

Nottebohm, F. 1980. Brain pathways for vocal learning in birds: A review of the first 10 years. In J. M. Sprague and A. N. Epstein (eds.), *Progress in Psychobiology and Physiological Psychology*, vol. 9. New York: Academic.

Nottebohm, F., and A. P. Arnold. 1976. Sexual dimorphism in vocal control areas of the songbird brain. *Science, 194*:211–213.

Ojemann, G. A., and C. Mateer. 1979. Human language cortex: Localization of memory, syntax, and sequential motorphoneme identification systems. *Science, 205*:1401–1403.

Ojemann, G. A., and H. A. Whitaker. 1978. The bilingual brain. *Archives of Neurology, 35*:409–412.

Oke, A., R. Keller, I. Mefford, and R. N. Adams. 1978. Lateralization of norepinephrine in the human thalamus. *Science, 200*:1411–1413.

O'Keefe, J., and L. Nadel. 1978. *The Hippocampus as a Cognitive Map*. London: Oxford University Press.

Olds, J. 1955. Physiological mechanism of reward. In M. R. Jones (ed.), *Nebraska Symposium on Motivation*, pp. 73–138. Lincoln: University of Nebraska Press.

Olds, J. 1958. Self-stimulation of the brain. *Science, 127*:315–323.

Olds, J. 1977. *Drives and Reinforcements: Behavioral Studies of Hypothalamic Functions*. New York: Raven.

Olpe, H. R., and M. W. Steinmann. 1982. Age-related decline in the activity of noradrenergic neurons of the rat locus coeruleus. *Brain Research, 251*:174–176.

Olton, D. S. 1977. Spatial memory. *Scientific American,* 236:82–98.

Olton, D. S., J. T. Becker, and G. E. Handelmann. 1980. Hippocampal function: Working memory or cognitive mapping. *Physiological Psychology,* 8:239–246.

Olton, D. S., and R. J. Samuelson, 1976. Remembrance of places passed: Spatial memory in rats. *Journal of Experimental Psychology: Animal Behavior Processes,* 2:97–116.

Oppenheim, R. W. 1981. Neuronal cell death and some related regressive phenomena during neurogenesis: A selective historical review and progress report. In W. M. Cowan (ed.), *Studies in Developmental Neurobiology.* New York: Oxford University Press.

Ordy, J. M., and B. Kaack. 1975. Neurochemical changes in composition, metabolism, and neurotransmitters in the human brain with age. In J. M. Ordy and K. R. Brizzee (eds.), *Neurobiology of Aging.* New York: Plenum.

Ordy, J. M., and K. R. Brizzee (eds.). 1975. *Neurobiology of Aging: An Interdisciplinary Life-Span Approach.* New York: Plenum.

Ornstein, R. 1978. The split and whole brain. *Human Nature,* 1:76–83.

Ornstein, R. 1977. *The Psychology of Consciousness.* New York: Harcourt.

Orton, S. T. 1937. *Reading, Writing, and Speech Problems in Children.* New York: Norton.

Overmier, J. B., and M. E. P. Seligman. 1967. Effects of inescapable shock upon subsequent escape and avoidance responding. *Journal of Comparative and Physiological Psychology,* 63:28–33.

Palmer, J. D. 1975. Biological clocks of the tidal zone, *Scientific American,* 232:70–79.

Papez, J. W. 1937. A proposed mechanism of emotion. *Archives of Neurology and Psychiatry,* 38:725–744.

Pavlov, I. P. 1927. *Conditioned Reflexes.* London: Oxford University Press.

Penfield, W. 1975. *The Mystery of the Mind.* Princeton: Princeton University Press.

Pengelley, E. T., and S. J. Asmundson. 1971. Annual biological clocks. *Scientific American,* 224:72–79.

Petersen, A. C. 1979. Hormones and cognitive functioning in normal development. In M. A. Wittig and A. C. Petersen (eds.), *Sex Related Differences in Cognitive Functioning—Developmental Issues.* New York: Academic.

Pfaff, D. W. 1980. *Estrogens and Brain Function.* New York: Springer.

Piaget, Jean. 1963. *The Origins of Intelligence in Children.* New York: Norton.

Pick, J. 1970. *The Autonomic Nervous System.* Philadelphia: Lippincott.

Platt, C. B., and B. MacWhinney. 1983. Error assimilation as a mechanism in language learning. *Journal of Child Language, 10:*401–414.

Ploog, Detlev, 1981. Neurobiology of primate audiovocal behavior, *Brain Research Review,* 3:35–61.

Popper, K. R., and J. C. Eccles, 1977. *The Self and Its Brain.* New York: Springer-Verlag.

Pratt, O. E. 1980. A new approach to the treatment of phenylketonuria. *Journal of Mental Deficiency Research,* 24:203–217.

Ratcliffe, S. G., J. Bancroft, D. Axworthy, and W. Mclaren. 1982. Klinefelter's syndrome in adolescence. *Archives of Disease in Childhood,* 57:6–12.

Raisman, G., and P. M. Field. 1973. Sexual dimorphism in the neuropil of the preoptic area of the rat and its dependence on neonatal androgen. *Brain Research,* 54:1–29.

Rakic, P. 1974. Neurons in rhesus monkey visual cortex: Systematic relation between time of origin and eventual disposition. *Science:* 183:425–427.

Rakic, P., and R. L. Sidman. 1973. Sequence of developmental abnormalities leading to granule cell deficit in cerebellar cortex of weaver mutant mice. *Journal of Comparative Neurology.* 152:133–162.

Rakic, P., J.-P. Bourgeois, M. F. Eckenhoff, N. Zecevic, and P. S. Goldman-Rakic. 1986. Concurrent overproduction of synapses in diverse regions of the primate cerebral cortex. *Science,* 232:232–234.

Reinberg, A., P. Andlauer, and N. Vieux. 1981. Circadian temperature rhythm amplitude and long-term tolerance of shiftworking. In L. C. Johnson et al. (eds.), *Biological Rhythms, Sleep and Shift Work.* New York: SP Medical and Scientific Books.

Reinberg, A., N. Vieux, P. Andlauer, and M. Smolensky. 1983. Tolerance to shift work: A chronobiological approach. In J. Mendlewicz and H. M. van Praag (eds.), *Biological Rhythms and Behavior Advances in Biological Psychiatry,* vol. 2, pp. 20–34. Basel: S. Karger.

Reinis, S., and J. M. Goldman. 1980. *The Development of the Brain.* Springfield, Ill.: Charles C Thomas.

Richter, C. 1965. *Biological Clocks in Medicine and Psychiatry.* Springfield, Ill.: Charles C Thomas.

Rife, D. C. 1950. Application of gene frequency analysis to the interpretation of data from twins. *Human Biology,* 22:136–145.

Risse, G. L., and M. S. Gazzaniga. 1978. Well-kept secrets of the right hemisphere: A sodium amytal study. *Neurology* 28:950–993.

Roffwarg, H. P., J. N. Muzio, & W. C. Dement. 1968. Ontogenetic development of the human sleep-dream cycle. In W. B. Webb (ed.), *Sleep: An Experimental Approach.* New York: Macmillan.

Rogers, J., G. R. Siggins, J. A. Schulman, and F. E. Bloom. 1980. Physiological correlates of ethanol intoxication, tolerance, and dependence in rat cerebellar Purkinje cells. *Brain Research, 196:*183–198.

Rogers, J., S. F. Zornetzer, W. J. Shoemaker, and F. E. Bloom. 1981. Electrophysiology of aging brain: senescent pathology of cerebellum. In S. J. Enna et al. (eds.), *Brain Neurotransmitters and Receptors in Aging and Age-Related Disorders.* (Aging, vol. 17). New York: Raven.

Rolls, E. T., and G. J. Morgenson. 1977. Brain self-stimulation behavior. In G. J. Morgenson, *The Neurobiology of Behavior: An Introduction.* Hillsdale, N.J.: Lawrence Erlbaum.

Rose, G. A., and R. T. Williams. 1961. Metabolic studies of large and small eaters. *British Journal of Nutrition, 15:*1–9.

Rose, S. P. R., and P. P. G. Bateson, and G. Horn. 1973. Experience and plasticity in the nervous system. *Science, 181:*506–514.

Rosenzweig, M. R. 1970. *Biology of Memory.* New York: Academic Press.

Rosenzweig, M. R. 1979. *Development and Evolution of Brain Size: Behavioral Implications.* New York: Academic Press.

Rosenzweig, M. R. 1984. Experience, memory, and the brain. *American Psychologist, 39:*365–376.

Rosenzweig, M. R., E. L. Bennett, and M. C. Diamond. 1972. Brain changes in response to experience. *Scientific American, 226:*22–29.

Rosvold, H. E., A. F. Mirsh, and K. H. Pribram. 1954. Influence in amygdalectomy on social behavior in monkeys. *Journal of Comparative and Physiological Psychology, 47:*173–178.

Routtenberg, A. 1978. The reward system of the brain. *Scientific American, 239:*122–131.

Rutishauser, V., R. Brackenburg, J. P. Thiery, and G. M. Edelman. 1976. Mechanisms of adhesion among cells from neural tissues of the chick embryo. *Journal of Cell Biology, 70:*A220.

Sagan, C. 1977. *The Dragons of Eden: Speculations on the Evolution of Human Intelligence.* New York: Random House.

Safanuma, S., and O. Fujimura. 1970. Selective impairment of phonetic and nonphonetic transcription of words in Japanese aphasic patients: Kana vs. kanji in visual recognition and writing. *Cortex, 6:*1–18.

Samuel, D., S. Algeri, S. Gershon, V. E. Grimm, and G. Toffano (eds.). 1983. *Aging of the Brain.* New York: Raven.

Schachter, S. 1971. Some extraordinary facts about obese humans and rats. *American Psychologist:26:*129–144.

Schachter, S., and J. E. Singer. 1962. Cognitive, social, and physiological determinants of emotional state. *Psychological Review, 69:*379–399.

Schaie, K. W. 1980. Intelligence and problem solving. In J. E. Birren and R. B. Sloane (eds.), *Handbook of Mental Health and Aging.* Englewood Cliffs, N.J.: Prentice-Hall.

Schemmel, R., O. Mickelson, and J. L. Gill. 1970. Dietary obesity in rats: Influence of diet, weight, fat accretion in seven strains of rats. *Journal of Nutrition, 100:*1041–1048.

Seligman, M. E. P. 1973. Fall into helplessness. *Psychology Today, 7:*43–48.

Seligman, M. E. P. 1975. *Helplessness.* New York: W. H. Freeman.

Seligman, M. E. P., and S. F. Maier. 1967. Failure to escape traumatic shock. *Journal of Experimental Psychology, 74:*1–9.

Selye, H. 1956. *The Stress of Life.* New York: McGraw-Hill.

Shaffer, J. W. 1962. A cognitive deficit observed in gonadal aplasia (Turner's syndrome). *Journal of Clinical Psychology, 18:*403–406.

Sheard, M. H. 1983. Aggressive behavior: Effects of neural modulation by serotonin. In E. C. Simmel et al. (eds.), *Aggressive Behavior: Genetic and Neural Approaches.* Hillsdale, N.J.: Lawrence Erlbaum.

Siffre, M. 1963. *Hors du temps.* Paris: Julliard.

Skinner, B. F. 1938. *The Behavior of Organisms.* New York: Appleton-Century-Crofts.

Slobin, D. I. 1979. *Psycholinguistics,* 2d ed. Glenview, Ill.: Scott-Foresman.

Sodersten, P., and K. Larsson. 1974. Lordosis behavior in castrated male rats treated with estradiol benzoate or testosterone propionate in combination with an estrogen antagonist MER-25, and in intact male rats. *Hormones and Behavior, 5:*13–18.

Sperry, R. W. 1945. Restoration of vision after crossing of optic nerves and after contralateral transplantation of eye. *Journal of Neurophysiology, 8:*15–28.

Sperry, R. W. 1951. Mechanisms of neural maturation. In S. S. Stevens (ed.), *Handbook of Experimental Psychology.* New York: Wiley.

Sperry, R. W. 1966. Brain bisection and consciousness. In J. Eccles (ed.), *Brain and Conscious Experience.* New York: Springer-Verlag.

Sperry, R. W. 1974. Lateral specialization in the surgically separated hemispheres. In. F.O. Schmitt and F. G. Worden (eds.). *The Neurosciences: Third Study Program.* Cambridge, Mass.: MIT Press.

Sperry, R. W. 1982. Some effects of disconnecting the cerebral hemispheres. *Science, 217:*1223–1226.

Spinelli, D. H., and F. E. Jensen. 1979. Plasticity: The mirror of experience. *Science, 203:*75–78.

Spinelli, D. H., F. E. Jensen, and G. V. DiPrisco. 1980. Early experience effect on dendritic branching in normally reared kittens. *Experimental Neurology, 62:*1–11.

Spooner, J. W., S. M. Sakala, and R. W. Balch. 1980. Effect of aging on eye tracking. *Archives of Neurology 37:*575.

Springer, S. P., and G. Deutsch. 1985. *Left Brain, Right Brain,* revised edition. New York: W. H. Freeman.

Squire, L. R. 1981. Two forms of human amnesia: An analysis of forgetting. *Journal of Neuroscience,* 1:635–640.

Squire, L. R. 1984. Memory and the brain. In S. Friedman et al. (eds.), *Brain, Cognition, and Education.* New York: Academic Press.

Staudt, J., and G. Dorner. 1976. Structural changes in the medial and central amygdala of the male rat following castration and androgen treatment. *Endokrinologie, 67:*296–300.

Stein, J., and S. Fowler. Visual dyslexia. *Trends in Neurosciences, 4:*77–80.

Steinberg, M. S. 1963. Reconstruction of tissues by dissociated cells. *Science, 141:*401–408.

Sternberg, D. B., and P. E. Gold. 1981. Retrograde amnesia produced by electrical stimulation of the amygdala: Attenuation with adrenergic antagonists. *Brain Research, 211:*59–65.

Strumwasser, F., J. W. Jacklet, and R. B. Alvarez. 1969. A seasonal rhythm in the neural extract induction of behavioral egg-laying in *Aplysia. Comparative Biochemistry and Physiology, 29:*197–206.

Strumwasser, F., F. R. Schlechte, and S. Bower. 1972. Distributed circadian oscillators in the nervous system of *Aplysia. Federation Proceedings, 31:*405.

Swanson, L. W., T. J. Teyler, and R. F. Thompson (eds.). 1982. *Hippocampal Long-term Potentiation: Mechanisms and Implications for Memory.* Neurosciences Research Program Bulletin, Vol. 20, No. 5. Cambridge, Mass.: MIT Press.

Takahashi, J. S., and M. Zatz. 1982. Regulation of circadian rhythmicity. *Science, 217:*1104—1111.

Tatlor, A. M., and J. E. Turnure. 1979. Imagery and verbal elaboration with retarded children: Effects on learning and memory. In N. R. Ellis (ed.), *Handbook of Mental Deficiency, Psychological Theory, and Research,* 2d ed. Hillsdale, N.J.: Lawrence Erlbaum.

Taylor, J. (ed.). 1958. *Selected Writings of John Hughlings Jackson,* vol. 2: London: Staples.

Teuber, H. L., B. Milner, and H. G. Vaughan. 1968. Persistent anterograde amnesia after stab wound of the basal brain. *Neuropsychologia, 6:*267–282.

Thompson, R. F., T. Berger, and J. Madden. 1983. Cellular processes of learning and memory in the mammalian CNS. *Annual Review of Neuroscience, 6:*447–491.

Thompson, R. F., L. H. Hicks, and V. B. Shryrkov. 1980. *Neural Mechanisms of Goal-Directed Behavior and Learning.* New York: Academic Press.

Thurstone, L. L., and T. G. Thurstone. 1941. Factorial studies of intelligence. *Psychometric Monographs.* No. 2. Chicago:University of Chicago Press.

Toivonen, S., and S. Saxen. 1968. Morphogenetic interaction of presumptive neural and mesodermal cells mixed in different ratios. *Science, 159:*539–540

Tomlinson, B. E., G. Blessed, and M. Roth. 1968. Observations in the brains of nondemented old people. *Journal of Neurological Science, 7:*331–356.

Tomlinson, B. E., G. Blessed, and M. Roth. 1970. Observations in the brains of demented old people. *Journal of Neurological Science, 11:*205–242.

Tordoff, M. G., J. Hoffenbeck, and D. Novin. 1982. Hepatic vagotomy (partial hepatic denervation) does not alter ingestive responses to metabolic challenges. *Physiology and Behavior, 28:* 417–424.

Trankell, A. 1955. Aspects of genetics in psychology. *American Journal of Human Genetics, 7:*264–276.

Trayhurn, P., P. L. Thurlby, C. J. H. Woodward, and W. P. T. James. 1979. Thermoregulation in genetically obese rodents: The relationship to metabolic efficiency. In M. F. W. Festing (ed.), *Genetic Models of Obesity in Laboratory Animals.* London: Macmillan.

Valzelli, L. 1981. *Psychobiology of Aggression and Violence.* New York: Raven.

Varon, Silvio. 1985. *Factors Promoting the Growth of the Nervous System.* Discussions in Neurosciences, Foundation for the Study of the Nervous System, vol. II, no. 3.

Vergnes, M. 1975. Déclenchement de réactions d'agression interspécific après lésion amygdalienne chez le rat. *Physiology and Behavior, 14:*271–276.

Volpe, B. T., J. E. LeDoux, and M. S. Gazzaniga. 1979. Information processing of visual stimuli in an extinguished field. *Nature, 282:*722.

Wada, J. A., R. Clarke, and A. Hamm. 1975. Cerebral hemispheric asymmetry in humans. *Archives of Neurology, 32:*239–246.

Watkins, L. R., and D. J. Mayer, 1982. Organization of endogenous opiate and nonopiate pain control systems. *Science, 216:*1183–1192.

Wehr, T. A., A. Wirz-Justice, F. K. Goodwin, W. Duncan, and J. C. Gillin. 1979. Phase advance of the circadian sleep-wake cycle as an anti-depressant. *Science, 206:*710–713.

Weiss, J. M. 1971. Effects of coping behavior in different warning-signal conditions on stress pathology in rats. *Journal of Comparative and Physiological Psychology, 77:*1–13.

Weiss, J. M. 1971. Somatic effects of predictable and unpredictable shock. *Psychosomatic Medicine, 6:*1–39.

Weiss, J. M. 1972. Psychological factors in stress and disease. *Scientific American, 226:*104–113.

Werner, E. E., J. M. Bierman, and F. E. French. 1971. *The Children of Kauai.* Honolulu: University of Hawaii Press.

West, D. B., R. H. Williams, D. J. Braget, and S. C. Woods. 1982. Bombesin reduces food intake of normal and hypothalamically obese rats and lowers body weight when given chronically. *Peptides, 3:*61–67.

West, D. B., J. Diaz, and S. C. Woods. 1982. Infant gastrostomy and chronic formula infusion as a technique to overfeed and accelerate weight gain in neonatal rats. *Journal of Nutrition, 112:*1339–1343.

White, C. T. 1974. The visual-evoked response and pattern stimuli. In G. Newton and A. H. Riesen (eds.), *Advances in Psychobiology,* vol. 2. New York: Wiley.

Whiting, B. B., and J. W. M. Whiting. 1975. *Children of Six Cultures: A Psychocultural Analysis.* Cambridge, Mass.: Harvard University Press.

Willen, J. C., H. Dehan, and J. Cambier. 1981. Stress-induced analgesia in humans: Endogenous opioids and naloxone-reversible depression of pain reflexes. *Science, 212:*689–691.

Wiesel, T. N. 1982. Postnatal development of the visual cortex and the influence of environment. *Nature, 299:* 583–592.

Winick, M., and R. E. Greenberg. 1965. Appearance and localization of a nerve growth-promoting protein during development. *Pediatrics, 35:*221–228.

Wisniewski, K. E., M. Laure-Kamionowska, F. Connell, and G. Y. Yen. 1986. Neuronal density and synaptogenesis in the postnatal stage of brain maturation in Down syndrome. In C. J. Epstein (ed.), *The Neurobiology of Down Syndrome.* New York: Raven.

Witelson, S. F. 1976. Sex and the single hemisphere: Specialization of the right hemisphere for spatial processing. *Science, 193:* 425–427.

Witelson, S., and W. Pallie. 1973. Left hemisphere specialisation for language in the newborn: Neuroanatomical evidence of asymmetry. *Brain:* 96:641–646.

Wood, F., D. Stump, A. Mckeehan, S. Sheldon, and J. Proctor. 1980. Patterns of regional cerebral blood flow during attempted reading aloud by stutterers both on and off haloperidol medication: Evidence for inadequate left frontal activation during stuttering. *Brain and Language, 9:*141–144.

Woods, S. C., E. Decke, and J. R. Vasselli. 1974. Metabolic hormones and regulation of body weight. *Psychological Review, 81:* 26–43.

Woods, S. C., G. J. Taborsky, Jr., and D. Porte, Jr. 1986. Central nervous system control of nutrient homeostasis. In F. E. Bloom (ed.), *Handbook of Physiology—The Nervous System IV.* Bethesda, Md.: American Physiological Society.

Woods, S. C., E. C. Lotter, L. D. McKay, and D. Porte. 1979. Chronic intracerebroventricular infusion reduces food intake and body weight of baboons. *Nature London* 282:503–505.

Woolridge, P. E. 1963. *The Machinery of the Brain.* Toronto: McGraw-Hill.

Woolsey, T. A., and J. R. Wann. 1976. Areal changes in mouse cortical barrels following vibrissal damage at different postnatal ages. *Journal of Comparative Neurology* 170:53–66.

Yates, C. M., J. Simpson, A. F. J. Maloney, A. Gordon, and A. H. Reid. 1980. Alzheimer-like cholinergic deficiency in Down syndrome. *Lancet:* 2:979.

Zaidel, E. 1975. A technique for presenting lateralized visual input with prolonged exposure. *Vision Research, 15:*283–289.

Zaidel, E. 1976. Auditory vocabulary of the right hemisphere following brain bisection or hemidecortication. *Cortex, 190:*191–211.

Zajonc, R. B. 1980. Feeling and thinking. *American Psychologist, 35:*151–175.

Zuckerman, M. 1979. *Sensation-seeking: Beyond the Optimum Level of Arousal.* Hillsdale, N.J.: Lawrence Erlbaum.

Credits

Several illustrations in Chapter 3 were adapted from *The Brain* (a collection of articles that originally appeared in *Scientific American,* September, 1979), W. H. Freeman and Company, New York, 1979. Many of the diagrams and line illustrations in Chapters 4 and 5 owe much to the admirable work found in R. F. Schmidt and G. Thews, eds., *Human Physiology,* Springer-Verlag, New York, 1983. In Chapter 9, a number of drawings were adapted from S. Springer and G. Deutsch, *Left Brain/Right Brain,* W. H. Freeman and Company, New York, 1981.

Drawings on pages xii–xv, 7, 8, 20, 21, 23, 24, 25, 31, 32, 34, 38, 39, 40, 42, 49, 52, 57, 58, 59, 75, 94, 95, 96, 99, 112, 114, 116, 117, 126, 127, 130, 132, 145, 148, 150, 186, 193, 199, 213, 222, 247, 277, 279, 283, 292, 314, 315, and 336 by Carol Donner.

Drawings on pages 47, 59, 61, 62, 65, 66, 69, 71, 72, 73, 77, 79, 83, 93, 98, 104, 109, 115, 118, 121, 122, 124, 141, 142, 147, 152, 158, 160, 171, 174, 175, 177, 180, 181, 182, 183, 185, 188, 189, 200, 202, 210, 211, 224, 230, 241, 242, 243, 244, 249, 257, 262, 264, 275, 279, 280, 281, 282, 289, 293, 298, 328, 334, 343, and 346 by Sally Black.

Chapter 1

page 4
bottom, from "Human Amnesia and the Medial Temporal Region," Stuart Zola-Morgan and David Amaral, *The Journal of Neuroscience,* October, 1986. Photograph by Kris Trulock and Marcia Lee Earnshaw.

page 13
The Granger Collection

page 14
Zentralbibliothek Zurich

page 15
New York Public Library

page 16
The Burndy Library

Chapter 2

page 30
Manfred Kage/Peter Arnold

page 33
bottom right The Granger Collection

page 35
The Granger Collection

page 51
Michael E. Phelps, Lewis Baxter, and John Mazziotta, UCLA School of Medicine

Chapter 3

page 56
Photo by Lennart Nilsson. From *Behold Man,* Little, Brown and Company, Boston.

page 64
From "The Development of the Brain," by W. Maxwell Cowan, *Scientific American,* September, 1979. Photograph by J. Michael Cochran and Mary Bartlett Bunge.

page 68
Travis Amos

page 70
Mia Tegner

page 78
Torsten Wiesel

page 80
Autoradiographs from D. N. Spenilli, F. E. Jensen, and G. V. DiPrisco, *Experimental Neurology,* 1980.

page 83
From *Human Development,* by Kurt W. Fischer and Arlyne Lazerson, W. H. Freeman and Company, New York, 1984.

page 84
Susan Schwarzenberg, Exploratorium

Chapter 4

page 89
Susan Schwarzenberg, Exploratorium

page 104
From the WNET series, *The Brain*

page 118
From *Tissues and Organs,* by Richard Kessel and Randy Kardon, W. H. Freeman and Co.

page 125
From the WNET series, *The Brain*

page 129
The British Museum (Natural History)

Chapter 5

page 139
NASA

page 153
From the WNET series, *The Brain*

page 162
From *The Psychology of Eating and Drinking,* by A. W. Logue, W. H. Freeman and Company, New York, 1986.

page 163
Schiffman/Gamma Liaison

Chapter 6

page 170
The Granger Collection

page 172
Travis Amos

page 173
Charles Arneson

page 178
Frank J. Miller/Photo Researchers

page 180
From the WNET series, *The Brain*

page 184
From the WNET series, *The Brain*

page 188
DREAMSCAPE © 1977 J. A. Hobson and Hoffmann-La Roche, Inc.

page 191
From the WNET series, *The Brain*

Chapter 7

page 208
John Storey/*San Francisco Examiner*

page 214
Warren Anatomical Museum, Harvard

page 218
New York Academy of Medicine Library

page 226
top Chuck Rogers

page 226
bottom J. P. Laffont/Sygma

page 227
James Olds

page 233
left George Holton/Photo Researchers

page 235
from *Darwin and Facial Expression,* Paul Eckman (ed.), Academic Press, 1973.

Chapter 8

page 240
Mickey Pfleger

page 244
Pierre Henkart

page 250
Primate Laboratory, University of Wisconsin

page 252
Thomas McAvoy/Life Magazine, © Time Inc.

page 258
From the WNET series, *The Brain*

page 259
New York Academy of Medicine Library

page 260
Barbara Phillips

Chapter 9

page 273
T. Urban, World Health Organization

page 286
From "Specializations of the Human Brain," by Norman Geschwind, *Scientific American,* 1979.

page 296
From "Brain Function and Blood Flow" by Niels A. Olassen, David H. Ingvar, and Erick Skinhoj, *Scientific American,* 1978.

page 302
Alinari/Art Resource

Chapter 10

page 309 top
American Museum of Natural History

page 309 bottom
Museo Nacional del Prado

page 310 left
The Granger Collection

page 311
Freud, The Granger Collection; Kraepelin, The Bettmann Archive; Bleuler, The Bettmann Archive; Jackson, The Granger Collection; Pavlov, The Bettmann Archive.

page 315 top left
Dr. Richard Wyatt

page 315 top right
Dr. John Mazziotta

page 315 bottom left
From *Pathology,* 3d ed. by Stanley L. Robbins, W. B. Saunders, 1981

page 320
Stedelijk Museum

page 323
Steve Uzzell

page 331
Drs. Michael E. Phelps, Lewis Baxter, and John Mazziotta, UCLA School of Medicine

page 338
From the WNET series, *The Brain*

page 340
Dr. Richard Wyatt

page 341
National Institute of Health

page 345
Dr. Arnold Scheibel

Index